PHILOSOPHICAL FOUNDATIONS OF CONTRACT LAW

Philosophical Foundations of Contract Law

Edited by

GREGORY KLASS,

GEORGE LETSAS,

and

PRINCE SAPRAI

OXFORD
UNIVERSITY PRESS

OXFORD
UNIVERSITY PRESS

Great Clarendon Street, Oxford, OX2 6DP,
United Kingdom

Oxford University Press is a department of the University of Oxford. It furthers the University's objective of excellence in research, scholarship, and education by publishing worldwide. Oxford is a registered trade mark of Oxford University Press in the UK and in certain other countries

First Edition published in 2014

Impression: 2

Published in the United States of America by Oxford University Press
198 Madison Avenue, New York, NY 10016, United States of America

British Library Cataloguing in Publication Data
Data available

Library of Congress Control Number: 2014942230

ISBN 978–0–19–871301–2

Printed and bound by
CPI Group (UK) Ltd, Croydon, CR0 4YY

Acknowledgments

The chapters that constitute this volume were first presented at the inaugural Bentham House conference at University College London in 2013. Thank you to the University College London Faculty of Laws for providing funding and a venue for this conference, and thank you in particular to the Dean of the Faculty, Dame Professor Hazel Genn, and Vice-Dean for Staffing at the time, Professor James Penner, for their unstinting support. Thank you to the conference participants for making the conference a success.

We would like to thank Alex Flach, Natasha Flemming, and Clare Kennedy from Oxford University Press for their support throughout this project.

The Georgetown Law Library provided much help with the manuscript. Special thanks on this front to librarians Morgan Stoddard and Esther Cho, as well as Georgetown Law student Joshua Slone.

Last but by no means least, thank you to the contributors to this volume.

Professor Gregory Klass
Dr George Letsas
Dr Prince Saprai

Table of Contents

List of Abbreviations

F.A.A.	Federal Arbitration Act
I.A.C.C.M.	International Association for Contract and Commercial Management
J.	Justice
L.C.	Lord Chancellor
L.J.	Lord Justice
P.I.R.C.	Valentine Shiffrin, *Promising, Intimate Relationships, and Conventionalism*
S.K.U.	stock keeping unit
T.G.F.A.	Texas Grain and Feed Association
T.O.S.	terms of service
U.C.C.	Uniform Commercial Code
V.O.	James Penner, *Voluntary Obligations*

List of Contributors

Aditi Bagchi is Associate Professor of Law at Fordham University School of Law.

Randy E. Barnett is Carmack Waterhouse Professor of Legal Theory at Georgetown University Law Center.

Lisa Bernstein is Wilson-Dickenson Professor of Law at the University of Chicago Law School.

Mindy Chen-Wishart is Reader in Contract Law and Fellow and Tutor in Law at Merton College, University of Oxford, and Professor of Law at the National University of Singapore.

Charles Fried is Beneficial Professor of Law at Harvard University Law School.

Avery W. Katz is Milton Handler Professor of Law at Columbia University Law School.

Dori Kimel is Reader in Legal Philosophy and Fellow and Tutor in Law at New College, University of Oxford.

Gregory Klass is Professor of Law at Georgetown University Law Center.

George Letsas is Reader in Philosophy of Law and Human Rights at University College London Faculty of Laws.

Daniel Markovits is Guido Calabresi Professor of Law at Yale Law School.

Liam Murphy is Herbert Peterfreund Professor of Law and Professor of Philosophy at New York University School of Law.

David Owens is Professor of Philosophy at the University of Reading Department of Philosophy.

James Penner is Professor of Law at the National University of Singapore.

Margaret Jane Radin is Henry King Ransom Professor of Law at the University of Michigan School of Law, and Distinguished Research Scholar, University of Toronto Faculty of Law.

Joseph Raz is Thomas M. Macioce Professor of Law at Columbia University Law School, and Research Professor at King's College London Dickson Poon School of Law.

Prince Saprai is a Lecturer at University College London Faculty of Laws.

Stephen A. Smith is James McGill Professor at McGill University Faculty of Law.

Charlie Webb is an Associate Professor at London School of Economics and Political Science Department of Law.

List of Contributors

1

Introduction to *Philosophical Foundations of Contract Law*

Gregory Klass

Contract theory is not one thing, but a collection of related inquiries. There is variety both in the questions theorists ask and in the methods they use to answer them. Among the questions are: What is distinctive about contract law? What are its core concepts? For what purpose do we enforce contracts? What justifies their enforcement? Given one or another function or justification, what should the rules of contract law be? What moral or political principles are relevant to the enforcement of contracts? There is also variety in method. Principled arguments of contract start from above. They ask first what justifies having a law of contract, and from that derive what the rules of contract law should be. Interpretive arguments begin from below. They examine the contract law we have, then ask what functions and justifications provide the best account of the practice. Critical analyses look for hidden purposes or unintended consequences, such as contract law's role in legitimizing or reproducing power relationships. Theorists also use a variety of analytic tools. These include moral and political theory, conceptual analysis, sociological theory, interpretation, neoclassical economic analysis, and empirical psychology.

This introduction sketches the field and locates in it the chapters that follow. We have organized those chapters into two large groups: essays that focus on general theoretical questions and essays that focus on more specific doctrinal questions. But this is a rough cut at best, and only one way to divide things up. Because they vary along multiple dimensions, contract theories cannot be ordered around or along any single line. So this Introduction will zigzag a bit.

It will help to define a few technical terms. Laws and collections of laws are instruments that society can employ to achieve one or more purposes. The purpose or purposes a law serves constitute its *function*. Because laws involve the deployment of collective resources and are ultimately backed by state coercion, they also require *justification*. That justification, if it exists, can be found in the moral, political, or other principles that render the use of collective resources and state coercion permissible.[1] Finally, it is sometimes argued that distinct areas of law, such as the law of contract,

[1] As Charlie Webb puts the point in this volume, "even where the law's technical rules are determinate and neither require nor invite [appeal to value judgments], these source-based norms earn a place in our reasoning and decision-making only on the back of norms which get there on their merits." Charlie Webb, *Contract as Fact and as Reason, in* Philosophical Foundations of Contract Law 134, 135 (Gregory Klass, George Letsas, & Prince Saprai eds., 2014).

have an internal logic or core set of commitments. Just as a language has a grammar, contract law might have basic rules or commitments that structure the practice as a whole. This immanent logic, if it exists, is contract law's *conceptual structure*. Noncritical general theories of contract typically focus on one or more of contract law's function, its justification, and its conceptual structure.

Much contract theory occupies itself one way or another with the relationship between contracts, which create legal obligations, and promises, which create moral ones. Contract law itself uses the language of promising. Courts and commentators regularly refer to the parties as "promisor" and "promisee," and the *Restatement (Second) of Contracts* opens by saying that a contract is "a promise or set of promises for the breach of which the law gives a remedy, or the performance of which the law in some way recognizes as a duty."[2] And no matter what words the law uses, there are obvious similarities between contracts and promises. Both are largely content independent, voluntarily acquired obligations owed to a particular person or persons.

Saying all that does not yet say what the relation between the legal obligation and the moral one is. One answer is that contract law functions to enforce certain promises. In contemporary Anglo-American scholarship, the thesis is most closely associated with Charles Fried's 1981 book, *Contract as Promise*. Fried's chapter in this volume updates that theory in light of subsequent work in the field. As Fried points out, dominant trends in contract theory have changed considerably in the past 30 years. The reliance-based and critical approaches that ruled when he wrote the book have been supplanted by economic analysis, corrective justice, and new autonomy theories. Fried's chapter discusses the relationship between his approach in *Contract as Promise* and subsequent work in the field. And he uses his chapter to provide new thoughts on topics such as the common law's preference for expectation damages, the consideration doctrine, unconscionability, the mitigation rule, contract interpretation, and the objective theory.

The claim that contracts just are legally enforceable promises has led many contract theorists back to moral theory and the analysis of promissory obligations. Fried, for example, argues that the institution of promising, and by extension contract, is built "on the deeper morality of trust and respect for persons."[3] Three chapters in this book focus on the morality of promising. Although they make different claims, each recommends paying attention not only to the new obligations a promisor acquires through her promise, but also to the normative interests or obligations of the promisee.

David Owens asks whether promises are properly characterized as transferring something from the promisor to the promisee. He argues against the common claim that a promise transfers the right to performance—that "[b]y promising, I transfer my... entitlement to act within a certain range of options, thereby giving that power to others."[4] Appealing to Hume's point that the mere fact of having a right does not entail the power to alienate or transfer it, Owens argues that right-transfer theories

[2] Restatement (Second) of Contracts § 1 (1983).

[3] Charles Fried, *The Ambitions of* Contract as Promise, *in* Philosophical Foundations of Contract Law 17, 21 (Gregory Klass, George Letsas, & Prince Saprai eds., 2014).

[4] Gary Watson, *Promises, Reasons and Normative Powers, in* Reasons for Action 155, 170 (D. Sabel & S. Wall eds., 2009), *quoted in* David Owens, *Does a Promise Transfer a Right?, in* Philosophical Foundations of Contract Law 78, 89 (Gregory Klass, George Letsas, & Prince Saprai eds., 2014).

cannot explain why promises bind. In Owens's view, the effect of a promise is rather to give the promisee the power to determine the promisor's moral obligations by deciding whether to insist on performance or to release the promisor from her obligation. Promises thereby serve what Owens calls the promisee's "Authority Interest." "By postulating an interest in the normative item that the promisee acquires we can identify the source of a promise's binding force."[5]

Joseph Raz's chapter explores several aspects of the reasons promises generate. Promises are generally content independent: the reason they bind does not depend on the act promised. Some acts, however, cannot be promised, such as selling oneself into slavery. Raz explains this fact by arguing that the power to promise exists only because, and to the extent that, it enhances our moral lives. There is no value to giving people the power to enslave themselves. Working from the same premise, Raz argues that promisors need not have the power to determine the strength of the reasons for performance that their promises create—to determine the strength of their promises. The fact that having the power to promise is valuable "does not mean that there is value in people being able to determine the strength of the reasons that promises generate."[6] Raz then asks how it is that the mere act of promising can create a new reason to act. He argues contra Owens that the reason to act is not a "bare reason" generated by the mere fact of the promise. Rather a promise gives the promisor a reason to perform because of the "normative assurance" that a promise provides the promisee, which is the promisee's opportunity to receive performance.

Dori Kimel also considers the normative position of the promisee. But where Raz and Owens emphasize the normative powers that a promise confers on the promisee, Kimel is interested in the promisee's moral duties in exercising those powers. Drawing from contract law, Kimel argues that promissory obligations are strict. Unless the promisor builds an excuse into the content of her promise, nonperformance is a breach of the promise, no matter what its reason or cause. This makes promising an especially risky business, in that a promisor might undertake obligations she later has reason to regret. If this is right, then "the capacity to self-create obligations owed to others may be thought of not only as a manifestation or an extension of personal autonomy, but also as something that can pose a particularly potent threat to it."[7] In fact, we might do better without the power to promise. The threat is reduced, however, by moral obligations of the promisee to sometimes exercise the power to release the promisor from her promise. Kimel argues that "promises are typically made or exchanged in... the sort of relationships that tend to generate a wealth of relationship-specific norms capable of supplementing, competing with, altering, or altogether defeating promissory norms."[8] The promisee's nonpromissory obligations of friendship, for example,

[5] Owens, *Does a Promise Transfer a Right?*, at 89. For a more thorough discussion of this claim, *see* David J. Owens, Shaping the Normative Landscape (2012).

[6] Joseph Raz, *Is There a Reason to Keep a Promise?*, *in* Philosophical Foundations of Contract Law 58, 64 (Gregory Klass, George Letsas, & Prince Saprai eds., 2014).

[7] Dori Kimel, *Promise, Contract, Personal Autonomy, and the Freedom to Change One's Mind*, *in* Philosophical Foundations of Contract Law 96, 99 (Gregory Klass, George Letsas, & Prince Saprai eds., 2014).

[8] Kimel, *Promise*, at 110.

can require her to excuse nonperformance when the promisor is not at fault, thereby reducing the risk attached to the unwise promise.

For those who believe that contract law functions to enforce promissory obligations, such arguments about the structure and scope of the moral obligation are highly relevant to understanding the structure and scope of the corresponding legal obligation. (I argue below that they might be relevant to other contract theorists as well, for other reasons.) If promissory obligations are the reason for enforcing contracts, we need to know what promissory obligations are and what they entail.

But promissory theories of contract are not without their critics. The critics can be divided into two broad camps: those who agree with Fried that contract serves moral ends, but reject his account of those ends, and those who reject moral accounts of contract law altogether.

Many who agree with Fried that contract serves moral ends do not agree with his claim that it serves to enforce promises. These theorists depart from Fried in two distinct ways.[9] First, some hold that the legally relevant moral obligations are not, or not only, promissory obligations. In his contribution to this volume, James Penner argues that contracts are best understood as involving agreements rather than promises.[10] Penner suggests several differences. First and foremost, whereas promises are unilateral acts, agreements are bilateral, involving active participation and commitment by all sides. In addition, agreements often arise in conditions where there is a preexisting obligation to coordinate behavior or a shared interest in accomplishing some project. And agreements are typically built on a shared foundation of mutual trust and an appreciation of one another's interests, whereas promises are often prompted by the promisee's mistrust of the promisor. On Penner's account, "promises are typically parasitic on prior agreements and are 'pathological' in the sense that they are typically only sought or given when a person already obliged is, for one reason or another, less than optimally likely to fulfill their obligations."[11] If Penner is correct, we should look for a moral basis for the law of contract not in the morality of promises, but in the morality of agreements more generally. Such a shift could shed new light on doctrines such as the requirement of good faith, the frustration and impracticability defenses, and the mitigation rule.

Other theorists question whether contract law's function with respect to the parties' moral obligations is one of simple enforcement. Liam Murphy's chapter distinguishes three functions contract law might play with respect to the moral sphere. First, contract law might enforce the first-order moral obligation to perform, as Fried suggests. Second, contract law might enforce second-order obligations that come into being only after the wrong of breach, as corrective justice theories claim. Third, contract law might be deployed instrumentally to increase social welfare, attending to the parties' particular obligations to one another only as a means to that broader end. Murphy discusses examples of the first two approaches, which he argues do not succeed.

[9] Both are discussed in Gregory Klass, *Promise Etc.*, 45 Suffolk U. L. Rev. 695 (2012).

[10] Penner's chapter updates and extends his earlier work on the subject in J. E. Penner, *Voluntary Obligations and the Scope of the Law of Contract*, 2 Legal Theory 325 (1996).

[11] J. E. Penner, *Promises, Agreements, and Contracts*, *in* Philosophical Foundations of Contract Law 116, 130 (Gregory Klass, George Letsas, & Prince Saprai eds., 2014).

Enforcement theories are difficult to square with the law's preference for expectation damages over specific performance, and they run contrary to a liberal suspicion of using state coercion "merely for the sake of improving a person's own welfare, or enforcing their obligations, or making them more virtuous."[12] Expectation-based corrective justice theories "offer[] no argument at all for the idea that all promisees have moral rights that it is the business of the law to protect."[13] Reliance-based corrective justice theories can explain neither why the law provides recovery for reliance on promises but not other sorts of reliance, nor the law's preference for the expectation measure. This leaves instrumentalist approaches, which "will not try to track the moral duties and interests of parties to particular agreements but will rather take a broader view, finding the point of the institution in the overall social good it produces."[14] Murphy's preferred instrumentalist approach is like economic analysis in that it identifies contract law's function as the promotion of social welfare. But Murphy takes a broader view of what constitutes social welfare. Whereas traditional economic analyses ask what remedies are likely to maximize the parties' joint profits, Murphy would ask what remedy is better for society as a whole, with a focus on contract law's role in supporting the social practice of making and keeping agreements.

Charlie Webb argues in his chapter that contracts necessarily give rise to promissory obligations, but that those obligations are not the reason for their legal enforcement. Contracts entail promises, according to Webb, because legal obligations claim to be moral obligations and so to voluntarily undertake a legal duty to perform a contract is also to voluntarily undertake a moral obligation to do so. "[I]f and insofar as contracts do involve the voluntary assumption of obligations—whatever their content—then these obligations are moral obligations."[15] It does not follow, however, that the promise is the reason for legal enforcement. "Whatever reasons we may identify for regarding promises as obligation creating may not be reasons to take them as creating *legal* rights and duties such as support state policing and intervention in the event of breach."[16] Webb does not fully articulate a theory of legal enforcement, but suggests that the relationship to the theory of promises is complex. On the one hand, the conditions of contractual validity clearly do not track the conditions of promissory obligations. On the other, the law can help to inform promisors as to the scope of their obligations. The morality of promising, in Webb's account, is relevant to the theory of contract, but the latter "need neither begin nor end with an account of promissory obligation."[17]

Penner, Murphy, and Webb do not deny that contract law might serve a moral function. They depart from Fried only in what each considers that function to be. Other theorists maintain that the function of contract law is not to be found in the parties' moral obligations at all. Like Fried, Randy Barnett is an autonomy theorist. But Barnett rejects

[12] Liam Murphy, *The Practice of Promise and Contract*, *in* PHILOSOPHICAL FOUNDATIONS OF CONTRACT LAW 151, 157 (Gregory Klass, George Letsas, & Prince Saprai eds., 2014).
[13] Murphy, *The Practice of Promise and Contract*, at 161.
[14] Murphy, *The Practice of Promise and Contract*, at 162.
[15] Webb, *Contract as Fact and as Reason*, at 145.
[16] Webb, *Contract as Fact and as Reason*, at 148.
[17] Webb, *Contract as Fact and as Reason*, at 150.

promissory or other moral theories of contract. In this volume, he argues that Fried's promise theory can neither explain the objective approach to contract interpretation nor guide lawmakers as to the appropriate default rules. More fundamentally, Barnett, like Murphy, argues that the law has no business enforcing the private morality of promising. Barnett would not agree with Murphy, however, that the function of contract law is therefore to support the moral practice more broadly. Rather than focusing on parties' moral relationships, contract law should ask only whether the parties to a transaction have consented to legal enforcement—whether at the time of formation they intended to be legally bound. Both Fried and Barnett are autonomy theorists. But where Fried's promise theory views contract law as imposing duties based on the parties' autonomous moral act of promising, Barnett characterizes it as conferring on them the legal power to autonomously undertake legal obligations to one another, no matter what their moral relationship.[18] For Barnett, "the private morality of promise resides in the realm of ethics," whereas "the morality of contract resides in the realm of justice."[19]

Barnett's consent theory of contract reflects his principled commitment to a libertarian theory of legal entitlements.[20] Other theorists provide other arguments for depicting contract as a sort of private legislative power that is independent of the parties' promise-based obligations. Dori Kimel has argued that contracts are not promises, but substitute for promises in situations where thicker forms of trust are not available.[21] Michael Pratt has constructed a thought experiment to demonstrate how one might undertake contractual obligations while at the same time effectively abjuring promissory ones.[22]

Another largely amoral account of contractual obligations can be found in economic analyses of contract law. The application of economic tools to legal questions is more common in the United States than elsewhere in the English-speaking world. Two chapters in this book provide windows into the approach. Avery Katz's chapter describes the basic concepts of economic legal analysis, such as the distinction between positive and normative economic analysis, how economists model decision making, and efficiency. Katz suggests several reasons to think that the normative economic analysis of contract law makes special sense, especially when it comes to contracts between sophisticated parties.

> In commerce, it is easier to value things in monetary terms and to calculate costs and benefits; and economic gain is usually the motivation for the transaction. In addition, contractual obligations are typically undertaken deliberately, at arms' length, and with managerial oversight if not professional legal assistance. The economic model of rational choice provides a more plausible descriptive account in such settings than it does when applied to less calculating actors such as negligent tortfeasors, divorcing spouses, criminals, or residential tenants.[23]

[18] For more thoughts on theories of contract law as duty-imposing and as power-conferring, *see* Gregory Klass, *Three Pictures of Contract: Duty, Power and Compound Rule*, 83 N.Y.U. L. Rev. 1726 (2008).

[19] Randy E. Barnett, *Contract Is Not Promise; Contract Is Consent*, *in* Philosophical Foundations of Contract Law 42, 57 (Gregory Klass, George Letsas, & Prince Saprai eds., 2014).

[20] *See* Randy E. Barnett, The Structure of Liberty: Justice and the Rule of Law (2d ed., 2014).

[21] Dori Kimel, From Promise to Contract: Toward a Liberal Theory of Contract (2002).

[22] Michael G. Pratt, *Contract: Not Promise*, 35 Fla. St. U. L. Rev. 801 (2008).

[23] Avery W. Katz, *Economic Foundations of Contract Law*, *in* Philosophical Foundations of Contract Law 171, 176 (Gregory Klass, George Letsas, & Prince Saprai eds., 2014).

Moreover, because such contracts involve exchanges between sophisticated parties to which they must consent, gains in overall efficiency are likely to be shared among them to make everyone better off. After mapping out three distinct approaches to economic analysis of the law, Katz provides the reader with examples of economic analyses of formation rules, the choice between private enforcement and state enforcement, contract interpretation, and the measure of damages for breach. Katz concludes with a discussion of where economic analysis stands with respect to other jurisprudential approaches to contract law. And he suggests that whether or not lawyers, judges, or legislators accept the prescriptive claims of normative economic analysis, they can and should employ the tools of economic analysis when performing their various roles.

My own chapter focuses on the best-known and most controversial example of the economic analysis of contract: the theory of efficient breach, which first appeared in the literature more than 40 years ago. After recounting a simple version of the theory and some common noneconomic criticisms of it, I describe four ways in which subsequent economic accounts have rejected and moved beyond the simple theory. Many non-economists critics of efficient breach, it turns out, are criticizing a theory that no serious economist would defend. But contract theorists should still pay attention to efficient breach theory. A more sophisticated version of the theory reveals three distinctive features of contract law that noneconomic theories often overlook: "First, remedies often affect other terms, including the price. Second, as a result, parties themselves often want efficient remedies. Third, lawmakers must decide whether, when, or how parties should be able to choose the remedy."[24] This claim is consistent with Murphy's suggestion that any instrumentalist theory should take economic analysis into account because economic analysis of the law offers "the only sustained attempt at explaining how legal rules affect behavior."[25]

Like consent theories, economic accounts view contract law as functioning primarily to confer on parties a private legislative power, rather than as taking account of independently acquired moral obligations. On these theories, contract law does not serve to enforce, support, or otherwise respond to the parties' moral obligations. The theories do, however, treat contract as a legal *analog* to the moral power of promising. Both contract and promise give persons the ability to voluntarily undertake new obligations—one legal, the other moral. This similarity provides an independent reason for contract theorists to pay attention to promise theory, whether or not they think that the point of contract is to enforce promise-based obligations. Thus Kimel, who believes that contracts are not promises but substitute for them, draws at the end of his chapter an analogy between contract and promise. Like promises, contracts can both expand autonomy and, when done wrongly, endanger it. Kimel suggests that this helps explain doctrines like the consideration requirement and the common use of money damages rather than specific performance. And Kimel's thoughts about a promisee's moral obligation to sometimes release

[24] Gregory Klass, *Efficient Breach, in* Philosophical Foundations of Contract Law 362, 363 (Gregory Klass, George Letsas, & Prince Saprai eds., 2014).

[25] Murphy, *The Practice of Promise and Contract*, at 163.

a promisor find their counterpart in George Letsas and Prince Saprai's observations, discussed below, about a nonbreaching party's obligation to mitigate damages. Similarly, Owens's analysis in this volume of transfer theories of promise has implications for transfer theories of contract. Raz's observations about the limits on a promisor's power to decide the strength of her promise suggest ways of thinking about whether parties should have the power to specify the remedy for breach. And the Owens and Raz chapters both suggest that contract theorists might pay more attention to the legal powers of the promisee, such as waiver, demanding adequate assurance, affirmation, cancellation, and a suit for breach. In short, one need not be a promise theorist to think that a clear understanding of the morality of promising is likely to cast new light on the law of contract.

The moral theories discussed above largely assume a sphere of moral obligations that exists and can be specified independently of the law of contracts. Other theorists argue instead for an intrinsic and distinctive morality of contract—one that might well be compatible with both consent and efficiency theories. Daniel Markovits has argued that contracts generate not promises but a distinctive form of moral relationship all their own.[26] In his chapter in this volume, Markovits argues that, properly understood, the obligation of good faith that attaches to every contract exemplifies a more general moral relationship of solidarity that contracts produce. The case begins with an analysis of the outer bounds of the duty. The duty of good faith is, Markovits argues, both "thin (being limited to respect for an antecedently and independently agreed surplus allocation) and flexible (being open to any surplus allocation on which the parties have so agreed)."[27] On this interpretation, the duty is neither a separate obligation nor a gap-filling rule, but simply the obligation to abide by the parties' shared intentions with respect to their agreement. A party's duty of good faith is her obligation not to "abandon her contractual intentions, including the intention to adjust to unanticipated contingencies in a fashion that secures the success of the contractual collaboration's shared plan."[28] This attitude and the distinctive form of solidarity it generates together define a moral perspective that underlies not only the marketplace, but liberal democratic societies more generally.

Markovits's project is to describe a moral relation distinctive of contractual relationships. That project involves abstracting from the various other moral relations in which contracting parties might find themselves. Thus Markovits goes so far as to suggest that "contract possesses the power to launder injustice, creating legitimate entitlements between parties where previously there were none."[29] Several other contributors emphasize instead ways in which nonvoluntary moral obligations apply to contracting parties in their relations with one another. Without denying that contracts are distinguished by voluntary obligations—moral, legal, or both—these authors argue that contracts also implicate other values or moral principles, and that a complete account of contract law must attend to those values or principles as well.

[26] *See* Daniel Markovits, *Contract and Collaboration*, 113 Yale L.J. 1417 (2004).

[27] Daniel Markovits, *Good Faith as Contract's Core Value, in* Philosophical Foundations of Contract Law 272, 282 (Gregory Klass, George Letsas, & Prince Saprai eds., 2014).

[28] Markovits, *Good Faith as Contract's Core Value*, at 292.

[29] Markovits, *Good Faith as Contract's Core Value*, at 291.

Aditi Bagchi argues that as a result of the exclusive focus on promise, "contract is not regarded as an elaboration of the standards of fairness in private exchange, which might plausibly involve a range of moral principles, but as only a deconstruction of the morality of promising."[30] Bagchi is interested in distributive justice, and especially the fact that the background conditions of many contracts involve unjust distribution. She allows that contract law is in several respects a poor tool for doing distributive justice. Contracts enforce particular agreements, whereas distributive injustice is systematic; the consent of the disadvantaged party might seem to vitiate broader claims of distributive justice; and there is a real worry that the attempts to regulate inequality in exchange will backfire and impose greater harms on disadvantaged parties, whether by producing iniquitous terms elsewhere in the transaction or by excluding disadvantaged parties from the market. But even granting these worries, Bagchi argues, distributive injustices should sometimes inform when society chooses to provide a party with the benefit of legal enforcement. And a complete account of contract law must attend to distributive justice, since "some of the background duties that infuse contract are derivative from principles of distributive justice."[31]

As already mentioned, George Letsas and Prince Saprai argue in their chapter that the mitigation rule is best explained by obligations that are neither promissory nor specific to contracts. They maintain that the rule is not, as Charles Fried has argued, grounded in a duty of altruism generated by the parties' relationship, but that it is a special application of a general principle of fairness. Although the nonbreaching party has no altruistic duty to avoid losses, it would be unfair for her to claim compensation for losses that she could have avoided without undue burden. Letsas and Saprai argue that the doctrinal elaborations of the mitigation rule found in English law largely conform to the requirements of the fairness principle. And, they argue, the appeal to fairness provides answers to Seana Shiffrin's claim that the mitigation rule is inconsistent with promissory morality and to Dori Kimel's argument that the mitigation rule is grounded in the harm principle. "[S]eemingly divergent doctrines of contract law can be justified if one considers the interaction between the promise principle and other moral principles."[32]

Mindy Chen-Wishart's chapter also describes a "conceptual space for the operation of principles beyond consent" in contract law.[33] Chen-Wishart's analysis focuses on vitiating factors such as incapacity, unconscionability, mistake, misrepresentation and duress, or what in the United States are commonly termed "formation defenses." She argues that these doctrines are structured to impose responsibility for reasonable expectations and reliance, to ensure fair dealing and withhold state support for exploitation, to advance both corrective and distributive justice, to advance community

[30] Aditi Bagchi, *Distributive Justice and Contract, in* Philosophical Foundations of Contract Law 193, 193 (Gregory Klass, George Letsas, & Prince Saprai eds., 2014).

[31] Bagchi, *Distributive Justice and Contract*, at 199.

[32] George Letsas & Prince Saprai, *Mitigation, Fairness, and Contract Law, in* Philosophical Foundations of Contract Law 319, 339 (Gregory Klass, George Letsas, & Prince Saprai eds., 2014).

[33] Mindy Chen-Wishart, *The Nature of Vitiating Factors in Contract Law, in* Philosophical Foundations of Contract Law 294, 294 (Gregory Klass, George Letsas, & Prince Saprai eds., 2014).

values, and to ensure administrability. After considering and rejecting consent-based accounts of these rules, Chen-Wishart argues that autonomy is a defeasible principle—one that can be overridden by other principles, policies, and values. Against the charge that such pluralism provides no guidance for courts when principles recommend different outcomes or rules, Chen-Wishart argues that the several values she identifies are complementary. More specifically, and echoing Raz, because "[t]he value of autonomy depends on the worthiness of its exercise," respect for autonomy requires also attending to the values that establish that worthiness.[34]

Letsas and Saprai's and Chen-Wishart's chapters each argue that consent- or promise-based principles fail to fully explain or justify the rules of contract law we find in the world around us. To the extent that their arguments start from the contract law we have, they can be classified as broadly interpretive. Stephen Smith's chapter on remedies also adopts an interpretive approach, though here Smith is interested less in the moral basis of contract law than in its function.[35] Smith poses a basic question about contract remedies: Is the reason for granting the remedy the parties' first-order duty to perform, as suggested by many corrective justice theories, or is it the fact that a wrong has been committed by that duty's breach? Smith argues for the latter interpretation, based on the structure and framing of common law damage awards, as well as more particular remedial rules such as the privity requirement and the ready availability of consequential damages. More broadly, the law does not impose a duty to pay damage upon breach, but does so only after a court ruling that identifies the appropriate remedy for the wrong. Together with additional theoretical considerations, these facts suggest that "the aim of damages is to provide redress for wrongs,"[36] and "damages orders create rather than confirm duties."[37] Like a fine or punitive damages, compensatory damages for breach mark that a wrong has been committed and shift responsibility for the consequences of that wrong to the wrongdoer. "[D]amages are the private law equivalent of punishment."[38]

Smith's analysis exemplifies a tradition of interpretive and conceptual legal analysis that is stronger in Commonwealth countries than in the United States. Such scholarship aims to uncover the law's immanent logic and the legal principles that a common law judge might rely on to extend an existing rule to a novel case or to resolve inconsistencies within the doctrine. To U.S. theorists and jurists steeped in the Legal Realist tradition, such arguments might appear formalist. But they can also figure into theories of the function or justification of contract law by suggesting alternative purposes the law might serve, and providing a better understanding of which theories fit with existing practice and which recommend revising it.

Much in contract theory depends on the choice of examples or paradigm cases. Those who find the function of contract in the parties' moral obligations often focus

[34] Chen-Wishart, *The Nature of Vitiating Factors in Contract Law*, at 315.

[35] Smith's interpretive argument for a rights-based promise theory of contract can be found in Stephen A. Smith, Contract Theory (2004).

[36] Stephen A. Smith, *Remedies for Breach of Contract: One Principle or Two?*, *in* Philosophical Foundations of Contract Law 341, 354 (Gregory Klass, George Letsas, & Prince Saprai eds., 2014).

[37] Smith, *Remedies for Breach of Contract*, at 356.

[38] Smith, *Remedies for Breach of Contract*, at 356.

on relatively low-stakes agreements between natural persons. Those who think of contract primarily as a private legislative power are more likely to emphasize high-stakes transactions between sophisticated parties, especially firms. (Barnett, whose consent theory is grounded in libertarian considerations, is an exception to the latter generalization.) The importance of examples can also be seen in the differences between the contributions of Lisa Bernstein and Margaret Jane Radin.

Working within a broadly instrumentalist framework, Lisa Bernstein explores the interaction between legal obligations and extralegal forms of assurance such as repeat-play, reputation, and nonlegal norms. Her thesis is twofold. First, she argues against attempts to give legal effect to customary business norms, commonly referred to as "trade usage." Using a mix of empirical and informal economic analysis, Bernstein argues that in many economic spheres there is no widespread agreement on trade usage, that where trade usage does exist it is often difficult to verify in court, and that most sophisticated parties do not want courts to use trade usage to interpret their agreements. Second, Bernstein criticizes courts' use of two other types of context evidence: course of dealings—the parties' actions in earlier similar transactions—and course of performance—how the parties performed under the contract at issue. One problem with using such evidence is that every deviation from contractual requirements then has the potential to change the parties' legal obligations. That result is likely to deter the flexibility in performance that many contemporary transactions require, which in turn can prevent the parties from utilizing "extralegal commitments backed only by reputation bonds and other types of nonlegal sanctions."[39] Another problem is that the use of such evidence increases a large organization's costs of doing business, as it must constantly monitor employees' actions to guard against unwanted changes to the organization's legal obligations. Again, Bernstein collects a range of empirical evidence that, for these and other reasons, sophisticated parties commonly craft their contracts to exclude such evidence from the interpretation of their contracts. If Bernstein is correct, no matter what the social interest in enforcing the obligations generated by parties' actual expectations and agreements, many sophisticated parties do not want such enforcement. And if given the opportunity, they will contract out of it.

Bernstein's arguments are an example of the new formalism in contract theory. "New" here refers not to the theory's vintage. The arguments have now been around for over 20 years.[40] It is used, rather, to distinguish the theory from an older formalism often associated with Christopher Columbus Langdell and Samuel Williston and sharply criticized by the first generation of Legal Realists. In contrast to the old formalism, the new formalism employs instrumentalist, economic, and empirical arguments, putting it squarely in the Realist camp.

Margaret Jane Radin's chapter also adopts a broadly empirical and Realist approach, but emphasizes the costs of formalism in other contracting contexts. Where Bernstein

[39] Lisa Bernstein, *Merchant Law in a Modern Economy, in* Philosophical Foundations of Contract Law 238, 258 (Gregory Klass, George Letsas, & Prince Saprai eds., 2014).

[40] For an early example, *see* Robert E. Scott, *A Relational Theory of Default Rules for Commercial Contracts*, 19 J. Legal Stud. 597 (1990); for a recent example, *see* Ronald J. Gilson, Charles F. Sabel, & Robert E. Scott, *Contract and Innovation: The Limited Role of Generalist Courts in the Evolution of Novel Contractual Forms*, 88 N.Y.U. L. Rev. 170 (2013).

is interested in the rules for interpreting valid contracts, Radin focuses on the rules that determine whether a contract is valid. And where Bernstein limits her analysis to contracts between sophisticated parties, Radin considers transactions with nonsophisticates. Radin's topic is transactions in which an unsophisticated party agrees to a form contract provided on a take-it-or-leave-it basis by a sophisticated party that engages in many similar transactions. Common examples of such "boilerplate" contracts include employment contracts, consumer contracts, and the licensing agreements to which users "agree" every time they choose to install or update a piece of software. The enforcement of these agreements in the United States turns almost entirely on the nonsophisticated party's formal act of agreement, without a significant inquiry into the quality of her consent or the fairness of the terms. The reason, Radin argues, is that in the United States the only mechanism for policing these agreements is the judicially developed unconscionability doctrine. After identifying several problems with that approach, Radin suggests a nonformalist framework for determining when to enforce boilerplate terms. Here Radin emphasizes not only the potential costs to the individual who agrees to unfavorable terms, but also the costs of the "large-scale remedy-deletion"[41] as terms proliferate, especially with respect to entitlements that are "components of public regimes underwritten by the polity for the sake of the structure of the polity itself."[42] Radin argues that we should not think of such entitlements as either alienable or inalienable. Rather, some entitlements should be made more difficult to sell than others. And if a contract purports to transfer such an entitlement, the legal rule should examine not only the quality of consent and the effects for the parties, but also the social and political effects of widespread use of the term at issue. Public structures such as tort, contract, and antidiscrimination law "should not be undermined by individual contracts, especially not when the contracts themselves may in fact be non-contracts."[43]

Several chapters in this book address metatheoretical issues, such as what is the question contract theorists should be asking and what sorts of arguments, analyses, or data can succeed in answering it. Charlie Webb spends a number of pages arguing for the possibility of nonevaluative accounts of legal practices generally.

> Legal practice... provides us with two distinct objects of inquiry: (1) we can inquire into how, as a matter of fact, decisions are and have been made within a particular community or across a set of communities; and (2) we can adopt the perspective of those acting within such a community, setting out to answer the same practical questions they face, identifying how they really *ought* to act.[44]

Webb deploys the possibility of nonevaluative legal theory to argue against the relevance of interpretive theory along the lines Dworkin describes and Smith and others practice.[45]

[41] Margaret Jane Radin, *An Analytic Framework for Legal Evaluation of Boilerplate, in* PHILOSOPHICAL FOUNDATIONS OF CONTRACT LAW 215, 217 (Gregory Klass, George Letsas, & Prince Saprai eds., 2014).

[42] Radin, *An Analytic Framework*, at 236.

[43] Radin, *An Analytic Framework*, at 237.

[44] Webb, *Contract as Fact and as Reason*, at 137 (footnote omitted).

[45] RONALD DWORKIN, LAW'S EMPIRE (1986). Jules Coleman, no Dworkinian, also defends the relevance of interpretive legal theory. JULES L. COLEMAN, THE PRACTICE OF PRINCIPLE: IN DEFENCE OF A PRAGMATIST APPROACH TO LEGAL THEORY 3–12 (2001).

> [W]hile we shouldn't deny that an inquiry into reasons which might be said to support these practices has the option not to consider those reasons on their merits, once we abandon the search for the reasons which have *in fact* guided these practices, it's not clear why this is an option anyone would want to take.[46]

Other chapters also address what makes for good contract theory. Murphy argues that contract theorists should attend to the normative structure of existing contract laws, but should not treat that structure as a limit on the contract law we might want. Katz's chapter on economic analysis is as much about the method of doing contract theory as it is about the purpose or design contract law. Bernstein's chapter illustrates ways contract theorists might engage more with empirical work. And Murphy and I both argue that they should engage more with economic analyses of contract.

In our attempt to capture both the substantive and methodological variety of contract theory within the space of a single volume we have had to omit examples of each. If Oxford University Press had given us two volumes for this project, we would also have included examples of reliance theories,[47] of corrective justice theories,[48] of civil recourse theories,[49] and of transfer theories.[50] We would also have sought out examples of critical theories of contract,[51] recent attempts to apply behavioral economics and the methods of empirical psychology to contract law,[52] and theories that draw from major philosophical frameworks such as those of Hegel or Aristotle.[53] We believe, however, that the selection presented here will provide the reader with a general introduction to the field. And we are enormously grateful to the contributors to this volume, whose novel works are significantly advancing our understanding of contract.

[46] Webb, *Contract as Fact and as Reason*, at 141.

[47] The classic reliance theorist was P. S. Atiyah. *See, e.g.*, P. S. Atiyah, *Contracts, Promises and the Law of Obligations*, 94 LAW Q. REV. 193 (1978). For more recent work along these lines, *see* T. M. Scanlon, *Promises and Contracts, in* THE THEORY OF CONTRACT LAW: NEW ESSAYS 86 (Peter Benson ed., 2001).

[48] *See, e.g.*, Ernest J. Weinrib, *Punishment & Disgorgement as Contract Remedies*, 78 CHI.-KENT L. REV. 55 2003; Curtis Bridgeman, *Reconciling Strict Liability with Corrective Justice in Contract Law*, 75 FORDHAM L. REV. 3013 (2007).

[49] *See, e.g.*, Nathan B. Oman, *Consent to Retaliation: A Civil Recourse Theory of Contractual Liability*, 96 IOWA L. REV. 529 (2011).

[50] *See, e.g.*, Andrew S. Gold, *A Property Theory of Contract*, 103 NW. U. L. REV. 1 (2009).

[51] *See, e.g.*, Duncan Kennedy, *Form & Substance in Private Law Adjudication*, 89 HARV. L. REV. 1685 (1976); Robert W. Gordon, *Unfreezing Legal Reality: Critical Approaches to Law*, 15 FLA. ST. U. L. REV. 195 (1987); Patricia J. Williams, *Alchemical Notes: Reconstructing Ideals from Deconstructed Rights*, 22 HARV. C.R.-C.L. L. REV. 401 (1987).

[52] *See, e.g.*, Melvin Aron Eisenberg, *The Limits of Cognition and the Limits of Contract*, 47 STAN. L. REV. 213 (1995); Tess Wilkinson-Ryan & David A. Hoffman, *Breach is for Suckers*, 63 VAND. L. REV. 1001 (2010).

[53] *See, e.g.*, Peter Benson, *The Unity of Contract Law, in* THE THEORY OF CONTRACT LAW: NEW ESSAYS 118 (Peter Benson ed., 2001); James Gordley, *Contract Law in the Aristotelian Tradition, in* THE THEORY OF CONTRACT LAW: NEW ESSAYS 265 (Peter Benson ed., 2001).

PART I

THEORETICAL APPROACHES

2

The Ambitions of *Contract as Promise*

*Charles Fried**

Contract as Promise[1] had as its overriding ambition connecting a number of salient doctrines of contract law to—indeed deriving them from—a central organizing moral and doctrinal principle: the promise principle. The burgeoning literature on contract practice and theory, and particularly the vast and sophisticated law-and-economics contribution to that literature, has cast doubt on the completeness and indeed the validity of that account. Particularly striking is the fact that the more or less utilitarian analyses of the law-and-economics school should often converge on the same conclusions as so Kantian a work as *Contract as Promise*. Other theorists, however, have criticized *Contract as Promise* as insufficiently faithful to its moral premises.[2] Still others have faulted the work for simply not accounting at all for important aspects of contract law. All this has caused me to think again. That reflection has led me to a less doctrinaire but more plausible account of topics such as consideration and contract damages. Also I was wrong to treat topics such as frustration, impossibility, and unconscionability as not belonging to contract law at all, gathered there only for indexical convenience because they come up to supplement or contradict contract law properly so called. Finally, I was wrong to take no account of the problems and practice of interpreting promissory and contractual undertakings. Most contract disputes have to do with disagreements about interpretation, and the topics of good faith and the effect of writing can be gathered under that rubric. Many of the deficiencies of my analysis can be attributed to my failure to take sufficient account of the evident fact that in passing from the realm of moral to that of legal obligation the predilections and obligations (moral and otherwise) of third parties (judges, jurors, legislators), who are not parties to the promise and not bound to its terms, are necessarily involved.

* This chapter revises, expands on, and changes focus from an essay responding to the many scholars who did me the honor of participating in a symposium, Contract as Promise *at 30: The Future of Contract Theory* in March 2011 at Suffolk University Law School. The papers presented at that symposium as well as my response to them are collected in 45 SUFFOLK U. L. REV. 601 *et seq.* (2012). Earlier versions of this chapter were presented at workshops at Harvard Law School, Columbia Law School, University College, London, and at a conference on The Philosophical Foundations of Contract Law at University College, London. I am grateful for the encouragement and many useful suggestions that emerged from those occasions and especially to John Goldberg, Avery Katz, Dori Kimel, Jeffrey Lipshaw, Daniel Markovits, and Robert Scott, and for the research assistance of Aaron Benjamin of the Harvard Law School class of 2014 and Ryan Galisewski of the Harvard Law School class of 2013.

1 CHARLES FRIED, CONTRACT AS PROMISE: A THEORY OF CONTRACTUAL OBLIGATION (1981).

2 *See* notes 34–6.

But at the end of the day (or 30-plus years) I still believe that *Contract as Promise* is correct to locate as the generating genius of this body of law the promise principle, the moral invention that facilitates human collaboration by self-imposed moral obligation.

I

In the late 1970s, when *Contract as Promise* was written, there were two views of contract in the field: a traditional, doctrinal, and not particularly theorized view that saw contract as the law's way of allowing private parties to create and enforce the terms that would govern transactions and long-term undertakings,[3] and a critical literature that saw contract law as a tool of social control imposing obligations on parties growing in part, but only in part, from dealings into which they had voluntarily entered. Of course, it was commonly recognized that society gains from the exchange of goods and services—not only immediately as with barter, but over time as with the system of credit and the stored value of money—and that therefore society was often justified in facilitating and enforcing the terms of such exchanges. But because promises are obligations freely chosen and undertaken, the aspect of social control on the traditional view was mediated by and responsive to the voluntary undertakings of the parties.

On the second view, the aspect of social control dominates—practically and theoretically. What we think of as contract law is in fact a system of government administration of the provision of goods and services—that present or future goods and services might in turn be allocated to the providers is a possible but not a foundational tenet. The government administrator (usually a judge) will make this allocation of burdens and benefits based on a variety of criteria: the relative virtues of the parties before him, the value they have or will provide to the state, their needs and capacities, their connections to members of the government. And, of course, the judge may—or may not—take into account what the parties have set out as their arrangement going into the relationship and the effect that any decision may have on incentives to cooperate in the future. The more or less explicit mode of deciding commercial and property disputes in the Soviet Union and the implicit but well understood method for resolving such disputes in the courts of contemporary China (and Russia) exemplify this system in action. (To be sure, as an instance of Rochefoucauld's maxim that hypocrisy is the homage that vice pays to virtue,[4] contemporary Chinese and Russian legal systems deploy the paraphernalia of the promissory system, but no party with the means and opportunity to address the real decision makers and the factors that motivate them will omit to do so as effectively as possible.) Those who proclaim the superiority and sometimes the inevitability of the administrative model rarely embrace it in its

[3] The Restatement defines a contract as a "promise or a set of promises for the breach of which the law gives a remedy, or the performance of which the law in some way recognizes as a duty." Restatement (Second) of Contracts § 1 (1981).

[4] François Duc De La Rouchefocauld, Moral Maximes 218 (Leonard Tancock trans., Penguin 1959) (1665).

full-blown form, preferring to see contract law as assimilable to other, more frankly administrative legal regimes, or at least doctrines within such regimes.

The signal work on this second view is Robert Lee Hale's *Coercion and Distribution in a Supposedly Non-Coercive State*.[5] Hale placed the concepts of duress and coercion, which the promissory regime treats as anomalies calling for occasional ad hoc administrative intervention and correction, at the heart of all supposedly voluntary transactions,[6] and reconceptualized them as covert exercises of power and dominance which the government (the courts) can either endorse or correct.[7] A later, less thoroughgoing variant sought to assimilate contract law to tort, which is more readily conceived of as a regime for adjusting—on grounds of perceived fairness, social utility, or redistribution—the burdens arising out of involuntary encounters.[8] The promissory model was associated (and on this view discredited by that association) with an individualistic ethos friendly to capitalism and free markets, the administrative one with a more socializing, communitarian ethos. The most prominent works in this genre were Grant Gilmore's *The Death of Contract*[9] and Patrick Atiyah's *The Rise and Fall of Freedom of Contract*.[10] Atiyah nicely captured the time's anti-individualist and anti-capitalist tone:

> Promise-based liability rests upon a belief in the traditional liberal values of free choice. Many still admire these values but they bring with them, inescapably, many other consequences which are today less admired, especially in England. They bring, in particular, the recognition that some individuals are better equipped to exercise free choice than others, through natural aptitude, education, or the possession of wealth. And the greater is the scope for the exercise of free choice, the stronger is the tendency for these original inequalities to perpetuate themselves by maintaining or even increasing economic inequalities.[11]

Atiyah is particularly concerned to associate with these—he thinks—increasingly obsolete values of promise-based contractual liability, the enforcement of purely executory contracts and a damage regime measured by the expectations that such contracts generate. To this purely promissory and forward-looking ground for contractual obligation, he contrasts more sympathetic, backward-looking grounds of liability based on the harm that a disappointed promisee suffered when he acted in reliance on the promise, or on the benefit that the disappointed promisee has conferred on the faithless promisor. These grounds of liability would cause contract law to disappear into

[5] 38 Pol. Sci. Q. 470 (1923).

[6] Hale's focus is primarily on property rights and the power dynamics created by property, but his logic may readily be extrapolated to contract. *See Coercion and Distribution* at 474.

[7] Hale, *Coercion and Distribution*, at 471–2.

[8] *See* John C. P. Goldberg & Benjamin C. Zipursky, *Seeing Tort Law from the Internal Point of View: Holmes and Hart on Legal Duties*, 75 Fordham L. Rev. 1563, 1571 n. 34 (2006).

[9] Grant Gilmore, The Death of Contract (1974).

[10] P. S. Atiyah, The Rise and Fall of Freedom of Contract (1979). Atiyah did acknowledge the inevitability of using the expectation measure in contracts whose purpose was the allocation of risks between the parties, but failed to *see* that most, if not all, contracts include exactly that purpose. *See* The Rise and Fall of Freedom of Contract at 5.

[11] The Rise and Fall of Freedom of Contract at 6. This was written before the Thatcher premiership.

the backward-looking grounds of tort and restitutionary liability, and that absorption of contract into tort was the thesis of Gilmore's book.[12]

The socializing thrust of Hale's, Gilmore's, and Atiyah's critiques of contract law was also associated with the post-1960s and often Marxist-tinged avatar of legal realism, the Critical Legal Studies movement. The critical legal theorists disputed, indeed mocked, the pretensions of standard contract doctrine as providing a neutral framework for discerning and implementing the terms of agreements freely arrived at. These scholars delighted in showing not only that these supposedly neutral doctrines were often contradictory and incoherent, but also that the real energy behind contract adjudication—as elsewhere in the law—was provided by powerful forces implementing their social agendas. Those agendas depended on the interests of those in power and those whom they represented or with whom they made common cause. The signal work in this genre was Duncan Kennedy's *Form and Substance in Private Law Adjudication*.[13]

Against these intellectual and cultural themes, *Contract as Promise* sought to assert the coherence of standard contract doctrine as providing the structure by which actors could determine for themselves the terms of their interaction and cooperation—whether in commercial or personal relations. The thesis was avowedly moralizing. It was based on a morality of autonomy, respect for persons, and trust. Promise is a kind of moral invention: its mode of causation is moral causation;[14] it allows persons to create obligation where there was none before, and thus it gives free individuals a facility for extending their reach by enlisting the reliable collaboration of other free persons. That we must not harm one another and that we must fulfill the terms of special relationships that may not have been of our choosing are moral obligations that are laid upon us. The obligation of a promise we lay upon ourselves. To be sure, this remarkable feature of promises can be trivialized by saying that the obligation of the institution of promising[15] precedes any particular promissory obligations we may assume; but the fact remains that until we invoke the institution and do so with the very purpose of activating its obligations, those distinct obligations do not exist. It is a remarkable feature of the institution that what before was—or may have been[16]—morally

[12] To the extent that the law of torts is more and more a law of insurance, it might be more apt to conclude that tort is being progressively absorbed into contract. *See generally* CHARLES FRIED & DAVID ROSENBERG, MAKING TORT LAW: WHAT SHOULD BE DONE AND WHO SHOULD DO IT (2003).

[13] Duncan Kennedy, *Form and Substance in Private Law Adjudication*, 89 HARV. L. REV. 1685 (1976).

[14] Charles Fried, *Moral Causation*, 77 HARV. L. REV. 1258 (1964).

[15] There has been a very large recent philosophical literature on the moral obligation of promises. Thomas Scanlon resists the argument—which goes back at least to Hume—that "promises. . . derive their moral force from a social institution." T. M. SCANLON, WHAT WE OWE TO EACH OTHER 315 (1998). His Principle *F* includes as a necessary element that "A acts with the aim of providing. . . [desired] assurance" that A will perform. WHAT WE OWE TO EACH OTHER at 304. It seems to me that a promise is a distinctive if not the paradigmatic way of providing that assurance. Scanlon's discussion of lying, with which I agree (*see* my text immediately below), strengthens my conviction in this regard, for lying (and truth-telling) paradigmatically depends on the institution of language, and in this sense language too may be taken as a human invention that creates the possibility of moral obligations and moral wrongs analogous to the institution of promising.

[16] I qualify here because it is quite possible that a person may unintentionally incur an obligation to another by acting in such a way that the other person has come to rely on him, and that he is obliged to avoid the harm that would be caused by the disappointment of that reliance. But that is not a promise. *See* FRIED, CONTRACT AS PROMISE, at 9–14. *Compare with* Thomas Scanlon and his Principle *L*. T. M.

indifferent or optional becomes nonoptional, and it becomes nonoptional because we want it to be so as a way of achieving our purposes.

This is not to say that promissory obligation in general does not have its roots in deeper moral soil. The institution is not an invention *ex nihilo*. It depends on the deeper morality of trust and respect for persons. It is an institution, like language, that allows us to accomplish an infinite variety of ends. But the efficacy of language depends on a morality of truth telling. If communications had no more than a random relation to the truth, language would be useless to accomplish its (our) ends. Truthfulness depends on trust, and trust on a morality of mutual respect. Trust may be (mis)characterized as merely providing a more or less secure prediction of another's future behavior. ("Trust him to lie, cheat and steal if he thinks he can get away with it.") But trust allows a particular kind of prediction, coordination, and collaboration based on a recursive and transparent mirroring of mutual recognition and respect. We start with respect, which allows trust, which allows language, which finally allows the institution of promising. At each step along the way our moral powers are amplified, as if each raised to a higher power the moral capacity of the one before. And, as I said in *Contract as Promise*, what starts as a means for enlarging human purposes becomes—perhaps only adverbially—an end in itself: it is desirable to attain our ends by the route of trust and promising, even if we could get there, and quite innocently, just as well without them.[17]

II

Thirty years later, the intellectual fashion that provoked *Contract as Promise* has faded from prominence. In its place has arisen a voluminous and often intricate literature offering alternative accounts and justifications for what might be called the classical law of contract. Indeed, the economic analysis of law may today be the dominant intellectual approach to legal institutions generally and to contract law in particular. Law and economics has evolved and ramified since 1973, when Richard Posner published *The Economic Analysis of Law*.[18] The empirical study of actual economic decision making is one example, which has been particularly important when applied to the economics of law. This ramification is the sign of a vibrant and dominant field. And whatever else may be the case, the law-and-economics movement certainly shares nothing of the nihilistic and anti-freemarket dispositions of the critical legal studies movement.[19] Work in the economic analysis of contract law takes three related forms: one analytical,

Scanlon, *Promises and Contracts, in* The Theory of Contract Law: New Essays 86, 92 (Peter Benson ed., 2001). Such an unintentionally incurred obligation, while not (I believe) promissory may yet be contractual as a result of the considerations I discuss in Section V. *See* Fried, Contract as Promise, at 9–11.

[17] Fried, Contract as Promise, at 16–17; *see also* John Rawls, A Theory of Justice, § 86, *The Good of the Sense of Justice* (1971); Seana Valentine Shiffrin, *Paternalism, Unconscionability Doctrine, and Accommodation*, 29 Phil. & Pub. Aff. 205, 221 (2000).

[18] Richard Posner, Economic Analysis of Law 15–20 (8th ed., 2011).

[19] For a concise and incisive statement of the economic point of view and a sharp critique of *Contract as Promise*, *see* Richard Craswell, *Contract Law, Default Rules, and the Philosophy of Promising*, 88 Mich. L. Rev. 489 (1989).

one empirical, and one normative. The analytical takes as its premise that rational actors seek to maximize their long-term advantage and will prefer legal arrangements that facilitate its attainment. In respect to contract, its institutions may be analyzed either as serving this disposition of the contracting parties or, if they do not, as serving the interests of some other class of actors, or finally as irrational. The empirical investigates actual economic decision making in particular contexts, as it often diverges from what the rational actor model posits. The normative law-and-economics account starts with a premise not dissimilar to that embraced by *Contract as Promise*: the law should be designed to allow people in a voluntary relationship to structure that relationship in the way that they judge will best serve their interests over the long run,[20] at least insofar as they may be deemed the best judges of their own interests. This premise builds on several background constraints that also accord with *Contract as Promise*: for instance, that the arrangement does not impose on third parties costs that those third parties have any moral right to complain about;[21] that the contracting individuals are ordinarily competent judges of their own welfare; and that neither individual has been forced or deceived into entering the relationship. Most distinctive for both the law-and-economics analysis of contracts and the morality of promising that underlies *Contract as Promise* is the assumption that individuals (promising or contracting) have a certain persistence as entities over time—what an individual chooses for his future he is choosing for himself and not for another person who will just happen to have the same name and D.N.A.; and what he gets by that choice he may not complain of as if it had been chosen for him by someone else.[22]

Law-and-economics analysis is avowedly utilitarian and proceeds from a premise of consumer sovereignty or subjective measure of welfare,[23] while *Contract as Promise*

[20] Professor Craswell argues, for example, that the point of law generally is enhancing social welfare, not by moral force but by facilitating investment in, and exchange of, better products and services; and contract law improves the quality of contract as a "product" in this sense. Richard Craswell, *Promises and Prices*, 45 SUFFOLK U. L. REV. 735, 738–9, 776 (2012). Daniel Markovits and Alan Schwartz justify expectation damages as the most likely to encourage the maximization of economic surplus, while George Triantis and Juliet Kostritsky question whether the expectation damage remedy truly reflects the choice of many contracting parties. *See* Daniel Markovits & Alan Schwartz, *The Expectation Remedy and the Promissory Basis of Contract*, 45 SUFFOLK U. L. REV. 799 (2012); George Triantis, *Promissory Autonomy, Imperfect Courts, and the Immorality of the Expectation Default Remedy*, 45 SUFFOLK U. L. REV. 827 (2012); Juliet P. Kostritsky, *The Promise Principle and Contract Interpretation*, 45 SUFFOLK U. L. REV. 843 (2012).

[21] For instance, if Dick and Jane agree to enter into an intimate relationship, this may cause considerable pain to Dick's disappointed rival, but it is not an effect the rival has any moral right to complain of. And more generally, disappointed rivals in a fair competition have no moral title to complain. There are exceptions to these generalities, as well as disputes about what constitutes fair competition, but the law ought to attempt to reflect these understandings as best it can.

[22] This last premise has been a concern of mine since writing *An Anatomy of Values*. CHARLES FRIED, *Life Plans and Mortality*, *in* AN ANATOMY OF VALUES: PROBLEMS OF PERSONAL AND SOCIAL CHOICE 155, 155–82 (1970). It takes on an institutional character in *Saying What the Law Is*. CHARLES FRIED, SAYING WHAT THE LAW IS: THE CONSTITUTION IN THE SUPREME COURT 6–10 (2004). It is the subject of the profound work of Derek Parfit. *See, e.g.*, Derek Parfit, *Personal Identity*, 80 PHIL. REV. 3–27 (1971). The recent development of what has come to be known as behavioral law and economics may be understood as questioning the premises of rationality and continuity. One is left wondering what the normative—as opposed to the purely descriptive—entailments of this move might be: a kind of paternalism for sure, but measured by what metric? *See, e.g.*, Richard Thaler & Cass Sunstein, *Libertarian Paternalism*, 93 AM. ECON. REV. 175 (2003) (arguing for a "libertarian paternalism" that preserves "free" choice but creates situations in which individuals are subtly pressured to make the "right" choice).

[23] *See, e.g.*, LOUIS KAPLOW & STEVEN SHAVELL, FAIRNESS VERSUS WELFARE (2002); POSNER, ECONOMIC ANALYSIS OF LAW.

is Kantian and more or less takes its cue from Kant's *The Metaphysical Elements of Justice*.[24] That the two should arrive at similar conclusions on many of the main points of contract doctrine[25] is striking. Differences come to the fore when the issue is the effect of social arrangements on the overall welfare of groups,[26] as opposed to the joint welfare of two contracting parties. The convergence is particularly salient in the design of institutions that facilitate the coordination, through agreements, of the energies of otherwise independent persons. Legal regimes by their nature are concerned with institutional design, and both the Kantian and utilitarian perspectives focus on maximizing the preferences of individuals *ex ante*;[27] that is, the two perspectives focus on the design of legal regimes and doctrines that collaborating individuals would themselves see as furthering the purposes they hope to achieve in their free collaboration. There may be regret *ex post*, but the Kantian perspective makes the individual responsible for his own regret; the premise of continuity and its entailment of self-respect require an individual to be willing to make commitments into the future, and the corollary of respect for others requires him to abide by those commitments made to others. The famous example is Kant's discussion of lying, and especially the lying promise.[28] Kant's test of universalization—would you be willing to propose the maxim of your action (i.e., the principle on which you act) as a universal law?—is quite congruent with the method of law and economics, which asks whether a rule of (contract) law is one that rational parties would accept *ex ante* to govern the arrangements on which they plan to embark.

That both the Kantian ethics of respect and the economic analysis of law concern themselves with general rules and proceed *ex ante* (i.e., before the parties know how a particular undertaking will work out) explains why the two methods arrive at similar, if not identical conclusions.[29] Utilitarianism and Kantian ethics diverge when

[24] Immanuel Kant, The Metaphysical Elements of Justice (John Ladd trans., The Bobbs-Merrill Co., 2d ed., 1999) (1797).

[25] The strongest and most comprehensive statement of this convergence, from which I have drawn wisdom and encouragement, is Jody S. Kraus, *The Correspondence of Contract and Promise*, 109 Colum. L. Rev. 1603, 1633–4 (2009. *See also* Jody S. Kraus, *Philosophy of Contract Law, in* The Oxford Handbook of Jurisprudence and Philosophy of Law 687 (Jules Coleman & Scott Shapiro eds., 2002).

Tort law is another matter. I had made a less comprehensive attempt at addressing the moral foundations of tort law in Charles Fried, Right and Wrong (1978) and Fried, An Anatomy of Values. In Fried & Rosenberg, Tort Law, our analysis and conclusions over a large range of topics coincided with those of the economic analysis of the subject.

[26] *See* Rawls, A Theory of Justice, §§ 5–6.

[27] It is an old, persistent, and sometimes willful misunderstanding of Kant to claim that he placed no value on the realization of a person's desires, goals, and preferences. From this misunderstanding Kant's critics gleefully conclude that his system is necessarily empty. In modern terminology, the categorical imperative is a constraint, so that only material ends pursued subject to that constraint are of value. An analogous misrepresentation is perpetrated by critics of John Rawls's *A Theory of Justice*, who claim that it is morally indifferent to what goals persons pursue, so long as they pursue them subject to the constraints of justice. This simply ignores the distinction between the right and the good. The ends persons pursue are judged by the theory of the good, but in Kantian fashion these goods only have value if they are pursued within the constraints of the right. Ronald Dworkin has presented a fairly detailed account of a theory of both the right and the good and of how the two relate to each other. This work is summed up in his magisterial, Ronald Dworkin, Justice for Hedgehogs (2011).

[28] Immanuel Kant, Groundwork of the Metaphysics of Morals 97 (H. J. Paton trans., Harper Perennial 2009) (1785).

[29] As John Rawls many times and in many places has acknowledged: the decision procedure by which individuals choose principles to govern their mutual interaction behind a veil of ignorance is very much

they advise particular persons how they should behave *ex post*; Kantian ethics and *Contract as Promise* require that promising (or contracting) parties fulfill the obligations they had embraced *ex ante*. But since the economic analysis of legal rules is an analysis of legal *rules*, it rarely diverges from Kantian ethics in this way. The way in which a divergence between the two might arise shows just how tight their convergence on this point is. Imagine a dispute in which the issue is inequality of bargaining power—for instance, where a consumer knowingly signs a standard contract containing a clause requiring that disputes be submitted to arbitration. There are those who hope the judge in a hard case will find some form of words to explain ruling for the more sympathetic party, even though no rule of law honestly applied would permit this.[30] Perhaps a utilitarian might applaud such judicial (mis)conduct, but the economic analysis of law and *Contract as Promise* would both insist that some rule reasonably applicable to all like cases be available to justify the ruling. They would both agree with Antonio in *The Merchant of Venice*:

> The duke cannot deny the course of law,
> For the commodity that strangers have
> With us in Venice, if it be denied,
> Will much impeach the justice of the state,
> Since that the trade and profit of the city
> Consisteth of all nations.[31]

III

Of particular interest is the large body of literature that claims to find a divergence between standard contract doctrine and *Contract as Promise*, insofar as *Contract as Promise* purports to derive contract doctrine as comporting with, and indeed issuing from Kantian moral premises. (The largest quarrel *Contract as Promise* has with standard doctrine is in the latter's doctrine of consideration.) There have been two strands in these critiques. Both strands insist that standard doctrine diverges from *Contract as Promise*, but they take opposite tacks. Utilitarian-minded economic critics complain that *Contract as Promise* is unsuccessful in accounting in its own moralizing terms for a number of important and practically sound contract doctrines—particularly the expectation measure of damages and the related rule requiring the victim of a breach to make efforts to mitigate his own damages. If promise really were at the heart of contract, then a promisor would be held to perform his exact undertaking—perhaps by a decree of specific performance or by the imposition of punitive damages. But instead, contract doctrine and *Contract as Promise* allow the party in breach to "get away" with

like Kant's formula: "Act only according to that maxim whereby you can, at the same time, will that it should become a universal law." *See* RAWLS, A THEORY OF JUSTICE, § 40.

[30] *See, e.g., Broemmer v. Abortion Servs. of Phx., Ltd.*, 840 P.2d 1013 (Ariz. 1992) (refusing to enforce an "adhesion contract"); *Richards v. Richards*, 513 N.W.2d 118 (Wis. 1997) (refusing to enforce a contract that was "void as against public policy"). This supposed divergence mirrors the well-known difference between act and rule utilitarianism and the controversy whether rule breaking can ever in the long run be truly for the best.

[31] WILLIAM SHAKESPEARE, THE MERCHANT OF VENICE act 3, scene 3 (Jay L. Halio ed., Clarendon Press 1993) (1600).

paying "only" the value of the expected performance.[32] Economists claim this shows that the law is more practical than moral: the law recognizes that a less rigid rule promotes social utility by encouraging a promisor to make the highest and best use of his resources, while awarding the disappointed promisee a money equivalent no greater than the worth of the promised performance. This is the much-mooted argument for the efficient breach. Related to efficient breach is the standard doctrine of mitigation.[33] Economic critics of *Contract as Promise* have been known to argue that if the moral obligation of promise really were the basis of contract, then insult would be added to injury—as it is in standard doctrine—by requiring that the victim of the breach extend himself to minimize the damage that the promisor has caused him.

These same instances are deployed against *Contract as Promise* by those who criticize standard contract doctrine as insufficiently faithful to the morality of promise and meretriciously swayed by (merely) economic arguments to loosen the rigors of promissory morality. They fault *Contract as Promise* for being untrue to its own moral premises by apologizing for these departures from what promissory morality requires. The leading critic along these lines is Seana Shiffrin, who concludes her important article, *The Divergence of Contract and Promise*,[34] by suggesting that the prevalence of expectation damages and the doctrine of efficient breach "may play a role in creating a wider culture in which pressure develops not to comply with the moral commitment, whether just because it is not legally required or because the legal permission spawns cultural habits that render moral compliance precious or alien."[35] Thus, she calls to mind a theme sounded by Atiyah, except that Atiyah celebrates what Shiffrin deplores.[36]

Both the moral criticism and the economic defense of expectation damages persuade me that the case I made for the connection between the promise principle and expectation damages is insufficiently nuanced:

> If I make a promise to you, I should do as I promise; and if I fail to keep my promise, it is fair that I should be made to hand over the equivalent of the promised performance. In contract doctrine this proposition appears as the expectation measure of damages for breach. The expectation standard gives the victim of a breach no more or less than he would have had had there been no breach—in other words, he gets the benefit of his bargain.[37]

Here is the standard example used to illustrate the theory of efficient breach and to justify the expectation measure of damages:

> Seller contracts to manufacture and deliver 14 gross of custom widgets to Buyer for $10 per gross for use as a necessary component in Buyer's unique gizmos. Just

[32] RESTATEMENT (SECOND) OF CONTRACTS § 347 (1981).

[33] RESTATEMENT (SECOND) OF CONTRACTS § 350.

[34] Seana Valentine Shiffrin, *The Divergence of Contract and Promise*, 120 HARV. L. REV. 708 (2007). Contra Kraus, *Correspondence*.

[35] Shiffrin, *Divergence*, at 740.

[36] *See* note 10 and accompanying text.

[37] FRIED, CONTRACT AS PROMISE, at 17. The endnote quotes the RESTATEMENT (FIRST) OF CONTRACTS § 329, cmt. a (1932): "In awarding compensatory damages, the effort is made to put the injured party in as good a position as that in which he would have been put by full performance of the contract. . ." The note also cites Charles J. Goetz & Robert E. Scott, *Enforcing Promises: An Examination of the Basis of Contracts*, 89 YALE L.J. 1261 (1980).

> prior to the date of delivery, Third Party offers Seller $25 per gross for immediate delivery to him of the widgets. Buyer will have to pay $15 per gross for the widgets from another manufacturer and will lose $5 in lost sales for each gross as a result of the delay.

Economists reason that Seller should sell the widgets to Third Party and pay Buyer the $5-per-gross difference in the price of the replacement widgets plus the $5 per gross in lost gizmo sales. Buyer will be no worse off financially than if Seller had faithfully performed, while Seller will be $5 per gross better off, which is roughly equivalent to the additional value to society created by Third Party receiving the early delivery of the widgets—the extra value exists because Third Party valued the widgets more than Buyer. Seller's move, compared to exact performance as promised, is not only Kaldor-Hicks optimal, in that there is a greater sum total of welfare, but also Pareto optimal, because none of the three is worse off and Seller and Third Party are better off. The rule is thus socially optimal because resources are directed without loss to their highest and best use.

Apart from Seana Shiffrin's concern that the efficient breach enabled by the expectation measure fosters a culture of faithless opportunism,[38] there is the objection raised by several contracts scholars[39] that the advantage reaped by the defaulting promisor (the $5 per gross in my example) really belongs to the promisee—Buyer and not the faithless Seller. This objection may be restated in terms that call to mind Kant's treatment of promises in *The Metaphysical Elements of Justice*: by promising, I give a notional property interest in my promised performance to the promisee.[40] And, of course, once viewed in property terms, any surplus would rightfully belong to the promisee.[41] Indeed, that is the legal regime that obtains in respect to contracts for the sale of real property, the standard buyer's remedy being specific performance.

But this line of argument founders—or at least begs the question—if one considers that, after all, the promisor is "master of the bargain" and the whole moral

[38] By contrast, Markovits argues—to my mind convincingly—that "it would be bad faith for a promisee to insist on specific performance, as this would give the promisee a benefit that he did not pay for. . ." Daniel Markovits, *Good Faith as Contract's Core Value, in* this volume, PHILOSOPHICAL FOUNDATIONS OF CONTRACT LAW, 281 (Gregory Klass, George Letsas, & Prince Saprai eds., 2014).

[39] *See* Richard Craswell, *Contract Remedies, Renegotiation, and the Theory of Efficient Breach*, 61 s. CAL. L. REV. 629, 640–2 (1988); Daniel Friedmann, *The Efficient Breach Fallacy*, 18 J. LEGAL STUD. 1, 13–18 (1989). Avery Katz's contribution to the Suffolk symposium takes an original approach to the problem of efficient breach. He notes that the payment of money damages in lieu of performance ought to satisfy deontological concerns in most cases, but wonders whether it makes sense to valorize, in pursuit of a *virtuous* (rather than a *moral*) society, the kind of promises that can be so satisfied. Avery Katz, *Virtue Ethics and Efficient Breach*, 45 SUFFOLK U. L. REV. 777 (2012).

[40] KANT, METAPHYSICAL ELEMENTS OF JUSTICE, §§ 20–1.

[41] The analysis is more plausible as one considers that the promisee can always sell his right to performance, and thus this issue boils down to who captures the surplus. This is illustrated by the leading case of *Groves v. John Wunder Co.*, 286 N.W. 235 (Minn. 1939) (remedy for failure to perform promise to improve land was cost of obtaining similar performance, over $60,000, not difference in value of land, only $12,160). "After the decision . . . the case was compromised and defendant paid $55,000 in a cash settlement." JOHN P. DAWSON, WILLIAM BURNETT HARVEY, STANLEY D. HENDERSON, & DOUGLAS G. BAIRD, CONTRACTS: CASES AND COMMENT 16 (9th ed., 2008).

case is built on respect for the promisor's autonomy, then the promisor should be able to specify not only the substantive terms but also what the bargain is worth in the event of default. Shiffrin's objection thus implies that a promisor should (morally) not be free to specify the remedy for his default, and that substance is for the parties to specify, and remedy for the state (and morality) to determine. This objection can be met by explicitly casting the promise in option terms. It would certainly be an odd kind of moral rigorism to allow freedom of contract to reign as to "substance" but to rule out option contracts.[42] And several commentators have pointed out that, as between sophisticated bargainers, the choice of damages from among the full range of consequences—from relatively small stipulated damages[43] to specific performance, and perhaps even to supercompensatory liquidated damages—will be reflected in the price that the promisee pays at the outset.[44] Indeed, as Avery Katz points out in his chapter in this volume, law-and-economics scholars have long moved beyond the staple efficient breach/widget example made famous by Richard Posner[45] to arguments focused on party-specified remedial regimes, recognizing that the scope of the remedy will enter into the price at the outset. Any rule like Posner's efficient breach rule would then come into play as one of several default rules, supplied by the court in the absence of party specification. The focus of recent law-and-economics literature in this, as in several other issues in contract law I discuss later in this chapter, has shifted to determining which default rules should be adopted and when.[46] The law does, it must be admitted, take Shiffrin's side to the extent that such remedial specification is subject to greater scrutiny and control by the courts than are substantive terms. Supercompensatory damages clauses may be struck down as penalties,[47] and undercompensatory provisions may be struck down as unconscionable.[48] But it is hard to see how such limitations—at least as applied to sophisticated parties—accord with the general principles of freedom of contract and party autonomy. As Judge Richard Posner, citing Goetz and Scott,[49] has said:

> Deep as the hostility to penalty clauses runs in the common law,... we still might be inclined to question, if we thought ourselves free to do so, whether a modern court should refuse to enforce a penalty clause where the signator is a substantial

[42] Indeed, Shiffrin herself works through the conceptual difficulty that the remedy affects the content of a promise—that a contractual promise, which includes for the promisor an effective legal option to perform as promised or pay expectation damages, is best characterized as a promise to perform or pay expectation damages. Shiffrin, *Divergence*, at 727–9.

[43] Such contracts are quite familiar: a contract for sale or for services that limits the remedy to a small sum—say the forfeiture of a deposit—but not so small that the law would treat the bargain as illusory.

[44] *See* Craswell, *Contract Remedies*, at 632; Markovits & Schwartz, *Expectation Remedy*, at 813.

[45] Posner, Economic Analysis of Law, at 149–51.

[46] *See* text accompanying notes 48–50 and 62–5.

[47] *See* U.C.C. § 2-718(1) (1977) ("A term fixing unreasonably large liquidated damages is void as a penalty"); Craswell, *Contract Remedies*, at 637–8; *see also* Restatement (First) of Contracts § 339 (1932).

[48] U.C.C. § 2-718 cmt. 1 ("An unreasonably small *amount*. . . might be stricken under the section on unconscionable contracts or clauses").

[49] Charles J. Goetz & Robert E. Scott, *Liquidated Damages, Penalties and the Just Compensation Principle: Some Notes on an Enforcement Model and a Theory of Efficient Breach*, 77 Colum. L. Rev. 554 (1977).

> corporation, well able to avoid improvident commitments. Penalty clauses provide an earnest of performance. . . .
>
> A better argument is that a penalty clause may discourage efficient as well as inefficient breaches of contract. . . .
>
> On this view, since compensatory damages should be sufficient to deter inefficient breaches (that is, breaches that cost the victim more than the gain to the contract breaker), penal damages could have no effect other than to deter some efficient breaches. But this overlooks the earlier point that the willingness to agree to a penalty clause is a way of making the promisor and his promise credible and may therefore be essential to inducing some value-maximizing contracts to be made. It also overlooks the more important point that the parties (always assuming they are fully competent) will, in deciding whether to include a penalty clause in their contract, weigh the gains against the costs—costs that include the possibility of discouraging an efficient breach somewhere down the road—and will include the clause only if the benefits exceed those costs as well as all other costs.
>
> On this view the refusal to enforce penalty clauses is (at best) paternalistic—and it seems odd that courts should display parental solicitude for large corporations.[50]

What remains of Shiffrin's point, I think, is that there is in this reasoning the danger of an infinite regress: if the remedy may be stipulated *ad lib* in the contract, what of the promisor's failure to comply with that second-order, remedial obligation? At some point, the law must step in and enforce the contract; and in doing so, it must take account of the costs imposed by the faithless promisor not only on his counterparty but also on the judicial system and the regime of confidence in contracts in general.

Critics of *Contract as Promise* also point to the rule requiring the victim of a breach to make reasonable efforts—the expense of which is to be charged to the party in breach—to mitigate his damages. So if the victim is a seller, the victim must try to find an alternative buyer, charging the repudiating buyer the difference.[51] Critics argue correctly that this rule cannot readily be deduced as a corollary of the promise principle. Some, who are hostile to the promise principle, argue that the mitigation rule shows that *Contract as Promise* is wrong to assert that the promise principle underlies contract law. As I have indicated, those who see contract law as insufficiently faithful to the promise principle, argue that the mitigation rule adds insult to injury by requiring the morally innocent injured party to take the initiative in salving his own wounds. The way *Contract as Promise* deals with the duty to mitigate is to treat it as another rule collected for convenience under the rubric of contract, although it is in fact imposed on the victim willy-nilly, not to affect the victim's preferences, but to avoid a waste of resources (as with efficient breach) or require a kind of altruism that is good for the soul. Recent scholarship quite reasonably identifies this as another default rule, which contracting parties can and regularly do reverse. Unlike expectancy as the default damage measure, it is not plausible to argue that contract law is simply choosing—for the convenience of the parties—the rule that they would have chosen had they thought about it. The moralists are more likely to be right in seeing as more

[50] *Lake River Corp. v. Carborundum Co.*, 769 F.2d 1284, 1288–9 (7th Cir. 1985).

[51] Restatement (Second) of Contracts § 350 (1981); U.C.C. § 2-706 (1977).

natural a "you broke it, you fix it" default. The mitigation rule is quite well supported, however, on efficiency grounds: the disappointed promisee is more likely to know what will best remedy the difficulties into which the breach has plunged him, and requiring him to take the initiative—though not at his own expense—is the best way to avoid a dead-weight loss.[52] Here too, however, the duty to mitigate is generally only a default rule, and the parties in most situations can specify what steps the breaching promisor must take to mitigate or cure the effects of his breach. Such a specification may take the form of an alternative performance obligation or of the payment of a liquidated sum. And here, too, the possibility of an infinite regress looms, although as the duties are more sharply defined—most clearly in the case of a liquidated damage clause—that possibility may shrink to nothing.

It is, of course, the case that many, perhaps most, contracts do not specify remedies in the event of breach. Indeed, all contracts fail to specify the parties' intentions in respect to many matters that *ex ante* seem quite remote and not worth spelling out. So courts are regularly called upon to fill in details that only *ex post* may loom large. This is a task that *Contract as Promise* discussed under the term "gaps," to which I return in detail in Section VII.

IV

Alan Schwartz and Robert Scott have considered at length another way in which the law of contracts seems to diverge from what an institution single-mindedly determined by the promise principle might look like.[53] As has many times been observed, the promise principle has a strong affinity to what has been called the will theory of contract, according to which the state's imposition of contractual liability is justified as a matter of political morality by the fact that the obligation is self-imposed. It is the supposed departure from fidelity to these premises by features of the standard contract law of damages that moralists like Shiffrin deplore and skeptics about the role of morality in law celebrate. Schwartz and Scott investigate a seeming divergence which goes much more to the heart of these premises. They point to doctrines that systematically decline to base legal liability on the fullest, most accurate inquiry into what the parties really intended (willed).[54] They point to them and leave us to conclude that if these doctrines do not accord with some moral theory (mine, for instance?) then so much the worse for that theory. Consider the rule that treats an agreement as fully integrated if from within its "four corners" the written agreement has the look and feel of an integrated agreement, and the parol evidence rule that excludes prior or

[52] The locution "duty to mitigate," though standard is misleading. There is no such duty. Rather, failure by the victim of the breach to take reasonable steps to mitigate her damages is factored into the calculation of the damages to be awarded.

[53] Alan Schwartz & Robert E. Scott, *Contract Interpretation Redux*, 119 Yale L.J. 926 (2010). This article builds on an earlier article. Alan Schwartz & Robert E. Scott, *Contract Theory and The Limits of Contract Law*, 113 Yale L.J. 541 (2003). It should be noted that the authors limit their analysis to contracts between businesspeople.

[54] E.g., Schwartz & Scott, *Contract Theory*, at 584–90 (majority-language linguistic default), Schwartz & Scott, *Contract Theory*, at 590–1 (parol evidence rule); *see also* Schwartz & Scott, *Redux*, at 945–6 (noting that parties will contract with these default rules in mind, thereby decreasing incorrect interpretations).

contemporaneous evidence that may suggest that the parties meant something more or different from what they have written down. Such doctrines would seem to violate both freedom of and freedom from contract. And predictably, promissory rigorists deplore as overly formalistic the textualist preferences of these doctrines.[55] The rejection of rules like the four corners rule is associated with the scholar A. L. Corbin,[56] the jurist Roger Traynor,[57] the Restatement (Second)[58] and the U.C.C.[59] (There is an irony here: Corbin is associated with the antiformalist realist school, while formalism is associated with Williston, who is in turn associated with the will theory of contracts.)

Schwartz and Scott untangle this skein of apparent contradictions in a way that bears a similarity to what I have suggested above in respect to remedies doctrine.[60] Parties considering the matter *ex ante* will often have reason to limit what evidence a court may look to in determining what were their contractual intentions. For instance, trials in which all evidence that may bear on the question of what were the parties' true intentions, trials in which the full truth of their states of mind is plumbed, would in most cases be long and costly. The four corners and parol evidence rules, in addition to limiting introduction of mounds of evidence, often allow a decision on summary judgment. Furthermore, since extrinsic evidence of intention is often ambiguous and/or contradictory, limiting what the judge and trier of fact may look to gives the parties greater assurance against surprising and anomalous decisions by decision makers with unexpected dislikes and predilections.

But this argument stinks in the nostrils of those who view contract as a moral institution and courts as instruments in the search for truth; on such a view, considerations of cost and efficiency are no more appropriate in the adjudication of contract claims than they would be in settling upon the best interpretation of a work by Bach or Shakespeare. Truth and justice are examples, as Michael Sandel might put it, of what money can't buy.[61] Just as money—perhaps accompanied by an appeal to the theory of efficient breach—shouldn't be allowed to buy you out of a promise you should be bound to keep, so the content of a promise is not what at a later time it seems efficient to prove, but the full truth of what you have pledged to perform. But if the limited truth of the original promise is exactly what you have bargained for, and if the written word and no more is all you want enforced, is it not odd that—in the name of your will, in the name of honoring bargains—your plea to respect those limits should not be heard?

[55] *See* Jody S. Kraus & Robert E. Scott, *Contract Design and the Structure of Contractual Intent*, 84 N.Y.U. L. Rev. 1023, 1046–8 (2009). Of course I do not suggest that either Kraus or Scott are promissory rigorists.

[56] *E.g.*, Arthur L. Corbin, *The Interpretation of Words and the Parol Evidence Rule*, 50 Cornell L.Q. 161 (1965).

[57] *See Pacific Gas & Elec. Co. v. G. W. Thomas Drayage & Rigging Co.*, 442 P.2d 641, 645 (Cal. 1968) ("[R]ational interpretation requires at least a preliminary consideration of all credible evidence offered to prove the intention of the parties" (citations omitted)).

[58] Restatement (Second) of Contracts § 201 cmt. b (1981) ("[T]he question of meaning in cases of misunderstanding depends on an inquiry into what each party knew or had reason to know. . ."); Restatement (Second) of Contracts § 209 rep. note, cmt. c (permitting introduction of extrinsic evidence to make a preliminary determination whether the parties intended an agreement to be integrated).

[59] U.C.C. §§ 2-202 (2003).

[60] *See* Schwartz & Scott, *Contract Theory*, at 587–90.

[61] *See generally* Michael Sandel, What Money Can't Buy: The Moral Limits of Markets (2012).

The confused distaste for arbitration displays some of this same incoherent moral rigorism: "people should keep their word, dammit, and no mere arbitrator should be able to get between a court of law and the deep down ascertainment of whether a person is welching on his bargain." But what if the arbitrator is part of that bargain? Moreover, Schwartz and Scott show that they are not efficiency fanatics: what they propose—be it the four corners rule or the parol evidence rule—are not categorical imperatives; they are defaults—*mere* defaults.[62] Their theory depends on the will of the parties in that they provide parties with a choice of interpretive strategy; under their system, if you don't want a formalist contract, don't have one.[63] Or, you can have as much of one as you want. In contrast, the opposite of formalism or textualism—let's call it purposivism[64]—leaves the parties no such choice of interpretivist strategies. For Schwartz and Scott, the only role that a predilection for efficiency plays is to stipulate formalism as a default. But once you see the choice between purposivism and formalism as a choice, one or the other has to be the default when the parties don't choose, and Schwartz and Scott make a pretty good argument that, at least between merchants, formalism is what most would choose—it is what they call a majoritarian default rule.[65]

But there is another problem of an infinite regress, one we have encountered in respect to remedies, but in the problem of interpretation it goes deeper: what if one party makes the contested claim that from the outset—*ex ante*—he had rejected formalism? How is that dispute to be adjudicated? (There is an analogous crux in respect to arbitration agreements, and whether the agreement to submit to arbitration is subject to arbitration.) After all, my argument depends on the premise that there is agreement—at least by default—to this higher-order rule about agreement. I am quite clear that this dispute must be adjudicated by the state on extrinsic grounds of political morality.

And in general, how are disputes about which style of interpretation to use to be adjudicated? It is standard doctrine that the parol evidence rule, the four-corners rule and the like have no application to certain claims of fraud: for instance imagine a purported obligee on a written instrument who claims that he was tricked into thinking that he was just signing his autograph. The law might take the line that the signer did at least voluntarily sign his name and that signing your name is an act so fraught with potential consequences that if you voluntarily do that, you must take on special burdens—either of proof if the claimant is the obligor, or of reasonable care if the claimant is an innocent third party, as for instance a holder in due course. But these are not arguments about real, though second-order, agreement; they are arguments about the efficiency or fairness of various benefits and burdens, or about the proper allocation of social resources in adjudicating disputes. Imagine the extreme case in which the purported obligee insists that it is not his signature on the document at all, that it is a forgery. There are burdens of proof, evidentiary rules, and limits to how much time a court will devote to resolving the issue. These procedural rules can be

[62] *See* Schwartz & Scott, *Redux*, at 946–7. [63] Schwartz & Scott, *Redux*, at 947.

[64] This is a bit of naughtiness on my part. I mean to draw an analogy between textualists in statutory interpretation and their counterparts who are called purposivists. *See, e.g.*, John F. Manning, *Textualism and the Equity of the Statute*, 101 Colum. L. Rev. 1, 3–5 (2001).

[65] *See* Schwartz & Scott, *Contract Theory*, at 568–9.

made to look like Schwartz and Scott's arguments about interpretive rules; but such agreement on background procedural matters is hypothetical, the kind that Robert Nozick has written are not worth the paper they are not written on. The two can be brought closer together, as in cases of what are called fraud not in the execution but in the inducement. The victim of the fraud does not claim, for instance, that he was told that he was just giving his autograph (the rest of the document artfully folded over). Rather he makes the more attenuated claim that he was led to believe that this mortgage agreement is just a formality necessary to obtain a loan on quite different terms. Schwartz and Scott carefully confine their argument to agreements between businesspeople—what the U.C.C. calls agreements between merchants—where the majoritarian default rule with considerable plausibility may be taken to be a rule of actual, second-order agreement. And in general, it is not possible to escape, even in the most thoroughgoingly subjective regime, the possibility of error and therefore the necessity of a rule that assigns the risks of such error without ultimate recourse to the parties' actual agreement. How could it be otherwise? At some point agreement between the parties, based only on the limited set of interactions leading up to the contract, runs out. To take from Wittgenstein in another context, at some point we hit bedrock and our spade is turned.[66] Or perhaps this is analogous to Weber's definition of the state as having the monopoly of coercive force. This is the notion of state and law writ not large but small.

V

Randy Barnett in *Contract Is Not Promise; Contract Is Consent*[67] and *A Consent Theory of Contract*,[68] goes much further on the textualist front. He argues that contract law not only favors formality and writing in agreements among merchants, as noted by Schwartz and Scott, but that the whole fabric of contract law is woven on the warp and woof of objectivity.[69] If, as *Contract as Promise* insists, promise is morally binding because it is the willing invocation by a free moral agent of a convention that allows him to bind his will,[70] and if promise were indeed the moral and political basis for contract law, as *Contract as Promise* also insists, then there should be no contractual liability for what the promisor's words would ordinarily be taken to mean in cases where the promisor had in fact meant something quite different. The prevailing objective doctrine shows, Barnett argues, that it is not promise but consent that is the underlying moral and political basis for contract law. It cannot be gainsaid that what has been called the will theory, to which as I have said *Contract as Promise* bears a close affinity, is incompatible with holding a promisor—contrary to his intent—to the

[66] Ludwig Wittgenstein, Philosophical Investigations ¶ 217, at 91 (G. E. M. Anscombe trans., Wiley Blackwell 4th ed., 2009).

[67] Randy E. Barnett, *Contract Is Not Promise; Contract Is Consent*, 45 Suffolk U. L. Rev. 647 (2012).

[68] Randy E. Barnett, *A Consent Theory of Contract*, 86 colum. l. rev. 269 (1986).

[69] *See* Barnett, *A Consent Theory of Contract*, at 302–3. Learned Hand wrote that the objective meaning binds the parties, even "were it proved by twenty bishops that either party, when he used the words, intended something else than the usual meaning which the law imposes upon them." *Hotchkiss v. Nat'l City Bank of N.Y.*, 200 F. 287, 293 (S.D.N.Y. 1911); *see also* Restatement (Second) of Contracts § 2 cmt. b (1981).

[70] Fried, Contract as Promise, at 7–17.

objective meaning of his words. The practical, economic, and utilitarian grounds for holding him to his words are obvious. And so is the moral argument that, as between the promisor who did not mean what his words plainly mean and the promisee who took him at his word, the former should—as in any accident—bear the cost of the harm he has caused. But these are not promissory, will-theory arguments.[71]

Barnett marks this divergence between contract and promise not just within but at the very threshold of contract. There are many promises in which the promisor does not intend, and cannot reasonably be understood as intending, to be legally bound.[72] Moral rigorists might deny the requirement of this meta-intention, just as they might deny the validity of meta-intentions regarding remedies, reasoning thus: a promise creates a moral obligation that is other-regarding—it creates a moral duty to another, and the promisor has no moral business denying the promisee the ability to enforce that obligation. This is indeed similar to the objections to contractual clauses limiting the remedy to the forfeiture of a small deposit or requiring arbitration before a religious panel. But just as I have argued that parties may, and by a morality of autonomy should, be able to agree not just as to the substantive terms of the promise but also as to its remedial implications, so that same morality requires, and the law (largely) agrees, that the parties may specify whether they want their promise to be legally cognizable at all. But Barnett points out that even this threshold question is determined on the basis of objective appearance, so that whether you are taken to have entered the contractual room at all, and so will be made to play by the rules of contract law, is not entirely a function of your will either. And from this he concludes that not promise but consent is the basis of contract. This is how he put it in a recent essay:

> [C]ourts should presumptively enforce private commitments when there exists a *manifested intention to create a legal relation*. ... [T]o determine the *prima facie* case of contract, we should determine whether there was a *manifested intention to be legally bound*. I refer to this criterion, in short, as *consent*.[73]

This does not solve but merely reproduces the puzzle posed by the objective theory of contract. Whether promise or consent is taken to be central to contract, there are occasions on which contractual liability is imposed (or denied) in contradiction to the actual will of one of the parties.[74] Switching from promise to consent invokes a different terminology, perhaps less individualistic and more wholesale, as in the presumed *consent* to be governed by the laws of a reasonably just polity in which we all participate and whose benefits we take. And like the general duty to obey the laws of such a polity, so the objective theory is a practical necessity. What Barnett's consent theory does—much in the way of social contract theory—is to suggest the fairness of holding

[71] *Accord* Shiffrin, *Divergence*, at 752–3.

[72] *See Leonard v. Pepsico, Inc.*, 88 F. Supp. 2d 116, 127–8 (S.D.N.Y. 1999).

[73] Barnett, *Contract Is Not Promise*, at 655 (emphasis in original).

[74] Barnett, like the law, allows subjective intent to control if it can be shown that in spite of the objective meaning of their words, *neither* party had a subjective intent to be bound, or that both parties understood a term of the contract to have a meaning other than the objective one. *See* Barnett, *Contract Is Not Promise*, at 307–9. I will not go into the wonderful intricacies occasioned by cases in which both parties had a subjective intent—though not the same one—that differed from the objective meaning of their words.

someone to legal obligations imposed by a regime with which—in one way or another, by his own actions—he has become enmeshed.

The law of contract is, after all, a practical institution involving lawyers, judges, documents, and third parties who make investments on the basis of what they have learned about other people's contracts, both those concluded and those not concluded. Such a regime cannot correspond exactly to what the morality of promising requires. The objective theory advocated by Barnett, like the regime of default rules, the requirement of mitigation, and much else, are practical necessities if the government is to become involved in enforcing agreements at all. (Think of the many technical, unsentimental, and unlovely but inevitable rules that come into being when the law becomes involved in the relations between lovers—whether as husbands and wives or otherwise.) Thus my claim in *Contract as Promise* about the relation of the legal regime of contract to the moral institution of promising was not so much wrong as overstated.

As Barnett also notes, the great difference between the moral regime of promise and the legal regime of contract is that the law (i.e., the state) threatens, and in the end will use, force to compel compliance. The use of force by the state is morally regulated under the concept of justice. Though the laws of a just state will not violate morality—that is, will not violate citizens' moral rights nor seek to compel citizens to violate their moral duties—neither can they protect all moral rights nor enforce all moral duties. All this is well known and quite obvious.[75] The economic analysis of law demonstrates how a well-functioning contractual regime increases the *ex ante* well-being of the contracting parties and social welfare generally. As I have argued, the moral regime of promising extends the moral autonomy of promisors—seemingly paradoxically—by giving them a means of putting themselves under moral obligations. To the extent that they are sufficiently moved by the moral sense alone[76] the moral regime will accomplish practical goods similar to those identified by the economic analysis of contract law. And conversely, to the extent that contract law imposes legal obligations that are congruent with moral obligations, the use of force it threatens or employs is morally justified and comports with the general criteria by which we judge that a legal system is just.[77] And so the relation between contract and promise is a good deal more complex than one of simple entailment.

VI

A promisee who seeks to enlist the help of the law to enforce a promise moves far beyond an appeal to the promisor's conscience and into a forum where he must persuade strangers to use force against his moral adversary. These strangers—judges, jurors, bailiffs, and so on—would themselves act unjustly and immorally if they descended upon the promisor just on the promisee's say-so. Not only does mobilizing

[75] Kant's *The Metaphysical Elements of Justice* is the canonical text explaining the relation between moral obligation and obligation in law.

[76] *See* Fried, *Moral Causation*, at 1260.

[77] Here we can *see* why there is a logical puzzle about promises otherwise sufficient to justify legal enforcement, which stipulate that they are not to be legally binding. A similar puzzle, this one noted by Shiffrin, obtains in respect to contracts that provide for what may seem like inadequate or excessive remedies. *See* Shiffrin, *Divergence*, at 734–7.

the ponderous and uncertain machinery of the law entail risks of error, but it also imposes significant costs on society—that is, on third parties not involved in the dispute. Even if all costs were assessed against the losing party—a regime that would have its own problems—the number of competent judges is limited: justice is a scarce societal resource.[78] The risks and costs of externalization (placing into the *forum externum*) of promissory obligation may explain the energy behind the doctrine of consideration, on which *Contract as Promise* pours so much scorn. The "owners" of the machinery of justice in addition to wanting to avoid mistakes may reasonably choose to focus their attention on the more serious cases and cases in which a regime of reliable enforcement will redound to the benefit of society as a whole. The doctrine of consideration accomplishes this triage in notoriously over- and under-inclusive ways and therefore has spawned whole treatises of exceptions and supplements. And other legal systems have used other devices, such as the formalities required by Continental jurisdictions, to answer the same difficulty. But grasping the nature of the problem should lead to greater indulgence of the law's unavoidably imperfect solutions than *Contract as Promise* displayed.

This line of argument also helps explain the law of unconscionability. If contractual obligation is based in promise—contract *as* promise—and promise implements and extends the autonomy of the parties, it is hard to explain the law's occasional refusal to enforce a promise, not because it is too trivial, nor because it is not clear enough, nor because a competent, adult promisor may not have fully understood or was misled about what his promise committed him to, but just because it seems harsh or unfair. In such cases the doctrine seems paternalistic and, as such, inconsistent with the promise principle, which is expressive of and implements the right of adult individuals to set their own goals and make such arrangements as seem best to them. In her magisterial treatment of this problem, *Paternalism, Unconscionability Doctrine, and Accommodation*, Seana Shiffrin identifies some typical cases in which enforcement has been denied:

> [C]ontracts that charge usurious loan rates, a contract paying a grossly inadequate sum for an annuity, a one-sided, mandatory employment arbitration agreement that heavily favored the employer, arbitration clauses that specify indeterminate or remote locations or that require high fees so as to discourage efforts at redress, contracts with people of modest means that feature aggressive repossession terms and very high interest rates, sales contracts that disclaim warranties and consequential damages, exclusive option contracts that permit a buyer both to refuse goods and to prevent the supplier from selling them elsewhere . . .[79]

Shiffrin acknowledges that in such cases the promisor understands just what he is getting into and that the denial of enforceability may in fact deprive that class of promisors of access to goods and services that they desire and may not get on better terms. She nonetheless concludes that the doctrine need not be paternalistic. It may override the promisor's wishes not because of some possible harm to third parties and also not

[78] Arbitration is an intermediate case. To the extent that arbitral awards are enforced by courts, an agreement to arbitrate is just a special kind of contract: a contract about a contract. If the parties stipulate against legal enforcement of the award, then this is another example of a promise that is not intended to create legal relations.

[79] Shiffrin, *Paternalism*,, at 205–6 (footnotes omitted).

on the ground that the paternalistic court or state knows better what is in the promisor's best interests.

Consider that in the case of gratuitous promises the law may simply wish to reserve its scarce resources for more serious matters, and what counts as more serious must inevitably be left to the law's and its officers' judgment. The law does not forcibly prevent the gratuitous promisor from doing as that promisor has promised, and usually would not lend its agency to recover the promised gift when the promisor repents. Nor does the law prevent the promisee from respecting the subjective meaning of the promisor's words. In much the same way, when the law for its own reasons imposes a statute of limitations on a promisee's ability to complain of disappointment or requires that certain promises be in writing, the law nonetheless will not prevent the promisor from paying a stale debt or honoring an unwritten obligation. And so it is with unconscionable bargains: the law will not prevent promisors from honoring them, but it will not lend its agency to what it believes is harsh, unfair, or just plain ugly. It says: "This is an awful way to treat another human being. Go ahead and do it if you want, but don't ask me to help." Imagine an agreement between adult, competent persons to engage in some degrading sexual practice. Respect for their autonomy may mean that the law will not interfere with their arrangement, but surely it does not require that judges, jurors, and bailiffs involve themselves in enforcing its implementation. We have just such an example in the case of racially restrictive covenants included in a deed of sale. Absent some antidiscrimination statute, voluntary compliance with such deeds is not unconstitutional, but in the leading case of *Shelley v. Kraemer*,[80] the Supreme Court ruled that the government must not be complicit in their enforcement.

VII

> [W]e have more laws in France than all the rest of the world put together, and more than would be necessary for the government of all the worlds of Epicurus:
>
> "Ut olim flagitiis, *sic* nunc legibus, laboramus."[81] and yet we have left so much to the opinions and decisions of our judges that there never was so full a liberty or so full a license. What have our legislators gained by culling out a hundred thousand particular cases, and by applying to these a hundred thousand laws? This number holds no manner of proportion with the infinite diversity of human actions; the multiplication of our inventions will never arrive at the variety of examples; add to these a hundred times as many more, it will still not happen that, of events to come, there shall one be found that, in this vast number of millions of events so chosen and recorded, shall so tally with any other one, and be so exactly coupled and matched with it that there will not remain some circumstance and diversity which will require a diverse judgment. There is little relation betwixt our actions, which are in perpetual mutation, and fixed and immutable laws; the most to be desired are those that are the

[80] *Shelley v. Kraemer*, 334 U.S. 1 (1948).

[81] *As we were formerly by crimes, so we are now overburdened by laws.*—Tacitus, Annal., iii. 25. Michel de Montaigne, *Of Experience, in* ESSAYS (Project Gutenberg ed., Charles Cotton trans., 1877).

most rare, the most simple and general; and I am even of opinion that we had better have none at all than to have them in so prodigious a number as we have.[82]

This reconsideration of damage rules of the objective theory of contract and of unconscionability prompts a more general reconsideration of my account of the promise principle and its articulation in contract law. In a chapter of *Contract as Promise* I took up the topics of mistake, frustration, impossibility, and good faith, which I gathered under the rubric "Gaps."[83] These topics all share the characteristic that the parties have not succeeded at the outset in making sufficiently explicit some aspect of their contractual relations that later turns out to be a crucial focus of dispute. The collector who buys a coin thinking it to be a valuable rarity but that is shown (to the surprise of both parties) to be a forgery,[84] the case of the cow presumed by the seller to be sterile and therefore worth only its weight as beef but that turns out to be pregnant,[85] the contract to allow the use of rooms with a fine view of a scheduled coronation procession which is cancelled because of the king's illness,[86] the charterparty to carry goods from Atlantic ports to Asia that unexpectedly requires a far more circuitous route because of a wartime closing of the Suez Canal,[87] all gave rise to disputes that a specific allocation of risk would have headed off.

In this respect these cases resemble the cases in which greater specificity would have made irrelevant disputes about whether or not a promisor should have the option to breach and pay expectation damages and whether or not a disappointed promise has what is called (erroneously, perhaps) a duty to mitigate.[88] To the same effect some of the cases Daniel Markovits uses to illustrate his inquiry in this volume into the concept of good faith[89] might have been headed off by more completely specified contractual terms. For instance, Markovits refers to the leading case, *Fortune v. National Cash Register*,[90] in which an employer "discharge[d] a sales employee who is paid on commission after the employee . . . obtained an extraordinarily large order but before completion of all the formalities required to make the commission come due."[91] There too one can imagine a contract that lays out in excruciating detail the point at which the right to the commission would vest. Some of these specifications would have alerted the parties to the risks they were assuming, while others set out in cold print might have seemed so one-sided as to be struck as unconscionable.[92] As with the damage cases, such greater specificity might have had an effect on the prices paid and in some cases might have allowed one or the other party to insure against the loss eventually suffered.

Such cases illustrate the general point that no contract can deal with all the contingencies that might in unlikely circumstances surprise and disappoint one or the other (or both) of the parties. Those who view this problem from an economic perspective point out the obvious, that there comes a point at which it is not worth the parties'

82 Montaigne, *Of Experience*.
83 Fried, Contract as Promise, ch. 5.
84 *Beachcomber Coins, Inc. v. Boskett*, 400 A.2d 78 (N.J. Super. Ct. App. Div. 1979).
85 *Sherwood v. Walker*, 33 N.W. 919 (Mich. 1887).
86 *Krell v. Henry*, [1903] 2 K.B. 740.
87 *Am. Trading & Prod. Corp. v. Shell Int'l Maritime, Ltd.*, 453 F.2d 939 (2d. Cir. 1972).
88 *See* Section III.
89 Markovits, *Good Faith as Contract's Core Value*.
90 *Fortune v. Nat'l Cash Register*, 364 N.E.2d 1251 (Mass. 1971).
91 Markovits, *Good Faith as Contract's Core Value*, 274.
92 *Gianni Sport Ltd. v. Gantos, Inc.*, 391 N.W.2d 760 (Mich. Ct. App. 1986).

time and effort to anticipate every remote contingency and that if a contract were treated as incomplete at the outset without such detail many fewer contracts would be concluded.[93] *Contract as Promise*, designating these disputes as falling in contractual "gaps," goes on to argue that as they are not the subject of explicit agreement they fall outside the purview of contract law altogether and must be dealt with—for they must be dealt with—under some other legal heading: perhaps as contractual accidents and therefore like other accidents under the law of torts, but also possibly requiring courts to lay on the hand of equity and simply devise and impose a resolution that seems fair to a disinterested observer. Roberto Unger[94] and others[95] have called such resolutions a duty of enforced altruism or sharing among persons brought together in a shared enterprise.[96]

There is something wrong about this. The clue to the error is the concept of language and of the proper interpretation of texts it betrays. Detour for a moment to the analogous domain of statutory interpretation. No statute can specify what effect it should have in all of the instances in which it may be invoked. John Marshall in *McCulloch v. Maryland* famously dismissed those who would insist that the Constitution's general language must set out all the instances to which its terms are to apply, so that the failure to include the power to charter a national bank among the powers of Congress would mean that it did not have that power. To demand such specificity would require that the Constitution "partake of the prolixity of a legal code and could be scarcely be embraced by the human mind."[97] But the fact of the matter is that a legal code also, if it is to do its job, cannot have "the prolixity of a legal code." Statutory interpretation requires ascribing rationality and purpose to the legislation (if not the legislators) in order to draw out the meaning of general terms and to resolve apparent contradictions and ambiguities. In the largest perspective not just constitutions, statutes, and contracts but all acts of communication require an interpretive stance that assumes some shared context of purpose, concepts, and experience. It is no coincidence that many of the maxims deployed in statutory interpretation (e.g., *eiusdem generis, noscitur a sociis, expressio unius est exclusio alterius*) do analogous service in the interpretation of contracts. And as with constitutions and statutes—but not necessarily with poems, novels, paintings, and music—the interpretive issue comes up in the context of a dispute after the text has been laid down (*ex post*), and not in the actual drafting, a dispute in the resolution of which there will be winners and losers, a dispute which by hypothesis has not yielded to the efforts of the parties to reach a resolution on their own.

Once again we are invoking the intervention of presumably disinterested third parties. What is their job? As Markovits explains, the job of the courts is *not* to impose some conception of generous, or virtuous or altruistic, or redistributive behavior on the parties. The courts must not make the parties fiduciaries for each other. It is, in the

[93] Steven Shavell, Foundations of Economic Analysis of Law 301–4 (2004).
[94] Roberto Mangabeira Unger, *The Critical Legal Studies Movement*, 96 Harv. L. Rev. 561, 639–46 (1983).
[95] *See, e.g.*, Kennedy, *Form and Substance in Private Law Adjudication*.
[96] Fried, Contract as Promise, at 76–7.
[97] *McCulloch v. Maryland*, 17 U.S. 316, 407 (1819).

first instance at least, the courts' job to interpret the contract, and that means to interpret *this* contract, not some contract that good or generous or socially minded people might have made. But nonetheless these authorized interpreters must assume that the contract had a purpose and that the parts of it fit together to serve that purpose—not because all contracting parties are rational, nor because all the parts of what they set down necessarily cohere, but because these are the only assumptions which we can ask courts and judges to make—they are neither historians nor psychiatrists.[98] Here we should generalize from what Markovits says about courts in imposing a duty of good faith on the parties to a dispute. His point just is that good faith is an interpretive concept,[99] a concept that excavates meaning from the actual agreement.[100] It is not the same as the judgment of substantive unconscionability. It requires the parties "to go only the distance, and only along the path, that the contract to which she and her collaborator agreed to."[101] He quotes the U.C.C.'s insistence that good faith "does not create a separate duty of fairness and reasonableness which can be independently breached,"[102] and thus keeps the courts' imposition of a duty of good faith within the confines of freedom of contract.[103]

And yet, if this excavation from the contract itself of the terms of the duty of good faith is not in fact to be an exercise in burying the courts' own ideas of virtue or fairness or efficiency and then with an interpretive flourish pulling them out again, we would do well to admit that there are times when the text, implicit and explicit, just gives out, and that then there is just no way to resolve the dispute from within the contract itself. But *non liquet* is not an option: even letting the loss lie where it falls (as the English courts thought they were doing in the early frustration and impossibility cases[104]) is also a disposition.

VIII

I have now several times invoked the third-party perspective of those who must administer the legal system to explain the divergence between what the promise principle entails and the actual functioning of the law. But the whole point of economic analysis—or, for that matter, a Marxist or critical legal studies or some other social science-based analysis—of contract *law* is to provide an account of the body of rules or doctrines or practices that these "third parties" institute and administer. And if I must turn to the economic/efficiency analysis to explain the *law*, say, regarding gratuitous

[98] Historians and psychiatrists are also interpreters, but theirs is a different interpretive task and they bring different points of departure to their work.

[99] *See* Dworkin, Justice for Hedgehogs, at 6–7.

[100] Curtis Bridgeman and John Goldberg argue that this stance is implicit in *Contract as Promise.* Curtis Bridgeman & John C. P. Goldberg, *Do Promises Distinguish Contract from Tort*, 45 Suffolk U. L. Rev. 873, 892–5(2012). Of course I do not quarrel with that. It is an illustration of the truth that interpretation—in this case of the author's text (mine)—is an interpretive, and not a psychological or historical exercise.

[101] Markovits, *Good Faith as Contract's Core Value.*

[102] U.C.C. §1-304 cmt. 1 (2003).

[103] Markovits, *Good Faith as Contract's Core Value.*

[104] *Chandler v. Webster,* [1904] 1 K.B. 493, *Krell v. Henry,* [1903] 2 K.B. 740, even *Fibrosa Spolka Akcyjna v. Fairbairn Lawson Combe Barbour, Ltd.*, [1943] A.C. 32 (H.L. 1942) (appeal taken from Eng.), though to a lesser degree.

promises or contract interpretation or unconscionability, then have I not just given the game away, lost the argument?[105]

Recall two examples. I have suggested that the doctrine of consideration may be seen as focusing scarce judicial resources on those promises that are likely to be most important to the functioning of market exchanges. Is that not a patently economic calculation? I have embraced Schwartz and Scott's account of why it makes sense for the courts to adopt a rather literalistic (New York rather than California) approach to the interpretation of promises between business entities. The sense that makes is economic sense: as rational economic actors, businesspeople by and large have good economic grounds to prefer *ex ante* such an approach in the enforcement of their engagements. Economic as those judgments are, they are of two different kinds. My account of the bargain theory of contracts emphasizes not the wishes of the parties[106] but the economic preferences of those who staff and pay for a public resource. On Schwartz and Scott's account, however, New York's "four corners" default rule serves the economic preferences of the contracting parties. And unconscionability practice quite often may not serve anyone's economic interest—at least not *ex ante*—but it is not for that reason necessarily irrational or wrong. *Contract as Promise* is a philosophical account of a central legal and political institution. It makes the *normative claim* that the moral and political principles of contract as promise are the correct, the best principles for understanding and applying the law, and that they should enjoy the prominence it attributes to them. It makes the *analytical claim* that existing institutions gathered under the rubric of contract can best be understood, explicated, and developed in terms of the promise principle. And it makes the *empirical claim* that the principal actors—contract parties, lawyers, and judges—on the legal and commercial scene do in fact refer to and are guided by the promise principle as they go about their legal and commercial business.

At the time of its formulation over 30 years ago, the principal challenge to this set of claims was a *gauchisant* if not *Marxisant* mix of legal realism, critical legal studies, and generalized allergy to free-market principles and analyses. Today, and for some decades past, the main competitor to the promise principle has been the economic analysis of law. Schwartz and Scott, for instance, state "that the law should pursue the first order goal of maximizing contractual surplus when it chooses rules to regulate merchant-to-merchant contracts."[107] By limiting their assertions to this context they put to one side arguments that the law of contract might be used to accomplish redistributional goals,[108] or that informational defects or severe disparities of resources or of rational ability to calculate advantage might justify paternalistic intervention. Other law-and-economics scholars have been willing to generalize much further.[109]

[105] I am grateful to Avery Katz for pressing this challenge.

[106] Although the bargain theory may do service as a default identifying those promises the parties wish to generate legal consequences.

[107] Schwartz & Scott, *Redux*, at 928.

[108] *See, e.g.*, Duncan Kennedy, *Distributive and Paternalist Motives in Contract and Tort Law, with Special Reference to Compulsory Terms and Unequal Bargaining Power*, 41 Md. L. Rev. 563 (1982); Anthony T. Kronman, *Contract Law and Distributive Justice*, 89 Yale L.J. 472 (1980). *But see* Louis Kaplow & Steven Shavell, *Why the Legal System Is Less Efficient than the Income Tax in Redistributing Income*, 23 J. Legal Stud. 667 (1994).

[109] *See* Craswell, *Promises and Prices*.

I have already argued that the considerable overlap between contract as promise and the economic analysis of contract is partly explained by the fact that both are concerned with fashioning rules and thus with the *ex ante* perspective of the parties.[110] Of these two theoretical accounts, contract as promise, by reason of its more familiar language and concepts, enjoys a certain advantage. But the partisans of the economic view might respond that, even if the vocabulary and conceptual structure of basic contract law correspond well to contract as promise, the law-and-economics approach overtakes contract as promise in explanatory power, in being able to explain the fringe, and even some of the central, doctrines of contract law. For example, in discussing topics like consideration and unconscionability, I have had to have recourse to explanations other than the morality of trust and the promise principle. Economic analysis is able to comprehend such topics and extend its explanatory framework to them as well. Is this greater generality not a sure sign of a better theory? Does not the promise principle drop out as less powerful and therefore otiose?

I think not. It is a proper accomplishment of the promise principle to root this crucial legal institution in the moral principles of mutual respect and trust, and through them to a general moral theory—in broad outline, Kantian—of the right and the good. My appreciation of important third-party concerns in matters like consideration and unconscionability, as well as the limits of the promise principle in dealing with cases of fraud and duress, does not undermine that connection to (what I call) Kantian moral theory. That theory claims to deal with such topics as part of a more general moral and political theory. It is a comprehensive theory. But so is the general utilitarian theory that underlies law and economics. The question then is—and it is an old one—which of the two is the better theory. The incompleteness of the promise principle does not reveal a weakness in Kantian theory, nor does it prove that utilitarianism's own comprehensive claims are somehow stronger. These moments of incompleteness, these occasions where we must go beyond the promise principle, show only that promise is not a general moral, legal, and political theory. It does not purport to be. Of course if utilitarianism really is the better general theory, then its account of the subsidiary issue of a legal institution like contract is bound to be better and deeper too. But that is a question for other days.

110 *See* notes 27–31 and accompanying text.

3

Contract Is Not Promise; Contract Is Consent

*Randy E. Barnett**

Introduction

Charles Fried's *Contract as Promise*[1] arrived on the scene in 1981 at exactly the right moment. In the 1970s, contract law scholarship had come to be dominated by two competing visions: the "contract as tort" vision associated with many scholars, but presented most pithily by Grant Gilmore in his highly influential *The Death of Contract*,[2] which appeared in 1974; and the "contract as efficiency" vision of law and economics scholars, especially the prolific and accessible Richard Posner in his book *The Economic Analysis of Law*,[3] the first edition of which was published in 1973.

Fried's "contract as promise" thesis was a welcome and much-needed defense of the traditional view of contract as protecting the "will" or choices of private parties. In his book, Fried defends what he calls "the promise principle," by which he meant "that principle by which persons may impose on themselves obligations where none existed before."[4] To make his case, Fried engaged in a *tour de force* march through the conundrums of contract doctrine, separating those doctrines that are best justified as consistent with the promise principle, those doctrines that could better be understood as resting on alternative justifications but are still consistent with the enforcement of voluntary transactions, and those doctrines that should be rejected because they are neither.

Perhaps due to Fried's systematic examination of the disparate contract law doctrines that so frustrate first-year law students, for a work of serious contracts scholarship, *Contract as Promise* has remained a remarkably popular book, even some 30 years after its appearance. And it also inspired a coterie of contracts scholars who, having taken contract law after its publication, have pursued and elaborated the "contract as promise" model.

By coincidence, in the fall of 1981, I began a one-year fellowship at the University of Chicago Law School, after having served four years as a criminal prosecutor for the Cook County State's Attorney's Office in Chicago. My research agenda was to retool as a contracts scholar, having been inspired to do so by taking Roberto Unger's contract class at Harvard Law School in 1974–5, the only time he ever taught Contracts. In his

* This chapter, which originally appeared in volume 45 of the *Suffolk University Law Review*, may be copied or distributed for classroom use. I thank Anastasia Killian for her research assistance.

[1] Charles Fried, Contract as Promise: A Theory of Contractual Obligation (1981).

[2] Grant Gilmore, The Death of Contract (1974).

[3] Richard A. Posner, The Economic Analysis of Law (1973).

[4] Fried, Contract as Promise, at 1 (defining promise principle).

course, Unger had effectively critiqued the "liberal" conception of contracts. We read, among other things, Gilmore's *The Death of Contract*, and Unger provided his own distinctive take on contract law. Later, I came to appreciate the extent to which Unger's critique of freedom of contract reflected that of Duncan Kennedy, who was then on the rise as a private-law legal theorist, but who taught Contracts in another section.

As a law student sympathetic to freedom of contract, I found myself unable to answer Unger's challenge, but at the same time unwilling to accept his critique, engaging as it was. Also unsatisfied was Unger's colleague (and my torts professor) Charles Fried. Fried's answer to Unger and others was *Contract as Promise*, but this answer, while a great step forward, did not fully satisfy me. With Fried's response in mind, I embarked on the writing that would lead to "a consent theory of contract," or what might be called "contract as consent."

I confess that I have not read *Contract as Promise* from cover to cover since my days at the University of Chicago. As a scholar, one has a tendency not to backtrack, which is why teaching is so valuable. It forces scholars to read, and reread, all the seminal cases and materials one might well never review. And that compels scholars to see these classic materials in a new light with each passing year. I accepted the invitation to participate in this symposium not only as an opportunity to pay homage to my professor Charles Fried, but as an inducement to revisit *Contract as Promise* to appreciate why it has endured so well for 30 years.

What I found upon my rereading was a book that exceeded my recollection of it. Not only does Fried's account of contract doctrine still seem fresh and insightful, it turns out that in several respects, he anticipated "contract as consent." Indeed, I can imagine that, if one changed its opening thesis from "contract as promise" to "contract as consent," much of the subsequent thesis could remain more or less intact, albeit with some important modifications and improvements.

In particular, one of the less satisfying aspects of *Contract as Promise*, and the reason it left me rather cold when it first appeared, is how willing it appears so quickly to shift away from the promise model to account for myriad doctrines. True, it claims that this shift does not undermine the promise principle. But it also insists that the promise principle does not account for many of the doctrines that are needed to supplement it. One comes away from the book, or at least I came away from the book, thinking that Fried opts for alternative principles on a seemingly ad hoc basis. Or at least, that the promise principle on its own appears unable to justify much of what he thinks of as justified contracts doctrine.

In my view, "contract as consent" explains and justifies far more of contract law doctrine than does "contract as promise." And it avoids some of the problems created by viewing promises as the core of contractual obligation. But because consent and promise are so close to each other—and both ground contractual obligations in the voluntary choices of contracting parties—it is hard for some to distinguish these two alternative defenses of contractual freedom.

In these remarks, I will not be able to mount a comprehensive critique of either "contract as promise" or *Contract as Promise*. Instead, I want to briefly summarize some of the difficulties of this model and describe how it differs from "contract as consent." But I also want to do one more thing I had not expected to do when I accepted the invitation to participate in this symposium. I wish to highlight the degree to which Fried's defense of "contract as promise" actually relies on arguments that are better understood as aspects of "contract as consent." In this regard, his instincts moved him in the direction of consent, even when his theory was ostensibly limited to promise. And his defense of contractual freedom was, I think, as a result, more powerful than it otherwise would have been.

I. Contract Is Not Promise

The thesis of *Contract as Promise* presents three major difficulties that undercut its claim to be either an explanation or justification of our law of contract. These concern: (1) its inability to explain contract law's objective theory of assent as contractual, (2) its inability to understand contract law's "gap fillers" as contractual, and (3) its moralizing the enforcement of contracts in the wrong way. In this section, I consider each in turn.

A. The problem of the objective theory of assent

In my 1986 article, *A Consent Theory of Contract*,[5] I presented a critique of "will theories" of contract that can be taken as a critique of Fried's "contract as promise" thesis as well. In my later writings, I refer to the "will principle" rather than will "theories,"[6] but I might just as well have called it the "promise principle" instead. According to the will or promise principle, commitments are enforceable because the promisor has "willed" or freely chosen to be bound by his commitment. Under the classical view, "the law of contract gives expression to and protects the will of the parties, for the will is something inherently worthy of respect."[7] In this approach, the use of force against a reneging promisor is morally justified because the promisor herself has undertaken the obligation in question. A promisor cannot complain about force being used against her, since she created the obligation being enforced. Or, as Fried puts it: "An individual is morally bound to keep his promises because he has intentionally invoked a convention whose function it is to give grounds—moral grounds—for another to expect the promised performance."[8]

In this way, the will (or promise) principle is able to distinguish contract law from tort law. In tort law, the source of the obligation or "duty" is the law. In contract, the source of the obligation or duty being enforced is the promisor herself. The spirit of the will principle may best be exemplified by the traditional sentiment, often expressed by nineteenth- and early twentieth-century courts, that contracts require a "meeting of the minds." That mutual "assent" is thought necessary to create a contractual obligation is quite harmonious with the will principle.

For its moral force, the promise principle depends upon the notion that contractual duties are binding because they are freely assumed by those who are required

[5] Randy E. Barnett, *A Consent Theory of Contract*, 86 Colum. L. Rev. 269 (1986). The next several paragraphs are based on this article from pages 272–4.

[6] *See* Randy E. Barnett, Contracts: Cases and Doctrine 586 (4th ed., 2008).

[7] Morris Cohen, *The Basis of Contract*, 46 Harv. L. Rev. 553, 575 (1933).

[8] Fried, Contract as Promise, at 16 (emphasis added).

to discharge them. This position leads quite naturally to an inquiry as to the promisor's actual state of mind at the time of agreement—the so-called "subjective" viewpoint—and indeed most important contractual duties probably are subjectively assented to by the promisor. However, what of those manifested commitments lacking subjective assent? Without a genuine commitment by the person who is to be subjected to a legal sanction, enforcement would seem to be unjustified by the "will" of the promisee and, hence, it seems unsupported by the promise principle. After all, enforcement can hardly be based on either will or promise if the obligation was not chosen by the individual but instead was imposed by law the way that tort duties are.

Yet, it has long been recognized that a system of contractual enforcement would be unworkable if it required a subjective inquiry into the putative promisor's intent. Where we cannot discern the actual subjective intent or will of the parties, there is no practical problem since we may assume it corresponds to objectively manifested intentions. But where subjective intent can somehow be proved, and is contrary to objectively manifested behavior, the subjective intent should prevail if the moral integrity of the will principle is to be preserved.

Of course, any legal preference for the promisor's hidden subjective intent would disappoint a promisee who has acted in reliance on the appearance of a commitment. Moreover, permitting a subjective inquiry into the promisor's intent could also enable a promisor to fraudulently undermine otherwise perfectly clear agreements by generating and preserving extrinsic evidence of ambiguous or conflicting intentions. Such a strategy might create a de facto option in the promisor. The promisor could insist on enforcement if the contract continued to be in her interest, but she could avoid the contract if it were no longer advantageous by producing evidence of a differing subjective intent.[9] In sum, because the subjective approach relies on evidence inaccessible to the promisee, much less to third parties, an inquiry into subjective intent would undermine the security of transactions by greatly reducing the reliability of contractual commitments. As philosopher David Hume, upon whom Fried relies,[10] observed over 200 years ago:

> If the secret direction of the intention, said every man of sense, could invalidate a contract; where is our security? And yet a metaphysical schoolman might think, that where an intention was supposed to be requisite, if that intention really had no place, no consequence ought to follow, and no obligation be imposed.[11]

Not surprisingly, despite the oft-expressed traditional sentiment that contracts require a "meeting of the minds," the objective approach has largely prevailed. A rigorous commitment to a will theory conflicts unavoidably with the practical need for a system of rules based to a large extent on objectively manifested states of mind. So too does the promise principle for the same reasons, unless it is qualified in some manner.

[9] For a case in which a court suspected a party of using the "mail-box rule" in such a fashion, *see Cohen v. Clayton Coal Co.*, 281 P. 111, 115 (Colo. 1929).

[10] *See* FRIED, CONTRACT AS PROMISE, at 1, 15, 137–8, 150–1.

[11] DAVID HUME, AN ENQUIRY CONCERNING THE PRINCIPLES OF MORALS 33 n. 1 (Eugene Freeman ed., 2d ed., 1966).

Of course, because a person's objective manifestations generally do reflect her subjective intentions, the doctrinal requirement of mutual assent tends, in the vast majority of cases, to honor the promise principle. And, consistent with these principles: (1) the reasonable or objective meaning of assent may be overridden by proof of a contrary subjective agreement between both parties; and (2) when a promisee has access to the subjective or actual understanding of the promisor, he may not rely on the "objective" or reasonable meaning of the promisor's conduct. In such circumstances, courts will enforce the subjective over the objective meaning of assent.

Nonetheless, the promise principle has difficulty explaining the enforcement of the objective agreement where it can be shown that the subjective understanding of a promisor differs from her objectively manifested behavior. Fried sees this all too clearly, but, with typical candor, he goes the other way: "Another of the classical law's evasions of the inevitability of using noncontractual principles to resolve failures of agreement is recourse to the so-called objective standard of interpretation."[12]

In short, Fried thinks that the objective approach to contract cannot be justified by the promise principle. "In the face of a claim of divergent intentions, the court imagines that it is respecting the will of the parties by asking what somebody else, say the ordinary person, would have intended by such words of agreement."[13] Instead, such an approach entails "imposing an external standard on the parties" based on "nonpromissory standards of justice."[14] However, if contract equals promise, and promise cannot justify this mainstay of contract law doctrine as "contractual," this is a major weakness of contract as promise. Contract as promise may not yet have been refuted, but this is strike one.

B. The problem of "gap filling"

A second serious problem is created by the promise theory's exclusive focus on promises once it is conceded—as it must be—that many real-world contract law problems arise precisely because parties have unavoidably left "gaps" in their promises. This has led some contracts theorists to argue that other nonpromissory principles must be used to determine the "gap-filling" rules of contract law.[15] In *Contract as Promise*, Fried takes exactly this position. Where gaps exist in a contract, "the court is forced to sort out the difficulties that result when parties think they have agreed but actually have not. The one basis on which these cases cannot be resolved is on the basis of the agreement—that is, of contract as promise."[16] In his analysis of the inevitable "gap-filling" that contract law provides, he readily concedes that the "gaps cannot be filled, the adjustments cannot be governed, by the promise principle."[17] When combined with its inability to justify the objective approach to contract, this inability to "fill gaps" is strike two for contract as promise.

[12] Fried, Contract as Promise, at 61.
[13] Fried, Contract as Promise, at 61.
[14] Fried, Contract as Promise, at 61.
[15] *See* Randy E. Barnett, *The Sound of Silence: Default Rules and Contractual Consent*, 78 Va. L. Rev. 821, 822–3 (1992).
[16] Fried, Contract as Promise, at 60.
[17] Fried, Contract as Promise, at 69.

C. The problem of moralizing contract

But there is one more problem that goes to the very heart of *Contract as Promise*: the claim that the obligation to keep one's promises is a moral one.

> An individual is morally bound to keep his promises because he has intentionally invoked a convention whose function it is to give grounds—moral grounds—for another to expect the promised performance. To renege is to abuse a confidence he was free to invite or not, and which he intentionally did invite. To abuse that confidence now is like (but only like) lying: the abuse of a shared social institution that is intended to invoke the bonds of trust.[18]

Recently, Fried has explained what he means by "morality," saying that "[m]orality is concerned with how people should lead their lives and how they should treat each other."[19] He further elaborated:

> Morality . . . condemns a way of life indifferent to the well-being of others, and even more strongly condemns pursuits that are constituted by the frustration, humiliation, or destruction of others. By contrast, it enjoins each actor to respect the other's humanity—that is, the feeling, judging, and striving nature of other persons—and celebrates pursuits that involve others not only without disrespecting them (that is, "using" them in Kantian terminology), but also by furthering their own pursuits as they further the actor's pursuit.[20]

But basing contracts on this capacious conception of morality invites courts to inquire into the moral merits of the respective parties.[21] Indeed, by justifying contract as a species of enforcing purely moral commitments, it seems tantamount to enforcing virtue.[22] Such an open-ended rationale leads to serious problems for the value of freedom of contract that Fried is defending in *Contract as Promise*. First, it commits courts to enforcing promissory commitments that the parties themselves may never have contemplated as "contractual" or legally enforceable, thereby undermining the value of freedom from contract. Second, once the moral behavior of the promisor is deemed relevant to the issue of enforceability, the promise theory also appears

[18] Fried, Contract as Promise, at 16 (footnote omitted).

[19] Charles Fried, *The Convergence of Contract and Promise*, 120 Harv. L. Rev. F. 1, 2 (2007).

[20] Fried, *The Convergence of Contract and Promise*, at 3.

[21] *See* Seana Valentine Shiffrin, *Could Breach of Contract Be Immoral?*, 107 Mich. L. Rev. 1551, 1567 (2009) ("I am not arguing that breach of contract is always immoral, just that it may sometimes be. Nothing I have argued precludes the judgment that some forms of breach are morally permissible"); Seana Valentine Shiffrin, *The Divergence of Contract and Promise*, 120 Harv. L. Rev. 708, 725 (2007) ("[W]hether it is morally wrong for the promisee to refuse [to mitigate] may depend on a number of factors to which the law is insensitive, including the closeness of the relationship, the history of the relationship, the reason for breach, the reason the promisor wants to shift the burden, and how cumbersome mitigation activities would be").

[22] *But see* Shiffrin, *The Divergence of Contract and Promise*, at 752 (denying that contract law is "an effort to get people to act virtuously, to prompt people to keep their promises for the right reasons, to ensure that private relationships go as well as possible, or to get people to make promises when morally appropriate to do so"). According to Shiffrin, contract law "is not an effort to legalize as much as possible the interpersonal moral regime of promising, but rather to provide support for the political and public values associated with promising." I view this effort by Shiffrin to distinguish the morality of contract that is the core of her approach from enforcing virtue as reintroducing into her analysis the distinction I make below between "public" and "private" morality.

to make relevant to the issue of enforcement other moral aspects of the promisor's behavior that may argue against enforcement, thereby undermining the value of freedom to contract. In this manner, the common law rights of contract can come to resemble the judicial discretion of a court of equity.

Those unsympathetic to freedom of contract will not be bothered by the implication of moralizing contract in this way. But Fried himself wrote *Contract as Promise* as a way to defend contractual freedom. "[T]he law of contracts facilitates our disposing of [our] rights on terms that seem best to us."[23] For those who share this view, this problem with contract as promise should be considered strike three.

II. Contract Is Consent

I do not intend to rehearse all the reasons I have previously advanced for why the overarching organizing principle of contract is not promise, but consent. My recent book, *Contracts*,[24] explains how and why discerning the existence and meaning of that consent comprises the core of the law of contract. Whereas the duties enforced by tort law may or may not be a product of the consent of the person on whom they are imposed, every contract begins with the consent of the parties.

I shall only briefly describe here the criterion of contractual enforceability that I have elaborated elsewhere over the past 25 years.[25] It is a criterion that is explicitly acknowledged in English law and underlies much of the doctrine of contract law we have inherited: courts should presumptively enforce private commitments when there exists a manifested intention to create a legal relation. Another formulation of this approach is that, to determine the prima facie case of contract, we should determine whether there was a manifested intention to be legally bound. I refer to this criterion, in short, as consent.

This special sense of "consent" is to be distinguished from promise. To promise is to commit to do or refrain from doing something. To consent to contract is to commit to be legally responsible for nonperformance of a promise. So consent is a commitment in addition to whatever moral commitment inheres in a promise.

[23] Fried, Contract as Promise, at 2.

[24] *See* Randy E. Barnett, The Oxford Introductions to U.S. Law: Contracts (2010). In a real sense, Contracts is my answer both to Fried's Contract as Promise and to Gilmore's The Death of Contract, although its survey of the principal doctrines of contract law resembles the former more than the latter.

[25] In addition to Barnett, The Oxford Introductions to U.S. Law, *see generally* Barnett, *A Consent Theory of Contract*; Randy E. Barnett, . . . *and Contractual Consent*, 3 S. Cal. Interdisc. L.J. 421 (1993); Randy E. Barnett & Mary E. Becker, *Beyond Reliance: Promissory Estoppel, Contract Formalities, and Misrepresentation*, 15 Hofstra L. Rev. 445 (1987); Randy E. Barnett, *Conflicting Visions: A Critique of Ian Macneil's Relational Theory of Contract*, 78 Va. L. Rev. 1175 (1992); Randy E. Barnett, *Consenting to Form Contracts*, 71 Fordham L. Rev. 627 (2002); Randy E. Barnett, *Contract Remedies and Inalienable Rights*, 4 Soc. Phil. & Pol'y 179 (1986); Randy E. Barnett, *Rational Bargaining Theory and Contract: Default Rules, Hypothetical Consent, the Duty to Disclose, and Fraud*, 15 Harv. J.L. & Pub. Pol'y 783 (1992); Randy E. Barnett, *Some Problems with Contract as Promise*, 77 Cornell L. Rev. 1022 (1992); Randy E. Barnett, *Squaring Undisclosed Agency Law with Contract Theory*, 75 Calif. L. Rev. 1969 (1987); Randy E. Barnett, *The Internal and External Analysis of Concepts*, 11 Cardozo L. Rev. 525 (1990); Randy E. Barnett, *The Function of Several Property and Freedom of Contract*, 9 Soc. Phil. & Pol'y 62 (1992); Barnett, *The Sound of Silence*; Randy E. Barnett, *Contract Scholarship and the Reemergence of Legal Philosophy*, 97 Harv. L. Rev. 1223 (1984) (book review). The next several paragraphs are based on Barnett, Contracts, at 602–4.

Moreover, contractual consent is to be distinguished from subjective assent. Consent is the voluntary communication by one person to another person of a particular message: that one intends to alter an already existing legal relation between the parties or to create a new one.[26] Some such criterion seems to have been incorporated into U.C.C. Section 2-204(3), which permits the enforcement of a contract with one or more open terms "if the parties have intended to make a contract and there is a reasonably certain basis for giving an appropriate remedy."[27]

A "consent theory" of contractual enforcement provides a general criterion of contractual enforceability that strikes a reasonable and workable balance among the party-based, substance-based, and process principles that comprise the core concerns of contract. Requiring a manifested intention to be legally bound facilitates the will or private autonomy of the parties, because one's manifested intention is highly likely to reflect an underlying subjective assent. The existence of a manifested intention to be legally bound also helps distinguish those commitments that merit legal protection, upon which reliance is justified, from those that do not. Although restitution-based liability is not limited to contract—it can provide an independent basis for legal enforcement apart from consent—the existence of a party's consent to be legally bound justifies forcing that party to disgorge her enrichment.

Adherence to a criterion of consent would tend to limit enforceability to value-enhancing or efficient commitments (whether gratuitous or as part of an exchange) in which, *ex ante*, the parties view enforceability to be worth more to them than its costs. To the extent that parties themselves are normally the best judge of their own interests, the substance of agreements that result from the parties' consent are also likely to be fair. But to the extent that normal conditions do not apply, the parties' consent provides only a prima facie basis for enforceability. Contract defenses that allow consent to be set aside or defeasible under a variety of circumstances—such as fraud, duress, various forms of incompetence, or undue influence—identify circumstances where the consent of the parties may not produce substantively fair or efficient agreements.

Finally, the criterion of consent helps place the bargain principle in proper perspective. The existence of a bargain in a commercial context is very likely to indicate the existence of an intention to be legally bound. The absence of bargains in noncommercial settings is apt to reflect the absence of such consent. Nonetheless, the existence of a bargain is not dispositive of the issue of consent. For example, the presence of a bargain in the commercial context could be negated by evidence that the parties did not intend to be legally bound. By the same token, the absence of a bargain in the noncommercial context could be compensated by the existence of some other indicia of intention to be legally bound—perhaps a formality such as so-called "nominal consideration."

[26] Because every person stands in some legal relation to every other person, analytically there is no real difference between altering a preexisting legal relationship and creating a new one. Still, it is useful to distinguish between creating a contractual relationship between parties who previously had no such relationship and altering a contractual relationship that already exists.

[27] U.C.C. § 2-204(3) (2003).

Furthermore, in many promissory estoppel cases, some indicia of consent other than bargain appear to be present. So we may be wrong to conceive of the doctrine of promissory estoppel solely in terms of reliance. And under some circumstances, consent of a promisor to be legally bound may be manifested by her silence in the face of substantial reliance by the promisee of the sort that would not be incurred without a commitment to be legally bound.

Like any rule of law, however, limiting even prima facie contractual enforcement to those commitments that are accompanied by some formal or informal manifestation of intention to be legally bound will lead to some cases of over- and under-enforcement from the standpoint of the underlying principles of will, reliance, fairness, restitution, and efficiency. On the one hand, if limited to highly formalized manifestations of consent, it will fail to capture all promises to which parties have actually consented. On the other hand, if expanded to include highly contextual indicia of consent such as those just discussed, it may lead to the enforcement of some commitments that should be left unenforced. Moreover, standing alone, consent to be legally bound does not immediately explain the limitations on its application; for example, in cases involving promises to perform illegal acts or consent to servitude.[28] Finally, although the consent criterion accounts for much of existing contract doctrine, this "fit" alone does not entirely justify a conclusion that it should be the sole criterion of contractual obligation.[29]

My purpose here is simply to compare "contract as promise" with "contract as consent." In particular, contract as consent better explains and justifies the objective theory of assent and the default rules that comprise the bulk of contract law.

A. The objective theory of assent

The law of contracts, property, and torts can be viewed as defining boundaries within which each person may make her own choices in pursuit of her own happiness.[30] You are allowed to do what you wish with what is yours (as defined by property law), provided that you do not infringe (as defined by tort law) on the property of others—including the inalienable property rights one has in one's own body. Contracts provide the means by which a person can transfer her property to another by her consent (although wholly gratuitous transfers are considered to be an aspect of property law, not contracts).

So contract, property, and torts—along with other subjects such as restitution—can be viewed as providing the legal boundaries that define the scope of individual liberty and distinguish rightful from wrongful conduct. To act rightfully is to remain within one's boundaries; wrongful conduct is when one crosses over into another's rightful

[28] My treatment of this subject examines the underlying entitlements that parties bring to transactions and that are transferred by their consent. Because some of these entitlements are inalienable, they cannot be transferred even with the consent of the parties. *See* Barnett, *Inalienable Rights* (defining inalienable rights as one that cannot be extinguished by right holder).

[29] For additional normative support of the consent criterion, *see* Barnett, The Oxford Introductions to U.S. Law, at 127–47 (discussing enforceability of contracts and consent).

[30] This section is drawn from Barnett, The Oxford Introductions to U.S. Law, at 72–4.

domain. These "boundaries" do not presuppose an atomistic individualism in which each person is an island. Contract, property, and torts are thoroughly relational or social. They address the fact that each person's actions can potentially affect others by distinguishing those actions that are nevertheless permissible from those that are not. In a world of atomistic individuals—or Robinson Crusoes on desert islands—no such concepts would be needed.

Fried agrees with this. "The law of property defines the boundaries of our rightful possessions, while the law of torts seeks to make us whole against violations of those boundaries, as well as against violations of the natural boundaries of our physical person."[31] And contract? "[T]he law of contracts facilitates our disposing of these rights on terms that seem best to us."[32] So far, so good. But this analysis leads not to enforcing our promises per se, but to enforcing consensual exchanges of entitlements—and an objective theory of contract, modified by a "subjective twist."

If the law is doing its boundary-defining job, each person should know, or be able to find out, what physical resources belong to her for her use, and what belongs to others, as well as how to use what is hers without interfering with the similar rights of others. In this way, the existence of these legal boundaries, or limits on the scope of rightful conduct, provides vital information to all those who might wish to avoid disputes and respect the rights of others, provided they know what those rights are. Potential conflicts between persons who might otherwise vie for control of a given resource are thus avoided, and society as a whole is rendered more harmonious.

In contract law, this informational or "boundary-defining" function is served by requiring that consent to alienate or transfer one's rights must be manifested by one party to the other in a manner that provides a criterion of enforcement. Without a manifestation of assent that is accessible to all affected parties, the law will have failed to clearly identify and communicate to both parties (and to third parties) the rightful boundaries that must be respected. Without such communication, parties to a transaction (and third parties) cannot accurately ascertain what constitutes rightful conduct and what constitutes a commitment on which they can rely. Disputes that might otherwise have been avoided will occur, and the attendant uncertainties of the transfer process will discourage beneficial reliance.

Although requiring the consent of one party to alienate or transfer her rights to another is essential to achieve the boundary-defining function of law, whether one has consented to a transfer of rights generally depends not on one's subjective opinion about the meaning of one's freely chosen words or conduct, but on the ordinary meaning that is attached to them. If the word "yes" ordinarily means yes, then a subjective and unrevealed belief that "yes" means no is generally immaterial. Only a general reliance on objectively ascertainable assertive conduct will enable a legal system to perform its boundary-defining function.

[31] Fried, Contract as Promise, at 1–2. He provides a nice, concise defense of property rights at 100–1.

[32] Fried, Contract as Promise, at 2.

It is true that, because one of the core concerns of contract is that the actual or inner subjective welfare of each party be increased,[33] contracts are interpreted with an eye towards honoring the actual intentions of the parties. In the main, genuinely consensual exchanges are value-enhancing. Because we cannot read each other's minds, however, only the "reasonable" or objective interpretation of the commitment will establish the clear boundaries that are required for persons to pursue happiness without interfering with the like pursuit by others of their happiness.

On the other hand, the "objective" approach to assent incorporates a subjective twist. Before one party may rely on the "objective" assent of another, that party must have subjectively understood the other party to have intended that meaning and actually relied upon it.[34] And, when it comes to discerning the meaning of the parties' agreement, where both parties subjectively agree on an idiosyncratic meaning—or when one party is subjectively aware of the idiosyncratic meaning held by the other—the idiosyncratic meaning will trump that of the reasonable person.[35]

There is nothing novel or revolutionary about contract law's concern for the protection of reliance by one contracting party on the commitment of the other. One of the most important functions of the institution of property rights is to legally protect certain expectations of the rights holder so that she may rely on the continued use of certain resources. For example, an owner of land relies upon her title when she invests in building a house or a factory upon it, because she expects that her title will be honored by a legal system in the future. She also relies upon her title when she leaves town on vacation, expecting her property to still be hers when she returns.

The alleged conflict in contracts between "will" and "reliance" results from focusing on one party to a transaction or the other. But, like property, the boundary-defining aspect of contract defines and regulates the relations between persons. Basing the prima facie case of contractual obligation on the manifestation of consent to be legally bound facilitates this relational quality of contract law.

B. From gap-filling to default rules

As seen in Section I, because he equates contract with promise, Fried concludes that an appeal to extra-contractual considerations becomes necessary when "gaps" arise in one's promise.[36] This stance stemmed not only from his commitment to contract as promise, but also from the "gap-filling" conception of contract law that was regnant when he wrote.

For a long time, many of the rules of contract law were called "gap fillers," which emphasized that they applied precisely when the agreement—or promises—of the parties did not address the issue governed by the rule. In short, the rules of contract law applied when there was a "gap" in the assent of the parties. By adopting this terminology, the consent of the parties could be cast as irrelevant to contract law because

[33] *See* Barnett, The Oxford Introductions to U.S. Law, at xix–xxi (discussing three core concerns of contract law).

[34] *See* Barnett, The Oxford Introductions to U.S. Law, at 71–2.

[35] *See* Barnett, The Oxford Introductions to U.S. Law, at 85–6.

[36] This section is based on Barnett, The Oxford Introductions to U.S. Law, at xxi–xxii, 99–100. For a much more extensive account of default rules and consent, *see* Barnett, *The Sound of Silence*.

contract law applied precisely when the consent of the parties did not exist. As we saw, this led Fried to conclude that much of contract law itself, not being based on the promises of the parties, was noncontractual.

Since *Contract as Promise* appeared, however, this "gap-filling" image of contract law has been supplanted to a great extent by the image of contract law as "default rules." The default rules of contract law are like the default margins supplied by your word-processing program that apply unless you change them. As such, the rules of contract law apply unless the parties "contract around" them by putting a different term in their agreement. Although some contract law doctrines cannot be contracted around, the great majority of contract law rules are default rules. Indeed, most of the cases studied in contracts courses would not be included had the parties simply inserted an express clause to cover the issue that later arose.

Whereas the image of "gap fillers" emphasized the discontinuity between contract law and the consent of the parties, the concept of default rules highlights an intimate connection between contract and consent. Notwithstanding that the rules of contract law are supplied by the courts or legislature rather than by the parties, under certain circumstances, the parties can be said to have consented to the application of those background rules by remaining silent and accepting their operation.

Some have maintained that the cost of contracting should be reduced by applying default rules that most parties would agree to, placing the onus on the minority of dissenting parties to expressly contract around the rules. While this may sometimes be a good way of selecting contract law rules, other considerations may also be taken into account. In particular, the background default rules can be chosen to reduce misunderstandings about the terms that will actually apply in the event of a dispute, even if that means applying default rules that all, or nearly all, parties expressly contract around. By contracting around the default rules, both parties become subjectively aware of the existence of the relevant term. When this happens, far from being inimical to consent, counter-majoritarian default rules can increase the likelihood that both parties are consenting to the same thing.

So far as freedom of contract is concerned, it sometimes does not matter what the "gap filling" default rule is, so long as the parties had access to it. It is rational for repeat players (or one-shot players in large transactions) to learn the content of the default rules via their lawyers. By remaining silent, they have consented to whatever term the law supplies as a gap filler and the conflict between freedom from and freedom to contract is ameliorated. Parties who do not contract around these default rules can realistically be said to have objectively manifested their consent to them.

But the default rules supplied by contract law will also apply when one or both parties are "rationally ignorant." It is rational to remain ignorant of the background rules of contract law when the cost of finding out the background rules that will be supplied by a court, for example by hiring a lawyer, is greater than the risk of agreeing to an undesired term. When this is the case, as it often is for one-shot players in low-stakes contracts, if courts supply a term that rationally ignorant parties would expect, the agreement is likely to be consistent with their consent.

For this reason, contract law should confine itself to common-sense default rules that unsophisticated parties would expect. When both parties are one-shot, rationally ignorant players, a common-sense default rule will likely reflect their tacit intentions. Repeat players who do not like the default rule are free to contract around it by inserting an express clause to the contrary in the agreement. By so doing, they will put the rationally ignorant party on notice that the term actually governing the transaction is not one that it would ordinarily expect, so they can decide whether to accept or reject the agreement with this unexpected term in mind.

In this way, default rules reflecting the conventional expectations of the less-sophisticated party will induce contracting behavior by repeat players that will minimize latent subjective disagreements, and thereby reduce the likelihood that the court will inadvertently impose upon the parties a term they did not expect, and to which it cannot be said they objectively consented.

Fried anticipated much of this analysis of the role of conventions in filling gaps. "Since actual intent is (by hypothesis) missing, a court respects the autonomy of the parties so far as possible by construing an allocation of burdens and benefits that reasonable persons would have made in this kind of arrangement."[37] He then immediately says this "treats the contract as a kind of charter or constitution for the parties' relation."[38] Had Fried not been blinded by his vision of contract as promise, he could have seen the next step: consent to the "charter or constitution" of the parties is simply consent to contract!

Yet his commitment to contract as promise leads Fried to shrink from this conclusion. After asserting that "contractual accidents occur precisely because no mutual engagements have been made," he concludes that contract law constructs "a kind of nonconsensual penumbra around the consensual core."[39] And how does it construct this penumbra? "Obviously some standard of sharing external to the intention of the parties must control."[40] By his account then, this standard is outside of contract as promise, and therefore outside contract.

But "contractual accidents" not covered by express agreements fill the pages of every contracts casebook. Indeed, very few of the classic cases of contract law would have existed had the parties expressly anticipated what precisely occurred. In effect, Fried must consider most of the actual law of contract to be noncontractual because it is not based on promise. He must abandon much of contract law to noncontractual considerations. This cannot be right.

Had the concept of default rules been available when he wrote, Fried might have been tempted to claim that the content of default rules is imported into the tacit understandings that surround an express promise. This would not have solved his basic problem, however, unless he conceded that there was not one, but two "promises:" the promise to perform, and the promise to be bound by the default rules supplied by the law of contract. This second commitment is not really a promise; it is simply the consent to be legally bound.

That consent to be legally bound is not a second "promise" was understood by Samuel Williston, the father of the modern promise theory of contract that, thanks to

[37] Fried, Contract as Promise, at 73 (emphasis added).
[38] Fried, Contract as Promise, at 73.
[39] Fried, Contract as Promise, at 72. Notice the use of "consensual" and "nonconsensual."
[40] Fried, Contract as Promise, at 72.

him, was embodied in the *Restatement of Contracts*. Williston made exactly this point when defending his proposed Uniform Written Obligations Act that would enforce a written promise without bargained-for consideration "if the writing also contains an additional express statement, in any form of language, that the signer intends to be legally bound."[41]

When asked by a commissioner whether, under Williston's proposal, "an express promise . . . would need another express promise added to that," Williston replied: "Another express statement that you intend to be legally bound. That is not another express promise, but it is a statement that you intend your promise not simply to create the moral obligation which attaches to every promise, but you intend that it shall create a legal obligation."[42] Although not a promise, such a statement would be a manifestation of intention to be legally bound, or what I call "consent."

Because it explains and justifies as contractual both the objective theory of contract along with its subjective twist, and the bulk of the default rules supplied by the law of contract, "contract as consent" is superior to "contract as promise." And, although Fried was right to shift our focus to moral concerns, his focus on contract as promise is problematic because it invites importing considerations of morality or virtue into the interpersonal law of contracts. This is because Fried mistakenly focused on what might be called "private" as opposed to "public" considerations of morality.

III. The Public Morality of Contract

The importance of "contract as consent" as opposed to "contract as promise" has come to be recognized by a new generation of contract scholars each of whom has questioned the model of contract as promise. I am thinking of such writers as Aditi Bagchi,[43] Andrew Gold,[44] Dori Kimel,[45] and my colleague Greg Klass.[46] I do not claim that each of these writers adopts what I call "a consent theory of contract" *in toto*. To the contrary, each has been critical of aspects of my approach. But each has also expressed grave skepticism of the "contract as promise" model and sympathy for a consent-based alternative to it. These scholars do not deny that there is a morality of contract, but insist it is not the same morality as promise.

[41] Uniform Written Obligation Act, No. 475, § 1, 1927 Pa. Laws 985, 985 (codified at 33 PA. STAT. ANN. § 6 (West 1997)).

[42] HANDBOOK OF THE NAT'L CONFERENCE OF COMM'RS ON UNIFORM STATE LAWS & PROCEEDINGS OF THE THIRTY-FIFTH ANNUAL MEETING (1925), reprinted in BARNETT, CONTRACTS, at 703.

[43] *See* Aditi Bagchi, *Separating Contract and Promise*, 38 FLA. ST. U. L. REV. 709, 754 (2011) ("It is appropriate to ask whether a party spoke and acted in a way that made it reasonable for the other party to believe that she intended to be bound. But the inquiry cannot end there").

[44] *See* Andrew S. Gold, *A Property Theory of Contract*, 103 NW. U. L. REV. 1, 61–2 (2009) ("A promisor's consent is necessary to a contractual obligation. However, contractual promises also depend on the acts of the promisee, and it is this feature that makes contracts binding").

[45] *See* DORI KIMEL, FROM PROMISE TO CONTRACT: TOWARDS A LIBERAL THEORY OF CONTRACT 136–42 (2003) (discussing "intention to create contractual relations").

[46] *See* generally Gregory Klass, *Intent to Contract*, 95 VA. L. REV. 1437 (2009) (examining doctrinal rules as reflecting in various ways the parties' intentions to be legally bound).

Charles Fried was entirely correct to notice something missing from the "law and economics" and "death of contracts" models of contract in vogue when he wrote *Contract as Promise*. And that something could be called "morality." But "morality" is ambiguous insofar as it has more than one aspect. And the morality of promise keeping is neither the only nor the best conception of morality to explain contractual obligation and distinguish contract from tort.

One way to express this is to distinguish "private" from "public" morality. Private morality governs the way one ought to live one's life. It identifies the duties one owes to oneself and to others. The term "ethics" perhaps best describes this moral domain. In contrast, public morality defines when coercion may be justifiably used against an individual for breaching a duty. The term "justice" best describes this moral domain. The old distinction between "perfect" and "imperfect" rights and duties also captures these two moralities. Perfect rights[47]—as in "I have a perfect right to that"—and perfect duties are enforceable; imperfect rights and duties are unenforceable and rely on moral suasion.

Lon Fuller offered a similar distinction between the "morality of aspiration" and the "morality of duty." "The morality of aspiration. . . is the morality of the Good Life, of excellence, of the fullest realization of human powers."[48] In contrast, the "morality of duty" provides "the basic rules without which an ordered society is impossible, or without which an ordered society directed toward certain specific goals must fail of its mark."[49] The morality of duty "does not condemn men for failing to embrace opportunities for the fullest realization of their powers. Instead, it condemns them for failing to respect the basic requirements of social living."[50] With respect to each other, "[w]here the morality of aspiration starts at the top of human achievement, the morality of duty starts at the bottom."[51]

Fried himself once offered a metaphor that distinguished between the realm of "philosophy" and the domain of "law." Philosophy, he wrote, proposes "an elaborate structure of arguments and considerations that descend from on high but stop some twenty feet above the ground."[52] In contrast, "[i]t is the peculiar task of law to complete this structure of ideals and values, to bring it down to earth; to complete it so that it is seated firmly and concretely and shelters real human beings against the storms of passion and conflict."[53]

According to Fried, "[t]he law is really an independent, distinct part of the structure of value."[54] Additionally, "[t]he lofty philosophical edifice does not determine what the last twenty feet are, yet if the legal foundation is to support the whole, then ideals and values must constrain, limit, inform, and inspire the foundation—but no more."[55] On this account, if the institution of "promise" lies within the realm of philosophy, as it

[47] *See* Adam Smith, Lectures on Jurisprudence 5 (R. L. Meek et al. eds., Liberty Classics 1982) ("The end proposed by justice is the maintaining men in what are called their perfect rights").

[48] Lon L. Fuller, The Morality of Law 5 (1964).

[49] Fuller, The Morality of Law, at 5–6.

[50] Fuller, The Morality of Law, at 6.

[51] Fuller, The Morality of Law, at 5.

[52] Charles Fried, *Rights and the Common Law*, in Utility and Rights 215, 231 (R. G. Frey ed., 1984).

[53] Charles Fried, *The Artificial Reason of the Law or: What Lawyers Know*, 60 Tex. L. Rev. 35, 52 (1981).

[54] Fried, *Rights and the Common Law*, at 231.

[55] Fried, *Rights and the Common Law*, at 231.

clearly seems to in *Contract as Promise*, then Fried's metaphor instructs that it is "independent" from and "does not determine" what constitutes the actual law of contract.

Viewed this way, the private morality of promise resides in the realm of ethics or what Fried calls "philosophy." In contrast, the morality of contract resides in the realm of justice to be governed by what Fried calls "law."[56] In Fullerian terms, whereas the ethical duty to keep one's promises is part of the private morality of aspiration, the duty to adhere to one's contractual commitments is part of the public morality of duty and is a requirement of justice. In his timely and worthwhile effort to ground contract in morality, Fried made a categorical mistake by focusing on the wrong moral construct. And this mistake resulted in his inability to reconcile much of the actual law of contract with the internal morality of contract.

Conclusion

Contract as Promise is a remarkable intellectual accomplishment of which Professor Fried should be proud. It made—and continues to make—a signal contribution to our understanding of contract law. For those who have accepted the contract as promise model, Fried correctly identified the core of contractual obligation. For those who, like me, reject contract as promise, Fried's contribution is twofold. First, he stood astride the momentum among contracts theorists to reject freedom of contract and collapse contract into tort and said "stop!" And stop it did. Second, his clear explication of the model of contract as promise, along with his candid admission of its limits, opened a theoretical space for a model of contractual obligation that better comports with the distinction in morality between the right and the good and that better explains and justifies the law of contract: contract as consent.

[56] I examine the relationship between justice and the rule of law at length in Randy E. Barnett, The Structure of Liberty: Justice and the Rule of Law (rev. ed., 2014).

4

Is There a Reason to Keep a Promise?

*Joseph Raz**

Recent times have seen the publication of a good number of articles and book chapters about promises and related normative phenomena like contracts, agreements, voluntary undertakings, and consent. Of these one may think that promises are the least important, and if we think of the kind of promises that moral and political philosophers write about this may be so. At least it is true that most undertakings and agreements are much less formally created, arising not so much out of explicit acts of commitment as out of the implied meaning and consequences of an interaction over time. Discussions of promises commonly aim to illuminate much more than promises. They aim to explain voluntary undertakings in general, and to shed light on consent, hypothetical consent, and agreements. That promises are undertaken (or are at least discussed by philosophers as if they are undertaken) in an act of commitment merely makes them clearer and easier to discuss, but *mutatis mutandis* they stand for the wider class.

But do they? Possibly the paradigm, and therefore the explanation, is radically different. It may be in the web of mutual obligations arising out of stable continuous interactions, of one or another of recognized kinds, among people, as in personal friendship, or in parent–child relations, or the relation between a client and his regular supplier of goods or services.

I will not discuss the claims of this second type of explanation. It seems to be credible, and of great importance to the understanding of social life. I doubt, though, that it can displace the accounts of promises and other undertakings generated by acts of commitment. They require a different explanation, and their explanation is also vital to an understanding of human interactions. The explanation of promises alone is the topic of this chapter.

The chapter discusses the bare bones of promises. Promises are made by acts of communication, but the content of the promise is not the same as what is said in making the promise. Much of it is implied rather than said (did I, when promising to water your garden daily during your trip away, promise to do so first thing in the morning, as we know that we know that you do?), and some of it is determined by the general moral principles governing the conditions that apply to promises (that they lapse if the promisor is paralyzed, that failure to perform the promised act because it could only be performed by killing someone is not a breach of the promise, etc.). They have different meanings in different contexts, though sometimes made almost useless when the context is too thin (a stranger comes up to me asking for a loan of a dollar, promising to return it the following day—if I give him the money this is only because I discount

* I am grateful to David Owens and to participants in my seminar at Columbia 2012, and in the Harvard Moral and Political Philosophy Workshop 2012 for helpful comments on earlier drafts.

the promise, though I am unlikely to reject it openly as this would openly display distrust of him). At the other extreme within a close intimate relationship promises may be out of place. Friends trust each other to act sensitively and the very fact that one promises an action whose performance should have been taken for granted may be inappropriate in that it conveys that one does not believe that the friend trusts one. And if one did promise and broke the promise it may be inappropriate for the other to express criticism invoking the promise, rather than the failure to act as one should have anyway, for that would show that one does not count on the other to be sensitive to the situation. I'm writing about the bare bones of promises, ignoring the rich contexts in which they occur, because the richness is based on familiarity with the bare bones and that enables the embedding of promises in the rich fabric of life.

If promises are binding, if they are cogent ways for people to bind themselves, there must be a reason to do as one promised. The chapter is motivated by belief that there is a difficulty in explaining what that reason is, a difficulty that is not often noticed. It arises because the reasons that promising creates are content independent. Similar difficulties arise regarding other content-independent reasons, though their solution need not be the same.

Section I introduces an approach to promises, and outlines an account of them that I have presented before.[1] It will form the backdrop for the ensuing discussion. The problems discussed in the chapter arise, albeit in slightly modified ways, for various other accounts as well. It is, however, helpful to use a specific account as a springboard leading to one explanation of promissory reasons, namely of the reasons that valid promises constitute for performing the promised act (Section II). We can call it the bare reasons account. Sections III and IV will raise difficulties with that account leading to its abandonment in favor of an alternative in Sections V and VI. Throughout I will avoid technicalities except when they matter to the issues under consideration. Thus I will refer indistinguishably to the promise, the promising, or the promising act as the reason or the source of the reason, or something that creates or establishes or provides a reason. I will not consider the conditions for a promise to be valid (can young children bind themselves by promising? Are promises to act immorally binding? Are promises binding after the death of the promisee, etc?), and will assume that they are fulfilled in the cases here discussed. And for the most part I will not comment about the special character of obligations, even though promisors have an obligation to keep the promise, and assume no more than that they are reasons. Nor will I say much about the fact that promisees have a right that the promise be kept.[2]

I. Promissory Reasons as Content-Independent Reasons

To see the difficulty think of an ordinary case: I have reason not to hit you, in fact there are a number of such reasons: it may injure you, it may cause you pain, invade your

[1] *See Promises and Obligations, in* Law, Society and Morality: Essays in Honour of H. L. A. Hart 210 (P. M. S. Hacker ed., 1977).

[2] Though to avoid misunderstanding it is worth remarking that on my view the right to have a particular promise kept is derivative from the general right to have promises made to one kept, and it is grounded on the general interest promisees have to have the promise-generated relation to promisors.

body, etc. They all depend on the nature of the action, its consequences and context. Now think of a reason arising out of a promise, say my reason to let you use my car tomorrow. The reason is that I promised to do so. But that very same reason applies to all my promises. If I promise to feed your cat next week, to come to your party, to send flowers in your name to your mother on Mother's Day, to lend you my new DVD, or whatever the action I promise to perform (or to refrain from) the reason is the same: my promise. Of course, these are different promises. But normatively speaking they are the same, they are all binding on me because they are promises I made, regardless of what is the act promised. This is why they are (called) content-independent reasons.[3] There are considerations that make them binding, that account for the fact that the promisor has a duty to perform the promised act. But these are reasons why a promise is binding as a promise. They have nothing to do with its specific content.

This last paragraph exaggerates. Some acts or omissions cannot be promised. One can mean to and even try to promise them, by communicating an intention that would have made a valid promise had it related to acts or omissions that can be promised, but the putative promise will not be binding.[4] If so, in what sense are promises content-independent reasons?

One simple idea is that promises are binding qua promises (or rather that that is the only ground for their binding character of relevance here), and that they are promises because they are communications of an intention to undertake an obligation by that very communication, regardless of their content, regardless of which act or omission they are about. I suggested that there are exceptions; acts that one cannot promise to perform. For example, a promise (given in current circumstances) to exterminate *homo sapiens* or all primate species would not be binding. One may think that so long as such exceptions are rare they do not undermine the suggestion that promises are content independent. Such classifications are commonly subject to exceptions. For example, most of his readers do not think that Nozick's idea of side-constraints is undermined by the fact that, as he allows, side-constraints are not exceptionless.[5]

We have, however, to say more in order to explain the kind of reasons we are talking about. We require an explanation on two grounds: (1) if the exceptions are not to undermine the cogency of the classification, there must an explanation of what it is that makes them exceptional. Perhaps there is no need for a special explanation when the suspected exceptions are borderline cases. But many, including my examples, are

[3] The term was coined by H. L. A. Hart. *See* H. L. A. Hart, *Legal and Moral Obligation, in* ESSAYS IN MORAL PHILOSOPHY 102 (A. I. Melden ed., 1958); H. L. A. HART, ESSAYS ON BENTHAM 254–5 (1982). For my own discussion *see* Joseph Raz, *Authority, Law, and Morality*, 68 THE MONIST 295–324 (1985), *reprinted in* JOSEPH RAZ, ETHICS IN THE PUBLIC DOMAIN (1995); JOSEPH RAZ, THE MORALITY OF FREEDOM (1986); JOSEPH RAZ, *Reasoning with Rules, in* BETWEEN AUTHORITY AND INTERPRETATION 203 (2010). For some other discussions *see* P. Markwick, *Law and Content-Independent Reasons*, 20 OXFORD J. LEGAL STUD. 579 (2000), and Stephan Sciaraffa, *On Content-Independent Reasons: It's Not in the Name*, 28 LAW & PHIL. 233 (2009). As these discussions illustrate there are other kinds of content-independent reasons. For example, whenever any person or institution has (normative) power to impose duties on some people those duties are content independent for they are binding not because of their content but because they are the product of the use of duty-imposing powers.

[4] "Promise" and its cognates are used to refer both to what I here called a putative promise, and to a binding promise. As is common I rely on context to disambiguate their meaning.

[5] *See* ROBERT NOZICK, ANARCHY STATE AND UTOPIA 29ff. (1974).

not. (2) The acts for which we have content-independent reasons are acts for which we have such reasons because of some of their features: they bring the acts within the ambit of those reasons. So in classifying the reasons as content independent we mean that some aspects of (the content) of the acts are irrelevant to the fact that they fall within the ambit of those reasons. But that is true of all acts: reasons apply to them because of some, not all of their features. We need an explanation of the special way in which these reasons are content independent.

We can proceed on the assumption that all content-independent reasons are generated by the use of normative powers. This is not entirely true but the explanation of why the other cases are cases of content-independent reasons is analogous to explanations that apply to reasons generated by the use of normative powers.[6]

Normative powers are the abilities of people (or institutions) to change normative situations or conditions (i.e., to impose or repeal duties, to confer or revoke rights, to change status, etc.) by acts intended to achieve these changes, where the ability depends on (namely is based on, grounded on, justified by) the desirability (the value) of those people (or institutions) having them.

In the case of promises the value of the power is that it expands people's ability to fashion their lives, or aspects of their lives, by their actions. Through their promises they commit themselves to others. Up to a point, promises are analogous to decisions that constitute reasons for the deciders to perform the act they decided to perform. Both are ways of opening up options through closing other options, normatively speaking. Decisions, as well as having goals, facilitate undertaking complex activities (giving a ball, writing a symphony, etc.) that require a series of actions or concerted actions. Promises, being commitments to others, facilitate cooperation, the forging of relations that presuppose dependence, trust and joint actions, and more. For the sake of brevity I will refer to the value of having these powers as the value of enhanced control (of one's life),[7] though a somewhat different explanation of their value is required when the powers are held by institutions.

Now we have the answers to our questions: The claim that some (putative) promises are not binding presupposes a distinction between binding promises that are overridden by conflicting reasons, and promises that are not binding, and therefore

[6] A typical and relatively well-known example concerns the making of the first laws of a new legal system, e.g., of its first constitution. In all respects it is just like the use of legislative power, except that as the original lawmakers established the first laws of the system there was at the time no law that conferred legislative power on them. They may or may not have had mere moral power, but they did not have morally valid legal power to make the laws that they did.

[7] Note that no claim is made that trust or cooperation etc. require promises. They do not, but often the ability to promise makes it easier to facilitate them, as well as—by refraining from promising—to make clear that they are not sought. However (these observations are prompted by a question of Selim Berker), would not the value of enhanced control be equally served if people believed that they have the power to promise even though they do not have it? False beliefs always lead to the conduct that the same beliefs would have led to had they been true until they collide with reality, a collision that if circumstances are propitious, leads to their abandonment. The same is true of normative beliefs. Those who know that they do not have the power to promise will not be able to make promises (unless they are willing to mislead the promisees) and those who discover that there is no power to make binding promises will realize that all the promises made to them are not binding, and the trust and reliance they inspired are ill-founded, or depend on the promisees remaining ignorant of the truth. Not only does the vulnerability of the falsely

do not constitute any reason at all. The difference is that the former do, and the latter do not serve the value that grounds the power to promise, giving promises their normative force, making them reasons for the promised acts. The assumption is that there are some undertakings, ability to make which does not serve the value of having enhanced control. Ability to promise to become a slave may be an example, as is a promise to destroy all primates. If the assumption is mistaken, and that is a substantive moral question, then we have power to make such promises, and when made they are binding and constitute reasons.[8]

The crucial point is that it is not having the obligations one undertakes by promising that is valuable, in enhancing people's control or in some other way. These obligations may or may not be valuable. Even when they are their value does not establish the existence of a normative power to undertake them by a promise. The power is grounded in the desirability of people being able to commit themselves by the relevant act of communication. For example, it may or may not be desirable that Jean will have a duty to serve in the army, or to do jury service. It is a separate question whether it is desirable that she should be able to undertake such obligations by promising to serve. So the value of the ability to promise to help a neighbor, for example, is the value of being able to fashion one's life in one's relations to one's neighbors, and it is as important to people to be able to decide to keep a distance from their neighbors as to get involved with them. The value is in being able to decide *whether* to commit to the neighbors, not in the value of committing to them. When you can commit, not committing is itself significant, and the ability to commit at will makes it so. And indeed, we know that people can gain by avoiding commitment (but only when that avoidance is optional, when they could have committed). For example, one person may reward an agent for not committing to another.

Therefore, if one does not have a power to promise to extinguish all bird species, that is not because it would be bad to extinguish them. That would only show that the obligation that the promise would have generated had it been binding, is overridden. What explains the absence of the power to make such a (binding) promise is that it

secured enhanced control lead to it not being as valuable as the one provided by the power to promise. It is also misguided to think that a significant good is systematically secured by continued false belief, especially when this implies, as it does here, that people unknowingly rely on the other not knowing the truth.

[8] The considerations help with the question what intention is required for the promise to be valid. Clearly, an intention to keep the promise is not a condition of its validity. But is an intention to undertake an obligation by the act of communication such a condition? Is an intention to communicate an intention to undertake an obligation? Some would argue that the value of having the power to promise is served only so long as one is bound only when the promising is done with the intention to thereby undertake an obligation. But arguably an intention to communicate, by the conduct that constitutes promising, an intention to undertake an obligation is sufficient for the promise to be binding, according to the explanation I gave. Others say that neither intention is needed for a promise to be binding. Promises are binding if the promisee would reasonably assume that the intention to undertake (or to communicate an intention to undertake) is present. This, if unqualified, goes too far. The consequences of even reasonable mistakes may justly have to be borne by those who make them. However, when a reasonable mistake is due to careless or negligent conduct of the promisor, the promisor will have a duty to compensate for any untoward consequences of the mistake, and that would often be the same as a duty to keep the promise (or to compensate for its breach). It would be pedantic to expect our concepts to be clear about whether that duty is the promissory duty or a separate one.

is not desirable that one should be able to decide whether or not to undertake such a commitment.[9]

That is why the value of the ability to bind oneself to others, in identifying the range of acts performance of which we have the power to promise, establishes the sense in which the reasons to perform them are content independent: it is not independent of their character as promised acts (whose performance was undertaken in binding promises), but it is independent of all their other features. The fact that they depend only on this one external property makes the use of the term content independence natural.

II. Promissory Reasons as Bare Reasons

Does this explanation of why promises constitute content-independent reasons answer the question of the title? It appears to do so: we have reason to act as we promised because we promised, and promises are such reasons because they are the product of the use of a valuable normative power. This may be true, but it also generates a puzzle.

Given that normatively all promises have the force of a promise, it must be, the argument goes, that their strength or stringency is the same. It does not matter whether the promise was to look after your children while you are away on a work-trip next week, or to lend you a copy of the new Murakami novel. The reason to keep either of these promises is the same because they are both promises, and have the so-called weight that all promises have. This may appear absurd. But perhaps it is not. Arguably as promises they all have the same force or weight. But once given they may affect the course of events in different ways. In the children promise my friend forgoes making alternative arrangements for looking after his children in his absence, in the Murakami case he forgoes buying the novel in a book sale. Given these facts the results of breaking the promises will be very different, and therefore the force of the promise is different, much greater in the children promise than in the Murakami one. But the difference in the strength of the reasons for keeping the promises is due not to the bare facts that I made the promises, but to events that happened as a result of promising, and for which I am responsible. Qua promises my reasons to do as I promised are indeed the same, the appearance of the difference is due to other events for which I am responsible. Of course, one may point out that the additional reasons, the ones that depend on the consequences and/or context of the promise, would not constitute the reasons that they are but for the promise. Therefore, they are promise-generated reasons. But they are contingently dependent on the promise. Let us call them secondary strength-affecting factors. The bare fact of the promise generates a reason of the same strength in all cases, never mind what is the content of the promise.

This argument is reinforced by the fact that what I called secondary strength-affecting considerations need not even be present. Possibly the promise

[9] How broad is the category of cases regarding which it is not desirable that one should have the power to bind oneself? It may relate to types of acts (self-enslavement, etc.) or duration or other aspects of the promise (cannot promise to obey forever, etc.), and it applies to the largest class of cases that does not include a subclass (demarcated in universal terms) such that it is desirable to have the power to promise regarding it.

was not relied upon and did not affect the course of events in any way. Nevertheless, even such promises are binding. That shows, the argument proceeds, that the very reason to keep a promise is independent of these strength-affecting factors. The strength-affecting factors are indeed secondary. The bare promise, shorn of all these contingent additions, is the reason to do what I promised, and it always has the same strength.

Perhaps this conclusion is premature. Perhaps the strength of the promise is determined by the promisor in the act of making the promise. "Why can't the promisor communicate an intention to create an obligation specifically of strength S?"[10] Perhaps promisors do so explicitly: "I promise to lend you my book, and that promise will have the strength S," but more commonly they may do so by their demeanor, or by making the promise in circumstances that imply that it has a certain strength.

The answer lies in the nature of promises. By promising we create a reason to act as promised. The nature of the promised act contributes to the determination of how much I am willing to give up to keep it. If I promise you $1,000 I create a reason that requires a greater "sacrifice" from me than if I promise you $1. I indicate that the promise has greater strength.[11] As each promise defeats "ordinary" self-regarding reasons against keeping it, the more it costs me the stronger it is: the more weighty reasons against keeping it that it defeats. So by making that promise I determine its strength at least to that extent. If promises are ever binding that is because of the value of people having the power to determine (up to a point) the strength of the promised act relative to their other interests. But that does not mean that there is value in people being able to determine the strength of the reasons that promises generate, or the strength of any other reasons, relative to the strength of reasons that arise out of the interests of others. There is not. I cannot make a binding promise to come to your party even if this will require me to injure or rob someone, or not to help a person just injured in an accident, etc. While it is, I assume, desirable that I should have some control over the strength of my promise relative to some of my own other interests, and the very making of a promise does just that, there is no case for letting me determine its strength relative to other people's needs, interests, etc.[12]

The strength of a reason is its standing when conflicting with other reasons. Assume that G has a general power to determine the strength of his promises. He can (a) promise to perform some action, and (b) determine that the promise will have a

[10] A question urged on me by David Owens.

[11] I have argued that promises have exclusionary force: They are reasons not to act for some reasons that apply to the promisor. More specifically, they are reasons not to act on some reasons that arise out of the promisor's convenience or his personal interests. That is why the reasons they provide are duties (roughly, exclusionary categorical reasons). This is consistent with the fact that the duty to act as promised can be overridden by some considerations relating to the promisor's interests or well-being.

[12] As always there are exceptions that confirm the underlying principle. Some promises are made in response to a request by the promisees that their interests or concerns shall not stand in the way: I may promise my partner that when choosing my next employer I will not be affected by her convenience, but by what is best for my own career. That promise binds me to downgrade reasons that concern her, but only in response to her own wishes.

certain strength, and he can do both by communicating an intention to do that by that very communication. He can of course promise to perform an act without determining what strength that promise has (beyond what is inherent in making a promise to perform that act). Can he also determine the strength of existing reasons without creating a new reason? Why not? He could, for example, do that by making the following promise: "Tomorrow I will do whatever serves my self-regarding interests regardless of whatever other reasons apply to me." That promise does not constrain him to perform any act he would not have reason to perform anyway (one's interests are reasons anyway). Its effect is merely to reduce to nothing the force of all reasons that derive from the interests of others applying to him. How much strength, if any, does this declaration have? I find nothing to suggest that there is any value in people having that power.

Two additional clarifications may be useful here. First, I ignore informal aspects of the manner of promising, those that convey sincerity, assurance of performance, etc., as they may affect trust in the promisor, but not the strength of his obligation. Second, different considerations apply to undertakings of different kinds, marked by their formal features. There are oaths of office (as a judge, etc.), and of loyalty (upon naturalization, etc.), vows of marriage, and more. These are voluntary undertakings that do or purport to affect the relative strength of reasons arising out of interests of people other than the person who undertakes them. Not all of them are normatively sound, and not all do yield valid undertakings. But some do, and those that do differ from promises in many ways, among them the fact that as they are established by law or custom: (a) people committing themselves do so in public; (b) they undertake duties whose content is determined by law or custom rather than by them; (c) there are restrictive qualifications for being able to undertake these obligations; and (d) strict conditions for being released from them; and all of these help explain why they do affect the strength of other people's interests. They establish, when sound, valuable optional patterns for structuring one's life, and relationships.

Back to the bare reasons account of promissory reasons. Though the reasons for embracing it may differ, it is often implicitly assumed, and has recently been explored by David Owens,[13] who traces it back to Hume's discussion of an analogue of the issue, applying to motives rather than to reasons.[14] According to it promising (when creating a binding promise) generates a bare promissory reason, which is the same reason with the same strength (relative to reasons relating to other people's interests and concerns) regardless of the promised act. However, the overall force of a promissory reason may be affected by secondary strength-affecting considerations, so that the case for keeping promises varies with these considerations.

[13] David Owens, *The Possibility of Consent*, 24 Ratio 402, 404 (2011). Rather than write about the obligations and reasons promises create he writes about the wrongings that (presumably only some) of their violations constitute. *See* his explanation of "bare wrongings" on p. 404 and on the relations between them and secondary reasons for keeping promisess on p. 405. These matters are explored in greater breadth in his Shaping the Normative Landscape pt. II (2012).

[14] David Hume, Treatise on Human Nature 482–3 (P. H. Nidditch ed., Oxford University Press 1978) (1740).

III. What is the Strength of Bare Promissory Reasons?

Later on I will argue that (a) while the reason for performing the promised act is the promise, (b) the strength of that reason is varied by factors that are not contingently related to the promising in the way that the secondary weight-affecting considerations are. But first, what is actually wrong with the thought that all promises qua promises have the same strength?

Imagine that I promised to do something today, and imagine that no secondary strength-determining factors apply. The promise was beyond doubt a binding one. Therefore, it constitutes a reason for performing the promised act. As is common, there are, however, also conflicting reasons. At the very least if the promise is to act, but sometimes even when it is to refrain from action, behaving as promised requires attention and effort that one could usefully put to other use. Hence the question: what is the strength of the promissory reason, how does it fare against the conflicting reasons?

Why not consider a case where there are no conflicting reasons?[15] Would not that reveal the true strength of the promissory reason on its own? No, is the answer. That would only establish whether the promise is binding at all. The strength, stringency, weight, importance, call it what you will, of a reason just is the case for conforming to it rather than to conflicting reasons.

So, what determines the bare strength of the promissory reason? As with all other practical reasons, it must depend on the considerations that make promises binding. At this point the content-independent character of our case complicates matters: The case for any particular promise being binding, thereby being a reason for the promised act, does not depend on the specific character of the action promised, but merely on the fact that it was promised. Therefore, it would appear that the case for keeping a promise must rest with factors that unite all binding promises regardless of their content. So, plausibly the factors that determine the strength of the reason to promise are to be found in the case for, the value of, possessing the power to promise. For example, given that I promised to let you use my car today, I have reason to let you use my car today. That reason does not depend on the wisdom or value of having made the promise, nor of your using the car, of having the chance to use it, nor of that chance being provided by me, nor on anything else to do with this particular promise and its content. It derives from the power to promise. Needless to say, I would not have the power if my promises did not bind me. They bind me because I have the power to bind myself, and I used it to make them.

Why not the other way round? Why not say that I have the power because my promises are binding? The order is the order of grounding or justification: as was suggested in Section II, we have the power to promise because it is valuable to be able to undertake obligations, of certain kinds and in certain conditions, and that value is sufficient to establish in us the normative power to do so. Powers, normative and otherwise, are not valuable unless some of their uses are. But their value is not in the value of their uses. It is in the value of the option to use them. Refraining from using them is one of

[15] We need not consider here whether a no-conflict situation is in principle possible.

the options that possession of powers provides, and indeed not using a power can be to the advantage of those who have it as much as using it. As was mentioned in Section II, they can earn money or other benefits by making it known (or by undertaking) that they will not use a power.

Here finally is the puzzle: I have a reason to let my friend use my car because I promised, and the promise is binding because that is the consequence of having and using the power to promise, and I have the power because of the value of the enhanced ability to shape my life that it provides. The value of that power should, I suggested, determine the force of the reason to keep the promise. But it does not seem to do so. My enhanced ability to control my life manifests itself in having the power to promise and in using it by promising. How does it reflect on the reason to keep a promise, and on its strength? Keeping the promise will not further enhance that ability, nor will breaking the promise undermine it. The normative case is a case for possessing the power to promise, not a case for keeping a promise, unless that is constitutive of or conducive to having the power. But is it? People who break their promises do nevertheless have the power to promise, as is evidenced by the fact that their promises are binding. If they were not there would be nothing wrong in breaking them.[16]

It is true that sometimes breaking promises will reduce the value of having the power to promise. Generally speaking the value of the power depends on the degree to which some people (those to whom we may wish to make promises) trust us to keep our promises. Sometimes, though far from always, breaking a promise undermines that trust. In such circumstances the case for protecting the value of the power to promise is one of the secondary strength-affecting considerations I referred to above. But in no case does it affect the strength of the bare reason to keep a promise, because it does not affect possession of the power to promise and the case for the power is the only resource that can provide bare promissory reasons for keeping promises.

It would, by this reasoning, appear that the value of having the power to promise is realized, and exhausts itself, by making binding promises. It does not determine the strength of the reason to keep one's promise. Worse still, it appears not to determine the strength of promissory reasons because it is powerless to give one a reason to keep promises.

IV. Is There a Bare Reason to Keep Promises?

I began with a puzzle about the resources available to determine the strength of the bare reason to keep a promise. In exploring it we discover that it goes further. It raises a question mark on the very existence of a reason to keep a promise. Earlier I assumed that the value of enhanced control over one's life, by providing an adequate case for having the power to promise, also constitutes an adequate case for the binding force

[16] Some people think that habitual promise breakers lose the normative power to promise. I think that they lose trust of others, and with it much of the value of having the power to promise, but they lose that power only if it is impossible for them to regain trust, and only if having the trust of others is the only way in which the power to promise is valuable to those who have it. Both conditions rarely materialize. It is true, though, that if a promise-breaker loses the confidence of people they will refuse to accept, or will rescind, any promise he may make.

of promises, for the power cannot exist without it, and thereby it establishes that there is a reason to keep them. But that may have been premature. Without resolving the puzzle about the force of bare promissory reasons, one may claim, there is no case for holding that there are any reasons for keeping promises. If so the reverse of the original argument holds: if one has power to promise one has reasons to keep one's promises. Therefore, since one does not have reason to keep promises one has no power to promise. Can it be that we have reason to keep our promises even though they do not have any strength? I doubt it. Here is an argument supporting the doubt:

First premise: The secondary strength-affecting considerations apply only if there is a bare reason to keep promises.

Of course there may be other reasons for performing the promised act. Letting you have my car today may express friendship or good will and trust, and there may be a case for lending you the car for reasons to do with these or similar considerations. But these are reasons to perform the promised act independently of whether or not there is a valid promise.[17] The same is true of reliance. Some writers have maintained either that people would not rely on promisors to perform the promised act, or that such reliance will not constitute a reason for promisors to perform it unless promises are binding and constitute reasons to act, at least if they were relied upon. But that is not true. People rely when they expect their reliance to be vindicated. This may be because they believe that binding promises were made, or more likely because they believe that the people on whom they rely think that they are bound by promises they made, but it does not presuppose that promises are binding. Nor is it the case that one has no reason to fulfil another's expectations when the other acted on them unless one made a valid promise to that person. The results of frustrating the reliance may be such as to require avoiding them. Besides, in many situations if the other innocently believed that I am bound by a valid promise that is a sufficient reason to behave as I would had I really been bound by such a promise. So, reliance can be an independent reason to behave as one promised. So can various other secondary reasons: where there is no binding promise they may be independent reasons in their own right. But they cannot be considerations affecting the strength of the reason to keep a promise, unless there is a binding promise that constitutes a reason, whose strength they affect.

Second premise: A reason that has no strength-determining factors is no reason at all. First, an aside: Could it be that it has some strength that we simply cannot know? Even if it has, the point is irrelevant here. The premise is about factors that make the strength what it is, regardless of our ability to know the strength. But throughout the discussion I assume that factors that ground reasons can in principle be known because reasons are factors that one can be guided by, one can act for, and that requires that they will be—in principle—knowable.[18] I further assume that not only can they be known, they can be understood. They are intelligible considerations, ones whose force and binding character can be understood.

[17] In saying that I am not denying that where there is a valid promise and a promissory reason to keep it some such considerations may affect its strength, may constitute strength-affecting considerations.

[18] *See* Joseph Raz, From Normativity to Responsibility, ch. 6 (2011).

Given that assumption, if a reason has strength or stringency there are grounds determining its stringency that can be known. And if there are none then either there is no reason or there is a reason whose degree of strength or stringency is zero. That possibility can be ruled out, given that the very idea of a reason is of a factor that militates in favor of some action (or omission), namely that lends some support to the possible conclusion that that action is the one to take.

But perhaps we should distinguish between two aspects of the normative force of reasons: the first is that they favor an action (or omission), the second that they have some strength or force. The first aspect is essential to all practical reasons, but the second is not. In its absence the reason cannot defeat any conflicting reasons, but it can (a) determine what is to be done in the absence of conflicting reasons,[19] and (b) be a tie-breaker. Can there be such reasons? They will be reasons that will be defeated if they conflict with another on their own,[20] however insignificant that other reason is. I find that hard to envisage: what could make it understandable that a consideration that militates for an action so that in the absence of any conflicting considerations one would have conclusive reason to perform it will nevertheless be defeated by even the most insignificant conflicting reason? I suspect that the distinctions on which we rely in deliberation and in reasoning cannot cut that fine. Therefore, I am inclined to conclude that: Unless there are factors that determine the strength of a bare reason it is not a reason, and we have discovered no such factors. Indeed, if all promises have the same strength it is difficult to see what could determine it.

This argument does not contradict any of the premises of the earlier argument that seemed to establish that there are binding promises. Rather, it points to a missing step: that argument relied on the fact that it would be good if people had the power to promise, and that there is no conflicting normative case sufficient to show that on balance people should not have that power. But that is not enough to show that people have the power to promise. It is impossible to have the power to promise, however good it may be to have it, unless that one promised is a reason to do as one promised, and it is impossible for there to be a reason to keep a promise unless it has strength. If promissory reasons have no strength they do not exist and however desirable it is to have the power to promise one cannot have it.

Yet we do have it. It would seem that I have failed to notice some factor that connects the case for the power to promise with the reasons to keep promises in each case in which one has promised. The fault may be in looking for too direct a connection. Here is one different approach, based on considerations of integrity: the power to promise serves and expresses one's ability to have some control over one's normative situation. Having exercised that power by making a promise it would show lack of integrity to deny that one is bound by the promise. Possibly, the degree to which

[19] I suggested above that that is hardly ever the case with actions. But perhaps it is not that rare with omissions.

[20] Note that the claim that any reason has some strength supporting the conclusion that the action it is a reason for is to be done is consistent with allowing that its existence makes no difference to the conclusion that the action is the one to be undertaken. It is possible that whenever that reason for doing Φ is present so is another reason for Φ-ing, and that the combined strength of both is no greater than the strength of either one of them in support of the action.

denying that a promise is binding compromises one's integrity varies with the content of the promise, and therefore while the reason is always the promise its strength varies with the damage to one's integrity of denying that it is binding.

But the argument is suspect for it merely shows that the promisor has reason not to deny that his promises are binding. Is that enough to show that they are binding (even assuming that the reasons not to deny that they are are conclusive)? Besides, the argument is guilty of *petitio principii*. Integrity is involved only regarding people's attitudes to obligations they have. It cannot establish the existence of those obligations, and therefore it cannot establish that promises create reasons.

The conclusion towards which we are driven is that there are no bare promissory reasons, and therefore no considerations that determine their strength. The thought that there are misunderstands promises because it misunderstands the point of promises. This conclusion can be reinforced by examples.

Consider the car-lending case with some additions. Abby promised to bring Ben her car and leave it in his garage for his own use for the whole of today. Yesterday Ben, who lives alone, was taken suddenly ill and is now in hospital unconscious, where he is expected to stay for at least a week. The example is meant to be one of a bare promise in that no conditions that could qualify as secondary strength-affecting considerations obtain.[21] Would Abby be breaking her promise if she fails to leave the car in Ben's garage, and instead uses it to do her shopping? Could it be that she would be breaking the promise and violating her duty to Ben, but that she is justified in doing so because the reasons to use the car for her shopping defeat the reasons for keeping the promise?

It is hard to think of any reasons that would not defeat the promising reason. Suppose it is just to save her the expense on petrol of driving the car to Ben's place, or suppose it is just saving herself the bother of getting out of bed in time to deliver the car. It appears that any reason against keeping the promise would in the circumstances override the promising reason. That makes it virtually impossible to maintain that the promise is a reason to perform the promised act. As we saw, to be a reason the promise must have some strength or force, and strength just is resistance to conflicting reasons. A reason that is defeated by any possible conflicting reason is (possibly apart from some exceptional cases) one without force and therefore is not a reason. That conclusion generalizes to all promises. The reason we are investigating is the reason provided by a bare promise according to the account that takes the strength of that reason to be the same regardless of the content of the promise. It is determined just by the fact that it is a promise, and is the strength of all bare promissory reasons (promises to counteract climate change, to provide pensions for the elderly, etc.). It appears that the bare reason account must be mistaken.

The way out is to deny that in the circumstances Abby is bound by the promise. Promises, like intentions, decisions, orders, vows, permissions, and the like are subject to conditions. These can be described as part of the content of the promise (I will give you the car so long as there is the slightest chance that having it will be of use to you,

[21] That means that it is assumed that Ben intended to use the car himself, made no arrangements for others to use it if he is prevented from doing so, that there is no one with the right to make such arrangements in his stead, etc.

or something along those lines) or they can be described as part of the ground rules that limit the kind of promises people can make: the limits can be conditions under which promises lapse, etc. (rather than merely specifying kinds of promises that can never be binding). In some cases one of those ways of perceiving the situation is better than the other. In some cases it matters not which way it is taken to be. What matters is that in some kinds of circumstances, and Abby's are one such kind, promises that appear to apply to them do not in fact apply.

This seems right, but it is also right that these background conditions eliminate the possibility of bare promissory reasons. It is plausible to think that in all situations to which no strength-affecting considerations apply there is no valid promissory reason. That casts doubt on the bare reasons account. It is time to consider an alternative account.

V. The Point of Promises and the Interests of Promisees

We have some building blocks: The point of the power to promise is to expand people's options by enabling them to undertake obligations at will, more specifically by communicating to the promisees an intention to undertake those obligations by that very act of communication. It is a valuable power, which is used (or not used) for many purposes. The value of having the power, and the fact that that value defeats contrary considerations, constitute the case for the existence of the power by showing that its existence is desirable.

The difficulty we encountered is that it is impossible to have the power unless promising creates a reason to perform the promised act. And so far we have found no way in which the value of having the power by itself generates such a reason. We need an account that shows how the exercise of the power changes the normative situation, most likely in different ways on different occasions, and how through that the value of the power to promise can explain why one has a reason to keep promises, the same reason, but possibly with a different strength on each occasion.

To find it we have to describe more fully what we do when we promise. One way to think of it is to think of the point, or purpose, of promises generally, meaning here not the point of having the power to promise (discussed earlier) but the point served by promises made. Different promises or classes of promises have, no doubt, different specific points or purposes. But all of them are particular instances of the general point of promises, and it determines what we necessarily do when we promise. For example, that general point cannot be to confer an advantage on the promisee, for while often this is the whole or part of the point of a promise, it need not be. It need not even appear or purport to be. I can promise my mother that I will look after my health, or that I will give money to Oxfam, or that I will never give her interests precedence over the interests of my father, for example. But something about promises being obligations undertaken *for the promisee* must be right. The question is how to understand the phrase "*for the promisee.*"

But why must it be that promises are obligations undertaken *for the promisee*?[22] There are two defining features of promises whose explanation establishes the point.

[22] There are marginal cases, but probably not clear counter-examples. I can promise my friend to diet if he sets me a weekly eating menu. Clearly that is a promise meant to help me rather than him. But it

First, obligations are binding only once communicated to the promisee. Second, the promisee has a right that the promise be kept, and a right and power to waive his right,[23] releasing the promisor from his undertaking, at any time and at his complete discretion. These features are not necessary elements of all undertakings. Vows do not require a recipient in the same way (though some have recipients). Undertaking an office, say of a judge, is not open to revocation at will by some recipients, etc. But the two are defining features of promises. Some writers add a third pointer in the same direction: the promisee, they say, has to accept the promise for it to be binding. This may be an exaggeration. I may promise someone in person, face to face, to come and visit him in hospital tomorrow. He receives the promise stone faced, saying nothing and moving not a muscle. My promise is binding, and it requires some imagination to claim that it has been accepted. It is merely that the promisee can release me from the obligation, at any time, including when it is undertaken. He did not do so, which is why I am bound by it.

That the promisee has a right that the promissory duty be kept, and a power to waive it and terminate the duty, reinforces the thought that the obligations are meant to be for the promisees. However, as we saw, being *for the promisees* does not mean conferring on them an advantage. It has to be understood more broadly, perhaps something like responding to something they are interested in or have an interest in, or may become interested in or develop an interest in (by relying on the promised act, betting on it, or some other way) once the promise is made.

The combination of the two factors, (a) the obligation is *for the promisee* and (b) he has the power to rescind it, implies a third (c) that the promisor relinquishes control over the question of whether it ever was or still is or is likely to become of interest to or in the interest of the promisee. It is up to the promisee to judge that and cancel it or not cancel it. Promising, we may say, relates to the self-governing ability of the promisor and the promisee alike, though in different ways. The promisor's interest in enhanced ability to control his life establishes his power to promise, and promising is an exercise of the power. On the other side, the promise once made enhances the power of the promisee by giving him *the normative assurance* of the promised act. I will use this expression to refer to the assurance, which can be overridden and is therefore not absolute, that a promise gives the promisee. It is normative for it is provided by the normative structure of a promise. It consists of (a) the obligation the promisor undertakes plus (b) the power of the promisee to terminate that obligation, plus, (c) the disability just noted of the promisor to terminate the promissory obligation on the ground that it is no longer in the interest of the promisee, and I will return to this point.

presupposes that he cares about my state of health, or just about me, and would be gratified if I keep my promise.

[23] Does it include the power to vary the terms of the promissory obligation? Possibly the matter is not completely determined—there may well be variations about which there is no fact of the matter whether the promisee has power to make them. But generally speaking promisees have the power to change the terms of the promissory obligation in ways that are clearly to the advantage of the promisor. But what these are may be very context dependent. Even a simple extension of the deadline for performance of the promised act will sometimes be against the interest of the promisor.

We can highlight the role of the promisee by contrasting a promissory obligation to my brother, with an obligation to do something for him arising in some other way. Suppose that my mother told me, and that I should obey her in this matter, to do something for my brother, who is finishing a grueling task at work. I intend to buy him a week in an Alpine hotel, judging that to be an appropriate gift. Until I actually buy the holiday (and possibly even for some time after that) I should change my intention the moment I realize that it never was, or no longer is, a suitable gift. But if I promised my brother the holiday (thinking that it is an ideal gift) I cannot change my mind. He has the normative assurance that he will have the holiday, and it is now up to him to decide whether to release me from the promise or not.

The general point of promising, I conclude, is to give promisees the normative assurance of the promised act. If that is *for the promisees* it must relate to their interests (in both senses of the word) that promises serve. The power to promise serves the interest of promisors in enhanced control. When wisely used, and subject to luck, etc., both making a promise and refraining from making one serve an interest of the promisor (or the one who might have been the promisor). Given that promises are *for the promisees* promisors are served by serving the promisees. They may do so in one or both of two ways. First, the promise or the keeping of the promise may serve, directly or indirectly, an interest of the promisee, or something the promisee is interested in, cares about. Second, the promise gives the promisee (as it were as a gift) an opportunity to develop an interest, one that it may not be sensible to develop or to have without the promise or the performance of the promised act being there.

I dwell on the second way of being for the promisee not only because it is sometimes ignored, but also because while it is contingent whether the promisee has an interest in the promised act, and whether it serves his interests, it is in the nature of promises that they (to use metaphorical language) extend an invitation (not always trustworthy) to the promisees to develop an interest that depends on the promised act. A book I will lend you may lead to developing new interests, as may a game of chess or an hour on the tennis court, or the loan of a sum of money, and so on. To the extent that a promise provides an opportunity, the opportunity will be there unless the promise is not kept. Often they can be used after the promises are kept. These opportunities may range from being of little value to being of very great value. The crucial point is that normally opportunities, options, for things or actions that may be of interest to a person have some value in themselves, that is qua opportunities, regardless of whether they are made use of or not. And it is that option that the normative assurance that the promise gives assures. It may do more, much more, but the rest is both specific to individual promises and contingent. If we are looking to what interest the normative assurance the promise is just about always serves—that is it.

Admittedly, even that option may be without value to the promisee. However, promises do not expire once they no longer serve the promisees. As I noted above, giving promisees the power to terminate the promissory reason implies that the continued normative force of the promise depends on the promisee's action—it is not merely that a promise may have lapsed but the promisor may not rely on his judgment on the matter. It does not lapse merely for the reason that it no longer serves the promisee, and the promisor is unable to terminate it on that ground.

Its continued existence is now in the promisee's hand. It binds so long as it was not rescinded, provided that the power of the promisee to waive it has not lapsed as well.

The promisee's power is neither unconditional nor absolute. For one thing, the reason to keep the promise may be overridden by conflicting considerations. Furthermore, if the promisee is disabled in a way that makes it impossible for him to waive the promise then if the promise no longer serves the promisee it lapses. That was the case with Abby's promise to lend Ben her car. Once he became ill in such a way that he could neither make use of the car, nor waive the promise to lend him the car, the promise lapsed and Abby had no promissory reason any more to lend him her car.[24] Finally, it is arguable that the power to rescind lapses if abused, that is if exercised for immoral purposes, or in an arbitrary way.

Is the power to rescind the promissory obligation a third kind of promisee's interest (in addition to the interest served by the performance of the promised act and the opportunities to develop new interests that it provides)? David Owens goes further. Seeking an explanation of the way promises are for the promisees, he claims that their function is to enhance an important individual interest: the interest of gaining authority over another.

> [P]romising exists because it serves our authority interest, our interest in having the right to oblige others to do certain things. My claim will be that human beings have an interest in the possession of authority for its own sake, regardless of any further purpose this authority might serve, and that this fact accounts for the distinctive features of a promise.
>
> The authority interest is a normative interest: it is an interest in the possession of a certain right, the right to impose an obligation.[25]

I doubt that there is such an interest, and if I am mistaken and people have that interest I doubt that there is a general reason to protect or serve it. But that is beside the point, as its existence is irrelevant to promises. Owens maintains that

> the fundamental promissory interest is an interest of the promisee. . . namely the promisee's interest in gaining authority over the promisor.

This suggests that the function of promises is to endow promisees with that authority. While not all promises are made in order to serve their function, given that they are made intentionally by people who know what promises are, it seems to follow from Owens's view that standardly promises are made when people intend to endow others with authority over them and they make them in order to endow those others with power over them, in order to submit themselves to such power. This is of course consistent with maintaining that promisors make promises in order to serve a goal that

[24] Two clarificatory points: First, that Ben's condition is not permanent does not matter. What matters is his ability to waive the promissory duty before or at the time its performance is due. Second, nor does it matter that Ben has an interest in being able to control the duty in the sense that it would have been good for him be able to waive it. The control or power to waive that we are concerned with is the power you have only if you (physically) can use it.

[25] Owens, Shaping the Normative Landscape.

they themselves are interested in. They aim to serve it by making the promise, namely by subjecting themselves to the power of another.

According to the account offered here matters are very different. The point of promises is to provide promisees with normative assurance that the promised act will be performed, thus enabling them to get the advantages and opportunities that that assurance can provide. Again, promises are not always made to serve the point, but standardly this is the intention with which promisors make them: to provide that normative assurance and enable the promisees to have those advantages and opportunities. The power to rescind is merely part of the normative structure that creates the normative assurance: promisees have a right that the promise be kept, and (as with many rights) a power to waive it, to terminate the promissory obligation. Furthermore, the promise can neither be cancelled by the promisor when it no longer serves the promisee, nor does it then lapse. The normative assurance would have been less secure if the promisor were free to conclude that in the circumstances the promise serves no point and is not (or no longer) binding.

In some cases one can imagine that one's interest in having power over another is not purpose specific. A hostage taker need not have an idea how to use his power over the hostage before capturing him. Once he has that power he may make the hostage clean his house or aim to secure some political objective by holding him, or releasing him, or just get ransom to release him, etc. With promises this is an implausible account. The power the promisee has is merely to rescind an obligation whose content and creation were not up to him. His interest in it is almost entirely derivative from his interest in the normative assurance of the promised act, and the advantages and opportunities that it serves. Hence the conclusion that the power to rescind is but an ingredient in securing normative assurance, which itself serves the point and purpose of the promise, rather than being an independent interest that promises are there to serve.

One final point before moving on: In asserting that promisees' interests are served by having the power to rescind the promise I was implicitly assuming that the case for that power is analogous to the case for the power to make promises. But there are important differences between them. We all have the power to promise. It merely depends on basic mental competence. But the power of promisees is had only by promisees, who are invested with it by promisors. Furthermore, in a significant number of cases, keeping promises disadvantages promisees. This need not be by damaging their independent interests. It may be because as things turn out keeping the promise imposes a considerable burden on the promisor, while doing little for the promisee. Promisees may prefer not to be in the situation where they impose the burden of keeping the promise on the promisors. But given that they have the exclusive power to release the promisor from the promise they find themselves with the burden of deciding whether to release the promisor and of communicating their decision to him. Most of the time this is hardly a burden at all, but at times it is. Can we still say that having the power to rescind the promise is of value to promisees? I think that we can. Considerations like the one I mentioned show that it is not an unmixed blessing. But it is of value on balance. Those who deny that do not believe that promises are normatively sound.

VI. Promissory Reasons

The explanation of the point of promises, the interests they serve, and the way they do so, when applied to each promise, yields an explanation of the reason to keep that promise and of the strength of that reason. The puzzle we started from resulted from the fact that as regards any promised act, the reason to perform it (the reason that applies to each and all of them) is that it was promised, namely the same reason in every case. However, initially we failed to find factors that determine the strength of the reasons and establish how they differ.

Promises are binding because there is normative power to make them, which is grounded in the interest for enhanced control. The question is how can that interest, seemingly affecting all promises uniformly, provide reasons of different strength regarding different promises, or indeed how does it provide any reason to keep promises, given that breaking the promise does not threaten that power?

There is, however, an inevitable and obvious connection between the value of the power to promise and the reasons to keep a promise: to repeat a triviality—the reasons are a result of the use of the power to promise, a result of the making of the specific promise made. All valid promises change the normative situation because they are the exercise of the same power, but they change it differently because they are different promises. In one regard promises are analogous to gifts: they give promisees the normative assurance of an action (or omission). Whenever I give a gift I change the normative situation by using the same gift-giving power, yet I change it differently by giving different gifts. My exercise of my power of making the promise changed the situation. Now the promisee has that normative assurance, namely I have a promissory reason to perform the promised act. Of course, gifts and promises are fundamentally different in other respects: When giving a gift I give the recipient something I had before. The gift was mine, now it is his. When making a promise I grant the promisee a right that did not exist before to a duty that did not exist before. There is nothing that was mine and is now his.

Promises may, in themselves or in combination with other factors, provide reasons, or affect the strength of reasons, for or against the promised act. But only those that relate to the point of the promise are promissory reasons, and these are the factors that make it a normative assurance meant to be for the promisee.

So that is how we can have our cake and eat it too. Promissory reasons derive from the value of having the power to promise, through its exercise. The exercise of the power introduces variability. All promises are the normative assurance of an act or omission, but the value of that assurance varies.

It is tempting to equate the strength of the reason to keep a promise with the value to the promisee of the promised act. But we already know that that is a mistake. For example, the promisor may perform the promised act anyway, regardless of whether the promise remains binding or whether it is waived by the promisee. The value of the promise is the value of the normative assurance it provides. In a case where the promised act will take place anyway that may be much less than the value to the promisee of the promised act. Besides, the promise is binding even if the promised act is of no value to the promisee. So, where performance of the promised act because it was promised serves the promisee, its value to him is just one consideration that affects the strength of the promissory reason. The opportunity value that the promise provides, its "invitation" to the promisee to developing interests based on the assurance of the promised act, is an independent consideration that is present in almost all promises, and affects their force. Yet there must be other strength-affecting factors present in all cases in which the promise is binding. This is where the power to terminate the promissory obligation, coupled with the fact that it does not lapse unless waived, are relevant. They exist in all binding promises, and their existence is of benefit to the promisee, enabling him to rescind the promise when it is to his advantage to do so, and disabling the promisor from escaping his promissory obligation without the promisee's consent.

As was explained, the promisee's interest in the power to rescind is secondary, being merely protective of the main ways in which the promise is for him. Only in exceptional cases would that be the only aspect of a specific promise that serves his interest, and thereby keeps the promise binding. There is, however, another doubt as to whether that interest can affect the strength of the reason to keep a promise (and if it cannot then in those exceptional cases just mentioned there would be no reason to keep it, it would not be binding). Does breach of the promise deny the promisee the power to terminate the promissory obligation?

I wish to avoid technicalities, and at this point they are hard to ignore altogether. I will simplify. We have to distinguish between a repudiatory breach and a nonrepudiatory breach.[26] Now consider the difference between a one-shot promise and a continuous one: between promising to water your plants tomorrow and promising to water them once a week for the coming year. Failure to water them once in the second case is a partial breach. Partial failure is possible regarding some one-shot promises as well: for example when time is not of the essence watering them a day late is not a complete breach. A complete breach is always repudiatory whereas a partial breach may or may not be, depending on the circumstances, including the intentions of the promisor. A repudiatory breach terminates the promissory obligation. It may give rise to a new duty, a duty to compensate for the breach.[27] In cases of nonrepudiatory partial breach the power to waive or rescind the promissory obligation lapses regarding the partial breach, and in repudiatory breach it lapses with the termination of the promissory duty altogether. Hence, even in the marginal cases where the only promisee interest a promise serves is due to the promisee's power to waive his right and terminate the promissory duty, breach affects that interest, and therefore there is reason to keep the promise.

[26] Which can be anticipatory, that is occurring before the time to keep the promise arrives, and can be by declaration: "I will not keep this promise;" such declaration deprives the promisee of the assurance that is the point of a promise, and is therefore a breach of the promise.

[27] The new duty comes with new powers to the promisee. But while they include a power to waive the duty to compensate that power differs, both in scope (the duty to compensate differs in content from the promissory duty) and in conditions of its exercise (communicating the waiver to the promisor is not constitutive of it). Hence its existence does not undermine the point in the text.

5

Does a Promise Transfer a Right?

*David Owens**

What do you give someone when you make them a promise? One popular answer is that you give them some information, specifically information about how you mean to behave in the future. On this view, the obligation to keep one's promises comes out of the same box as the obligation not to lie, not to mislead, and so forth. This idea lies behind both Hume's conventionalist theory of promise and Scanlon and Thomson's anti-conventionalist expectation theory.

On this informational account of promising there is no suggestion that a promise need transfer anything from the promisor to the promisee. True the promisor *gives* their word and *offers* their assurance, but their word, their assurance are not things which they have prior to their promise and which they lose to the promisee in making their promise. When a promise works as it should, the promisee ends up with the same information as the promisor: they both know what the promisor is going to do. And when the promisee is misled, they end up with something that the promisor never had, namely a false assurance, a mistaken belief, and so forth. In neither case is there any item the promisor relinquishes and the promisee acquires.

Nevertheless, the idea that a promise transfers something from promisor to promisee has informed much theorizing about both contracts and promises. Grotius, Pufendorf, Locke, and Hobbes all affirm that something is transferred or translated by a promise or a contract and the transfer theory is currently experiencing a revival. Several recent critics of the expectation theory of promissory obligation have adopted a right-transfer model and used it to explain the binding force of a promise.[1]

In the first section of this chapter, I'll raise some difficulties for the idea that a promise involves the literal transfer of a right. In the second section I formulate the main idea behind the transfer theory without the metaphor of transfer whilst in the third section I subject the reformulated theory to further criticism. In the final section I sketch my own view, one that rejects both informational theories and the reformulated right-transfer view.[2]

* Thanks to Chris Essert, Andrew Gold, Peter Graham, Daniel Markovits, Joseph Raz, Gregory Klass, Prince Saprai, Seana Shiffrin, and Robert Stevens for comments.

[1] Right-transfer may also be an element in various "property-transfer" theories of contract. Recent examples include Peter Benson, *Contract as a Transfer of Ownership*, 48 Wm. & Mary L. Rev. 1673 (2006) and Andrew S. Gold, *A Property Theory of Contract*, 103 Nw. U. L. Rev. 1 (2009). For skepticism about property-transfer theories of contract, *see* J.W. Harris, Property and Justice 19–20 (1996) and Stephen A. Smith, Contract Theory 97–103 (2004).

[2] Seana Valentine Shiffrin, *Immoral, Conflicting and Redundant Promises, in* Reasons and Recognition: Essays on the Philosophy of T.M. Scanlon 156 n.7 (R. Jay Wallace et al. eds., 2011) and Thomas Pink, *Promising and Obligation*, 23 Phil. Persp. 389, 405 (2009) both cite David

I. Promise and Property

All parties should agree that a successful promise changes the normative situation. After the promise, there is something the promisor is bound to do that they were not previously bound to do. Furthermore, if they break their promise and breach their obligation, they are thereby wronging the promisee. To wrong someone is to do something that tends to render it apt for them to blame you and which puts them in a position to forgive you for what you did, should they so choose.[3] Nothing more should be read into the notion of wronging. In particular, there is no implication that the wronged party (or anyone else) is entitled to vindicate their rights by force or receive any particular remedy.

Does this normative change, this creation of a wronging involve a transfer of some normative item from promisor to promisee? Suppose I promise you that I'll be at the bus stop at noon. And suppose that neither you nor I have any prior obligations with respect to the bus stop. What right, liberty, or power is such that I possess it prior to my promise and you possess it once the promise is made? My promise deprives me of the liberty not to appear at noon since it means I would be wronging you if I failed to show up. But you acquire no liberty in respect of my nonappearance (it was already the case that you wouldn't be wronging anyone if I didn't appear). Furthermore you acquire no claim-right that I not appear. If I show up, I'm not wronging you; on the contrary, I'm fulfilling my obligation. Of course, you do acquire a claim-right that I show up, but this is not a right that I lose in making the promise; if anything it is a right that I exercise in fulfilling it.[4]

In pressing this objection, are we being rather literal minded, treating talk of right-transfer more seriously than was intended? Perhaps all that was meant was this: the right the promisor loses stands in some interesting explanatory relation to the right that the promisee acquires? In Section II, I reinterpret the theory along these lines but we should first ask why the image of a transfer has proved attractive to so many writers.

I'll start with a characterization of the promissory transaction that is, I hope, common ground between myself and the transfer theorist:

> *Power Generation*: Before promising I have the power to determine whether or not I would be wronging you by failing to show up, that is I possess the power to promise to appear.[5] This is a *normative power*, that is a power I exercise *by declaration*,

Owens, *A Simple Theory of Promising*, 115 PHIL. REV. 51 (2006) as an instance of the right-transfer theory, a theory Shiffrin endorses and Pink rejects. At one point in the chapter I do employ the transfer metaphor but, as Joseph Raz pointed out to me, the main claims of the chapter do not depend on the metaphor and are better stated without it.

[3] The point of "tends to" in the first clause is to allow for excuses and justifications; the point of talking about forgiveness is to distinguish the wronged party from indignant bystanders. Here I am oversimplifying the connection between wronging and forgiveness; *see* DAVID OWENS, SHAPING THE NORMATIVE LANDSCAPE 57–8 (2012).

[4] For related worries about transfer theories of contract *see* SMITH, CONTRACT THEORY, at 101–2 and Gold, *A Property Theory of Contract*, at 50–3.

[5] To be more precise, I have the power to determine whether or not I would be wronging you in a particular way, namely by breaching the promise I am now making. Where I have some prior obligation to do what I am promising to do, things get more complicated.

by communicating the intention of hereby exercising that power. Having successfully promised, I can no longer determine by declaration whether or not I would be wronging you by failing to show up.[6] I can't rescind my promise. Furthermore once I have successfully promised, you *thereby* acquire the power to determine whether or not I would be wronging you by failing to show up, for you have the power to release me from my obligation (or not as the case may be). This again is a power you exercise by declaration, by communicating the intention of hereby exercising that power.[7]

I'll call powers exercised by declaration *normative powers*. According to *Power Generation*, the promisee gains one normative power and does so because the promisor cedes another normative power. I leave it open how similar the power the promisee ends up with is to the power the promisor relinquishes.[8]

Power Generation goes beyond the platitude that a binding promise gives the promisee a right to performance. It identifies a normative power relinquished by the promisor and another acquired by the promisee and postulates an explanatory connection between them. Many writers would not accept *Power Generation* since they deny that promising could involve the exercise of normative power.[9] Since these doubts are not shared by advocates of the transfer theory, I shall set them to one side. Instead I'll ask why one might seek to ground *Power-Generation* in the transfer of a normative item from promisor to promisee.

Some see a close parallel between making a promise and giving away something you own.[10] Here is Grotius:

> And this is a compleat promise, as having the same effect as the alienation of a man's property. For it is either the introduction to the alienating of a thing, or the alienation of some part of our liberty. To the former belong our promises to give, to the latter our promises to do something.[11]

For Grotius, the power of transfer by declaration is involved in the very idea of ownership:

> Men who are masters of their own goods have by the law of nature a power of disposing of or transferring all or any part of their effects to other persons; for this is in the very nature of property.[12]

[6] A successful promise is a promise that binds, i.e. a promise not invalidated by deception, duress, nonacceptance, and so forth.

[7] The powers in question are powers to create and rescind particular obligations: the general power to make promises or waive them is not in play.

[8] Pete Graham and Daniel Markovits pointed out one potential difference between these powers: whilst the successful exercise of the power of release does not require the promisor's acceptance, a promise may need to be accepted by the promisee before it binds.

[9] For example T. M. Scanlon, What We Owe Each Other 295–327 (1998). Hume maintains that because promisors do think of themselves as exercising a normative power, the practice of promising rests upon an illusion: David Hume, A Treatise on Human Nature 523 (L. A. Selby-Bigge ed., 1978).

[10] The property-transfer analogy informs some contemporary right-transfer theory (e.g., Watson) and is taken literally by property-transfer theorists of contract, e.g., Benson, *A Property Theory of Contract*, and Gold, *A Property Theory of Contract*. The latter have reasons of their own for endorsing the theory (i.e. the need to explain the characteristic remedies for breach of contact).

[11] Hugo Grotius, The Rights of War and Peace 704 (Richard Tuck ed., 2005).

[12] Grotius, The Rights of War and Peace, at 566.

And by interpreting our rights of self-government as rights of self-ownership, Grotius gives us the power to transfer those rights by declaration:

> There is the further fact that ownership of property can be transferred by an act of will which is sufficiently manifest, as we have said above. Why then, since we have equally right over our actions and over our property, may there not be transferred to a person also . . . the right to do something?[13]

When I own my car, I am in possession of a set of claims, liberties, and powers with respect to the car. Among these is the power of sale, namely the power to transfer this set of claims, liberties, and powers *en masse* to another person. Upon the completion of the sale, the buyer acquires the very claims, liberties, and powers that the vendor used to possess. Here the idea of a literal transfer of normative items (perhaps embodied in the physical transfer of a non-normative item, namely the car) gets a firm grip. Grotius suggests that we own ourselves as we own our cars and that our power of promise or contract is the power to transfer some elements of the rights of self-ownership ("some part of our liberty") to another. For Grotius, our property includes ourselves and our power to promise is one aspect of our power to transfer our property to another.

As we have seen, it is hard to specify the normative item(s) transferred by a promise but even those willing to give Grotius the benefit of the doubt on that point may still baulk at the notion that we have property in ourselves, property which can be transferred to another just like our cars and our houses. Isn't it much more obvious that we have the power to promise than that we own ourselves? If so, the power to promise shouldn't be defended against Hume and other skeptics by invoking the idea of self-ownership. In Section II, I'll introduce a contemporary version of the right-transfer theory, one that does not rest on the idea of self-ownership.

II. Promise and Autonomy

Here is Shiffrin:

> *Passage A*: the rights-transfer theory claims that a binding promise effects a transfer from the promisor to the promisee, through the communicated intent to do so, of the promisor's right to decide to act otherwise than how she promised to act . . . The transfer explains why the promisor is bound to perform: he no longer has a (moral) right to decide whether to do otherwise. It further explains why the promisee has the power to waive performance: the moral permission of the promisor to decide to act otherwise now lies in the hands of the promisee and the promisee may exercise this permission. The theory thereby explains the basic structure of the promissory relationship with satisfying simplicity.[14]

[13] Quoted in Pink, *Promising and Obligation*, at 404. Hume would agree that property transfers raise the same issues as promises and they receive a similar treatment at his hands but he denies that we can render promissory obligation any more intelligible simply by portraying it as a species of property transfer. Hume, A Treatise on Human Nature, at 477–516.

[14] Shiffrin, *Immoral, Conflicting and Redundant Promises*, at 157. Shiffrin herself would not endorse the theory in precisely this form. *See also* Seana Shiffrin, *Promising, Intimate Relationships and Conventionalism*, 117 Phil. Rev. 481, 517 (2008).

The model of promising described in Passage A has several features worthy of note. Shiffrin begins her story not with a power but with a right, namely (broadly speaking) the promisor's right to decide how they will act. The subject matter of this right is non-normative: for example it is the right to show up or not as you choose. But we are given to understand that the promisor's right to control this aspect of their non-normative situation somehow involves a power over the normative. The promisor can "through the communicated intent to do so" ensure that they are bound to perform, that they no longer possess the right to control that aspect of the non-normative situation implicated in their promise. Furthermore, once the promise is made (a) the promisee will have acquired a power over the normative situation, namely the power to release the promisor from the obligation to perform and (b) their acquisition of this power of release is explained by the fact that the promisee now has the right, previously possessed by the promisor, to control those aspects of the non-normative situation relevant to the fulfillment of the promise.

Passage A raises three questions. First, what exactly is the content of the right transferred from promisor to promisee by the promise? Second, how does the transfer of this right explain the transfer of the associated normative power? Third, why does anyone bother to make such transfers? Why renounce your rights in favor of another?

As to the first, Shiffrin tells us that the promise effects a transfer of "the promisor's right to decide to act otherwise than how she promised to act." As we have seen, the idea that the promisee acquires the promisor's "right to decide to act otherwise than how she promised to act" is hard to elucidate further. I suggest we give up on the attempt to identify some act or acts that the promisor used to have a right to perform (or omit), which right the promisee now possesses. Rather the transfer theorist should seek to defend a conjunctive claim of the following sort:

> *Right Base*: First, I no longer have the liberty to not show up at the bus stop because I exercised a power to deprive myself of this liberty by declaration, a power that I have *in virtue of* having that very liberty. Second, you now have the power to determine whether I am obliged to show up and you have that power because I exercised (in your favour) my power to deprive myself of the liberty not to show up.

The second clause here is simply an abbreviation of *Power Generation*: there is no implication that the promisee has this power of release because they now possess some right that the promisor used to have. Our attention should instead focus on the claim implicit in the first clause: *I have the power to ensure by declaration that I would be wronging you by failing to appear in virtue of having the liberty to show up or not show up as I please.* On the transfer theory, a binding promise transfers a right that one possesses prior to the promise. *Right Base* drops the idea of a literal transfer whilst preserving the notion that the power to promise depends on a prior right to fulfill the promise.[15]

[15] Many transfer theorists deem promises to do what one has no right to do invalid because there is no prior right to fulfill the promise for the promise to transfer. For example, *see* Grotius, The Rights of War and Peace, at 714. *Right Base* preserves this feature of their theory. For discussion of whether such promises should be deemed invalid, *see* Shiffrin, *Immoral, Conflicting and Redundant Promises*, at 159–65 and Owens, Shaping The Normative Landscape, § 48.

Having addressed the first of our questions by dropping the transfer metaphor, an analog of the second question now confronts us. It is unclear why the fact that I have the right to show up or not as I please should give me the power to ensure, just by declaration, that I would be wronging you by not showing up in the future. For example, we can't infer that I have the power to promise you my life from the fact that I am now at liberty to kill myself. There is a gap here that needs to be filled, a gap perhaps concealed by the metaphor of right-transfer. Can the gap be bridged without it?

Shiffrin offers us the following line of thought about consent:

> *Passage B*: The idea that an agent can intentionally form an obligation through the exercise and expression of her will alone (and not by first transforming the state of affairs around her) comes part and parcel with any plausible conception of an autonomous agent. When an agent gives consent to another—to a doctor to perform an examination or to a worker to enter the agent's apartment—she transforms, in the way intended, the moral situation between the parties simply through the transmission of her will to do so. Prior to conferring consent, the agent's right to control her body, and her property, forbade touching or entering as forms of assault and trespass. Simply by expressing her will, the consenting agent morally transforms the situation as intended, thereby generating a permission for another.[16]

As "autonomous agents" we start out with a right to exercise control over what happens to our bodies and to our property. This means that others are excluded from our bodies and our property; they cannot enter this protected realm without wronging us. But mere exclusion will not give the autonomous agent all they need:

> *Passage C*: One could imagine a conception of autonomy without consent in which an agent exercised complete sovereignty over her body and other personal spaces, such as the home, but had no ability to share or transfer these powers to others. That is, the agent could not grant consent to others to exercise these powers in lieu of or alongside herself. . . . Rights of autonomous control that were inalienable to this degree would render (morally) impossible real forms of meaningful human relationships and the full definition and recognition of the self (not to mention making medical and dental care cumbersome, dangerous, and awfully painful). To forge meaningful relationships, embodied human beings must have the ability to interact within the same physical space, to share the use of property, and to touch one another.[17]

In Shiffrin's eyes the rationale for the rights we have in respect of our "personal space" lies in the importance of control for autonomy, a need that also justifies our being able to modify these rights should we so wish. So the very consideration that explains our enjoyment of these prior rights also explains our posterior ability to vary them.

Having made the case that the rights of autonomous agents involve such a "power of consent," Shiffrin generalizes to promise. A meaningful human life requires the ability to commit ourselves to others and thereby renounce a part of our liberty in their favor.[18] Thus, our power to make promises is no more mysterious than our ability to

[16] Shiffrin, *Promising, Intimate Relationships and Conventionalism*, at 500.

[17] Shiffrin, *Promising, Intimate Relationships and Conventionalism*, at 501–2.

[18] For a related line of thought, *see* Gary Watson, *Promises, Reasons and Normative Powers*, *in* Reasons for Action 165–6 (David Sobel and Steven Wall eds., 2009).

consent. The gap between right and normative power has apparently been bridged. Furthermore it has been bridged in a way that suggests an answer to our third question also. We can now see why people should wish to make and accept promises, and what interest they have in making use of this procedure.[19]

What of promises to kill yourself, slavery contracts, and the like? Were the right to promise grounded in the fact that we own our lives, our bodies, etc., it would remain unclear why we should lack the power to enslave ourselves. Since Shiffrin instead grounds our natural rights and powers in the value of autonomy, she can respond that the reach of our normative power is restricted by the underlying value. We possess rights and powers because of the significance of our capacity for autonomous agency and slavery contracts etc. are ruled out because they involve a denial of the value of personal autonomy. Even if we have the right to kill ourselves, or work ourselves to death should we so choose, we may lack the power to sell ourselves into slavery.[20]

Before concluding our discussion of the right-transfer theory, we should note that its advocates reject the Humean idea that promissory obligation is conventional, that is the idea that promises bind only in a social context in which people generally treat them as binding.[21] According to both Shiffrin and the Natural Lawyers, we possess a right to control what we do regardless of whether this right is recognized by those around us and we have the power to make binding promises in virtue of having this natural right. Since the power to make promises is implicit in that natural right, our promises bind regardless of whether their binding force is recognized by those around us. In exercising our normative powers we acquire, relinquish, and modify our rights. Linguistic convention may be needed to facilitate the relevant communications but convention is not required to underwrite the normative force of the agreements they enable.

III. Hume's Point

Let's begin our assessment of Shiffrin's theory with her account of the binding force of a promise and, in particular, with the parallel she draws between promise and consent. Shiffrin claims (a) that consent is a normative power, (b) that our ability to consent can be grounded in our need for autonomy, and (c) that the normative power of promise can also be grounded in our need for autonomy. I suspect that the word "consent" is being used to cover two different phenomena here only one of which, like promise, involves an exercise of normative power. We can't assess Shiffrin's claims

[19] Shiffrin can allow that both the right of autonomy and the consequent power to consent or to promise go well beyond the body. But she will presumably ground both our power to make promises whose fulfillment will involve an exercise of bodily control and our power to consent to manipulations of our body in our natural right to control our own bodies. *See* Shiffrin, *Promising, Intimate Relationships and Conventionalism*, at 501.

[20] Grotius, The Rights of War and Peace, at 556–8 has a more equivocal attitude to voluntary servitude.

[21] Shiffrin, *Promising, Intimate Relationships and Conventionalism*, at 482–5. John Locke, Two Treatises on Civil Government 277 (Peter Laslett ed., 1988), Judith Jarvis Thomson, The Realm of Rights 303–4 (1990) and Scanlon, What We Owe Each Other, all reject conventionalism.

about consent, promise, and their connection with autonomy until we have made the relevant distinctions.

Shiffrin tells us that both promise and consent:

> alter moral status without a change in circumstances that is independent of the parties' wills. Why then has consent seemed so unexceptional, sufficiently invisible so as to render sensible the idea that promises are unique in this respect? Perhaps it is because this moral power flows so naturally from a plausible understanding of a meaningful right of autonomy.[22]

But what exactly is needed to furnish us with a "meaningful right of autonomy"? We could hardly have such a right unless our choices were normatively significant but *normatively significant choice* need involve no exercise of normative power, no ability to change the normative situation by declaration. The true analog of promise is something much more specific, namely the *power of consent*, a power that, like the power to promise, is exercised by declaration alone and is directed specifically at the normative situation. It is not immediately obvious that any "meaningful right of autonomy" requires such a normative power.

Speaking, in Passage A, of the power of promise, Shiffrin is clear that promising involves the communication of the intention to transfer a right to the promisee and to do so in virtue of this very communication. Thus the analogous normative power of consent must be a device that communicates, say, the intention of hereby making it the case that you are permitted to stick a knife into me and thereby makes it so. Now couldn't an agent change their normative situation, and do so "at will," without exercising such a power of consent? Shiffrin appears to deny this. In Passage C she implies that without the ability to consent to medical procedures, we'd be left to operate on ourselves. But again this is far from obvious. My having a right that others not invade my body space could consist in the following sort of fact: you would be wronging me by sticking a knife into me unless you do so only when I have chosen this (non-normative) outcome. That way of specifying the right would give me the ability to ensure, and to ensure "at will," that you can operate on me without wronging me. It would give me a meaningful right of bodily autonomy. Yet it need give me no power of consent.

Passage B states that when promising and consenting, the agent changes the normative situation "simply by expressing her will." Here Shiffrin intends to distinguish the normative changes effected through promising and consent from those which result when I (perhaps deliberately) alter my rights and obligations by changing the objective circumstances, as when I incur an obligation to remain sober by driving off in my car. But that is not the only distinction that needs to be made here. We must also differentiate (a) the case where someone acquires either a right or an obligation to ϕ because

[22] Shiffrin, *Promising, Intimate Relationships and Conventionalism*, at 501; *see also* 517. Hume was well aware of the parallel between promise and consent. *See* David Hume, Enquiry Concerning The Principle of Morals 208 (Selby-Bigge ed., 1975). Thomson compares consent and promise, with a view to making promising seem unproblematic Thomson, The Realm of Rights, at 350–1. *See also* Herbert Hart, *Are There Any Natural Rights?*, 64 Phil. Rev. 175, 184 and Watson, *Promises, Reasons and Normative Powers*, at 165.

I choose that they ϕ from (b) the case where they acquire either a right or an obligation to ϕ because I communicate the intention of hereby making it the case that they acquire such a right or such an obligation.[23]

What is choice? What is involved in "choosing that someone ϕ"? One instance of choice is where one intends to ϕ, or else intends to bring it about that someone (either oneself or someone else) ϕs. Here one has made up one's mind to effect the result once the moment arrives. But I doubt intention is the only normatively significant form of choice. It is often in our interests for what happens to depend on our intentions, perhaps because of our need for autonomy. But we also have an autonomy-interest in whether what happens to us depends on our *judgments* about what ought to happen (or else on our all-things-considered desires). Different forms of choice are normatively significant in different situations and perhaps in different ways. A comprehensive treatment is impossible here.[24] Instead I shall run through a series of examples intended to illustrate the complexity of the phenomena. All these examples have one thing in common: they are cases in which a normatively significant choice is made but no power of consent is exercised.

Let's start with a choice that may well involve an intention. Michael Thompson gives us the following example:

> In a traditional Jewish wedding, the bride is not among the signatories of the ketubah, but she is studied for signs of despair or opposition to the advancing proceeding. If they are found, the wedding is off. Though everything depends, in a sense, on the bride's will, the arrangement seems not to give her a (Mosaic-legal) *potestas* over the groom and her father. Her will does not enter into the matter in the right sort of way, as directed consent.[25]

Here the bride might protest with a view to aborting the wedding by conveying her unhappiness. Under Jewish law her protest is decisive and presumably she is granted this influence (in part) out of respect for her autonomy i.e. to give her some control over whom she lives with. But she is given no power of consent since she can't call off the wedding simply by communicating the intention to hereby call it off. Of course, Jewish law (as Thompson represents it) does not go far enough: full respect for the bride's autonomy also requires that she be given direct control over the marriage contract but it is an interesting question why that further power should be needed. Why isn't the normative significance of her choice enough?

Now let's consider choice that involves no intention because the subject thinks they can do nothing to bring about the desired result; rather they simply judge that the result ought to be brought about (or else desire that it be brought about all things considered). Suppose I need an operation and judge that this surgeon ought to operate on me were they available, which they are not. I then fall unconscious. The surgeon's

[23] In the philosophical literature on promising, it is widely accepted that a communication of the intention to ϕ is importantly different from a communication of the intention to hereby undertake an obligation to ϕ. The analogous point is not so well appreciated in the literature on consent.

[24] For a fuller discussion *see* Owens, Shaping The Normative Landscape, ch. 7.

[25] Michael Thompson, *What is it to Wrong Someone? A Puzzle about Justice*, *in* Reason And Value: Themes From The Moral Philosophy Of Joseph Raz 351 n. 25 (M. Smith et al. eds., 2004).

knowledge of this judgment of mine might be crucial to whether they are entitled to operate on me should they then become available. But there is no question of my consenting to the operation. Some may suppose that I have "hypothetically" consented in such circumstances but the only basis for thinking that I *would* consent is my actual judgment. Were I to regain consciousness, my consent would now be sought even if my judgment were known and the operation might be permissible only once I had actually given it.

Another kind of normatively significant choice involves no intention because the chooser neither wishes to bring about the desired result themselves nor wishes to communicate the intention to oblige (or permit) anyone else to bring about that result. I am obliged to buy my partner the birthday present they think I ought to buy them and I am supposed to know (or at least to find out) what present that is without the benefit of requests, promises, consents, and so forth. Here my respect for their choice is, in part, an expression of respect for their autonomy—I should not allow my own judgment of what would be best for them to override theirs. And should I need to be *told* what to buy them, that would indicate a lack of interest in and respect for their choices.

Could Shiffrin concede my point? True, some portion of a meaningful right of autonomy could be based on the normative significance of choice alone. Yet, she might urge, the very same need for autonomy gives us good reason to wish to be able to influence people's rights and obligations through declarations explicitly concerned with the normative situation. Indeed we very often think mere choice is insufficient to authorize an invasion of personal space. A surgeon is expected to get the patient's consent before operating, not just to divine their intentions.

It is true that we need both ways of influencing our normative situation. This is because (as I shall urge in Section IV) we have both normative and non-normative interests. Furthermore these two modes of influence may pull in different directions, sometimes in a useful fashion. For example, I may invite you to our party whilst making it clear that I don't intend you to come (you'd have come had my partner invited you but by doing so myself I mean to put you off). And I can communicate that I intend you to be at the party without inviting you myself (I'd prefer that my partner invite you and urge you to ask them). Given this, we should not assume that we can look to the normative significance of choice to ensure the intelligibility of the power of consent (and promise).

Hume for one argued that *nothing* can render such normative powers intelligible. Suppose I have a natural right to control what happens to my body. There must be something about me in virtue of which I have that right. For example, I might possess the right to control my body because it is in my interests to control my body, because my life goes better in various ways if I control my body and worse if I do not. Alternatively I might possess that right because rational agents have a dignity that demands respect and excludes interference with their agency. Let us call the basis for my natural right to control my own body, whatever it may be, the *Foundation*. I lose much or all of this natural right if the Foundation is altered or disappears (perhaps I become magically invulnerable to the actions of others, perhaps I suffer a lobotomy and lose my reason). But if the right is indeed a natural right, it can't be degraded or lost unless the Foundation is somehow affected. And—here is *Hume's Point*—how could any plausible Foundation be affected simply by the fact that someone (anyone) has spoken with the intention of hereby making it the case that I no longer possess some portion of my right to control my body?[26]

Plausible foundations for the normative significance of choice are close at hand; for instance it is often in one's interests to have whether one goes under the knife or whom one lives with depend on one's intentions or judgments on the matter.[27] But our interest in the potency of these choices grants no authority to the simple communication of an intention to change the normative situation by means of this very communication. For example, if it is in my interests to exercise a given degree of control over what you do to my body, I cannot make it otherwise just by communicating the intention to make it otherwise (and thereby consenting). And this remains the case whatever the shape of our story about the value of control. Suppose the value of control over my body and so forth derives not from some interest of mine but rather from my inherent dignity as a rational agent. Again, I cannot deprive myself of any element of this dignity simply by declaration.[28]

True, consent is frequently an expression of choice. Your consenting to the operation is very often an expression of your intention that the operation should happen. Here your declaration has extrinsic normative significance since it informs us of your choices. Because choice and consent usually go together, it is not hard to see why foundations available to one should be thought to support the other. But, if Hume is right, your communication of an intention to hereby ensure that I can operate without wronging you has, in itself, no normative significance whatsoever. This mumbo-jumbo might have communicated the fact that you'd rather like an operation and *that* fact may well be normatively significant but this is irrelevant. Until we distinguish choice from consent, Hume's Point will escape us.

Hume's Point is, I maintain, a conclusive objection to all those versions of the right-transfer theory so far considered. Advocates of informational theories (from Adam Smith and Richard Price onwards) take Hume's Point and infer that a promise can't be what it seems to be, namely an attempt to change the normative situation by declaration. So what explains the insouciance of contemporary right-transfer theorists in the face of Hume's observation?[29] Shiffrin may be concealing the difficulty from herself by equating consent with normatively significant choice and then modelling promise on consent. In other authors, the idea of self-ownership is playing a role.

In a recent discussion of promising which is in many respects close to Shiffrin's, Watson says that

[26] Hume, A Treatise on Human Nature, at 516–25.

[27] The non-normative interests in play here may give choice both an instrumental and an intrinsic importance. *See* Owens, Shaping The Normative Landscape, at 166–8.

[28] In Owens, Shaping The Normative Landscape, at 127–9, I formulate Hume's Point as a worry about bare wrongings, i.e., wrongings that involve no action against a human interest. Since the right-transfer theorist may not share the assumption that wrongings involve acting against some human interest, I here formulate the point without it.

[29] "I have never felt the magnetism of the problem nor the attraction of the conventionalist solution, despite their distinguished careers." Shiffrin, *Promising, Intimate Relationships and Conventionalism*, at 482. *See also* Thomson, The Realm of Rights, at 303.

> Prior to promising, I am free to engage in any number of optional performances. By promising, I transfer my ownership of some alternatives, my entitlement to act within a certain range of options, thereby giving that power to others.[30]

The idea that we "own" our rights to control our performances tends to obscure Hume's Point because, in Grotius' words, it is "in the very nature of property" that we are able to transfer or otherwise modify our property rights by declaration. In fact Hume's Point calls the possibility of property (so understood) into question quite as much as the possibility of promise. Why should I have *both* the right to decide whether or not to drive my car and the power to give that right away by declaration? How does the former right explain the latter power? Indeed how can the latter power be explained at all?

In this section, I've made Hume's Point and offered a diagnosis of the resistance to it but there remains the conviction, which I share, that promise and consent can indeed change the normative situation by declaration and so any argument that makes this seem impossible cannot be sound. One of the main attractions of the right-transfer theory is that it preserves appearances here, offering to make sense of our attempts to exercise normative power. We won't have laid the right-transfer theory to rest unless we can accommodate Hume's Point without it.

IV. The Authority Interest

A promise grants the promisee a right to performance: the promisor would be wronging the promisee by failing to perform unless the promisee releases the promisor from their promise. Let's call this right to performance *authority.* A successful promise gives the promisee authority over the promisor. Why should any promisor seek to do so? On the face of it, the promisee is the primary beneficiary of the transaction—they acquire authority from the promisor. And so, it is natural to suppose, the promisee must (at least on occasion) have some interest in acquiring this power, in having authority over the promisor, an interest that the promisor has a secondary interest in satisfying. Call this an *authority interest.* And if authority can be worth something to the promisee, mightn't that explain the bindingness of the promisor's promise? We need not suppose that each individual promise is made to serve the promisee's authority interest, merely that promises serve this interest often enough to explain why promises bind.[31] By postulating an interest in the normative item that the promisee acquires we can identify the source of a promise's binding force.[32]

Should a theory of the binding force of a promise take this form? Should it appeal to the *value* of a promise, to some *interest* we have in giving and receiving promises?

[30] Watson, *Promises, Reasons and Normative Powers*, at 170. *See also* Hart, *Are There Any Natural Rights?*, at 323.

[31] I do not say that promises are standardly used to serve the authority interest or even that they are more often used to serve this interest than any other interest. I say only that they are used to serve the authority interest as often as is needed to explain the continued existence of promising. On this point *see* Owens, Shaping The Normative Landscape, at 143–5.

[32] I would argue that the primary normative interest grounding the power of consent is an interest of the consentor. *See* Owens, Shaping The Normative Landscape, at 181–2.

Some might think that we are confusing two different questions: (a) why do people bother to make and accept promises? (b) why does a promise bind once made? People make and accept promises for all sorts of reasons, good and bad but, the objection goes, their reason for making and accepting a particular promise might have little to do with why that promise binds once made.

I agree that the question of why one has a certain right and the question of whether it is in one's interests to have that right are distinct. There may be rights that exist regardless of whether it is ever in the right holder's interests to have them. Suppose, for example, I possess a right to go on living purely because of my dignity as a creature capable of rational decision making. Or suppose I possess this right because I have an interest in remaining alive. Either way, my having this right to life is not grounded in my interest in having that *right*; I have this right to life regardless of whether I benefit from my possession of that right. My right to life is grounded rather in my non-normative interest in remaining alive or else in the inherent value of my remaining alive.[33]

Promissory rights are different. Promissory rights don't exist at all unless someone intentionally brings them into existence by making the relevant declarations. And this will happen only if that person or persons sees some point in bringing them into existence. And this will be so only if they see some value in a binding promise, either for themselves or for someone else. So the right acquired by the promisee can't be a right that exists regardless of whether it matters to anyone that the promisee possesses that right. True specific promises may matter to different people in different ways but on my hypothesis one of these interests, the authority interest, is special: promises would not be made and would not bind when made unless people wanted authority for its own sake. A full defense of this hypothesis can't be attempted here but in the rest of this section I shall highlight some of its more attractive consequences.

On my hypothesis, we can see why it has seemed so natural to model promissory rights on property rights. Even if I own some things as a matter of innate right (e.g., my body) most of my property is not like that. Nobody thinks that I have an innate right to my car, my house, and so forth; rather I own these things because someone gave them to me by gift, sale, bequest, etc.[34] Furthermore such transactions occur because one or both parties have an interest in transferring ownership of the relevant things. In order to explain why I have a right to life, we need not suppose that I have any interest in having a right to life, that it will do me any good to have such a right. But in order to explain how we come to own cars and houses, we *do* need to suppose that people have an interest in ownership of cars and houses, that ownership of these things somehow serves their interests.

What interest does ownership serve? Those who purchase and sell are exercising normative powers, are acting with the intention of changing the normative situation by declaration. When I buy your car, I communicate the intention of hereby acquiring

[33] Non-normative interests are often normatively significant in that they help to determine our rights and obligations but they do not take such normative phenomena as their objects; they are not interests *in* rights and obligations.

[34] There is also ownership by original acquisition etc., but this too (I would argue) involves the exercise of normative power and so presupposes normative interests.

the claims, liberties, and powers associated with ownership of the car and you communicate the intention of hereby granting me those items. This suggests that the interests most directly served by such transactions are normative interests. Of course, we may be interested in the normative situation here only because we are interested in the non-normative situation i.e. in who has physical control over the car. But sometimes those involved in the exchange of physical goods have an interest in ownership that goes beyond any interest they have in making use of the thing owned. For example, the purchaser may be concerned solely with the car's future resale value and thus in having the power to sell it on.

Promissory rights, like property rights, are acquired by declaration. Where a right is acquired by the communication of an intention to acquire it (a) the receiver has some interest in acquiring it and (b) such interests must be capable of explaining their acquisition of that right. The right must be the kind of thing that one can acquire *because* one has an interest in acquiring it. Rights acquirable by declaration are what I'll call *interested* rights, rights that people can possess in virtue of having an interest in possessing them. The interest in play might be a purely instrumental one: I might be interested in your promise simply because it will give me control over what you'll actually do. Yet, on my hypothesis, promises bind because people also have specifically normative interests, interests in being invested with certain rights and powers for their own sake, and they sometimes seek a promise in the service of those interests.[35]

The transfer theorist fell victim to Hume's Point because the natural rights allegedly transferred by a promise (or relinquished by consent) had a foundation that would not allow them to be moved from one person to another simply by declaration. If rights of bodily control etc. are grounded in one's rational personality or in one's (non-normative) interests, it is hard to see how mere declaration could affect the extent of such rights. By contrast, such declarations can intelligibly engage with interested rights, rights whose possession depends on whether it is (or seems to be) good for me to have them. Why shouldn't I be entitled to control whether I have such rights by making declarations directed at those rights, as I am entitled to control various non-normative phenomena that matter to me by making choices directed at those non-normative phenomena? Both entitlements are grounded in my interest in having control over things that matter to me.[36] Once we ground normative power in normative interest, Hume's Point no longer applies.

Can the transfer theorist take advantage of my reply to Hume's Point by invoking an interest in autonomy? Shiffrin tells us that we'd be unable to form "meaningful human relationships" and so forth unless we were able to waive our rights and impose obligations on ourselves by declaration. Though Shiffrin overstates her case here, such normative powers would undeniably give us a useful form of control over our social environment. Mightn't that suffice to make sense of our claim to exercise such control?

[35] To address Hume's Point effectively, we must suppose that our interest in controlling rights and duties is not purely instrumental. *See* Owens, Shaping The Normative Landscape, at 148–9.

[36] There are things (including obligations) that we have no interest in controlling even though they matter to us, e.g., surprise parties and the obligation to hold them. But many things (including obligations) matter to us in such a way as to give us an interest in controlling them.

There is a crucial ambiguity in the idea of an autonomy interest: are we dealing with an interest in normative or in non-normative phenomena? On the one hand, the phrase "interest in autonomy" might refer to an interest in having the kind of physical control over what we do or what happens to us that (e.g.) the rights of bodily integrity are meant to protect. So understood an interest in autonomy is a non-normative interest. And since these rights of bodily integrity are based on the human need to control various non-normative phenomena (e.g., whether a knife goes into my body) they are surely *noninterested* rights, rights we have regardless of whether it does us any good to have them. But to take this line is to expose oneself to Hume's Point. How can rights so understood be varied merely by declaration? The alternative is to treat our "interest in autonomy" as a normative interest, as an interest in the possession of (and control over) certain rights. So understood the proposal does address Hume's Point but not in a way that the transfer theorist would find congenial for it also undermines the idea that our power to promise and consent are natural powers, i.e., powers that we have independently of social convention.[37]

Where rights (like promissory rights) are the products of an exercise of normative powers, those rights must be interested rights. Now the idea of an interested right makes sense only if we think of the right in which I have an interest as having some social reality. For it to be in my interests to possess a certain right, possession of that right must (in at least some respect) make my life go better and it can do so only in so far as this right is recognized by the people around me.[38] Interested rights are conventionally recognized rights (and more generally normative interests are interests in conventionally recognized norms). For example, it can't be in my *interests* that some act be an appropriate object of blame (etc.) unless its being so makes a difference to what actually happens or is likely to happen.[39] True my possession of this right alone hardly ensures that the right will actually be respected: even rights established by convention are frequently violated. Perhaps my possession of the right need make no difference to the probability of its violation. Nevertheless it must at least make a difference to people's likely reactions to that violation, reactions which cast a pall of disapproval over acts of this sort. Interested rights cannot be items that we

[37] Shiffrin formulates a moderate form of conventionalism according to which, though promises do not bind until they are socially recognized, we all have a pre-conventional obligation to accord them social recognition. She comments: "once conventionalism has transformed itself so completely, it loses moral distinctiveness." Though I agree that we all have an important pre-conventional interest in the establishment of a social practice of promising, I remain uncertain whether this generates an obligation to establish such a practice. Even if it does, I doubt that this obligation (as opposed to the underlying authority interest) is the source of our promissory obligations. *See* Shiffrin, *Promising, Intimate Relationships and Conventionalism*, at 521–3 and Owens, Shaping The Normative Landscape, at 153.

[38] Nagel maintains that we are all better off simply in virtue of being possessors of "moral" rights and regardless of whether these rights are recognized but he does not explain how the fact that we are wronged by torture and so forth could make our lives go better. He says that the relevant notion of well-being presupposes the possession of moral status but that implies only that nothing counts as better or worse for us unless we have moral status, not that possession of moral status makes things go any better (Thomas Nagel, *Personal Rights and Public Space*, 24 Phil. & Pub. Aff. 83, 92–3 (1995)).

[39] Here we must distinguish what is in my interests (i.e., what is good for me) from what interests me. I may take an interest in things that do not bear upon my interests, e.g., in the fact that I have certain natural or innate rights.

possess regardless of whether anyone ever has or ever will recognize the fact.[40] Hume is quite correct that "a promise would not be intelligible before human conventions had established it."[41]

I have sketched a theory of promising which vindicates the idea that, in making a promise, we are changing the normative situation by declaration but I have not argued that the normative character of a promise can be explained *only* on the hypothesis that promises are here to serve the promisee's authority interest in particular.[42] A full discussion is beyond the scope of this chapter but I shall conclude by highlighting one essential feature of the promise that my hypothesis is well placed to explain, namely the fact that the promisee is the only party necessarily wronged by a breach of the promise.

It might be thought that this feature of promising can be explained without invoking any normative interest. Perhaps we need only suppose that the promisee wants control over the non-normative situation and in particular over the behavior of the promisor. For example, the promisee might wish to be able to determine whether the promisor will appear at the bus stop at noon and seeks a promise for that reason. A valid promise gives the promisee's choice in this matter a certain normative significance: if, at noon, the promisee intends the promisor to appear and the promisor does not appear, the promisor will have violated an obligation and committed a wrong. Furthermore, they will have wronged the promisee in particular. Isn't this last fact best explained by the nature of the interest that led the promisee to seek the promise, namely the promisee's need to control the promisor's behavior "at will"? Things are not so simple.

People often seek promises with a view to giving some third party control over what will happen. For example, I might ask you to promise to mow my mother's lawn on a certain date. Most such promises are implicitly conditional on the agreement of the purported beneficiary: you are meant to mow my mother's lawn only if she wishes to have it mowed. So, once you have promised, my mother can determine "at will" whether or not you would be committing a wrong in failing to mow her lawn. Your promise gives her choice in the matter the sort of normative significance that, we were supposing, it is the point of a promise to secure. It gives her "moral control" over your behavior and thereby serves her interest in controlling the non-normative situation. Still it does not ensure that, were you to breach your promise, you would thereby be wronging *her*. The only person necessarily wronged by breach of promise is the person to whom the promise was made, namely myself. My mother may also be wronged but if so that is only in virtue of some further fact (harm, disappointed expectations) beyond the mere breach of promise. Thus, we cannot identify the person wronged by breach of promise as the

[40] Owens, Shaping The Normative Landscape, at 9–10 and 150–1.

[41] Hume, A Treatise on Human Nature, at 516.

[42] For example, someone might endorse the general notion that normative powers are to be grounded in normative interests (plus social convention) whilst arguing that I have misidentified the normative interest or interests at stake. *See* Raz's contribution to this volume in which he highlights the promisor's interest in being able to shape their lives, as well as the promisee's interest in "normative assurance." I suspect that what Raz calls "the value of normative assurance" depends on what I call the authority interest. The material that follows may be relevant to this point.

person whose interest in controlling the promisor's behavior "at will" is served by the promise.[43]

One might respond that there is a crucial difference between my mother and me. My mother does not have the power to release you from your promise by declaration; rather she is able to determine by choice whether the conditions of the promise apply and this is so in virtue of the content of the promise. To equate the two is like confusing normatively significant choice with consent. That's all perfectly true but the question remains: Why should this difference matter on the view under consideration, namely that the interest served by promising is an interest in having the right to control what happens "at will"? Both my mother and I are granted *that* right by the promise and so, on this view, both of us should be equally wronged by the breach of it.

All becomes clear once we allow that the promisee might have a specific interest in controlling the *normative* situation by declaration, quite apart from any interest they may have in controlling the non-normative situation. Perhaps my mother too has such a normative interest but a promise made to me does not serve that interest. Like Thompson's Jewish bride, it gives her choice normative significance without granting her any normative power. That difference matters because human beings have what I call authority interests distinct from any interests they might have in exercising control over the non-normative situation. If we suppose that promises are here to serve these authority interests, we can explain (amongst other things) why the promisee is wronged by the breach of promise. Promising exists to serve people's interest in controlling whether they would be wronged by nonperformance, not their interest in controlling whether performance actually occurs.

Conclusion

It is not hard to see why the transfer theory has proved so attractive over the centuries despite the difficulty we found in identifying the item supposedly transferred by a promise. First, the transfer theory preserves the appearance that those who make and accept promises are changing the normative situation by declaration. Second, the transfer theory seeks to ground this power to change our obligations by declaration in a prior natural right (which many believe we have) to control various aspects of our own lives. In this chapter I have argued that appearances can be preserved here only once the attempt to base our power to promise on such a prior natural right has been abandoned.

Perhaps we do have such a right but, as Hume showed, any attempt to ground the power to promise in natural rights must fail. Expectation theorists respond to this failure by dropping the whole idea of normative power and seeking to rebuild promissory obligation on the quite different foundation of harm avoidance. They affirm that promissory obligation is grounded in our natural right not to be harmed in certain ways whilst denying that it either involves a transfer of this right or originates in an

[43] Hart, *Are There Any Natural Rights?*, at 180–2, discusses such examples to make a related point. For present purposes it does not matter whether my mother will either benefit from performance of the promise or be harmed by nonperformance. All that matters is that the obligation is conditional on her choice.

exercise of normative power. I suggest that we rescue normative power by acknowledging normative interests, by adding to the familiar list of human goods (knowledge, beauty, pleasure, etc.) normative phenomena such as rights and obligations. Our interest in rights and obligations involves an interest in controlling them and that normative control interest is what underwrites our possession of the normative powers of promise and consent.

6

Personal Autonomy and Change of Mind in Promise and in Contract

Dori Kimel

Introduction: Promise and Personal Autonomy

For those who see value in personal autonomy, one of the supposed great mysteries of moral philosophy—the binding force of a promise—turns out to be far less mysterious. At least for those who also believe that the desirability of a state of affairs whereby people can bind themselves in a promise is the basis on which to explain promissory obligations, the value of personal autonomy has been key in solving that supposed mystery, as it constitutes the broadway to explaining the desirability of that very state of affairs. Personal autonomy concerns people exerting control, through the exercise of free choice, over a significant proportion of fundamental aspects of their lives. At its core, it is an ideal of self-authorship; what better manifestation of that ideal than a person acting, *inter alia*, as the author of her own moral obligations?

Autonomy-based accounts of the value, and hence the binding force of promises, have come to dominate the philosophical understanding of this domain, and that is perhaps not surprising in view of the depth of this idea's philosophical roots. Indeed, the capacity to self-impose an obligation—to self-legislate, to be the willing author of significant dimensions of one's own normative environment—has long been seen by many not just as *an* important freedom, but possibly as some sort of a paradigmatic, logically antecedent freedom—a freedom capable of providing an explanation and a foundation to all other freedoms, and a freedom such that, when present, its bearer is seen as "free" even when its exercise, actual or hypothetical, has seemingly rendered her, and in fairly obvious ways, far less free than she would have been otherwise. This idea has long gained perch in political thought, informing much of what has become known as social contract theory (if political obligations, no matter how onerous, can be construed as self-imposed, their legitimacy is all but guaranteed) and, somewhat less extravagantly, has gained much prominence in promissory theory, and in the theory of contract law. The modern canonical statement of the position I have in mind is probably Charles Fried's, for whom promise (and hence also contract) is explicable as a freedom-maximizing device in the most straightforward way:

> In order that I be as free as possible, that my will have the greatest possible range consistent with the similar will of others, it is necessary that there be a way in

> which I may commit myself. It is necessary that I be able to make nonoptional a course of conduct that would otherwise be optional for me.[1]

Fried's treatment of the value, and ultimately the binding force of promise as *the* device which secures this crucial freedom subsequently places some emphasis on the reciprocal or bilateral potential that it holds: the motive for the kind of commitment it facilitates need not be altruistic, and it is just as valuable—just as "worth facilitating," as he put it[2]—when deployed with the aim of receiving the promisee's own commitment in return, which is of course the norm in the domain of contract. Nevertheless for him, to recognize the binding force of a promise—even quite regardless of reciprocity or bilaterality—is to show respect for the promisor's standing as an autonomous moral agent, whereas a failure to so recognize—for instance, by allowing a promisor who regrets the promise to renege—amounts to doing the opposite:

> If we decline to take seriously the assumption of an obligation because we do not take seriously the promisor's prior conception of the good that led him to assume it, to that extent we do not take him seriously as a person. We infantilize him, as we do quite properly when we release the very young from the consequences of their choices.[3]

This last quote may seem to apply with equal force to nonpromissory undertakings just the same; yet when it comes to promises, as a particular form of a voluntary assumption of obligations, the link to the ideal of personal autonomy can be shown to be particularly natural and particularly strong. By exploring the special bond-creating dimension of promises, Jospeh Raz has shown that particularly well. Unlike, say, a vow, or other putative forms of personal undertakings, a promise is made to someone; it involves a promisee. When successful, a promise places the promisor under an obligation that is owed, at least primarily, specifically to the promisee; it creates a special relationship between two agents. It creates, as Raz put it, "a special bond, binding the promisor to be, in the matter of the promise, partial to the promisee. It obliges the promisor to regard the claim of the promisee as not just one of the many claims that every person has for his respect and help but as having peremptory force."[4] On this basis, Raz went on to explain that the moral principles which govern the binding force of promises "can only be justified if the creation of such special relationships between people is held to be valuable."[5] And personal autonomy can indeed play a central role in explaining why it is valuable. Human relationships feature prominently in any plausible account of personal autonomy. The control over one's life that personal autonomy prizes concerns primarily the meaningful, the lasting, the profound—those choices that can truly be said to be the ones through which a person's life acquires the particular character and meaning that it has. These are choices that concern matters such as long-term projects, careers, and relationships. By promising, a person elevates some

[1] Charles Fried, Contract as Promise: A Theory of Contractual Obligation 13 (1981).

[2] Fried, Contract as Promise, 13. [3] Fried, Contract as Promise, at 20–1.

[4] J. Raz, *Promises and Obligations*, *in* Law, Morality and Society 210, 227–8 (P. M. S. Hacker & J. Raz eds., 1977).

[5] Raz, *Promises and Obligations*, at 228.

future conduct for which she might at best have an ordinary reason, into something which she bears an obligation to do, and an obligation owed specifically to another at that. Thus beyond the natural affinity of obligations (as opposed to ordinary reasons) to the stable, the long term, here we have (self-created) obligations that, by their very nature as obligations owed to another, establish special relationships. And interpersonal relationships are not only one of those central dimensions of life over which self-authorship is called for from the perspective of personal autonomy; rather, they are often the bedrock of other such central dimensions just the same: careers, long-term pursuits, serious hobbies, and the like are usually significantly constituted by the interpersonal relationships involved in their pursuit.

So the capacity to promise makes us freer, and freer in a sense which is particularly germane to the ideal of personal autonomy: through it we become part-authors of our own moral obligations, and, moreover, the obligations we author, bond creating as they are, are particularly conducive to autonomy-related interests. Might that be a bit too easy? Might personal autonomy-based accounts of the value—and hence also, by implication, the binding force—of promise have been too casual in assuming that the ability to create obligations for one's self in general, and create those so that they are owed to others in particular, is, overall, beneficial to one's propensity to be autonomous? Might there be another side to things?

We could envisage an attempt to reduce the reasoning by which self-imposed obligations are some sort of a pinnacle of self-authorship, and hence a requirement as well as a most natural extension of personal autonomy, to absurdity. Taken at face value, this reasoning may inform the view that the more one promises, thus exercising more authorship over one's own normative environment, the more autonomous one is. That may ring true particularly when it is noted that promissory obligations can not just add to, but sometimes displace nonpromissory, nonself-created moral obligations (let alone nonobligatory norms): the prolific promisor may not just bear more obligations, but a greater proportion of obligations which she herself has authored, and a smaller proportion, perhaps even a smaller number, of obligations over which she has exercised no control. Does that invariably make her more autonomous?

Of course not. When someone promises willy-nilly, makes promises that it is not in her interests to make, or makes promises to the wrong people or at the wrong time (etc.), she may be authoring more of her own obligations, but authoring them badly—and, most likely, "badly" precisely in the relevant sense: to the detriment of her personal autonomy. Yet this is by no means an embarrassment to the original contention. Personal autonomy in general depends for its value on the worthiness of its exercise,[6] and its exercise through promising may be more or less worthy. The capacity to self-author obligations to others may be of great value, autonomy-wise and otherwise; but like most other capacities, it can be used and it can be misused, and it can indeed be misused in a way that undermines the very goals that (when used prudently) it is particularly suitable for promoting. There is nothing unique about that.

[6] The benchmark argument for this position is Joseph Raz. *See* Joseph Raz, The Morality of Freedom 378–81 (1986).

But perhaps there is something unique, not in the mere fact that the capacity to self-author obligations can be misused, but in the magnitude of the risk inherent in such an occurrence? In this line of thought, I believe, lurks a more serious anxiety. In light of certain prominent features it has or may plausibly be thought to have, the capacity to self-create obligations owed to others may be thought of not only as a manifestation or an extension of personal autonomy, but also as something that can pose a particularly potent threat to it. Once its nature and magnitude are understood, it may be asked rather credibly: is it possible that the removal of that threat, albeit at the cost of removing the autonomy-enhancing potential inherent in promises, would leave us with no net detriment in terms of personal autonomy and the capacity to enjoy it, or even with a net gain? Is it possible that, in a world without promise, people would be just as likely, or perhaps even more likely, to be autonomous?

This is the main question to be addressed in this chapter. I will begin by animating it a little further, by reference to the autonomy-related value of a change of mind, and by reference to some (perceived) qualities of promises that may be thought to render the practice exceptionally hostile to a change of mind. Having done that, I will argue to the contrary, and aim to restore the notion that the autonomy-enhancing potential of promises outweighs the autonomy-curtailing risk they create. I will conclude with some observations concerning the difference between contract and promise, and the case for treating the former as a device for the legal enforcement of the latter.

I. Personal Autonomy and a Change of Mind

The control over one's life that personal autonomy prizes concerns, in particular, not the trivial or the transient but the meaningful and lasting. It concerns those aspects of a life that endow it with the particular meaning and character that it has as a whole; it places particular value on free choice when it comes to significant decisions—those decisions that have the propensity to shape a life, make it into the kind of life that it is. Therefore it is not surprising that much of the emphasis, in discussions of personal autonomy, its exercise, and the conditions that must obtain in order for people to enjoy it, revolves around the long term, the stable, the unchanging. The range of options people must have so as to have the opportunity to live truly autonomous lives primarily concerns the big themes—careers, deep relationships, abiding passions; the background conditions must include, beyond a range of valuable options from which to choose, the normative transparency and stability required for long-term planning and enduring commitment.[7] Indeed, inasmuch as commitment and spontaneity are viewed as (potentially) contrasting dispositions, or the propensity to display them as contrasting virtues, the emphasis in discussions of personal autonomy, notwithstanding it being *a freedom*, tends to be on the former, and not the latter: the commitments in question ought to be of one's own making, but the freedom in question is the freedom to shape one's own life as a whole, not to do as one pleases at any given moment. This is why, when instantiations of both types of freedom come into conflict, curtailment of the latter kind of freedom, even when done against the present

[7] This theme is often explored in discussions of the rule of law as a condition for personal autonomy.

wishes of a person, can be viewed as manifestations of respect for her personal autonomy, whereas, as we have seen, the opposite can be described as her infantilization.[8]

Again we can see, now perhaps with greater clarity, how naturally promises may seem to fit within the general scheme of reverence for personal autonomy. By placing herself under a self-created obligation, the promisor may impose a weighty restriction upon the prospect of deviating from a course of future conduct, but that is precisely what personal autonomy routinely calls for; it is part and parcel of the idea of freely chosen commitments, so central to the very possibility of personal autonomy—and promises are a particularly useful means to just that end. Thus, as Fried put it, the supposed "mystery that surrounds increasing autonomy by providing means for restricting it" turns out to be "a pseudomystery:" "the restrictions involved in promising are restrictions undertaken just in order to increase one's options in the long run, and thus are perfectly consistent with the principle of autonomy."[9] Those restrictions, moreover, are conceived and undertaken by the promisor, who is in control over their timing, their content, and their context (when to promise, what to promise, to whom). All that is missing for the air of mystery to be dispelled altogether is an assumption of "the continuity of the self and the possibility of maintaining complex projects over time"—an assumption in the absence of which, as Fried has observed correctly, "not only the morality of promising but also any coherent picture of the person becomes impossible."[10]

Does this picture leave any meaningful moral space for a change of mind? That is, can the freedom and the capacity to change one's mind, at least in circumstances where the change in question is relative to a past commitment of the agent's own making, ever have a distinct value, appreciable by those who see personal autonomy as key to the good life? I think so. One way to articulate what I have in mind here involves that underlying assumption we have just encountered. Yes, a certain conception of the continuity of the self invariably underpins any plausible account of personal autonomy. Yet the continuity of past commitments may exceed that of the relevant self. The continuing self, that is, may also continue to evolve. Particularly over extended periods of time, tastes develop, priorities change, temperaments mellow or intensify, new passions are ignited, old ones extinguished. Still without straying into the realm of conceiving the self as perpetually fragmented, we can sometimes observe that certain choices that a person has made at some point in the past are now, in quite a profound sense, "no longer hers;" or indeed, consider a person who remains unwaveringly true to past commitments which no longer meaningfully relate to her present vision of how she ought to live as anything but a model of personal autonomy in action.

Perhaps the quality at stake is authenticity. The example around which Fried has offered his observations concerning the right way to treat the regretting promisor is that of a person who concludes, shortly after the act, that the purchase of an expensive antique was an unnecessary extravagance. In a case such as this, it seems quite right to suggest, as Fried has done, that a refusal to release the promisor is entirely consistent with, and may indeed be required by, respect for his standing as an autonomous agent,

[8] *See* Fried, Contract as Promise, at 20–1.

[9] Fried, Contract as Promise, at 20–1.

[10] Fried, Contract as Promise, at 20–1.

and thus as someone whose own commitments ought to be taken seriously; in any event, such a refusal would not represent much of a setback to the promisor's personal autonomy. But things are not always like that. Particularly when it is remembered that personal autonomy consists primarily in long-term endeavors and relationships, it becomes natural to think of it as involving not only *original* authorship of fundamental aspects of one's life, but also a continuing sense of authorship—a striving, if you like, towards authenticity in one's pursuits. Buyer's regret following the purchase of an expensive antique ought not render a person dissociated from the life she is living or from any significant dimension of that life, or make that life any less authentic, or less authentically *hers*. But other types of regret, other types of issue over which a change of mind may occur, can do just that.

Changes of mind of the latter sort, it should be noted, need not always be the product of some profound evolution of character, as I may have been taken to imply thus far. This kind of development only tends to take place over lengthy periods of time, and usually in a manner so piecemeal as to rarely manifest itself by way of a discrete change of mind over a particular matter (although sometimes it does). But frequently, limitations of self-knowledge, or knowledge other than of the self, or limitations of imagination (and the like) are at stake. Sometimes, it is only through immersion in a career, a relationship, a project (etc.), no matter how profoundly appealing or suitable it appeared to be or how earnestly a person chose to embark upon it in the first place, that the realization emerges as to its unsuitability or undesirability for that person. Once some idea of authenticity in one's pursuits and relationships is accepted as a vital quality of the truly autonomous life, not just the ability to choose, to commit, to persist... but also the occasion to stop, to reappraise, to break from the past, to veer into a new path—to change one's mind—emerges as crucial for personal autonomy.

Indeed, it may be thought that a considerable freedom to change one's mind is just as essential for the ongoing pursuit of personal autonomy as is the capacity and the willingness to make long-term commitments or to persevere with past choices. The notion that there is always tension between these two sets of conditions and (corresponding) personal attributes may itself emerge as highly exaggerated, perhaps altogether misleading: a change of mind is not always the antithesis of planning, controlling, self-authorship; sometimes it is part and parcel of those. Pathology, to put it differently, can be found on either ends of the spectrum: a person who cannot make long-term commitments cannot be autonomous, but nor can a person who never has the opportunity or the disposition to experience, and where appropriate to act on a change of mind.

Once this is taken into account, the capacity facilitated by promise to bind one's self to another may begin to appear in a slightly different light. There is clearly a danger here, not just a potential. There are, of course, numerous other ways in which people place themselves, voluntarily, under obligations which are owed to others. Most if not all types of personal relationships, to take one example, tend to generate their own norms, including mandatory ones; so by choosing to enter or to remain in a relationship, a person renders herself bound by norms which would not bind her otherwise. Yet there is something different about a promise: you say something, and you are bound—possibly in perpetuity; there is probably no easier way to incur a new obligation, there is barely a limit on its possible content and scope, and it is an obligation which, once incurred, may prove particularly tricky to shake off. By stark contrast to that earlier caricature—the more you promise, the more autonomous you are—the carefree promisor can begin to look anything but truly autonomous; instead, it is a person shackled to past decisions, mired in other people's expectations—legitimate expectations, at that!—with her ability to respond to changes in outlook, temperament, desires, interests, or priorities, and to maintain a sense of authenticity and true engagement in her life, severely curtailed. That may seem true particularly when it is remembered that an obligation excludes counter-reasons for action by type,[11] and the type most trivially excluded is a simple change of mind: if that is not excluded, what is?

Of course, not all changes of mind are the same. A change of mind that is truly relevant to personal autonomy, or to the safeguarding of authenticity in one's pursuits, would be, for the most part at least, rational. It would be a response to reasons, which happen to be (among other things) reasons to break from a past commitment. Obligations may always exclude a random, capricious change of mind as ground for nonconforming action, but not necessarily exclude those proper, potentially weighty reasons for action informing what may be thought of as a *reasonable* change of mind; occasionally, acting on such reasons may be morally permissible after all. Still, it remains the case that existing moral obligations can pose a significant restriction on the latitude for changing course, and the capacity to create new ones by one's mere say-so increases the span of such a restriction to a potentially limitless extent.

It is time to focus on those characteristics of promises, as a particular (although not unique) device for the voluntary assumption of obligations, which may give the impression that they pose the risk in question in a particularly acute way. Some such characteristics have been touched upon already: promissory obligations are easy to assume, and their content (and timing, scope, etc.) is within the control of the promisor. I have also mentioned the notion that, once incurred, such obligations may prove particularly tricky to shake off—why is that? In what follows, I will focus on three sets of considerations which may contribute to this impression, or something like it. First, the issue of fault, and, in particular, the notion that promissory obligations *exclude* fault—that they are, by their very nature, strict liability. Second, the notion that a failure to discharge a promissory obligation typically triggers other obligations—obligations which often are just as onerous as the promissory obligation by the breach of which they are triggered. Finally, considerations relating to the role of the promisee, and, in particular, the notion that whilst the promisee is granted the unique prerogative and with it the discretion to release the promisor (or to alter the terms of the obligation, or the terms of the reparative obligation that a breach carries in its wake, etc.), the exercise of this discretion is ungoverned by any binding norms.

If sound, these considerations are mutually reinforcing: that a promise is strict liability means that a broader range of possible scenarios would involve a breach, thus triggering (potentially equally onerous) reparative obligations; that, in turn, shows the power the promisee has over the promisor to be even greater, and the apparent dearth

[11] *See* Joseph Raz, The Authority of Law 22 (1979).

of norms governing its exercise all the more troubling. I will, however, aim to show that the first and the third type of consideration, or the anxieties to which they give rise, are rather exaggerated if not altogether misplaced. If so, then their relationship may in fact prove to be mutually weakening, perhaps with the overall effect of restoring promises to their status as enhancers of personal autonomy more than they are a threat to it.

II. Are Promissory Obligations Strict?

Contract law—thought of by many as, simply, the law of enforceable promises—is often distinguished from other branches of the law by reference to the strict liability nature of the obligations arising and enforced within it.[12] Promissory liability can similarly be thought of as strict. Indeed, it is usually thought of as such. Few have endorsed this view explicitly, but it seems to be at least implicitly implicated in many standard philosophical accounts of promising, if only through the sort of examples which are most commonly used to animate them. These are examples of promises as undertakings, sometimes conditional (on the future conduct of the promisee, or on some other future eventuality), to do something or to refrain from doing something, such that an eventual failure to do the thing promised—turn up someplace, render some service, pay—is a breach, no matter what the surrounding circumstances are, what reasons there may have been for the failure, or whether those reasons have been in any way within the control of the promisor. In such scenarios it may of course be acknowledged, where appropriate (e.g., when the frustrating circumstances are truly beyond the control of the promisor: an unforecast storm has blocked her path, or some emergency required her attention) that the breach "wasn't her fault"; that "she is not to blame," or even that "she did nothing wrong;", but even so, the breach means that she has committed one distinct wrong—indeed, she wronged the promisee—she broke the promise. The breach, in other words, may happen to be unavoidable, or justified, or excusable, but such considerations would not affect the issue of its very occurrence, nor its status as a wrong.

Does that matter? Especially as I have just endorsed the view that conceptually dissociates the wrong from fault, or any other notion of blameworthiness, it may be thought not to matter one bit. If the wrong of a breach does not, in and of itself, entail the conclusion nor presupposes the premise that the promisor has been in any way blameworthy, life can simply go on, with no moral blemish attached to anyone and nothing more to be said or done. For that matter, even inasmuch as some sort of a moral blemish does happen to attach to the promisor, that in and of itself may seem to matter little: either way, the breach has terminated the promise, it has now been discharged. The moral blemish need not be too grave, and life can still go on.

Yet it does matter, since, being a wrong, a breach of promise always leaves something in its wake—a certain moral residue, if you like—and something which can be far more burdensome than moral blemish alone: it may give rise to reparative obligations.

[12] For an influential critique, *see* George M. Cohen, *The Fault Lines in Contract Damages*, 80 Va. L. Rev. 1225 (1994). For a recent volume collecting diverse contributions on the topic *see* Fault in American Contract Law (Omri Ben-Shahar & Ariel Porat eds., 2010).

So once a wrong has been committed, whether its commission was attended by fault may indeed matter little; but the fault dimension of the obligation itself is part of what determines whether the wrong—the breach of the obligation—has been committed in the first place, so that the moral residue in question, possibly in the shape of reparative obligations, comes into existence.

This is probably true of all wrongs, but when it comes to broken promises, the nature and scope of the so-called moral residue is particularly straightforward to establish. A promissory obligation is typically owed to a specified person—the promisee; its breach is therefore not just a wrong, but it wrongs someone—there is an aggrieved party, and its identity is readily ascertainable. The obligation's precise content is also readily ascertainable. So a reparative obligation arises in the wake of a broken promise, and *its* content as well as would-be beneficiary can be ascertained straightforwardly by reference to the content of the primary obligation, the promise.

Whereas lawyers and philosophers alike have always shown interest in promises (or, for that matter, agreements), lawyers, much more so than philosophers, have always paid particularly close attention to the normative aftermath of a breach. This is probably only natural, given that the law of contract primarily expresses itself, so to speak, in this very domain—that is, by responding to a breach, or anyway by responding to "things going wrong" with agreements: mistakes being made, parties coming under undue influence, etc. And in practically all jurisdictions, the norm, when it comes to the choice of remedy for a breach of contract, is to opt, other things being equal, for that remedy which would place the aggrieved party in as good a position, or as close as possible to the position in which it would have been absent the breach. Moreover, at common law, at least, considerations relating to fault in breach play an extremely limited role in the selection of the appropriate remedy to be awarded; even when truly without fault, the leading consideration in responding to a breach is the need to secure for the plaintiff, as much as possible, if not the very performance of the promise made to her then the benefits that performance would have brought.[13]

Is the morality of promise different, in this regard, from the law of contract? I do not think so. Neil MacCormick, and more recently John Gardner, have both argued that when a promise is broken, an obligation arises in its stead, the content of which is largely determined by the content of the promise. MacCormick's treatment of this particular issue was encapsulated in an example of a (justifiably) broken promise to take the children to the beach on a particular afternoon, and the judgment he offered that, in such a case, the promisor "now owes it to his children as soon as possible to make good their disappointment by taking them to the seaside."[14] Gardner, for his part, has explicated that judgment by way of offering a thesis explaining the emergence, in the wake of a failure to perform an obligation, of an obligation to do the "next best," which is rooted in the need to satisfy the same reasons that ground the original obligation:

> Once the time for performance of a primary obligation is past, so that it can no longer be performed, one can often nevertheless still contribute to satisfaction of some or all

[13] For my own explanation, *see* Dori Kimel, *Fault and Harm in Breach of Contract, in* Fault in American Contract Law, at 271.

[14] Neil MacCormick, *The Obligation of Reparation, in* Legal Right and Social Democracy 212 (1982).

> of the reasons that added up to make the action obligatory. Those reasons, not having been satisfied by performance of the primary obligation, are still with us awaiting satisfaction and since they cannot now be satisfied by performance of that obligation, they call for satisfaction in some other way. They call for next-best satisfaction, the closest to full satisfaction that is still available.[15]

Gardner's thesis concerns the foundations of corrective justice in general, and is not limited to promissory obligations; but in the promissory domain, as MacCormick's example (and Gardner's deployment of the same example) illustrates, its application appears to be particularly straightforward. The example also illustrates that it is by no means unusual for the reparative obligations that arise in the wake of a broken promise to be just as onerous as the promissory obligation was. And if promissory obligations are always strict—if fault has no necessary bearing not only on the nature of the reparative obligation that arises in the wake of a breach, but also no bearing on the question of whether a breach has taken place in the first place—then promissory obligations emerge as quite a burdensome affair indeed. A promisor may do all she can to keep the promise, and fail to do so for reasons that are entirely beyond her control, or that entirely justify the failure; nevertheless she now owes the promisee an "obligation of reparation" (to use MacCormick's language) the content of which may differ little from the content of the promise. This has little to do with a change of mind as such, of course, but it does show promissory obligations to be burdensome in a way which is clearly pertinent to the assessment of their likely impact on the (future) autonomy of those who undertake them: anything short of actual performance leaves the promisor still bound to the promisee, the magnitude of her debt to him (potentially) barely diminished.

As far as it goes, I think the upshot of this analysis is correct. Whether for the reasons captured in Gardner's continuity thesis, or for the reasons offered by MacCormick, the conclusions they both draw—when a promise is broken, the promisor incurs an obligation to do the "next best" for the promisee, and that need not depend on fault in breach—are sound.[16] The one qualification I would offer concerns the notion that promissory obligations themselves are necessarily strict; that is, that the fact of a breach (and hence, also, the emergence of those reparative obligations) is a matter in which fault can play no role.

My point is not that promissory obligations necessarily are *not* strict. They can be. But equally, promissory obligations can be fault based, and the fault element—so long as it "matches" the wrong in terms of its inherent logic[17]—can be any of the types of fault which may attend the commission of a wrong: intention, knowledge, inappropriate motive, recklessness, negligence, or as the case may be. My point, in other words, is that promissory obligations do not have a fixed fault element; that, like much else to do with the content of the promise, the fault element is essentially

[15] John Gardner, *What Is Tort Law for? Part 1. The Place of Corrective Justice*, 30 L. & PHIL. 1, 33 (2011).

[16] Why "as far as it goes?" I return to this question in Section III, arguing that, for reasons that do not originate in the morality of promise itself, what the promisor ends up owing the promisee in the aftermath of a breach may depend on fault after all.

[17] For example, recklessness, or unreasonable risk taking, can only attend certain types of conduct but not others; some things can be done with or without knowledge, but knowledge or its absence is not a dimension of others; etc.

under the control of the promisor. And that, I believe, softens the picture painted up to this point a great deal.

Philosophical discussions of promises (and, similarly, contracts) tend to place considerable emphasis on the control the promisor has over the content of the promise—"content," that is, in terms of the subject matter of the promise: can one promise to do that which is not morally permissible? Promise the impossible? Etc.—as well as over various aspects of its normative implications, yet tend to pay little attention to the promisor's (or the contract parties') control over the fault dimension of the undertaking. But the fault dimension is, in fact, a dimension of the content. That the promisor, as a matter of principle, has as much control over that dimension of the content as she does over others—still limited, of course, by the bounds of logic, moral permissibility, perhaps the wishes of the promisee,[18] but not otherwise—is, in fact, a proposition I would find difficult to defend in isolation from a comprehensive account of promise as a whole, as it strikes me as a rather obvious implication of any such plausible account: if there is a point to and a justification for the institution of promise as a whole, why would the promisor *not* have such control?

Indeed, I can only advance the proposition that the fault dimension of promissory obligations, rather than fixed (at strict liability, or otherwise) is something which can be freely determined by promisors, by way of defending it against possible objections, and the only objections I can anticipate would take the shape of denying either the possibility, or the desirability of such a proposition. So: can it plausibly be argued, first, that something about the nature or the method of promissory undertakings somehow makes it *impossible* for promisors to introduce a fault element into that which they undertake? I cannot see why. A famous British chain of department stores, for example, has been trading for decades under the motto "Never Knowingly Undersold." This statement can be understood as a promise to customers, not to overcharge them with knowledge. This promise is not broken *whenever* customers are overcharged—it is not broken when, unbeknownst to the store, a rival store starts selling the same product for less, and, strictly speaking, it is not broken even if the pricing procedure deployed by the store involves the known risk of overcharging. Similarly, a person can promise to make an effort to bring (although not to succeed in bringing) about some state of affairs, or to refrain from doing something intentionally (although not accidentally or negligently or through risk taking) or for a certain motive (though not necessarily for others), and so on. To say "I promise I'll try to be there" is not the same as to say "I don't promise I'll be there:" in the first instance, but not the second, a promise has been made, albeit one that does not create a strict liability for not being there, but merely an obligation to make some reasonable effort towards that end. If the effort has been made yet the being there has not been achieved, the promise has been performed, and no reparative obligations need kick in. Similarly if I borrow something and promise not to take unreasonable risks with it, so long as I refrain from taking unreasonable

[18] Whether the wishes of the promisee matter in this way in controversial. *Compare* John R. Searle, *The Structure of Illocutionary Acts*, *in* Speech Acts 54 (1969); G. J. Warnock, The Object of Morality 99–101 (1971); Raz, *Promises and Obligations*, at 213; Dori Kimel, From Promise to Contract: Towards a Liberal Theory of Contract 21, 24–5 (2003).

risks I will have kept my promise even if I break it through the materialization of some reasonable risk I take.

Can it be argued that making the promissory obligation fault based rather than strict liability, or that giving the power to make them so to promisors is morally (or otherwise) *undesirable*? Or, at least, that a state of affairs in which all promissory obligations are treated as strict liability is somehow preferable to one in which the fault element is left to be determined by the promisor? If something like this could be established, it would make it plausible to insist that promissory obligations are strict liability even when they do not look or sound like that: if making the obligation fault based is not within the control of the promisor, then attempts by promisors to make it that way would simply fail,[19] in much the same way that attempts to promise that which simply cannot be the subject of a moral obligation would fail. But again, I cannot see how any variation on the theme that the practice as a whole becomes more valuable or desirable if the promisor's control over the fault element is removed could possibly be established. If anything, by exploring the anxiety that the notion that promises *are* always strict liability may generate, we have already encountered a powerful reason to think otherwise. The ability to make promises fault based moderates the combined implications of the facts that broken promissory obligations carry reparative obligations in their wake, that those reparative obligations can be and often are just as onerous as the original obligation, and that their incidence once a promise has been broken need not depend on fault. By making their promises fault based, promisors can protect themselves, to a degree, from a certain kind of over-exposure to the future claims of promisees: inasmuch as the fact of the breach depends on fault, at least those promisors who have failed to secure the ends of the promise—a rival store charges less; I did not make it there; the borrowed object broke—but with no fault (or with fault below the specified type) are now free to move on. This is desirable, and desirable precisely on the basis of concern for personal autonomy: the ability to introduce a fault element into the structure of promissory obligations allows promisors to strike a better balance between present commitment and future freedom.

I can think of two possible objections to the conclusions thus far. The first is a technicality: promissory obligations, so the objection goes, are strict liability after all: if I promise not to knowingly overcharge, I am strictly liable for knowingly overcharging. Of course, in a particular sense, that is true—I have indeed endorsed the view by which, *once the wrong has been committed*, reparative obligations may arise irrespectively of fault. If that makes promises strict liability, then they are indeed, as are, probably, all moral obligations. Or criminal offences, for that matter: the offence of murder can be said to impose a strict liability for killing with intention, "gross-negligence manslaughter" imposes a strict liability on those who kill through gross negligence, and so on. I am not convinced that the distinction between strict liability and fault-based liability remains of much interest or analytical import if it is understood exhaustively in this manner, but be that as it may, my point could be put thus: promissory obligations

[19] Although if that were the case, it would also be open to argument that the result of the failure is not a strict-liability obligation but a failure to assume an obligation altogether. Either way, all promissory obligations would be strict liability.

are strict liability in terms of the incidence of reparative obligations, but not necessarily strict liability in terms of what constitutes the commission of the wrong. Moreover, they are probably unique amongst moral obligations in the sense that the fault element is under the control of the bearer of the obligation, who is also its author.

The second objection concerns the notion that when a fault-based promissory obligation has been kept only in the sense that the fault condition has not been satisfied—that is, the promisee did not receive the performance she hoped for, but the promisor acted without the requisite fault for that to constitute a breach—no moral residue remains, no secondary obligations kick in, and the promisor is free from the claims of the promisee. Reparative obligations, so the objection goes, may still kick in in such a scenario. The fault element, after all, is just a modifier of performance. Performance can be modified in other ways; it can be made conditional, for instance—and then, too, if the condition fails to materialize, something may still be owed to the promisee. Perhaps not when the condition concerns the conduct of the promisee; but take a modified version of MacCormick's example: if the father promises "I'll take you to the beach tomorrow unless something important comes up at work," and something important does come up at work, is it not plausible to think that he now owes his children something very similar to what he ended up owing them in the original example?

In a scenario such as this, he may indeed; even though he has not broken the promise, he probably does owe his children precisely the same debt MacCormick identified in his discussion of the original example, "as soon as possible to make good their disappointment by taking them to the seaside."[20] Yet in the modified example, I would argue, the new obligation to do the next-best thing for the promisee originates elsewhere. It would probably be an instantiation of some parental (or general) obligation not to disappoint small children, particularly having first raised their hopes. So the fact of the promise and its particular aftermath forms part of the scenario that triggers the new obligation (an obligation which could, of course, be triggered in any number of different ways), but it is not its source: by failing to take the children to the beach in the first place, the father committed no wrong; relative to the promise itself, there is nothing to remedy.[21] The same would be true in a case where the promisee is similarly disappointed, but the promise has not been broken since the promisor has not acted with the kind of fault specified in the promise as the standard by which her conduct is to be judged.

This last objection and its refutation bring to the fore an important prospect: that norms that originate elsewhere—that is, originate in the background relationship between promisor and promisee—can interact with and supplement promissory norms, and end up playing a significant role in governing what the promisor and the promisee own each other in and around the promise. This theme will take central stage in Section III, with the focus shifting from the promisor to the promisee.

[20] MacCormick, *The Obligation of Reparation*, at 212.

[21] Does Gardner's "continuity thesis" support this conclusion? Does it discriminate between the original and the modified example? I think so, even though the earlier quote, text accompanying note 15, perhaps leaves it somewhat ambiguous. If it does not, however, this can only be a flaw in the thesis: a specific duty of corrective justice must be distinctly attached to an ascertainable wrong; if the wrong in question is the broken promise, yet the duty can emerge in the same way and for the same reasons even if it has not been committed, the distinctiveness of correcting a wrong has not been captured.

III. The Morality of Being a Promisee

The rules of promise seem to constitute the role of the promisee in quite a limited way. What do we know? The promise places the promisee in a uniquely privileged position relative to the promisor. We know it is the promisee who is owed performance. We know it is the promisee who is owed reparation (or an apology, an explanation—whatever is owed) if the promise is broken. We know that the promisee, and the promisee alone, has the power to release the promisor—either from the promise altogether, or from parts of it, or, following a breach, from any or all of the reparative obligations. But promissory norms seem to tell us very little besides. They are unclear, for instance, on whether the promisee can refuse that power altogether. And, more significantly in the present context, they are silent on the manner in which this power is to be exercised. Thus, viewed in the abstract, the promisee appears to have *unlimited* power over the promisor—one that is not governed by any binding norms. The promisee may show compassion or generosity in exercising this power, but she may not. She may simply refuse to release the promisor from the promise, or refuse to forgo or discount her reparative entitlements; for all we know, she may behave this way even in the face of the weightiest reasons to release or discount and in the absence of any reason not to, or for the worst motives imaginable.

That the power of the promisee over the promisor may be unlimited in this way is probably the most potent consideration informing the view that promissory obligations, compared to all other types of voluntarily assumed obligations, are uniquely difficult to shake off. The obligations of friendship, for example, may not be the easiest to set aside; but setting them aside is just as hard as it is to exit a friendship—often a tricky feat, admittedly, but not one that usually involves one person in a position of unlimited normative power to stop another from accomplishing it.[22]

This picture, however, is somewhat simplistic, and for a reason I hinted at earlier. In fact, promisees hardly ever operate in such a normative vacuum. Usually they are bound by a multitude of norms that govern their power over the promisor, and are capable of comprehensively curtailing it. These are, however, for the most part not promissory norms as such, but norms that constitute, or originate in, the background relationship between promisee and promisor.

Such norms need not, in fact, obtain exclusively in the context of particularly rich or meaningful relationships. Even when the promisor and promisee are complete strangers, brought together by the bond of promise and not much else, certain norms—perhaps the general obligation to treat all others with decency, or some particular implication thereof—may come to curtail the promisee's power to refuse a complete or partial release, or to insist on (full or even partial) reparation; it may come into direct conflict, in other words, with the promisee's promissory rights, and may indeed

[22] There are some exceptions. I am told that under Jewish law, for example, each party to a marriage must assent to her or his counterpart's request for a divorce, and although the party who refuses to grant it may come under judicial pressure to do so, its power to continue to refuse cannot be taken away under any circumstances, no matter how unreasonable or badly motivated the refusal is deemed to be. Relationships that are constituted in such a way can perhaps be defended, but I suspect that their autonomy-enhancing potential would not be a central feature of any plausible defense.

erode them, possibly to a vanishing point. For this to happen, however, the circumstances must be quite exceptional indeed. And when we try to assess the overall effect of promises (or the capacity to make them) on personal autonomy, not just the logical possibility but the prevalence and scope of such norms should concern us. It then becomes crucial to note that complete strangerhood between the parties to the transaction is not the typical habitat for promises. Rather, promises are typically made or exchanged in the context of already existing, well-established, personal relationships[23]—friendships, collegiate relationships, family ties, etc.—indeed, precisely the sort of relationships that tend to generate a wealth of relationship-specific norms capable of supplementing, competing with, altering, or altogether defeating promissory norms, and by no means only in extreme or highly exceptional circumstances.

Let us persevere with the example of friendship. There are, of course, endless permutations on the theme of friendship; perhaps not two friendships are exactly alike. But I think it is true of all friendships (and, of course, many other types of interpersonal relationship) that the parties are—that they must be—to some extent attuned, and responsive, to each others' well-being, interests, desires, dreams, and aspirations in a way that transcends their preoccupation with or responsiveness to their own. The completely self-serving, or hermetically self-regarding friend is, in fact, not a friend at all. And many of those norms that govern true friendship are nothing short of mandatory. They can be binding on the parties in much the same way that promissory norms may bind them. And, of course, when friendship norms and promissory norms conflict, the upshot of the conflict is anything but a forgone conclusion; there is no telling in the abstract which are likely to triumph, or be modified or weakened or strengthened or outweighed.

The scope for conflict, or for some sort of coming-into-contact or interaction between friendship norms and promissory norms is wide indeed. Friendship norms can apply to all aspects of the promissory transaction, and apply to either of its parties. They may determine, or, at least, have a bearing on issues such as when it is right, and when it is wrong, to ask for a promise, to expect one, or to accept it; or when it is right to offer a promise and what linguistic conventions would be appropriate for the task, what needs saying and what goes without; how to interpret a promise when interpretation is called for, or how to debate the choice between rival interpretation; and of course, there are norms that govern the question as to when it is right to expect or ask for a release, when to grant it, when to discount, when to insist.

The list goes on, of course; and studying the particular implications of every item on it—the particular ways, that is, that all possible interactions between promissory and nonpromissory norms may turn out—would be a hefty and inevitably rather speculative undertaking indeed. But I think that the general observation suffices to show how the prospect and indeed the reality of such interactions ought to moderate, and quite significantly, the perception of promissory obligations as exceptionally hazardous to personal autonomy, particularly to the extent that such a perception is informed by anxiety over the seemingly unlimited power of the promisee over the promisor: in the real life of promises, this power is in fact limited in a plethora of ways.

[23] I have defended and elaborated on this proposition. *See* Kimel, From Promise to Contract, ch. 1.

As the hazard in question has been animated by reference to the potential significance of a change of mind, let us return for a moment to that theme. The discussion thus far, it should be recognized, does not produce the conclusion that the promisee-friend must always see a change of mind, even a reasonable one, as reason to release or to forgo reparation, fully or even partially. Far from it. The balance of considerations applicable in every case may be complex and quite delicate. Certain actions which would usually be taken to exhibit exceptional generosity, thoughtfulness, or compassion when aimed at strangers, are nothing other than the norm between friends. That can push things one way when it comes to norms governing the role of the promisee. Yet even in the context of friendship, by releasing too easily the promisee may infantilize the promisor, in much the same way that may be the case in general;[24] and in the context of friendship, infantilization of this sort usually would be more egregious, not less—and that can sometimes push things the other way. Nevertheless, the requisite balancing of considerations, and the complex weighing up of norms of different origins and pedigree that the role of the promisee-friend calls for, would often discriminate, in terms of its overall conclusion, between different types of change of mind, different reasons for it, different types of circumstances in which it occurs and the likely ramifications of allowing or not allowing it, with the likely gains and the likely losses in terms of the personal autonomy of the promisor inevitably central to any such reasoning.

The main argument of this section, it may be noted, has a direct bearing on the question of the previous section—the role of fault—and in two different ways. First, it shows how fault can find its way back into the picture, and prove relevant after all for the identity of the reparative obligation arising in the wake of a breach. That is, some of the nonpromissory norms that govern the role of the promisee at this juncture—that govern, if you like, the exercise of her discretion to forgo reparation, or to settle for less (etc.), or that possibly remove that discretion altogether and make it mandatory for her to do so—may well be sensitive to fault. They may well *require* the promisee to take fault into account, and, in certain circumstances at least, to treat a justified breach one way, an excusable breach another, and so on. They may even require her to take repentance or the (additional) fault exhibited by its absence into account.

Second, when promises are given, received, or interpreted in the context of certain kinds of personal relationship—friendship would again be a sound example—a fault element may often be read into their content even when it is not explicitly articulated. In such contexts, that is, it may be particularly natural to resist an interpretation of a promissory undertaking as rendering the promisor strictly liable for a failure to secure the ends of the promise—her failure to *be there*, in the earlier example—irrespective of the presence of excusatory or justificatory factors. So in the abstract, it remains true that when a person says, "I promise to be there by three o'clock" and ends up being late, she broke the promise; by then explaining that the car broke down she is not arguing to the contrary. Yet if the promisee is her partner, things may be different: the norms governing that relationship may inform the very way in which the

[24] *See* text accompanying notes 3, 8.

original undertaking is understood by both parties, to the extent that "the car broke down" may be an account of how, despite appearances, the promise has not been broken after all.[25]

Conclusions: Promise

Recall the earlier question: is it possible that, in a world without promise, people would be just as likely, or perhaps even more likely, to be autonomous? I would say that if this question, or anyway its second permutation, were to be answered in the affirmative, then morally-speaking the world we live in *is* a world without promise. The existence of promise, as a moral phenomenon, depends on its desirability; and its desirability depends on its effect on personal autonomy.

It turns out, however, that promises do not endanger personal autonomy to the extent that it might be thought. They allow those who make them to render the obligation they assume fault based. And they operate predominantly within relational contexts, in which parties relate to each other not just as promisor and promisee but also as actors within a relationship, and a relationship comprising of norms capable of having the effect of considerably softening, to put it loosely, the apparent firmness of promissory obligations: such norms may increase the incidence of fault-based (as opposed to strict liability) undertakings, and increase the significance of fault for the emergence and character of reparative obligations in the aftermath of a breach; and, more importantly, they govern, and significantly limit, the power of the promisee over the promisor.

I do not think, however, that those anxieties we have examined, concerning the autonomy-related risks inherent in the capacity to promise, have gone away altogether. Besides the great autonomy-enhancing potential encapsulated in the capacity to promise, there remains a particularly potent risk. There is an art to promising; when mastered, its autonomy-enhancing potential can be realized, and in an infinite number of ways. But mistakes can be costly: the autonomy of the carefree promisor can indeed be very severely curtailed. It is crucial to know when to promise, what to promise, and to whom; and just as crucial to know when to withhold a promise, resist pressure or even a temptation to promise, not be seduced by the immediate gratification to be had.

When contemplating this equilibrium, it is perhaps worth noting that the capacity to promise, when present, adds more to the available spectrum of modes of commitment than just the one option—*to promise*. That option itself, we have seen, encompasses a range—the obligations assumed may be conditional in numerous different ways, or unconditional; and they can span the entire menu of fault conditions, from strict liability to intention or motive. But beyond that, the capacity to promise makes the whole range of dispositions in between the two ends—no commitment whatsoever, and full-blown moral obligation—that bit finer grained. It allows people to articulate to themselves, and to communicate, intermediate levels of commitment by reference

[25] Of course it would be quite perverse, in the context of an intimate relationship, for this to matter, in terms of the normative aftermath of the event: no-breach and excusable breach would mean the same; the explanation would do the trick, no matter which of the two tricks it is.

to, but short of deploying that capacity. It allows people to say distinctly meaningful things such as "I can't promise, but I'll do my best."

Finally, the promisee. Being a promisee, it turns out, is a serious business. There is an art to that, too. In exercising her unique power over the promisor, the promisee often has a wide range of options to choose from, and must attend to a delicate and complex balance of considerations before she can make the right choice. That, incidentally, informs my view that it is a role that cannot be thrust upon a person without her consent; that it is possible to refuse it, reject a promise, prevent it from coming into existence.[26] A full defense of this view must await another day; if I am right, however, then here we have yet another feature of promise that renders it attractive for those who value personal autonomy: not just the role of the promisor, but also that of the promisee involves self-authorship of significant dimensions of one's normative environment.

Conclusions: Contract

I have said little about contract thus far, other than mentioning, in passing, that the law of contract is commonly thought of as the law of enforceable promises—or, at any rate, as the legal iteration of the moral institution of promise;[27] and that philosophical theory of contract, just like that of promise, has come to be dominated by the view that the key to the desirability of the institution lies in its personal-autonomy-enhancing potential. Yet much the same anxieties over the likely effect of promise on personal autonomy may be felt in relation to contract; in light of the role of the state in enforcing contracts, perhaps even more strongly. Moreover, parties to contract are invited to relate to each other predominantly as parties to contract; the relational background, in this instance, is at best a contingency: much of the very point of the institution is the way in which it avails itself to those who are not already interlocked in meaningful personal relationships.[28]

Indeed, in contract, the risk of excessive restriction of the freedom to change one's mind, and various other dimensions of the inherent, potentially excessive risk to personal autonomy this institution could pose, are addressed, inasmuch as they are, differently. It is true that in contract, too, parties can sometimes create a fault condition for an obligation they assume. Yet it is not surprising that creating such fault conditions is not a very pervasive practice in this domain, nor that, in the absence of an explicit contractual provision to such an effect, contracts are usually interpreted (and rightly so) as excluding it.[29] There are, however, various other ways in which the law of contract may be understood, or indeed *justified*, as setting out to moderate such risks. Focusing on the common law of contract, I will list three, in an ascending order of generality and scope.

[26] Although in cases such as this, some sort of an obligation (a vow?) may still come into existence.

[27] The moral institution of agreement is, in fact, the better analogy. I have argued along such lines in Dori Kimel, *The Morality of Contract and Moral Culpability in Breach*, 21 K.L.J. 213, 215 n. 2 (2010).

[28] *See* Kimel, From Promise to Contract, at 57.

[29] Some very specific exceptions may be found in "vitiating" doctrines such as frustration and impossibility; these, by their nature, are limited in application to highly exceptional circumstances.

1. The common law of contract is generally averse to recognizing and enforcing unilateral undertakings. There are specific ways in which to create unilateral, legally binding obligations, but the norm in contract law is bilaterality. The formation requirement of consideration, while not coming close to ensuring that every contract represents an equally beneficial bargain to all parties, prevents entirely unreciprocated undertakings from acquiring legal force. It is plausible to think that entirely unreciprocated undertakings are particularly likely to become the object of a change of mind, or that the capacity to act on a change of mind of this sort merits particularly robust protection.

2. The common law of contract does not enforce promises, or indeed agreements, per se; rather, it protects the performance interest that agreements generate. To non-lawyers, this distinction may seem trivial; however, it has numerous, far-reaching doctrinal and practical implications. It manifests itself most palpably in the area of remedies for breach of contract: whereas the protection of the performance interest sometimes calls for the actual enforcement of contracts, very frequently it does not—for instance, in all cases where the award of a certain measure of monetary damages suffices to place the plaintiff in as good a position as that in which it would have been had the contract been performed.

This, of course, is a feature far greater in doctrinal scope, as well as theoretical significance. It is a feature of the law of contract that has always attracted a great deal of critical attention, particularly by those who, for a wide range of reasons, think that the enforcement of promises *is* in fact a proper role for the law of contract to fulfil. But the analysis I have offered gives us one more reason to be wary of all such views. It suggests that if contract law set out to systematically enforce promises (or even, for that matter, just agreements), what it would end up enforcing is something far less autonomy enhancing, far more autonomy endangering than the moral institution of promise: it would end up enforcing promissory norms in a relative normative vacuum, that is, absent the myriad relationship-derived norms which supplement and often supplant promissory norms in the normal, nonlegal habitat for promissory activity.

3. The freedom of contract appears to be significantly narrower than the freedom of promise. Numerous forms of restriction on the freedom of contract, that is, go far beyond excluding from the realm of contract that which it would be morally impermissible for parties to contract to undertake, and much further, often on straightforwardly paternalistic grounds, towards the removal of those options which are likely to cause particularly acute regret, or prevent parties from acting on such regret.[30] Curtailed as it is, the freedom of contract is not quite as limited as to ensure that every contract represents a net gain for the personal autonomy of its parties, or indeed that the very capacity to make contracts ends up representing a net gain for the personal autonomy of all those who may deploy it—far from it; yet the observable trend, in virtually all legal systems which are the product of a moral-political outlook that prizes personal autonomy, can be understood, and by and large justified, as one orientated towards some more modest iteration of such a goal.

[30] For a classic discussion, *see* Anthony T. Kronman, *Paternalism and the Law of Contracts*, 92 Yale L.J. 763 (1983).

It remains the case that, just as with promises, there is an art to making contracts. With contracts, too, there is scope for making mistakes, and mistakes that can be costly, and can be costly in terms of the personal autonomy of those who make them. It cannot be assumed too casually that by facilitating the capacity to make legally binding agreements—by creating *a* law of contract—the state invariably enhances rather than endangers the personal autonomy of those who may deploy it. The historical as well as ongoing trajectory of the law of contract in autonomy-prizing cultures attests to that: tilting the overall balance away from the endangerment of personal autonomy and in favor of its enhancement has been the most enduring challenge, and the endeavor to meet it the most powerful engine of development and reform.

7

Promises, Agreements, and Contracts

*James Penner**

This chapter is both a development of the views I first expressed some 15 years[1] ago on the nature of promises, agreements, and the law of contract, and a response to the recent work of Shiffrin on the same subject.[2] There are a number of points I intend to discuss, so I hope the reader will forgive something of a preliminary outline by way of introduction.

I shall begin by giving reasons for taking agreements, rather than promises, as the kind of voluntary obligations which help us make sense of both the voluntary undertakings between those whom Shiffrin calls "intimates" as well as those in contracts between strangers. I will briefly reprise the reasons I gave for this preference in *V.O.*, but here I will give a couple more reasons that have been prompted by Shiffrin's work. The general argument will be that our collective practical reason is typically organized around agreements, not promises, and so understanding agreements is essential if we want to understand the normative relations between intimates as well as contracts between strangers, for both of these are kinds of agreements, not promises. I take this not to be a matter of semantics, but one of substance. But I shall build upon both Raz's and Shiffrin's work here to try to establish the truth of this "agreement" thesis.

I then turn to an examination of Shiffrin's work, in particular her treatment of certain examples where she argues for the importance of the facility that individuals have to make promises. Arguably, Shiffrin errs in failing to distinguish sufficiently clearly the facility to enter into agreements with the facility to make promises, and this has consequences for understanding the lessons she draws from these examples. The principle reason for that judgment can be stated as follows: promises are voluntary obligations that principally address what might be regarded as pathological failures properly to respond to reasons, as in the case of akrasia. By situating her analysis of intimate voluntary obligations in the province of promises, Shiffrin explains the normative function of voluntary joint action as essentially the prevention of the negative, as the prevention of exploitations of vulnerability. Focusing on this negative aspect, she fails

* I owe a great debt of gratitude to Pat Gudridge, Gregory Klass, George Letsas, Prince Saprai, and Seana Shiffrin for comments on earlier drafts. Of course they bear no responsibility for any remaining idiocies.

[1] J. E. Penner, *Voluntary Obligations and the Scope of the Law of Contract*, 2 Legal Theory 325 (1996) [hereinafter *V.O.*].

[2] In particular Seana Valentine Shiffrin, *Promising, Intimate Relationships, and Conventionalism*, 117 Phil. Rev. 481 (2008) [hereinafter *P.I.R.C.*]; *but see* Seana Valentine Shiffrin, *The Divergence of Contract and Promise*, 120 Harv. L. Rev. 708 (2007). *See also* Seana Valentine Shiffrin, *Could Breach of Contract Be Immoral?*, 107 Mich. L. Rev. 1551 (2009).

to grasp the positive, facilitating aspects of agreements. As she realizes,[3] this prioritization of the negative over the positive distinguishes her account of promising from her account of consent (with which I entirely agree), but, at least on the assumption that her account of promising would also color her account of agreements between intimates, I think her reason for this prioritization is inadequate. I shall argue that agreements are typically facilitative, not preventative, whereas promises are typically preventative, dealing, as I have said, with "pathological" personality aspects which interfere with a person's doing what they realize they should do.

Following this I shall turn to the question whether contracts, agreements between strangers, are dependent upon a convention. I shall argue that the strongest argument that they are derives from Kant's attitude to rights in the state of nature, and his conventionalist explanation about the transition to a civil condition. I shall argue that this conventionalist explanation is wanting, largely for the sorts of reasons that Gardner gives: roughly, as (normal) human beings are responsive to reasons, something like a duty of humanity operates even in a state of nature. If this is right, then voluntarily undertaken obligations of cooperation between strangers (as in Scanlon's example of the spear and boomerang throwers[4]) can genuinely arise in the absence of conventions. After all, there is *some* truth in the treacly sentiment, as I understand Will Rogers put it, "a stranger is just a friend I haven't met."

I. Contracts are Agreements, not Promises

In *V.O.* I argued that contracts are agreements, not promises, and I gave two distinct reasons for that. The first argument turned on the claim I make that promises and agreements are conceptually distinct. By "promise" I mean to indicate a voluntarily undertaken obligation which is unilateral in character, and by "agreement" voluntarily undertaken obligations which are bi- or multilateral in character. I should say at the outset that by drawing this distinction I do not intend in any way to distinguish agreements from promises on the basis that promises, but not agreements, are to be understood to be morally binding, agreements (especially agreements recognized as legally binding contracts) to be understood to be binding only in law[5] or only on some other normative basis. I see no sense in such a distinction; if agreements are true examples of voluntarily undertaken obligations, which they are, then the obligations in question are to be conceived of as morally binding for the same sorts of reasons promises are. That is, to put this in Razian terms, to the extent that by making a promise one can acquire a morally binding exclusionary reason to do what one promises, to just that same extent one can acquire a morally binding exclusionary reason to do what one agrees to do with or for another. The unilateral/bilateral distinction between promises and agreements parallels the unilateral/bilateral distinction between gifts and exchanges, the latter (gifts and exchanges) concerning transfers of property, the

[3] *P.I.R.C.* at 504 n. 39. [4] T. M. Scanlon, What We Owe to Each Other 296–7 (1998).

[5] Shiffrin explores this possible motivation for distinguishing agreements from promises in Seana Valentine Shiffrin, *Is a Contract a Promise?*, *in* The Routledge Companion to Philosophy of Law 241 (Andrei Marmor ed., 2012).

former (promises and agreements) the undertaking of obligations. In the same way that we distinguish between gifts and exchanges, and regard the latter, not the former, as possible transactions under the law of contract, it seems to me rather intuitive, even obvious, that agreements, not promises, are the obvious candidate for the kind of voluntarily undertaken obligations which fall within the province of contract. This is a point to which I shall return in a moment when I look at the formation of contracts, and why that is unfortunately described as an "exchange of promises." Another way of putting this point is to speak in terms of normative powers and what is required for their exercise. The power to promise, and the power to make a gift, are powers that an individual is capable of exercising on their own; by contrast, the power to enter into an agreement is one which can only be exercised jointly by the prospective parties to that agreement, and similarly, the power to exchange this for that is a power that can only be exercised jointly by the prospective parties to the exchange.

One issue which is sometimes thought to impair the distinction I have just drawn is this: it may be argued that since gifts and promises need to be accepted to be effective, even gifts and promises are necessarily bilateral in character, and so any distinction by which gifts and promises are conceived as unilateral is misconceived. On this view, every gift is a kind of exchange, every promise a kind of agreement, and the exercise of normative power to make a gift, or undertake a promise, is a joint exercise, by that of the donor and donee or the promisor and promisee respectively. This is wrong-headed. Whilst one does have a right to refuse a gift or a promise, this does not turn gifts or promises into exchanges or agreements. Indeed, even if one holds, as some do, that "*acceptance* is to be construed as a necessary *complement* of the promisor's or the donor's act"[6] so that, for instance, a promisor by his speech act alone cannot undertake a voluntary obligation unless his intended promisee responds with a speech act of her own, that does not erase the conceptual distinction between unilateral transfers (gifts) or unilateral undertakings of obligations (promises) on the one hand, and bilateral (or multilateral) transfers (exchanges) or bilateral (or multilateral) undertakings of obligations (agreements) on the other. As I said in *V.O.*,[7]

> To hold otherwise is essentially to deny the *conceptual possibility* of unilateral acts or unilateral undertakings of obligations that are intended to benefit someone else. There is, as far as I know, no reason for thinking such a view even plausible.

To put this the other way round, to allow that you must participate in my promise or gift to the extent of not blocking it or even of having to allow it is an essentially *passive* participation as a *recipient* of the normatively significant act or undertaking of another; or to put this in another way again, to exercise the normative "power" to receive or allow is not to be taken as, in some sense, sharing the exercise of the donor's or promisor's power to give or promise. To have a power to promise is to have a power to do something oneself; similarly with the power to give. It is *my* promise *to* you, or *my* gift *to* you, after all. Under both a promise and an agreement, of course, one can individuate a promisor's and a party's[8] personal obligations, obligations which they

[6] *V.O.* at 328–9. [7] *V.O.* at 329.

[8] For the sake of clarity I will call the individuals involved in a promise the "promisor" and "promisee," and those involved in an agreement "parties."

individually have to carry out.[9] It is just the brute conceptual fact about the "ownership" of the act—that gifts are acts of mine irrespective of your participation as a recipient in a way that is not true of exchanges, and that promises are undertakings of mine irrespective of your participation as a recipient in a way that is not true of agreements—that makes the distinction intuitive and resonant. Compare: it may be the case that for what I say actually to be *said* to be an act of communication—I must have an auditor who attends to my words, grasps them, and so on. Well, fine, but that does not mean that your listening to me makes what I said something you said too. My words were my own, however much communication conceptually depends upon there being an audience.[10]

Having set out the distinction between promises and agreements along these lines, I then claimed that contracts, involving the participation of two (or more) persons who stand on an equal footing to determine a future outcome which they both undertake obligations to secure and/or not undermine,[11] look much more like agreements than coincidental promises, in the same way that contracts of sale seem to be exchanges and would be misdescribed as coincidental gifts.

The second argument I made was essentially an argument against conceiving of contract formation as the "exchange of promises." Everyone knows that under a contract the obligations of the parties are linked in substantial ways. Whilst I have an obligation under a contract from the outset of its formation, it is defeasible. The most important cases of this are when I am entitled to terminate the contract for breach, or when I am relieved of performance by the contract's being frustrated by some event. Under the "exchange of promises" theory of contract, however, these sorts of doctrines are difficult to make sense of, because under that theory parties to an agreement are treated as promisors and promisees, and nothing in the behaviour of A qua promisor, such as a breach of A's promise, would appear to relieve B of any obligation to perform B's promise to A. This is made clear by pursuing the model of contractual promises as conditional promises. Let me offer a modified passage from *V.O.*:[12]

> Take the case of an executory contract of sale in which A wants to buy B's book. Framed in terms of a promissory characterisation of offer and acceptance, contract formation is initiated by a conditional promise, say by A: "if you promise to transfer the book to me, then I promise to pay you £10." When B promises to transfer the

[9] Similarly, I do not distinguish between promises and agreements on the basis of whether one or both or all persons involved undertake obligations to perform, although that is typically the case. An agreement between husband and wife that the husband will look after the kids this week is just as much an agreement despite the fact that only the husband acquires an obligation to do something. This last example should not be construed as the husband promising, and the wife accepting the promise, for the fact of the matter is that the husband has no power to make such a promise in this case; both wife and husband need to come to a meeting of minds and together make the agreement; it would mischaracterize the situation to conceive of the husband having the unilateral right to undertake such an obligation, for that would be to usurp the power that they share and must exercise jointly. Furthermore, in this example it is not the case that the wife undertakes no obligations; it is just that she undertakes no positive obligation to perform in some way. She would, implicitly if not explicitly, undertake the "negative" obligation not to undermine or thwart the husband's performance of his "positive" obligation.

[10] The analogy can be extended of course; when we have a back and forth, it is *our* conversation, though our words remain each of ours; certain speech acts are clearly conceived to be unilateral, as when I order you to do something, when I warn or inform you, etc.

[11] *See* note 9. [12] *V.O.* at 333–4.

> book, he undertakes the obligation to transfer it, and the condition on A's promise is met, so he now has the obligation to pay £10. But the obligations are not linked any more than that. A and B now merely have separate unilateral obligations. It is no answer to B's claim for £10 from A that B has not transferred the book, for the promise to pay £10 is now absolute. The condition for the coming into being was not that B transfer the book, but that he promise to do so, and that B has done. This result of the promissory analysis cannot be avoided or patched up by incorporating conditions which last for the life of the contract, for that renders all contractual obligations merely conditional, and they are not. Try it out: What would constitute the offer? A's first stab might be something like, "I promise to create a conditional promise to transfer £10 to you conditional on your transferring the book to me if you promise to transfer the book to me." But B would not accept this offer, for it would leave him under an unconditional obligation to transfer the book, but A only under a conditional obligation, an obligation which only comes into existence when an event occurs, ie to make payment only once the book is transferred, so if, prior to the time of B's performance, A was unable to pay, say because of his insolvency, or unwilling to pay, as when A repudiates,[13] B would still be obliged to transfer the book. B wants to be in a position to say that A has an obligation to pay B *when* B performs, not *if* B performs, and this rendering of A's offer as a conditional promise fails to provide that for B.[14] The problem is obvious: promises are unilateral obligations. As such, they are conceptually unlinked to the obligations of other persons, and conditions do not frame that linkage. The bilateral character of agreements comprises more than the coincidental or bi-conditional creation of otherwise independent obligations. An agreement comprises a future state of affairs both parties to which are bound to bring into existence, though their actions in doing so are differently defined and set out.

Prince Saprai has suggested to me that treating contractual obligations as promises can be salvaged by, rather than treating offer and acceptance in terms of conditional promises, treating offers and acceptances in terms of defeasible promises, perhaps drawing upon the property law distinction between conditions precedent and conditions subsequent, something along the lines of: "I promise to transfer you this book on Tuesday if you promise to pay me £5 on Tuesday *unless* you fail to pay me £5 on Tuesday in which case I won't have an obligation to transfer the book to you." I don't think this ultimately works because the notion of defeasibility underlying, say, the doctrine of frustration, cannot in principle be recast as the explicit or implicit introduction of corresponding "unless" conditions on each party's individual obligations under the contract. What is special about the doctrine of frustration of contracts is that whilst one party may be entirely capable of fulfilling her contractual obligations, she is relieved of doing so not simply because the other party may not be able to perform—that would normally just signal a case of breach of contract—but because the nature and sense of the contractual agreement itself is regarded as being undermined; the *contract* is frustrated, not just the individual party's particular obligations to

[13] If B accepts A's repudiation, then A is no longer bound to perform (neither is B, of course), but A is still liable for damages for breach of contract.

[14] Contract lawyers distinguish between an obligation to perform and the *time* of performance under the contract.

perform, conceived separately. Thus the linkage between the two parties' obligations is not one of there being corresponding "unless" clauses, such unless clauses alone making the performance of one party's obligation dependent or conditional upon the performance of the other party's obligation; rather, the parties' individual obligations are conceived of as the means of achieving the particular result or goal or state of affairs the agreement contemplates.

Whilst I stand by both of these arguments, they make a negative, rather than a positive case for the agreement analysis of contracts. That positive case, as I shall now set out, is, in essence, that agreements are morally prior to promises in an important sense. By morally prior, I mean that understanding the mutual or joint undertaking of voluntary obligations would appear to be the normal, or typical, means by which individuals act in order to manage their interactions, whereas relying upon individual's exercising their individual powers to undertake voluntary obligations by promising is an obviously less satisfactory means for doing so. In order to show this I shall draw upon both Raz's and Shiffrin's work. Let's start with Raz.

II. The Moral Priority of Agreements over Promises

The Razian perspective (which I take to be a development of Hart's) is so well known that I can be brief.[15] This is that voluntarily undertaken obligations are a type of exclusionary reason, which facilitate the coordination of behavior, and as such are an aspect of what I like to call "collective" or "communal" or "social" practical reason. A simple example might be the unanimous agreement within a family to go to Edinburgh on holiday. Once the agreement is formed, each member of the family will have various positive and negative obligations which, if fulfilled, will make the holiday a success. Such an agreement allows cooperation, typically by permitting a sensible "division of labour," without which the individuals could simply not act together (act *in agreement* or *in concert*) to achieve their goal. By entering into the agreement, each member of the family binds themself to perform whatever tasks fall to them, as well as (usually implicitly) undertaking not to act in a way which undermines the enterprise. Though these obligations can be specified as the individual obligations of each particular person, they are not promises in the sense of unilaterally undertaken obligations. What I want to emphasize about this way of conceiving agreements is that under it agreements are seen to be both *positive*, or *facilitative*, and completely *natural*.

As to the facilitative aspect, this is blindingly obvious. The benefits of social cooperation are all around us for everyone to see. Very little in the way of complex enterprises could get off the ground if individuals could not act in concert with others. And the fact is that in many cases, one hopes in most cases, the tasks that one is under obligations to perform as part of a joint enterprise are not onerous. I am obliged to do all the things that go with my contract of service at my university, and whilst some are irksome, in total they are not. We can quibble about whether the modern world demands us to be busier than we should be (I think it does), but humans mostly like

[15] H. L. A. Hart, The Concept of Law (P. A. Bullock & J. Raz eds., 2d ed., 1997); J. Raz, Practical Reason and Norms (1999).

doing valuable things, and just because achieving those things may involve acting in concert with, and therefore under an obligation to, others, does not transform the required performances into drudgery. If we agree to go to dinner together, my interest and pleasure in doing so is not diminished in the least because attending is a subject of agreement with attendant obligations. Indeed, because I trust you to come to dinner, I have the added pleasure of anticipation, which gets me through the long afternoon hours editing a paper on the philosophy of agreements. This is why when I apologize for not being able to comply with my obligation to come to dinner I normally not only express regret for your inconvenience, but also *my own disappointment*.

As to agreements of this kind being *natural*, we can draw upon Shiffrin, who explains the plausibility of humans having the power to consent to being touched in this way:[16]

> One could imagine a conception of autonomy without consent in which an agent exercised complete sovereignty over her body and other personal spaces, such as the home, but had no ability to share or transfer these powers to others. That is, the agent could not grant consent to others to exercise these powers in lieu of or alongside herself. Such a structure is imaginable but so impoverished as to be utterly implausible. As Joseph Raz has argued, the development and realization of our central autonomous capacities requires a diverse and rich set of meaningful options. Rights of autonomous control that were inalienable to this degree would render (morally) impossible real forms of meaningful human relationships and the full definition and recognition of the self (not to mention making medical and dental care cumbersome, dangerous, and awfully painful). To forge meaningful relationships, embodied human beings must have the ability to interact within the same physical space, to share the use of property, and to touch one another. They must therefore be able to empower particular people. A plausible account of autonomy would have to reject the isolation the constricted model of self-sovereignty would enforce as inconsistent with affording opportunities to lead a decent life and realize one's central capacities. It would have to include the power of consent to share at least some of the powers associated with self-sovereignty.

Although one might quibble with some of the details,[17] this is one of the best statements of the "social thesis" I have ever encountered. The "social thesis" is the thesis that the "default" characterization of human existence for the purposes of exploring interpersonal (including political) morality is not that of a hermit in some state of nature who shares no interests with others, but one in which interpersonal relations of real significance are native or natural to human existence. As such, those normative means, like the power to consent or to make agreements, are not some cultural

[16] *P.I.R.C.* at 501–2.

[17] I am not sure how much weight Shiffrin wishes to place on the Razian considerations of autonomy she cites; I would not place much. It seems to me that, considerations of the value of autonomy to one side, what her characterization of the importance of the power to consent makes plain is the ability of different individuals to respond to the same reason, not only when the interest is one they might share (forming a meaningful relationship), but even where the reason in question is an interest of only one of them (to have some dental work done). If this is right, then in order to explain the norms of agreements, all we have to do is make plausible that these norms are exclusionary reasons to which we would naturally respond in the appropriate social context.

achievement which we could plausibly be without, but are part and parcel of our natural endowments, in the same way as our basic responsiveness to reasons[18] makes us (in part) the kind of creatures that we are. Indeed, as I shall argue below in the last section on bargain agreements, the power to enter into agreements *just is* an aspect of our basic responsiveness to reasons.

In *V.O.*, I, like Shiffrin, examined voluntary obligations, taking first the case of "intimates," not strangers, though I took agreements (not promises) to be fundamental. The analysis went something like this: I divided voluntary obligations between intimates into two kinds. One, which I called "mutual obligatory agreements," are those agreements that parties are obliged to come to, not in the sense that any one particular agreement is necessarily obligatory, but obligatory in the sense that some agreement as to how they will coordinate their behavior is necessary. The most obvious examples are agreements between parents and other care givers to coordinate their behavior so as to provide care to those needing it. There may be any number of ways of dividing up the various tasks that need doing, but in order that the tasks get done there must be that coordination. Notice that the good achieved by the coordinated actions agreed upon here is a good for all concerned, including those obliged to come to agreement. I take it that parents have an interest in the welfare of their children, and that interest is one that they share.

The second sort of agreement I called "mutual agreements," and these differed from those just set out in not being the result of an obligation to come to an agreement (or are at least not dominated by an independent obligation to agree on a course of action). The case of the family holiday to Edinburgh above is, I think, an example, though if you think that does not work because parents and children have an obligation to go on holiday together, it is easy to come up with your own example. These agreements attend to joint projects in which the interest in the project is one which all parties value (not always necessarily to the same extent), and which deepen, redefine, or express the relationship between the parties. Whilst I have taken the family context as the obvious one, relations of friendship also display agreements of the two kinds. Friends have an obligation to see each other when they can, and this will involve cooperation, but friends also deepen or express their relationship by undertaking joint activities which they are able to agree to, but not ones which they are required to undertake.

If this is right, then the idea of "offer and acceptance" as the way in which we conceive the formation of agreements has to be explained in a different way than the stating of conditions upon which one will be bound. On the view of agreements as being matters of communal or collective practical reason, an offer is a statement of the terms of engagement proposed by one party, i.e., proposed as terms of engagement they are willing to agree to, and acceptance is the acceptance of this proposal, meaning the acceptor agrees that this will be the basis upon which they proceed. The mutuality of this notion of agreement formation is seen in the handshake, which joint act is seen as the sign that the parties are bound.

Understood in this way, it seems to me that the bilaterality or multilaterality of agreements shows them in one sense to be morally prior to promises qua unilateral

[18] John Gardner, *Nearly Natural Law*, 52 Am. J. Juris. 1 (2007).

voluntary undertakings, in the sense of being the more obvious and natural normative device to promote the flourishing of those involved, at least in the context of intimates. Whilst agreements are just as voluntaristic as promises in the sense that they equally are acts of the individual wills of the parties, they express, or are explained by, the social thesis in a much more straightforward way. Let me explain.

To understand the typical voluntarily undertaken obligation as agreements treats the sociability of humans, their shared fate and their shared interests, which typifies the condition of intimates, as being a core feature of their existence as humans. (The situation is, after all, that if you had no intimates, you would not survive childhood.) An adult who is responsive to the reason that is the interest of a dependent child will regard themself as being obliged in some sense to respond to that interest. And presumably more than one person with that same responsiveness to reasons will be around, each having the same obligation because they will share the same interest in the child's interest. Now, the natural way in which these adults will respond to their situation is not that each one will *promise* to do whatever respecting that child's interest requires them to do (whatever that might be), for example unilaterally promising to look after the child on every second Tuesday on the assumption that, on their own, each individual has a power to determine without consulting any others what "share" of the workload he or she will bear. Rather, these individuals would seek to come to an agreement[19] to coordinate their behavior to achieve the shared end of advancing the child's welfare. Promises, as well as oaths and vows, seem a singularly odd way of aiming to meet one's obligations or advance one's relationships with intimates if the reality of the social thesis is appreciated. Indeed, as I shall now go on to show, independent of the claim I have just made about the way in which agreements are more naturally and plausibly taken to be the sorts of voluntarily undertaken obligations which would typify those of intimates, promises are largely untypical between intimates, and essentially deal with human frailties and pathologies which would otherwise work to undermine agreements.

I am going to begin with my own case, as it is most familiar to me, but not for that reason, I think, atypical. Now it seems to me that I rarely make promises. I enter into agreements with people all the time, to go for coffee, to go for dinner, to throw the frisbee around, to go on holiday, to plan a party, to do things at work such as teach this course rather than that, become chairman of the undergraduate exam board rather than vice-dean for teaching, and on and on. Now of course when I enter into these agreements I am undertaking personal obligations, most of which I do not regard as onerous (indeed, typically the opposite), and some of which may be more or less trivial. The point about these undertakings, however, is that they are overwhelmingly agreements, not promises; they are inherently particular agreements dependent upon a sharing of purposes, interests, and goals, and an underlying network of agreements which form the context or backdrop to all of these particular agreements. Even when

[19] Pat Gudridge has suggested to me in conversation that a better term is "arrangement." We make arrangements to meet for dinner, about who is going to do the laundry, about who is looking after the kids this weekend, etc. The reader who prefers to think of the exercise of jointly undertaking obligations in these sorts of contexts as entering into "arrangements" rather than "agreements" can do so, without loss of the points I am making.

I voluntarily undertake to do something "on my own" as it were, this is better conceived as *the exercise of a power to specify* an obligation that I have under a preexisting agreement, not the exercise of a power to promise to do something that, prior to making the promise, I had no obligation to do. It would seem to me to be silly to say that when I specify my teaching obligations, insofar as I have free choice in the matter, e.g., by saying that I will teach first year property, I am in any genuine way making a promise. What I am doing is exercising a power as to the way in which I fulfill my obligations under the agreement that makes me a law teacher in the Faculty. There might be all sorts of good reasons that *I* have this power which I can in one sense exercise unilaterally—but it is not a power to promise, but a power to specify the way in which I fulfill my preexisting obligation, and my exercise of that power must, to be reasonable, be responsive to the rationality of the underlying agreement which coordinates my activity with others. In that sense, there is nothing *unilateral* at all about my exercise of the power.

The relatively rare occasions when I do promise are when I want to assure people that I am responsive to those sorts of underlying reasons. Guess when I am most likely to make a promise? Well, if you are at all like me you will guess that it is when I have, and am about to miss, a deadline, or have just missed one. Even if there is nothing in the world that I would rather do than meet a deadline I have agreed to but am about to miss, I have failed in my obligation, and it is natural to assure the publisher or whomever that this *is* something I take seriously, and I may promise to get the piece to him or her by the end of the week. By making this promise I "gild the lily," undertaking to do what I already value and desire, and which I already understand myself to be obliged to do. It assures my promisee that I do respond properly to the reasons that apply to me, expresses my disappointment in my failure, and commits me to attend as assiduously as I can, "re-double my efforts," to complete. I am not denying that promises in these contexts create new obligations. Nothing I have suggested says that one cannot undertake more than one obligation to do the same thing, even to the same person. My claim is that typically the creation of a new obligation on a unilateral basis reinforces a prior obligation upon which, again typically, it is dependent or parasitic in the sense that the existence of the prior obligation is the main reason for the undertaking of the second, promissory one.

As I read her, following on from and in keeping with her analysis of consent, Shiffrin begins her explication of promising by citing the facilitative, positive possibilities that the power to promise (though I should say the power to agree) opens up for the coordination of behavior.[20] But then she takes us to her examples, and here she emphasizes the way in which promises can be preventative of the negative consequences of power imbalances between intimates. I want to take some time on these examples, for here I think it is clearest that she characterizes promises correctly but, without I think meaning to do so, shows them at the same time to be incapable of performing the role of the typical voluntary obligation that is found amongst intimates, which is the agreement.

[20] *P.I.R.C.* at 502–4.

III. Shiffrin on the Functions of Promises

Her first example is that of Bernard and Amy. Bernard wants Amy to listen to an album that Bernard admires but which Amy expects not to enjoy. Nevertheless, Amy promises to do so to avoid a tedious discussion about the merits of the artist, whilst Bernard is happy to have the promise, not because he wants to avoid such a discussion—there is nothing he would like better—but because he is hopeful that Amy will find the album enjoyable and then come to change her mind about the artist. This example sets up Shiffrin's discussion of promises between intimates, and of this example she says:[21]

> While they don't share an end because of or through the promise, the promise allows Amy to commit to pursue an end that is not actually held or valued by her. This is an important feature of the power to promise. To be able to commit to a course of action, without valuing it as the promisee does, can facilitate healthy dynamics within relationships . . .

This passage reveals what will be an important difference between Shiffrin and me in our analysis of voluntary obligations in the context of intimate relationships. I agree with the function of the promise in this example. But I want to argue that this sort of circumstance, whilst typical of the use of promises, is atypical of the sorts of voluntary obligations which intimates undertake, because typically, perhaps even paradigmatically, those voluntary obligations are ones framed against interests that are shared. The Bernard and Amy example shows how promises may be engaged to negotiate what would otherwise be a stumbling block in their relationship, viz. their very different tastes in music. Now, spouses, brothers and sisters, and very good friends can have very different tastes in music without that being such a stumbling block, but it is in this case because Bernard wishes so much that Amy and he shared his interests in music, or at least in this artist. By promising Bernard that she will listen to the album, Amy assures him that his interest in her interest in music is something she takes seriously, seriously enough to listen to the album, though not seriously enough to persist in a conversation about the artist's merits. So the promise has an "assurance" function here, but does so in response to a pathology, a dysfunction in their relationship, albeit perhaps a minor one. The example as written seems to indicate that Amy is not similarly concerned that they share the same interests in music. If this is right, the promise is merely a stopgap. (If there is only one artist about which they disagree, but share their musical tastes more generally, then a stopgap when that artist's music comes up may be all that is required.) If other similar sorts of case arise frequently, where Bernard wants to insist that Amy spends her time listening to music the merits of which Amy cannot herself appreciate, then it will undermine their relationship; in such circumstances whilst promises like Amy's may work as temporary stopgaps, they cannot forestall the inevitable. If there is a genuine absence of sharing of significant interests, or worse, an actual and significant antipathy of interests between them, the exercise of the power to promise in the way that Amy does might actually be regarded

[21] *P.I.R.C.* at 496.

as itself pathological, in that it perpetuates a dysfunctional relationship which should really be brought to a dignified end. Of course all this depends on how much Bernard's and Amy's friendship turns on a shared appreciation of music. If this is more or less a trivial matter between them, then the "pathology" or "dysfunction" may be assuaged by Amy's making promises of this kind, and indeed, it may not matter very much whether she keeps these promises. Making the promise alone might ease the tension, and they can "move on," so to speak.

However, Shiffrin's next several examples are more serious, and, it is submitted, they strengthen the analysis I am suggesting.

Shiffrin's next example is a case of A and B (whom I shall call "Anna" and "Ben") who are in a conflict about whether they should move to another city in some months' time.[22] Anna's interest in moving with Ben to the new city is much greater than Ben's interest in moving with Anna to the new city because Ben has other attractive options which Anna does not. Therefore, in terms of determining how to act prior to the move, Anna is more vulnerable than Ben. If Ben cannot commit to making the move because there is no facility to promise, but is only able to state a present intention to move that he can revise later, then any prior investment in making the move with Ben that Anna makes is liable to be wasted, and the danger is real, since Ben has less interest in the move. As a result, Anna may underinvest in making the move, or may sweeten the pot by doing other things to entice Ben not to change his mind, transforming Anna's vulnerability into a real loss. Furthermore, Anna may become frustrated and feel powerless and resentful, so that the relationship sours, all this because Ben cannot make a promise to Anna and thereby undertake a binding obligation to Anna to go to the new city, not just announce his present intentions. Shiffrin concludes from this analysis[23] that "for moral agents acting in moral character, promises provide a unique and indispensable tool to manage and assuage vulnerabilities."[24]

I would put this another way, following on from my discussion of Amy and Bernard: for moral agents acting in moral character, promises provide a questionable tool which can at times be used to manage and assuage the pathologies of relationships, although there are usually better ways forward. The reasons for this substantial revision is that I think there is a lot going on in the example of Anna's and Ben's move to a new city, and I am not very hopeful about Anna's and Ben's prospects, whether or not Ben is able to and does promise Anna to go with her to the new city. What Anna and Ben need to do is to agree, not promise each other, to move to the new city (or not to do so), and this must express a joint commitment based upon the interests that they share. Relationships do come to turning points, in which life throws up an opportunity, sometimes a challenge, to one member of the relationship which changes its dynamic. But the way to deal with such turning points, however heart-wrenching it may be, is to express where one thinks one's interests lie honestly to the other party(ies) to the relationship. This, by the way, will not be simply a report of preferences. People who

[22] *P.I.R.C.* at 504–9.

[23] The analysis, running to six pages, is obviously more nuanced than I can do justice to here, but I do not think I misrepresent the quoted sentence as her main conclusion about the function of promises that she takes away from the example.

[24] *P.I.R.C.* at 508.

are interested in each other are entitled, and indeed to some extent have an obligation, to help shape that other's appreciation of his or her own interests, drawing upon their own experiences, but often more crucially, their intimate understanding of what that other is really like, what he or she really values, what he or she really is capable of, in short, what really makes that other prosper or founder. It seems to me that this is the sort of chat that Anna and Ben need to have. If after that chat a way forward is found, they can agree how to proceed. If not, then their relationship may necessarily have to become less consequential for them, as they move apart to pursue a range of interests less involving of the other. Again, this is not to deny the particular bond of a love relationship, in which the interest is most tangibly, if I can put it that way, an interest *in* the interest of the other, in the sense that one's own interest in flourishing is one of flourishing with that other, and whose own flourishing depends on that other's flourishing. But if that is the situation with Anna and Ben, then they should be able to work out whether the move to the new city is one which is good or bad for them (accepting that there are always uncertainties and disagreements that arise as a consequence).

This is why I think Ben's use of a promise in this case is questionable, if not actually problematic. If what Ben really wants to express is that he intends to go with Anna to the new city because he agrees with her that it is the best option available *to them*, despite the fact that, considering his self-interests, narrowly conceived, staying put would be roughly as good, or even a little better, then he should say so, and then they could *agree* to move to the new city. But by making a promise in this way, it appears that Ben is expressing much the opposite, something like, "I promise to go though although I don't see the advantage in doing so. I am doing it for your sake, not mine." If I were Anna, I should think myself a fool to be happy with this sort of promise. Rather than assuaging a vulnerability or an inequality, it positively entrenches it. By accepting the promise, Anna is in the unhappy position of one who can only maintain a relationship by extracting promises, promises that *ex hypothesi* are grudgingly given (otherwise there would be an agreement between them), and what sort of relationship *that* is going to be going forward.

The last example Shiffrin gives is that of young children extracting promises from their parents.[25] Shiffrin again:

> Their need for promises arises independently of the quality of parenting and is directed at even the most loving, nurturing, devoted parents. It is implausible to attribute children's strong desire for promises predominantly to parental failures to attend to their needs or even to their insecurity about whether they are loved and important. The parent–child relationship, though, does carry an important, emotionally charged, power imbalance. What happens to children is largely determined by their parents; children have little official power. In seeking promises, they seek some measure of acknowledged control over their experience. To promise a child is, in a limited domain, to share power with him or her.

I don't actually recall my children regularly getting me to make promises to them when they were little, but I do recall that their promising behavior struck me as along the same lines as adults. One of the functions of promises is to make a person who has

[25] *P.I.R.C.* at 497, 509–10.

already agreed to do something, but is weak-willed or is in some other way in danger of not acting on his intentions, to reassure the other. Shiffrin gives just the right sort of example:

> [Y]ou and I plan to review the department's job applications tomorrow. We concur that we should get an early start and that 9 a.m. would be a civilized, sensible time to begin. In a conversation confirming our plan, you say "I'll see you at 9 a.m.," and I reply "Yes . . . Do you *promise* to be on time?" You respond, "Yes, I'll be on time." We have not created or generated any new shared end through this exchange, at least not in any interesting way; our ends remain the same. By asking for the promise, I communicate perhaps a concern about your past tardiness and a desire for you to acknowledge the special significance of resisting your tendency to interpret starting times in a loose way. You undertake a special obligation to be on time and therefore to pay close attention to the temptations and habits that have previously led you astray. The promise alters our moral situation, but does not add a new end. We already had the end of meeting for a shared purpose at a specific, agreeable time. Further, I may regard it as regrettable, rather than valuable, that a promise need be sought or relied upon.

I agree here with the essentials of Shiffrin's analysis. This promise is regrettable, because we normally expect people to be motivated by the agreements they make. But experience tells us that sometimes they are not. So we seek a super-strong, added obligation to pile on top of the one they already have. Promises can provide this. But it is not clear to me that insisting to X that one will comply with the obligations one already has could be other than dealing with a parasitic or pathological case. If it were a normal case, surely this would lead to a regress. Thus, if having an obligation to do *y* did not sufficiently motivate me in the general case, so that in order truly to motivate myself I needed to come under an obligation to comply with my obligation to *y*, then why should this second-order obligation motivate me any more? Let's suppose that in this example that even having given the promise one's colleague shows up late after all? What does one ask for next time? "Now, I don't want you just to promise me, but promise me that you'll keep your promise." And so it would go, I suspect.[26]

I think the case with children is basically similar. I agree with Shiffrin that the promising behavior of children does not correlate with an absence of care or affection. And I think Shiffrin's analysis is along the right lines, but just needs a bit of tweaking. The powerlessness children often feel is that they are unable to predict and anticipate the frequent changes of plans that occur almost every day in adult life for one reason or other. Just like for adults this gives rise to disappointment, but in view of their relative powerlessness, it is easy to reconfigure this justified disappointment into resentment, and a desire to have (more of) a say in the change of plans in future. And to be fair, every parent has to let his or her children know, perhaps indirectly, on numerous occasions that the child's own priorities, its appreciation of its own interests, must give

[26] The terrain here is difficult. I agree with Shiffrin's sentiments when she terms her illuminating examination of redundant promises "tentative" and finds this frustrating. *See* Seana Valentine Shiffrin, *Immoral, Conflicting, and Redundant Promises, in* Reasons and Recognition: Essays on the Philosophy of T. M. Scanlon 155, 170 (R. Jay Wallace, Rahul Kumar, & Samuel Freeman eds., 2011).

way to its parents'. That, no doubt, is one of the frustrating aspects of childhood, and a natural response is to extract a promise from a parent when the possibility of some upcoming event or activity that is important to the child is at issue. By the way, the promising behavior in families tends to undergo a reversal as children age. When children become teenagers, their parents start extracting promises *from them* for much the same reasons. Teenagers let their parents know directly and indirectly in countless ways whose priorities they truly regard as the more important. (And perhaps that's as it should be.)

I have been explaining why, in my view, promises are typically parasitic on prior agreements and are "pathological" in the sense that they are typically only sought or given when a person already obliged is, for one reason or another, less than optimally likely to fulfill their obligations. In this sense, I think promises are a bit like oaths.

Consider the oath given by witnesses in court. Everyone has an obligation to tell the truth in circumstances in which honesty can reasonably be expected; that is true of a court of law where people's lives and fortunes are at stake. I have no obligation as a witness to tell the truth in a kangaroo court or show trial, of course, but let us assume that we are not dealing with that sort of court. Why the oath? Why aren't witnesses motivated by the obligation of truthfulness that they already have? The reason is obvious; this is a classic case in which an individual witness's loyalties, and perhaps obligations, may conflict. By requiring the oath, we insist that the witness swear that he will comply with his obligation of truthfulness, in preference to his other loyalties, obligations, or all-things-considered judgments. The oath is probably pointless in the case of a neutral witness with a good reputation to protect, but we swear everybody out of a concern for equal treatment or just *ex abundante cautela*.[27]

The last thing I want to touch on is the unilateral nature of promises and gifts, and the relation between them. Let me say at once that I think gifts are not pathological at all. Gifts are not one-half of some *sotto voce* or "implicit" bargain, whatever the more psychopathic sort of economist might tell you, but are perfectly normal expressions of the fact that people share interests, that is, can be interested in the welfare of others.[28] Promises, that is, *unilateral* undertakings of obligations to be bound, on the other hand, are odd sorts of creatures. It is difficult for me to think of circumstances where these arise in a healthy relationship. Take the case of a promise to make a gift. Who would seek or desire such a promise? I am speaking of a genuine gift here, not a gratuitous transfer I might be obliged to make, say a transfer of money to my child for a school book.[29] When I make a gift to you, part of the meaning of that act is that I am under no obligation to do so. Otherwise it wouldn't express the fact I am interested

[27] In some cases oaths are formal declarations of role and allegiance, which we do not really think "up the ante" when someone takes them. I think this is true of the U.S. president's oath of office. No one would elect a president who was prone to subverting the U.S. Constitution in the belief that swearing the oath would turn him or her around. The same thing, I think, could be said of wedding vows, without at the same time denying their performative function in creating the contract of marriage. As Shiffrin reminds me, oaths may have a multiplicity of functions. For example, the oath a witness gives in court may also establish a context for the testimony; that the setting is serious and that certain communicative purposes, e.g. humour, irony, are not to be indulged.

[28] For discussion *see* J. E. Penner, The Idea of Property in Law 88–90 (1997).

[29] There is a sense in which some gifts have an obligatory quality, such as making a birthday present to one's child in a culture in which this is the recognized way to express affection on such an occasion.

in your welfare as an aspect of my welfare, of my flourishing, not because I am bound by obligations to you.[30] So any gift that I make *because* I promised to make you a gift fails to do what a gift ought to do. Think about it; when an "obligatory" gift arrives, it doesn't feel much like a gift, does it? The only nonpathological cases of "promising" in respect of gifts are really cases of agreeing, to my mind. I might get in touch with you about a gift I intend to make to ensure that it can be delivered when it is convenient for you, or in the case of one's children, if the gift is of a substantial sum of money I will get them to confirm their bank details, tell them when I can move the money to them, and so on. I think this comes out in the sense we have that there is something odd about regarding as legitimate an expectation interest in gratuitous promises. If someone is unable to make the gift they intended and said they would, because, perhaps, of changed circumstances, then to the extent the intended recipient *reasonably* relied to their detriment, then the intending donor might have something to answer for. But if there was no reliance, and yet the intended recipient feels wronged, rather than just disappointed, then to my mind there is something wrong with the sensibility of that intended recipient.

In this section, I have traded upon examples devised by Shiffrin in order to explore differences in the way I think agreements and promises operate in relations between intimates. I am fully aware that this was not Shiffrin's purpose; she was interested in showing (and to my mind, succeeded in showing) how a nonconventional faculty to undertake voluntary obligations could be both elaborated and justified in regard to relations between intimates. In particular it was no part of her project to distinguish between promises (unilateral undertakings), and agreements (joint undertakings) as I have described them. Nevertheless, I do think the lessons I have drawn about the distinction between the two are robust even though I have turned these examples to my own purposes.

IV. The Nature of Bargains and the Conventionality (or not) of Contract

In *V.O.*[31] I described bargain agreements as agreements between strangers, which I explained to be cases where the parties did not share interests in each other's welfare or in some shared joint project (though I did question, given that there are all sorts of contracts where this is not the case—such as contracts of employment, long-term supply contracts, relational contracts of various kinds—whether the bargain between strangers should be the paradigm it seems to be in contract law theory).[32] Nor in the case of bargains are parties usually in a position to help shape or reveal the interests of the other (the patter of certain sales people notwithstanding). Nevertheless, it

A parent who failed in the past to make such a gift could promise to make a gift at their child's upcoming birthday. But then this case is no different from the case of the redundant promise to meet a deadline one was already bound to meet, discussed above.

[30] Intimates, friends, and family members do of course owe each other obligations, but I am concerned with generous acts between them which are not matters of obligation.

[31] *V.O.* at 337–9. [32] *V.O.* at 341–3.

would be a mistake to characterize bargains purely in terms of self-interest, narrowly conceived:[33]

> It is often assumed that in a true bargain, one is supposed to disregard the interests of the other party, paying attention only to one's own. As a practical matter, in the limiting case of some simple transaction, such as the purchase of an umbrella, the interests of the other part hardly rise to consciousness; one simply goes through with the transaction. But generally, not only is this a poor bargaining strategy, it involves a misconception of the relationship bargainers have to each other's interests. In a bargain, parties do serve the interests of another, by acting in accordance with the normative character of the transaction (e.g. selling only what one has title or power to sell) or by performing executory undertakings. Each party therefore must "take on board" the interests of the other—as defined by the agreement—by treating the agreement as an exclusionary reason guiding his or her behaviour. The value of bargains, indeed their nobility, is that this relationship of obligation and trust permits strangers voluntarily to treat the interests of each other as reasons guiding their behaviour.

I now want to deal with a sort of Kantian challenge to the plausibility of this picture. As is well known, Kant has an extremely austere notion of what rights individuals, that is, strangers, have in a state of nature. In that section of the *Metaphysics of Morals* called "The Doctrine of Right," Kant describes the innate right a person holds in the state of nature as essentially the right not to be shoved off or out of the space one currently occupies.[34] No one has any property rights, and of promises Kant has this to say:

> Freedom (independence from being constrained by another's choice), insofar as it can coexist with the freedom of every other in accordance with a universal law, is the only original right belonging to every man by virtue of his humanity.—This principle of innate freedom already involves the following authorizations. . . his being authorised to do to others anything that does not in itself diminish what is theirs, so long as they do not want to accept it—such things as merely communicating his thoughts to them, telling or promising them something, whether what he says is true and sincere or untrue and insincere, for it is entirely up to them whether they want to believe him or not.

Thus, prior to entry into a civil condition there just is no facility for promising or agreeing, since *ex hypothesi* the declarations of one's intentions cannot be assured to be binding. Since a person is always free to disregard what one has said, *ex post facto* one can never be bound by one's communications. One can *always* say to some complaining other who has relied upon what one said, "you did not have to take what I said seriously." And, very importantly, because of this formal freedom, there is *no way* to assure anyone that you won't take this "out."

[33] *V.O.* at 338.

[34] Immanuel Kant, *The Metaphysics of Morals*, *in* Practical Philosophy (The Cambridge Edition of the Works of Immanuel Kant) 393, 394 (Mary J. Gregor ed., 1999); *See also* Arthur Ripstein, Force and Freedom: Kant's Legal and Political Philosophy 30–56 (2009).

Kant, however, does allow individuals to escape the state of nature, and enter into what he calls a "civil" or "rightful condition," one in which, roughly, people live under a rule of law. But our interest here is that although Kant claims that individuals who cannot avoid interacting with each other have a duty to enter into a rightful condition, the rightful condition itself seems strongly conventional (that is, entered into to generate a practice for the advantage of each), for under the rightful condition property rights, which are only "provisional" in the state of nature, become fully recognized and enforced.

The conventionality of the transition to the civil condition is brought out in Kant's famous "assurance" argument:[35]

> When I declare (by word or deed), I will that something external is to be mine, I thereby declare that everyone else is under obligation to refrain from using that object of my choice, an obligation no one would have were it not for this act of mine to establish a right. This claim involves, however, acknowledging that I in turn am under obligation to every other to refrain from using what is externally his; for the obligation here arises from a universal rule having to do with external rightful relations. I am therefore not under obligation to leave external objects belonging to others untouched unless everyone provides me with assurance that he will behave in accordance with the same principle with regard to what is mine.

I have discussed the merits of this argument at some length elsewhere,[36] but what I want to point out here is that, whether or not interacting individuals have an obligation to enter into a civil condition, their doing so is nonetheless "voluntaristic" in the sense that it seems *everyone's* willingness to play the game, *everyone's* assurance to each other that he will play by the rules, is what secures the state in which right and duty genuinely exist, and that is, at base, what a conventional explanation of right and duty does. The fact that Kant conceives this "everyone-ness" of the assurance as an "omnilateral" (all vis-à-vis all) form of assurance does not undermine the point. The question with which I want to close is whether Kant's characterization of those in a state of nature, whom I shall treat as the equivalent of strangers, i.e. not intimates, for my purposes, is plausible. The question is whether, given the existence of interactions between strangers, we are in some sense *required* to treat them like people coming into interaction in a state of nature—that is, in the absence of any conventions of agreement or rights enforcement and so on—and then conclude, as Kant seems to do, that in the absence of those conventions such strangers could not enter into agreements, for they could not give commitments.

It seems to me that the Kantian rationale for a conventional account of promising can be undermined, and I want to do so by drawing once again upon that aspect of human nature that Gardner emphasizes, our responsiveness to reasons. Consider Scanlon's example[37] of two hunters in a state of nature. They are on opposite river banks, and one has thrown his spear to the opposite bank, the other his boomerang.

[35] Kant, *The Metaphysics of Morals*, at 409.

[36] James Penner, *The State Duty to Support the Poor in Kant's Doctrine of Right*, 12 Brit. J. Pol. & Int'l Rel. 88, 94–6 (2010).

[37] Scanlon, What We Owe to Each Other, 4.

Can they cooperate, promise each other, agree, so that they return their weapons to each other? I want first to say that I am a little put out by the set-up to this story. Why not start (surely more plausibly) with the case where one hunter, standing on his side of the river with his spear, sees the other chap's boomerang sail over the river and land on his side. Now the boomerang hunter appears, seeking his boomerang. It seems obvious to me that what the other hunter should do is just toss it back to him. Humans are responsive to reasons, and this includes the interests that others have.[38] Whilst on occasions one might have reasons for not doing this (the other hunter is a warrior intent on harming one, one simply hasn't the time, etc.), it is implausible that the other hunter would, as a constitutive matter of his strangerhood, be *unable to appreciate* the interest of the boomerang hunter, and thus not be able take it on board as a reason for his action. Similarly, he would be able to realize his mistake if, after throwing it over to the chap who appeared on the other side, a third hunter turned up beside him and jumped up and down, mimicking that he had thrown it, and thus that it was his (the other hunter now sheepishly recalling that boomerangs tend to return in an arc). None of this requires any convention.

Now, the further question is whether this appreciation of the interests of others, which I take to be necessary for the formation of agreements, is sufficient in the absence of conventions for individuals to be able to enter binding agreements. I think it is. Consider another state of nature case. Child minder Andrew is walking along the river past Brenda, a stranger, when Andrew's child falls into the water. If hunters can appreciate the interests of stranger hunters in their weapons, then I take it as given that Brenda, another human, can recognize stranger Andrew's interest in retrieving the child. Now let us assume that the only way in which Andrew can retrieve the child is with the cooperation of Brenda; say Andrew needs Brenda to hold onto a branch at the side of the river and hold her hand out to Andrew so Andrew can reach the child. I don't see how we could doubt the possibility of this cooperation taking place. It seems like the most natural thing in the world, this cooperation forced by circumstances. Assuming that it is not perverse for Brenda to consider the interests of the child and Andrew as sufficiently motivating for her to act the way she does, what motivation is there for denying Brenda the facility of assuring Andrew that he can trust her? If there is such a facility we can easily account for the intuition that Brenda would do wrong if, just when Andrew was about to reach the child, Brenda wrested her hand from Andrew's grasp, sending Andrew into the river himself.

Thus—in the same way that Shiffrin argues that, given the value we place on the ability to interact with others in terms of our own bodies, an inability to consent to being touched is just implausible—I should argue that given the human capacity to respond to reasons, an inability to agree with others so that we could respond to reasons in a coordinated fashion, *in concert* as it were, is equally so.

[38] I am assuming there is no obvious hostile intent in this situation; but Scanlon assumes this as well.

8

Contract as Fact and as Reason

Charlie Webb

I. Facts and Reasons

Legal reasoning is, in its principal forms, practical reasoning: reasoning towards choice and action, to determining what one ought to do. In these forms, legal reasoning is, in common with all examples of practical reasoning, always normative, always evaluative. This is so notwithstanding that legal reasoning is in many respects technical, involving the application of rules and procedures identifiable simply by their "sources" rather than their "merits" and so insulated from broader questions of value. In part this is because these technical rules leave some questions unanswered, meaning that the choice between those options not excluded by these rules can only be made on other grounds and by the application of other factors. At other times these posited rules might expressly direct the decision maker to give consideration to such factors. But more than this, even where the law's technical rules are determinate and neither require nor invite any such supplement, these source-based norms earn a place in our reasoning and decision making only on the back of norms which get there on their merits. For the question of when positive law lets us look *beyond* law arises only if we have a reason to look *to* law in the first place. If the fact that a community's legal institutions have identified a particular rule as determinative of a particular practical problem is to have any bearing on—let alone to be truly determinative of—how any person (official or citizen) *ought* to act, this can only be in light of the values served by complying with rules settled in this (or some such) way. No ought from a mere is.

There are often good reasons to comply with the law's directives. For one thing, all communities require some scheme of arrangement, allocating roles, responsibilities, and resources among its members and otherwise providing a set of conditions which facilitate and accommodate their diverse projects. Yet there are any number of ways such a community might reasonably arrange itself so as to surmount the challenges and exploit the opportunities communal life provides. To this extent, there is simply a range of alternative, mutually incompatible arrangements a community might adopt, each reasonable but no more reasonable than the others still in play, yet each plainly more reasonable than leaving these matters unsettled. There is a value, therefore, in a choice being made and so in such matters being settled, even if reason alone cannot determine which one we should choose. In turn, once a choice has been made or once some such arrangement emerges, it means we then have good reason to stick with it. Given that these sorts of questions are not one-offs, arising not simply at the outset of any communal enterprise, but are ongoing, there is a need for a mechanism, for institutions and processes, which can provide and keep on providing authoritative solutions to the many coordination problems communities face. In light of the benefits that can thereby be secured, members of those communities will typically have good reason to do as these institutions direct, notwithstanding that there existed no reason so to act prior to and independently of the directive being issued.[1] Moreover, such laws, at least when enforced and applied with some regularity, then create expectations in those to whom they are directed and who makes plans in their light. The knowledge that the law will apply as advertised, and that others will likewise tailor their actions to keep within its limits, provides a level of security when making such choices, opening up options which are otherwise unavailable or would come at too high a cost.

In such ways, law merits not only a place in the deliberations of citizens and officials alike but a place which is often decisive; what we have good reason to do is what the law directs that we do and that reason derives from the fact that it is the law telling us to do it. So the priority in fact given to these posited norms in the reasoning of legal officials and of other acting and choosing under law is a priority which is often rightly earned. But it does have to be earned. And it is earned not just by identifying what reasons exist for having and following this or some such system of posited rules but also by weighing these against reasons we may have for disregarding those rules and acting instead on other considerations. Though it may be that the positive law can always be identified without evaluation, law's place in our practical reasoning always depends on evaluation, on an assessment of what really are *good* reasons for action.

Nonetheless, the fact that evaluation is in this way essential to any decision made by or under law does not itself mean that an account of these decisions and practices must likewise be evaluative. The various evaluations made by various individuals at various times and places are all matters of social fact and can be identified and reported without their having to be evaluated in turn. If we are seeking a faithful description of the reasoning and judgments of legal officials and of the associated facts of a community's legal practices, there should no question of revising these facts such that they better fit some idea of what may be good or valuable.[2] No doubt any description of any subject matter requires a selection of what facts about that subject matter to include in one's description and how to present them. But again to make these choices we don't need to take any view of the value of the practices we are describing, but rather to consider what and whom this description is for, what of the countless facts about these practices are most relevant or salient *for these purposes*. And so while we must indeed identify what makes for *good description* of the law, this typically won't require us to consider what makes for *good law*.

It shouldn't be thought that the possibility of an (in this sense) evaluation-free account of legal practice is a consequence of or is otherwise tied to the positivity, and so evaluation independence, of positive law. We can provide such an account whatever role positive law in fact plays in the decision making of legal officials and so even if it

[1] *See* John Finnis, Natural Law and Natural Rights 231–54 (2d ed., 2011); John Finnis, *Law as Co-ordination*, 2 Ratio Juris 97 (1989).

[2] As Hart put it: "Description may still be description, even when what is described is evaluation." H. L. A. Hart, The Concept of Law 244 (3d ed., 2013); *see also* John Finnis, *On Hart's Ways: Law as Reason and as Fact*, 52 Am. J. Juris. 25, 27–8 (2007).

turns out that the law is radically indeterminate and so requires supplementation with additional "merit-based" norms or indeed even if the law's posited rules are frequently disregarded and decisions made on other grounds. Again, in all cases these evaluations—what these individuals *consider* or *adjudge* to be reasonable—are, like the acts and statements they ground, social facts and can, *as* matters of fact, be identified and reported without needing to be evaluated in turn. It follows that, while the positive law is inevitably indeterminate and gappy, an account of legal practice need not be or at least need not to the same extent. We can identify and describe how, say, courts have proceeded where the law runs out, what arguments they have then employed, what reasons they have then acted on. Just as lawyers can provide advice on points of law which have as yet received no authoritative resolution in the courts or by statute not by themselves assessing the reasonableness of alternative solutions but by considering how courts are likely to resolve these questions, an account of a community's laws and practices can look to draw out their implications and likely development without consideration of the goods these practices can serve but rather by attending more closely to the facts of these practices, to their processes, and to the attitudes and understandings of those operating within them.

II. Legal Theory and its Objects

Legal practice therefore provides us with two distinct objects of inquiry:[3] (1) we can inquire into how, as a matter of fact, decisions are and have been made within a particular community or across a set of communities; and (2) we can adopt the perspective of those acting within such a community, setting out to answer the same practical questions they face, identifying how they really *ought* to act. If our inquiry is directed to decisions *in fact* reached and norms *in fact* identified and applied then, as we have seen, we need undertake no evaluation of those decisions and norms, no assessment of what are good reasons for decision and action. For an account which aims to capture these practices as they are, nothing should make its way in other than by virtue of its unqualified "fit" with these practices. By contrast, if we want an account which addresses and answers the sort of questions members of such a community themselves face, then our inquiry is directed to what are truly *good* reasons for action, reasons which determine what they really *ought* to do. And so, for this sort of inquiry and this sort of account, the sole measure is, in the end, one of reasonableness or moral soundness, with the facts of past practice relevant only where reason makes them so.

The distinctiveness of these two objects of inquiry is, however, masked or simply neglected in much work on contract law, not least in those accounts of the law which we now see labelled interpretive.[4] For the object of much contract theory is to offer an account of legal practice—decisions in fact made, concepts in fact employed, rules in fact endorsed and applied—which doesn't simply fit these facts but which brings out

[3] *See also* John Finnis, *Natural Law: The Classical Tradition, in* THE OXFORD HANDBOOK OF JURISPRUDENCE AND PHILOSOPHY OF LAW 11–12, 16 (Jules Coleman & Scott Shapiro eds., 2002).

[4] *See, e.g.*, STEPHEN A. SMITH, CONTRACT THEORY (2004). The inspiration, sometimes distant, often tacit, is RONALD DWORKIN, LAW'S EMPIRE (1986).

whatever common ideas or principles underpin them and hold them together. And to this extent, so it is thought, such accounts cannot be *simply* descriptive but involve at the very least some reconstruction or rationalization of the relevant decisions and doctrines. Where many of these accounts fall down is in failing to maintain a clear distinction between: (a) providing an account of legal practice which works through the implications of and broader normative commitments reflected in the decisions and evaluations of legal officials, (b) evaluation *of* those practices and evaluations, and (c) identifying what, for those operating within such practices and against their backdrop, are good reasons for decision and action.

We can indeed ask what goods or goals ground that particular set of ideas and practices we call the law of contract. Since the laws of any community will derive from a series of decisions made by different individuals at different times, it is inevitable that they will, at least on occasion, express different reasons and priorities. An examination of these practices is, therefore, unlikely to express a single, coherent set and ranking of goods and value. Nonetheless, whatever differences and inconsistencies may exist at the surface, in the individual decisions and determinations of particular officials, we may find a greater stability and unity in the basic structures and ideas which are taken to underpin these practices. Bodies of law, such as the law of contract, may demonstrate a basic and established form lawyers recognize. So too may we find common understandings of the sorts of problems to which they are addressed, whatever differences we may also find in the way these problems are then solved. Similarly there will be features of these practices—aspects, say, of contract doctrine—which lawyers take as foundational, as characteristic of that body of law. In light of these facts, we can then ask what these basic structures and ideas reveal, or at least suggest, about that community's normative commitments, what might explain its choice to do things *this way*.

An account of contract can proceed in just this way, fleshing out an understanding of the nature of this particular concept or category by seeing what ideas or commitments appear to be implicated by its role in legal practice. To what extent does this take us beyond fact finding, beyond mere description? Many accounts which take something like this approach deny that they are offering any endorsement of the principles or goals they identify as grounding this body of law; they are explanations, not justifications. This contrast of explanation and justification has its doubters. John Gardner puts the challenge this way:[5]

> The choice [between explanation and justification], it seems to me, is a false one. True, not all explanations are justifications. But all justifications are explanations. To justify something is to explain it rationally. It is to set out some or all of the reasons why it is as it is. Anyone who tries to explain anything in terms of reasons for it cannot but be concerned with the justification of that thing.

For Gardner such "non-justificatory" explanations are really provisional, non-committal justifications. On this view, the question these accounts are really

[5] John Gardner, *What is Tort Law for? Part 1. The Place of Corrective Justice*, 30 LAW & PHIL. 1, 2–3 (2011).

concerned with is how can we defend or legitimate this practice or this body of law. We can then either do this straight off, identifying what good reasons exist for doing things this way. Or we can ask whether a particular reason would, if sound, support this way of doing things, but leaving the question of whether that reason *really is* sound to be settled at some other time. Accounts of contract (or tort or unjust enrichment etc.) which describe themselves as providing explanations but not justifications are taking this latter route.

Perhaps Gardner is right to read these accounts in this way. But it is clear that there is another sense of explanation, one which does not entail even a detached interest in the merits of the acts or practices it seeks to account for. Often when we look for explanations what we want to know is why—for what reasons—someone did as he did. Why did he leave the party early? Because he wasn't feeling well. Why did she send the defendant to prison? To send out a message that this sort of behavior will not be tolerated, etc. Of course, we can, if we want, go on to ask whether these reasons are good reasons, or perhaps whether there were other, better reasons for doing as they did. But it would be a mistake to think of these explanations as simply provisional conclusions on the merits of these actions. If the reasons on which someone in fact acted turn out to be unsound, we don't start again in a bid to find *better* reasons for explaining why he did what he did. The explanation is complete.

So, while we might say that all such explanations involve an inquiry into the reasons for a particular act or activity, the question "What reason did A have for φ-ing?" is ambiguous between two different inquiries. One asks: what reasons *in fact* guided A to φ? The other: what reasons were available to A for φ-ing (whether or not these were reasons he grasped and acted on)?[6] The same is true for law and legal practice. We can ask why this community developed this way of doing things (these rules, these classifications and concepts, etc.): an inquiry into the reasons which in fact, for better or worse, guided these people to make these decisions. And we can ask what reasons there are or were for doing things this way, why one might choose these rules and concepts. Of course these inquiries might provide the same answer: the reasons there are for doing things this way are the reasons which in fact led these people to this way of doing things. But they needn't. There may be good reasons for a practice which differ from the reasons which in fact guided those engaged in it.

These inquiries are distinct and an explanation of some body of law can seek to answer either one. But this difference is often elided in accounts which seek to identify the goods and values which ground some body of law. Perhaps it is thought that any such account is compelled to look beyond whatever goods and values are in fact identified by legal officials as the grounds of their decisions. After all, the reasons which in fact guided the various acts and determinations which make up a community's legal practices will often be opaque or confused or simply incomplete. It is likely that many, perhaps most, decisions in legal practice are made without reflection on the basic goods and values to which the practice is directed. Precedents are followed and

[6] The distinction I'm drawing here is sometimes framed in terms of "explanatory" and "guiding" reasons, the former being those that did in fact guide an agent's actions, the latter those which were applicable to them: Joseph Raz, Practical Reason and Norms 15–20 (1999).

statutes applied without pause to consider their purpose or rationale. Even law-*making* will often be motivated by the need to fashion a workable solution to some immediate practical problem, without any broader survey of the law's aims and values. And often this is a reasonable way to proceed. The conclusion that, say, A should be ordered to pay the £100 he promised to pay to B is a conclusion we can reach without first reflecting on what values promise keeping serves. Indeed the judgment that people should generally keep their promises is one most come to without any such reflection. Of course we can also recognize that a challenge to the validity of this judgment requires that we address the question of what these values might be. But the order of justification need not be the order in which these conclusions are arrived at and one's conviction that promises should be kept may be more secure than one's commitment to whatever account of the morality of promising might be offered in its support.

It seems likely then that few judges or legislators have worked-through theories of contract, expressing a commitment to a particular understanding of this concept and to its normative foundations. Moreover, insofar as officials do engage with this question, we are likely to find no small amount of disagreement and uncertainty. As such, any attempt to explain these practices slips easily from the apparently hopeless task of locating the reasons (goods, values) which *in fact* guided officials' decision making to the seemingly more fruitful option of identifying reasons which are, broadly, in line with what these people have been saying and doing—and which might, therefore, be said to support these practices—but which may have played little or no role in their reasoning. All the more so if our aim is not simply to capture the laws and practices of a given community at a given point in time but instead to provide what we might call a general theory of contract applicable across communities and across times.

Nonetheless this elision is one we should resist. True, the line between—on the one hand—uncovering goods and values *in fact* identified, if only imperfectly and inchoately, by officials as the grounds of their acts and choices and—on the other—reading some such scheme of goods and values into these decisions and practices is one we will sometimes draw with little confidence. True too, any attempt to locate the reasons in fact adopted and endorsed through the practices of a community or set of communities will encounter much uncertainty and disagreement. Still we can be clear that attempts to establish the reasons which in fact led a given community to adopt a given set of practices are not attempts to justify these practices and require no assessment of their merits. For, once again, while the goods and values identified in and expressed through the reasoning of legal officials are goods and values those officials take to justify their decisions and practices, their identification and description involves no assessment of the merits of these purported justifications.

By contrast, once an explanation of some body of law or aspect of legal practice detaches itself from the reasons in fact offered by legal officials and the normative commitments their decisions in fact express, there is little sense in it *not* going on address the merits of these practices and of the goods and values by which it chooses to explain them. For if we ask not what reasons officials in fact *have given* but what reasons one *could give* for adopting a particular set of practices, why would we be concerned with anything other than *good* reasons? The search for goods and values that are implicit in the law makes sense as a historical inquiry into the considerations which have guided official decision making and it makes sense too as part of an assessment of what these practices have going for them. But it's doubtful what use there is in an account which explains a body of law by reference to considerations which no official either does or ought to endorse. So, while we shouldn't deny that an inquiry into reasons which might be said to support these practices has the option not to consider those reasons on their merits, once we abandon the search for the reasons which have *in fact* guided these practices, it's not clear why this is an option anyone would want to take.

In these ways, we can seek to identify from a community's legal practices a scheme of goods and values which can be said to be, in one sense or another, implied in or by those practices. We can then work from these implicit goods and values to see what implications they in turn have for concrete disputes and decisions within these practices: to see how certain contested questions might be resolved in keeping with the goods and values to which the law appears already to be committed, to check what features of legal practice might be out of line with what is done elsewhere. It is tempting then to see these accounts as providing not only an account of the law of contract as it is but also a steer to judicial decision making and to the law's future development. But for those making decisions within these practices and in light of these laws—whether as officials or citizens—the question they face is not "what would others do?" or "what would others have me do?" but "what ought I to do?" And to answer *this* question, what matters is not what others have considered good reasons for action nor even what good reasons might best explain what others have said and done in the past but what are, for this person making this decision here and now, good reasons for action.

So we come back to the point with which we started: there is no requirement of fit for (good) judicial decision making which is independent of and to be weighed alongside the requirement of reasonableness. If the fact that deciding a case one way rather than another would fit better or worse with a community's past legal practices is relevant to how a judge really *ought* to decide that case, then it is relevant only because there is reason why we should value such consistency. If judges should limit themselves or otherwise accord priority to norms and reasons which are found in or can be squared with the decisions of other officials then this can only be by virtue of other reasons and norms which point us *to* those decisions in the first place. Now, as we have seen, such reasons exist and so officials and citizens often have good reason to comply with the law's posited norms. But these reasons don't exist in isolation and in all cases must be considered alongside other reasons, expressing other goods and values, which at least on occasion point in other directions. So, while legal reasoning, when undertaken as a form of practical reasoning, cannot get by without some inquiry into the facts of legal practice, it is never reducible to such an inquiry. And so if we want an account or theory of contract which aims not to describe but to guide legal reasoning, our starting point is not the legal practices and doctrines of a given community but the goods and values which gives that reasoning its point and direction.

III. Promises and Contracts

The same duality of inquiry as exists with law exists too with promising: (1) we can inquire into the practice of promising, looking at how promises are understood within a particular group or community, what obligations they are taken to generate, the conditions in which such obligations are thought to arise, and so on; and (2) we can inquire into the goods and values served by the making and keeping of promises, how promises affect our reasons for action, what obligations promisors *do*—and not just *are thought to*—owe. So promises exist as expressions of an intention to assume an obligation to do what is promised; an obligation taken, by promisors and promisees alike, to arise from this act of communication alone. Any account of the practice of promising fails insofar as it fails to fit these and other such facts about the attitudes and understandings of those who make and receive promises. But any such account leaves wholly open the question of what obligations promisors really do owe, what reasons for action promises really do provide or invoke. That promisors take themselves to be obligated to keep their promises is compatible with their owing some other obligation or none at all. And even if promisors aren't wrong to think that promising triggers an obligation to keep that promise, that the promise is the only thing that needs to happen for the obligation to arise does not mean that the reason for this obligation is to be found in the promise alone. Again: no ought from a mere is.

There are two senses then in which an account or theory of contract may be promissory. It may be promissory simply on the basis that it takes contracts to be or to involve the making of promises. Alternatively, it may be promissory not only on the basis that it takes contracts to be or involve promises but also because it takes contracts to generate, by the very making of these promises, obligations to perform the promised/contracted act. An account of contract might be promissory in the first sense but not in the second either because it rejects the idea that the mere act of promising does in fact provide the promisor with a reason to keep his promise or because, though it accepts that such reasons exist, it concludes that these are insufficient to justify legal enforcement of the promise or legal redress in the event of its breach. Reliance theories of contract, for example, are not committed to denying that contracts involve promises and so these theories may be promissory in the first sense, just not in the second. All this means that asking whether contracts are promises is not the make or break question when it comes to adjudicating between different theories or contract. If, or to the extent that, contracts are or involve the making of promises all plausible candidates for what might ground the rights and obligations of contracting parties remain in play. The most we might say is that, if it does turn out that contracting parties aren't making promises when they enter into contracts, we can narrow down the list of viable options by one, counting out any theory which seeks to tie contractual obligations to the morality of promising.

So are contracts promises? It's not hard to find examples of cases conventionally classed as contracts which are not. When I buy a drink from a vending machine no promises are made.[7] Some conclude from this that cases such as this should be treated

[7] *See also* Smith, Contract Theory, at 62–3, 176–9; J. E. Penner, *Voluntary Obligations and the Scope of the Law of Contract*, 2 Legal Theory 325, 330–1 (1996).

as falling outside contract law, others that this illustrates that contracts are not, or need not be, promises. The disagreement here is apparent rather than real. If we understand contracts to be legally enforceable promises, these aren't contracts; if we take contract to describe a broader class of voluntary transactions, they are. All this tells us is that there exist not simply different conceptions but different *concepts* of contract, different ideas which from time to time are labelled "contract."[8] Those who would reserve the label "contract" for cases involving true promises are not thereby committed to denying the affinity these might have with other consensual transactions. Likewise those who use "contract" to describe some such broader class of transactions need not deny that within that category exists a subclass of binding *promises*, nor need they deny that, where a contract *does* involve promises, these promises play their part in justifying the parties' obligations. In other words, these non-promissory contracts, by themselves, tell us nothing about how we should understand those contracts which do involve or derive from promises. The idea that they do rests on the assumption that all those obligations or cases which are described as contractual share a common basis, so that, if some contracts can be shown to be independent of promise, it follows that all must be. But the rational unity of contract isn't something an inquiry into the grounds of contractual obligation can take as a given; rather it is something a fully worked-out theory of contract might reveal or refute.

More significant would be if it could be shown that, even in those contracts which have the appearance of promises, no promises are in fact made or whatever promises the parties do make are extraneous to their contractual obligations. So a standard contract of services looks a lot like an exchange of promises: one party promising to do the relevant work, the other to pay. Of course, contracts are frequently entered into without either party saying "I promise." But the same is true of promises too, which can be expressed in various forms. What makes all these forms of expression promises is that all carry the same meaning, signifying the same intention on the part of the speaker: an intention to assume, by that very act of communication, an obligation to perform the specified act.[9] Perhaps many promisors, and many contracting parties, do not think in these terms. Take the following example. Erika calls me one afternoon to ask me what we shall be doing for dinner that evening. I know she is busy, so I promise to stop by the shops and pick something up on the way home. Why do I make the promise? Not in the first instance *to* assume this obligation. The obligation is neither here nor there to me. I'd decided already to go the shops and I see no circumstances arising in which I might want to revisit that decision. Granted, I understand that by making the promise I will indeed come under some such obligation. But it is not my object to bring this about. Rather I make the promise to assure Erika that she doesn't have to go to the shops herself and can plan the rest of her day accordingly.

[8] *Cf.* Hugh Collins, The Law of Contract 1 (4th ed., 2003): "The law of contract states the fundamental rules governing market transactions."

[9] *See* Finnis, Natural Law and Natural Rights, at 298–9; Charles Fried, Contract as Promise: A Theory of Contractual Obligation 9–11 (1981); Joseph Raz, *Promises in Morality and Law*, 95 Harv. L. Rev. 916, 927 (1982).

But how is it that my promise can provide this assurance? Not simply by conveying my present intention to go to the shops, nor even when combined with my further present intention not to reconsider this plan, both of which are consistent with my intending something different later on. I provide this assurance only if my words express a *commitment*, presenting my going to the shops as not just intended but settled, as good as done. I can do this only by treating my not going to the shops as non-optional. And, since this was an option open to me before making the promise, albeit one I didn't plan on exercising, my promise must involve the *assumption* of an obligation. So here too my promise communicates an intention to assume an obligation to perform the specified act, this being the necessary means to my chosen end. Most contracts might be thought to tell a similar story: each party's object is not to undertake an obligation to his counterpart but to secure some sort of performance from him. However, since neither party is willing to provide his performance without the other providing his, each can secure the other's performance only by an assurance that his own performance will be forthcoming.

So there seems no reason to doubt that most standard contracts, like contracts of sale and of services, do involve the making of promises. Is it possible to enter into such a contract without promising? One thought experiment asks us to consider the situation where the contracting parties explicitly disclaim that they are thereby promising to do what the contract provides.[10] Is the statement "I contract to do the work but do not promise to do it" intelligible? Perhaps. One way we could make sense of it is to see the contractual "undertaking" as narrower in scope than a promissory undertaking of the same form.[11] It may be that (some) promises carry with them—or at least are taken to carry with them—obligations beyond the obligation to perform the promised act, so that the statement "I contract to do the work but don't promise" really means "I promise to do the work but no more." Or it may be that the contracting party shares the view of contractual obligation taken by Holmes, granting the obligor the option to perform or pay damages.[12] A contractual undertaking to "do the work" is in truth an undertaking either to do the work or to pay over a sum of money as damages. So here too the upshot is that the apparent denial of any promise is in fact a clarification of what exactly the obligor *is* promising.

But these revisions only sidestep the challenge the example of the non-promising contractor is intended to set. For the point of the example is not to show how a contract and a promise of the same form might nonetheless differ in their content, but to show that it is possible to contract without making any promise at all. How? Because—so the argument goes—contracts involve the assumption of a specifically *legal* obligation, an obligation which can but need not be accompanied by the assumption, through the making of a promise, of a parallel moral obligation.[13]

[10] Michael G. Pratt, *Contract: Not Promise*, 35 Fla. St. U. L. Rev. 801 (2008).

[11] *See generally* Seana Valentine Shiffrin, *Is a Contract a Promise? in* The Routledge Companion to Philosophy of Law 245–7 (Andrei Marmor ed., 2012).

[12] Oliver Wendell Holmes, The Common Law 301 (1881).

[13] *See* Pratt, *Contract: Not Promise*, at 811. The idea that contract involves the undertaking of specifically legal obligations is common: *see, e.g.*, Randy E. Barnett, *A Consent Theory of Contract*, 86 Colum. L. Rev. 269 (1986); Gregory Klass, *Promise Etc.*, 45 Suffolk U. L. Rev. 695 (2012).

This, I think, is a mistake. There is perhaps a sense of legal obligation which is not even putatively moral. So we can say there is a legal obligation wherever positive law identifies some act or forbearance as obligatory.[14] Obligatory in what sense? In the first instance, obligatory under the rules and for the purposes of the legal system. The law is providing: if you are to act in accordance with law, this is what is required of you. In this way, we could think of the obligation-imposing rule as identifying what is the legally right way for people to conduct themselves, in the same way as the rules of Monopoly set out the right way of playing Monopoly. But the claims made by and on behalf of law go beyond this for, unlike a game of Monopoly, the law requires no opt-in and permits no opt-out. It addresses our choices and actions whether we like it or not, and it addresses them not by setting out one way by which choices can be made and evaluated but *the* way, seeking (at least ordinarily) the first and last word in our practical deliberations. The law's message is not simply: if you are to act in accordance with law, this is what is required of you, but: this is what is required of you *full stop*. And so, in this way, when the law designates some act or forbearance as obligatory, it is identifying it as not simply *legally* (i.e., intra-systemically) obligatory but truly—and so *morally*—obligatory.[15]

Of course, not everything the law designates as obligatory is truly, morally obligatory. Though, as we saw at the outset, there are often good reasons to conform with the law's directives, this isn't always the case. And, where there are not, we can say that there exists a legal obligation—in the sense that it remains true that the law has indeed identified this conduct as obligatory—but not a moral obligation. But in such cases, for someone deciding what he truly ought do, this legal obligation is no obligation at all. Conversely, where there are good reasons to treat what the law holds out as obligatory as morally obligatory, we don't then have two obligations, a moral obligation sitting on top of a legal obligation. Rather the legal—and hence putatively moral—obligation *is* a moral obligation. In short: for those deciding what they ought in full reasonableness to do, the law provides either moral obligations or no obligations at all.

As such, there is simply no space for an undertaking of legal but not moral obligation, for there are not two kinds of obligation here but one. One cannot voluntarily assume an obligation without believing that one really is assuming, and not just purporting to assume, an obligation; and hence the nonpromising contractor cannot voluntarily assume his "legal" obligation without believing that the obligation he is assuming is a true, and not just purported, obligation. So "legal" here cannot mean simply "intra-systemic" or "according to rules posited by legal officials" but must also convey ". . . and truly binding on *my* deliberations." The proper conclusion then is that if and insofar as contracts do involve the voluntary assumption of obligations—whatever their content—then these obligations are moral obligations. And, where these obligations are assumed by communicating the intention to assume those obligations to one's contractual counterpart, these contracts are or arise from promises.

[14] *See* Finnis, Natural Law and Natural Rights, at 314–20.

[15] *See also* Joseph Raz, The Authority of Law: Essays on Law and Morality 28–33 (2d ed., 2009); John Gardner, *How Law Claims, What Law Claims*, *in* Institutionalized Reason: The Jurisprudence of Robert Alexy (Matthias Klatt ed., 2012).

IV. Reason, Obligation, Coercion

Promises are just one mode of voluntarily assuming obligations. We can, or at least it is common to think we can, assume such obligations other than by communicating such an intention to someone else. So we can make vows, oaths, and other commitments, which even if communicated to another person, need not involve an assumption of an obligation owed specifically *to* that person. It is reasonable to assume that whatever reasons we have for treating these commitments as obligation giving apply too to promises. But it doesn't follow that the reasons we have for keeping promises will all extend to these other modes of obligation assumption.

One argument for taking these other forms of committing as creating obligations mirrors the argument for taking laws to be obligation creating we looked at earlier. So one reason we have to comply with the law's directives derives from law's capacity to solve coordination problems, settling questions which require some answer but where no one possible answer is more reasonable than the others. Just as any community face challenges which can be surmounted by any one of a menu of alternative reasonable measures from which that community must simply choose, so too there are questions we as individuals must answer which are likewise left underdetermined by the reasons which apply to them. So we must all decide how we should live our lives: what projects we shall take on, what goals we shall adopt, what relationships we shall foster, and so on. Since there are countless ways of living well, far more than we can pursue in any one lifetime, any choice will involve prioritizing some projects and opportunities over others. And yet often no one course of action and so no one choice is, or stands out as being, more reasonable than all others. Nonetheless, since none of these projects will be achieved if no choice is made, nor if the choice of *this* project is repeatedly revisited, we need to choose and, having chosen, to move on.

There is then a value both in committing to certain goals and certain routes to those goals *and* in abiding by those commitments, even where the courses of action we have committed to are no more reasonable than other courses of action we could take instead. This then provides a possible explanation of how the simple fact of commitment, of binding oneself to a certain course of conduct, may—like the simple fact of an authority positing *this* norm or ruling—create an obligation to do that which was merely optional before that act.[16] So too it shows how limiting our options now may expand our options down the line. If this reasoning is sound then it applies too to promises which are likewise commitments but have the additional features that the commitment is made and communicated specifically *to* some other person.

This argument then identifies a reason for promisors to keep their promises which is grounded in their own self-interest, showing how their own lives go better if they both make and keep their commitments. This differs from the argument for laws being obligation creating with which we started, for here the claim is that it is in all of our interests to have an effective resolution to the various coordination problems thrown up by communal life and hence in all of our interests that each one of us complies with the directives issued by an authority as a means to resolve such problems.

[16] *See also* Joseph Raz, *Reasons for Action, Decisions and Norms*, 84 Mind 481, 494 (1975).

The fact that the community as a whole stands to lose out if these directives are disregarded means the state has reason to take steps, on our behalf, to see that we comply and to take measures against those of us who do not. It's rather more doubtful that the state has any business in policing our commitments in the same way, compelling us to be resolute, to stick to the plans and projects we have taken on, even if this does in the long run serve our interests. No surprise then that the law does not in fact hold us to the vast majority of our commitments.

Yet, as we have noted, promises have additional features which distinguish them from other sorts of commitment. These added features are important for they may provide additional reasons for taking promises to be obligation creating, reasons which may present a stronger case for state regulation of (some) promises. So the argument just rehearsed provides a reason why making and keeping promises, as with other such commitments, is in a promisor's interests. But unlike these other forms of commitment, promise making is not simply, or perhaps even primarily, in and for the promisor's interests but (also) in and for the interests of the *promisee*. So as we have seen, promises are typically made to provide assurance, inviting the promisee to take the promisor's performance of that promise as a given, as something the promisee can safely assume will be done. This is valuable to the promisee since, if she takes the promise seriously and trusts in the promisor's performance, it allows her to plan her affairs subject to one less uncertainty. Erika now knows that she can get on with the rest of her day, devoting her time to whatever other projects she has set herself and meeting whatever other responsibilities she has, safe in the knowledge that she doesn't need to set aside time to get dinner.

In contrast then with other commitments, it is not simply my interests and my projects which are implicated in my promising but (in the usual case) my promisee's too. My promise to Erika is made not to settle some question for me—to my mind it had already been settled—but to settle it for her. Promises such as this are made to give promisees reasons for belief (e.g., that I will go to the shops) and, usually, for action (e.g., to spend the rest of her day getting on with work or whatever else she has planned). As such, if I break my promise I both falsify a belief I have intentionally created and I undermine any decisions and actions of hers she has taken on the back of it, often decisions and actions which my promise was designed to encourage. And so though it may be that I lose out, in the end, by not keeping my promises and not abiding by my commitments more generally, the increased options this gives me in the short term outweighed by the options this shuts down later on, each broken promise does an immediate harm to my promisee.

This harm will vary in kind and in degree. Sometimes it will simply lie in the disappointment of the expectations created by the promisor: the belief that the promised performance was as good as done now revealed to be false, my promise a deception. At other times, however, the promisee will have made decisions and taken action on this belief, committing herself to acts and projects to which she would not have committed had she known the promised performance may not be forthcoming. There may be other harms too: in the parties' wider relationship to one another, in the promisee's willingness to trust—and so to benefit from—the promises of others. That promises exposes promisees to the risks of these harms, and that promisors do this by design (though it is rarely their design to bring such harm about), provides further reasons to keep promises. In turn, when promises are not kept, the responsibility promisors bear for these harms may ground obligations of apology and reparation.

The avoidance and compensation of these harms, unlike an agent's wavering commitment to his own plans, look more like the sorts of things that the state should take an interest in, at least where these harms are sufficiently serious and state intervention does not come at too high a cost.[17] Here then is one reason to think that promises merit special treatment in law as against oaths and vows and other forms of voluntary obligation. Moreover, it gives a reason why the law might be particularly concerned with promises that have in fact prompted some act or commitment on the part of the promisee—as, for instance, is required by the common law doctrines of consideration and estoppel—since this is where the harms caused by breach stand to be greater, and why it might take compensating such harms rather than securing performance as the principal objective of any relief accorded in the event of breach. In this way, the obligations in fact endorsed and enforced through the legal regulation of promises may reasonably differ from and be more limited than the obligations promisors themselves intend to undertake.

V. Who is Contract Law for?

The preceding sketch offers no more than the barest skeleton of an account of how the reasons which promises give and the goods and values that are implicated in their making and breaking bear on the sorts of practical questions addressed by the law of contract. But what it does show is that there is both more and less to the morality of promising than there is to the morality of contract. The conclusion that contracts involve or arise out of promises is really only the beginning of an inquiry into the reasons which properly bear on the decision making of contracting parties and those charged with resolving contractual disputes. The fact that promisors take themselves to come under obligations to perform does not, by itself, establish that they do indeed owe these or any obligations. Whatever reasons we may identify for regarding promises as obligation creating may not be reasons to take them as creating *legal* rights and duties such as support state policing and intervention in the event of breach.

The idea that an account of contract must go beyond an account of promises and of promissory obligations is, I'd have thought, by and large uncontroversial. But it may be that we should go further than this and say that to focus on theories of promissory obligation when looking for a theory of contract is a failure to grasp the task at hand.[18] For in many ways the distinctive practical question to which the law of contract is addressed is not the promisor's question, "Should I keep my promises?," but the official's question, "When should I, on behalf of the state and backed by its coercive machinery, order that promises be performed or take measures against those who have broken them?" This is not to say the law of contract has nothing to say to

[17] *See also* Joseph Raz, *Promises in Morality and Law*, 95 Harv. L. Rev. 916, 937 (1982).

[18] *Cf.* T. M. Scanlon, *Promises and Contracts, in* The Theory of Contract: New Essays 99–100 (Peter Benson ed., 2001).

promisors, simply that it is a stretch to see contract law—or at least the common law of contract as developed by English judges—as attempting any sort of thoroughgoing answer to the promisor's question. One way to see this is by considering what sort of direction the law would be giving to promisors were its rules to be read with this purpose in mind. So no contract will arise if the promise was not supported by consideration or if the promise was made in such circumstances as support the conclusion that the promisor had no intent to create legal relations. If we take these rules as setting down the circumstances in which the law directs that we should be keeping our promises, the upshot is that the direction the law offers is that a significant class of promises—including pretty much all those made between family and friends—not only need not be kept but generate no obligations whatsoever.

The more plausible reading of these rules is that they are answers to the question of when it is reasonable for officials to intervene where promises are broken. We seen this in the reasons given for the intent to create legal relations rule: that state enforcement or policing of these arrangements would be heavy-handed and intrusive, that state enforcement or policing would often damage these typically long-standing and valuable relationships, that providing claims to such promisees would lead to a flood of litigation, and so on.[19] None of these identifies a reason why promisors in such situations should not keep their promises; each is a reason for the courts not to intervene in the event that they don't. The same goes if we see the rule not as an expression of these policy concerns but as reflecting what the parties intend when they enter into such arrangements. For what these parties typically intend is that no dispute that might arise from their arrangements should end up in court, not that the law shouldn't endorse the obligation to perform they themselves voluntarily undertook.

Indeed not only does the law appear, to this extent, not to be taking on the job of directing promisors but, for many purposes, such guidance would be redundant. As we have seen already, one cannot consciously and sincerely make a promise without believing that one thereby comes under an obligation to do what one promised. So most promisors don't need the law to tell them to keep their promises. Not only do they know it, the fact of their promising shows they embrace it. Of course, it's possible to communicate an intention to assume a particular obligation while lacking that intention and even those who made their promises sincerely may have second thoughts by the time it comes to performance. But here too one might think the law has little to offer. For second thoughts about whether one really needs to keep a given promise are second thoughts about whether this promise really did generate an obligation. And one cannot revise one's attitude to *this* promise—concluding on balance that one need not perform—without thereby revising one's attitude to promises generally. So the stakes here are high. One cannot, in honesty, go on making promises, knowing that promises are presented as and are understood to be assumptions of an obligation, without acknowledging the reality of this obligation.[20] Acknowledging the

[19] *See* for instance the judgment of Atkin L.J. in *Balfour v. Balfour,* [1919] 2 K.B. 571.

[20] Or more precisely, given that this obligation may not be a "reality," one cannot go on making promises without committing, rightly or wrongly, to the idea that it *is* a reality, that promises *really do* give rise to obligations to perform.

reality of this obligation means taking it as binding even where the keeping of the promise no longer suits one's immediate purposes.

These arguments go only so far. The obligation to keep one's promises which all sincere promisors accept is not accepted as indefeasible, yet promisors will often have no clear sense of the circumstances in which this obligation may be defeated. There will often be uncertainty too over when coercion or mistakes may justify treating an apparent promise as non-obligation generating. Here the law has a role to play in providing answers to these questions, setting out what obligations promisors in these situations really do owe, and it seems likely that these questions cannot be answered well without getting clear on what goods and values the practice of promising serves. Similarly, these goods and values are likely to be relevant too when it comes to addressing the official's question—when is it reasonable for me, as a state official, to take action against those who break or threaten to break promises?—since, or to the extent that, such action may support and reinforce the practice of promising. A clear understanding of the reasons for action promises provide is thus essential to the sound reasoning of those entering and enforcing contracts.

Nonetheless, the preceding account does show why contract law and contractual obligation may often reasonably depart from the morality and practice of promising, and that these departures needn't be seen as a subversion of or threat to that practice. Contracts *are* (in the main) promises and contracting parties do, in these cases, come under the same obligations promisors generally owe. But if our concern is with the law of contract and the practical questions it distinctively raises, our inquiry need neither begin nor end with an account of promissory obligation.

9

The Practice of Promise and Contract

*Liam Murphy**

I. Contract Theory

A philosophical theory of promising attempts to justify some account of promissory obligation. It does not, at the outset, attempt to justify any particular social practice or set of prevailing ethical commitments. This is why the dependence of promissory obligation on an actual social practice is a discovery worth remarking upon.[1] Of course, one's beliefs about promissory rights and obligations—beliefs embedded in a social practice—are the initial data from which any theory of promise is constructed. There is nowhere else to start. But in most philosophical reflection about substantive moral issues the prospect of revisionary conclusions is part of the point of engaging in the inquiry. Few philosophers believe that pretheoretical moral commitment or "intuition" should be treated as sacrosanct.

Whatever the right methodology in moral theory may be, it is clear enough that normative legal theory should not treat existing law as presumptively good and seek only to show why this is so. Law is obviously a social, indeed a political, artefact. We don't need critical theory to tell us that law has a certain genesis and serves certain functions and that it would be perverse simply to *assume* that it deserves our approval.[2]

Of course, it is an essential project to uncover the internal normative structure (if there is one) of a particular branch of law in a particular place. Such an understanding is obviously crucial for the making of arguments within that legal practice. But it's also the right starting point for normative legal theory.[3] Though the main point of normative legal theory as most see it is evaluative, aiming at least to produce criteria

* Thanks to Oren Bar-Gill, Kevin Davis, Martijn Hesselink, Lewis Kornhauser, George Letsas, Seana Shiffrin, Alan Schwartz, and audience members at the University College London conference and a seminar at the Center for the Study of European Contract Law at the University of Amsterdam for comments and criticism. The support of the Filomen D'Agostino and Max E. Greenberg Research Fund of New York University School of Law is gratefully acknowledged.

[1] *See* David Hume, A Treatise of Human Nature (P. H. Nidditch ed., Oxford University Press 1978) (1740); Liam Murphy, The Practice of Promise (2014) (unpublished manuscript, on file with author).

[2] The formalist approach to legal theory of Ernest Weinrib, The Idea of Private Law (1995), and Peter Benson's work on contract theory may seem to reflect a different view. But in the end I do not believe this is the best way to understand their work. On Benson, see note 3.

[3] For some, for example Jules Coleman in tort theory and Peter Benson in contract theory, it is also the endpoint, at least of their inquiry. Having presented an analysis of the normative structure of tort law, Coleman leaves it to others to determine whether such an institution is worth having; *see, e.g.*, Jules Coleman, Risks and Wrongs (2002). And Benson, while arguing that uncovering the implicit normative structure of contract doctrine provides a "public justification of contract," leaves it open whether this justification can be given a deeper philosophical or moral foundation. See Peter Benson, *The Unity of Contract Law*, *in* The Theory of Contract Law 118, 124 (Peter Benson ed., 2001).

by which particular legal doctrines and practices can be judged, it would obviously be a waste of time to try to design an ideal system of contract law (or even to try to come up with a set of goals contract law should serve, leaving the problem of concrete institutionalization to someone else) in ignorance of how societies have been thinking about the topic over the centuries. Though it is possible that all actual contract law is all wrong, it is very unlikely to be so, and any theory claiming this has the burden of explaining how we all went astray. (I think it quite likely that New Zealand was right to abandon the whole of accident law, but we do need an account of why the rest of the world is unmoved by this revolution.) In any event, as with the moral case, where else can we start than with existing ideas about why and how law should enforce agreements?

In practice, the connection between normative legal theory and actual law is often stronger than this.[4] It is typical for writers to attempt to fit a theory of, say, contract, as closely as possible to some particular actual legal system, even if their ultimate motivation is critical.[5] This is in a way surprising, since if one sees existing law as just initial data for theory construction, a comparative approach—drawing on as wide a variety of legal systems as possible—would clearly be preferable. But existing English-speaking legal theory, at any rate, is notably parochial. This is probably partly attributable to the prevailing monolingualism of contemporary scholars in the English-speaking world—in stark contrast with what seems to have been the norm a hundred years ago. But it is also surely partly because legal theorists typically have mixed aims. They mostly do wish to advance a normative and not just a descriptive or explanatory legal theory. But by training and profession they also tend to be experts on a particular legal system and so have a natural interest in making reformist proposals that have a chance of success in their own legal world; the closer the evaluative theory matches existing law in a particular place, the more likely arguments for or against reform made in its name will be heeded.

The approach of Stephen Smith deserves special mention.[6] Smith's discussion of contract theory is offered as an interpretation of existing law, along the lines of Dworkin's theory of how to figure out the content of the law in force. Such an interpretation, simplifying greatly, aims both to fit the existing legal materials and show them in their morally best light. Smith therefore aims to go beyond uncovering the normative structure of contract law; he aims to provide the best available justification for the way that it is. Now Dworkin's theory of how to determine the content of the law may be correct.[7] But if it is evaluative contract theory we are doing, rather than trying to make the best sense of the law we have, the method of showing existing legal materials in their best light is inappropriate. Evaluative or critical legal theory is not constrained to fit existing materials. Though existing materials are the starting point

[4] *See also* Jody Kraus, *The Philosophy of Contract Law, in* The Oxford Handbook of Jurisprudence and Philosophy of Law 687 (Jules Coleman & Scott Shapiro eds., 2004).

[5] A good example is Charles Fried, whose theory in Contract as Promise (1981) leaves him with no choice but to repudiate the doctrine of consideration but who strives to justify as much as possible of the rest of U.S. law on the contract as promise model.

[6] Stephen Smith, Contract Theory (2004).

[7] For discussion, *see* Liam Murphy, What Makes Law (2014).

of the discussion, there is no loss, so far as the theory is concerned, if it explains why some well-established feature of the law should simply be dropped; less fit is not in itself a count against the theory. To use Smith's helpful taxonomy, I am interested in "prescriptive" rather than "interpretive" contract theory.[8]

II. Legal Enforcement of Agreements

The basic question to ask about contract law is why (some) agreements or promises should be enforced by the state. An answer to this question will provide criteria for determining which agreements and promises should be enforced, and which should not. It will also carry with it an account of what enforcement amounts to: an account of the appropriate remedy for breach.

It might seem that in stating the problem in this way, I have already restricted myself to the common law world, where it is entirely natural to lawyers and theorists to think of contract law in terms of the enforcement of agreements and promises, and left behind the civil law tradition, in which the question is typically posed as one about the conditions under which a person has taken on a legal (contractual) obligation. But the difference is actually superficial, since even if we don't think of contract law in terms of the enforcement of independently existing promises or agreements that might have moral force, contractual obligations everywhere are legal obligations to perform one's side of an agreement or stand-alone commitment. Whether or not we think of contract law as arriving on the scene of a moral practice of making promises and agreements and choosing to add legal force to some of them, we can agree that contract theory aims to provide normative foundations for the type of legal institution that enforces (some) agreements and unilateral undertakings.

For a body of law as comparatively settled as contracts, it is perhaps surprising that so many very different answers to the basic questions have been proposed. But then perhaps it is not surprising: like property, contract is a fundamental legal category and a lot is at stake here for a society's moral and political self-understanding.

We can organize the most important options in contract theory into three broad camps. First, there are *moralistic* accounts—those that see contract law as aimed at either enforcing moral obligation or promoting a virtuous character. Second, there are *corrective justice* accounts, according to which the aim of contract law is to allow the victims of a certain kind of wrongdoing to extract compensation (rectification) from the wrongdoers. Last, there are *instrumental* accounts, which find the point of contract law in the morally significant social effects that flow from it. One might of course subscribe to some pluralistic mix of some or all of these basic types, but I will first introduce each type in its pure form.

The labels could mislead. Though I label only the first view (and this somewhat tendentiously) moralistic, all the contract theories I consider are grounded in considerations of political morality. Even the economic theory of contract, despite the ideological disavowals of some of its practitioners,[9] depends on the assumption that

[8] Smith, Contract Theory, at 4.

[9] *See, e.g.*, Richard Posner, Problematics of Moral and Legal Reasoning (2002).

economic efficiency is a value legal institutions should promote. And of course all corrective justice views are moral views. What makes the first group of views worthy of the label "moralistic" is that they understand the point of contract law to be the enforcement of moral obligation, or the promotion of virtue, for their own sake. The distinction is familiar from criminal law theory. All accounts of criminal law attempt to provide moral justification for this most coercive branch of the law. And all agree that most defensible criminal prohibitions dovetail with what most people would acknowledge as their moral obligations. But only the kind of view H. L. A. Hart called legal moralism will hold that the point of the criminal prohibition is to enforce the associated moral obligation.[10] On instrumental accounts, to take one contrasting case, the content of the law is justified because and to the extent that enforcement of these criminal duties does some good.

If all contract theories are at the broadest level grounded (in part) in moral theory, it is also true that there is a sense in which they are all instrumental: They hold not that the legal regulation of agreements has intrinsic value but rather that it is valuable as a means to certain good effects—including, perhaps, the enforcement of moral obligation.[11] Those theories I label instrumental are so in a more particular, narrower sense: they reject the idea that the point of contract law is to do justice to the moral dimensions of the relationship between the parties. Thus they deny that the point of contract law lies with the moral standing of the promisor (the moralistic view) *or* with the rights and legitimate interests of the promisee (the corrective justice view). Rather, they find the point of contract law in society-wide morally significant consequences. It is appropriate to call such theories instrumental, because they treat as mere instruments in service of an entirely distinct goal legal rights and duties that most people, on first thought, would treat as tracking real and significant moral rights and duties held by the parties to the agreement against each other.

I favor an instrumentalist contract theory, though not of the narrowly economic variety. I begin with a review of the most important alternatives on their own terms. Much of the argument that follows does not depend upon any particular account of promise.

III. Moralistic Contract Theory

Charles Fried's main aim in *Contract as Promise* is to establish the centrality of promise to contract theory. He sets himself against those who downplay the importance of promise to contract either by taking a purely instrumental view in which the morality of promise does not figure, or by explaining contract in corrective justice terms but with reference to the promisee's reliance rather than expectation interest.

In Fried's account of promise, the value of the practice lies in its contribution to human autonomy: In providing a mechanism whereby people can secure others'

[10] *See* H. L. A. HART, LAW, LIBERTY, AND MORALITY (1963). For defense of legal moralism in the criminal law, *see* MICHAEL MOORE, PLACING BLAME (1997).

[11] Even Ronald Dworkin's theory of law, which perhaps has more to say about the value of law than any other, is instrumental in this sense: the ordering of social life through law is not intrinsically valuable, rather, its value lies in its role in creating a certain kind of political community. *See* RONALD DWORKIN, LAW'S EMPIRE (1986); Ronald Dworkin, *In Praise of Theory*, 29 ARIZ. ST. L.J. 353 (1997).

trust and therefore cooperation, the practice expands freedom. But Fried does not explain the obligation to keep promises instrumentally, in terms of the promotion of autonomy.[12] Rather he gives a deontological account of why it is wrong to violate the rules of the practice. To do so is to intentionally invoke another's trust and then abuse it, and to do that is to use a person, in the Kantian sense—to fail to show them appropriate respect.[13] Now this account of promissory obligation is subject to essentially the same circularity problem faced by nonpractice accounts.[14] We might think that trust can be invoked out of thin air if a promisor can give moral grounds for the promisee to expect performance.[15] Fried claims that this happens automatically. "An individual is morally bound to keep his promises because he has intentionally invoked a convention whose function it is to give grounds—moral grounds—for another to expect the promised performance."[16] The trouble, the circle, is that there are no moral grounds to expect performance unless the individual is already bound to keep his promise.[17]

Be that as it may, it is plain that Fried takes the conclusion of his account of promise to be that promisors have a deontological obligation to perform and that promisees have the correlative right to performance. Fried's discussion of contract law starts downstream of this moral conclusion. And is not undermined by his unpersuasive argument for that conclusion, since there are other ways to argue for a deontological basis of the duty to keep promises—even others, such as Rawls's, that also invoke the value of the practice of promise.[18]

What is most important in Fried's contract theory, and what justifies treating his as the exemplary moralistic account, is the focus on the moral obligation of the promisor as the main justifying ground of contract law.

> The moralist of duty thus posits a general obligation to keep promises, of which the obligation of contract will be only a special case—that special case in which certain promises have attained legal as well as moral force. But since a contract is first of all a promise, the contract must be kept because a promise must be kept.[19]

The message is clear enough. Just as legal-moralist theories of criminal law hold that the legal duty not to murder has as its point the enforcement of the moral duty not to kill, moralistic contract theory holds that the legal duty of contractual performance has as its aim the enforcement of the moral duty of performance of promise.

[12] Thus Richard Craswell's characterization of Fried's theory of promise (and contract) as an "autonomy" theory, in *Contract Law, Default Rules, and the Philosophy of Promising*, 88 Mich. L. Rev. 489 (1989), is misleading. Unfortunately, this terminology has been widely adopted by contract theorists.

[13] Fried, Contract as Promise, 16–17. For sympathetic discussion, *see* Dori Kimel, From Promise to Contract 7–31 (2003).

[14] *See* Niko Kolodny & R. Jay Wallace, *Promise and Practice Revisited*, 31 Phil. & Pub. Aff. 119 (2003); Murphy, The Practice of Promise.

[15] Though even in that case I do not believe that trust will automatically be generated.

[16] Fried, Contract as Promise, at 16.

[17] Stephen Smith makes essentially the same objection to Fried's account of promise in *Towards a Theory of Contract, in* Oxford Essays in Jurisprudence, 4th series 107 (Jeremy Horder ed., 2000). But he takes it to undermine Fried's contract theory, which I do not.

[18] *See* John Rawls, A Theory of Justice 93–8 (rev. ed., 1999).

[19] Fried, Contract as Promise, at 17.

Fried believes that the standard common law remedy for breach of contract, expectation damages, achieves this aim: "If I make a promise to you, I should do as I promise; and if I fail to keep my promise, it is fair that I should be made to hand over the equivalent of the promised performance."[20] Fried's advocacy of expectation damages has drawn considerable criticism, not all of which is effective.[21] The main question to ask is why, if enforcement of moral obligation is the aim, the appropriate remedy is not to be figured out on retributive and/or deterrence grounds. Whatever normative force we give to the boundary between criminal and civil law is irrelevant here, since the civil law does have the option of punitive damages.

An argument can be made for the nonpunitive remedy of specific performance. In the case of a promise, there is a very straightforward way in which the obligation can be enforced by law: the state can force the promisor to perform. In this respect promissory obligation differs from most of the obligations the legal moralist takes to be the business of the criminal law, which may only be "enforced" by way of deterrence and retribution. Though in some cases the time for performance without loss to the promisee has passed by the time of litigation, when that is not the case the injunction simply *is* the legal enforcement of the moral obligation. Of course, one could go further and argue for a punitive sanction for all who waver in the performance of their obligation, but the very idea of legal enforcement of moral obligation does not require that purely retributive element.

Moralistic theories do face a further decision: Should the court's order of performance be backed up with the full range of criminal sanctions, including imprisonment, as is the case in Germany and, in principle, in the common law world via the mechanism of criminal contempt of court, or should only some weaker civil enforcement of the injunction be available, as in France?[22] But this is a choice about the lengths to which the law should go in enforcing courts' injunctions, or this one in particular, not a choice about whether the enforcement of contractual obligation should be inherently punitive, since in all cases the promisor will be in the clear if she complies with the injunction.

So a good case can be made for a natural association between moralistic contract theory and the remedy of specific performance. Whether or not legal enforcement of promissory morality should go beyond this, it should do at least this much. The relevant complaint to make against Fried's discussion in *Contract as Promise* would seem to be that he ignored the important differences between specific performance and expectation damages from the promisee's point of view.[23] Expectation damages aim to put the promisee in as good a position as she would have been in had the promise been performed, and so in that sense they are ideally the financial equivalent of the

[20] Fried, Contract as Promise, at 17.

[21] *See* Craswell, *Contract Law, Default Rules, and the Philosophy of Promising*; Richard Craswell, *Against Fuller and Perdue*, 67 U. Chi. L. Rev. 99 (2000); Gillian Hadfield, *Of Sovereignty and Contract: Damages for Breach of Contract by Government*, 8 S. Cal. Interdisc. L.J. 467 (1999). Craswell's well-known complaint that the remedy of expectation damages "cannot be derived solely from the value of individual freedom and autonomy," Craswell, *Contract Law, Default Rules, and the Philosophy of Promising*, at 517, misreads Fried as offering an instrumental account of promise and contract.

[22] On France and Germany, *see* Hein Kötz & Konrad Zweigert, Introduction to Comparative Law (1998).

[23] *See* Louis Kaplow & Steven Shavell, Fairness Versus Welfare 161 n. 18 (2002).

promised performance for the promisee. But in a situation where a promisor could commit the promised performance to a higher-paying third party, pay expectation damages to the original promisee, and still come out better off, paying expectation damages is not the equivalent, for the promisee, of performing as promised.

In his most recent writing on this issue Fried suggests that expectation damages are best understood as a default rule, justified as the rule that most parties would choose or on instrumental grounds.[24] (I discuss the idea that the remedy for breach is for the parties to determine *ex ante* in Section VII.) This does not mean that Fried thinks that nonperformance is not always morally and legally wrong.[25] The promisor should keep his promise. But if he does not, and legal enforcement is required, and the parties have not stipulated specific performance in advance, then an accurate award of expectation damages gives the promisee no more nor less than was agreed to.[26]

In any event, the important objection to the moralistic theory lies not with its implications for the remedy, but in its very foundation as an application of legal moralism to contract law.[27]

Fried writes that, "Law can be, should be, but need not be a set of institutions that underwrite, facilitate, and enforce the demands and aspirations of morality in our dealings with each other."[28] It is this view about the proper role of legal coercion that sets Fried's contract theory apart in a special category and, for many of us, allows us to set it aside. For Millian liberals, who reject coercion merely for the sake of improving a person's own welfare, or enforcing their obligations, or making them more virtuous, the moralistic view of contract law does not get off the ground.[29]

Having said this, it seems clear that Fried does not regard the enforcement of people's obligations just for its own sake as the *sole* point of contract law. He clearly regards more ordinary instrumental benefits as part of the point.[30] Perhaps if it did not also produce significant economic benefits a legal apparatus that enforced promissory obligation would not be worth the cost. Furthermore, much of what Fried writes aligns him closely with the broadly Kantian, expectation-based corrective justice view defended by Ernest Weinrib, discussed in Section IV. So we should class Fried as a pluralist contract theorist—but as one who nonetheless stands out for holding that one

[24] This volume, Charles Fried, *The Ambitions of* Contract as Promise, *in* PHILOSOPHICAL FOUNDATIONS OF CONTRACT LAW, 17, 24–8 (Gregory Klass, George Letsas & Prince Saprai eds., 2014).

[25] Courts typically do not have to take a stand on that precise issue, since, in the common law world, the expectation damages rule is so well entrenched. But there is usually a way for foundational issues to make it to the surface of doctrine: In the wonderful case of *Anguilla v. Estate & Trust Agencies (1927) Ltd.*, [1938] A.C. 624 (P.C.) (appeal taken from Sing.), the question was whether the executor of an estate was required to breach a contract when this would have left the estate better off even after paying expectation damages. The Privy Council held that "the breaking of an enforceable contract is an unlawful act, and... it can never be the duty of an executor or an administrator to commit such an act." [1938] A.C. 624 at 635.

[26] Fried acknowledges that expectation damages frequently undercompensate in practice. Charles Fried, *The Convergence of Contract and Promise*, 120 HARV. L. REV. F. 1, 6 (2007).

[27] *See* Joseph Raz, *Promises in Morality and Law*, 95 HARV. L. REV. 916 (1982).

[28] Fried, *The Convergence of Contract and Promise*, at 3.

[29] But not because it imposes an obligation to benefit others—as Smith, *Towards a Theory of Contract*, argues. Mill has no objection to positive legal duties; in fact, he explicitly embraces a legal duty to rescue in *On Liberty*. JOHN STUART MILL, ON LIBERTY (1859). For further discussion, *see* Liam Murphy, *Beneficence, Law, and Liberty: The Case of Required Rescue* 89 GEO. L.J. 605 (2001).

[30] *See* Fried, *The Ambitions of* Contract as Promise, this volume.

aim of contract law, an aim that constrains its content, is the enforcement of promisors' moral obligations.

IV. Corrective Justice I: The Promisee's Right to Performance

Corrective justice views of private law see the point of contract, or tort, as the righting of wrongs in the particular sense of compensation for, or undoing of, the harm suffered as a result of another's wrongdoing. Taking this perspective on contract law, our focus is on the promisee. As we know, corrective justice accounts of contract could understand the wrong done to the promisee as lying with his expectation or performance interest or instead with his reliance interest.

There are at least two importantly different ways a performance-interest account could be further spelled out. The first is that promises transfer property rights from the promisor to the promisee.

Peter Benson's brilliant, though to my mind Quixotic,[31] reconstruction of common law contract doctrine along these lines—finding the essence of contract in the transfer of personal proprietary rights[32]—is limited in its justificatory aims, since his project is to uncover the normative structure of contract doctrine.[33] To take this line of thought further, so that it generates standards for the evaluation of contract law rather than a thick description of it, we would have to agree that the transfer of rights recognized by contract law flows from the morality of property. I have rights to my person and my legitimately acquired holdings, and implicit in these rights is the right to alienate them. Two wills are required for the effective transfer of the right, since we cannot force property rights on others without their consent. When two wills have joined in an agreement, or a gratuitous promise (on this view, gratuitous promises must be accepted by the promisee to take effect, as Kant emphasizes and civilian contract law requires), the promisee acquires a new right, and if the promisor fails to perform, she violates that right. Contract law ensures that such wrongdoing is appropriately compensated. There is no mystery about what form that compensation should take: it should undo the violation of right by requiring performance or something just as good, along with disgorgement of any profit made by the promisor from violation of the promisee's property right.

My own objection to this approach is again fundamental: I reject moral property rights in the Lockean sense, and especially the idea of self-ownership.[34] So though it is true that if natural property rights along Lockean lines made sense, then the right to alienate would be a natural implication that would offer a straightforward justification for contract law, I cannot accept the foundations of this argument. A defense of this rejection of the Lockean view is obviously beyond my scope here. But even apart from this theoretical objection, there is a prima facie oddness to the assimilation of contract

[31] Benson goes so far as to attempt to provide an independently plausible normative rationale for the common law doctrine of consideration. Peter Benson, *The Idea of Consideration*, 61 U. Toronto L.J. 241 (2011). For many contract scholars, this is almost a *reductio ad absurdum* of Benson's project.

[32] *See* Peter Benson, *Contract as a Transfer of Ownership*, 48 Wm. & Mary L. Rev. 1673 (2007).

[33] *See* Benson, *The Unity of Contract Law.*

[34] For discussion, *see* G. A. Cohen, Self-Ownership, Freedom, and Equality (1995).

to property since contracts for services are not most naturally thought of as transferring a property right to (some part of) a person's freedom of action.

The second possible expectation-focused corrective justice account is on its face much more plausible. Instead of locating the relevant moral interests of promisees in the morality of property, it lays out an independent morality of contract.

The kind of view I have in mind is set out with exemplary clarity by Ernest Weinrib.[35] The aim of providing a remedy for breach of contract, on this view, is to restore to the plaintiff that which is rightfully his; specific performance or expectation damages do this, and are thus the proper remedies. The promisee's right under a contract is not a property right, or any kind of right to the subject matter of the contract. Rather, as Kant emphasizes, the promisee's right is to the promisor's performance.[36]

Now this kind of view makes excellent sense of the structure and content of contract law as it is found virtually everywhere, including the fact that contract remedies are not generally aimed at punishment of the promisor, or disgorgement of her gains. Contract remedies simply require the promisor to give to the promisee what was rightfully his all along, the promised performance or its monetary equivalent. But such a view depends upon an independent account of why exactly a promisee acquires a right to the promisor's performance.

The inspiration for this kind of view is Kant's remarks on contract in the *Metaphysical Principles of Justice*. But what Kant writes is very disappointing, since it too is heavy on form and light on justification. We are told that the simultaneous joining together of two wills in contract transfers a right. (Kant's philosophical exertion is limited to an almost parodic transcendental argument that two empirically nonsimultaneous assents must be conceivable as noumenally simultaneous, lest contract be impossible.) While contract as the joining of wills may be a satisfactory descriptive account of some legal regime, it fails to explain why such a regime would make sense or be desirable.

The natural place to look for such a justification would be in the morality of promise. But there is no plausible deontological account of promise that would establish that promisees have a right to the promised performance.[37] Rawls's practice-based account of promise does provide a deontological reason for keeping a promise: someone who makes, and then breaks, a promise can be seen as free-riding on a beneficial social practice in which he participates voluntarily. This is an attractive account of the morality of promise and it does ground a deontological reason for fidelity to promise. But that reason relates to the interests of everyone engaged in the practice; it does not ground an account of why breach violates the rights of a particular promisee. And of course a practice-based account of the purely consequentialist variety does not ground a deontological reason for fidelity to promise: the reason to perform promises made, if there is one, turns on the harm that noncompliance would do to the valuable social practice.

[35] Earnest Weinrib, *Punishment and Disgorgement as Contract Remedies*, 78 Chi.-Kent L. Rev. 55 (2003).

[36] Weinrib, *Punishment and Disgorgement as Contract Remedies*, at 67; *see* Immanuel Kant, The Metaphysics of Morals § 6:273 (Mary Gregor ed., Cambridge University Press 1996) (1797).

[37] *See* Murphy, The Practice of Promise.

For all practice-based accounts (other than Fried's, discussed in Section III) the reasons to keep a promise—one made at arm's length, at any rate—relate to the practice of promising at large, and are not grounded on the rights or interests of the promisee. In the case of promises made to intimates there can be special kinds of expectations the disappointment of which would do significant harm. But there is no reason to think that the harm nonperformance would do is just the same as the loss in value to the promise from nonperformance.[38]

It is no doubt because Fuller and Perdue did not consider the possibility that promisees simply had a right to performance that they believed expectation damages to be, on the face of it, an unjustified remedy. They declare that the expectation interest of promisees has very little moral importance.[39] The way they write about it, it is as if unfulfilled expectations on the part of all promisees should be likened to a child's disappointment at not getting an anticipated ice-cream. But on the corrective justice view, the remedy of expectation damages is appropriate not because the promisee has a specially valuable interest, or because she will suffer a loss from nonperformance, but because she has a right to performance. Just as, if we believe in property rights, restoring my stolen property is morally appropriate (since I have a right to the property) even when the loss did not set back my welfare interests at all.

Similarly, Joseph Raz argues that expectation damages for the sake of the promisee alone (as opposed to the social good) are incompatible with Mill's harm principle.[40] As with Fuller and Perdue's discussion, Raz here seems to believe that expectation losses, since they are in an important sense hypothetical, measured against a baseline of what might have been, are not real harms. On the corrective justice view now being considered, we are not looking to prevent material harm, but protect rights.

It is worth pointing out that Fuller and Perdue's skepticism about the importance of the promisee's expectations is fully compatible with recognizing that promisees under a valid contract have a legitimate expectation of performance. A promisee's legitimate expectations can be understood to flow not from the promisor's natural duty to perform, but from her participation in a legitimate practice justified on other grounds. Where contract law must be justified on other grounds, promisees' expectations, even though they are legitimate once the system is up and running, do not provide any additional justification for having such a system. We mustn't confuse a moral side-effect of the system with its underlying justification. Take a welfare system that is justified by some account of social justice. Individuals living under that scheme have a legitimate expectation to the delivery of what they are legally entitled to. But those expectations do not explain why the welfare system is a good idea. The key point to make about Fuller and Perdue, then, is that they simply did not consider that contract law might be justified as a way to enforce the independently generated right of promisees to the promised performance.[41]

I conclude that Weinrib's Kantian corrective justice account is the most eligible candidate noninstrumental contract theory, particularly in making sense of

[38] *See* Murphy, The Practice of Promise.

[39] *See* L. L. Fuller & William R. Perdue, Jr., *The Reliance Interest in Contract Damages: I*, 46 Yale L.J. 52 (1936).

[40] *See* Raz, *Promises in Morality and Law.*

[41] *See* Weinrib, *Punishment and Disgorgement as Contract Remedies*, at 63–4.

existing law in such a clear and compelling way. As a normative reconstruction of the law—which may also be all that either Kant or Weinrib believed they were offering—it is far superior to accounts that link contract to property, or, the account we turn to next, those that focus on reliance. The problem with this account is where it stops. It offers no argument at all for the idea that all promisees have moral rights that it is the business of the law to protect. I cannot defend the claim here, but it is my view that promisees have no such rights.

V. Corrective Justice II: Compensation for Detrimental Reliance

Though in the end I agree with Fuller and Perdue in rejecting an expectation-focused corrective justice account, I cannot see any plausibility in the view they put in its place—the idea that contract law is about compensation for detrimental reliance.

Despite its popularity in the twentieth century, and despite its affinity with the U.S. doctrine of promissory estoppel, the "reliance theory" of contract is perhaps the least plausible of the views considered so far. The only way it can be saved from incoherence is by transforming into a view that no one could accept.

In a nutshell, the theory is that breach of promise (usually) causes reliance losses, that the wrong inflicted on the promisee just is the infliction of these losses, and that therefore corrective justice requires their compensation, which is what contract law aims to ensure. In justification of this account, one could put forward the moral view that any induced reliance is the responsibility of the inducer, independent of promise. If Bruce induces Alice to buy an airplane ticket to Australia by saying in public that he is on his way there, Bruce is responsible for Alice's loss if he fails to go. But it's pretty clear, I think, that this is an unacceptable moral view—our responsibility for losses others incur in reliance on their expectations about what we will do cannot possibly be as extensive as this.[42] There are legal doctrines, such as the recently forged Australian doctrine of "equitable estoppel" which recognizes a (very limited) cause of action for reliance damages in the absence of promise, and some have defended this doctrine by appeal to an entirely general principle of responsibility for induced reliance.[43] But if ever a flood-gates objection were appropriate in legal argument, it would be here. (The Australian doctrine stops the flood by including unconscionability as a condition of recovery.[44])

The way reliance theorists of contract typically limit the scope of compensatory responsibility is by insisting that it is only reliance on promises that counts. Not all reliance is the responsibility of the inducer of it, only that induced by promise. But this, presumably, can only be because the promisor ought to keep his promise.[45] And if that is right, it is hard to see why the responsibility of the promisor is limited to reliance losses—if the promise is the ground of the responsibility in the first

[42] *See* Murphy, The Practice of Promise.

[43] *See* Michael Spence, Protecting Reliance (1999).

[44] *See Waltons Stores (Interstate) Ltd. v Maher* (1988) 164 C.L.R. 387, 62 A.L.J. 110 (Austl.)

[45] Fried, Contract as Promise, at 10–11, 20, makes all the important points about reliance theories with great clarity.

place, why is the promisor not responsible for the promisee's expectation losses? So the problem with the reliance theory is not just that it implies a remedy, reliance damages, that is nowhere awarded for breach of contract (the U.S. doctrine of promissory estoppel providing only a partial exception), though that is very important; the problem is rather that the very idea that promises (alone) generate responsibility for reliance losses makes little sense.

Patrick Atiyah attempted to avoid this problem by taking a formal view of the role of promise in contract.[46] Atiyah recognized that not all induced reliance could be the responsibility of the inducer of it; on his view, responsibility is limited to cases of reasonable reliance. And the relevance of a promise, on his account, is not that the moral force of the promise itself generates responsibility for reliance, but rather that to make a promise is to "admit" that reliance is reasonable. But a promise doesn't at all seem like an admission. And even if it were, admitting one is responsible doesn't make it so. Generally, one's responsibility is not determined by what one declares one is responsible for.

VI. Instrumental Contract Theory

If contract law is not grounded in the idea that the moral obligation to keep promises should be enforced by law, or that the law should protect and compensate for the violation of the rights of promisees, we are left, by process of elimination, with instrumental accounts. Contract law does not have as its main justification some goal of policing the moral significance of the relationship between promisors and promisees, but rather one of promoting, protecting, and policing the social practice of making and keeping agreements and promises.

The most popular instrumental theory is that of the economic analysis of law. Many articles on contract theory contrast the economic approach with that of the philosophers. That is seriously misleading, since the economic approach needs to be just as philosophical as any other if it is to provide a justificatory or critical account of contract law. Defense of the economic approach requires an argument of relative plausibility: Do we have more reason to embrace this particular instrumental contract theory as opposed to some other, or some noninstrumental account? The answer to this question cannot be determined by declaring disciplinary affiliation.

I agree with economic analysts that the best contract theory will not try to track the moral duties and interests of parties to particular agreements but will rather take a broader view, finding the point of the institution in the overall social good it produces. What is wrong with the traditional economic approach is its impoverished criterion of the social good—that of economic efficiency. Economic contract theory is a very strong theory, in the sense that it tries to justify a lot with extremely little; on the face it, it would be surprising if the resulting account were adequate.

This is not the place to review the deficiencies of economic efficiency as a social aim. There are reasons why economists abandoned a more plausible version of welfarism

[46] *See* Patrick Atiyah, Promise, Morals, and Law 177–215 (1983).

that allowed for comparisons among people's absolute levels of welfare and thus also distributive information—reasons having to do with misguided worries about the "meaningfulness" of interpersonal comparisons of welfare and excessive appreciation for the theorems of welfare economics.[47] But suffice it to say that the instrumental approach to contract theory I embrace does not limit itself to economic efficiency as the proper aim. The aim of contract law, on any instrumental theory, is to make things go better. In my view the proper aim is plural, comprising total or average welfare and its distribution along with nonwelfarist aspects of social justice such as equality of social status, as well, perhaps, as the prevention of the unfairness that results from free-riding on a fair practice.[48]

Economic analysis of law makes its invaluable contribution to instrumental contract theory not by postulating an impoverished account of the social good, but in offering the only sustained attempt at explaining how legal rules affect behavior.[49] Any instrumental theory of any area of law requires a theory of how law achieves good things. The only way changing law can make things better is by inducing people to act in ways that make things better; so any instrumental theory of contract law requires a theory of behavior. Only economic theory has attempted to explain just how legal rules affect people's decisions about how to act. It is here also that contemporary economic analysis is making the most progress in recent years, moving beyond the implausible assumption that people always react to legal rules as prices affecting their rational calculations of self-interest. Behavioral law and economics attempts to take into account the rather obvious fact that we are not always fully rational.[50] And very recently Rebecca Stone has made the crucial step of acknowledging the equally obvious fact that people don't always simply react to legal rules as prices. Stone offers us a theory of how to model behavior of those who accept legal rules, in H. L. A. Hart's sense of treating them (for some reason or other) as providing standing reasons for action.[51]

Any instrumental contract theory must draw heavily on the contributions of the economic analysis of contract law as many of its results are easily generalizable to instrumental accounts generally. But on one topic—the foundational topic of remedies for breach—the influential idea of efficient breach has led many astray. The points I will make about efficient breach are not especially novel, but it is worth rehearsing them to highlight the danger of myopia in instrumental legal theory—by which I mean a tendency to apply the analysis retail, forgetting that it is always the entire scheme that requires justification.

[47] *See* AMARTYA SEN, ON ECONOMIC INEQUALITY, 1–23 (2d ed., 1997).

[48] From the point of view of individual morality, a deontological duty not to free-ride on a fair practice may have great weight for a participant in the practice. But from the point of view of third parties and the law, the importance of preventing the unfairness that results from free-riding may be insignificant compared to the beneficial effects of the practice itself. A full account of the social goods contract law should be aiming at, including their relative weights, is beyond the scope of this chapter.

[49] *See* Lewis A. Kornhauser, *An Introduction to the Economic Analysis of Contract Remedies*, 57 U. COLO. L. REV. 683 (1986).

[50] For a state of the art study, *see* OREN BAR-GILL, SEDUCTION BY CONTRACT (2012).

[51] Rebecca Stone, Economic Analysis of Contract Law from the Internal Point of View (2013) (unpublished manuscript, on file with author).

VII. Instrumental Remedies

There are two rather different ways of conceptualizing the issue of the choice of contract remedies. We could, first, see the remedy as supplied by the law in just the way tort remedies are: this is what you get if the other side breaches. Call this the fixed remedy approach. The alternative is to regard the enforcement of agreements—specific performance—as the inescapable background remedy. We then allow that parties have the option to choose *ex ante*, within limits, a noninjunctive remedy, or the *ex post* option of one, as a term of their contract. Call this the model of remedies by agreement. (Though that is potentially misleading in that the model of course builds on the fixed remedy that the agreement will be enforced as written. The idea that the remedy for breach is or should be entirely up to the parties—all the way down, as it were—is incoherent.[52]) The two models can overlap. Suppose it is said that the fixed remedy supplied by law is expectation damages. We could also present this in terms of the model of remedies by agreement by saying that expectation damages is a mandatory term of all agreements.

On the whole, since contract law in most places allows some control over remedies by the parties, the model of remedies by agreement allows for more clarity. Recent economic analysis of contract remedies tends to employ this model.

There is a potential problem, however, with the remedies by agreement model, which is that it might be thought to countenance unjustified interference with the judicial role. Parties might agree to punitive damages but, it could be said, courts cannot simply be required to honor that agreement. But it is implausible to think that any agreement on remedies is an infringement on the proper authority of the courts. When the U.S. government enters into procurement contracts, it generally insists on a "termination for convenience" term that stipulates that the government can cancel at any time, incurring liability for reliance losses only.[53] There is nothing objectionable about the courts honoring such a term. The concern about judicial authority is better expressed this way: the law can always legitimately set limits to what terms (remedial or otherwise) it will enforce.

Now the termination for convenience clause found in government contracts might be understood not as an agreement about the remedy for breach, but as a promise in the alternative: the government will either perform or cover its contract partner's out of pocket expenses. Perhaps. But not all limitations on damages can be seen that way—thus for example the very common exclusion of consequential damages is clearly an agreed limitation on the remedy available in the event of breach.

Using the model of remedies by agreement, what remedy does the economic analysis of contract law recommend? It was once thought that since expectation damages gave efficient incentives for the decision whether to perform or breach, economic analysis supports the common law's mandatory remedy of expectation damages. (More fully, the mandatory remedy is expectation damages or less, as the parties might agree *ex ante*, with injunctive relief potentially available at the discretion of the court where

[52] *See* T. M. Scanlon, *Promises and Contracts, in* The Theory of Contract Law 86, 107 (Peter Benson ed., 2001).

[53] For discussion, *see* Hadfield, *Of Sovereignty and Contract.*

money damages are clearly inadequate.) But it was quickly pointed out that the decision whether to perform or breach was just one decision contract parties or potential parties had to make; others include how much to spend in reliance on the other party's performance, with whom to contract, whether to enter a contract at all, and so on. Work has been done on what might be the efficient remedy in respect of the incentives provided for these other decisions. It seems clear that it will be impossible to come up with an answer to the question of what remedy is efficient, all relevant decisions considered. But the main point to make about the economic theory of contract remedies is not that it is indeterminate, but rather that, as Craswell has so clearly explained, there is no reason to expect that the efficient remedy will line up with one of those standardly discussed by contract theorists.[54] In particular, there is no reason to think economic analysis would be able to justify the performance or expectation damages remedies provided for breach of contract everywhere. For all we know, Craswell writes, the most efficient remedy, all things considered, might be 66 percent of expectation damages.

Be that as it may, there is a fundamental and important problem in the textbook presentation of the argument that expectation damages is efficient with respect to the decision whether to perform or breach.

The textbook argument that expectation damages provide the right incentives for the decision whether to perform or breach is familiar. The right incentive is one where a party will be moved to breach just in case breach leaves at least one person better off and no person worse off than performance would; that will be a Pareto improvement. Under the common law, this is exactly the incentive parties have, since they will be moved to breach just in case this will leave them better off even after paying damages that aim precisely to leave the promisee no worse off than performance.

Now there is considerable discussion about whether specific performance would do just as well as expectation damages, since the original promisee may be able to deal with a higher-valuing third party, and even if not, the two original parties may be able to reach a deal that will release the original promisor. Everything turns on what we believe about the ability of courts accurately to determine expectation damages, relative to the outcome of the parties' bargain over release from an injunction, and the relative costs of these two processes.[55] But my issue with traditional efficient breach analysis is different. It is that there is no reason why the interests of the original promisee should be singled out as especially important.

Under either the Pareto or Kaldor–Hicks criteria of efficiency, an efficient breach is one that yields enough surplus to the promisor that would enable him to fully compensate the promisee for his lost expectancy. But the question is this: Why should the promisee's expectancy as measured against a baseline of the contract be of any significance at all? Here we find another respect in which Fuller and Perdue got it right. Leaving aside hurt feelings, or any kind of psychic harm of disappointment, denying

[54] *See* Craswell, *Contract Law, Default Rules, and the Philosophy of Promising* and *Against Fuller and Perdue*; Richard Craswell, *Two Economic Theories of Enforcing Promises, in* The Theory of Contract Law 19 (Peter Benson ed., 2001).

[55] *See* Alan Schwartz, *The Case for Specific Performance*, 89 Yale L.J. 271 (1979).

a promisee his expectation interest is not to make him worse off. Denial of the expectancy makes a promisee worse off relative to a baseline of performance of the contract. But that baseline cannot simply be taken for granted; it is a product of the very system of contract law that we are trying to justify. We cannot help ourselves to the idea that the promisee has an entitlement to performance when trying to give an instrumental justification for contract remedies.

There are two aspects to the objection I am raising: Why the promisee's interests only? And why measure these against the baseline of the contract? When making her decision about breach versus performance, the promisor is supposed to be concerned that the promisee can be made indifferent between performance or breach. But what about anyone else who might be interested in the subject matter of the contract? The promisor could give the goods away to a bystander; that bystander prefers breach and gift to him to performance, so why does that not figure in the calculation? And when thinking about the promisee's preferences, why is the contract price assumed to be the right baseline? Suppose the promisee values the good at $10, but the contract price is $2; we say he needs a full $8 before he is indifferent between performance and breach. But the baseline of the contract price has significance only on the assumption that the promisee is already in some way entitled to performance of the contract.

The story of efficient breach takes the structure of contract law for granted, and helps itself to the idea that a promisee is entitled to his expectancy, since that, after all, is how we all see it.[56] But we only see it that way because we take for granted that enforcement of contracts is a good idea. Considered as a stand-alone defense of expectation damages, the standard theory of efficient breach is entirely question begging.

An analogy can be drawn here to standard discussions of tax justice in public finance economics. In those discussions, it is said that tax fairness consists in criteria of vertical and horizontal equity in the burdens of taxation, where those burdens are measured against a baseline of pretax income. To use that baseline is myopic because taxation is only one part of the whole set of economic and legal institutions that structure a market economy. We cannot treat pretax income as if it were in some sense an entitlement within the system, against which tax burdens can properly be assessed, since pretax incomes are affected by legal rules, including rules of taxation.[57]

The fundamental insight of Fuller and Perdue was that an account of the significance of the expectation interest is required, since lost expectancy is not, as it were, a natural loss; it is a theoretically constructed loss. Treating it as a loss requires justification for the entire system of contract law or else some account of the moral rights of promisees. It is therefore a mistake to argue for a particular remedy—a foundational element of the overall system—by simply assuming that it is a loss. It is a loss from the perspective of a system of contract rules of which the rule governing remedies is a central part. If we are going to justify expectation damages, we have to lift our eyes from particular transactions, and argue that it finds its place in an overall scheme of contract law that produces the best results.

[56] *See* Melvin Eisenberg, The Foundational Principles of Contract Law (2013) (unpublished manuscript, on file with author).

[57] *See* Liam Murphy & Thomas Nagel, The Myth of Ownership (2002).

If we do lift our eyes, it is obvious that the most important reason to protect promisees' performance or expectation interests is to give people reason to enter into mutually beneficial agreements that otherwise, for want of confidence in performance, would not be entered into. I thus agree with economic analysts Schwartz and Scott, who write:

> Contract remedies are thought to protect injured promisees . . . by awarding the expectation interest. This view is true but shallow. If contracts were not enforceable, sophisticated commercial parties seldom would put themselves in positions where they needed the law's aid. . . . Enforcement . . . in sum, permits parties to make believable promises to each other when reputational or self-enforcement sanctions will not avail.[58]

Now, the textbook account of why expectation damages give efficient incentives over the decision whether to perform is not the only argument that economic analysis offers for expectation damages. The alternative approach adopts the remedies by agreement model. The fundamental idea is that, within limits, it makes sense to enforce whatever rational parties do or would agree to by way of remedies for breach. So we should not think of contract remedies as *compensatory* of a harm we can independently make sense of. What we are doing is enforcing agreements.[59] Of course, there are limits. Two days in the stocks as a penalty for breach is presumably out, and perhaps penalty liquidated-damages clauses should not be enforceable in consumer contracts.

An argument can be made that rational contracting parties will elect expectation damages rather than specific performance in the standard case, since the additional costs to a breaching promisor of bargaining her way out of an injunction will lead her to demand a higher price, *ex ante*.[60] If that is so (and much could be said about the assumptions this argument requires), then we have a case for expectation damages as a default rule, since that would save rational parties the trouble of writing down what they want. (Such an argument cannot justify the common law rule, however, since if in a particular case the parties prefer specific performance *ex ante*, the common law will not necessarily enforce that preference.)

It would be good to have some evidence that in legal systems where specific performance is the background remedy but parties can choose damages *ex ante* as a term of their contract and have that choice honored by the courts—Germany, for example—sophisticated parties do choose damages in order to lower the price. I have not been able to find any such evidence, even anecdotal. Be that as it may, there is a more general concern about an approach that puts all the weight on what rational contracting parties do or would have agreed to.

[58] Alan Schwartz & Robert E. Scott, *Contract Theory and the Limits of Contract Law*, 113 Yale L.J., 541, 562 (2003).

[59] *See* Robert E. Scott & George G. Triantis, *Embedded Options and the Case against Compensation in Contract Law*, 104 Colum. L. Rev. 1428 (2004).

[60] *See* Steven Shavell, *Damage Measures for Breach of Contract*, 11 Bell J. Econ. 466 (1980). For a recent statement of this argument, *see* Daniel Markovits & Alan Schwartz, *The Myth of Efficient Breach: New Defenses of the Expectation Interest*, 97 Va. L. Rev. 1939 (2011), though Markovits and Schwartz further argue that the rationality of choosing expectation damages *ex ante* justifies interpreting the content of the agreement as perform or pay.

Once again, the approach is myopic. Why would the appropriate rule be the one that particular parties might choose, rather than the one that does best overall, for society at large? Most commentators simply take for granted that these are equivalent. Steven Shavell, the pioneer of this approach, does not. But he writes that the "utility of damage measures to contracting parties themselves is no doubt a and perhaps *the* major aspect in which the social advantage of damage measures inheres."[61] This seems plausible but, mostly, I believe, because we take for granted the ongoing stability of the system of private ordering without which we cannot even make sense of what two parties to a contract might rationally agree to.

There is no guarantee that what is best for each contracting pair is best for all of us. Suppose expectation damages are best for each contracting party. Suppose further that parties cannot simultaneously hold in their minds the knowledge that if they breach they are legally liable for expectation damages only and the thought that it is a norm, a requirement of the social practice they are engaged in, that they perform their agreements. No harm is done to anything if one contracting pair start to believe that performance is optional, so long as the legally required compensation is paid. But if everyone believes that, then things have gone badly awry.

Now in fact unless the unfortunate idea of efficient breach is in the air, there is no reason why contracting parties cannot regard themselves as obliged to perform while fully aware that if they do not perform, all that will happen to them is that they will have to pay damages which may be less than the gains from breach. This is the situation, for example, of participants in the American cotton industry as described by Lisa Bernstein, where the damages awards provided by the private arbitral tribunals are undercompensatory, but the norm of performance remains extremely strong.[62] The important point here is that this is the level at which instrumental analysis must focus: the level of generally accepted norms and overall social practice.

VIII. Contract and Promise

Against the textbook efficient breach analysis, I have said that an evaluation of contract remedies cannot assume that promisees are entitled to their expectation when discussing whether that is what they should get. It is only once we have concluded that promisees are entitled to their expectancy that it makes sense to regard denying it as a harm to them. Against economic arguments for expectation or other damage measures that turn on what rational parties would agree to, I have argued that this analytic framework risks losing sight of the normative significance of the social and legal practice within which it makes sense to discuss what rational pairs might choose. The first order of business, when thinking about remedies, and rationales for them, is the health of that background practice.

The most obvious way to support the practice of making and keeping agreements is to enforce them—by ordering performance or something just as good. Absent special

[61] Shavell, *Damage Measures for Breach of Contract*, at 489.

[62] Lisa Bernstein, *Private Commercial Law in the Cotton Industry: Creating Cooperation through Rules, Norms, and Institutions*, 99 Mich. L. Rev. 1724 (1991).

circumstances such as a close-knit commercial community where nonlegal sanctions are especially effective, any remedy short of performance or expectation damages seems very likely to lead to fewer agreements being made. This, of course, is not something the economist need disagree with. It seems unlikely that the choice between performance or expectation damages would have any effect on the background practice one way or another. But it does seem likely that general recognition of the idea of a good—because socially beneficial—breach would do so. Here disagreement is reached.

The simplest way to state the point of contract law is that it supports and shapes the social practice of making and keeping promises and agreements.[63] And within that social practice, the expectation is that when people make agreements, they should keep them. My claim is that while departures from a performance remedy may do no harm, a publicly accepted justification of a such a legal regime according to which breach is often the right thing to do from a social point of view will tend to undermine the practice of promise and contract.

My argument resembles that of Seana Shiffrin, especially in its reference to the effects of certain understandings of the justification of legal rights and obligations on the political and legal culture.[64] But Shriffin's concern lies with the effects of departures in contract law from the morality of promise on moral agency. I see promissory morality as itself largely of instrumental significance, to be promoted because of its overall good social effects, and my claim is that departures from the conventions of the practice of promise within contract law will tend to undermine the former, and thus also the point of the latter—which is to strengthen, not weaken, the socially beneficial practice of making and keeping agreements.

The mere fact that the common law remedy is not a performance remedy is not itself, in my view, a departure from the practice of promise. After all, in our ordinary ethical lives, we do not have an account of *remedies* at all. If you make a promise you should keep it.[65] What if you don't? Here there is no clear answer. Certainly there is no clear practice of providing compensatory damages. What we expect in the moral domain is performance, and it is hard to see how this practice could be made more sophisticated.

This point immediately brings to mind an objection, however. Let's forget about informal promises, or noncommercial promises that might be legally enforceable. Let's restrict contract theory to commercial transactions between medium-sized sophisticated firms.[66] Such actors need not confuse contract law with any moral practice; they are quite capable of distinguishing the two domains. Even if in a broad sense both the legal and nonlegal practices aim to bring about some good through facilitating beneficial cooperative arrangements, there is no reason why they should take exactly the same form. For such parties, who may insist on performance when the promisor is

[63] *See* Raz, *Promises in Morality and Law*, at 933.

[64] *See* Seana Valentine Shiffrin, *The Divergence of Contract and Promise*, 120 Harv. L. Rev. 708 (2007).

[65] Within limits, of course. Even in the absence of excusing conditions such as duress, misrepresentation, mistake, and impracticability, the informal practice does not always demand performance where that would involve, for example, enormous expense to correct a minor mistake. Most legal systems reflect this common-sense view.

[66] *See* Schwartz & Scott, *Contract Theory and the Limits of Contract Law.*

their friend, there may be no harm done to the moral practice if they believe that it is all right to breach commercial agreements so long as damages are paid. For that matter, damages of 66 percent of the promisee's expectancy may be enough to encourage them to deal with others in the first place.

It cannot be denied that this is a possibility. My main reaction to it is that there is ample evidence that sophisticated commercial parties expect performance from their promisors. Economists rightly emphasize the role of reputational factors, even among sophisticated parties. If harm is done to your reputation when you breach an agreement, that simply shows that what is expected is performance. Hugh Collins's discussion of these issues is especially illuminating.[67] Collins's account closely resembles that of Hume, according to which legal sanctions are a back-up system of enforcement, to ground confidence when informal sanctions turning on reputation would not be sufficient to generate confidence in performance.[68] For Hume, the need for coercive enforcement by the state only arises when societies become big enough to make it plausibly rational not to perform your side of an agreement. But the role of nonlegal sanctions doesn't disappear once government appears on the scene to enforce agreements. The two systems of enforcement work together in tandem. The "construction of markets," to use Collins's phrase, is a social process that take place both outside of law and within it.

Now none of this so much as proves that it would not be better for contract law to break free from nonlegal expectations regarding decent commercial behavior. Perhaps it could be done, but the result would be a very different social world, and there is no reason to think it would be a better one. Absent a compelling reason to make this drastic change, it is overwhelmingly plausible to insist that in our thinking about what the best legal remedy would be, and what the proper public justification for that remedy would be—both by legal theorists and judges—we should count as a serious cost any tendency to undermine the banal but beneficial disposition to regard breach of contract as bad practice.

[67] Hugh Collins, Regulating Contracts 97–126 (1999).
[68] Hume, A Treatise of Human Nature.

10

Economic Foundations of Contract Law

*Avery W. Katz**

Since at least the time of Lord Mansfield, it has been commonplace to view the law of contracts as an important tool for facilitating and regulating economic activity. But in order fully to understand this basic function, it is not possible to treat the law as an autonomous system. Rather, one must understand the substance of the human activity that contract law aims to govern, and the meaning of the communications that arise out of that activity. The economic approach to contract proposes to use the tools and methods of economics as the means toward such understanding.

This chapter discusses the role of economic analysis in explaining, justifying, and critiquing the law of contracts and its effects on private exchange. It discusses both positive issues (e.g., what motivates the practices regulated by contract law; what effect does law have on contracting behavior) and normative ones (e.g., is the law properly designed in light of such effects; to what extent should interpretation of legal rules and the design of legal institutions be based on economic as opposed to noneconomic considerations). Finally, it will discuss whether an economic approach to contract law can be squared with other paradigms, and to the extent it cannot, how such inconsistency might be dealt with.

The first section of the chapter deals with some basic methodological issues inherent to the economic approach to law that must be addressed up front; while the second section discusses jurisprudential issues that arise when applying that approach to contract law in particular. Section III then illustrates the approach with reference to a standard set of doctrinal issues within the law of contract. With the basic outlines of the approach thus set forth, Section IV compares it to accounts of contract law based on consent, deontological morality, corrective justice, and virtue ethics. Finally, Section V offers a pragmatic assessment of the economic approach to contracts, with primary emphasis on how it might be used by lawyers and legal officials in the performance of their professional duties.

I. Basic Methodological Issues in the Economic Approach to Law

A. Positive versus normative economics

As an initial matter, it is useful to discuss some methodological issues relating to economic analysis generally. The first of these is how modern neoclassical economics addresses questions of value.

* This chapter was initially prepared for presentation at the Bentham House Annual Conference on The Philosophical Foundations of Contract Law, held at University College London, May 10–11, 2013. I am grateful

In modern economics, it is conventional to distinguish between two modes of analysis: positive economics and normative economics. Positive economics focuses on explaining and predicting economic behavior: for example, how do farmers determine which crops to produce given the relative cost of productive inputs, the uncertainties of weather, and their desires for diversification; or how will the quantity of crops brought to market be affected by a change in the price of fertilizer, the imposition of an excise tax on trucking, or the unionization of farm workers. Normative economics, in contrast, focuses on evaluative and prescriptive matters: for instance, whether agricultural price supports should be maintained at their current level, given the costs to consumers and taxpayers and the economic benefits to farmers, along with their possible role in protecting traditional rural culture against the incursions of a globalizing market.

The distinction between positive and normative economics has roots in moral philosophy and epistemology going back at least to Hume's distinction between is and ought.[1] The substantial history of contestation of the fact/value distinction within philosophy and in other disciplines, however, has largely escaped the attention of most professional economists. Of course, most economists accept that these two perspectives cannot be entirely untangled: to evaluate the desirability of a proposed policy change, one must have some way of predicting how people are likely to react to it; conversely, to predict economic actors' behavior, it is necessary to have some appreciation of their goals and purposes. If pressed, many economists would further concede that their own personal choices of which phenomena to study are influenced by their normative priorities and commitments. Nonetheless, the discipline has for the most part drawn the distinction sharply. The reasons are largely pragmatic ones; methodological positivism has proved a useful strategy in putting aside economists' political disagreements so that they can focus their efforts on shared goals of analytical and empirical progress.[2]

The jurisprudential scholars for whom this volume is primarily intended may find it natural to view the distinction between positive and normative economics through the lens of their own long-standing debates over legal positivism, which in Anglo-American circles are most notably exemplified by the Hart–Fuller exchange.[3] Such an interpretation is likely helpful, but it is important to recognize that most economists (and most academic practitioners of law and economics) come down very decidedly on Hart's side of the controversy. Much of the controversy over the academic law and economics movement arises from that very fact.[4]

to the organizers and participants in the conference, and to students and colleagues at Columbia, Georgetown, and Michigan law schools, for helping me work out my thoughts regarding these issues over the years.

[1] See Mark Blaug, The Methodology of Economics: Or How Economists Explain 112–34 (1980).

[2] Though some would claim that obscuring (and thus shielding from critique) the profession's normative commitments are equally important motivations. *See, e.g.*, Duncan Kennedy, *Distributive and Paternalist Motives in Contract and Tort Law, with Special Reference to Compulsory Terms and Unequal Bargaining Power*, 41 Md. L. Rev. 563, 603–4 (1982).

[3] Lon Fuller, *Positivism and Fidelity to Law—A Response to Professor Hart*, 71 Harv. L. Rev. 630 (1958); H. L. A. Hart, *Positivism and the Separation of Law and Morals*, 71 Harv. L. Rev. 593 (1958).

[4] *See generally* Avery Katz, *Positivism and the Separation of Law and Economics*, 94 Mich. L. Rev. 2229 (1996).

B. Theory of constrained optimization

In addition to taking a distinctive position on the relationship between positive and normative analysis, most positive economic analysis continues to be based on a specific and distinctive account of human behavior: that of constrained optimization. This theory posits that economic actors are best described as pursuing a consistent set of goals as fully as possible within the constraints of time, money, attention, and other relevant resources. The paradigmatic example of such an actor is a consumer choosing expenditures limited by the constraint of a fixed budget. Elucidation of the theory in this example yields the standard predictions of microeconomics, including the fundamental law of demand, which posits that an increase in an item's price, other things being equal, results in a decline in consumer demand for the item.

The theory of constrained optimization (sometimes referred to by the ambitious title of "rational choice theory") does not require that the actor only be interested in material benefit; nor does it require that she have access to all relevant information or calculate without error, or that her goals be determined in isolation from the influence of others. It only presumes that she has a coherent and well-defined set of goals, together with preferences for choosing among goals in the event they come into conflict. What the theory does require, however, is that the actor's preferences remain stable over the period of observation and prediction, and most importantly, that such preferences are determined independently of the constraints that limit them. Preferences that are formed in adaptation to the relevant constraints (or for that matter, out of resentment to and rebellion against them) are ruled out of the model.

Not even the most narrow-minded economist believes that the model of constrained maximization provides a perfectly accurate description of human behavior in markets or in law. But, to the extent that legal actors do have coherent wishes of their own and react to legal rules and institutions as if they were constraints (in the manner of Holmes's "bad man"[5]), the insights and predictions of economics can be used to generate analogous insights and predictions in legal settings.

C. Economic efficiency

Just as the economic approach brings a distinctive positive perspective to legal analysis, it also brings a distinctive normative perspective. Economists use efficiency as their principal normative criterion, and by "efficiency" they mean something different than laypeople do when they use the term. Specifically, economic efficiency is a term of art that follows the definitions of Pareto, Kaldor, and Hicks, who identified an allocation of resources as efficient if and only if there is no way to rearrange resources

[5] Oliver Wendell Holmes, Jr., *The Path of the Law*, 10 HARV. L. REV. 457, 462 (1897). ("The duty to keep a contract at common law means a prediction that you must pay damages if you do not keep it—and nothing else. If you commit a tort, you are liable to pay a compensatory sum. If you commit a contract, you are liable to pay a compensatory sum unless the promised event comes to pass, and that is all the difference. But such a mode of looking at the matter stinks in the nostrils of those who think it advantageous to get as much ethics into the law as they can.")

among the actors in a way that makes at least one of them better off while making none worse off. To illustrate, suppose that by breaching a contract to deliver goods a seller will cause the buyer to suffer a monetary loss of $1,000, but at the same time will reap a personal benefit of $2,000. In this case an economist would say (putting aside considerations external to the two contracting parties) that continuing with the contract as originally planned would be inefficient, because it is possible to design an outcome that leaves at least one of the parties better off while holding the other harmless. (For instance, the seller could pay the buyer $1,500 in exchange for rescission.[6]) In contrast, the outcome where the buyer receives $1,500 in compensation for nonperformance is efficient, in that it would be possible to improve the buyer's position by providing for a larger sum in compensation, but only at the cost of worsening the seller's position.

Note, however, that it is also efficient for the seller to cancel performance and to pay $1,000 of compensation, just as it would be for the seller to cancel and pay no compensation at all. Once the decision not to perform has been made and the efficiency gains pocketed, how the gains are divided between the parties is a matter of distributional equity, not efficiency. And on matters of distributional equity, economists qua economists have nothing to say; or at least that is the conventional position of neoclassical welfare economics (that is, the branch of economics devoted to measuring gains and losses as opposed to prices and quantities).

The economist's technical definition of efficiency must be contrasted with the common meaning of the term in ordinary discourse, where it typically connotes the effective pursuit of any instrumental goal. On this colloquial usage, an unscrupulous businessman might assert that it is efficient to dump industrial waste in a public waterway, because it is personally cheaper for him to do this than it would be to pay the costs of ecologically secure disposal. Such usage conflicts with what economists mean by efficiency, however, because it excludes the very real costs suffered by neighboring landowners and other users of the polluted water. The economist's view would be that dumping industrial waste could sometimes be efficient, but only if it is the cheapest alternative considering the interests of all parties put together. If the costs of ecologically secure disposal (or of abstaining from the activity that generates the industrial waste) are greater than the social costs of pollution, only then would pollution be the economically efficient alternative.

The economist's definition of efficiency does share one important feature with the unscrupulous businessman's, however: both are instrumental concepts as opposed to substantive ones. Efficiency does not tell us whether we should wish to pursue material gain, private profit, protection of the environment, social justice, or any other substantive goal. It merely tells us how best to pursue the goals we have, or more precisely, how to pursue them in such a way that performs best on a cost–benefit test. When efficiency and distributional equity come into conflict (for instance, if a program of redistributional taxation were to lead to a reduction in work effort or capital investment,

[6] Whether this outcome is appropriately achieved by having the seller breach the contract and pay $1,000 in expectation damages is discussed at greater length in Greg Klass's chapter in this volume. *See* Gregory Klass, *Efficient Breach, in* Philosophical Foundations of Contract Law (Gregory Klass, George Letsas & Prince Saprai eds., 2014).

thus reducing the total societal product to be shared), some other normative criterion will be needed to choose among them. Economists do not propose to offer such a criterion, though they sometime have proposed ways to determine whether a given proposed criterion is internally consistent.[7]

II. Application to Contract Law in Particular

The economic approach to law has been controversial ever since its intellectual rise in the 1960s and 1970s. One reason for this controversy is that law and economics, like legal realism and other social science-based approaches to law, asserts that law is not an autonomous discipline. As a result, jurisprudential traditionalists concerned to maintain the irreducibility of legal reasoning to other more general forms of analysis will naturally want to resist this assertion.[8] But it is also the case that scholars who have made their peace with basic claims of legal realism, or who have accepted the application of sociological and political ideas to legal analysis, often continue to object to the economic approach to law. Such objections can in large part be understood as arising from the particular methodological features outlined in Section I. This is because those features often stand in tension (or are seen to stand in tension) with the values and assumptions of traditional jurisprudence.

Such tensions arise along both positive and normative dimensions. On the positive side, the standard economic assumption that human goals are determined independently of external constraint stands in obvious contrast with the law's important role in reinforcing social solidarity and the internalization of ethics. Similarly, a descriptive strategy that depends on a model in which people relentlessly pursue a set of fixed and coherent goals fails to match up with many of the empirical behaviors that law seeks to regulate.

On the normative side, conversely, economics' inattention to matters of distributional and corrective justice renders it at best an incomplete guide for officials and scholars who seek to promote equity and the rule of law. A theory that purports to demonstrate that a tortfeasor and his victim are equally responsible for the negative consequences of their interactions (as in Coase's classic analysis of social cost[9]) or that professes indifference to whether a promisor performs her contractual obligations, so long as the outcome passes a cost–benefit test (as in the literature on efficient breach[10]) will be ruled out by many traditional jurisprudes from the start.

In the field of contract law, however, such objections are substantially diminished. Putting specialized categories such as consumer and employment contracts to the side, much of contract law has been developed with the goal of facilitating exchange between business firms or commercial professionals.

[7] *See generally* Arthur Okun, Equality and Efficiency: The Big Tradeoff (1975); Steven Shavell & Louis Kaplow, Fairness versus Welfare (2002).

[8] *See* Richard A. Posner, *The Decline of Law as an Autonomous Discipline: 1962–1987*, 100 Harv. L. Rev. 761 (1987).

[9] Ronald Coase, *The Problem of Social Cost*, 3 J.L. & Econ. 1 (1960).

[10] *See, e.g.*, Richard Posner, Economic Analysis of Law 55–9 (1973); Robert L. Birmingham, *Breach of Contract, Damage Measures, and Economic Efficiency*, 24 Rutgers L. Rev. 273 (1970); Charles J. Goetz & Robert E. Scott, *Liquidated Damages, Penalties and the Just Compensation Principle: Some Notes on an Enforcement Model and a Theory of Efficient Breach*, 77 Colum. L. Rev. 554 (1977).

In commerce, it is easier to value things in monetary terms and to calculate costs and benefits; and economic gain is usually the motivation for the transaction. In addition, contractual obligations are typically undertaken deliberately, at arms' length, and with managerial oversight if not professional legal assistance. The economic model of rational choice provides a more plausible descriptive account in such settings than it does when applied to less calculating actors such as negligent tortfeasors, divorcing spouses, criminals, or residential tenants. From a normative perspective, furthermore, it is easier to justify applying the efficiency norm to commercial agreements than to the typical tort case involving persons drawn together involuntarily and outside of market institutions. This is not just because one can plausibly claim that the contracting parties have consented to have their affairs be governed by economic criteria. Various features of the commercial setting also make it more likely that efficiency gains will be shared, rather than being appropriated by one of the parties. The main reason for this likelihood is that contracts are largely based on voluntary exchange; and self-interested actors do not knowingly enter into voluntary exchange unless the expected benefits of the exchange are greater than those of the available alternatives.

Specifically, changes in legal rules or contract terms that benefit one side of the transaction at the expense of the other (for example, providing an implied warranty in a sale of goods), will increase the amount the benefited party is willing to pay to enter into the deal, as well as the exchange value that the burdened party will insist on receiving. Because the agreed price must necessarily fall somewhere between the buyer's and seller's reservation prices for trade, a legal rule that alters reservation prices will tend to move the exchange price in the same direction.[11] In the involuntary setting, in contrast, a rule change that alters the relative rights of exchange will typically result in a material redistribution as well.[12]

For these reasons, an efficient change in applicable legal rules (or modification of contract terms) will tend to increase the returns of both parties to the exchange. But even when this is not the case in every transaction—for example, if the rule change is minor enough that it is not worth redrafting existing standard forms or spending the additional time dickering over the issue, or if the price is rigidly determined by convention or law, as with real estate commissions and contingent fees for plaintiff's attorneys in the U.S.—both parties may well gain over the

[11] *See* Richard Craswell, *Passing on the Costs of Legal Rules: Efficiency and Distribution in Buyer–Seller Relationships*, 43 Stan. L. Rev. 361 (1991). The exception would be where one or both parties lacks good market alternatives to the transaction, so that the bargaining range between seller's and buyer's reservation prices is large, and when the change in legal rule also affects the parties' relative bargaining power. Accordingly, a rule change that limits or enhances the parties' ability to shop around for alternatives, or that prescribes who must make the first or the last offer, may well have distributional consequences that outweigh the efficiency gains for the disadvantaged party.

[12] This is so notwithstanding the potential for contractual interactions of the sort discussed by Coase, *The Problem of Social Cost*. While Coasian bargaining can redress inefficiencies by allowing injured parties to bribe their injurers into better behavior, it cannot redress distributional outcomes. Whether farmer pays rancher or rancher pays farmer may not make a difference in terms of whether we reach the optimal tradeoff between beef and cabbage production; but it still makes a difference in terms of whether both parties profit from the interaction.

run of transactions. In particular, in a mercantile setting where parties anticipate being on both sides of a transaction with roughly equal frequency, they may well prefer an efficient rule rather than the one that protects them from possible loss in every instance. It is very difficult to predict, for instance, whether commercial buyers will benefit in the long run relative to their sellers from a change in the common law mailbox rule, or even from a change in rules governing the battle of the forms. As a result, a regulatory strategy that chooses rules based on their efficiency alone will probably benefit all concerned and in any event may be the best that we can do.

Although it cannot be denied that the economic approach to contracts has over the years been associated with a program of economic liberalism, it is important to recognize that it need not lead inexorably to a deregulatory agenda. In its development over the last four decades, law and economics has been deployed by scholars of varying political, philosophical, and ideological perspectives; and both progressive and conservative scholars have found support for their arguments within its framework.[13] Within this history, however, it is possible to identify some more specific patterns, including what might usefully be viewed as three distinct modes of intellectual argument.

The first mode of argument focuses on explaining and justifying legal principles in economic terms. Richard Posner's analysis of efficient breach,[14] his joint work with Rosenfield on impossibility and change of circumstances,[15] and Goetz and Scott's articles on the just compensation and mitigation principles[16] exemplify this approach. All of these authors suggest that traditional legal doctrines are best understood in terms of an underlying economic logic that can be used to organize lines of cases and to resolve doctrinal inconsistencies and ambiguities.

A second mode of argument, exemplified by Ayres and Gertner's analysis of default rules[17] and by Shavell's work on money remedies and on information disclosure,[18] aims less at justifying traditional principles than at identifying opportunities for superior alternatives. These authors in these articles are most concerned with analyzing which legal rules are more efficient than others and under which conditions; their conclusions are addressed implicitly to those with the power to change the rules and often explicitly to social planners.

[13] *See, e.g.*, Duncan Kennedy, *Cost-Benefit Analysis of Entitlement Problems: A Critique*, 33 STAN. L. REV. 387 (1981).

[14] *See* POSNER, ECONOMIC ANALYSIS OF LAW.

[15] Richard A. Posner & Andrew M. Rosenfield, *Impossibility and Related Doctrines in Contract Law: An Economic Analysis*, 6 J. LEGAL STUD. 83 (1977).

[16] Goetz & Scott, *Liquidated Damages, Penalties and the Just Compensation Principle*; Charles J. Goetz & Robert E. Scott, *The Mitigation Principle: Toward a General Theory of Contractual Obligation*, 69 VA. L. REV. 967 (1983).

[17] Ian Ayres & Robert Gertner, *Filling Gaps in Incomplete Contracts: An Economic Theory of Default Rules*, 99 YALE L.J. 87 (1989).

[18] Steven Shavell, *Specific Performance Versus Damages for Breach of Contract: An Economic Analysis*, 84 TEX. L. REV. 831 (2005); Steven Shavell, *Acquisition and Disclosure of Information Prior to Sale*, 25 RAND J. ECON. 20 (1994).

Finally, a third mode of argument focuses less on how state actors might create or apply legal rules, and more on how the private actors who are subject to those rules actually conduct their affairs. This approach is illustrated by the work of Lisa Bernstein[19] and some of the more recent work of Robert Scott and his various co-authors;[20] these authors explore, often with thick description, how commercial parties manage to create their own contractual enforcement institutions, in addition to or in substitution for the law.

These three modes of argument overlap; and one sees particular authors making use of more than one of them, sometimes in the same book or article. Indeed, Section III of this chapter, which presents some illustrative applications of the economic approach to contracts, uses all of them. But they have quite different ideological implications. The first mode of argument is essentially conservative; it suggests that the common law judges basically got things right from an economic point of view. On this view, economic analysis does not much require lawyers to change what they have been doing, but rather offers a vocabulary and method of discourse to help them do it more clearly and consistently. From an institutional perspective, the strong implication is that legislative incursions on the common law are to be avoided.

The second mode tends to be reformist and progressive; it suggests that traditional legal rules are only sometimes economically rational, but that more rigorous use of economic tools can improve matters for the benefit of all. Accordingly, enlightened legislators can improve on the work of common law judges. And the third mode is potentially radical, even anarchistic. It emphasizes the limitations of state-provided law and the advantages if not the inevitability of decentralized private ordering.

Traditional legal scholars have often accused practitioners of law and economics of intellectual imperialism; and it is true that economic methodology, because of its canonical model of constrained optimization and its emphasis on the instrumental value of efficiency, has reductionist tendencies. But these three modes of intellectual argument differ substantially in their imperial ambitions. The first mode aims at most at a sort of intellectual syncretism, in which lawyers are encouraged to continue much of their traditional practice while rationalizing it in new terms. The second mode proposes to displace traditional legal practices only where they are economically dysfunctional, and to retain them otherwise. Only the third mode advocates a wholesale deference to private economic norms, and only then for certain types of actors: those who are full participants in the private governance regime and who have the power and sophistication to protect their interests within it. Like the traditional law merchant, this mode seeks not to entirely replace traditional

[19] In addition to Bernstein's chapter in this volume, *see, e.g.*, Lisa Bernstein, *Merchant Law in a Merchant Court: Rethinking the Code's Search for Immanent Business Norms*, 144 U. Pa. L. Rev. 1765 (1996); Lisa Bernstein, *Opting out of the Legal System: Extralegal Contractual Relations in the Diamond Industry*, 21 J. Legal Stud. 138 (1992).

[20] *See, e.g.*, Ronald J. Gilson, Charles F. Sabel, & Robert E. Scott, *Contract and Innovation: The Limited Role of Generalist Courts in the Evolution of Novel Contractual Terms*, 88 N.Y.U. L. Rev. 170 (2013); Ronald J. Gilson, Charles F. Sabel, & Robert E. Scott, *Contracting for Innovation: Vertical Disintegration and Interfirm Collaboration*, 109 Colum. L. Rev. 431 (2009); Robert E. Scott & George G. Triantis, *Embedded Options and the Case against Compensation in Contract Law*, 104 Colum. L. Rev. 1428 (2004).

legal categories, but rather to grant autonomy to a discrete group of actors who are argued to be best governed by the norms of their own private communities.[21]

III. Application to Specific Principles of Contract Law

In this section, which is intended to offer a sort of proof of the pudding, we consider a few concrete illustrations of how the economic approach can clarify our understanding of contract law, recommend reforms, or identify occasions where private contracting can improve on the background established by default legal rules. Due to length limitations it is not feasible to present even the beginnings of a complete doctrinal survey, but the examples provided should be enough to demonstrate the spirit of the approach.[22]

A. Freedom of contract

All legal systems draw some line between those voluntary private agreements that are enforceable judicially, and those that are not. The reasons for the line can be divided into two categories: those arising from properties of the parties to the agreement, which one might call issues of freedom of contract, and those arising from properties of the judiciary and of society more generally, which one might call issues of justiciability. The economic approach suggests a distinctive way of looking at both, based on the subfield of economics known as welfare economics, which focuses on the question of when and how state intervention can improve on allocations produced by an unregulated market.

One of the main achievements of welfare economics has been to identify conditions under which market interaction will lead to an efficient outcome; these include the existence of markets for all tangible or intangible resources relevant to human welfare, enough market competition that individuals regard market prices as exogenous to their own actions, full and symmetric information and the capacity to act on it for all market actors, and the absence of any third-party effects. When these conditions fail to obtain, market efficiency can no longer be presumed; thus each of these categories of market failure helps justify one or more of the standard list of limitations on freedom of contract.

It makes sense on economic grounds, for instance, to deny enforcement to agreements entered into by persons who lack the capacity to look out for their own interests or by persons who are defrauded or mistaken as to some fundamental aspect of

[21] *See* Robert D. Cooter, *Decentralized Law for a Complex Economy*, 23 Sw. U. L. Rev. 443 (1994); Robert D. Cooter, *Structural Adjudication and the New Law Merchant: A Model of Decentralized Law*, 14 Int'l Rev. L. & Econ. 215 (1994). For a discussion of the limitations of this approach, *see* Zipporah B. Wiseman, *The Limits of Vision: Karl Llewellyn and the Merchant Rules*, 100 Harv. L Rev. 465 (1987).

[22] For examples of economic analysis of other bodies of contract doctrine, *see* Richard Craswell, *Insecurity, Repudiation, and Cure*, 19 J. Legal Stud. 399 (1990) (anticipatory breach); Avery Katz, *The Strategic Structure of Offer and Acceptance: Game Theory and the Law of Contract Formation*, 89 Mich. L. Rev. 215–95 (1990) (contract formation); Posner & Rosenfield, *Impossibility and Related Doctrines in Contract Law* (change of circumstance). For an introductory survey written for an audience of economists, *see* Avery W. Katz, Benjamin

the contract. In the ordinary case, we can reasonably presume that if two people agree on an exchange, the result will be welfare improving for both and hence for society at large; for children, drunkards, persons subject to undue influence or fraud, and the like, such a presumption is not warranted.

Similarly, the presumption of efficiency does not apply when one party to the transaction is able to strategically manipulate the other's opportunity to consider market alternatives. Thus, an economic approach would generally support the existence of doctrines such as undue influence and duress.[23] It would also support the traditional common law rule limiting the negative freedom of contract of common carriers.

The law of contracts also recognizes the problem of third-party effects in refusing to enforce illegal contracts, contracts in restraint of trade, and contracts against public policy. However, contract law is likely to be a highly imperfect regulatory tool in this regard, because the cases in which one of the parties seeks to avoid liability *ex post* are only loosely correlated with those in which the collective gains to the parties are outweighed by the losses to outsiders. Thus it makes good economic sense that agreements that impose adverse effects on third parties are regulated primarily by tort, criminal, and public law, and not by the law of contracts.

Not all limitations on freedom of contract, however, can be understood in efficiency terms. For example, Richard Epstein has argued that the unconscionability doctrine is justified only in cases of procedural unconscionability—that is, where the court detects or strongly suspects some defect in the bargaining process, but cannot easily fit it into the categories of capacity, mistake, fraud, or duress.[24] Voiding a contract in cases of pure substantive unconscionability, in contrast, does not fit this model; but it is unquestionably the law, at least in the United States.[25] Similarly, some contracts that might currently be voided for duress under the law of contracts, for example, a seller who took advantage of straitened market conditions in a public emergency, might not be voided under a system based strictly on the efficiency norm.[26]

B. Managing relational contracts

Traditional limits on the justiciability of contracts can also be analyzed in economic terms. For instance, courts in the U.S. would not traditionally enforce an agreement under which one party promised to purchase the entire output or supply the entire requirements of the other party's business, although both types of agreements would

Hermalin, & Richard Craswell, *The Economics of Contract Law, in* 1 Handbook of Law and Economics 102–14 (Steven Shavell & A. Mitchell Polinsky eds., 2007).

[23] *See generally* Robert Cooter, *The Cost of Coase*, 11 J. Legal Stud. 1 (1982).

[24] Richard A. Epstein, *Unconscionability: A Critical Reappraisal*, 18 J. Law & Econ. 293 (1975).

[25] *See* U.C.C. § 2-302 (1990); Restatement (Second) of Contracts § 208 (1981).

[26] *See, e.g.*, Oren Bar-Gill & Omri Ben-Shahar, *Credible Coercion*, 83 Tex. L. Rev. 717, 755 (2005); Oren Bar-Gill & Omri Ben-Shahar, *The Law of Duress and the Economics of Credible Threats*, 33 J. Legal Stud. 391 (2004); John P. Dawson, *Economic Duress: An Essay in Perspective*, 45 Mich. L. Rev. 253 (1947); Robert A. Hillman, *Policing Contract Modifications under the UCC: Good Faith and the Doctrine of Economic Duress*, 64 Iowa L. Rev. 849 (1978).

be enforceable today in sales cases governed by the Uniform Commercial Code.[27] Similarly, agreements to modify an existing contract, which may be thought to pose special risks of opportunistic behavior, were traditionally policed by the preexisting duty rule, which required both parties to offer fresh consideration in order for a modification to be enforceable; and contracts which left too many terms open to be decided after the fact were traditionally unenforceable on grounds of indefiniteness.[28] Today in the U.S., in contrast, courts are generally willing to enforce incomplete contracts if it is clear the parties intended them to be enforced and an administrable remedy can be found;[29] and the problem of opportunistic modification is handled in sales cases by the duty of good faith and in other cases by Restatement § 89's requirement that all such modifications be fair and equitable in view of circumstances not anticipated by the parties when the contract was made.[30]

Modern economic commentators would analyze such doctrines in terms of the cost of writing down the complete set of conditions and promises that delineate the precise scope of the parties' agreement and then verifying after the fact whether those conditions have been met and those promises have been kept.[31] While it is apparent that there could be economic value in an arrangement under which one party promises to insure the other against market variations that affect the optimal contract terms, or in partially negotiating a contract and binding oneself to complete the negotiation after more information is available, it is not apparent that this value exceeds the transaction costs of formal contracting and enforcement in court. In addition, since contracting parties do not pay the full costs of litigating their disputes in court (overhead costs of operating the civil judicial system are partially subsidized by the public fisc, and the costs of crowding are imposed on other litigants waiting in the queue, some of whom are involuntary tort victims or plaintiffs pursuing rights under public law) the fact that the contracting parties wished their agreement to be judicially enforceable does not necessarily imply that it is socially optimal to follow their wishes. If litigation costs are relatively high, it may be more economically efficient to leave the parties to enforce their obligations privately through inducements of repeat business or commercial reputation.[32] The answer depends on empirical evidence which has yet to be conclusively established and which could differ across time and place; but the traditional jurists who refused to recognize such contracts may well have been right in efficiency terms.

[27] *Compare Wickham & Burton Coal Co. v. Farmers' Lumber Co.*, 179 N.W. 417 (1920) with U.C.C. § 2-306 (1990).

[28] *See, e.g., Varney v. Ditmars*, 217 N.Y. 223, 111 N.E. 822 (1916) (indefiniteness doctrine); *Lingenfelder v. Wainwright Brewing Co.*, 15 S.W. 844 (1891) (preexisting duty rule).

[29] *See, e.g., Teachers Ins. & Annuity Ass'n of Am. v. Tribune Co.*, 270 F. Supp. 491, 498 (S.D.N.Y 1987); U.C.C. § 2-204 (1990).

[30] *See* U.C.C. § 2-209 (1990); RESTATEMENT (SECOND) OF CONTRACTS § 89 (1981).

[31] *See, e.g.*, Charles J. Goetz & Robert E. Scott, *Principles of Relational Contracts*, 67 VA. L. REV. 1089 (1981); Alan Schwartz & Robert E Scott, *Contract Theory and the Limits of Contract Law*, 113 YALE L.J. 541 (2003); Alan Schwartz, *Relational Contracts in the Courts: An Analysis of Incomplete Agreements and Judicial Strategies*, 21 J. LEGAL STUD. 271 (1992).

[32] As in Arthur Allan Leff, *Injury, Ignorance and Spite: The Dynamics of Coercive Collection*, 80 YALE L.J. 1 (1970); Stewart Macauley, *Non-contractual Relations in Business: A Preliminary Study*, 28 AM. SOC. REV. 55 (1963); and Bernstein, *Extralegal Contractual Relations in the Diamond Industry.*

C. Interpretation

The question of implied terms leads naturally to the general problem of contract interpretation: an issue that ranges across many separate doctrines and that is probably the locus for a majority of contract disputes. Interpretive doctrines drew relatively little focused attention in the early years of the law and economics literature but have more recently been the subject of more sustained analysis. Because of the breadth of the topic and the complexity of interpretation as a human activity, there has been relatively less consensus among commentators in this branch of the literature, but several important lessons come through.

First, interpretive problems arise from the brute fact that the transmission of information is costly. In order for parties to form a contract they must communicate with each other, and for them to enforce the contract they must communicate with a third-party tribunal. The cost of such communication rises with the complexity and idiosyncrasy of the transaction, and also with the margin of error that the parties are willing to tolerate. Because of these costs, actual contracts are always less than fully complete; and some agreements that would be reached in an ideal world where communication is costless are not reached (and should not be reached) in the real world. For this reason, the claim that courts do not complete contracts for the parties cannot be taken literally. Instead it needs to be understood in relative terms, reflecting the tradeoff between the cost of providing clearer and more thorough instructions *ex ante* (the cost of which is borne largely by the parties) and the cost of conducting a fuller inquiry into the substance of the transaction *ex post* (a cost that is in significant part borne by the legal system).[33]

Second, courts and other lawmakers, by setting up general rules of interpretation that they commit to following in subsequent cases, can lower the private cost of contracting and thus increase the potential social surplus from exchange. One way in which they may do this is by establishing default terms that the parties know will be followed in the event that they do not specify otherwise. For instance, Article 2 of the Uniform Commercial Code provides that if the parties do not specify the price at which they intend to conclude their exchange, the court will interpret their contract as if they had agreed that the contract price be determined by the market price prevailing at the time of delivery.[34] Default terms might be chosen according to various criteria, but if one focuses simply on the immediate cost of contract writing, the term that most parties would prefer is a straightforward choice, since (assuming that the costs of contracting in or out of that term are symmetric) that will minimize the sum total of transaction costs incurred by parties who would prefer different terms.[35]

[33] *See generally* Avery W. Katz, *The Economics of Form and Substance in Contract Interpretation*, 104 Colum. L. Rev. 496 (2004); Richard A. Posner, *The Law and Economics of Contract Interpretation*, 83 Tex. L. Rev. 1581 (2005); Steven Shavell, *On the Writing and the Interpretation of Contracts*, 22 J.L. Econ. & Org. 289 (2006).

[34] U.C.C. § 2-305 (1990). Similarly, Article 2 provides that if the parties do not specify a place for tender and delivery of the goods, the default is that it is seller's place of business (§ 2-309); that if the parties do not specify a time and method for payment then the default is that it is cash on delivery (§ 2-310); and that if the parties do not provide any express warranty, the default is that the goods are warranted to be fit for the ordinary purposes for which they are used (§ 2-314).

[35] *See* Charles J. Goetz & Robert E. Scott, *The Limits of Expanded Choice: An Analysis of the Interactions between Express and Implied Contract Terms*, 73 Calif. L. Rev. 261 (1985).

Third, rules of contract interpretation will affect not only the amount of resources that parties devote to contract writing *ex ante* and to litigation *ex post*, but also to other dimensions of contracting behavior. For instance, Ian Ayers and Robert Gertner have argued that when parties are asymmetrically informed about the subject of their transaction, courts can and should induce fuller disclosure by prescribing a "penalty default" which fills in contractual gaps and resolves ambiguities with the terms that the relatively informed party least prefers.[36] Conversely, Charles Goetz and Robert Scott have argued that in order to induce optimal innovation of contract terms, courts should be sparing in their willingness to fill contractual gaps, since the terms they provide will crowd out privately designed terms that would be based on superior information and that therefore would likely be more efficient.[37] And more narrowly, various commentators have explained how relatively formalistic interpretation rules can reduce the cost of monitoring organizational agents[38] and the cost of recruiting third parties to provide financing and other assets complementary to the underlying transaction.[39]

Finally, because the economic effect of interpretation rules are so complex, a legal regime in which contracting parties are allowed to specify which rules of interpretation will apply to their agreement will produce more contractual value than one in which interpretation rules are mandatory. Accordingly, courts should defer to parties' instructions to interpret their contract more or less formally, or to incorporate (or exclude) parol evidence, trade usage, and course of dealing—provided of course that these instructions are mutually assented to and are sufficiently clear according to the standard default rules of interpretation, and that none of the standard reasons for restricting the parties' freedom of contract are present.

D. Damages for breach

The area of contract law that has attracted the most attention over the years from economically influenced commentators is that governing damages for breach. For this reason, it is probably one of the few applications of economics to law (in addition to Posner's "Hand formula") that most traditional legal scholars have heard of and possibly even assimilated. The literature on this topic, however, has developed well beyond the simple lessons regarding "efficient breach" which many traditional scholars associate with the approach. The concept of efficient breach nonetheless remains important, not least as a teaching tool, because it clarifies two fundamental lessons: first, that remedial rules have important consequences for *ex ante* primary behavior, and second,

[36] Ayres & Gertner, *Filling Gaps in Incomplete Contracts*. The conditions under which this advice is sound as a matter of welfare economics, however, has proved particularly difficult to pin down. *See* Barry E. Adler, *The Questionable Ascent of* Hadley v. Baxendale, 51 Stan. L. Rev. 1547 (1999); Jason Scott Johnston, *Strategic Bargaining and the Economic Theory of Contract Default Rules*, 100 Yale L.J. 615 (1990); Eric A. Posner, *There Are No Penalty Default Rules in Contract Law*, 33 Fla. St. U.L. Rev. 563 (2005).

[37] *See* Goetz & Scott, *The Limits of Expanded Choice*; Robert E. Scott, *The Case for Formalism in Relational Contract*, 94 Nw. U. L. Rev. 847 (1999).

[38] Kevin Davis, *Licensing Lies: Merger Clauses, the Parol Evidence Rule and Precontractual Misrepresentations*, 33 Val. U. L. Rev. 485 (1998); Katz, *The Economics of Form and Substance in Contract Interpretation*.

[39] *See* Katz, *The Economics of Form and Substance in Contract Interpretation*; Henry Smith, *Modularity in Contracts: Boilerplate and Information Flow*, 104 Mich. L. Rev. 1175 (2005).

that our concerns for those consequences may come into conflict with our concerns for corrective justice. For that reason, like the negligence/strict liability debate in tort law and like the Trolley Problem in the field of ethics, it offers a locus for the law's two main normative traditions—deontology and consequentialism—to join issue.[40]

Traditional legal scholars should understand, however, that "efficient breach" is not the state of the art in the economic analysis of contracts and has not been for a very long time. Contemporary law and economics scholars are much more likely to advocate that contracting parties should arrange for liquidated damages than they are to argue in favor of the expectation principle. The logic underlying this modern view is that the performance/breach decision is only one aspect of contractual efficiency; and it may be far from the most important one. The extent of contractual surplus, rather, depends on numerous aspects of the parties' behavior, including their decisions to invest in their relationship, to allocate and insure against external risk, to take precautions against contractual failure, to disclose relevant information to their counterparties, to mitigate losses in the event of nonperformance, and to investigate whether it is worth getting into the contract in the first place.

Remedial doctrines affect parties' incentives along all of these dimensions and in different ways. For example, economic analysis suggests that full expectation damages, if properly measured, will provide efficient incentives with regard to the performance decision and the promisor's decision to take *ex ante* precautions against nonperformance, but inefficient incentives with regard to pre-contractual investment, disclosure of information, *ex post* mitigation of losses, and pre-contractual investigation.[41] And expectation damages may or may not provide for efficient allocation of risk, depending on the parties' relative risk aversion and the configuration of public and private information relevant to the provision of insurance. Choosing a damage rule that draws an efficient balance across all these dimensions of behavior, accordingly, is necessarily an exercise in the second best, in which one must sacrifice efficiency along one margin to achieve more of it along another. And this tradeoff does not even take into account the costs of litigation, measurement error, and the possibility that contract breach will pass undetected by the injured party.

The performance/breach decision, however, is relatively amenable to solution through *ex post* renegotiation between the original contracting parties. Such renegotiation is far from costless; and it is subject to problems of asymmetric information and strategic behavior. But investment and insurance decisions cannot be addressed by renegotiation at all, because those decisions are complete and irrevocable before any *ex post* bargaining starts. For that reason, it may be second best for lawmakers interested in efficiency to place relatively less emphasis on promoting

[40] Additionally, within the jurisprudence of law and economics more generally, the concept of efficient breach has been important because it fits nicely into larger theoretical frameworks that cut across multiple fields of law. *See* A. Mitchell Polinsky, An Introduction to Law and Economics (4th ed., 2011); Robert Cooter, *Unity in Tort, Contract, and Property: The Model of Precaution*, 73 Calif. L. Rev. 1 (1985).

[41] *See* Katz, Hermalin, & Craswell, *The Economics of Contract Law*, at 102–14.

efficient performance, and relatively more emphasis on promoting efficiency along other dimensions of contracting.[42]

Given the complexity of determining what measure of damages is most efficient in the second-best sense, however, and the difficulties of applying any particular measure on a given set of facts, the increasing trend in the law and economics literature has been to suggest that the matter simply be left to the parties, either by encouraging greater use of and deference to liquidated damage clauses, or in cases where this option is not available, by applying more mechanical formulas such as the difference between contract and market.[43] For the parties to take advantage of such encouragement and liquidate damages most effectively for their own purposes, of course, they will need to take the foregoing considerations into account.

Even putting efficiency considerations aside, however, economic analysis remains important in giving practical meaning to basic concepts of reliance and expectation. To illustrate, consider the case of anticipatory repudiation, where a promisor announces well in advance of the time of performance that she intends to breach. Under modern doctrine an early repudiation is treated as a breach entitling the promisee to seek damages; but given the dynamic nature of markets and the length of time it takes for cases to reach trial, courts are typically faced with two possible measures of expectation: one based on market conditions prevailing at the time of the promised performance, and another based on market conditions prevailing at the time of breach. Courts and commentators have disagreed which measure is proper, sometimes with incongruous results. For example, the case law in sales cases under U.C.C. Article 2 appears to establish one rule when sellers breach, and a different rule when buyers breach.[44]

One might suppose that if the purpose of contract damages is to put the aggrieved party as close as possible to the position he would enjoy in the event of performance, then contract-market must similarly be measured at the time of performance. But economic analysis (and specifically, the economics of options pricing) reveals that this is not the case. Measuring contract-market at the time of performance overcompensates the promisee relative to his actual losses, by giving him a free speculative opportunity for the period between repudiation and the promised time for performance. If market conditions move against the promisee during this period, he is completely protected from any loss; while if conditions turn in his favor, he does better than he would have

[42] Similarly, given the existence of nonlegal sanctions for breach of contract such as loss of reputation and withholding of repeat business, it may be second best for courts to place less emphasis on aspects of contractual inefficiency that are well policed by such sanctions, and more emphasis on aspects of inefficiency that are not. *See* Avery W. Katz, *Contractual Enforcement Institutions and the Structure of Information*, 164 J. Institutional & Theoretical Econ. 134 (2008).

[43] *See* Aaron S. Edlin & Alan Schwartz, *Optimal Penalties in Contracts*, 78 Chi.-Kent L. Rev. 33 (2003); Katz, *Contractual Enforcement Institutions*; Scott & Triantis, *Embedded Options*. Similarly, some have argued on the same grounds for greater use of specific performance. *See, e.g.*, Thomas S. Ulen, *The Efficiency of Specific Performance: Toward a Unified Theory of Contract Remedies*, 83 Mich. L. Rev. 341 (1984).

[44] *Compare* U.C.C. § 2-708(1) (1990) (standard measure for buyer's breach is difference between contract price and market price prevailing at the time for tender) with U.C.C. § 2-713 (1990) (standard measure for seller's breach is difference between contract price and market price prevailing at the time buyer learned of the breach). Most courts interpreting the latter provision have held that the buyer learns of the breach at the

under the original agreement. His private incentive, therefore, is to speculate at the breacher's expense by waiting to see which way prices move. In contrast, a rule that measures market price at the time of repudiation, but that awards incidental damages incurred if the promisee does decide to cover or hedge, completely protects the promisee's economic interest in performance without encouraging inefficient speculation.[45]

IV. Comparison with Other Paradigms

The discussion in Section III demonstrates the potential for economic theories of contract to illuminate legal and jurisprudential questions. A jurisprudential discussion of the economic approach would be highly incomplete, however, if it did not evaluate its claims in light of those of other leading perspectives. Four such perspectives are considered here: those based on consent, deontological morality, corrective justice, and virtue ethics.

A. Consent

Consent-based theories of contract emphasize individual liberty and self-governance over more collective concerns such as social welfare and the promotion of virtue or justice.[46] Such a perspective has considerable affinity with the economic approach, which is grounded in both normative and methodological individualism. As we have seen, standard economic measures of welfare are based on aggregates of individual benefit and burden; the model of constrained optimization places at its center a choosing individual actor; and as discussed in Section III.A, the conventional assumptions of welfare economics imply that liberal freedoms will tend to promote economically efficient outcomes.

There will be tension between libertarian and economic approaches, however, whenever market failures or other transaction costs prevent the completion of efficient exchange. In such cases, it may not be logically possible to promote both efficiency and self-governance.[47] While many economically oriented commentators would use arguments of hypothetical consent to close the gap, principled libertarians would not accept hypothetical consent as a substitute for the real thing. Conversely, some libertarians would argue that the law should protect even anticompetitive agreements such as price fixing, on the basis that the conduct is voluntary and that consumers have no inherent

moment that repudiation is communicated. *See, e.g., Oloffson v. Coomer*, 11 Ill. App. 3d 918, 296 N.E.2d 871 (1973).

[45] *See* Thomas H. Jackson, *Anticipatory Repudiation and the Temporal Element of Contract Law: An Economic Inquiry into Contract Damages in Cases of Prospective Nonperformance*, 31 STAN. L. REV. 69 (1978). Jackson's argument depends on the availability of either cover or hedging opportunities in the relevant market at the time of repudiation; in the absence of these, a risk-averse promisee who entered into the original agreement for the purpose of price protection would be forced into an undesired gamble.

[46] *See, e.g.*, Randy E. Barnett, *A Consent Theory of Contract*, 86 COLUM. L. REV. 269 (1986); Randy E. Barnett, *Contract Is Not Promise; Contract Is Consent*, 45 SUFFOLK U. L. REV. 735 (2012).

[47] For a formal demonstration, *see* Amartya Sen, *The Impossibility of a Paretian Liberal*, 78 J. POL. ECON. 152 (1970).

right to trade with producers on any particular terms; but efficiency proponents clearly would not.

B. Deontological morality

Legal scholars working in the Kantian tradition have often claimed that the economic approach to law, being purely consequential in nature, cannot be squared with a deontologically grounded moral obligation to keep one's promises. The inconsistency, however, is less fundamental than is commonly asserted, particularly in the field of contracts. Deontologists and efficiency theorists agree on many doctrinal issues in contract—for example, on most of the standard limits on freedom of contract, which can be justified either on grounds of efficiency or on the morality of promising. On many other issues, however, especially in the areas of contract formation and interpretation where legal rules in large part reflect social conventions, deontological morality has less to say; it can tell us why failing to keep a promise is wrong, but absent some additional theory of conventional meaning it cannot tell us how we know what a promise means or whether one has been made at all.[48] While people may well have a moral right to what they have relied upon or been promised under the prevailing conventions of interpretation, no one has a right to have any particular convention chosen as the prevailing one to begin with.

More generally, because deontological theories depend on the existence of an established set of rights to get off the ground, they are less helpful in telling us what rights to establish initially. Charles Fried's theory of promissory morality, for instance, does not prescribe what promises parties should make in the first place except within very broad limits. Obviously parties should not make promises that require them to violate third parties' rights (as in the case of conspiracies to commit fraud) and they should not make promises that undermine their own human dignity (as in the case of promises to sell oneself into slavery). But beyond such limits it is not clear, for instance, why sophisticated parties should not agree to limit their contractual remedies for breach of warranty to repair-and-replace (as in standard business-to-business sales contracts) or to relieve their counterparties from the ordinary duty to mitigate (as in standard take-or-pay option contracts) if doing so serves their purposes in contracting.[49] On such questions, the economic approach to contract has an advantage over deontological theories, because it does provide a guide to which promises are worth making and how best to design the transactions in which they are embedded.

[48] Richard Craswell makes this point with regard to the specific phenomenon of default rules in *Contract Law, Default Rules, and the Philosophy of Promising*, 88 MICH. L. REV. 489 (1989); but an analogous argument carries over to formation and interpretation rules more generally.

[49] This, indeed, is the best defense of the efficient breach principle against the standard deontological objections to it—that it embodies the remedial principle that, as a default rule, best suits the typical parties' purposes in contracting. *See, e.g.*, Steven Shavell, *Contracts*, *in* THE NEW PALGRAVE DICTIONARY OF ECONOMICS AND THE LAW 436, 439 (P. Newman ed., 1998).

A further advantage of the economic approach is that it provides a clear principle for which promises are worth enforcing in court: namely, those for which the efficiency gains achieved by public enforcement outweigh the costs of operating the judicial system. Deontological theories have a harder time with this question; they can explain when breach of contract is morally wrong, but not when it is worth enforcing that moral obligation in state institutions funded out of public resources, obtained from individual citizens through the state's coercive taxing powers. There may well be good noneconomic answers to this latter question, but these implicate matters of distributive justice and political morality. They do not arise out of deontological obligations between promisor and promisee.

C. Corrective justice

The conflict between corrective justice and economic efficiency is more fundamental than the conflict between deontology and efficiency. Because corrective justice focuses on redressing past wrongdoing (in particular, by restoring a past or proper state of affairs that has been disrupted by the defendant's behavior), those who view it as the primary purpose of the legal system have typically rejected the claims of the economic approach. Conversely, proponents of the economic approach, which regards past gains and losses as mere sunk costs (that is, distributional rents that are irrelevant to incentives for future behavior), have generally had little use for the prescriptions of corrective justice.[50]

Such conflict is primarily limited, however, to normative applications of economic efficiency in the judicial setting. When economics is used for positive analysis, it can often be put to the service of corrective justice: for example, by helping to calculate the amount of damages that are needed to redress past wrongs or to determine the content of contractual obligations so as to decide whether there has been a wrong that needs redressing at all. And in legislative and transactional settings, there need be no conflict at all, at least if one subscribes to an institutional theory under which judges confine themselves to matters of principle when retroactively deciding disputes under existing law but legislators are free to consider matters of policy when deciding whether prospectively to change the rules of the game.[51] Indeed, it is unclear whether a corrective justice approach has any implications at all for *ex ante* analysis of legal problems.[52]

D. Virtue theory

Finally, some jurisprudential theorists have argued implicitly or explicitly that contract law should be judged in terms of how well it promotes virtuous moral behavior and human flourishing. The relevant moral behavior could include promise keeping, but as

[50] *See, e.g.*, Frank H. Easterbrook, *Foreword: The Court and the Economic System*, 98 HARV. L. REV. 4 (1984).

[51] *See* Ronald Dworkin, *Hard Cases*, 88 HARV. L. REV. 1057 (1975).

[52] Note that even Dworkin, who excoriates the use of economic analysis in judicial decision making, accepts it as a legitimate policy tool in the legislative setting. *See* Ronald Dworkin, *Is Wealth a Value?*, 9 J. LEGAL STUD. 191 (1980); Ronald Dworkin, *Why Efficiency? A Response to Professors Calabresi and Posner*, 8 HOFSTRA L. REV. 563 (1979).

often as not it incorporates the value of making the right kind of promises; that is, of entering into contractual relationships that are authentic and mutually satisfying, and avoiding those that are degrading and mutually exploitative. Such theories are based on the normative premise that it is better to live one's life in certain ways than in others, and that following the path of virtue is objectively better than following one's base desires. Daniel Markovits's contribution to this volume focuses explicitly on such an argument,[53] and while Margaret Jane Radin's contribution to this volume chooses a different focus, it incorporates resonances of her influential work in this normative tradition.[54]

The economic approach to contracts is more in tension with this way of looking at the law than with any of the other perspectives thus far discussed. The reason is that contemporary economics, in contrast to the historical tradition of political economy out of which it developed, proceeds from a distinctive rhetoric and culture that runs counter to the aretaic tradition.[55] Following in the tradition of Benthamite subjective utilitarianism, most economists working today renounce interest in the content of individual preferences. Instead, they take those preferences as both exogenous to their descriptive theories and as the fundamental normative basis for social welfare calculations. As discussed in Section II, they also have a methodological preference for reductionist theories over holistic ones, for formal analysis over narrative, and for sharply distinguishing between fact and value.

There are exceptions to this generalization, especially among scholars working on the borders of economics, law, sociology, and psychology.[56] But as a general rule, these methodological commitments combine to result in a professional culture that pays little attention to moral improvement. In addition, the socially libertarian inclinations of most economists leave them skeptical of claims that government power should be used to promote virtuous behavior, except when ostensible defects in virtue can be ascribed to cognitive or emotional limits on people's capacities to behave rationally.[57]

This tension between economic analysis and virtue ethics, however, is more cultural than conceptual. The classical and utilitarian forebears of modern economics were highly concerned with questions of moral development, and there is no logical reason that modern economic analysis could not be turned to the same purpose.[58] The field of behavioral law and economics has developed rapidly over the past 20 years as scholars have grown more interested in investigating the limitations of the standard economic model of rational choice. If virtue ethics continues to gain influence in the legal scholarly

[53] Daniel Markovits, *Good Faith as Contract's Core Value, in* PHILOSOPHICAL FOUNDATIONS OF CONTRACT LAW (Gregory Klass, George Letsas & Prince Saprai eds., 2014); *see also* Daniel Markovits, *Contract and Collaboration*, 113 YALE L. J. 1417 (2004).

[54] Margaret J. Radin, *Market-Inalienability*, 100 HARV. L. REV. 1849 (1987).

[55] *See generally* Donald McCloskey, *The Rhetoric of Law and Economics*, 86 MICH. L. REV. 752 (1988); James Boyd White, *Economics and Law: Two Cultures in Tension*, 54 TENN. L. REV. 161 (1987); Avery Katz, *Positivism and the Separation of Law and Economics.*

[56] *See, e.g.*, George A. Akerlof, *The Economics of Caste and of the Rat Race and Other Woeful Tales*, 90 Q. J. ECON. 599 (1976); George A. Akerlof, *Social Distance and Social Decisions*, 65 ECONOMETRICA 1005 (1997).

[57] *See, e.g.*, RICHARD H. THALER & CASS R. SUNSTEIN, NUDGE: IMPROVING DECISIONS ABOUT HEALTH, WEALTH, AND HAPPINESS (2008); Richard H. Thaler & Cass R. Sunstein, *Libertarian Paternalism*, 93 AM. ECON. REV. 175 (2003).

[58] Occasional examples do arise; *see, e.g.*, Robert D. Cooter, *Lapses, Conflict, and Akrasia in Torts and Crimes: Towards an Economic Theory of the Will*, 11 INT'L REV. L. & ECON. 149 (1991); Thomas C. Schelling,

community more generally, one may expect that some version of aretaic law and economics will follow in its wake.

V. Conclusion: A Pragmatic Assessment of the Economic Approach

In the end, whether and how economics can be used by lawyers and legal scholars will depend on the professional role they are playing, and on whether they are using economics for positive or normative reasons. For legislators (or for lawyers and scholars who are advising legislators), whether to use economics in setting the framework for contract law depends on all the usual determinants of state policy, including the interests of their constituents.

While there are surely good reasons for legislators to subordinate economic efficiency to other normative considerations in many policy settings, it would be a serious mistake to assume that such a choice requires disregarding the lessons of economics as a whole. That's not to say that lawmakers don't sometimes make that mistake (for example, when budget austerity is recommended on moralistic grounds rather than on the best understandings of macroeconomic evidence), but when they do the result is likely to be bad policy that fails to take into account the neutralizing or even perverse effects resulting from ordinary economic behavior.[59]

For judges and administrative officials acting in an adjudicative role—the audience toward which most scholarly discussions of law and economics have been directed—the situation is more complicated. For those who view at least some judicial lawmaking as legitimate, inevitable, or both, economic analysis of law is appropriate for the same reasons as it is in the legislative setting: on positive grounds, because it helps predict contracting parties' likely response to changes in legal rules, and on normative grounds, because it helps assess who is likely to gain and lose from those rules and whether the aggregate social balance of gains and losses is favorable. In particular, economic models may be particularly useful in helping a court see how a ruling undertaken to settle a dispute immediately before it may spread more generally to influence behavior in future cases.

It is possible, however, that institutional limits on jurisdiction or judicial fact finding might militate in the direction of either more attention to the efficiency norm or less. For instance, Louis Kaplow and Steven Shavell have argued that because legislatures have a comparative (and perhaps also an absolute) advantage over judges in redistributing income as a result of legislative jurisdiction over the general system of tax and transfers, a division of labor in which courts focus on efficiency considerations and legislatures on distribution will better promote both efficiency and distributive justice.[60] Perhaps more controversially, Richard Posner has argued that courts will best preserve their legitimacy and political capital by focusing on efficiency, because efficiency enjoys

Egonomics, or the Art of Self-Management, 68 Am. Econ. Rev. 290 (1978); Thomas C. Schelling, *Self-Command in Practice, in Policy, and in a Theory of Rational Choice*, 74 Am. Econ. Rev. 1 (1984).

[59] *See, e.g.*, John Maynard Keynes, The General Theory of Employment, Interest and Money 383 (1935) ("Practical men, who believe themselves to be quite exempt from any intellectual influence, are usually the slaves of some defunct economist. ... I am sure that the power of vested interests is vastly exaggerated compared with the gradual encroachment of ideas").

[60] Louis Kaplow & Steven Shavell, *Why the Legal System Is Less Efficient than the Income Tax in Redistributing Income*, 23 J. Legal Stud. 667 (1994).

greater acceptance as a neutral standard while redistribution is an inherently divisive matter best left to the more democratically branches of government.[61] And as argued in Section II, attempts to achieve distributional ends through contract law are likely to be particularly ineffective, because changes in legal entitlements tend to be neutralized by corresponding changes in parties' reservation prices for exchange.

Conversely, if one believes that judges should decide cases according only to legal principle while leaving policy matters to the legislature, economic analysis still remains relevant to their task, though in a more narrowly cabined way. One way in which it is relevant is when economic analysis is needed to discern legal principles, as it clearly is in the case of statutes passed with the purpose of economic regulation (e.g., the Securities and Exchange Act and the Sherman Antitrust Act in the United States), and as Posner and others have claimed with regard to the common law more generally. Indeed, Posner's well-known claim that the common law tends to the promotion of economic efficiency is perhaps best understood as responding to the desire to justify economic norms in terms of traditional legal principle, and not just on grounds of policy.

Another way in which economic analysis may be used in the traditional judicial context is in applying law to facts. The classic example of this approach in American jurisprudence is Judge Learned Hand's application of cost–benefit analysis as a metaphor for negligence in *U.S. v Carroll Towing*.[62] But many doctrines in the law of contracts and commercial law lend themselves to an economic interpretation, including basic doctrines of consideration, mutuality, expectation damages, and the traditional prohibition on contractual penalties.

Perhaps most importantly, in order to apply a contract it is first necessary to determine its meaning; and in many if not all contractual disputes this meaning is at issue. In such cases, economic analysis can be a critically useful interpretive tool. This is especially so when the contract governs a complex business relationship, since the adjudicator will hardly be able to understand the contract without understanding the relationship itself. But even when the contractual exchange is a simple one, some interpretations of the agreement will make more economic sense than others.

For example, in the well-known *Frigaliment Importing* case,[63] the parties differed over whether the seller was obligated to supply the higher-quality broiling chicken (*Brathuhn*) or only the lower-quality stewing chicken (*Suppenhuhn*). In deciding for the seller, the court relied in part on the fact that the high-quality interpretation would result not just in a contract price in excess of the market price prevailing at the time the deal was signed, but in the seller expecting to lose money on the deal *ex ante*.[64]

The *Frigaliment* opinion turned on a distributional economic analysis, but efficiency analysis can equally be relevant to contract interpretation. When the purpose of a contract is economic exchange, it can fairly be presumed (absent some countervailing factor) that the parties will want to make their gains from trade as large as possible. For this reason, courts should not construe contracts to promote or require economic waste, or more generally to require one party to undertake a burden the cost

[61] *See generally* Richard A. Posner, The Economics of Justice (1981).

[62] *United States v. Carroll Towing Co.*, 159 F.2d 169 (2d. Cir. 1947).

[63] *Frigaliment Importing Co. v. B.N.S. International Sales Corp.*, 190 F. Supp. 116 (1960).

[64] *Cf.* U.C.C. § 2-314, cmt. 7 (1990) ("In cases of doubt as to what quality is intended, the price at which a merchant closes a contract is an excellent index of the nature and scope of his obligation. . .").

of which exceeds the benefit to the other, unless there is reason to think that the parties actually intended an inefficient outcome.

In the leading US case of *Peevyhouse v Garland Coal*,[65] for example, a young farmsteading couple sued a coal company for failing to restore their property after the end of a strip-mining lease. The coal company admitted breach, but introduced evidence that the cost of the restoration would be $29,000, which was far greater than the established reduction in value of the land if not restored. The court rejected the plaintiff's demand for cost-of-completion damages, reasoning that the restoration of the land was only a secondary purpose of the contract (the primary purpose being mining), and that completion in accordance with the contract would involve "unreasonable economic waste."[66] As a result, the plaintiffs received only $300—the court's measure of the diminution in value of their land.

There is good reason to think that the damages awarded in *Peevyhouse* were inadequate in economic terms. In particular, the jury had measured the plaintiff's losses at $5,000, and evidence introduced at rehearing showed that diminution-in-value losses were likely greater than $300 because the farm consisted of other lands beyond the 60 acres covered by the coal-mining lease.[67] Additionally, the court's opinion focused more on the supposedly undeserved windfall the plaintiffs would have received under the cost-of-completion measure, rather than on the inefficiency of completion. Nonetheless, the court was correct that completion would have been inefficient, reducing the economic surplus available to both parties. For that reason, it would not have promoted the parties' purposes either to specifically enforce the restoration of the land, or to award damages large enough to induce the defendants to complete.[68]

Ultimately, however, the most relevant arena for the economic analysis of contracts is likely to be found not in governmental venues, but in the private transactional setting. Attorneys representing clients in business transactions are much likelier to have access to the detailed, individualized information that is necessary to implement an efficient contractual arrangement; and they are also better motivated to pursue efficiency as a goal. In practical terms, being able to identify whether a legal rule is efficient is the key step in determining whether it is worthwhile trying to contract around it. If the background rule is inefficient, then there is mutual profit in changing it when legally permissible; leaving it alone is leaving money on the table.[69] For that reason, adjudicators and legislators who are able to anticipate such private activity will be able to make better laws in the first place; but it is the private contractors themselves who are most likely to find value in the economic approach to law.

[65] *Peevyhouse v. Garland Coal & Mining Co.*, 382 P.2d 109 (Okla. 1962).

[66] *Peevyhouse v. Garland Coal & Mining Co.* at 113.

[67] In addition, the Peevyhouses had specifically negotiated for Garland's promise to restore the land, and in so doing gave up an advance payment of $3,000 that they would have otherwise received. *See* Judith L. Maute, Peevyhouse v. Garland Coal & Mining Co. *Revisited: The Ballad of Willie and Lucille*, 89 Nw. U. L. Rev. 1341, 1358–63 (1995).

[68] For a formal demonstration that supra-compensatory damages reduce the *ex ante* value of the contract to both parties, *see* Avery W. Katz, *Virtue Ethics and Efficient Breach*, 45 Suffolk. U.L. Rev. 777, 782–4 (2012).

[69] It's for this reason that good transactional lawyers need to look out not just for their clients' interests, but also for the interests of the clients' counterparties. *See generally* Ronald J. Gilson, *Value Creation by Business Lawyers: Legal Skills and Asset Pricing*, 94 Yale L.J. 239 (1984).

11

Distributive Justice and Contract

Aditi Bagchi

Every subject of law raises concerns of fairness and many involve efforts to induce and reward right behavior. Common law subjects like contract may be unusually open to moral theorizing because legal rules evolve organically and legal claims are often stated and evaluated in apparently moralistic language. The express language of equity in the common law of contract could be read to invite parties and judges to invoke a range of moral considerations so as to ensure fairness all things considered.

The normative framework most often invoked to flesh out the morality of contract is the practice of promising.[1] A normative power that creates moral obligation between private persons, promise seems to track the moral relations created by contract. With a few exceptions, most recent philosophical thinking about contract has been within the promissory framework.

The result has been that the morality of contract is not regarded as an elaboration of the standards of fairness in private exchange, which might plausibly involve a range of moral principles, but as only a deconstruction of the morality of promising. Since the morality of promising does not obviously have anything to do with distributive justice, philosophical writing about contract has largely ignored matters of distribution even though they are intuitively related to the fairness of exchange.

Contract as promise has either distracted us from distributive justice or revealed its irrelevance. In this chapter, I argue the former. Principles of distributive justice may have a number of implications for contract law. They are among the moral considerations that appropriately inform rules of validity, interpretation, and remedy.

It is useful to distinguish among distinct possible claims. First, distributive justice may make categorical demands on the *legal rules* governing private exchange. It may also constrain *individuals* engaged in private exchange.

We usually take those questions to operate in ideal theory. Contracts that take place against a backdrop of distributive *injustice* may be subject to further (or different) constraints. That is, even if the first-order demands of distributive justice do not implicate contract, contract law might be drawn into a second-best or remedial scheme. Relatedly, collective failure to achieve distributive justice may inform individual rights and obligations in exchange. Even if distributive justice does not constrain

[1] *See* Charles Fried, Contract as Promise (1981); Jody Kraus, *The Correspondence of Contract and Promise*, 109 Colum. L. Rev. 1603 (2009); Daniel Markovits, *Contract and Collaboration*, 113 Yale L.J. 1417, 1448 (2004) (arguing that "[c]ontract presents a special case of promise" and that contract is a "class of promises"); Seana Valentine Shiffrin, *The Divergence of Contract and Promise*, 120 Harv. L. Rev. 708 (2007).

individuals engaged in private exchange against a background of distributive *justice*, parties to contract may be morally constricted in a state of distributive injustice.

Many people have the view that principles of distributive justice impose all or none of these possible constraints on contract, under ideal or imperfect conditions, on individuals or policymakers.[2] But at least the reasons we give for invoking or dismissing distributive justice as among the equitable principles that inform contract will turn on the particular question at hand. In this chapter I focus on the legal question of how regulation of private exchange is informed by distributive justice and consider questions of individual morality in contracting only inasmuch as they inform legal rules. Without attempting to settle on a single conception here, I take distributive justice to constrain our choice of social institutions in favor of ones that distribute material resources more equally than other social interests, such as efficiency, might dictate standing alone. Within the legal domain I focus on the moral consequences of distributive injustice (which results from institutions that do not distribute resources equally enough) but will suggest that it has some implications for how we think about the scope of contract law even in an ideal world. The ultimate question here is whether reasons relating to the distribution of material goods in a society are among those we properly invoke to favor any one rule of contract over another.

Most scholars exclude reasons of distributive justice from the set of reasons we should consider in choosing the rules of contract. Although their affirmative focus is on either the efficiency of exchange or the morality of promising, legal economists and legal philosophers tend to agree that contract law is not an appropriate means by which to advance distributive justice. They imply further that distributive justice has no implications for the substance of contract law.

Any attempt to incorporate claims of distributive justice into contract faces three problems. First, it can be arbitrary to impose the burden of redistribution on a party to contract when the underlying injustice is systemic.[3] Second, the disadvantaged party has consented to the terms of the agreement and these terms might exhaust obligations between the parties with respect to the transaction. That is, even if the disadvantaged party had any claims arising from distributive injustice, she waives them vis-à-vis particular individuals by agreeing to contract on particular terms. Third, any

[2] *See* A. Mitchell Polinsky, An Introduction to Law and Economics 124–7 (2d ed., 1989); Michael J. Trebilcock, The Limits of Freedom of Contract 97–101 (1993); Ernest J. Weinrib, The Idea of Private Law 80 (1995); Peter Benson, *The Basis of Corrective Justice and Its Relation to Distributive Justice*, 77 Iowa L. Rev. 515, 607 (1992); Louis Kaplow & Steven Shavell, *Why the Legal System Is Less Efficient than the Income Tax in Redistributing Income*, 23 J. Legal Stud. 667, 677 (1994); Stephen R. Perry, *On the Relationship between Corrective and Distributive Justice, in* Oxford Essays in Jurisprudence: Fourth Series 237, 247 (Jeremy Horder ed., 2000); Arthur Ripstein, *Private Order and Public Justice: Kant and Rawls*, 92 Va. L. Rev. 1391, 1395 (2006).

[3] *See* Jules Coleman & Arthur Ripstein, *Mischief and Misfortune*, 41 McGill L.J. 91, 93 (1995) ("Corrective justice concerns the rectification of losses owing to private wrongs. In contrast, distributive justice concerns the general allocation of resources, benefits, opportunities, and the like. The duty to repair under corrective justice is agent-specific—only wrongdoers need make up the losses of others. The duties imposed by distributive justice are, in contrast, agent-general—everyone has a duty to create and sustain just distributions"); Melvin A. Eisenberg, *The Theory of Contracts, in* The Theory of Contract Law: New Essays 206, 257 (Peter Benson ed., 2001) (rejecting redistribution in contract law as "completely haphazard"); Eric A. Posner, *Contract Law in the Welfare State: A Defense of the Unconscionability Doctrine, Usury Laws, and Related Limitations on the Freedom to Contract*, 24 J. Legal

attempt to correct distributions through contract adjudication or even regulation of classes of contract may be futile, or worse, counterproductive.[4]

A few liberal theorists, economists, and critical legal scholars have attempted to rebut one or more of these serious challenges to the significance of distributive questions to contract. Their arguments and others show that background distributions inform the content of private obligations, even in the context of agreement. Section II argues that the terms on which individuals are free to contract may depend descriptively, morally, and legally on the socio-economic positions of the parties. There is nothing arbitrary about recognizing those distribution-sensitive constraints in the liability conditions of contract law.

Section III argues that the fact of consent in contract also fails to insulate contract from distributive considerations. Consent does not foreclose either allocation of economic losses from contract for distributive ends (e.g., in exceptions to the normal rules of remedy) or interpretation of ambiguous agreements to be consistent with distributive preferences. Objections to distributive considerations in contract that rest on the institutional advantages of redistributive taxation sometimes exaggerate those advantages, but are in any case highly contingent on other social facts. Section IV shows the limitations of arguments from futility.

Most of this chapter is devoted to developing the three major strands of the standard critique against considerations of distributive justice and rejecting each in turn. Before turning to this substantive discussion, I will first consider the boundaries of the subject—the scope of contract law—and the implications for its permeability by distributive concerns.

I. Regulating Private Exchange

"Contract law" can refer to the common law of contracts or it can encompass the entire body of law that governs private exchange. The more narrow meaning is unhelpful; even ordinary courses in contract cover some statutes, like the Uniform Commercial Code in the United States. So many types of exchange are regulated by statute that the common law is a mere default regime. Since in each departure from it policymakers appear to have concluded that the common law regime was inadequate to the task, focusing on the common law at the expense of other forms of contract regulation skews one's perspective on how we use legal rules to facilitate and shape transactional activity.

On the other hand, the more expansive meaning of contract law, which includes every statute regulating terms and results of exchange, may seem unwieldy. It might seem implausible that any unifying principles underwrite regulation of all forms of private exchange, no matter the subject matter. Indeed, the codification of rules

STUD. 283, 284 (1995) ("Critics further argue that the welfare system provides a more equitable way to redistribute wealth than legal rules do, because legal rules redistribute wealth only to people who happen to be injured or people in the class of those likely to be injured in a way that can be redressed by courts—a small and arbitrarily selected portion of the needy population").

[4] *See* POLINSKY, AN INTRODUCTION TO LAW AND ECONOMICS; Kaplow & Shavell, *Why the Legal System Is Less Efficient than the Income Tax in Redistributing Income*.

governing particular classes of transactions might be taken as indication that policymakers believe each to be essentially distinct, subject to unique concerns and dynamics.

However overwhelming the entire class of transactions governed by contract law, taking anything less than the broader view of contract distorts a discussion of its underlying principles and what those may include. To be sure, the particular concerns of public policy will vary across transactional context. So, for example, background distributions may be central to the regulation of healthcare and ordinary consumer contracts, distributional outcomes may be central to the regulation of employment and mortgage contracts, and neither may be important to the regulation of jewelry sales. But there are some goals common to regulating all manner of exchange and some meta-rules that determine the most appropriate regulatory approach in a given context. For example, across subject matters, policymakers tend to prefer contracts that can be expected to benefit both the parties involved and maybe others affected. They also prefer terms that are clear, in that the terms are understood by (or at least unsurprising to) the parties and transparent to third parties like the courts. The content of fairness will depend on a range of considerations, as will the best method for measuring and inducing efficient exchange, but these are policy goals that apply more or less across the board. Even at a high level of generality, goals and principles are both intelligible and contestable.

Some aspects of contract regulation are especially salient in the common law's treatment of contract. These have in turn been highly salient to contract scholars, in part because unlike most other areas of contract regulation, the common law purports to speak in general terms about exchange. Some important features of common law contract, which it does not necessarily share with other forms of contract regulation, are the pervasive language of voluntary obligation and its emphasis on individual right and wrongdoing. The result has been a scholarly focus on the scope of promise and consent, and the conditions of responsibility and entitlement. The explicit invocation of these concepts in common law does not imply that they are irrelevant to how we should regulate contracts by statute; it may be illiberal to mandate the terms of exchange for certain kinds of reasons and it may be unfair to impose certain terms. Policymakers debating the merits of intervening in this or that class of contract regularly invoke principles of freely given consent and individual responsibility, even when the proposed intervention is statutory. Moral concepts that are salient in common law reasoning about contract have permeated public discourse about contract regulation more broadly.

Unfortunately, public discourse on statutory regulation has been more receptive to the normative commitments of common law contract than the common law has been receptive to the relatively new public policy goals embodied in statutes. Hundreds of statutes overtly and obviously invoke distributive concerns to justify regulation of contract, from housing to employment to financial derivatives. Yet this new reality of contract law has not legitimated distributive justice as an ambition of contract. In fact, distributive justice is still perceived as not just misguided but *alien* to contract. There has been little reverse permeation from public discourse about contract regulation into either philosophical thinking about contract or the contract cases still governed by common law.

Given the abundance of legislation regulating contract that is animated by principles of distributive justice, scholars of contract must either revise our normative account of contract or reject whole categories of modern contract law. Some scholars are indeed prepared to reject large swaths of the contemporary legal landscape.[5] But most private law theorists today understand their task to illuminate legal practice in a way that makes sense of it, on terms that are recognizable to its ordinary practitioners.[6] I take that to be the task of contract theory and my aim here is to show how distributive justice can fit into an already rich normative scheme.

II. Arbitrariness

Distributive justice, like justice writ large, is a property of social institutions.[7] When a society fails to meet the requirements of distributive justice we might describe the society as unjust, at least along this dimension. But we would not describe its members as unjust. Even those individuals who enjoy or benefit from the injustice are not culpable for it. We might feel guilty or ashamed about social injustice in our society because we identify with the society and its government but this identification is not literal. The wrong of distributive injustice is collective and does not trickle down to each of its members. If it did, even those disadvantaged by distributive injustice would be guilty of wrongdoing.

We sometimes describe individuals as possessing the virtue of justice or as acting justly but individuals are not positioned to bring about justice per se. Because individuals lack the capacity to effectuate distributive justice, and because control is usually thought a prerequisite to responsibility, distributive injustice is not a state of affairs for which any particular person is uniquely responsible.

Rawls plausibly suggested that though justice is a property of social institutions individuals have a duty to support just institutions.[8] This duty to support just institutions appears to consist in a duty to comply with the rules of just institutions and perhaps an imperfect duty to reform institutions in order to make them more just. It seems unlikely, however, that cooperating with or complying with the rules of unjust institutions implies complicity in their injustice except in the extreme circumstance where their injustice exceeds the (admittedly controversial) duty to obey the law, or the duty to otherwise defer to collective decision making or appropriate authority on matters of collective living.

Again, even if individuals were complicit in the injustice of their society, this complicity would not differentiate most citizens from one another. One might argue that

[5] *See, e.g.*, Richard A. Epstein, *A Common Law for Labor Relations: A Critique of the New Deal Labor Legislation*, 92 YALE L.J. 1357 (1983).

[6] *See* Jody Kraus, *Legal Theory and Contract Law: Groundwork for the Reconciliation of Autonomy and Efficiency*, *in* LEGAL AND POLITICAL PHILOSOPHY 385, 395–410 (E. Villanueva ed., 2002) ("[C]onceptual explanation" aims "to identify a concept or set of concepts that render the phenomena sought to be explained maximally 'coherent' " so as to capture its "immanent, inherent, intrinsic, or internal rationality or intelligibility, deep structure, animating or underwriting principles, logical consistency, or theoretical or conceptual unity"); JULES COLEMAN, THE PRACTICE OF PRINCIPLE: IN DEFENSE OF A PRAGMATIST APPROACH TO LEGAL THEORY 3–12 (2001).

[7] JOHN RAWLS, A THEORY OF JUSTICE (1971).

[8] RAWLS, A THEORY OF JUSTICE.

only individuals who benefit from the injustice are complicit, especially since wealth and income in excess of what one would be entitled to under a just scheme are benefits individuals are able to forgo. But even if we were to agree on what distribution would result under more just institutions we would not know what any individual's entitlement would be under that just scheme. It is implausible that a general sense that a society is morally imperfect renders its winners complicit in wrongdoing against its losers where any particular winner and loser might still be winner and loser, respectively, under a more just arrangement.

If there is arbitrariness in pinning responsibility for distributive injustice on particular parties to contract, it is also arbitrary to award compensation for it to particular individuals through the law of contract. Again, we do not know how much better or worse particular individuals would fare under improved social institutions. They have not been injured by distributive injustice more (and possibly less) than others who happened not to be in contract or who lack a colorable claim in contract. Using distributive justice to adjust liability and remedy on the margins might deprive individuals who fare worst under an unjust distribution of remedy for distributive injustice because they fail to meet other requirements of a contract claim. And it might confer a windfall on those who have a colorable contract claim "enhanced" by their low socio-economic status. Even if distributive injustice gives rise to corrective compensation, that compensation would be arbitrarily distributed among those with valid claims if distributed through adjudication of private contract disputes. In fact, this aspect of the arbitrariness objection applies even to legislative schemes that are motivated by distributive concerns. Mortgage relief for low-income homeowners who are unable to repay their loans may unfairly benefit them over those with income too low to qualify for a mortgage in the first instance. It may unduly burden banks prepared to lend to low-income borrowers relative to banks that deal exclusively with the rich.

If individuals are not uniquely responsible or deserving as a result of distributive injustice then private law appears a poor instrument with which to pursue that type of justice (as opposed to, for example, corrective justice). Private law is the law governing private obligations and recourse for their breach. One of its distinctive features is bilateralism: the linking of plaintiff-victim with defendant-wrongdoer (even where wrongdoing and victimhood are expansively conceived).[9] While private law might be theoretically used to efficiently incentivize actors in various domains, the internal language of private law suggests that plaintiffs are expected to have claims against the particular defendants against whom they bring suit. For a claim to be valid, the actions of that defendant must breach a duty she owed to plaintiff in particular. Private law seems to require a moral linkage between plaintiff's claim and defendant's liability.

Contract law is of course one substantial pillar of private law. In fact, contract law is often regarded as more radically private than torts. While torts involve involuntary duties owed to many private individuals, obligation and entitlement in contract not only attach to private persons but are their own creation. On the classic view, individuals entering contract understand themselves to be engaged in a strictly bilateral

[9] *See* Weinrib, The Idea of Private Law, at 63–6; Jules L. Coleman, *The Structure of Tort Law*, 97 Yale L.J. 1233 (1988).

exchange to which the parties jointly (and exclusively) control the terms. Upon breach, the plaintiff party brings suit based on breach of the contract alone, without reference to outside legal or social norms. The breaching party, in turn, is bound only if she failed to fulfill an obligation she communicated an intention to assume, and is excused only where there was a defect in the process by which she consented—her best shot is where the nonbreaching party in some way induced her error. Other people do not appear in this narrow picture of contract. Neither do values that expressed only in our manner of collective living. In this picture, there is no moral link between particular individuals and principles of distributive justice and drawing such a line in the law is morally arbitrary.

The Arbitrariness Problem described above ultimately rests on two assumptions about contract: Contracts involve just two people and distributive justice involves many. It is because of this apparent dissonance that moral claims arising from distributive justice are perceived not to translate in any principled way into claims arising in contract.

Neither assumption holds. There is of course an important sense in which contracts are private. Contractual obligations run directly between private individuals and that is sufficient to explain their status as private obligations within the domain of private law. Beyond this feature that contract has in common with torts, in contract—*as compared to other legal obligations*—individuals play an outsized role in shaping the content of their obligations to particular other persons. Notwithstanding this uniquely private dimension of contract, contract law is not exhaustively private in the sense of *insular*. Contracting parties do not encounter each other in a moral or legal vacuum. In leaving some portion of the transactional landscape to contract law policymakers create important space for individuals to navigate the ethics of exchange on their own. But individuals owe a number of duties to each other independent of their (even objective) intent to do so. That is, though contractual obligation is bilateral and runs between private individuals, it is not wholly private in its source.

Kevin Kordana and David Tabachnik have argued that, because the rules of contract are among the rules that determine the allocation of basic resources, contract law falls within the bounds of distributive justice on a Rawlsian account.[10] But because the entitlements that individuals have against one another in contract are understood by contracting parties to reflect bilateral moral obligations, and because the language of contract law continues to invoke obligation in those terms, a better account of the role of distributive justice in contract will show how it *informs* the legally enforceable obligations that run directly between private persons. Even if distributive justice is not appropriately implemented via contract law, it shapes the kinds of bilateral obligations that are the stuff of private law. I will argue further below that some of the background duties that infuse contract are derivative from principles of distributive justice. Although these duties are ultimately interpersonal moral duties, their content turns on the normative state of the world (i.e., distributive justice or injustice) and related facts about distribution.

[10] Kevin A. Kordana & David H. Tabachnik, *Rawls and Contract Law*, 73 GEO. WASH. L. REV. 598 (2005).

Before we consider the particular logic that links distributive justice to interpersonal duties, we should distinguish two senses in which distributive justice might constrain contract law and the mediating role of interpersonal duty. First, as Kordana and Blankfein-Tabachnik suggest, the claims of distributive justice might require that we enlist contract as a tool with which to pursue more equitable distributions. A related but weaker claim would be that we should interpret interpersonal entitlements in such a way that they do not exacerbate distributive injustice. On the stronger view, contract is essentially *instrumental* while on the latter it might be animated by other principles; it is, though, constrained by exogenous principles of distributive justice. On even the weaker claim the focus is on the effects of contract on distribution rather than the effect of distribution on the independent morality of contract. Critics of "using" private law for distributive justice usually chafe at just this sort of account of the relation between distributive justice and private law. Because instrumental accounts do not make interpersonal morality central to their account of contract, the institutional features that make private law bilateral seem to render ad hoc its allocation of liability.

There is, though, another kind of accounting of the relation between distributive justice and contract that does not conceive of contract as merely hedged in, more or less severely, by distributive justice. It is this alternative type of argument that I pursue here. On these accounts, distributive justice operates through interpersonal duties by determining their content. The morality of exchange, agreement, and even promise is misconceived when treated as prepolitical; each is *contingent* on institutional arrangements. We can only do justice between persons after situating them in a political economy; political justice conditions private morality, especially (or at least) within the domain of commercial exchange. Unlike instrumental accounts, contingent accounts do not treat the language of responsibility and wrongdoing in private law as epiphenomenal; whether particular acts create responsibility or constitute wrongs depends on social context. The value of promise depends on the kind of relation from which it arises and that it might further. The efficacy of permission depends on the kind of relation from which it arises and that it might further. The normative power of parties to revise their rights and duties depends on their social starting points and background involuntary duties. The effect of their words and acts depends on the social forces they are acting with or against. The content of interpersonal duties is not "set" instrumentally with an eye to distribution but actually turns on background distribution, as well as prospective effects on distribution. Distinguishing between the instrumental and contingent views of contract and its relation to distributive justice, we can now turn to two accounts that substantiate the linkage. Both accounts cast contract as contingent, not instrumental, and they avoid the Arbitrariness Problem.

Anthony Kronman proposed one link between the morality of contracting and broader principles of distributive justice by framing the question as which advantages individuals should be allowed to exploit in contract.[11] His is a contingent rather than a merely instrumental account. He argues that liberals and libertarians should

[11] Anthony T. Kronman, *Contract Law and Distributive Justice*, 89 Yale L.J. 472 (1980).

both be committed to enforcing a contract only where parties have voluntarily consented to its terms. On both views, he argues, meaningful consent is absent where one party exploits certain types of advantage. Which advantages may a party legitimately exploit and which others render the resulting agreement unworthy of deference (or enforcement) by courts and policymakers? He suggests that we should permit parties to exploit only those kinds of advantages which both parties generally benefit from allowing the exploitation of.[12] What he calls the Paretian principle incorporates the distributive concerns of Rawls's difference principle. It is concerned with the distributive consequences of a rule but it gives rise to a standard for evaluating the conduct of individual parties to contract.

Kronman is persuasive on the fundamental point that there is no categorical reason for barring distributive considerations from the calculus of contract regulation. However, the Paretian principle he endorses is difficult to apply because its outcome turns on the level of generality with which one identifies the kind of advantage taking at issue. In particular, many legal economists argue that allowing parties to take advantage of disparities in information and resources consistently (across types of transactions) produces better long-term welfare outcomes for disadvantaged parties. In that case, permitting such advantage taking is not just a welfare-maximizing strategy but is morally acceptable on a Paretian standard. While Kronman makes the point that it is implausible that every regulation of contract for distributive purposes will be less efficient than pursuit of that end through tax and transfer, the moral test for advantage taking in particular types of transactions depends on how one groups transactions. Since the grouping of transactions is under the control of the state and will turn on a host of details relating to regulatory infrastructure, individuals exploiting particular advantages seem to lack notice or control over whether their advantage taking qualifies as morally acceptable under this test. The result is that it is difficult to use this standard to characterize individual behavior as wrongful. Although the Paretian principle seems to generate an important guideline for policymakers deciding when to regulate exchange, it does not fully avoid the Arbitrariness Problem as its focus on the morality of advantage taking at first seems to promise.

However, there are other ways in which principles of distributive justice might generate or influence standards of right conduct between contracting parties, which should in turn affect the enforceability of agreed terms. For example, this author has argued the state's duties in regard to distributive justice correspond to imperfect rights in individuals to such justice.[13] Individuals are not entitled to particular amounts from particular others but that a range of possible allocations is compatible with distributive justice does not imply that individuals are entitled to nothing—at least where zero is surely outside the range of morally plausible entitlements.

Private law is not the best venue in which to vindicate most imperfect rights. But imperfect rights correspond to perfect rights which are amenable to enforcement in private adjudication. Specifically, an imperfect right to distributive justice gives rise to a perfect right against other individuals not to have that distributive injustice

[12] Kronman, *Contract Law and Distributive Justice.*
[13] Aditi Bagchi, *Distributive Injustice and Private Law*, 60 Hastings L.J. 105, 122–4 (2008).

exacerbated or exploited by their actions.[14] That perfect and private right correlates with a corresponding duty not to exacerbate or exploit distributive injustice. Such a rule may generate results similar to Kronman's Paretian principle in that it too turns on whether enforcement of certain terms will leave disadvantaged parties worse off but it also incorporates a retrospective element that turns on whether the advantage taking at issue is possible only because of distributive injustice. Because the focus is on the marginal effect of individual advantage taking, contract rules that expand and limit responsibility to reflect duties not to exacerbate or exploit distributive injustice are not subject to the Arbitrariness Problem.

The ordinary conditions of responsibility may be met on either Kronman or my own account of how the enforceability of terms depends in some way on distributive considerations. In Kronman's account it is implicit that individuals can foresee and control how their advantage taking will adversely affect the other party. Although the margin of control and the ascertainability are both limited by the institutional questions on which the permissibility of advantage taking depend, individuals do decide whether to exploit advantages and they can foresee how the consequence for their share of transactional surplus. And while Kronman does not propose that the advantaged party be deprived of the benefit of his bargain on each occasion that he can foresee and control harm, responsibility is present in those subset of cases where we would decline to enforce.

In my own account, perhaps because it is more oriented toward common law adjudication than public regulation of contract, liability tracks moral responsibility more closely. Enforceability turns primarily on facts that speak to a party's moral responsibility. The advantaged agent uses contract in a way that harms a disadvantaged party and the question is whether contract should be available as a tool for such exchange. Withholding contract—or remedies in contract—does not unfairly surprise an unsuspecting contracting party. The absence of remedy reflects the respective moral position of breaching and nonbreaching parties against a backdrop of distributive injustice. Although our moral position always reflects a host of arbitrary factors, there is nothing distinctively arbitrary about either liability or compensation in this account.

III. Consent

Although incorporating distributive aims into tort law is thought to be subject to the Arbitrariness Problem discussed in Section II, considerations of distributive justice face an additional hurdle in the context of contract. Unlike those at the losing end of involuntary "transactions" in tort, contracting parties have consented to the sometimes onerous terms on which they are dealt. Consent thus poses a second and distinct challenge to incorporating even bilateral duties deriving from distributive justice.

Indeed, background duties of all sorts fare poorly in Anglo-Saxon theories of contract. Most famously, the common law does not recognize a general duty to negotiate

[14] Bagchi, *Distributive Injustice and Private Law.*

in good faith.[15] Once parties enter contract, they must bring claims relating to the transaction based on the contract alone; with a few exceptions, they cannot invoke overlapping tort claims.[16] Contract *replaces* tort as the governing legal regime; accordingly, the voluntary obligations assumed by the parties are thought to exhaust obligations between the parties. Because contract is regarded as *quintessentially* voluntary (and not merely relatively voluntary), we (talk as if we) define the scope of contractual obligation by the scope of obligation that parties intended at the moment of contract formation.[17] Courts and scholars alike tend to see the world of contract as immune from the moral claims that may torpedo about outside it. Entering the bubble of contract cleanses the parties of the claims they had before contract and they are left only with the entitlements for which they bargain within the bubble.

The Consent Problem too rests on a fantastic view of the moral insularity of contract. It overestimates the *power of consent* as well as the *scope of consent*. We should not construe the normative powers invoked in contract as capable of overriding completely every background duty that might apply between contracting parties. Moreover, even if contracting parties have such power, in the usual case, we have no reason to regard them as having exercised their normative powers in that way.

A. Consent and surviving moral responsibility

Outside of contract, it is implausible that consent renders ill-treatment of another person without moral consequence. We can distinguish between stronger and weaker versions of this claim. The stronger claim is that inflicting some kinds of harm results in culpability even where the victim consents.[18] On this strong version, individuals simply lack the normative power of consent in some contexts.

Because contract liability is not normally concerned with culpability, more relevant here is the weaker version of the claim: Moral responsibility for injury may survive consent even where permission effectively renders risk-creating conduct blameless in itself. The power of consent is limited to making an act permissible that was otherwise impermissible; it does not immunize individuals of responsibility for outcomes which otherwise meet ordinary conditions of responsibility.

[15] *See* Friedrich Kessler & Edith Fine, Culpa in Contrahendo, *Bargaining in Good Faith, and Freedom of Contract: A Comparative Study*, 77 Harv. L. Rev. 401, 408 (1964); John Klein & Carla Bachechi, *Precontractual Liability and the Duty of Good Faith Negotiation in International Transactions*, 17 Hous. J. Int'l L. 1, 16 (1994); Ralph B. Lake, *Letters of Intent: A Comparative Examination under English, U.S., French, and West German Law*, 18 Geo. Wash. J. Int'l L. & Econ. 331, 346–8 (1984).

[16] *See All-Tech Telecom, Inc. v. Amway Corp.*, 174 F.3d 862 (7th Cir. 1999).

[17] *See, e.g., Schering Corp. v. Ill. Antibiotics Co.*, 62 F.3d 903, 909 (7th Cir. 1995) (aiming for "a proper reconstruction of the parties' intentions"); *United Rentals, Inc. v. RAM Holdings, Inc.*, 937 A.2d 810, 829 n.92 (Del. Ch. 2007) ("Fact finding leads to the best reconstruction of the parties' intentions while drafting the contract, and the purpose of contract interpretation is to discover the common intent of the parties"); *Shannopin Mining Co. v. Commonwealth, Dep't of Labor & Indus., State Workmen's Ins. Fund*, 556 A.2d 488, 491 (Pa. Commonw. Ct. 1989) ("Our appointed task is to reconstruct the intention of the two parties").

[18] For example, Dennis Baker has argued that one cannot waive rights steeped in human dignity, though one can waive rights of personal autonomy. One can also argue that our ability to consent to harms is limited by the independent interests of our future selves.

In particular, shared responsibility for an economic injury, as through joint drafting of contract terms, justifies sharing in the losses. Shared responsibility of this sort does not *require* sharing in the losses—indeed, in the usual cases we have abundant reason not to allocate losses in contract primarily by reference to moral responsibility for them. But assigning risk for certain losses to a party A by contract does not absolve the other party B of responsibility for those losses when they materialize. The fact that A agreed to proceed on certain terms, or to bear a certain risk, is usually but not *always* reason for the state to assign her that risk. Our sound reasons for not imposing losses on B in the usual case do not rest on his lacking responsibility for those losses. And where there is reason to assign losses differently—e.g., on distributive grounds—the parties' decision to assign risk to A does not make it unfair to make B bear losses because A's consent did not absolve B of responsibility. This view of the parties' "ownership" of economic losses is reflected in recent statutory and regulatory moves to adjust mortgage balances and interest rates in the face of foreclosure.

Why should the power of consent be regarded as limited in this way? Our normative interest in the scope of outcome responsibility competes with our normative interest in the scope of the normative power of consent. The gist of outcome responsibility is that individuals do not fully control even their own responsibility. We might tie certain robust variants of culpability to blameworthy mental states but our more general moral responsibility does not depend on our intentions. Foreseeability and (a modicum of) control are adequate to give rise to basic responsibility on the most familiar, and perhaps ultimately attractive, picture of moral agency.[19]

If an agent's intentions (or lack of culpable intent to produce an injury) do not limit her own responsibility, her communication of an intent to limit another agent's responsibility does not plausibly limit his responsibility either. We hold agents morally responsible irrespective of their intentions because it helps construct them as moral agents who make imprints on the world when they act on it. Failing to recognize an imprint (or responsibility) where an agent has not intended an outcome (and perhaps intended the opposite) shrinks the scope of her agency. It compromises a picture of her as a person acting on the world all the time, and always at its mercy. Failing to recognize an agent's imprint where *another person* agreed to allow the action shrinks agency still further in that it removes responsibility from the agent's control altogether. Allowing that outcome responsibility attaches even where individuals do not intend injuries they cause commits us to the proposition that intentions may control culpability but not responsibility. It is only consistent to treat consent, or the communicated intent to make an act permissible, as similarly limiting culpability for an act but incapable of immunizing the agent of responsibility for its outcomes.

At first blush the idea that both parties to contract share responsibility for losses may seem distinctly unhelpful given that the decision facing a court is precisely to whom it should assign responsibility. But the idea that shared responsibility deprives courts of good reason—even moral reasons—to assign liability to one party or the

[19] *See* Tony Honoré, *Responsibility and Luck*, 104 Law Q. Rev. 530 (1988); Stephen R. Perry, *Responsibility for Outcomes, Risk, and the Law of Torts*, *in* Philosophy and the Law of Torts 72 (Gerald J. Postema ed., 2001).

other demonstrates the outsized role that responsibility plays in explaining liability in contemporary private law theory. Responsibility may rightfully operate as a *constraint* on the assignment of liability but other compelling reasons justify withholding liability even where responsibility is present.

In contract, consent to terms has a double significance. On the one hand, as discussed above, it alters the moral relations of parties to each other. But consent to contract also gives *the state* reason to defer to the allocation chosen by parties in the usual case. In particular, it indicates that each party expects her position to improve by way of the agreement. Liberal states stand in a special relation to citizens that may require deference to an individual's own assessment of her welfare. Denying the power of contractual consent in particular cases may undermine the utility of contract as a social tool and withholding remedy against certain groups may actually reduce their access to good and services. The state thus has contingent but normatively compelling reasons for treating a party's consent to contract as binding on her, regardless of how consent operates on the responsibility of the other party for economic losses.

The claim that responsibility for economic loss survives consent by the other party to bear that loss therefore does not imply that consent is inconsequential for how states should enforce contracts. The affirmative plausibility of the claim is evident outside of contract, where the significance of consent to the state is not at issue and does not spill over to our assessment of its effect on the bilateral relations between private individuals.

Consider the case of a bad friend. If friendship entails certain measures of support, withholding such support from a friend who agrees that you need not provide it remains a breach of the friendship. Recall the strong version of the claim would hold that the friend who fails to abide by the norms of friendship has wronged her friend within the friendship, irrespective of whether her friend acknowledges those norms, invokes them as binding, or purports to excuse her friend from them. On such a view, the friend whom one mistreats lacks the power to excuse and more generally may lack normative power over her own moral claim against you.

The weaker version of the claim relevant here would hold that though you cannot wrong a friend who excuses you from a duty that normally attends friendship, you retain a special responsibility for the harms that might result from failure to follow through on the duty. The effect of excuse would be to obviate culpability but not responsibility. While you may not be culpable for not visiting your lonely friend in the hospital where she has credibly released you from this duty, you remain responsible for her loneliness in a way strangers never subject to the duty are not.

Consider next the act of hitting someone in the face. Even absent any special relation, hitting someone is wrong. Here the strong version of the survival thesis is especially plausible: Hitting someone in the face may be blameworthy even if he allows you to do it—possibly even where you are playing a game that leads you to believe he wants you to try. The weak version of the claim is still more plausible: Even if a person grants you permission to hit him in the face, you have a special moral responsibility for any injury that results.

Finally, consider the case of a doctor who operates on a patient while drinking heavily. If operating on a person while drunk is wrong, it does not become right because the patient agrees not to insist on sobriety. Even if culpability does not survive permission, at least responsibility persists. That is, even if the doctor is not culpable for operating while drunk because the patient permitted him to do so, he has greater responsibility for the harms that result from his drunken efforts. We recognize this persistence in tort, which does not grant immunity to a doctor for reckless negligence even where a patient appears to have signed away her right to sober treatment.

The limited significance of consent is most evident where the wrong is most grievous because in some of those cases consent may not even obviate culpability. But in none of these cases does the persistence of responsibility (or *ex ante* risk of it) after consent depend on the magnitude of the prospective wrong. In the friendship example, depending on the details, the possible wrong and the resulting harm may both be quite minor.

One might argue that contract is different from these examples, not because the significance of consent to the state is distracting but because one's choice of terms merely creates a risk of harm. Moreover, the risk is symmetrical in two respects. The terms which ultimately result in economic loss for one party may have resulted in economic gain for her instead. Also, each party bears potential risk so the terms do not represent a unidirectional imposition of risk. Depending on alternatives, it may not be irrational for a party to agree a term that comes with a non-negligible risk of economic loss and it may be part of a transaction that is equitable. That is, the moral merits of a contract term cannot be assessed just by reference to the probability of loss for one party.

In most contracts, moral responsibility may result from a choice of terms that produce economic harm for one of the parties but economic harm is unlikely or at least unexpected. By contrast, in the first example above, in which a person chooses not to visit her friend in the hospital, the wrong at issue (failing to perform a plausible duty of friendship) seems only tenuously related to the potential harm (loneliness). Failure to visit, especially without the friend's consent, might be wrong even where the friend is not lonely at all.

In the second example above, the wrongfulness of hitting is closely connected to the potential injury but the injury is very likely. In fact, bringing about such injury is the usual purpose of the act. By contrast, a party to contract rarely enters into agreement with the aim of creating a substantial risk of injury for the other party. The injury is not only perceived as unlikely but is in any event incidental to the primary aim of securing some benefit for oneself. Like the hitting example, the risk of injury in the third example is also high. We do not assume that someone operating while drunk intends harm in the way that we assume someone hitting another person in the face intends harm, but we tend to assume there is no good reason for operating drunk either. In none of these examples is potential harm the basis for any potential negative moral responsibility, risk of that harm low, and that risk incidental to the pursuit of a legitimate interest.

Although contract is distinguishable from the examples in this way, the significance of the difference is that negative moral responsibility is less likely in the ordinary contracts case; it does not show that consent is uniquely effective in that context.

Because moral responsibility for a wrong that does not turn on harm is less contingent, moral responsibility is not subject to the uncertainties that apply in contract. Because contracts do not usually result in economic loss for one of the parties, there usually is no injury for which to share responsibility. And because contract losses are usually incidental to the pursuit of a legitimate economic interest, rather than deliberately or recklessly inflicted, mere responsibility rather than culpability is at issue. My claim here is not that contract will ordinarily result in negative moral responsibility in the way it might in other intuitive examples, only that in those cases where it does, that responsibility is not negated by virtue of the other party's consent to terms.

The relevance of responsibility is negative here. The argument is not that parties should be "compensated" for losses they incur in contract or that any skewed distribution of risk in a contract is problematic. The question I am addressing here is whether courts or regulators are barred from imposing losses differently than parties contemplated because the consent of the parties to the transactions absolves one of those parties of responsibility for the other's losses.

Courts and regulators are not barred from reassigning losses on equitable grounds, including reasons relating to the initial or resulting distribution. The Consent Problem rests on an exaggerated notion of what consent achieves. The fact of consent gives states many reasons to defer to parties' allocation of losses but as a normative power it does not inoculate either party from responsibility for the other's misfortunes under the jointly produced agreement. It does not create a dispositive reason why one party is barred from laying her injury at the foot of the other even in those cases where her permission to the other not to proceed on terms more favorable to her is crystal clear. In the next section I consider how courts should construe her consent in the frequent cases where the scope of her consent is unclear.

B. Consent and the best reading of contractual intent

The above discussion of consent pertains to a contract that definitely allocates a certain risk to one party over the other, or clearly articulates performance obligations in a way that implicitly assigns risk of some event to one party. Many contracts lack such clarity and courts must interpret the document to decide what each party owes under the agreement.

Because the principle of objectivity requires that courts ask how each party could reasonably have understood the other, courts already prefer reasonable and fair reading of terms over harsh or surprising interpretations.[20] Distributive considerations are among those relevant to reading ambiguous contract terms in a way that renders them reasonable.

[20] *See, e.g., Schwartz v. Family Dental Grp., P.C.*, 943 A.2d 1122, 1126 (Conn. App. Ct. 2008) ("[I]ntent… is to be ascertained by a fair and reasonable construction of the written words and. . . the language used must be accorded its common, natural, and ordinary meaning and usage where it can be sensibly applied to the subject matter of the contract;" alteration in original), quoting *Phillips v. Phillips*, 922 A.2d 1100, 1106 (Conn. App. Ct. 2007); *Dickenson v. State, Dep't of Wildlife*, 877 P.2d 1059, 1061 (Nev. 1994) ("An interpretation which results in a fair and reasonable contract is preferable to one that results in a harsh and unreasonable contract"); *Wilkes-Barre Twp. Sch. Dist. v. Corgan*, 170 A.2d 97, 98–9 (Pa. 1961) ("Where the language of a contract is contradictory, obscure, or ambiguous, or where its meaning

Reasonableness in contract encompasses multiple meanings. First, a party's understanding of terms may be *empirically* reasonable in that it is consistent with how most parties would interpret agreements under comparable circumstances. Second, her understanding may be *normatively* reasonable in that as a substantive matter the agreement is equitable on that reading. Third, it may be *procedurally* reasonable to privilege one party's understanding of terms over that of the other party because of their relative expertise or control over the agreement. Finally, one understanding of a term may be more *publicly* reasonable in that it may be desirable as a matter of public policy that obligations be construed in that way.

Sometimes courts directly employ one of these conceptions of reasonableness in their characterization of a particular bargain. At other times, courts may explicitly or implicitly invoke a default, which may be motivated by an array of reasons that roughly correspond to the considerations that bear on the reasonableness inquiry.[21]

Only empirical reasonableness, or majoritarian defaults, are designed to reconstruct bargains as they might have been, if unobservable directly. Each of the other interpretive motivations above may invite consideration of distribution. Courts can prefer contracts that achieve more equitable distributions (e.g., they may gravitate toward market price where a pricing mechanism fails), especially where contracts are patterned. Courts might take into account differences in the resources parties bring to contract. And finally, courts might favor one interpretation of a contract term over another because of its impact on third parties and the terms likely to be available to them; and its interest in third parties may have to do with the cumulative distributive consequences of private contracting. Each of these judicial preferences are expressed in the default rules courts use to interpret ambiguity.

We often refer to contractual obligation as voluntary, and indeed, contract relies on the exercise of normative powers of promise and permission in a way that distinguishes it from almost all other areas of law. In that way, contract is relatively or distinctively voluntary. But it is not quintessentially or wholly voluntary, in the sense that parties' obligations to each other are entirely a product of their undertaking. People in a legally organized society owe each a great deal in the absence of any communicated intent to assume obligation. These duties attach by virtue of their status as members of a political economy, and more particularly in the course of exchange.[22] If contractual obligation were fully voluntary, intent to assume contractual obligation would control the precise boundaries of contractual obligation. In that world, it would be inappropriate to reference the other dimensions of reasonableness described above. But because contract is the combined result of voluntary obligation and the involuntary background duties that citizens owe one another, it is appropriate for courts to construe agreements by reference not

is doubtful, so that it is susceptible of two constructions, one of which makes it fair, customary, and such as prudent men would naturally execute, while the other makes it inequitable, unusual, or such as reasonable men would not be likely to enter into, the interpretation which makes a rational and probable agreement must be preferred. If one construction would make it unreasonable, while another would do justice to both parties, the latter will be adopted").

[21] *See* Alan Schwartz, *The Default Rule Paradigm and the Limits of Contract Law*, 3 S. Cal. Interdisc. L.J. 389, 390 (1993) (describing types of defaults).

[22] *See* Aditi Bagchi, Promise and Permission in Contract (February 26, 2014) (unpublished working paper) (on file with author).

only to the words and acts of the parties but also the duties they owe each other and third parties, as those duties are expressed in identifiable sources of public policy.[23] As argued above, even if principles of distributive justice primarily regulate public law institutions, they also give rise to limited duties between private persons and those are relevant to how we understand the obligations parties effectively assume in contract.

IV. Futility

The harms occasioned by contract are wide ranging. They extend beyond those quantifiable and predictable material harms that might be compensated by legal remedy. Lending money at high or highly variable interest rates with a security interest in the borrower's home makes more likely that her family will face financial devastation and social dislocation. Employing someone on terms that limit their recourse for grievances burdens their daily experience of employment with fear and powerlessness. Selling goods or services to people on terms that make those goods and services less valuable than buyers foresaw implies that people will allocate their limited resources suboptimally and may forego otherwise attainable pleasures and joys as a result.

These contract-based harms are not trivial. If they are more likely or more severe for some segments of the population, it might be that the public institution of contract serves them less well in their private pursuits than it does those who begin with more. The relevant comparisons are between how well they are served by contract law as compared to those more socially advantaged, and between how well off they are under present contract law and some recognizable but reformed variant of it. On this standard, we should regard our contract law as morally inadequate even if socially disadvantaged people are better off with contract law as we know it than without contract at all, and even if they are better off under particular contracts than they would be were those transactions not to take place at all. If those who do least well under existing contract law could do better all-things-considered under some modified regime, the modification is commendable.

Of course, the difficulty is separating those modifications which will benefit parties in the short term but worsen outcomes for the least disadvantaged in the long run, from those which gain them more than they lose. Legislatures arrive at conclusions—or make gambles—about particular reforms. In some cases, we make certain contracts more difficult, as in subprime lending, or actually impossible, as in waivers of all liability for personal injury. In most cases, as with arbitration clauses in employment and consumer contracts, we come to tolerate their harmful effects. We enforce those contracts because the social losses from banning them appear to exceed the gains from prohibition.

There is no question that the basic economic logic of contract implies that regulating terms risks increasing transaction costs for some parties and making impossible a Pareto-superior bargain for others. Where a regulation alters the default away from the one preferred by most parties, parties will either incur the costs of opting out or, if

[23] *See* Aditi Bagchi, 'Normative Triangulation in Contract Interpretation' (February 26, 2014) (unpublished working paper) (on file with author).

those are prohibitively high, they will either forgo contract altogether or operate under the inferior term. If a regulation imposes a mandatory term, some parties may find it is not worthwhile to contract or will at least forgo the additional transactional surplus that would have been achieved on alternative terms. Rules intended to advance distributive justice exact a cost.

The economic cost of distributive justice is not so alarming in itself, as there is no variety of justice that is achieved without substantial cost. The costs are perverse, though, if they are disproportionately borne by the socially disadvantaged. For example, if prohibiting certain terms in high-risk loans actually reduces available credit, then a measure intended to benefit a disadvantaged group will actually worsen their financial situation.

Whether a distributively motivated default or mandatory term will actually deliver a benefit to the intended group is a highly contingent question. It will depend on how a variety of market actors value exchange on a variety of terms, and regulators will never know definitely in advance how each market actor will respond. But regulators do have some information about gains from trade or the profitability of some transactions relative to others. A regulation that will put credit out of reach for some number of consumers with respect to some credit suppliers may increase the gains from trade for many other consumers.

Although simpler economic theories of exchange predict that parties will always maximize gains from trade, the many varieties of transaction costs, asymmetric information, and cognitive error suggest otherwise. Again, whether a particular regulation will deliver more to disadvantaged parties than it will take away is highly fact intensive, and whether it will do better for her than an alternative tax-and-transfer regime is also uncertain.[24]

In the face of epistemic constraints, a policymaker might be risk averse and shy away from intervening in the private market only to make things worse. But the private market is after all not truly private but sustained by at least contract law, and the unavoidable question is what kind of contract law the state should offer. A simpler and doctrinally consistent policy may be more attractive than a more cumbersome and context-sensitive one. But given the empirical reality of factual variety and the moral reality of distributive injustice, a regulatory approach that ignores matters of distribution lacks the moral virtue of either simplicity or consistency.

If policymakers were ever to find themselves in the situation of revising all economic laws—from contract through tax—all at once, they might very well abandon some regulatory interventions in favor of tax and transfer. But the decisions policymakers face are always on the margin. Just as they must take distributive injustice rather than an ideal state as the backdrop for their policymaking, so too must regulators of exchange take a given regime of tax and transfer as largely fixed in the medium term.

[24] *See, e.g.*, Bruce Ackerman, *Regulating Slum Housing Markets on Behalf of the Poor: Of Housing Codes, Housing Subsidies and Income Redistribution Policy*, 80 Yale L.J. 1093, 1096–7 (1971); Christine Jolls, *Behavioral Economics Analysis of Redistributive Legal Rules*, 51 Vand. L. Rev. 1653, 1656–7 (1998); Chris William Sanchirico, *Deconstructing the New Efficiency Rationale*, 86 Cornell L. Rev. 1003, 1008–14 (2001).

The choice of time frame also attenuates the distinction between ideal and nonideal theory. Even a society that is essentially compliant with principles of distributive justice will be in constant flux. Not only outcomes but institutions evolve organically and in ways that make any one institutional cocktail unstable over time. Especially where the institutions we rely upon in pursuit of distributive justice are corrective rather than preventative (tax and transfer may be regarded as more corrective, regulation of private exchange more preventative), at any given moment in time, some persons will stand in problematic relation to others. Although we can expect ideal institutions to push entitlements back into alignment, some transactions will take place outside of ideal conditions even under ideal institutions.

This raises a more tentative issue about the scope of distributive justice. It is likely that even in political economies endorsable from the standpoint of distributive justice there are individuals who at times experience just those social harms that would compromise actual wrongs in an inferior political environment. For the most part I have taken distributive justice to generate strict imperatives, primarily for the state but also for individuals. But we can also take it to identify a softer imperative. It elevates a class of human concerns that have to do with inequality. Given the limitations of law, only some of the problems with inequality amount to actual injustice. Others are merely tragic. It might be that acknowledging the human reality of inequality and its effects on private exchange softens how people experience inequality of even the tragic variety in a way that a progressive regime of tax and transfer does not.

PART II

DOCTRINAL ANALYSES

12

An Analytical Framework for Legal Evaluation of Boilerplate

*Margaret Jane Radin**

I. Background Considerations

A. *Boilerplate and those who receive it*

Boilerplate is a name commonly used to denote fine-print (purported) contractual terms that cannot be altered by a party to a transaction, particularly as such terms are deployed in mass markets. In this chapter I focus on boilerplate used by firms in their dealings with consumers (or indeed with firms in the position of customers, but for convenience I will use the term consumer to apply to both). So for my purposes I will consider that the boilerplate is chosen by the firm, and the consumer cannot alter it. It is true that commercial parties also use boilerplate between themselves, but that is not my focus here.[1] For my purposes, therefore, I shall call the consumer party the "recipient." The recipient receives the boilerplate and (supposedly) has the choice whether or not to buy the product or service, but not the choice to change the terms. For each set of boilerplate terms, there are typically large numbers of recipients.

There are many different species of boilerplate clauses that consumer advocates and their sympathizers find troublesome, including contracts that are modifiable at the will of the firm, onerous choice of law/choice of forum clauses, and mandatory arbitration clauses with class action waivers. These clauses are variously defended by business advocates and their sympathizers, primarily by claiming that firms save money by deploying these clauses, which savings they pass on to consumers; and that consumers "would" or hypothetically "do" choose the lower price over the legal rights.[2] These clauses are also defended, weakly, by others, who essentially throw up their

* This chapter is based in part on chapter 9 of MARGARET JANE RADIN, BOILERPLATE: THE FINE PRINT, VANISHING RIGHTS, AND THE RULE OF LAW (2013). Permission of Princeton University Press to use this material is hereby gratefully acknowledged.

[1] Interesting recent work on commercial boilerplate shows that in some cases sophisticated commercial parties do not read boilerplate. *See* MITU GULATI & ROBERT E. SCOTT, THE THREE AND A HALF MINUTE TRANSACTION (2012). *See also* Stephen Choi & Mitu Gulati, *Contract as Statute*, 104 MICH. L. REV. 1129 (2006). This work argues, at least implicitly, that the basic model of contracting, the model of individual negotiated deals, is not suitable for sophisticated financial markets.

[2] *See, e.g., Carnival Cruise Lines, Inc. v. Shute*, 499 U.S. 585 (1991). This argument makes empirical assumptions that cannot be true in all (or even many) markets, to arrive at the assumption that firms pass on whatever they save, rather than just pocketing the money. This argument also assumes that the amounts passed on are exactly the amount that is sufficient to compensate recipients for loss of their

hands and say it would cause too much disruption to alter the widespread use of boilerplate in today's market environment.[3]

In many jurisdictions—the prime example being the European Union—these clauses are largely unenforceable against consumers,[4] but that is not the case in the United States. In the U.S., the primary avenue for legal oversight of boilerplate is the doctrine of unconscionability, and an important secondary doctrine is voidness as against public policy. My focus in this chapter is not primarily to rehearse the debates about whether boilerplate should be routinely enforceable, as is the case in the U.S., but rather to try to develop a better analytical framework that could help legal analysts—especially common law judges—make better decisions about it. In a sense, this chapter is a second-best effort, because, in my view, a great deal of mass-market boilerplate should not be treated as contractual. But if courts insist on treating boilerplate as contractual, invoking the doctrines of unconscionability and voidness as against public policy, they should implement an improved analysis. That analysis will be the focus of this chapter. (One result of the improved analysis will indeed be more focused attention on which alleged contracts should not be enforceable.)

B. *Remedy deletion (a core case for analysis)*

My niece, the mother of a 3-year-old, was asked to sign a release in order for her child to be admitted to a birthday party being held at a children's recreational facility. The clause that troubled my niece read:

> The undersigned agrees to defend, indemnify, and hold harmless [this facility], its officers, managers, members, employees, servants, agents and coaches/instructors and their successors and assigns from and against all legal liability, claims, suits, damages, losses, and expenses, including attorneys' fees, threatened or incurred, and arising from the child's participation, or from any cause whatsoever.

My students who are parents tell me that they have met almost identical clauses when enrolling their children in a day-care facility or in a school or recreational program. Such clauses are widely deployed in the U.S., often in near-identical wording. They purport to delete all remedies for harm to the consumer caused by the firm.[5]

rights. This argument also assumes that it is justifiable for recipients' property-rule entitlements to be transformed into liability rules that can be condemned by a firm. And it also assumes that recipients' entitlements are actually alienable. For discussion of the flaws in this argument, *see* RADIN, BOILERPLATE. It is the type of argument for which the economics joke, "Assume a can opener..." was invented.

[3] *See, e.g.*, Brian Bix, *Contracts, in* THE ETHICS OF CONSENT 251 (Franklin G. Miller & Alan Wertheimer eds., 2009).

[4] *See* Council Directive 93/13, Directive on Unfair Terms in Consumer Contracts, 1993 O.J. (L 95) 29 (E.C.), whose annex included an "indicative" list of unfair terms, together with further E.U. developments which tightened this to "presumptive" unfairness and in some cases per se unfairness (black listing); *see, e.g.*, PRINCIPLES, DEFINITIONS AND MODEL RULES OF EUROPEAN PRIVATE LAW: DRAFT COMMON FRAME OF REFERENCE (Christian von Bar & Eric Clive eds., 2010); and Jules Stuyck, *Unfair Terms, in* MODERNISING AND HARMONISING CONSUMER CONTRACT LAW 115, 134–6 (Geraint Howells & Reiner Schulze eds., 2009). *See also* the "grey list" of presumptively unfair terms in the comprehensive Australian Consumer Protection Law of 2010. *Competition and Consumer Act* (Cth) s. 25(1) (Austrl.), *available at* <http://www.comlaw.gov.au/Details/C2011C00003>.

[5] When exculpation is folded into an indemnification clause, as here, it adds insult to injury. Now someone who dares to challenge the clause in court will, if the clause is actually honored against her, have to pay the firm's expenses for beating her.

In this chapter, in order to develop an analytical framework suitable for evaluating the enforceability of boilerplate, I will often use as a test case boilerplate that deletes redress of grievances: boilerplate that eliminates all remedies for harms, freedom from which is otherwise a right of the recipient, or boilerplate that effectively eliminates remedies for breach of contract, which is otherwise a right of recipients as contractual parties. As I will elaborate shortly, large-scale remedy deletion is particularly suspect from the point of view of political theory. It is also particularly difficult to adjudicate on an individual basis. The exculpatory/indemnity clauses represent outright rights deletion, whereas other widely used clauses may have the same practical result, but do not literally proclaim it.[6]

The analytical framework I will suggest in this chapter is not proposed solely to address remedy deletion, but remedy deletion is a good illustration of how the proposed framework can function.

C. *Boilerplate and the political functions of remedies*

Why is boilerplate that deletes legal remedies particularly suspect from the point of view of political theory?[7] With respect to deletion of remedies by means of (purported) contracts—such as deploying choice of forum clauses to select a particularly remote forum or class action waivers in situations of recurring small injuries that cannot otherwise be redressed—I suggest the following considerations.

Begin with the basic claim that the institution of contract underwrites a regime of private ordering. In standard liberal stories, the creation and maintenance of the institution of contract is a primary justification for the existence of the state. Exchanges in a regime of private ordering are legitimate only within a polity that underwrites a background public legal infrastructure by which contracts that lack consent or are obtained by force or fraud will be denied enforcement, and by which contracts that are legitimately made will in fact be enforced. Because of the necessity of creating and maintaining a system of rules and practices that differentiate between contracts to be enforced and noncontracts to be refused enforcement, and that specify how enforcement must be managed, remedies are central to the idea of contract. They are of its essence.

To this basic claim add another: some functions of the polity are situated in the public realm and may not be privatized, or at the very least not without special justification and limitation. Excessive privatization of those functions that are situated in the public realm—whether by private armies, private prisons, or private police—erases the safeguards that are afforded by the polity. Establishing and maintaining these safeguards can be theorized as the reason that those functions were situated within the control of the polity in the first place. Excessive privatization of the legal infrastructure of contracts—such as mass-market deletion of the background rules

[6] Other clauses may in practice have the same result, or close to it. Mandatory arbitration clauses that eliminate aggregate remedies may in effect eliminate remedies for small recurring losses. Choice of forum clauses that mandate legal redress in a place far away from a consumer's home may also make remedial action so difficult as to be rare.

[7] For further thoughts on this topic, *see* Margaret Jane Radin, *Boilerplate: A Threat to the Rule of Law?*, *in* PRIVATE LAW AND THE RULE OF LAW (Lisa Austin & Dennis Klimchuk eds., forthcoming 2014).

of legal rights to redress in case of breach—undermines the possibility of private ordering by contracts as envisioned in the basic liberal story. Firms that deploy boilerplate in order to erase the legal rights that form the infrastructure that makes contractual private ordering possible are using contract to destroy the underlying basis of contract.

To enforce a contract, the state must divest an entitlement from one holder and deliver it to another, which is a form of coercion in the name of private ordering. The state must also refuse to enforce alleged contracts that do not meet its rules of contractual validity, meaning it must countermand instances of alleged private ordering. Since justification of state enforcement is apparently dependent on versions of the traditional liberal story, what happens if the story is not plausible for a large percentage of alleged contracts?

This question brings up the problem of "fit" between an ideal justification and a set of nonideal circumstances. The traditional story provides an ideal justification: what justifies state enforcement is instantiation of free will furthering mutually beneficial exchanges. How far can a practice diverge from this story (fail to be described by this story) and still be considered justified as an instance of it? That is, how good a "fit" do we need in order for a practice in nonideal circumstances to be considered justified?

I cannot deliver here a general theory of "fit." My view is that, at any rate, at least mass-market boilerplate rights deletions of certain kinds clearly do not fit the justification for state coercion, and thus should not be held to qualify as enforceable contracts. What kinds of rights deletions are those? At least those rights deletions that are constitutive of civil society, and especially if the rights are not salient for individuals, and especially if the deletions affect millions of recipients, not just one individual. Thus, remedy deletion becomes a core case to consider.

The situation with deletion of remedies for harm to others, such as with the exculpatory/indemnity clause that worried my niece, is likewise an assault on the underlying structure of the polity.[8] In most stories of political justification, safety from continuous susceptibility to harm imposed by others—and safety from continuous fear of such harm, and from continuous need to protect oneself against it—is another primary justification for the existence and powers of the political state. Criminal law is in the province of the polity. That is the reason why courts would not enforce the literal meaning of the clause that worried my niece: one cannot use contract to immunize another from deliberately inflicting harm. Nor would courts enforce such a clause to the extent that it would excuse harm caused by reckless behavior towards others, or gross negligence.

The battleground in the U.S. has been whether one can exculpate for one's own negligence, and many states have drifted toward this position. In the mass-market boilerplate context, the arguments for this position do not survive scrutiny.[9] First, we

[8] As my proposed analytical framework will emphasize, a judge should give attention to the nature of the right when an alleged contract in the form of boilerplate comes before her.

[9] There could be a different conclusion in the case of negotiated contracts between sophisticated parties. Commercial partners may engage in cognizant risk allocation, with the risk-bearing firm either self-insuring or purchasing insurance. That is different from what is happening with mass-market boilerplate rights deletion. The fact that the boilerplate is routinely copied from other firms' boilerplate is

ought to grant that everyone bears a social responsibility not to harm others, usually expressed in tort law. It should not be so easy to shuck this responsibility by deploying boilerplate; to make oneself nonresponsible and one's customers super-responsible. Second, a rationale for tort law that one often meets is the idea that liability for negligently causing harm deters firms from being lax about the responsibility not to harm others. If the deterrence rationale is accepted, and if we assume that tort liability deters firms from negligently causing harm, then we should infer that that deterrence is eliminated where widespread boilerplate exculpation prevails, and thus infer that firms will cause more harm than would be inflicted on society if deterrence were in place. In other words, ability to exculpate oneself on a mass-market basis enables a variety of moral hazard. Firms are free to save money by behaving badly, by omitting precautions and safety controls.

Third, it is said that recipients should walk away, that is, not deal with the firm that deploys onerous boilerplate. But recipients cannot always walk away, because sometimes the product or service is a necessity, and sometimes the market is monopolized, or cartelized, or there is industry-wide boilerplate for some other reason. Fourth, it is also said that recipients should insure themselves. But the firm is almost always the best cost avoider (to invoke a prevalent rationale for who should insure), so the firm should be the insurer, or the insurance purchaser.[10] Parents cannot investigate the screening of employees, the managerial practices, the equipment maintenance, etc., of every firm. To talk in economic terms, that would be wastefully costly. More important, that is exactly the kind of super-responsibility necessitated on the part of individuals that the polity precludes by upholding rights against harm. Widespread use of boilerplate to delete basic rights of civil society undermines the rule of law.[11]

D. *The problem of salience*

The right to meaningful remedy, while it is central to civil society, is not salient for individuals. Issues that are salient for humans are those that our intuitions and habitual reasoning processes make us likely to consider when evaluating a situation or making a decision. The lack of salience with regard to legal remedies makes the situation with boilerplate remedy deletion difficult. Individuals do sometimes push back against firms with regard to rights deletions that they experience as salient, especially if they can aggregate, which has become feasible online in some kinds of situations.[12] Individuals are unlikely to push back against firms that engage in wholesale remedies deletion. Rights that undergird the polity, the collective, tend not to be salient to individuals.

enough to show that cognizant risk allocation is not what is going on when firms deploy boilerplate against consumers.

[10] And insurers should not be allowed to condition insurance of firms on the firms' using boilerplate to shunt liability to their customers. That amounts to the insurer insuring against harms whose costs are going to be borne by someone else. (Nice work if you can get it.)

[11] *See* Radin, *Boilerplate: A Threat to the Rule of Law?*.

[12] For example, in January 2013, Instagram, a photo-sharing site affiliated with Facebook, announced it was instituting new Terms of Use. Users interpreted the new terms as in effect confiscating their rights

Moreover, individuals tend not to take seriously any risk that they will need to invoke their legal rights. It might be rational sometimes to consider that the risk of needing to use legal rights to redress is slim and worth taking. Even so, it may not be rational when the risk is extremely serious, such as death, even if few recipients are killed by the negligent acts or omissions of a firm. More important, psychology has shown that humans tend to be irrational when it comes to risk estimation.[13] Some risks are overestimated (such as how often planes will crash), and some risks are underestimated (such as how dangerous it is to drive on worn tires). Many risks are experienced as likely to materialize for others, but not for oneself (such as the risk that one's marriage may end in divorce).

II. Current Issues for Judicial Oversight Based on Unconscionability

In the U.S.—and to some extent in other common-law jurisdictions that have not enacted comprehensive regulatory control of fine-print clauses used against consumers—the responsibility to decide which boilerplate rights deletions against consumers to enforce often falls to the courts.[14] The primary doctrine used is the doctrine of unconscionability.[15] Here I want to mention three serious problems for the doctrine of unconscionability as currently practiced, which I hope the analytic framework I will propose can help to alleviate. These problems are: (1) the relentlessly case-by-case discretionary nature of unconscionability evaluation; (2) the ambiguous use of the idea of consumer "expectation" in unconscionability evaluation; (3) the use in unconscionability evaluation of a distinction between "procedural" and "substantive" evaluation of a purported contract.

under copyright (though not explicitly saying this). *See, e.g.*, Mike Tomkins, *Instapanic: New terms grant Instagram right to sell users' photos, share data and more*, Imaging Resource (December 18, 2012, 7:53 p.m.), <http://www.imaging-resource.com>. After massive protest by users, Instagram withdrew the revised clause that was protested. But users apparently did not protest Instagram's promulgation of a mandatory arbitration clause, and Instagram did not walk that one back.

[13] *See generally*, Daniel Kahneman, Thinking, Fast, and Slow (2011).

[14] The common law provinces of Canada form one such jurisdiction (or set of jurisdictions). *See, e.g.*, Stephen Waddams, *Adhesive or Unconscionable Clauses from a Common Law Perspective*, 49 Canadian Business L.J. 378 (2010). *Cf.* Sebastien Grammond, *The Regulation of Abusive or Unconscionable Clauses from a Comparative Perspective*, 49 Canadian Business L.J. 345 (2010) (arguing that judicial interpretation of the Quebec Civil Code provisions on abusive contracts against consumers is tending toward alignment with the unconscionability doctrine as practiced in the common law provinces). Although unconscionability is a common judicial doctrine for evaluating boilerplate, it should be recognized that jurisdictions using it have many consumer protection statutes and regulations as well. Even the U.S. has many consumer protection laws on the books, as has been ably pointed out by Jean Braucher, *Form and Substance in Consumer Financial Protection*, 7 Brook. J. Corp., Fin. & Com L. 107, 111–18, 125–8 (2012).

[15] Secondarily, the doctrine of voidness as against public policy is also used. It is currently less often invoked than the doctrine of unconscionability, but my impression is that it was more frequently used in the past. Common law courts have the power to declare a contract void because it undermines public policy, but most courts today are conservative in using that power. A common position today is that in order for a court to find that a contract violates public policy, there must be a statute or some other kind of authoritative legal directive that explicitly supports that result. *See* David Adam Friedman, *Bringing Order to Contracts against Public Policy*, 39 Fla. St. U. L. Rev. 563 (2012).

A. *The discretionary nature of unconscionability review*

The doctrine of unconscionability has a long pedigree in equity. It answers the need for a common law judge to try to do justice in the case before him. The ever-present dilemma is that a judge must also try to maintain a system that is consistent and predictable for everyone subject to it. That much is demanded by the ideal of the rule of law and the ideal of equality before the law. The dilemma between doing justice to the party before the court and maintaining a consistent and predictable system is at the core of unconscionability adjudication.

Between the horns of this jurisprudential dilemma, application of the doctrine of unconscionability is a process of relentless case-by-case adjudication, with many discretionary judgment calls in each case. Perhaps with the exception of truly egregious cases, outcomes are unpredictable. Moreover, the fact that the doctrine is formulated so as to address particulars of individual cases makes it impossible or at least very difficult to apply to mass-market contracts in the aggregate. It is not, therefore, a judicial oversight method well suited to evaluating and limiting large-scale boilerplate rights deletion schemes. Although thousands, hundreds of thousands, or even millions of people may be subject to a particular boilerplate scheme, only a few will bring suit challenging it, and the results in different courts may be half for and half against the challengers. This kind of jurisprudence neither validates nor invalidates such a scheme for everyone else who is subject to the scheme. It is a wild card.

It would be difficult to use the doctrine of unconscionability in a way that gets around this wild-card problem, so it is likely that comprehensive regulation of boilerplate will often be a better solution than leaving the evaluation to common law courts and purported contracts between two individuals. Especially in the U.S., however, where comprehensive regulation is politically precluded for the foreseeable future, it is important to seek other avenues of amelioration of legal evaluation of boilerplate, whether by courts (or indeed, agencies). The second and third of the three issues with the doctrine of unconscionability as it is now practiced relate to conceptions that cause needless confusion and could be changed more readily than the underlying dilemma inherent in the doctrine, and could be accomplished more readily than a switch to comprehensive regulation. To these issues I now turn. If these defects are ameliorated, as I hope my proposal would do, then concomitantly there may be some alleviation of the underlying jurisprudential dilemma, even though that problem—because it is inherent in the nature of equity judgment—would not be completely overcome.

B. *The ambiguity of "expectation"*

The second pressing issue for unconscionability evaluation is the problematic use of the notion of recipients' expectation, a notion that features prominently in unconscionability jurisprudence. Karl Llewellyn applied a notion of "blanket assent" to fine-print terms that were "not unreasonable or indecent."[16] Leaving aside the question of what Llewellyn meant by "indecent," blanket assent plays out in subsequent

[16] Karl N. Llewellyn, The Common law Tradition: Deciding Appeals 370 (1960).

attempts to provide for exceptions to enforceability for unknown terms not within the recipient's "reasonable expectations," or (as Randy Barnett would have it) not "radically unexpected."[17] The notion of expectedness, or radical unexpectedness, creates a big problem for courts. When a recipient who has been harmed by an unread boilerplate clause presents the purported contract to a court and asks that the clause be excised, what principles or procedures can the court use to decide whether the term is unexpected? For a recipient wishing to excise an onerous clause, radical unexpectedness seems to be a more stringent standard than not reasonably expected, but either way, these expectation theories do not make for a predictable jurisprudence.

Perhaps worse than the mere fact of unpredictability is this: the more widespread the use of a clause, the more a judge is likely to think that the clause is acceptable and should be validated, whereas the opposite may well be true. The prevalence of the clause may signify a massive taking advantage of recipients.[18] This tendency of many judges to rubberstamp boilerplate that is widespread raises the issue that I wish to draw attention to here.

The issue is a serious ambiguity in the idea of expectation. The ambiguity is a wavering between positive and normative, between an "is" and an "ought." From a positive or empirical point of view, the more prevalent a bad clause (or any unjust practice is), the more people reasonably expect it. The more instances I know about in which it turns out the police are invading people's bedrooms and the legal system under which I live is permitting it, the more I should reasonably expect that the police will invade my bedroom.[19] And had I lived in the early nineteenth century, I would have reasonably expected that women and black people had very few rights compared to white men. But from a normative point of view, expectation can characterize the honoring of rights that a citizen has a right to expect. From a normative point of view, I have the expectation that my right to privacy must be honored, even if I am living in a draconian regime that fails to do so. From a normative point of view, I have the expectation

[17] Randy Barnett, *Consenting to Form Contracts*, 71 Fordham L. Rev. 627 (2002).

[18] For example, in the U.S. the Uniform Commercial Code (U.C.C.) provides that a court may take commercial setting into account in deciding whether a contract is unconscionable. U.C.C. § 2-302(2) (2002). (The U.C.C. is a model law under the supervision of two nongovernmental organizations, the National Conference of Commissioners on Uniform State Laws and the American Law Institute. The model provisions of the U.C.C. have been widely enacted by state legislatures in the U.S.. Article 2 of the U.C.C., in which section 2-302 appears, applies only to sales of goods. There is no analogous general model law for service transactions.) The U.C.C. drafters probably intended widespread commercial use of a clause to be a defense for the firm using it, and it is often thought that widespread commercial use signifies efficiency. *See, e.g.*, Douglas Baird, *The Boilerplate Puzzle*, 104 Mich. L. Rev. 933 (2006). But the opposite may be true: widespread use of a clause that unjustly deletes a legal right may be a greater wrong than using it against only one or a few individuals. By now we are aware that industry-wide standardization by no means indicates that a clause is either efficient or what consumers "would" have chosen. *See* Radin, Boilerplate, at 99–120.

[19] The U.S. Supreme Court struggled with this very is/ought problem in its rulings on "reasonable expectation of privacy." The phrase made its appearance in *Katz v. United States*, 389 U.S. 347, 360 (1967) (Harlan, J. concurring). In later cases the court backed away to some extent from any strictly positivist interpretation of reasonable expectation, because there has been a gradual and incomplete realization that that would mean that the more police intruded in people's bedrooms, the more it would be constitutionally permissible to do so. *See, e.g.*, *Rakas v. Illinois*, 439 U.S. 128, 143 n. 12 (1978) ("Legitimation of expectations of privacy by law must have a source outside of the Fourth Amendment, either by reference to concepts of real or personal property law or to understandings that are recognized and permitted by society").

that as a human being I should have equal rights with other human beings, even if the current social order does not honor this principle.

It may be that what is routine in practice is that firms use onerous boilerplate to cancel consumers' rights of redress. If this is what exists, then this is what people will expect (in the empirical sense), the "is." Yet the more that something normatively inappropriate is happening to people, the more that society is deviating from what is justified (the "ought"). Thus, even if this becomes what is expected (empirically), it is nevertheless a form of defeat for the normative aspect of expectation, the right to expect the treatment that the polity is committed to, the commitment that undergirds the polity's existence and justifies its power.

Without adverting to the ambiguity in the meaning of expectation, some judges intuitively interpret expectation at least partly in the normative sense of what a recipient has a right to expect; others are resolutely empirical in their interpretation (because it could be said, "Surely everyone knows by now that unpleasant clauses lurk in boilerplate"). The empirical interpretation simply finesses the problem of whether merely knowing that a wrong is widespread can somehow indicate that a wrong does not exist or can erase the wrong. The "Everybody does it" defense must be questioned. It didn't work in the case of right to privacy, and (ultimately) it didn't work in the case of gender and race. If proponents want to argue that it should work in case of widespread boilerplate, more will be required than mere pointing to how widespread the boilerplate is.

C. *The procedural/substantive dichotomy and its truncated analysis*

The third pressing issue in unconscionability adjudication as it is currently practiced is the use of a procedural/substantive doctrinal template.

In evaluating whether or not a contract appears unconscionable, common law courts almost always look for both procedural and substantive unconscionability. U.S. courts have often defined unconscionability as "an absence of meaningful choice on the part of one of the parties together with contract terms which are unreasonably favorable to the other party."[20] Procedural unconscionability refers to the notion that the way in which the contract came into being looks somehow improper ("absence of meaningful choice"); it refers to defects in bargaining such as coercion or deception, or their penumbras,[21] not defects in the bargain. By contrast, substantive unconscionability refers to defects in the bargain itself: the notion that some contracts may look so one-sided, unequal, or oppressive that the court in good conscience simply should not tolerate enforcing them ("contract terms which are unreasonably favorable to the other party"). As this doctrine has developed, many courts declare that both prongs must be satisfied in order to find unconscionability. Thus, if the court decides that "consent" passes muster, the court will simply not evaluate the nature of the right that the recipient has given up.

[20] *Williams v. Walker-Thomas Furniture Co.*, 350 F.2d 445, 449 (D.C. Cir. 1965).

[21] I include in the penumbra of coercion or duress the related (and more disputed) doctrines of economic duress and undue influence; I include in the penumbra of deception, fraud, and misrepresentation the related (and more disputed) doctrines of mistake and failure to disclose.

In effect, the substantive question eludes the courts. It is understandable how this situation came about. Procedural unconscionability can be interpreted as countenancing court intervention only within the standard realm of preventing subversion of a party's will, whereas substantive unconscionability, because it allows courts to look into the basis of a bargain, has always appeared more questionable to common law courts. Because a finding of substantive unconscionability may appear to substitute the judgment of a court for the will of a party, many courts are happy to evade it. Nevertheless, judges when they are sympathetic to the recipient's case may reason from substantive one-sidedness of the deal to an inference that the deal must have been procedurally improper. (She can't have consented to *that*!) And some jurisdictions adopt a sliding scale in which the worse the deal looks, the less strong a case is needed for the procedural prong.

In spite of this type of doctrinal adjustment, the outcome is quite prevalent in which a court will erase the substantive question. Once the judge looks at consent and finds that there is no procedural unconscionability, there will be no inquiry into whether substantive rights were violated.[22] Moreover, even when a judge has the intuition that a purported contract is substantively unconscionable, the evidence taken into account is almost always about excessive price. Substantive unconscionability cases do not usually advert to loss of basic legal rights, such as meaningful access to redress of grievances.[23]

III. The Proposed Framework: Three Issues for Analysis

The considerations I have mentioned above are the backdrop for the analytical framework I want to propose. The framework could alleviate some of the difficulties with the current form of judicial oversight, though I am not under the illusion that it would be a panacea. A root difficulty, as I mentioned in Section II, is that unconscionability adjudication is relentlessly case by case, and indeed contract is conceived of as being a matter between just two parties; whereas imposition of boilerplate is a mass-market phenomenon, for which some kind of aggregate consideration is needed.[24] Later in this chapter I will put forward some tentative thoughts about how to move some awareness of the mass-market aspects of the problem into explicit judicial consideration, but here I do want to flag this as a continuing issue. Because most recipients will not take a mass-market clause to court—because the clause is not salient, because they don't notice it, because they don't understand it, or because the harm is

[22] *See, e.g., Loychuk v. Cougar Mountain Adventures Ltd.*, 2012 BCCA 122. Although this case came before an appellate court in British Columbia, there are numerous cases like it in the U.S.

[23] After a finding that the consent prong of the procedural/substantive test is satisfied so that there is no need to proceed further with unconscionability analysis, it would be possible for consideration to switch to analysis under public policy, which indeed happened in *Loychuk*, but in a truncated manner. Public policy is likely to produce a truncated analysis for the many jurisdictions that now require that an adjudication of voidness based on public policy must be based on a particular statute, regulation, or well-established authoritative directive. *See* note 15 and accompanying text.

[24] More than the "Everybody does it" defense mentioned earlier—though I suppose that that is a form of aggregate analysis. In fact, it is no accident, I venture to say, that some form of aggregate analysis sneaks its way sub rosa into adjudication of boilerplate, because boilerplate is a mass-market phenomenon that doesn't fit the template of contract, which relates to the rights of two individuals.

too small—and because the cases that do get adjudicated are unpredictable and inconsistent, the mass-market phenomenon is more amenable to statutory or administrative regulation than it is to case-by-case adjudication. In spite of the continuing issue posed by case-by-case consideration, I have some confidence that an analytical framework consisting of three parameters would improve matters, and that such a framework should now supersede both the trope of expectation and the application of a procedural/substantive distinction. Here are the questions posed by the three parameters I want to consider:

> *Question 1.* The ideal of private ordering often assumes a universe of default rules that individuals are free to alter by contract. Thus, a primary question for evaluating boilerplate rights deletion schemes can be framed this way: Are all of the rights granted or maintained by the state appropriately considered default rules? If not, then how does the analysis of whether and to what extent a right exists as a default rule figure in an analysis of whether a particular boilerplate deletion scheme should be enforceable? This is the question of the analytical role of the degree of alienability (vel non) of the right in question in a boilerplate rights deletion scheme.

> *Question 2.* Another primary question for evaluating boilerplate rights deletion schemes can be framed this way: How does the presence or absence of actual consent to waiver of individual rights affect the analysis of enforceability? How should problematic or unclear consent figure into the analysis of enforceability? This is the question of the analytical role of quality of consent of recipients of a boilerplate rights deletion scheme.

> *Question 3.* A third primary question with respect to boilerplate rights deletion schemes can be framed this way: To what extent should the number of recipients affected by a particular rights deletion scheme affect the analysis? Might deleting the rights of thousands or even millions of consumers be properly analyzed differently from deleting the rights of just one? This is the question of the analytical role of the extent of social dissemination of a particular rights deletion scheme.

These three analytical categories should be understood to reflect three continua. Whether or not a right is waivable by contract can range from treating the right as inalienable or market-inalienable[25] to treating the right as fully alienable.[26] Whether or not there is consent to waiver of a right can range from clear and informed consent to obvious nonconsent, such as sheer ignorance that anything was purportedly waived. Whether a waiver is widely socially disseminated can range from only one individual relinquishing her right to a situation where millions of people are purportedly relinquishing a right. Between clear inalienability or market-inalienability and

[25] In earlier work I developed the concept of market-inalienability to denote things that are not tradable for money, though they may be alienable in gift transactions. *See* Margaret Jane Radin, *Market-Inalienability*, 100 Harv. L. Rev. 1849 (1987); further developed in Margaret Jane Radin, Contested Commodities (1996).

[26] In accordance with the popular argument involving rights traded for lower prices, one would ask whether the right is tradable in nature.

clear alienability of a right there may exist a grey area of partial market-inalienability ranging from not-quite inalienable or market-inalienable to not quite fully alienable; and between clear consent and clear nonconsent there can exist a grey area ranging from consent that is not quite clear to nonconsent that is not quite clear; and between imposition of onerous boilerplate on one individual and large-scale social dissemination there can exist a grey area in which multiple individuals are affected but not large swaths of the public.

To put my critique of current doctrine in a nutshell, that doctrine has overvalued consent (often a seriously attenuated version thereof) while ignoring the other two parameters of concern.

A. *Market-inalienability*

The classic debates about market-alienability involve such transactions as sale of children or selling oneself into slavery. Although boilerplate does not contain, as far as I know, selling one's child or selling oneself into slavery, market-inalienability often should figure in decisions about boilerplate. As I mentioned earlier, the difference between market-inalienability and full alienability is that full alienability describes situations in which all relinquishment of a right is prohibited, not just sale. There may not be many instances of boilerplate attempting to accomplish the waiver of a right that is fully inalienable, though the purported waiver of tort remedy for intentional bodily harm could be such an instance.

The category of market-inalienability, that is, disallowance of market trading, is more useful in evaluating boilerplate, because rights that should be market-inalienable occur with some frequency in boilerplate. If we accept the prevalent argument that recipients are compensated for loss of their legal rights by lower prices charged by the firm, and that recipients "would" or hypothetically "do" choose this tradeoff,[27] we have thereby assumed that recipients are being paid in return for divesting themselves of legal rights. This assumption squarely invokes the question of market-inalienability. Rights that cannot be relinquished for pay cannot be "traded" either hypothetically or actually, no matter what level of consent exists. A prime candidate for market-inalienability is the basic right to legal redress, because legal redress is foundational for civil society.[28]

A court that invokes the procedural/substantive gloss of unconscionability to find that consent exists will often deem that, since both prongs of the doctrine must be satisfied, and it has decided that one of them (consent, "meaningful choice") has been satisfied, *ipso facto* there is no unconscionability. The inquiry whether the right impacted is market-inalienable is one that such a court is not going to reach. It is precisely an inquiry that is most needed. Market-inalienability negates the possibility of valid contract.

[27] *See* note 2 and accompanying text.

[28] Indeed I think that contractual ordering is a hallmark of civil society in traditional liberal conceptions, and that contractual ordering, with its backdrop of legal infrastructure governing state enforcement and nonenforcement, cannot exist outside of civil society. If a purported contract explicitly withdrew all remedies for breach, I would think courts would be reluctant to call it a contract, and surely that they should.

Recognizing that market-inalienability is at one pole of a continuum and the market-alienability represented by pure default rules is at the opposite pole, we can see that along the continuum between them are various situations where a right may be alienable, but only with individualized investigation of the appropriateness of that alienation under the circumstances. These situations I call partial market-inalienability. Although market-inalienability may apply to various widely deployed boilerplate clauses that result in remedy deletion, partial market-inalienability may apply to even more of them, such as situations where it is not clear whether in practice curtailment of remedies is equivalent to remedy deletion.

The level of review or oversight by public institutions reflects the appropriate place of a right on the continuum between market-inalienability and easily waivable default rules. It is important to recognize that courts as well as legislatures have the power to decide what is market-inalienable and what is partially market-inalienable, as well as where on the continuum of stringency of review or oversight such partially market-inalienable rights should fall. Courts may decide that an entitlement can be waived but only after the court performs a more stringent analysis, which will usually be called application of stricter scrutiny. Stricter scrutiny may include requirements of more decisive evidence, clearer arguments, or other specific legal prerequisites.

B. *Quality of consent*

Consent by a party to a purported contract may be unquestionably present (clear consent) or unquestionably absent (clear nonconsent). Even in a case of clear consent, as I have argued, a purported contract must be disallowed if the right that is transferred or waived is inalienable or market-inalienable, so courts should not allow consent to trump this consideration, or other considerations concerning the nature of the right.

Clear nonconsent likewise negates the existence of contract. If an exchange or waiver of rights is sought, but consent is unquestionably absent, then, whatever else has taken place, a contract has not come into being.[29] Like market-inalienability, nonconsent trumps other parameters in evaluating the appropriateness of enforcement as a contract. In a situation I will call sheer ignorance, in which those who are the targeted recipients of boilerplate containing rights deletions do not know that anything is happening, much less that they have purportedly "agreed" to cancel rights, a contract does not come into existence. (Examples of sheer ignorance may be found in the purported contracts of the form that are called "browsewrap."[30])

[29] When a contract does not come into being, can boilerplate nevertheless be validated under some other form of analysis? I leave aside this question here, but believe a *sui generis* regime should be considered, based upon background public policies and rights. When contract drops out of the analysis, boilerplate could (for example) be regulated in ways analogous to product safety or public health.

[30] What is "browsewrap"? Most websites have a small link called something like "terms of service" (T.O.S.). If one were to click on it, which most users don't (in fact, most probably don't even see the link), one would see pages of boilerplate open out, telling the user that she is bound to these terms, that she has "agreed" to them simply by the act of looking at the site through her computer's browser, and, moreover, that the owner may change the terms from time to time and that the user will then be bound by the new terms as well. This type of purported contract is called "browsewrap," by lineal derivation from "shrink-wrap," a method of (purported) contract formation when a buyer broke the plastic wrap of packaged software through which boilerplate terms could be seen. Compare the term "click-wrap," also

In the abstract there may be no conceptual space between the notions of consent and nonconsent, at least if one adopts a philosophical view that consent versus nonconsent is inherently or in principle a binary, either/or, phenomenon. In practice, however, because consent must be judged by whatever evidence of behavior (words and actions) we have, plus whatever we can make of the contexts in which the behavior occurred, there is a large grey area in between these poles. And indeed a more pragmatic philosophical view of consent would take account of these parameters that affect our understanding of consent in practice. Consent in practice—at least an observer's evaluation of consent—forms a continuum from only slightly doubtful to not quite clearly absent. Consent is going to be problematic to varying degrees in the many contexts when we must ask whether consent existed. In those cases we are actually asking to what extent we lean toward believing consent did or did not exist.

What shall we make of situations in which it is claimed that recipients are consenting to boilerplate rights deletion, but consent looks problematic? I take unawareness that boilerplate exists (sheer ignorance) as nonconsent, but there are many situations in which recipients do know that boilerplate exists but do not read it or take any action to understand what it means. I take these situations to be problematic on the issue of consent. For example, consent looks problematic with so-called "rolling contracts," when it is argued that recipients either are consenting to terms that haven't arrived yet, or are consenting to terms *sub silentio* by not trying to return the product or cancel the service.

Moreover, consent is also problematic when recipients do have some opportunity to see the terms. Many recipients just sign papers that are put in front of them, or just click "I agree" when the box appears online. What are they thinking, if anything? We certainly lack data on that question. They could be thinking, "I don't understand this legalese anyway," or "I don't have the time and energy to try to go elsewhere for this transaction," or many other possibilities; but it is even more likely that they aren't thinking anything, other than perhaps "Let's get on with this transaction." Those who click are almost certainly not thinking about, or intending to consent to terms that may deprive them of important legal rights that they might not know they have and probably (if they thought about it) would not think they will ever need.

Proponents of boilerplate might want to support their case with the objective theory of contract rather than trying to analyze what recipients really are thinking. The objective theory of contract relates to the reasonable understanding of the firm deploying the boilerplate, the party who wants to construe clicking "I agree" as consent to the terms.

derived from the original "-wrap," referring to the procedure of requiring users to click an "I agree" box after boilerplate is shown (or perhaps referred to) on-screen before proceeding to a transaction.

A contract does not come into existence merely because unseen browsewrap exists. (Unless those who wish to defend such a rights deletion as contractual can succeed in arguing for hypothetical consent, by which the unknowing [non]recipient "would" have consented to loss of her rights had she known about the offer to trade those rights for an allegedly cheaper price). (Or unless those who wish to defend such a rights deletion as contractual can succeed in arguing that anyone who had enough opportunity to see terms deleting his rights—whatever level of opportunity a judge may decide is "enough"—should be treated as if he consented to the deletion.) Although U.S. courts are often willing to take up these constructive (fictional) views of consent, my view is that hypothetical consent is not consent, and neither is as-if consent.

My view is that a firm does not have a basis for reading the meaning it wants into the fact that its recipients click. It may be relevant that firms know that people don't read these things and wouldn't understand them if they did read them, and that in many cases we might infer that firms intend this.

More clearly relevant is that we do not have a well-understood meaning of clicking "I agree" online to proceed with a transaction, such that any hearer socialized into our language and culture could be expected to take that meaning at face value. Rather the meaning of clicking "I agree" is more analogous to a contested concept; something that can have different meanings. In other words, a firm cannot "reasonably" understand all of its recipients to be consenting to its terms, because no one can "reasonably" understand that.

In fact, everyone, including a reasonable person in the position of the firm, should be able to infer that recipients will not properly evaluate cancellation of legal rights. The use of the trope of "expectation" may be understood as a vague way of groping for this conclusion. But it would be better to take the bull by the horns and dig more deeply into the contestedness of consent and how that meshes with other parameters of analysis. One could begin by asking why so much less is required of consent when we are considering a contract than when we are considering permission to perform surgery. Informed consent requires a lot more knowledge of information actually available to the consenting party. No one is arguing that consent to surgery would be implied by "I realize you are going to operate on something, and that there may be risks involved, so go ahead and operate on anything, with any degree of risk." Yet boilerplate supporters routinely argue that one may consent to bear risks of which one lacks any knowledge.

If we were to look to the analogy of informed consent when we reconsider consent to boilerplate, we would have to investigate the issue of salience. It is (perhaps) salient for someone about to undergo surgery to pay attention to the risk of surgery, even though the risks may be unlikely to materialize in every case, whereas it is less likely to be salient for an individual recipient to consider loss of legal rights when confronted with boilerplate. When a right is important to the structure of civil society, and when salience is lacking (perhaps not the case with informed consent to surgery), those considerations might suggest that more information is required to find consent to boilerplate, not less.[31]

C. *Extent of social dissemination*

Evaluation of waivers in mass-market boilerplate rights deletion schemes should often (though not always) take into account a third factor: the extent of social dissemination of the terms deleting legal rights.[32] That is, how large a portion of the polity is affected?

[31] The question of how much information is required on the part of a recipient before consent can be inferred remains a live one. Perhaps analogously, economists have studied the problem of information asymmetry (which means that the firm has more information than the recipient) and have realized that it can lead to a bad outcome such as a "race to the bottom" even where a market is competitive. I leave aside further investigation here.

[32] If we are sure that a right is alienable by contract, and if we are sure that there exists a contract with the requisite consent to waive that right, then the existence of multiple contracts would not be problematic. This situation would be rare or nonexistent in cases of mass-market boilerplate. It is dubious at best

Amazon is estimated to have over 100 million customers, AT&T about 107 million. Facebook has about 163 million U.S. users. Firms with broad reach over large swaths of the public are deploying boilerplate that restructures recipients' legal rights. They are in effect replacing the law of the state with the "law" of the firm for substantial portions of the populace.

Any instance of depriving someone of a right without consent—such as mistaken contract enforcement—is wrong, a normative wrong. Construing rights deletions as involving consent where the consent is nonexistent or problematic, or where the consent should have been trumped by market-inalienability, becomes more troubling for democratic ordering than the wrong against an individual, because boilerplate rights deletion schemes undermine the significance of political debate and procedures.

Some of the rights that boilerplate erases are often thought to be prepolitical and to underwrite the organization of a polity in order to maintain those rights. In this category, for example, could be placed the right to be free from (nonaccidental) bodily harm inflicted by others. Other rights have been enacted through democratic processes, often after extended debate and fierce political struggles.[33] Yet erasing these rights only requires drafting boilerplate (or indeed, just copying someone else's boilerplate).[34] When firms can easily divest recipients of rights that are part of the infrastructure of polity, that is threatening to the continuing necessary infrastructure of private ordering. When firms can easily divest recipients of rights that are part of a legislative regime arrived at only with much difficulty, debate, and compromise, it makes a sham of the apparatus of democratic governance. All of the public input and hard-fought compromises and tradeoffs seem like an ironic form of kabuki theatre. Worse, well-funded interests lobbying in the legislative arena could be merely feigning legislative horse trading and could be entering into compromises just for show, because these firms would be reasonable in expecting that whatever political compromises they enter into can be rescinded by deploying boilerplate.

Consent that is problematic or nonexistent becomes democratically more troubling as it becomes more widespread. Undermining of entitlements that should be market-inalienable becomes progressively more troubling as well. As assessment of the social prevalence of any particular rights deletion scheme becomes more urgent because the democratic degradation that replaces the law of the state with the "law" of the firm becomes a more and more serious concern as the number of people who are subjected to the firm's alternative legal universe increases.

whether mass-market boilerplate deployed against a wide group of recipients exhibits an appropriate level of consent. Moreover, even if appropriate consent is present, an important question remaining here is what rights are alienable by contract. My view is that certain rights should be understood as permanently situated in the public realm and not waivable by individuals. *See* Section I.C.

[33] U.S. intellectual property reform is a good example: Both the Copyright Act of 1976 and the America Invents Act of 2011 were debated and amended for years before finally being enacted. *See* Joe Matal, *A Guide to the Legislative History of the America Invents Act: Part I of II*, 21 Fed. Cir. B.J. 435 (2012); Jessica D. Litman, *Copyright, Compromise, and Legislative History*, 72 Cornell L. Rev. 857 (1987).

[34] For example, sets of terms on websites (T.O.S.) and many End User Licensing Agreements (E.U.L.A.s) deploy boilerplate to delete user rights provisions of U.S. copyright law.

The extent to which the alternative universe prevails depends both on how many people are recipients of a particular boilerplate scheme, and the extent to which those recipients could perhaps escape from the alternative scheme by buying the product or service from a different firm or by doing without the product or service. Necessities of life cannot be done without, and that comes close to applying to near-necessities, such as provision of childcare for workers. Especially when goods or services cannot be forgone, it matters whether there is only one provider; or whether, if there are multiple providers, all of the firms providing the good or service use identical boilerplate. In these cases, the recipient is stuck with the terms, and thereby with the firm's alternative legal universe.

The situation is different if the product is available with different terms from different sellers—especially if shopping around for terms is easy, and especially if there is a subset of recipients who will do the shopping and the firm must charge the same price to all, thereby giving the benefit of the savvy consumers' researches to everyone. These inquiries depend upon market structure, and the degree of information asymmetry, and the degree of transaction costs for acquiring information, and the possibilities of arbitrage, etc., so it must be recognized that these inquiries would not be easy (and maybe not even feasible) for a reviewing court to undertake. Possibly a court could appoint a special master to develop a rough estimate of the extent to which we should consider the alternative universe to be inescapable in real-life conditions.

Just because an inquiry is not easy does not by itself render it irrelevant. That is, courts should not blindly sign off on widespread boilerplate rights deletion schemes just because they don't have an easy way of investigating whether recipients can escape them. At least, they should attempt to investigate which way the risk of error runs. When the right in question might be at least partially market-inalienable and is most likely not salient for recipients, I suggest that the risk of error should go against the firm deploying the scheme.

Many boilerplate schemes purport to bind millions of people. How many people would such a scheme have to bind in order for it to count as a rights deletion scheme that is likely to create significant democratic degradation? It is not going to be possible to answer this question with a number, at least not by using abstract reasoning. The question regarding the extent to which people can escape the imposed clauses must interact at some level with the number of people affected. If it seems easy to escape the clause because the clause is salient to consumers, and because the product or service is not an essential or because the product or service is readily available from competing providers without the onerous boilerplate, then perhaps even if large numbers are recipients, the large numbers do not lead to democratic degradation (replacing the law of the state with the "law" of the firm). Even in this case, some investigation about whether consumers really are escaping the clause would be warranted, because that might reveal whether the loss of the right really is salient to individuals, as many rights that are important to civil society or the public as a whole are not. As larger numbers of people are affected, the risk of democratic degradation rises, and the question whether people can escape and would consider the clause salient enough to do so becomes more important to attend to by investigation rather than brushing off with presumption.

A legislature or administrative agency could set a threshold number of recipients for invoking disqualification of a boilerplate scheme on the basis of widespread social dissemination of an onerous clause, because it has the power to use estimates that it decides serve the public interest. A legislature or agency could decide, for example, to consider a boilerplate scheme to be a troublesome rights deletion scheme when there are likely 100,000 or more people covered by the scheme, and where the right is not likely to be salient to motivate recipients to push back against it, and where there is evidence of market structure that makes it impossible or very difficult for recipients to escape the scheme. A court could also come to a decision in a particular case on a similar pragmatic basis. Courts do not draw lines by applying numbers the way legislatures and agencies do. But courts could—and should—be attentive to the problem of democratic degradation. They could—and should—understand that the problem deepens as the number of recipients of a particular clause rises, and that the problem is particularly acute when recipients cannot (due to lack of available alternatives) or will not (due to lack of salience) vote with their feet.

IV. The Proposed Framework: Further Considerations

To recapitulate, I am proposing that courts—and also legislatures and agencies—should evaluate boilerplate rights deletion according to an analytical framework including three main inquiries: (1) the nature of the divested right; (2) the quality of recipients' consent; and (3) the extent of social dissemination of the scheme that imposes an alternative legal universe on recipients. When a court is faced with a boilerplate scheme, this framework can be used for unconscionability evaluation. It should replace the use of recipients' expectations as a guide to enforceability, and it should also replace the use of the procedural/substantive distinction. As we have seen, the expectation trope is subject to a deeply mischievous ambiguity between empirical and normative understandings; and the procedural/substantive distinction has in practice caused foreclosure of any inquiry into the nature of the right being purportedly waived by recipients.

This analytical framework can also be used for evaluation under public policy, in which individual consent would play less of a role, or perhaps no role. It should replace the prevalent idea that public policy depends upon particularized legislative or authoritative regulatory declarations. Public policy would be a good arena in which to take up the cause of democratic degradation owing to loss of rights that are central to democratic ordering and to the maintenance of civil society. These rights are truly public in nature, but they tend not to be salient to individual recipients, which makes them more difficult to safeguard.

Under the proposed analytical framework, as long as we are sticking with a contract paradigm, the appropriate response to a question whether a waiver is valid or invalid may often depend upon a reasoning process that takes into account all three parameters of analysis. In many situations this evaluation cannot be an exclusively rule-driven endeavor, but rather must be a process of pragmatic judgment. That is why this proposed analytical framework does not do away with the problem of discretion-based jurisprudence and its tendency to be unpredictable. Discretion is equity's virtue.

Nevertheless, by clarifying the parameters to be considered, this framework may alleviate the problem to some extent, because the framework reveals that under some circumstances there are conclusions that rely in large part on rules.

If the nature of the right is such that after due consideration it must be recognized as fully inalienable or market-inalienable, then, whatever else is happening, there is not an enforceable contract. Two important examples are: (1) the purported relinquishment of an employee recipient's right not to be discriminated against on the basis of race, sex, religion, or national origin; and (2) the portion of a blanket exculpatory clause that purports to delete one's right to tort damages or injunction for the intentional or reckless infliction of harm.

Whether or not a right is fully inalienable, market-inalienable, or partially market-inalienable depends on reasoning and argument about the purpose of the right and its function in civil society, rather than on contested issues of fact in a given case. Because it is primarily contested fact issues that render discretionary doctrines unpredictable in outcome, decisions about inalienability may not seem as unpredictable. Moreover, the reasoning in one case can more readily be carried over into other cases than can fact-based individual decisions. This means that precedent will have more force, and more uniformity may result, as well as more transparency to recipients.

If consent is totally lacking, then whatever else is happening, there is not an enforceable contract. In contrast to decisions about market-inalienability, or indeed partial market-inalienability, there is a contested factual decision to be made about consent. But perhaps situations in which consent is not merely problematic but rather is totally lacking should not prove to be difficult or unpredictable. Sheer ignorance that there is a purported contract in the vicinity—as is most often the case with "browsewrap" terms interior to websites—is an example of clear nonconsent.[35]

Social dissemination need not be taken into account in either the case of nonconsent or the case of inalienability. (Of course, democratic degradation is worse if such clauses are allowed to govern a wide swath of recipients.) There may also be situations in which questionable alienability should be understood to interact with questionable consent to render a specific contract unenforceable, without regard to the number of people affected.

Attention to the nature of the right, especially attention to inalienability or market -inalienability, as well as attention to nonconsent or very minimal quality of consent, will clarify some important cases. Nevertheless, many cases that come before courts

[35] *See* note 30. Insistence that hypothetical consent amounts to consent, or insistence upon gerrymandered definitions of agreement, cloud the picture. My view is that these workarounds should be rejected, but I will not elaborate these arguments here. *See* Radin, Boilerplate, at 82–98. With browsewrap, what I say in the text is controversial because U.S. judges are willing to assimilate an opportunity to read something to actually having read that thing, as well as willing to assimilate actually having read something to having consented to that thing. They are willing to assimilate sheer ignorance to consent. The "opportunity to read" or "reasonably communicated" doctrine gets the learned judges into debates about whether a link to unread terms was or was not situated such that it provided an appropriate opportunity to have clicked on it, even though recipient didn't. My view is that doctrines such as duty to read, reasonable communication or reasonable opportunity to read, which amount to fictional or constructive consent, are relics of a bygone era when contracts were theorized as taking place between traders who were socialized into a particular culture and language of trade. A relic of that culture that still exists is the notion of usage of trade. Again, I will not argue for these views here.

will be less than clear-cut and still require a pragmatic judgment. Perhaps consent is problematic, but not totally absent; perhaps the right being purportedly waived is a significant political or legal right, but not one that appears to be fully inalienable or market-inalienable. For such cases, courts should consider imposing or recognizing a partial market-inalienability. Partial market-inalienability means some restraint on alienation, some variety of stricter scrutiny.

A partial market-inalienability may be declared by a legislature or a court. There is a broad range of possibilities. A statute could say, as the Uniform Commercial Code in the U.S. does,[36] that waiver of consequential damages for personal injury caused by a product is prima facie unconscionable, thereby placing a difficult burden of proof on the firm deploying the waiver to justify it. Or it could say, as the U.C.C. also does, that waiver of protection under the implied warranty of merchantability must be in writing and use certain words,[37] thereby placing a much less stringent burden of proof on the firm deploying the waiver. My term, partial market-inalienability, as exemplified by these U.C.C. provisions, is meant to direct decision makers' attention to the continuum of levels of scrutiny or requirements of justification that is open to them. Courts can implement partial market-inalienability in various ways. They can vary burdens of proof. They can require particular evidence. They can adopt appropriate rebuttable presumptions. They should become more aware of the range of possibilities in the grey area of the continuum between full alienability and market-inalienability.

V. Reconsidering Redress of Grievances

The wrong of depriving individuals of their right to meaningful legal redress of grievances is especially apt to grow in severity as the number of affected individuals increases. That is because if large numbers of people have no realistic recourse when harmed in a transaction, the rule of law is undercut. Moreover, equality before the law ceases to exist in practice when those who are not recipients of the widespread rights deletion scheme have better legal rights than those who are recipients. Widespread exculpatory clauses such as the one that I used for illustration at the beginning of this chapter divide the public into those who have tort remedies available and those who do not.

A. *Other problematic clauses*

Other clauses that call into question the background right of redress of grievances include, first and foremost, mandatory arbitration clauses; and also choice of law/ choice of forum clauses.

[36] *See* U.C.C. § 2-719(3) (2002) ("Contractual Modification or Limitation of Remedy").

[37] *See* U.C.C. § 2-316 (2002) (to disclaim the implied warranty of merchantability "the language must mention merchantability and in case of a writing must be conspicuous").

1. *Arbitration clauses*

In the U.S., but not in other countries, the existence of a Federal Arbitration Act dating from 1925, coupled with the Supremacy clause in the U.S. Constitution and the current U.S. Supreme Court majority's apparent desire to eliminate collective legal actions, has caused mandatory arbitration clauses to proliferate.[38] Mandatory arbitration clauses erase the right to jury trial. They are widely deployed to preclude collective relief, and in doing so they thereby preclude—in practice, much of the time—any legal remedy. The preclusion of collective relief (class action or classwide arbitration) undermines the possibility of relief for small repetitive harms from which firms might harvest large profits.[39]

The analytical framework I have proposed suggests that mandatory arbitration clauses should be disallowed in mass-market deletion schemes—schemes that satisfy a criterion of widespread social dissemination—where their practical effect is to deny any remedy. A core case is the situation where only a class action would be effective, because a firm has inflicted small losses on many people. A fortiori, mass-market arbitration clauses at least should be disallowed where such clauses are deployed to prevent employees from trying to enforce other rights that are market-inalienable, such as, in particular, the right not to be discriminated against on the basis of race, sex, or another invidious category.[40]

2. *Choice of forum/choice of law clauses*

The analytical framework I have proposed also suggests stricter scrutiny of choice of forum/choice of law clauses. Clauses of this kind may make sense for sophisticated commercial parties. When extended to boilerplate schemes used by firms with consumers,

[38] The U.S. Supreme Court has been expanding more and more the situations in which firms may deploy boilerplate to make arbitration mandatory and exclude any aggregate relief. The court has accomplished this result by interpreting the Federal Arbitration Act of 1925 (F.A.A.) as preempting state law that would retain litigation remedies, jury trial, and aggregate remedies. These holdings are based on an interpretation of U.S. Const. art. VI, cl. 2 ("the Supremacy Clause") stating that federal law is the supreme law of the land. The court has used a super-expansive interpretation of the F.A.A., which was originally intended to eliminate courts' hostility to arbitration in order to permit commercial firms to take their disputes to arbitration, to preclude many state courts' attempts to protect their citizens from boilerplate schemes that they consider unconscionable. Probably the only way to escape this situation is for the U.S. Congress to amend the F.A.A. to make clear that civil rights actions by employees are not preempted, class actions by recipients injured by small losses are not preempted, etc. An Arbitration Fairness Act has been introduced in Congress several times, but so far has died in committee each time. For an update on how far the U.S. Supreme Court has now gone with mandatory arbitration, and the court's seeming unconcern with state public policies of redress, *see* David Horton, *Mass Contracting and Democratic Legitimacy*, 84 U. Colo. L. Rev. 459 (2014).

[39] It is commonly said in the U.S., usually in a vituperative tone of voice, that greedy class action lawyers and litigious plaintiffs are attacking innocent businesses, which must defend themselves by cutting out consumer remedies. I think recipients who are without remedy far outnumber any litigious recipients. And even if most of the recovery goes to lawyers and little goes to the recipients who were cheated out of small amounts, it is still the case that legal remedies might be used to deter further overreaching behavior, and might not be expected or required to be purely compensatory.

[40] Needless to say, the framework I propose cannot now be implemented in the U.S. with respect to arbitration clauses. Nevertheless, other jurisdictions do disallow arbitration clauses in consumer contracts, and perhaps others might be encouraged to do so by what I argue here.

however, they are often problematic. Requiring a recipient to litigate somewhere far away from home may in effect deprive the recipient of any reasonable opportunity to obtain a legal remedy (or as traditional language puts it, "to have her day in court").

Here again, explicit attention to the nature of the right in question may aid analysis. The operation of forum selection is at least theoretically limited by the U.S. constitutional guarantee of due process of law, which is a bulwark of the rule of law. The constitutional requirement of due process is usually stated in terms of a guarantee that those who invoke the law through courts will be treated in accordance with "traditional notions of fair play and substantial justice."[41] Yet U.S. courts, especially federal courts, have endorsed the rationale that firms save money by forcing litigants to come to their home jurisdiction and pass the savings on to consumers, and have allowed this rationale in many instances to trump constitutional review.[42]

Constitutional due process in the case of mass-market choice of forum/choice of law clauses seems to be under a shadow. When U.S. courts hold that choice of forum clauses are almost per se valid, even those that render litigation almost impossible for claimants and thus deprive them of any viable opportunity to have their day in court, the mere existence of boilerplate can have the effect of negating a constitutional limitation. This constitutional limitation remains viable in other aspects of due process adjudication. Thus, it looks as if U.S. federal courts have allowed purported contractual agreements to trump a constitutional right of due process, the right to have a reasonable opportunity to pursue one's day in court. If courts adopt a serious consideration of the nature of the right in question, they will perhaps not be so hasty in allowing a contract to trump it. This conclusion should result a fortiori where consent, and therefore existence of a contract, is dubious.

B. *Maintaining public legal infrastructure*

Entitlements that should be interpreted to be inalienable or market-inalienable, or at least not readily alienable, may be components of public regimes underwritten by the polity for the sake of the structure of the polity itself. The idea of redress of grievances through law is primary among them. The underlying structure of due process of law, the rule of law,

[41] The notion of "fair play and substantial justice" has been developed in cases involving a defendant being haled into court in a remote jurisdiction. In such a case, the courts say that "fair play and substantial justice" requires that a defendant not be haled into court in a jurisdiction in which she does not have enough relationship (minimum contacts). (For an example, *see* Legal Info. Inst., *Minimum Contacts*, <http://www.law.cornell.edu/wex/minimum_contacts>.) But it seems the underlying notion should also apply to situations in which a plaintiff wants to bring suit in a jurisdiction in which she does have contact, especially if the defendant also has contact, but the defendant wants to force the plaintiff to defendant's home jurisdiction. *See, e.g.*, Linda S. Mullenix, *Carnival Cruise Lines, Inc. v. Shute: The Titanic of Worst Decisions*, 12 Nev. L. J. 549 (2012). In *Carnival Cruise*, the due process standard may have been alluded to, because the court considered "fairness" to be the appropriate standard, but the constitutional due process standard was not officially invoked. The court implicitly decided that (assuming that the plaintiffs actually consented, so that a contract actually existed) the choice of the defendant's home forum did not violate an underlying constitutional standard. Thus did contract trump due process. In that case, to make matters worse, it seemed that the assumption that plaintiffs consented was clearly wrong. The question of when consent, even if actual, should be able to trump due process rights needs more investigation, which should take serious account of the nature of the rights.

[42] *See* note 2 and accompanying text.

equality before the law, and the shared responsibility to avoid harming others are part of this public political structure. Such public structures should not be undermined by individual contracts, especially not when the contracts themselves may in fact be noncontracts. At least, much more thought is required before enforcing such individual contracts than the rubberstamp enforcement of boilerplate that now prevails in the U.S.

It bears repeating that the narrative of traditional liberalism implies that individuals cannot be divested of their rights to redress of grievances without undermining the very structure of rights that the state is charged with maintaining in order to foster individual freedom. Freedom of contract is of course among these rights. If either the remedies for breach of contract or for purported contractual exchanges that are instead instances of coercion or deception or other forms of nonconsent are nonexistent or inadequate, then the liberal ideal of private ordering cannot be implemented. If we were to reach a situation in practice in which the ability of a party to claim coercion or deception or nonconsent was routinely waived, we would not have a regime of contract or of private ordering compatible with our received understanding of freedom of contract and the enforcement of those and only those contracts that accord with it.

Conclusion

When mass-market purported contracts exclude litigation and thereby exclude class actions; when they purport to waive all recipient rights to hold the firm responsible for harm it causes; when they limit legal action to a forum that is too inconvenient for claimants, they are using "private" tools to do away with "public" avenues of redress. The framework I have offered here can, I hope, help the legal community take account of the important considerations relating to maintaining the structures underlying contractual ordering, such that those structures will not be readily eliminated by mass-market boilerplate.

Firms should be free to maximize profit, of course, but within the limits of the legal infrastructures that make private ordering possible. If a firm exceeds those limits, then it is maximizing its own profit at the expense of everyone's ability to rely on the background legal infrastructures. If all firms did this, the background structures that enable private ordering would collapse. If many firms do this, as now seems to be the case in the U.S., the legal infrastructure that supports private ordering is rendered shaky and trust is undermined. We could take firms that undermine private ordering in this way to be defecting from an underlying social contract. Then we should interpret that underlying social contract so as to prevent these defections. Firms should be prevented from extending their profit-maximizing strategies to deletion of the background infrastructure that makes private ordering possible.

A standard type of coordination argument has it that tying firms' hands is to their own ultimate benefit, and a restriction to which firms would agree in an original position. Instead of interpreting *recipients* as having hypothetically consented to deletion of their own legal rights, then, we would interpret *firms* as having hypothetically consented to society's prevention of such attempted deletions. By deploying such attempted deletions, firms are attempting to defect from the social contract to which all firms are presumed to have agreed.

13

Merchant Law in a Modern Economy

*Lisa Bernstein**

Introduction

The Uniform Commercial Code ("Code"), the statute that governs transactions in the sale of goods in the United States, adopts a highly legal realist jurisprudential approach that gives great weight to context, applies a lax parol evidence rule, and looks to usage of trade, course of performance, and course of dealing to interpret contracts, fill contractual gaps, imply warranties, modify agreements, waive obligations, and give meaning to many of the Code's own standard like default rules. This adjudicative approach (with some nuanced variations) has been widely adopted the world over. It is at the heart of many continental legal systems as well as the United Nations Convention on the International Sale of Goods and the recently proposed Common European Sales Law.

The Code's contextualized adjudicative approach was designed to provide a set of off-the-rack contract default rules that would "simplify, clarify and modernize the law governing commercial transactions."[1] By directing courts to look to trade practices and the contracting context to give meaning to both parties' agreements and the Code's standard-like defaults, the Code's drafters sought to provide defaults that would, by virtue of their reflection of the contracting context, be better tailored to parties' transactional needs than any possible set of clear and definite rules designed to apply across a wide range of transaction types. In adopting this approach, the drafters also sought to create a semi-permanent piece of legislation. A piece of legislation that when applied by courts in a purposeful way that took account of its reason would "provide its own machinery for the expansion of commercial practices... through custom, usage and agreement of the parties" thereby ensuring that the Code could adapt itself to "unforeseen and new circumstances and practices"[2] without the need for legislative amendments.

This chapter explores the Code's adjudicative architecture from both an empirical and a theoretical perspective. Its goal is to assess whether the Code will be able to successfully adapt American commercial law to meet the challenges created by

* I would like to thank Douglas Baird, Brian Bix, Patrick Barry, Robin Effron, Emily Kadens, Shai Dothan, Matthew Jennejohn, Avery Katz, Steve Burton, Tim Cummins, Nicole DeHorasis, Jean Braucher, Stewart Macaulay, Brad Peterson, Connie Fleisher, Hagay Volvovsky, Bill Schwesig, Margaret Schilt, Sean Ghoetz, Douglas Baird, David Zarfes, Richard Epstein, and Philip Hamburger for interesting comments and conversations. Portions of the research discussed here were sponsored by NSF Grant SBR-9422795.

[1] U.C.C. § 1-102(2)(b). [2] U.C.C. § 1-102(b) & cmt. 1.

the structural changes in the American economy that have taken place over the past 20 years.

The chapter begins by exploring the best available evidence on the validity of the empirical assumptions that are central to the Code's jurisprudential approach and its machinery for adapting to change. The primary focus is on the assumptions that unwritten usages of trade that are widely known across the relevant geographic boundaries of trade exist, that these usages can be found by courts, and that contextualized adjudication is a majoritarian default rule from the perspective of business transactors.

After presenting empirical evidence that suggests that the truth of these assumptions is questionable at best, the chapter draws on arguments developed by neoformalist scholars to explore the reasons that the Code's adjudicative approach is ill-suited to transactions between both merchants and sophisticated business entities. It begins by suggesting that the Code prevents transactors from contracting using their preferred mix of legal and extralegal terms, impedes the very types of flexible work-a-day contractual relationships it was designed to encourage, and encourages certain types of strategic behavior. It then suggests that in transactions between large multi-agent entities, the Code's contextualist interpretive approach imposes significant additional costs on business transactors: it creates or exacerbates *intra-firm* agency costs, increases both information transmittal costs and operating costs, and leads parties to use complex transactional structures that they could more easily forgo if the law gave primacy to the terms of their written agreements and adopted a more formalistic adjudicative approach. In addition, and of increasing importance to the modern economy, the Code's adjudicative approach makes what scholars have termed "contracting for innovation"[3] more expensive and difficult than it would be in a more formalist, agreement-centric, interpretive regime.

The chapter concludes that given the fundamental changes in the American economy and the structure and operation of firms that have occurred over the past two decades, it is very unlikely that the Code will be able to successfully adapt to the demands of the modern economy. Rather, for sales law to successfully respond to these changes, reformers will need to rethink commercial law from the ground up. They will need to recognize that recent changes in the structure, organization, and operation of large multi-agent firms pose contract governance challenges that cannot be adequately met through a contextualist approach to adjudication that relies on the gradual evolution of usages and practices to respond to economic change. The complexity of modern contractual relationships together with the high levels of coordination and innovation (both inside and outside of the firm) that are needed for economic success, suggest that written contracts that are interpreted as written will (except when the parties specify otherwise) provide businesses, and by implication markets, with a faster and more tailored way of responding to economic change, than will the continued incorporation of usages and practices, especially in light of changes in the technology of contracting.

[3] Ronald J. Gilson, Charles F. Sabel, & Robert E. Scott, *Contracting for Innovation: Vertical Disintegration and Interfirm Collaboration*, 109 Colum. L. Rev. 431, 432 (2009).

I. The Empirical Basis of the Code's Jurisprudential Architecture

The Uniform Commercial Code was drafted by Karl Llewellyn, one of the leading legal realists of his time and an outspoken advocate of the social scientific approach to law making. Llewellyn sought to draft a statute whose rules were "designed to adapt rules of law to the way that business is actually carried on,"[4] and that drew on "the practices of businessmen and business houses [as] important factors in construing their contracts and actions and in determining their rights and liabilities."[5] Given this goal it is tempting to assume that the Code's assumptions about the business/merchant world and merchant preferences were based on solid empirical evidence. However, as a leading historian of the Code creation process concluded, "it must be conceded that there was virtually no systematic project research of the kind postulated by the scientific method. There were no orderly research designs, disciplined sampling, or carefully tested questionnaires."[6] In drafting the Code, Llewellyn relied primarily on his knowledge of the medieval law merchant,[7] his own business intuitions and conversations with bankers and lawyers.[8] "Such fieldwork as was done tended to be adhoc."[9]

Llewellyn's failure to conduct social scientific research to inform the Code drafting project has long been dismissed by his supporters who claim that despite his methodological lapses, "critics who have been suspicious of his alleged 'unscientific' 'impressionistic' or 'anecdotal' approach to facts have yet to point to any major factual assumptions of the code that were misleading or inaccurate."[10] In recent years, however, an increasing body of historical and empirical evidence has begun to raise serious questions about the soundness of the Code's empirical assumptions. This section draws on the best (though limited) historical and empirical evidence available to explore whether usages of trade actually exist in merchant communities, whether courts can determine the existence and content of usages with reasonable accuracy, and finally, whether there is any reason to question the widely shared assumption that contextualist adjudication is a majoritarian default rule.

A. Do usages of trade exist?

1. *The law merchant*

A fundamental starting point for defenders of the proposition that meaningful merchant customs and usages exist is the history of the so-called medieval law merchant of sales. According to the accounts of the law merchant relied upon by

[4] Walter D. Malcolm, *The Proposed Commercial Code*, 6 Bus. Law. 113, 126 (1951) (quoting the report of the Committee on the Proposed Commercial Code).

[5] Malcolm, *The Proposed Commercial Code*, 126.

[6] William Twining, Karl Llewellyn and the Realist Movement 316 (1973).

[7] *See* James Q. Whitman, *Commercial Law and the American Volk: A Note on Llewellyn's German Sources for the Uniform Commercial Code*, 97 Yale L.J. 156 (1987) (concluding that Llewellyn's thinking was deeply influenced by the account of the law merchant given by Levin Goldschmidt).

[8] Twining, Karl Llewellyn and the Realist Movement, at 316.

[9] Twining, Karl Llewellyn and the Realist Movement, at 316.

[10] Twining, Karl Llewellyn and the Realist Movement, at 319.

Llewellyn,[11] during the Middle Ages supra-local transactions in the sale of goods were governed by unwritten customs of trade that were widely known, widely followed, and used by merchant arbitrators to decide cases in specialized merchant courts that operated wholly outside of the purview of the state. This image of the operation of the law merchant had a powerful effect on Llewellyn's thinking. In fact, early drafts of the Code provided for "mercantile facts," including trade usages and commercial practices, to be found by panels of merchant experts.[12] More generally, as one of Llewellyn's assistants in the Code-drafting process explained, "[i]t is fair to say that the draftsmen of the Code... wanted to correct some false starts... and to restore the law merchant as an institution for growth only lightly kept in bounds by statute."[13]

Although Llewellyn relied heavily on the history of the law merchant in drafting the Code, recent historical scholarship casts doubt on the claim that medieval law merchant—in the sense of a generally accepted set of unwritten sales-related customs—actually existed.[14] Indeed the account of its operation that Llewellyn himself relied on (that of Levin Goldschmit) has been largely discredited,[15] and recent research on medieval commerce has concluded that "we lack evidence that [sales-related gap filling customs] became a uniform and universal part of the *lex mercatoria* other than, perhaps, at a very high level of generality. Instead, the evidence suggests that substantive customs remained geographically local or confined to a particular network of repeat players."[16] To the extent that robust commercial customs existed in the Middle Ages, they were not part of "sales" law, but rather dealt with bills of exchange. Yet even in this area, usages did not emerge through the evolution of unwritten practices and understandings. Rather, they emerged through the repeated use of written standard form contracts and the emergence of transactional intermediaries like notaries. As a consequence, the history of the so-called medieval law merchant of negotiable instruments cannot be said to provide empirical evidence that the types of unwritten usages of trade that the Code relies on so extensively actually existed in the Middle Ages. It does, however, illustrate the power of written agreements to support trade and

[11] The idea of the law merchant continues to influence American commercial law. *See, e.g., revised* U.C.C. § 1-301 cmt. 3 (2001) ("Application of the Code... may be justified by... the fact that it is in large part a reformulation and restatement of the law merchant...").

[12] *See* NAT'L CONFERENCE OF COMM'RS ON UNIFORM STATE LAWS, REPORT AND SECOND DRAFT: THE REVISED UNIFORM SALES ACT § 59 (1941), *reprinted in* 1 UNIFORM COMMERCIAL CODE: DRAFTS 269, 534 (Elizabeth Slusser Kelley ed., 1984).

[13] Homer Kripke, *The Principles Underlying the Drafting of the Uniform Commercial Code*, 1962 U. ILL. L.F. 321, 331 (1962).

[14] *See* Celia Wasserstein Fassberg, *Lex Mercatoria: Hoist with Its Own Petard?*, 5 CHI. J. INT'L L. 67, 67–8 (2004) (The "idyllic image of an international community of merchants interacting on the basis of shared values," cannot be reconciled with the historical evidence that "the law merchant was not substantive, but rather procedural law, that it was neither transnational nor personal, [and] that it was very probably not customary").

[15] *See* Charles Donahue, Jr., *Medieval and Early Modern Lex Mercatoria: An Attempt at the Probatio Diabolica*, 5 CHI. J. INT'L L. 21, 23, n. 8 (2004) (arguing that the account of the law merchant given by Levin Goldschmidt was highly inaccurate).

[16] Emily Kadens, *The Myth of the Customary Law Merchant*, 90 TEX. L. REV. 1153, 1177 (2012); *accord* Donahue, *Medieval and Early Modern Lex Mercatoria*, at 36 ("These customs did not... add up to a mercantile legal system...").

introduce contractual innovations, even in an environment where both writing and transmitting a writing were more time consuming and expensive then they are today.

2. Trade Association codification attempts at the turn of the twentieth century

In an effort to conduct the type of social scientific studies that Llewellyn might have conducted had he applied his ideas about social science research to the Code-drafting project, one study looked at the efforts of trade associations in five merchant industries—grain, feed, hay, textiles, and silk to codify their customs into written trade rules in the 50 years prior to the start of the Code project.[17] All of the industries studied were ones where the preconditions for the emergence of customs were met—transactors interacted on a repeat basis in relatively similar transactions over a long period of time. Nevertheless, the debates leading up to the adoption of these rules revealed that transactors did not agree about the meaning of even very common trade terms and that there was no consensus about the ways that common aspects of business were generally conducted.

In the hay industry for example, before the first set of national trading rules was adopted the "packaging, shipping and handling [of] hay was an irregular business. There were no established customs to govern, and every transaction was typical of the parties engaged in it."[18] Transactors did not even agree about the meaning of the term "bale" of hay, for "the large bales of New York and New England means a different bale from the large bale in the Western States."[19] Even within local areas no uniform definitions emerged. As participants at the fourth convention of the National Hay Association discovered, "in Chicago at present there is a lack of definition of small bales."[20] Attempts to develop rules on the reasonable time for payment also led to contentious debate. As one participant in the debate aptly observed, "that reasonable time business will not [tell you] anything. You might as well leave it out."[21]

Disagreement about the meaning of terms and the content of usages was also rampant in the grain industry. Shortly before the rules-drafting process began the trade press concluded that "there are customs in the grain trade that are supported to be established, but the trouble in respect to them is, [that] they are not fixed, [and] are not understood alike, some understand them in one way and others in another way, and for that reason, if for no other [they] cause difficulty."[22] The national grain rules were adopted in 1902 after only a two-year drafting process. However, it took much longer for them to supplant the rules of local associations. As late as 1928, the chairman of the national rules committee observed that "uniformity in the rules is a matter

[17] Lisa Bernstein, *The Questionable Empirical Basis of Article 2's Incorporation Strategy: A Preliminary Study*, 66 U. Chi. L. Rev. 710 (1999).

[18] Bernstein, *Questionable Basis*, at 720 (citing Nat'l Hay Ass'n, Report of the Eighteenth Annual Convention 3 (1911)).

[19] Bernstein, *Questionable Basis*, at 721 (citing Nat'l Hay Ass'n, Report of the Fourth Annual Meeting 40 (1897)).

[20] Bernstein, *Questionable Basis*, at 721.

[21] Bernstein, *Questionable Basis*,. at 722 (citing Nat'l Hay Ass'n, Report of the Sixteenth Annual Convention 229 (1909)).

[22] *Bernstein, Questionable Basis*, at 727 (citing Minutes of Meetings, The Secretary's Book (Nov. 9, 1896)).

of slow growth as the different markets are very conservative in making changes in rules of years standing."[23]

In the textile and silk industries, the disagreements about the content of customs were even more significant and the debates over the creation of rules were even more heated. This is not surprising because the rules in these groups did not govern transactions between merchants who were buyers one day and sellers the next, but rather transactions between merchants who played a fixed role in the chain of production and distribution and therefore had industry-segment level interests.

The drafting of the textile rules, known as the Worth Street Rules, "was fraught with conflict, involved negotiation among numerous trade associations,"[24] and took 18 years to complete. Consensus was so difficult to achieve that the drafting committee ultimately decided to create several different sets of codified customs for different segments of the industry; yet even with this high degree of particularization, many terms remained uncodified since a consensus on their meaning could not be reached. In the silk industry, the creation of rules was equally hard fought and, as in textiles, many different sets of rules governing different stages in the chain of production and distribution were adopted. Interestingly, silkmen did not revere usages. As one silkman put it "huge question marks are boldly inscribed on the walls of custom, hoary with age, and covered with the ivy of reverence."[25] And, as one of the association's annual reports explained, silkmen were reluctant to codify usages because "when a business routine is established in an organization it often requires... a so-called shake up to introduce innovations."[26]

Eventually, each of these industries shifted their efforts from codifying customs, to negotiating agreed meanings of common terms (frequently in ways that revealed a desire to change not to harmonize local meanings).[27] Although the trade rules they adopted might have been loosely informed by practices prevailing in different parts of the country, they were not mere codifications of common understandings. The process by which they were drafted and adopted was quasi-legislative in nature. Rules-drafting committees actively sought to consider practices and policy considerations so as to better promote trade. As the by-laws of these associations and other trade associations made clear, their goal was to "*promote* uniformity" of practices and "to seek certainty in usages," all in an effort to avoid "misunderstandings."[28]

[23] *Bernstein, Questionable Basis*, at 728 (citing *Trade Rules: The Chairman Replies*, 17 Who's Who in the Grain Trade 28–9 (February 20, 1923–4)).

[24] *Bernstein, Questionable Basis*, at 732.

[25] *Bernstein, Questionable Basis*, at 739 (citing Silk Ass'n of Am., Annual Report 145 (1914)).

[26] *Bernstein, Questionable Basis*, at 739. [27] *Bernstein, Questionable Basis*, at 719–40.

[28] *See, e.g.*, Am. Fats and Oils Ass'n, By Laws of the American Fats and Oils Association, Inc., art. I, § I (1994) (noting that a goal of the organization is to "work towards uniformity and certainty in the standards of such products and in the customs and usages of the trade"); Am. Spice Trade Ass'n, Handbook of the American Spice Trade Association, by-laws, art. I, § 2 (1925) ("The object of this Association shall be to maintain just and equitable principles and establish uniformity of commercial usage among its members..."); Baltimore Butter & Egg Exchange Inc., 15 Butter, Cheese & Egg J., no. 26, 17 (1924) (noting that an important function of the group is "to promote uniformity in the customs and usages of trade"); Ass'n of Food Indus., Constitution and Bylaws, art. III (1992) (noting that one purpose of the association is to "seek uniformity and certainty in the customs and usage of the trade"); Nat'l Hay Ass'n, Constitution and By-Laws Preamble, *reprinted in* Report of the Second Annual Meeting 29 (1985) (a goal of the association is to "use our best efforts to have established and maintained a uniformity in commercial usages and in the grades of hay and straw in the

Some critics have characterized these studies as "highly controversial."[29] They have variously argued that the individual case studies of particular industries do not shed light on the contracting preferences of businesses in general;[30] that the period chosen for study had not given transnational usages long enough to evolve;[31] and that evidence from the turn of the nineteenth century is of little importance today.[32] Critics also point out that even if usages are uncommon, evidentiary rules provide sufficient protection against courts looking to nonexistent unwritten usages.[33]

The first of these objections is certainly true. Extreme caution is always warranted when extrapolating from case studies. However, it is notable that the contextualists have not identified any studies that contradict the findings of the case studies discussed here. Rather, they justify their positions by reference to the "pre-theoretical empirical presumption that widespread, identifiable, and effective commercial practices do exist,"[34] and by proffering ad hoc examples like the fact that a 2 × 4 is not a board measuring two inches by four inches.[35] It is, however, unclear what a "pre-theoretical

different markets of the country"); 51 The Tea & Coffee Trade J. 321 n. 3 (1926) (noting that the Tea Association of the United States was formed in part to "procure uniformity and certainty in the customs and usages of said trade and commerce, [and] to settle differences between the members of the association"); 43 Tea & Coffee Trade J. 207–8 n. 2 (1922) (The Green Coffee Association of New York was organized in part to "establish uniformity of commercial usage among its members... and to adjust controversies and misunderstandings").

[29] Catherine Mitchell, Interpretation of Contracts 122 (2007).

[30] Jody S. Kraus & Steven D. Walt, *In Defense of the Incorporation Strategy, in* The Jurisprudential Foundations of Corporate and Commercial Law 201 (Jody S. Kraus & Steven D. Walt eds., 2000); Clayton Gillette, *Harmony and Stasis in Trade Usages for International Trade*, 39 Va. J. Int'l L. 707, 710 n. 10 (1999) ("[E]ven if some industries [studied by Bernstein] did not have customs, that tells us nothing about industries that might have had customs or about Article 2's application to such industries"); William J. Woodward, *Neoformalism in a Real World of Forms*, 2001 Wis. L. Rev. 971, 984 ("[G]eneralizing from [Bernstein's] observations in discrete, relatively homogeneous business areas to the broad spectrum of contracts covered by the Uniform Commercial Code is unjustified at this point").

[31] *See* Gillette, *Harmony and Stasis in Trade Usages for International Trade*, at n. 10.

[32] Kraus & Walt, *In Defense of the Incorporation Strategy*, at 202 ("The dearth of uniform, trade wide customs in the early part of the century provides poor evidence that such customs do not exist now"); *see* David V. Snyder, *Language and Formalities in Commercial Contracts: A Defense of Custom and Conduct*, 54 S.M.U. L. Rev. 617, 627 (2001) (noting that "there is the problem of extrapolating from codification debates [described by Bernstein] that took place in the first decade or two of the last century," to the present).

[33] *See* Stewart Macaulay, *Relational Contract Theory: Floating on a Sea of Custom? Thoughts about the Ideas of Ian Macneil and Lisa Bernstein*, 94 Nw. U. L. Rev. 775, 778 (2000) (The "empirical findings [of Bernstein's studies] raise questions of evidence rather than challenge the entire approach of the U.C.C. Why isn't it enough to say that one who wants to rely on a usage must prove it?").

[34] Kraus & Walt, *In Defense of the Incorporation Strategy*, at 201.

[35] *See* Steven L. Harris, *Rules for Interpreting Incomplete Contracts: A Cautionary Note*, 62 La. L. Rev. 1279, 1281 (2002) ("[A]nyone with any familiarity with a [contract for the sale of two-by-fours]... knows that [the parties did not contemplate] boards that are two inches by four inches"); Macaulay, *Relational Contract Theory*, at 787 (an example of business custom is the fact that "if you go to a lumber yard and ask for a 'two-by-four,' the board tendered will not measure two inches by four inches. It will be approximately one-and-one half inches by three-and-one half inches"); John E. Murray, Jr., *Contract Theories and the Rise of Neoformalism*, 71 Fordham L. Rev. 869, 913 (2002) (noting that the "two-by-four" is "an example [of a usage of trade] that has occurred to neoclassicists for the last fifty years"); Snyder, *Language and Formalities in Commercial Contracts*, at 651 n. 218 (using the fact that a two-by-four does not measure two inches by four inches as an example of usage and noting that "this fact can be proved with testimony from people in the trade, not to mention actual two-by-fours, and birdfeeders made to be mounted on two-by-fours"); Franklin G. Snyder, *Clouds of Mystery: Dispelling the Realist Rhetoric of the Uniform Commercial Code*, 68 Ohio St. L.J. 11, 47 (2007) (noting that "[t]he classic example is the trade usage that says a "two by four" [*sic*] piece of lumber will actually measure 3.5 × 1.5 inches").

empirical assumption" is, and as discussed further below, the example of the 2 × 4 actually undermines the claim that unwritten usages that are coextensive with the extent of trade (or important and delineated subsets of it) evolve over time and coalesce into workable trading norms in merchant communities.

During the last decades of the 1800s, as trade in lumber became national in scope, lumber industry participants soon realized that there were different understandings of lumber size and grading designations in different parts of the country, and even within some local areas.[36] These differences led to many disputes, and were viewed by lumbermen as a major impediment to trade; yet by the early 1920s no consensus on the meaning of lumber size and grade designations had emerged. Lumber dealers widely agreed that the term 2 × 4 did not mean a board that measures two inches by four inches, but there was no consensus about the actual dimensions that a board described as a 2 × 4 should have. For example, the Northern Pine Manufacturers Association defined a 2 × 4 as measuring 1⅝ × 3⅝, while the North Carolina Pine Association defined it as 1¾ × 3¾.[37]

When an industry wide definition finally emerged (which even today is different for dry and green lumber),[38] it came about through a quasi-legislative effort, rather than through the evolution of customary practices. In 1919, under the sponsorship of the Commerce Department,[39] lumber associations representing different regions of the country and segments of the industry negotiated and codified definitions of the 2 × 4 and other common size designations. In the course of their deliberations these groups did look at the prevalence of different meanings across the country,[40] many of which had already been codified by regional associations, local associations, and individual sawmills. Yet they also took into account the functional uses to which boards of different sizes were commonly put, and tailored the definitions they adopted to reflect the minimum engineering standards needed to accomplish these various ends.[41]

Today, the meaning of 2 × 4 and other common lumber size designations is codified in a voluntary product standard put out by the National Institute of Standards and Technology. In sum, the history of the 2 × 4 suggests that it is a poor example of an unwritten and generally understood trade usage that emerged over time through an informal and gradually evolving industry consensus.

The second objection to the case studies is that at the time the codification efforts began the industries studied had not been national for long enough for customs to evolve. This objection is difficult to evaluate as critics do not put forth any metric for assessing the expected pace of customary evolution. However, the grain trade had been national in scope for over 60 years before the first trade rules were adopted,[42]

[36] Forest Prod. Lab., Forest Serv., U.S. Dept. Agric., History of Yard Lumber Size Standard app. A (1964) (hereinafter "Yard Sizes") at Appendix A.

[37] Yard Sizes.

[38] Nat'l Inst. of Standards and Tech., Voluntary Product Standard PS 20-10, at 9 tbl. 4 (2010).

[39] Royal S. Kellog, Lumber and Its Uses (4th ed., 1931).

[40] *See Recommendations as to Standard Sizes and Grades of Lumber Are Explained by the Central Committee*, The American Lumberman, 44 (1923) (reporting the results of surveys of 12 sets of trade association rules that included softwood sizing standards for yard lumber).

[41] *See* The American Lumberman at 44–5 (discussing the considerations the committees relied on in defining the nominal designation of size 2 inches, and the nominal designation of size 4 inches).

[42] *See* William Cronon, Nature's Metropolis: Chicago and the Great West ch. 3 (1991) (noting that cross country trade in grain had emerged by 1840s).

and the hay trade had been interregional and at least partially national 30 years before the rules codification process even began.[43] Even more strikingly, important parts of the American textile trade were centered in New York City for over 300 years before the process of creating trading rules even began. Indeed, they were concentrated on Worth Street itself for 75 years prior to the adoption of the Worth Street Trading Rules.[44] Similarly, the American silk industry had been centered in the northeast since the mid-1840s with a significant concentration of silkmen in New York and Patterson, New Jersey. These silkmen met with one another on a regular basis and also formed a variety of clubs and associations to further their business interests.[45] The industry was thus organized into meaningful groups/associations for over 50 years before the Silk Association of America's trade rule codification process even began.

In light of these facts, the claim that the codification efforts began before national—or in the cases of textiles and silk, local—customs had had sufficient time to develop, cannot provide a plausible account of the lack of agreement on the meaning of terms that everyone acknowledged were in wide spread use. Regardless, the important point for commercial law and commercial law reform is that even if usages might have emerged in the long run, however defined, usages had not evolved quickly enough to meet the needs of commerce. Otherwise codification, an expensive and time-consuming enterprise would not have been needed.

Finally, in assessing the relevance of the case studies to contemporary commerce, it is important to note that the conditions for the emergence of usages were more nearly met in the contexts studied than they are in most industries today. Although the studies do not (and do not purport to) prove that usages do not exist today, their evidence is powerful enough to suggest that those who continue to advocate incorporating trade usages into commercial contracts should be moved to provide proof of their existence.

3. *Usage in the contemporary Texas cattle feed market*

In a follow-up to the case studies discussed above, and to begin to explore whether usages exist in modern merchant industries, a pilot case study of transactional practices in the contemporary cattle feed market in and around Amarillo Texas was conducted.[46] This market is characterized by the preconditions typically associated with the emergence of well-developed trade usages. Most transactors have relatively few trading partners[47] and most of their contracting relationships are long-standing and

[43] *See* Bernstein, *Questionable Basis*, at n. 30.

[44] From 1635 to 1835, the textile trade was centered on New York's Pearl Street. However, a fire and changes in the real estate market forced it to disperse throughout lower Manhattan. In 1853, the trade decided it should again locate in one geographic area and it chose Worth Street, less than a mile and a half from Pearl Street. The first large merchants moved there in 1857. By 1861 it was recognized as "the primary mill agency market in the United States" and by 1870, it was considered the "textile center" of the country. *See* Frank L. Walton, Tomahawks to Textiles: The Fabulous Story of Worth Street, 61, 62, 102, 104 (1953).

[45] *See* Silk City: Studies on the Patterson Silk Industry 1860–1940 (Philip B. Scranton ed., 1985).

[46] This survey was conducted and designed by Martha Van Heitsma and Virginia Bartot of the Small Survey Lab at the University of Chicago. The raw data and research protocols for the study are on file with the author (hereinafter *NORC Survey*).

[47] Just over half of the firms surveyed had 27 or fewer such partners.

repeat.[48] Most transactions take place in a geographically limited area characterized by a high degree of social and ethnic homogeneity.[49] The firms surveyed were mostly well-established market participants.[50] All were members of either the Texas Grain and Feed Association (T.G.F.A.), an organization that runs the private legal system that governs transactions in this market, or the Texas Cattle Feeders Association, an association of feedlot owners and feed brokers, who view themselves as being part of a close-knit group.[51] As a consequence, the entities studied were quite likely to be well versed in any trade usages that were indeed widely followed; yet the study found that even under these near ideal conditions, unwritten work-a-day practices varied widely with respect to aspects of exchange where the Code would look to usage to give meaning its own standard like default rules.

For example, transactors widely (though not universally) agreed that giving a grace period for payment was appropriate,[52] yet they did not agree on the proper length of the grace period which differed for new and old transactors.[53] Moreover not a single respondent indicated that they would determine the appropriate grace period by an industry norm or practice. Most of those who commented on the subject indicated that their actions would be determined by the identity of their contracting partner and the reason for the delay.[54] Transactors were also split about how frequently they would accept nonconforming tender with a price adjustment,[55] and how that price adjustment was to be determined—some thought it should be individually negotiated while others thought that it should be determined on the basis of a regional scale of discounts, or a local scale of discounts.[56]

[48] Fifty-four percent of transactors reported that their contracting relationships usually lasted more than ten years, 32 percent reported they lasted five to ten years, and 12 percent two to five years. Only one firm reported that its relationships tended to last less than two years.

[49] Responses to Question 7. Among their Texas trading partners 86 percent were based in the "Lubbock, Amarillo, Abilene, Wichita Falls" areas, a radius of about 500 miles.

[50] In addition, the majority of firms in the study were quite mature. Sixty percent of the firms had been in business for more than 20 years, while only 10 percent had been in business less than six years.

[51] Interview with Panelists at T.G.F.A. Meeting. *See also* Resp. 81.

[52] Among the firms surveyed, 68 percent gave a grace period for new partners, and 72 percent did so for old partners.

[53] The mean grace period for a new partner was 13.8 days while for an old partner it was 20.4 days.

[54] *See*, e.g., Resp. 0005 (noting they would give no grace period for a new trading partner, but for an old trading partner "it might be 10 days depending on the relationship and the reason," and they would "call up that firm and ask what the problem was. If they have a reason—someone was sick—might possibly extend more time, if no satisfactory answer, turn it over to the credit people in Kansas city"); Respondent 024 (explaining that he gives at most 4–5 days grace to new and old trading partners alike, but noting that whether they would get it would "depend on the reason" noting that it must be a "reasonable excuse"); Resp. 025 (grace period, up to ten days for a new trading partner and up to a month for an old trading partner, "depends on circumstances," the "action [I take] depends on the explanation given by the trader"); Resp. 029 ("[R]eally depends on circumstance, judgment call"); Resp. 030 (if time for payment passed "I'd be knocking on his door or ringing his bell," and action "could depend on what he'd say"); Resp. 031(explaining that if the grace period passed for an old trading partner, "I'd commence to find out if there was some kind of problem").

[55] Among the firms surveyed, 20.4 percent *never* accept nonconforming tender, 20.4 percent *frequently* do so, and 59.2 percent *sometimes* do so.

[56] Among the 92 percent of respondents who said that a discount was reasonable when goods below the expected quality were accepted, there was no agreement about either the size of the discount or the method of determining it. 41.3 percent of the respondents said that the discount should be individually

Finally, although most contracts in the market contained an F.O.B. delivery term, transactors could not agree about its meaning, or even what the acronym stood for.[57]

More generally, the study also sought to explore whether the transactors themselves thought that unwritten customs and usages of trade exist. They were asked "[w]hen you use written contracts, or purchase and sale orders, are there some unwritten rules or customs or practices that you expect your trading partner to follow even though they are not explicitly written down?"[58] Initially, 72 percent of the respondents said unwritten practices existed, although four changed their minds when asked to give an example. Among the 65.3 percent who ultimately answered that these usages existed, all but two eventually provided an example,[59] but most did so only after a follow-up probe that attempted to focus their attention on "quality or time or cost considerations."[60]

Interestingly, most of the examples given by respondents would not have qualified as unwritten usages under the Code.[61] Half of the respondents either described practices that were set out in one of the two relevant sets of written trading rules (the T.G.F.A. Trading Rules or the Southwest Scale of discounts),[62] or referred to these sets of rules themselves as customs.[63] Twenty-five percent made references to "old boy" rules of thumb,[64] and

negotiated, 50 percent said it should be determined on a regional scale, and 8.7 percent on a national scale.

[57] When asked what the term F.O.B. meant, 6 percent said they did not know, 2 percent said "factory on balance," 32 percent said "free on board," 22 percent said "freight on board," 2 percent said "freight on delivery," and 34 percent responded in other ways.

[58] *NORC Survey*, at Q14.

[59] Resp. 049 and Resp. 020.

[60] *NORC Survey*, at probe to question 14.

[61] The only exception was Resp. 019 who asserted that "everybody [knows] to order for Friday give a weeks notice."

[62] The T.G.F.A. Trading Rules are the rules used to resolve disputes in the association's private legal system. The Southwest Scale of discounts is a document setting out standardized deductions for particular types of quality and quantity deviations.

[63] The examples given were as follows: Resp. 007 (mentioning protein contents and other quality specifications that are defined in the Southwest Scales); Resp. 047 (same); Resp. 017 (the Southwest Scales); Resp. 046 (same); Resp. 83 (same) Resp. 023 (following the written trade rules is a usage); Resp. 001 (describing several practices relating to grading times, and buying in that are set out in the T.G.F.A. Trade Rules); Resp. 050a (observing that most trade practices are spelled out in the contract, and giving as an example of an unwritten practice a definition of a delivery term that is in accord with the T.G.F.A. Rules); Resp. 081 (noting that the grain quality standards set out in the rules are generally understood and taken for granted); Resp. 021 ("if feed is sold on standard terms, I expect them to replace it if it is a mess," which is just a restatement of T.G.F.A. R. 17); Resp. 015 (after being pressed to give an example of a usage in a follow-up interview, the respondent gave a long discourse on converting truck measure to rail measures whose content is extensively covered in the T.G.F.A. rules); Resp. 008B (the need to observe state laws on truck weight); Resp. 068 (the right to reject for bad quality which is codified in the Trading Rules). In addition, three buyers mentioned being able to reject hay that was either moldy, wet, or foul smelling, but this is just a particularization of the rule that the buyer may reject off grade goods. Resp. 058 (even if a written contract is not used, wet hay can be returned); Resp. 061 ("sure there are some. Can't think of any... if you buy a load of alfalfa hay and its moldy you can turn it down"); Resp. 063 ("There are some things we take for granted that you just expect. There a legal term—normal trade practices that you don't have to spell out," and noting you may reject wet hay).

[64] Resp. 010 (when the market shifts, you have to see what your competitors are doing because if you "don't word gets out real quick"); Resp.024 ("giving the people you deal with courtesy of understanding," and noting he will pay return freight if something is rejected to keep his customers happy); Resp. 045 ("I expect that they'll do what they say and visa versa"); Resp. 054 ("everyone stands on honor to a certain

19 percent noted aspects of agreements that were sometimes left unwritten without noting whether they were given meaning through usages or bilateral understandings.[65]

More broadly, the study suggests that merchants have a very inaccurate understanding of the concepts of custom and usage, a finding that raises questions about the reliability of merchant testimony (whether expert or lay) about the content of trade usages. As discussed further below, in most trade usage cases this is the only type of usage evidence introduced in court.

In sum, the studies of merchant industries discussed here suggest that the types of trade usages the Code relies on so heavily may not in fact exist in merchant communities. They do not seem to have existed in the Middle Ages, they did not exist in important American industries at the turn of the twentieth century, and the Texas study provides some limited evidence that they do not presently exist even in a market as small and homogeneous as the feed trade within 500 miles of Amarillo Texas, a context where unlike most modern contexts, the preconditions for the emergence of usages are largely present. Although these studies and historical investigations are not perfect, it is notable that there are no studies documenting that usages do exist. Contextualists repeatedly dismiss the importance of investigating this issue, explaining that if usages do not exist or are far less prevalent than commonly believed, the rules of evidence can be relied on to ensure that nonexistent usages will be excluded so they will play no role in contract adjudication.[66]

This argument assumes, however, that courts and juries will do a relatively good job distinguishing extant from nonexistent usages, and that courts will not permit mere assertions that a usage exists to defeat motions for summary judgment unless meaningful evidence of its existence and scope is introduced. These are assumptions that need to be evaluated not in the abstract, but rather in light of the way the Code's trade usage provision operates in practice. Interestingly, while the Code drafters were concerned that courts would set the evidentiary bar for establishing usages too high,[67] schooled as they were in the stricter requirements for establishing a custom, precisely the opposite occurred. As discussed further below, a recent study found that in practice the evidentiary requirements for establishing a usage in court are, in fact, quite lax.

extent"); Resp. 056 ("the basic rule of thumb is that its got to be feed quality"); Resp. 066 ("Be on time, honor their end of the deal" are standard expectations); Resp. 030 ("There are generally accepted rules of conduct in the business that we're in... We sort of expect people to go with the flow," noting sometimes people do not "holler" if average grade is okay even if some is off); Resp. 76 ("I am sure there is no way you can write everything in a contract. You still deal with someone you trust" so you can work things out).

[65] Resp. 052 (noting that the term "on demand" could have many different meanings, but that "our partners know what we mean"); Resp. 029 (noting that it expects those it deals with to observe its rules, but not specifying what the rules were); Resp. 072 (noting that delivery time and quality are not always specified in a contract, but not saying how they are set); Resp. 031 (noting that when transactors dealt on a repeat basis, some quality and delivery terms were not written down); Resp. 84 (sometimes shipping method isn't written down and is understood); Resp. 036 (sometimes extra charges were added when shipping terms changed, but noting this was varied and local).

[66] *See, e.g.*, Macaulay, *Relational Contract Theory*.

[67] U.C.C. §1-205 cmt. 4 (2010) (distinguishing the Code's concept of usage from the common law conception of custom).

B. Can courts find usages

In defending the Code's reliance on trade usage, contextualists have long assumed that to prove a usage a party will have to introduce "objective" evidence that the usage exists, in the form of either "expert testimony and evidence about [the] statistical regularity of observance," or the submission of a "considerable mass of behavioral data,"[68] meaning "evidence of statistic norms—mere frequency of a given behavior in the trade."[69] This assumption is echoed in the leading Code treatise, which opines that to prove a usage "a party must usually call on an expert," or introduce a written trade code.[70] Similar assertions are made in most formbooks and practice manuals.[71]

However, a study of all of the trade usage cases digested under the Code's trade usage provision from 1970 to 2000 demonstrates that in practice the evidentiary requirements for establishing the existence of a usage at trial are far less stringent.[72] The study found that nonparty testimony (a category that includes both lay and expert witnesses) was introduced in less than 30 percent of the cases and that parties sought to introduce trade codes in only 11 percent. In cases that both went to trial and found a custom to exist, nonparty testimony was introduced by 16 percent of plaintiffs and 28.2 percent of defendants. In over 50 percent of these cases, the testimony of the parties and/or their employees was the *only* evidence of usage introduced. Moreover, there was not a single case in which statistical information about the regularity or frequency with which the usage was followed was introduced. To the extent that regularity of observance was mentioned at all in witness testimony, it was most almost always simply asserted. There were only a few cases where evidence of even a few actual transactions in which the usage was followed was introduced.

The study also found that similarly thin evidence was all that was needed to demonstrate the existence of a usage with enough plausibility to defeat a motion for summary judgment. Nonmovants were successful in using usage-related arguments to defeat the motion 70 percent of the time; and in 83 percent of the cases in which they did so, the only evidence they introduced was a cursory affidavit from a party or a party's employees.

These and other findings of the study suggest that court determinations relating to the existence, content, and scope of usages are likely to be both inaccurate and highly unpredictable, as they are typically made on the basis of very limited information.[73]

[68] Matthew C. Jennejohn, *Contract Adjudication in a Collaborative Economy*, 5 VA. L. & BUS. REV. 175, 207 n. 142 (2010) (citing Charles Goetz & Robert Scott, *The Limits of Expanded Choice: An Analysis of the Interaction between Express and Implied Contract Terms*, 73 CAL. L. REV. 261, 275–6 (1985)).

[69] Kraus & Walt, *In Defense of the Incorporation Strategy*, at 213.

[70] JAMES WHITE & ROBERT SUMMERS, UNIFORM COMMERCIAL CODE 140 (6th ed., 2010).

[71] *See* GREGORY M. TRAVALIO, ROBERT J. NORDSTROM & ALBERT L. CLOVIS NORDSTROM ON SALES & LEASES OF GOODS, para. 3.14[c], ("[P]resumably expert testimony will be necessary to establish a trade usage").

[72] *See* Lisa E. Bernstein, *Trade Usage in the Courts: The Flawed Empirical Basis of Article 2's Incorporation Strategy* (forthcoming in the NORTHWESTERN LAW REVIEW (2015)) (available at <http://papers.ssrn.com/sol3/papers.cfm?abstract_id=2366533>).

[73] Similar results were found in a recent study of the use of custom and usage in reinsurance litigation, *see* William Hoffman, *On the Use and Abuse of Custom and Usage in Reinsurances Contracts*, 33 TORT & INS L.J. 1 (1997). ("[C]ounsel asserting a reinsurance usage often do not present, nor do the courts require, the evidence necessary to support a finding that a reinsurance usage affects the meaning of a contract... [T]hese cases often lack any reference whatsoever to the applicable rules for proof of a reinsurance usage,"

This study also raises, though does not answer, the question of why, if usages are as well established and well known as the Code assumes, more robust evidence of their existence is not introduced in court, especially since most of the sources consulted by practicing lawyers would suggest (albeit incorrectly) that introducing such evidence is a necessary precondition to a finding that a usage exists.

C. Do transactors clearly prefer contextualized adjudication

The contextualized interpretive approach reflected in American commercial law is often defended as a majoritarian default rule that reflects the hypothetical bargain that transactors would have struck with regard to interpretation had they been able to costlessly negotiate over it.[74] There are, however, no studies documenting that such an approach actually corresponds to transactors' preferences.[75]

It is impossible to measure the extent of parties' preferences for formalistic adjudication by looking at their contracts. This is due, in part, to the fact that the Code's contextualist interpretive approach is, in practice, quasi-mandatory.[76] Nevertheless it is useful to explore common contracting practices. A careful review of major supply agreements reveals that certain types of contracts commonly include a variety of provisions designed to ensure the primacy of the contract's written terms and to constrain the types of contextual considerations courts can take into account.[77] The inclusion of these provisions is particularly notable because, under current law, some of them are not consistently enforced. The enforceability of others is either unclear or remains untested despite their apparent conflict with the Code and its Official Comments.[78]

Consider, for example, the Master Vendor Agreements used by large Big Box retailers in their relationships with the vast majority of their suppliers. These agreements typically contain provisions attempting to negate the Code's formation rules

and information about its prevalence in a local market and evidence of actual instances in which it was observed are rarely presented.)

[74] *See* Gillette, *Harmony and Stasis in Trade Usages for International Trade, supra* note 30, at 708.

[75] Modern contextualists point to the fact that the Code has not been amended to justify the conclusion that transactors view its adjudicative approach as desirable, explaining that "[I]f, as has been alleged, business lawyers dominate the U.C.C. revision process, one might interpret the reaffirmation of the Code's approach as a "vote" against a more formal approach by those whose clients are affected by the law." Woodward, *Neoformalism in a Real World of Forms*, at 958; Robert A. Hillman, *More in Defense of U.C.C. Methodology*, 62 La. L. Rev. 1153, 1157 (2002) ("I am unaware of any effort by business to overturn the Code's use of trade custom"). However, even if business interests were opposed to the Code, business lawyers would not necessarily choose to advocate for their clients' preferences during the ALI/NCUSSAL law reform process. Article 2 is good for law firm revenue and the ALI process is far from transparent. In addition, the political economy of private legislatures like the ALI, suggests that such groups are strongly inclined to adopt the types of vague standard-like provisions that are so ubiquitous in the Code. *See* Alan Schwartz & Robert E. Scott, *The Political Economy of Private Legislatures*, 143 U. Pa. L. Rev. 595 (1995).

[76] *See* Bernstein, *Trade Usage in the Courts*; Alan Schwartz & Robert E. Scott, *Contract Theory and the Limits of Contract Law*, 113 Yale L.J. 541, 585 n. 84 (2003) (concluding that the Code's interpretive rules are "quasi-mandatory").

[77] *See* notes 78–92 and accompanying text; *also* Alan Schwartz & Robert E. Scott, *Contract Interpretation Redux*, 119 Yale L.J. 926 (2010) (suggesting that the terms of alliance agreements reflect transactors' preferences for formalistic adjudication).

[78] The enforceability of some of these provisions has not been tested, yet a close reading of the Code and its Official Comments suggests that they might not be enforced by a court that sought to follow both the letter and/or the spirit of the Code.

(including but not limited to the battle-of-the-forms);[79] clauses making clear that no courses of dealing,[80] courses of performance, actions, inactions or trade usages, are to be construed as waivers or modifications of the agreement's written terms;[81] provisions negating the applicability of usages and industry standards to interpretation of the contract;[82] clauses noting that no estimates of future needs are to be relied on or considered relevant in determining the scope of the agreement;[83] time is of the essence clauses requiring strict compliance with delivery dates;[84] provisions stating

[79] Most of the contracts state that contracts cannot be created verbally, Nordstrom, Terms and Conditions of Purchase Order, cl. 2 ("Verbal orders will not be valid unless confirmed with a written or electronic purchase order"), while others go further emphasizing that email orders are also considered invalid and noting that only orders submitted on a signed copy of the buyer's standard purchase order or through the company's Electronic Data Interchange system will be binding. Most of these agreements also all contain language attempting to contract out of the battle of the forms, *see, e.g*, Burlington Coat Factory, Express Terms and Conditions, cl. 2 ("THE TERMS STATED IN THIS ORDER ARE THE ONLY AGREEMENT BETWEEN PURCHASER AND VENDOR RELATING TO THE GOODS AND SHALL NOT BE VARIED BY ANY ADDITIONAL OR INCONSISTENT TERMS CONTAINED IN ANY LATER INVOICE, CONFIRMATION OR OTHER MATERIAL OF VENDOR"); Radio Shack, Terms and Conditions of Purchase, cl. 1 ("Any document of Seller [that] conflicts with, contradicts or adds to any provision, terms or conditions of this Agreement... is hereby rejected (unless specifically agreed to in a separate document executed by the Buyer) and the provisions, terms and conditions of this Agreement and the PO by such acceptance shall constitute the whole contract between the parties. Any statement purporting to make Seller's acceptance conditional on Buyer's assent to additional or different terms are hereby rejected and shall be of no effect. Buyer shall have the right to make reasonable changes to any PO from time-to-time... To the extent that Buyer and Seller are parties to Buyer's form of Vendor Agreement and any of the terms and conditions of such Vendor Agreement conflicts with the terms of this Agreement the Vendor Agreement shall govern").

[80] *See, e.g.*, Target Supply Agreement, Conditions of Contract, Partnersonline.com, cl. 21 & 20b [hereinafter Target Contract] (the "Purchaser's right to require strict observance of the terms of the Contract shall not be waived by course of dealing" and "[t]he Contract may not be modified by course of dealing, course of performance, or any oral communication between Purchaser and Vendor. The Contract may only be modified by (i) a separate written agreement signed by Vendor and an authorized agent or officer of Purchaser, or (ii) Purchaser providing Vendor, with respect to future Purchase Orders, with advance written or electronic notice"); *see also* Kohl's Terms and Conditions at 20 (providing that course of dealing may not create a waiver... [and that] "Kohl's' rights herein are reserved and may be exercised at any time as long as any breach of any of the terms or conditions hereof shall continue, and shall not be deemed waived by delay or by waiver of such condition or any other condition hereof in previous transactions between the parties").

[81] Radio Shack Corp. Purchase Order Terms and Conditions, cl. 19, 21 ("No course of dealing or course of performance between Buyer and Seller nor any delay or omission of Buyer to exercise any right or remedy granted under this Agreement shall operate as a waiver of any rights of Buyer," nor shall any "trade custom or practice, course of dealing or course of performance between Buyer and Seller... operate as a modification or amendment of this Agreement").

[82] Clauses opting out of usage for the purpose of interpretation are not uncommon in Supply contracts generally, *see* Purchase and License Agreement between VLSI Libraries and Eki Electronics (1996) ("THIS AGREEMENT MAY NOT BE... INTERPRETED BY ANY TRADE USAGE OR PRIOR COURSE OF DEALING NOT MADE A PART OF THIS AGREEMENT BY ITS EXPRESS TERMS"); Purchase Agreement between Gillette Co. and 123 Systems cl. 12.4.2 (2008) ("[N]o trade usage shall be used to explain... this AGREEMENT even if either or both PARTIES were aware or should have been aware of such trade usage"); Development and Product Supply Agreement (2000) between S3 Inc and Intellon Corp. cl. 7.1 ("This Agreement shall not be... interpreted by any trade usage or prior course of dealing not made a part of this Agreement by its express terms"); Master Supply Agreement between Berkeley Heartlab Inc. and Diadexus, Inc. (April 1, 2009) ("No trade customs, courses of dealing or courses of performance by the parties shall be relevant to... explain any term(s) used in this Agreement").

[83] Target Contract, at cl. 1 ("Any forecasts, commitments, projections, representation about quantities to be purchased or other estimates provided to Vendor are for planning purposes only and shall not be binding upon Purchaser, and Purchaser shall not be liable for any amounts incurred by Vendor in reliance on such estimates").

[84] *See, e.g.*, Burlington Coat Factory, Express Terms and Conditions, at cl. 1 ("Time of delivery is hereby made of the essence").

that perfect tender is required;[85] provisions defining cure quite precisely or noting that no cure will be acceptable;[86] provisions making clear that any terms in purchase orders or commitments made (either orally or in writing) during the life of the parties' contracting relationship are unenforceable unless memorialized in a signed amendment to the Master Agreement;[87] and, finally, a variety of merger, integration, and entire agreement clauses that are not mere boilerplate but rather vary considerably in their specificity and seek to exclude from consideration not only pre-contractual considerations, but some post-contract ones as well.[88] The widespread use of these clauses, which are also common in the Master Supply Agreements between manufacturers and the suppliers of their component parts, suggests a strong preference on the part of these transactors for opting out of the context-specific Code provisions that are at the core of the statute's jurisprudential approach. Together these clauses can be understood as a direct rejection of the Code's central assumption that "the course of actual performance by the parties is the best indicator of what they intended their writing to mean,"[89] and that "the course of prior dealings between the parties and the usage of trade were taken for granted when the document was phrased."[90]

More generally, a look at a wide variety of Material Contracts filed in the EDGAR system reveals that sophisticated transactors often use the clauses described above, as well as an array of other types of clauses that can fairly be understood as attempts to constrain the extent to which courts will contextualize the interpretation of their written agreements in the event of a dispute. The most extreme such provisions, while not in widespread use, require arbitration and direct arbitrators to rule on the basis of the written agreement's "plain meaning."[91] A more tempered approach, used in a

[85] *See, e.g.*, Target Contract, at cl. 5(v) (defining a breach to include "any deviation from or variation in quantities, assortments, prices, or other terms or conditions specified in the Contract").

[86] *See, e.g.*, Kohl's Terms and Conditions, at cl. 2 ("Seller hereby waives any right to cure improper tender which might otherwise be available under law").

[87] Kohl's Terms and Conditions, at cl. 21. Courts differ in their treatment of no oral modification clauses. *See, e.g.*, Akash Sethi, Derrick Carson & Brad Whitlock, *Boilerplate Provisions*, 44 Tex. J. Bus. L. 158, 159 (2012) (noting the inconsistent positions taken by Texas state courts with respect to clauses limiting modification to written amendments).

[88] Courts' approaches to enforcing these clauses vary both across and even within jurisdictions. *See* Geoffrey P. Miller, *Bargains Bicoastal: New Light on Contract Theory*, 31 Cardozo L. Rev. 1475, 1507–8 (2010) (noting that merger and integration clauses are "accorded nearly conclusive deference by the New York courts," while in California, they are "not conclusive but rather considered along with other evidence of contract integration," and "even if an integration clause is present and respected regarding the original terms of the contract, California recognizes relatively easy modification by course of dealing among the parties"); Schwartz & Scott, *Limits*, at 589 at n. 94 (citing cases that illustrate that courts' attitudes towards merger clauses and integration clauses vary widely and that such provisions are not automatically enforced without question).

[89] U.C.C. § 2-202 cmt. 4. [90] U.C.C. § 2-202 cmt. 4.

[91] *See, e.g.*, Master Sales Agreement between Telecommunication Systems, Inc. and Vonage Network Inc. cl. 14 (2006) (providing for arbitration and noting that the "arbitrator's award shall adhere to the plain meaning of this Agreement and to applicable law"); Supply Agreement between Akorn Inc. and Novadaq Technologies cl. 12.9 (2002) (providing for arbitration and directing that "arbitrator(s) shall apply first the plain meaning of this Agreement, but in matters not fairly provided for in this Agreement, shall apply the substantive law of the State of Illinois"). Such "plain meaning" provisions can also be found in smaller contracts, *see, e.g.*, Growfoo Vendor Agreement (2012) (providing for arbitration and requiring that "The arbitrator's decision shall follow the plain meaning of the relevant documents and shall be final and binding."); Planters Rural Tel. Coop., Service Terms and Conditions of Service, <http://www.planters.net/docs/service_terms_conditions.pdf> (same), and are quite common in website statements of their terms and conditions of use.

variety of agreements for complex services, attempts to assert the primacy of both the scope and meaning of the agreement's written terms by directing that they be given their "plain meaning," while providing a detailed preamble describing the purpose and goals of the transactors business relationship that courts are directed to take into consideration if, and only if, the provisions are found to be ambiguous or the agreement fails to deal with a contingency.[92] These clauses reflect transactors' preferences for the terms they write to be enforced *as written* with a strong presumption that their plain meaning was intended, as well as their recognition that contextualized interpretation may be unavoidable in the case of an ambiguity or a contractual gap. Nevertheless, despite transactors' seeming acceptance of the necessity of contextualist interpretation, the detail in these preambles together with the directive that all gaps are to be filled and ambiguities resolved so as to "give full effect to the provisions of th[e] preamble," without "expanding the scope of the Parties direct obligations,"[93] suggests that transactors want to constrain the court's discretion when it engages in even this highly limited type of contextualized purposeful interpretation. Finally, it is interesting to note that attempts to opt out of contextualism are not limited to the largest contracts. Provisions attempting to opt out of or limit the role of trade usage, course of performance, and course of dealing are also common in the standard Terms and Conditions of small- and medium-sized product buyers and sellers.[94]

The transactor preferences expressed in these Master Agreements and Terms and Conditions of Trade are consistent with those reflected in the jurisprudential approaches adopted by trade association-run private legal systems. In these systems contract disputes are resolved by panels of merchant arbitrators who do not apply the Code, but rather the Trade Rules developed by and voted on by the very transactors whose contracts they govern.[95] Arbitrators do not look to course of performance,

[92] *See* SmartMeter Program Upgrade Supply Agreement with Pacific Gas and Electric ("This preamble is intended to provide a general introduction to the Agreement. It is not intended to alter the plain meaning of the Agreement or to expand the scope of the Parties' express obligations under it. However, to the extent the terms and conditions of the Agreement do not address a particular circumstance or are otherwise unclear or ambiguous, such terms and conditions are to be interpreted and construed so as to give full effect to the provisions of this preamble"); Master Services Agreement by and between ACI World Wide and International Machines (same). One lawyer interviewed about this clause noted that his firm had dropped it in information technology outsourcing contracts because it was making preambles too difficult to agree on.

[93] Smartmeter Program Upgrade Supply Agreement with Pacific Gas and Electric, at cl. 1.2.

[94] *See, e.g.*, The Miniature Garden Shoppe, General Terms and Conditions, <http://www.miniaturegardenshoppe.com/termsandconditions.html> ("This agreement may not be explained or supplemented by any prior course of dealings or trade by custom or usage"); Hauser Packaging, Terms and Conditions, <http://www.hauserpack.com> ("Trade usage shall neither be applicable nor relevant to this agreement, nor be used in any manner whatsoever to explain, qualify or supplement any of the provisions hereof," and that "[i]n the event of any ambiguity or inconsistency in these terms and conditions of sale, said terms shall be given their literal or intended meaning and will not be strictly construed against or to the detriment of the seller"); Consolidated Elec. Distribs., Terms and Conditions ("Any representation, promise, course of dealing or trade usage not contained or referred to herein will not be binding on Seller. No modification, amendment, rescission, waiver or other change shall be binding on Seller unless assented to in writing by Seller's authorized representative"); Noble Polymers, L.L.C. Standard Terms and Conditions of Sale ("Prior courses of dealing, trade usage and verbal agreements not reduced to a writing signed by Seller, to the extent they differ from, modify, add to or detract from the contract, shall not be binding on Seller").

[95] Most of these systems opted for formalistic approaches long before the Code was adopted so cannot properly be viewed as a reaction to it.

course of dealing, or usage of trade to interpret contracts. They only look to usages when faced with a contractual gap, a concept they define far more narrowly than courts applying the Code. Good faith and fair dealing provisions are also conspicuously absent from the trade rules and play no role in the resolution of cases. In the main, these private legal systems have adopted a highly textualist approach to contractual adjudication.

Although there are a number of reasons that the costs of textualism may be lower in private legal systems than in the public legal system, the consistency of this preference across most merchant-run systems suggests that at the time the Code was adopted, merchant transactors preferred clear, definite, and specific rules together with a formalistic adjudicative approach. Indeed, at the New York Law Reform Commission's hearings on the adoption of Article 2, representatives of the Commerce and Industry Association specifically objected to some of the Code's most contextualist provisions. They objected to its lax formation rules and its lenient statute of frauds on the grounds that "you may find you have an unintended contract on your hands even though the 'memorandum' concerning a 'sale' omits all of the following: price, time and place of payment, time and place of delivery, general quality of goods, and warranties!"[96] They also opposed the Code's nonwaiveable obligations of good faith, commercial reasonableness and reasonable care, explaining that looking to these considerations will "not tend to greater precision in the law... the determination will result in much litigation."[97] They also strenuously objected to the definition of the merchant's duty of good faith, explaining that it made "a merchant... guilty of breach of contract if he does not observe reasonable commercial standards," yet "[t]he usages, customs, and practices of business are far from being uniform, and the determination of whether a merchant has conformed to reasonable commercial standards would be difficult and would produce excessive litigation."[98] Additional examples abound.

Although caution is warranted in abstracting from the trade association context and there are no studies of the frequency with which the contract provisions discussed here are included in commercial agreements, some systematic evidence about whether sophisticated transactors prefer highly contextualist or more formalist adjudicative approaches can be found in studies of choice-of-law provisions in large commercial contracts.[99] A recent study looked at whether transactors entering into a variety of types of large commercial agreements (not exclusively sale of goods transactions) preferred to be governed by relatively contextual California law or relatively formalist New York law that is more protective of the terms of written agreements. It found a marked preference for New York law concluding that "the testimony of the marketplace, the verdict of thousands of sophisticated parties whose incentives are to maximize the value of contract terms—is that New York's formalistic rules win out over California's contextualist approach. As predicted by theory, sophisticated parties

[96] State of N.Y., Law Revision Comm'n, Study of the Uniform Commercial Code 23 (1954).

[97] Study of the Uniform Commercial Code, at 25.

[98] Study of the Uniform Commercial Code, at 29.

[99] Theodore Eisenberg & Geoffrey P. Miller, *The Flight to New York: An Empirical Study of Choice of Law and Choice of Forum Clauses in Publicly-Held Companies' Contracts*, 30 Cardozo L. Rev. 1457 (2009).

prefer formalistic rules of contract law."[100] The generality of this conclusion is buttressed by the findings of two studies. One looked at the choice of law provisions in European business transactions subject to International Chamber of Commerce arbitration; it found a strong transactor preference for British Law, which is considered the most formalist of the EU countries.[101] The other surveyed contract managers about the types of contract provisions they thought would be most "proactive in supporting successful relations;" it found that "entirety of agreement clauses," were the second most common response.[102]

In sum, the types of contract provisions discussed here, together with the adjudicative approaches of merchant tribunals and the choice of law provisions in corporations' material contracts, suggest that both merchant transactors engaged in the sale of cash commodities and sophisticated transactors entering into complex supply chain transactions attempt to reject the Code's contextualist adjudicative approach. In its place, transactors attempt to contract for an interpretive approach that both gives primacy to the terms of their written agreement and protects those terms from erosion,[103] modification, or waiver through the actions, inactions, and communications (both written and oral) of either transactors' employees that occurred before and after their written agreement was signed.

It is impossible to determine from the empirical evidence currently available whether contextualism or formalism is a majoritarian preference. The evidence discussed here, however, is nonetheless strong enough to suggest that transactors do not have a uniform preference for contextual adjudication. Together with the theoretical arguments presented below, this evidence suggests that the Code's adjudicative approach, which is, in practice, a quasi-mandatory rule rather than a pure default rule, should be turned into a pure default that transactors can opt out of either on a contract-by-contract basis or, as some commentators have suggested, on a term-by-term basis.[104]

II. Contextualism and the Modern Economy

Over the past few decades the structure of important sectors of American businesses have undergone a shift from large vertically integrated concerns to large multi-agent firms who keep only their "core competencies" in house. These firms outsource the production of important components of their products, many of which are specially manufactured and thus involve specific investment. A number of these firms

[100] Miller, *Bargains Bicoastal*, at 1478.

[101] Stuart Popham, Clifford Chance LLP, The View of European Business: Survey Results 6 (Mar. 14, 2008), *available at* <http://denning.law.ox.ac.uk/news/events_files/Popham_-_presentation.PPT>.

[102] Int'l Ass'n of Contract and Commercial Managers, 2012 Top Terms in Negotiation 11, 12 (noting that the importance attached to these provisions might be because "the tendency of courts—and in particular regulatory authorities—to view any communication (including social media) as relevant to [its] investigations has impacted sensitivity in this area.")

[103] *See* Bernstein, *Trade Usage in the Courts* (exploring the ways that the Code's interpretive approach induces parties to fortify their contracts with terms that attempt to constrain the courts' recourse to contextual considerations in the event of a dispute).

[104] *See* Avery Weiner Katz, *The Economics of Form and Substance in Contract Interpretation*, 104 Colum. L. Rev. 496 (2004).

also adopt some variant of just-in-time inventory practices. This section explores the uneasy fit between these types of supply relationships and the jurisprudence of the Code. It begins by suggesting that the Code's contextualized adjudicative approach is ill-suited to these transactions for many of the same reasons that it is ill-suited to the simple merchant transactions in industries that have created private legal systems—it stifles work-a-day flexibility, prevents firms from contracting using their preferred mix of legal and extralegal terms, and facilitates strategic behavior. It then identifies additional respects in which the Code is particularly ill-suited to transactions among multi-agent firms paying special attention to its impact on intra-firm agency costs, intra-firm information costs, operational costs, and the costs of entering into contracts for innovation.

A. Flexibility

The Code's provisions on course of dealing and course of performance were designed to encourage work-a-day contractual flexibility; yet they are likely to have precisely the opposite effect. In the course of business operations, there are adjustments that transactors find it worthwhile to make at a particular point in time that they would, for any of a number of reasons, be unwilling to promise to make in a legally enforceable agreement. Sometimes these adjustments implicitly condition on information that is observable but not verifiable (such as whether or not one's contracting partner is trustworthy). Other times they simply reflect on the spot compromises that seem reasonable (or necessary) to the employee making them at the time they are made, but that might not be desirable on a go forward basis under all circumstances. Because the Code creates a risk that these actions, if taken more than twice, will be considered binding courses of performance or dealing (or, at a minimum, be looked to understand what the parties intended their written agreement to mean), transactors are less likely than they would be in a more formalist system to behave flexibly and make value creating on the spot adjustments; they know that if they do so and a dispute arises, they may no longer have a right to insist on compliance with their contract's written terms.

Under the Code, firms can take action to reduce this risk by sending letters stating that any concessions are on a one-time basis only. However, to ensure that letters were sent where needed, firms would have to educate employees at many levels of their organization about the terms of the firm's written agreements (so they would at least be aware when they do something nonconforming). This process would be quite expensive. The firm would also have to put monitoring systems in place to ensure that actions at variance with the contract's written terms were detected and the proper letters sent. In addition, in certain types of contractual relationships (such as highly personal long-standing relationships between smaller firms), the sending of these letters might result in significant relational costs.[105] Recognizing the costs and difficulty of making these decisions on an occurrence-by-occurrence basis helps explain the ubiquity of anti-waiver provisions in these agreements.

[105] *See* Lisa Bernstein, *Social Norms and Default Rules Analysis*, 3 S. Cal. Interdis. L.J. 59 (1993).

In recent years, however, firms have begun to use automated systems to detect certain types of deviations from their contracts' written terms and generate these letters automatically. For example, many big box retailers have programmed their contract administration software to generate these notices whenever a delivery ticket is scanned into the system that indicates a delivery is late or the quantity on the ticket does not match the quantity in the relevant purchase order. The depersonalized nature of these letters and the widespread adoption of this software has made the sending of these notices so routine that they no longer seem to result in relational costs.

B. Preferred mix of legal and extralegal terms

In some contracting contexts (often, though not exclusively, when reputation information is widely available) parties may find it desirable to supplement the terms of their written legally enforceable contracts with extralegal commitments backed only by reputation bonds and other types of nonlegal sanctions. These commitments can add significant value to transactions. For example, in certain types of feed transactions where reputation is important, contracts often specify that a federal weight must be obtained at the shipment's destination. However, actually getting a federal weight is both time consuming and expensive. As a consequence, transactors who trust one another often agree to waive this requirement and use one another's in-house weights so long as each believes the other is acting in good faith. If one or the other becomes suspicious, they can simply demand a return to the contract's written terms, confident that in the event of a dispute the industry's private legal system will not find their course of conduct to have altered the terms of their written agreement. If, however, these transactions were covered by Code, the parties would be much less likely to enter into these value-creating extralegal agreements, since the Code would likely wind up enforcing them in the event of a dispute.

An example of a value-creating extralegal commitment in the context of the modern supply chain can be found in buyers' written commitments to provide their suppliers with regularly updated forecasts of their purchasing needs, while at the same time making it abundantly clear in their contracts, service level agreements, and vendor guides that these forecasts are not to be relied on, are not guaranteed to be accurate, and do not commit the buyer firm to purchase a specified or even any amount of goods.[106] This type of extralegal commitment creates value by enabling the seller to engage in better planning and giving the buyer greater confidence that the seller will produce enough to meet its orders in a timely fashion; yet it is precisely the type of commitment a buyer would be much less likely to make, were it legally enforceable.

[106] *See* Target Contract, at cl. 1; *see also* Liebert eProcurement Vendor Guide 9 (Liebert provides suppliers with data on historical forecasts and usage, as well as current forecasts on a weekly basis, but noting that "it is not a commitment by Liebert to purchase"); OshKosh, Commercial Terms and Conditions: Commercial Purchase Orders cl. 2 (2013) ("From time to time, Buyer may, in its sole discretion, deliver non-binding 52-week forecasts to Supplier. Notwithstanding any such forecast delivered by Buyer, all purchases of Products shall be governed by this Purchase Order and Supplier agrees that any such forecast is intended solely to assist in planning Buyer's production schedules and is not a commitment to purchase any minimum volume of Products from Supplier").

Additional examples of value-creating but legally unenforceable commitments in business relationships are common.[107]

The significance of preventing transactors from structuring their contracting relationship using their preferred mix of legally enforceable and legally unenforceable terms depends on the contracting context. In the context of discrete one-time contracts for the purchase of standard goods in a market the buyer rarely enters, the loss may be small or nonexistent. In contrast, in markets where reputation information is widely available and parties deal with one another or within a segment of a market on a repeat basis over a long period of time, the losses occasioned by Code's adjudicative approach may be significant.

C. Strategic behavior costs

Neoformalist scholars[108] writing in the law and economics tradition have suggested that the Code's contextualized approach to interpretation together with its trade usage provision encourage strategic behavior by enabling a party who is seemingly disadvantaged by the ordinary meaning of a contract's explicit terms to strategically claim that the contract was written in an industry-specific (usage-based) "private language" that favors his position.[109] They argue that replacing the Code's quasi-mandatory contextualist interpretive approach with a textualist default (which they maintain is the clear majoritarian preference), while permitting transactors to explicitly opt into contextualism, will largely eliminate this type of behavior. When textualism is the default, transactors who want a court to look to a private language will have to specify this choice *ex ante*; if they don't they will be barred from raising this type of argument *ex post*. The rule will therefore eliminate purely strategic *ex post* claims that the contract was written in a private language. At the same time, it will enable transactors who genuinely want a court to interpret their contract on the assumption that it was written in a private language to easily select this option simply by including a provision saying something like: "this contract is to be governed by the usages in the widget industry," a provision that under the proposed approach would be summarily enforced.

Although this proposed switch to a textualist default would largely eliminate private language-related strategic behavior when transactors opt for textualism, it will not (as some theorists suggest)[110] do so as effectively when parties opt for contextualism, even

[107] Value creating extralegal promises are not uncommon in commercial relationships. *See* Scott E. Masten & Edward A. Snyder, *United States Versus United Shoe Machinery Corporation: On the Merits*, 36 J.L. & Econ. 33, 62–3 (1993) (discussing the efficient extralegal promises made by the United Shoe Machine Company to its shoe machine lessees); Lisa Bernstein, *Merchant Law in a Merchant Court: Rethinking the Code's Search for Immanent Business Norms*, 144 U. Pa. L. Rev. 1765, 1790–4 (1996) (providing additional examples of value creating extralegal promises in computer software and commodities sales).

[108] *See* Melvin A. Eisenberg, Foundational Principles of Contract Law 13 (forthcoming) (observing that commentators who report the "birth of neo-formalism in contract law usually point to the work of only three scholars: Lisa Bernstein, Alan Schwartz, and Robert Scott").

[109] Schwartz & Scott, *Limits*.

[110] Schwartz and Scott assume that when contextualism is selected, a party disadvantaged by the private-language meaning of a term will only engage in *ex post* interpretation-related strategic behavior in the rare case where a contract's plain meaning (or one of a relatively small number of plain meanings

if they include a clause specifying the private language in which their contract is written. As the case studies of codification revealed, even within highly local areas, and trades narrowly defined, there is much disagreement about the meaning of even basic terms of trade. Consequently, unless the private language selected is codified in a written set of rules (such as the Incoterms) *ex post* a party will almost always be able to plausibly assert the existence of a different private meaning that supports his interpretation, thus reintroducing the strategic behavior problem.[111]

Nevertheless, the adoption of a textualist default is superior to the current contextualist interpretive regime for several reasons. First, it is far less costly for transactors who want contextualized adjudication to include a provision opting for it than it is for transactors who want to opt out of the Code's approach to do so (even to the arguably limited extent that this is possible).[112] Second, requiring transactors to opt in to a private language alerts them to what they are doing and creates an incentive for them to specify the particular private language they are choosing. Although, as noted above, they will still be able to engage in strategic behavior as to private meanings, making this designation may at least partially cabin the range of private meanings they can plausibly assert. This suggests that strategic behavior costs may be lower and, in any event, are unlikely to be higher, than they are under the present rule. Third, reversing the default will eliminate issues surrounding the question of whether a transactor knew or had a reason to know the content of these private languages, since the issue will be resolved by contract. Finally, if neoformalist theorists are correct that businesses prefer a textualist default (which can be defined in many ways other than the caricature of plain meaning or "hard literalism" asserted by most contextualists as the relevant alternative),[113] the interpretive default approach of commercial law will again reflect majoritarian preferences.

The benefits of adopting a more textualist default rule are even greater once the effects of the new rule on motions for summary judgment are taken into account. As the study of usage in the courts discussed above revealed, under the Code's approach, even if a private language does not exist, a party can claim it does, introduce nothing more than a cursory affidavit from one of his employees asserting its existence, and thereby (with a significantly high probability) defeat a motion for summary judgment, a move that greatly reduces the settlement value of a claim[114] as well as the value of any judgment the moving party eventually receives. Under the textualist default, in contrast, transactors opting for textualism will have more ready access to summary judgment, and for those who prefer contextualism summary judgment will be no less available then it is under the current interpretive regime.

it might be viewed to reference) by mere happenstance turn out to favor the position he wants to espouse *ex post*.

[111] Schwartz & Scott, *Limits*, Bernstein, *Trade Usage in the Courts*.

[112] *See* Schwartz & Scott, *Limits*, and Bernstein, *Trade Usage in the Courts* (exploring the many barriers to effectively opting out of the Code's contextualized adjudicative approach).

[113] *See, e.g.*, Eisenberg, Foundational Principles of Contract Law. Cf. Steven J. Burton, Elements of Contracts Interpretation (2009) (presenting the interpretive theory known as objective contextualism).

[114] Bernstein, *Trade Usage in the Courts*.

A final benefit of the proposed change to a textualist interpretive default and the one that is most important to the law's ability to adapt to support complex private commercial contracting, is that when transactors opt for textualism, the return they receive from careful contractual drafting will increase because the terms they write will be enforced as written and will not be eroded or undermined by usage-based interpretation. Although the Code's hierarchy of authority states that express terms trump conflicting usages, in practice courts routinely permit usages to override or erode written provisions. Usages are commonly found to be "consistent" with seemingly contrary express provision unless the usage is found to "totally negate" the express provision,[115] a finding that is very rarely made. As one court observed, "[i]n cases governed by the Uniform Commercial Code, the courts have regarded the established practices and usages within a particular trade or industry as a more reliable indicator of the true intentions of the parties than the sometimes imperfect and often incomplete language of the written contract. The courts have allowed such extrinsic evidence to modify the apparent agreement, as seen in the written terms, so long as it does not totally negate it."[116] And, as another explained "the trend has been for judges, looking beyond written contract terms to reach the 'true understanding' of the parties, to extend themselves to reconcile trade usage and course of dealing with seemingly contradictory express terms. They have permitted course of dealing and usage of trade to add terms, cut down or subtract terms, or lend special meaning to contract language."[117] By removing the interpretive discount on written terms, the neoformalist proposal will increase the return to contract drafting, which will likely lead to clearer contracts, fewer disputes occasioned by misunderstandings, and a decrease in the social costs of disputing.

Contextualists oppose a shift to a more textualist default on the grounds that it will greatly increase the specification costs of entering to a contract because transactors will choose to spell out more aspects of their agreement. However, the widespread use of master agreements, standard purchase orders, and detailed vendor guides (which are routinely incorporated into contracts), together with the availability of model contracts from both the internet and law firms specializing in particular sorts of outsourcing contracts (such as technology outsourcing), suggests that any increase is likely to be small on a per contract basis. The shift in default rule will also decrease the specification costs occasioned by transactors' desire to fortify their contracts against contextualist interpretation, a saving that may not be insignificant. Finally, as discussed further below, once it is recognized that firms need to memorialize both the explicit

[115] *See, e.g., Michael Schiavone & Sons, Inc. v. Securalloy Co.*, 312 F. Supp. 801 (D. Conn. 1970) (where the contract called for the delivery of 500 tons of steel, the court permitted evidence in the form of testimony by the defendant's employee that there was a usage of trade whereby a fixed quantity term in a contract meant an amount up to that quantity, explaining that such a usage did not contradict the term, and that summary judgment was therefore inappropriate); *Heggblade-Marguleas-Tenaco v. Sunshine Biscuit*, 59 Cal. App. 3d 948 (Cal. Ct. App. 1976) (where a contract had a fixed quantity provision that was held not to contradict a usage proffered by the plaintiff seller who drafted the contract that all stated quantities were mere estimates); *Crest Ridge Constr. Group v. Newcourt, Inc.*, 78 F.3d 146 (5th Cir. 1996) (contract term "subject to credit department approval," was held not to contradict a usage giving 45-day credit terms).

[116] *Campbell Farms v. Wald*, 578 N.W.2d 96 (1998).

[117] *American Mach. and Tool Co., Inc. v. Strite-Anderson Mfg. Co.* 353 N.W.2d 592 (Minn. Ct. App. 1984).

and implicit terms of their agreements in writing so that they can be disseminated throughout the firm's organizational hierarchy, it becomes clear that any savings from omitting terms in the contract between the parties is likely to be slight.

Wholly apart from its effects on drafting costs, a switch to a more formalist default rule may produce a variety of other cost savings and transactional benefits for firms, many of which stem from enabling them to use both legal and extralegal commitments and sanctions to structure their transactional relationship. In addition, as discussed further below, the availability of a textualist default will save firms the cost of adopting a variety of agency cost reduction mechanisms that the Code's contextualism makes it necessary for them to implement and will enable them to adapt more effective and less expensive contract governance structures.[118]

More generally, an interpretive approach that encourages transactors to invest in improving their written contracts will do more to support trade in the face of changing conditions and complex interdependent agreements than any system based on the incorporation of gradually evolving usages. As the case studies discussed above revealed, convergent understandings of trade usages are slow to evolve and consensus on the meaning of terms and industry practices is difficult to achieve even through negotiation among industry participants. This process is especially slow and difficult in contexts where the relevant usages apply to transactions across stages in a chain of production and distribution. Given these difficulties, the complexity of modern outsourcing transactions, and the fact that these transactions typically take place between large multi-agent firms (an aspect of these transactions discussed further below) the evolution of usages related to outsourcing transactions is likely be highly problematic, making the Code a poor vehicle for responding to the contract governance challenges these transactions create.

D. Intra-firm agency costs

In thinking about the ability of the Code to support contractual relationships between multi-agent firms, it is important to focus not only on how the Code affects the costs of firm A dealing with firm B, but also the way these considerations affect the intra-firm agency and transactions costs *within* firm A and *within* firm B. These intra-firm costs are not part of the standard analysis of the costs and benefits of different types of contract rules and interpretive approaches—which typically compare the effect of a particular approach on specification costs and litigation costs respectively—and have received only sporadic mention in the legal literature.[119] However, they need to be systematically taken into account in any future efforts at legal reform. As the examples below illustrate, the functional consequences of contextualist adjudication for the management and operation of multi-agent firms may be significant.

[118] *See* Bernstein, *Trade Usage in the Courts.*

[119] *See* Weiner Katz, *The Economics of Form and Substance in Contract Interpretation* (noting that when firms do not have effective internal controls over the actions of their employees, but feel their legal staffs adequately represent their interests, they will prefer relatively formalist types of contract interpretation).

To get a feel for the way the Code creates and/or exacerbates internal firm agency costs, consider its provision on contract formation which states that "a contract for the sale of goods may be made in any manner sufficient to show agreement, including conduct by both parties which recognizes the existence of such a contract."[120] This provision creates a risk that an employee may, through her words, actions, and/or written communications, knowingly or unknowingly bind the firm to contractual obligations. Large firms routinely hold seminars to educate employees about this aspect of the Code in an effort to prevent them from inadvertently binding the firm. In addition, given the especially large financial exposure the Code's formation rules create, firms also attempt to control this risk through explicit contractual provisions.

One common method is for the buyer-firm to post a Master Agreement (or a set of Standard Terms and Conditions) on its supplier portal website along with a prominent statement that these are the only terms on which it will do business.[121] These agreements typically set forth an exhaustive list of the ways the buyer-firm is and is not willing to enter into binding agreements. For example, Dollar General's Master Agreement states that "in no event will an e-mail or other communication, regardless of its content, that is not a signed paper purchase Order or electronic Order issued via Buyer's EDI system, constitute an Order for the purposes of this Agreement... [Neither] Buyer and/or its affiliates have any obligation or liability with respect to such an email or other communication."[122] In addition to limiting its exposure when its employees fail to stay in line with the company's contracting policies, this provision shifts the burden of monitoring compliance with the company's policy to its vendors—because vendors will not be paid for unauthorized orders, they have an incentive to closely monitor the province of the orders they do receive.

Firms also use these master agreements/standard terms to attempt to opt out of the Code's battle-of-the-forms provision,[123] a provision that also gives rise to agency problems within both buyer and seller firms. These agreements typically categorically reject any additional or different terms that might be introduced by a trading partner's standard forms, the firm's own service level agreements and purchase orders, or any oral or side understandings. They state very clearly that the firm will not do business on any terms other than their standard posted terms. Although this approach is likely to be effective when the transactors have both signed a master agreement or only one of them has posted a master agreement or set of terms and conditions on the web, it is not uncommon for both buyers and sellers to both post similar statements, a practice that simply recreates the potential for a battle-of-the-forms when the website of suppliers and buyers conflict.

[120] U.C.C. § 2-204(1) (2010).

[121] In practice, however, large firms dealing with especially important suppliers (or suppliers with a great deal of bargaining power) will enter into specially negotiated transactions with different terms. These are referred to as exempt transactions.

[122] Dollar General, Master Supply Agreement, cl. 4.1.

[123] When these opt-outs are included by buyers they are designed to prevent the acceptance of additional or different terms that might arise when a supplier sends a confirmatory memorandum prior to shipment that the buyer does not object to. Conversely, when used by sellers, they guard against the legal consequences that would otherwise flow from the sellers' employees shipping against a purchase order with additional or conflicting terms.

The Code's course of dealing and course of performance provisions create analytically similar agency problems in the performance phase of an agreement. Together they give a firm's employees the power to modify, waive, and alter the meaning of the firm's written contracts; they can do this through their words, their written exchanges with their counterparty, their actions, and their inactions. Large multi-agent firms are highly unlikely to want their employees to have this power. These firms go to extraordinary lengths to adopt explicit written internal policies that carefully articulate the contours of the explicit contractual authority (if any) delegated to managers/employees at different levels of the corporate hierarchy.[124] Given these (costly) efforts to control the explicit contracting authority of their employees, it seems highly unlikely that these firms would want their employees to be empowered to do indirectly what they are explicitly prohibited from doing directly. Indeed, the difficulty firms face in trying to eliminate the risk of employees affecting the legal meaning of their written contracts, may be one reason for the ubiquity of anti-waiver, anti-modification, and merger/integration clauses in these agreements. However, the interpretive protection offered by these clauses (even in jurisdictions where they are enforceable) is far from complete. Well-drawn clauses may prevent employee's actions from modifying or waiving contractual provisions, but the actions of a firm's agents will remain relevant to interpreting the meaning of the firm's contract if a court finds a contract provision to be ambiguous. In addition, while "entire agreement" clauses sometimes try to make these considerations irrelevant to contract interpretation generally, the enforceability of this aspect of these provisions does not appear to have been tested.

Other Code provisions may introduce agency problems that are even more difficult to eliminate or reduce through intra-firm policies or contractual provisions. For example, the Code's provision on demands for adequate assurance of performance can be triggered by the off-hand remarks of an employee indicating financial problems at the firm or the mention of problems the company is having in a contract with an entirely other firm. Similarly, the time for cure may extend beyond the delivery date if the seller makes a nonconforming tender but had a reasonable belief (perhaps based on comments from the buyer's personnel) that it would be acceptable to the buyer with or without a price adjustment. The applicability of these Code provisions can be triggered by a wide variety of statements by employees at many levels of a firm's organizational structure and is difficult to control through intra-firm monitoring and/or company policies. As a consequence, to guard against the significant legal implications of statements made by its employees, firms might find it necessary to limit employee access to information that it might otherwise be desirable for employees to have. Alternatively, within limits, transactors might be able to contract for a

[124] For example, many large firms produce internal policy manuals that set out who may sign particular types of contracts, the maximum length of commitments and/or the total value of commitments certain employees can make, and many other details about the constrained menu of provisions that managers at different levels may include in the agreements they sign. These internal policy documents also commonly set out the authority or lack thereof of particular employees to approve change orders and alterations of existing agreements. In firms that use primarily master agreements, similar constraints are placed on managers charged with negotiating and drafting service level agreements.

limited and exclusive list of events that may trigger a demand for adequate assurances and/or can try to contract out of the Code's cure provisions.

More generally, recognizing the existence of these intra-firm agency costs suggests that in assessing the costs of contextualism, it is important to take into account the costs, including the inflexibility costs, oversight costs, and information flow costs, of the policies, contract provisions, and other mechanisms firms must adopt if they want, as most business concerns do, to control the existence, performance, and meaning of their contracts.

E. Information costs

Within large multi-agent firms, the people entering into contracts are not, for the most part those who carry them out. In order for a deal to be administered within a large organization, the purchasing managers and their subordinates in the buyer's organization, as well as the selling agents and production managers in the seller's organization, all have to understand the quality, quantity, and delivery specifications (including timing, packaging, and labeling) of the contract. The "key to a successful outcome," is said to be "carrying out a detailed contract handover session from the bid/negotiation team to the post-award management team."[125]

According to the International Association for Contract and Commercial Management, "for a complex outsourcing contract... this might be a half a day of the pre-award and post award teams sitting together in a meeting room, each with a copy of the contract, going through page by page."[126] In addition, the bid/negotiation team is advised to provide a great deal of background on the deal. This is often viewed as "more important than handing over documents," because "the interpretation and history of how we ended up where we did in negotiations is key to understanding the risks and opportunities arising and which need to be managed during contract management."[127] They will also, in the absence of a contract provision to the contrary, have to recount any prior courses of dealing between the parties, something that will be costly and, in the event of a change in personnel, also quite difficult to do with accuracy.

Incident to these handover sessions, and in recognition of the fact that the oral communication of this information about contract terms is subject to considerable error, most firms require the bid/negotiation team to fill out a template form summarizing the key terms of the deal from various financial and operational perspectives.[128] As a

125 *See* I.A.C.C.M., Contract Briefing Template 1 (Version 7 July 2011).

126 I.A.C.C.M., Contract Briefing Template 1.

127 I.A.C.C.M., Contract Briefing Template 1.

128 I.A.C.C.M., Contract Briefing Template 1. The template includes: "Goals of the Customer (summarise the outcomes sought from this deal)... Goals of supplier (summarise the outcomes sought from this deal)... Scope—what is in, anything specific that is out (but could be a source of confusion)... Beneficiaries (ie who is eligible to participate)... Performance measures/KPIs (including any specific obligations re: on-going price reductions, performance improvements)... Consequences of non-performance (in particular areas such as LDs)... Change procedures (and major sources of anticipated change)... Review, reporting communication procedures (internal and external)... Responsibilities of Customer [including contract page number, name of lead person, and date for performance]... Responsibilities of the Supplier... Active Terms [including page number, lead person, and date for performance]... Milestones [same]...Time-bound activities and responsibilities [same]... Risks (noted during the bid and negotiation phase [including 'mitigation/management/allocation assumed when contract signed']...

consequence, even if the principals to the contracting relationship had implicit understandings based on usages of trade or prior courses of dealing, or were simply willing to let the Code's context-dependent default rules fill the gaps in their agreement, they would still need to memorialize many of these understandings in writing as part of the contract hand-off process, thereby greatly reducing any specification cost saving benefits created by the Code's gap fillers and its contextualized interpretive approach.

Moreover, because firms are aware that this type of deal hand-off process will be followed, they will have an increased incentive to include these understandings in their writings. The marginal cost of including them in the contract over and above the cost of memorializing them for its own employees will be small, at least with respect to many types of provisions, such as those related to operational specifications and acceptable deviations from quality/quantity provisions. In addition, as contract coding software (which enables users to pull up all operational specifications, all financial specification, or all production metrics with one mouse click) comes into wider use, the contract provisions dealing with these aspects of the deal can be captured by the software and provided directly to operations, thus creating a cheaper more seamless transfer of information that is both less expensive and less prone to error, than the current contract hand-off process.

Indeed, even with all of the efforts firms make to disseminate contract information through these detailed handover sessions, firms report that among those charged with implementing contracts, there remains a well-documented "lack of consensus over what constitutes the contract," and "the extent to which it includes emails, oral communications, SOWs [scope of work], SLAs [service level agreements] as well as invoices, operational reports, and other communications within and between firms."[129] This confusion, which contract managers work hard to eliminate, is nonetheless entirely understandable given the Code's broad definition of agreement and its lax parol evidence rule.

More generally, the need for the terms of a contract to be disseminated through various levels of a firm's hierarchy suggests that contrary to the implicit assumption of contextualists, the principals to a transaction and the court are not the only audiences for the contract's language. Indeed, taking into account the need to inform agents of the contract's content undermines contextualists' main defense of the methods cost-saving benefits—namely, that transactors will save on specification costs by relying on default rules and usages rather than spelling out their understandings in explicit contract provisions, while any increased litigation costs contextualism may create will only be incurred if a dispute goes to court, something that occurs with a low probability. Once the cost of the bid/negotiation team summarizing and describing to the operations team what a contract that relies on usages and default rules actually requires is taken into account, most if not all of the specification cost savings from the availability of contextualist defaults is likely to disappear. Moreover, given the

Opportunities noted during bid negotiation phase [and designations for follow through]... Useful information discovered concerning customer/supplier organization and personalities, relevant to managing the contract... Governance Requirements [including manager names and committee names]... Other relevant information we already obtained that will help with interpretation of the contract (e.g. Legal Advice)... [and] Subcontract details").

[129] I.A.C.C.M., The State of Sales Contract Management 9–10 (2011).

uncertainty introduced when translating the tacit elements of the transaction into the firm's template term sheet, and the greater likelihood that a dispute will arise due to a misunderstanding of what the contract requires, it is also important recognize that when transactors rely on the availability of the Code's defaults and trade usages, the likelihood of a dispute requiring court adjudication also increases.

F. Operational costs

Many large organizations adopt contracting policies that are not tailored to individual agreements, but rather are optimized over a larger set of the firm's contracting relationships. Large big box retailers for example, typically memorialize their policies in vendor guides which apply to the vast majority of the firm's routine transactions. These guides cover the extent of permitted quality deviations, what constitutes on time delivery, the types of paper work and S.K.U. codes that must be used, and dozens of different dimensions of logistics (which have a significant impact on the profitability of a deal). The policies set forth in these guides are optimized over a large number of the company's contracts; they are not tailored to the purchase of any particular input and do not take into account usages of trade that might exist in particular industries. As a consequence, if a dispute were to arise and go to court, it would be open to the seller to argue that the buyer is a merchant in the type of goods at issue and should be bound to the usages common in the trade; that the buyer's specifications are unreasonable applied as to the transaction at issue; or that the usage is relevant to interpreting the contract's written provisions, even if they are not ambiguous.[130] These concerns are quite real to firms; as the Target Master Vendor Agreement states: "Regardless of industry standards, no variances with respect to quality, quantity, size, capacity, volume, content or other standard measure of Goods are allowed."[131]

More generally, there is a fundamental tension between the Code which looks at the usages related to the particular contract at issue, and the policies of large firms, which are developed to be optimal over a large number of contracts that may involve a variety of markets with vastly different practices. Moreover, given the number of individuals within the corporate hierarchy who would have to have actual knowledge of usages in order to operationalize them, the cost to bigger entities of usages being read into their agreements is potentially large.

G. Innovation costs

Contract theorists, writing about the economics of supply chain relationships, have suggested that many such contracts involve "contracting for innovation,"[132] which

[130] Even if the contract is clear, evidence of these usages will be admissible to supplement or explain the written terms, as under the Code trade usages are not parol evidence.

[131] Target Contract, at cl. 13.

[132] Gilson, Sabel, & Scott, *Contracting for Innovation*. In the modern economy many of even the most straightforward sales transactions have a contracting for innovation component, reflected in the supply chain philosophy of "continuous improvement," in which vendor and supplies work together to achieve gains "in the form of improved product quality, delivery, part pricing and service." NAT'L INSTRUMENTS,

they describe as a situation where the transactors' relationship is not mediated "by fully specified explicit contracts... nor by entirely implicit relational contracts supported only by the norms of reciprocity and the expectation of future dealings."[133] Rather, in these contracting contexts, "the explicit and implicit obligations interact within a formal governance structure that regulates the exchange of highly revealing information but does not necessarily impose legally enforceable obligations to buy or sell anything," and thereby supports "iterative collaboration between firms [in creating or improving products and systems] by interweaving explicit and implicit terms that respond to the uncertainty inherent in the innovation process."[134] The success or failure of these ventures is said to depend critically on the parties' ability to achieve deliberate and delicate "braiding"[135] of legal and extralegal obligations and sanctions.

Given the structure and operation of these collaborative ventures, the Code's adjudicative approach (which as discussed above transforms many legally unenforceable aspects of the transactors' agreement into legally enforceable contract provisions and many of their work-a-day actions into legally enforceable obligations) is likely to both increase the cost and impair the operation of these types of contracting relationships. Among other things, it will decrease the work-a-day flexibility and free flow of information that is essential to the success of such ventures and greatly increase the likelihood that courts will make interpretive errors when disputes arise. As innovation theorists have noted, the Code's course of dealing and course of performance provisions undermine collaborative activities, because "there is a constant risk that a collaborators' experimentation will be interpreted as a modification of the contract,"[136] and errors are likely since "courts [will] have insufficient information from which to glean patterns in the disputants' behavior," given the "[t]he constant experimentation that generative contracts institutionalize."[137] The Code's usage of trade provision is viewed as similarly disruptive to contracting relationships (especially if, as the evidence presented above suggests, the information base available to the court to distinguish extant from nonexistent usages is thin) because the invocation of concepts like "trade usage, which use wider industry norms to interpret the meaning of a contract, will likely lead the court astray since collaborators are often actively trying to forsake industry conventions as they innovate."[138] In addition, and perhaps most importantly, the Code's overall contextualized approach will increase the cost of entering into "contracts for innovation," as parties will need to use both complex agreements (with many clauses whose legal enforceability is doubtful) that are costly to draft and adapt to the particular context, as well as detailed governance structures to create zones of collaborative interaction that can operate free from legal intervention.

NI Supplier Handbook 5 (2013), *available at* <http://www.ni.com/pdf/misc/en/supplier_handbook.pdf>.

133 Gilson, Sabel, & Scott, *Contracting for Innovation*, at 435.
134 Gilson, Sabel, & Scott, *Contracting for Innovation*, at 435.
135 Gilson, Sabel, & Scott, *Contracting for Innovation*, at 492.
136 Jennejohn, *Contract Adjudication in a Collaborative Economy*, at 179.
137 Jennejohn, *Contract Adjudication in a Collaborative Economy*, at 207.
138 Jennejohn, *Contract Adjudication in a Collaborative Economy*, at 179.

In sum, the types of conceptual, institutional and operational considerations discussed here, along with a recognition of the role nonlegal sanctions and extralegal agreements and adjustments can play in even the most complex and institutionalized agreements, suggests that the contextualized jurisprudence of the Code is unlikely to qualify as a majoritarian default rule in a twenty-first-century, highly outsourced economy. The Code's adjudicative approach has the effect of both undermining the value of written contracts and impeding the creation and implementation of institutional structures that are designed to create zones of contracting behavior that operate free from judicial oversight or legal consequences yet nevertheless add tremendous value to some of the simplest and most complex contracting relationships alike.[139]

Industries and firms have devised a sophisticated array of methods for minimizing or avoiding the effect of the Code's default rules and adjudicative approach and increasing the value of the terms of their written contracts. These range from the private legal systems and trading rules created by trade associations in merchant industries, to a variety of mechanisms used in more complex outsourcing transactions that enable transactors to conduct important parts of their contracting relationships largely (though not entirely) outside of the shadow of the legal system. These mechanisms include: supplier qualification processes and vendor scorecard programs that are used to create nonlegal sanctions and harness the forces of repeat dealing to support cooperative contracting relationships; the creation of interior remedies in Service Level Agreements and Scope of Works; easy to exercise termination rights in Master Agreements that provide parties with "self-help" options that reduce the need to rely on legal remedies for breach of contract; and a variety of mechanisms (such as audit rights[140] and the right to demand a root cause analysis[141]) designed to enable buyers to determine (without filing a suit for breach of contracting and engaging in civil discovery) whether problems that arise over the life of the contract reflect failed attempts at cooperation or deliberate acts of defection. Although these contracting practices and structures might survive even if the law were moved in the direction of giving greater primacy to written contracts and respecting transactors' desire for freedom

[139] *See* Lisa Bernstein, *Private Ordering, Social Capital, and Network Governance in Procurement Contracts: A Preliminary Exploration*, forthcoming in the Journal of Legal Analysis (2015).

[140] These audit provisions tend to be quite broad and give the buyer the right to inspect the seller's plant, its books and records, its quality control documentation, and the like, information that, for the most part, firms do not usually have access to unless they file a suit for breach and obtain the right to conduct discovery. Like the right to demand root cause analysis, audit provisions enable the seller to better understand both whether certain types of breaches have occurred (such as not meeting most favored nation pricing provisions), and why, without the need to file a lawsuit, thereby opening the door (though by no means ensuring) that corrective actions can be taken. These types of provisions also help transactors figure out whether or not a bad outcome is due to opportunism or inadvertent error; they thereby make it less likely that cooperative contracting relationships (once established) will break down.

[141] "Root cause analysis" is a semi-structured method of determining the cause of a problem in performance. The information generated by this process can be used to maintain cooperation by helping a firm figure out whether a bad outcome should be classified as an act of deliberate defection, or chalked up to an inadvertent mistake, the actions of a rogue agent, or a problem in the seller's production process that it can commit to change. This process is especially important in transactions between entities who have so many agents involved in the execution of a single contract that an entity's intent to cooperate or defect cannot be discerned merely by looking at outcomes or through one entity's understanding of the other (as is possible in smaller, more personal contracting relationships).

from contract (for the law is limited in its ability to create value for contracting parties), such a change is nevertheless important to the future success of American business. It would not only reduce the agency costs, operational costs, and information costs within firms, but would also eliminate some of the inflexibility costs created by firms' attempts to minimize the negative effect of the Code on their operations. More generally, while the type of change contemplated might not entirely eliminate some of the institutional structures, contractual arrangements, and operational processes that were created to better support trade in the shadow of the Code, it would very likely improve their functioning and enable firms and industries to adopt them at a far lower cost than they can in the shadow of the Code.

Conclusion

This chapter has explored the questionable empirical basis of the Code's adjudicative architecture. It has also suggested that even if the Code worked in practice the way Llewellyn and modern day incorporationists thought it would work in theory, its highly contextualized adjudicative approach, its reliance on unwritten usages, and its insistence that parties' actions under a contract are the best indication of what they intend their writing to mean, would make the Code ill-suited to the needs of important sectors of the modern, highly outsourced, economy, even if it were extensively amended.

These reasons for suggesting that the Code's "machinery" for adapting to change is broken, and that an entirely new approach to the content and theory of sales law is required, are curiously parallel to Llewellyn's reasons for advocating the adoption of an entirely new commercial code rather than proposing extensive amendments to the Uniform Sales Act. As Llewellyn explained, the Sales Act was based on "concepts that took shape on the basis of a face-to-face dealing with present goods," whereas the American economy in the 1920s and 1930s was increasingly dominated by the emergence of a "nationwide indirect marketing structure" in which most contracts were executory and a large portion of trade was mediated by brokers and factors of various sorts. Llewellyn concluded that these structural changes were so significant that the "present trends and present needs" of commerce could not be met through amendments to the Sales Act, but rather required a fundamental reconceptualization of the role of law in commercial life and the adoption of a statute that was responsive to and reflective of those changes.

The ground up reimagining of sales law suggested here would require reformers to recognize that the contracts play many roles in transactions (especially in multi-agent firms) beyond merely regulating the terms of exchange *between* the parties and providing rules in the event of a dispute. They play a significant role in influencing the information flow throughout the firm's organizational hierarchy and provide a framework that enables firms to use the law to create contract governance structures that use interior remedies and nonlegal sanctions much as trade association-run private legal systems do, thereby creating flexible, cooperative contractual relationships that are capable of meeting the needs for precision in quality and timing, as well as the need to respond to changes and make corrections mid-course, that are the hallmarks of successful manufacturing outsourcing transactions.

Most fundamentally, however, reformers would have to accept that the institutional structures created by market transactors are far more likely to respond efficiently to changes in business needs than are unwritten customs and judicial conceptions of commerce. This is especially true if the institutions are free to adopt their own rules and courts give primacy to the terms of written agreements, turning to other considerations only in the case of a true contractual gap, narrowly defined. Just as the medieval law merchant of bills and notes—the only law merchant that ever really existed—evolved from the use and adaption of standard-form contracts over time, aided by the rise of institutions like notaries and registrars,[142] so too American commercial law can best and most quickly adapt to the changes it must confront now and in the future, by recognizing the central importance of enforcing the explicit written terms of private agreements and encouraging the emergence and endurance of private institutions that support trade.

[142] *See* Kadens, *The Myth of the Customary Law Merchant.*

14

Good Faith as Contract's Core Value

*Daniel Markovits**

The common law of contract has long recognized a duty of good faith in performance.[1] This chapter argues that this duty is contract's core value—that good faith *constitutes* the distinct form of legal obligation that contracts establish. An initial section introduces the duty of good faith in performance through a series of doctrinal examples. Subsequent sections examine the metes and bounds of good faith and elaborate a theory of this duty. The theory explains that the duty of good faith in performance neither adds to the obligations that contracts impose nor recasts the substantive terms of actual contracts to fit any ideal. Instead, good faith is an attitude that contracting parties might take to the agreements that they have in actual fact made. When contracting parties approach their agreements in good faith, they at once respect freedom of contract and establish their contractual relations as sites of intrinsically valuable reciprocal recognition. Good faith thus constitutes contracts as what I have elsewhere called *collaborations*.[2]

I. Good Faith in Contract Doctrine

In the United States, the Uniform Commercial Code imposes a mandatory duty of good faith in performance on "every contract" within its scope.[3] The *Restatement (Second) of Contracts* similarly says that "[e]very contract imposes upon each party a duty of good faith and fair dealing in its performance and its enforcement."[4] Moreover, the two authorities elaborate good faith in similar terms. The U.C.C. thus adds that "good faith" means "honesty in fact and the observance of reasonable commercial standards of fair dealing."[5] The comments to the Restatement explain that good faith "excludes a variety of types of conduct characterized as involving 'bad faith' because they violate community standards of decency, fairness or reasonableness."[6]

* This chapter derives from Chapter 19 of my Contract Law and Legal Methods (2012). I would like to thank Gregory Klass, George Letsas, and Prince Saprai for inviting me to participate in this volume and in the conference devoted to the papers collected in it. In addition, the chapter benefited substantially from the engagement of many other conference participants.

[1] A seminal authority is Lord Mansfield's opinion in *Boone v. Eyre*, (1777) 126 Eng. Rep. 160 (K.B.); 1 H. Bl. 273. An early case imposing this duty in an American Jurisdiction is *Kirke La Shelle Co. v. Paul Armstrong Co.*, 188 N.E. 163, 167 (N.Y. 1933).

[2] Daniel Markovits, *Contract and Collaboration*, 113 Yale L.J. 1417 (2004).

[3] Uniform Commercial Code § 1-304 (2003) [hereinafter U.C.C.]

[4] Restatement (Second) of Contracts § 205 cmt. [a] (1981) [hereinafter Restatement].

[5] U.C.C. §§ 1-201, 2-103.

[6] Restatement § 205 cmt. [a].

While the Restatement sensibly takes the position that a "complete catalogue of types of bad faith is impossible," it nevertheless provides representative examples. These include: "evasion of the spirit of the bargain, lack of diligence and slacking off, willful rendering of imperfect performance, abuse of a power to specify terms, and interference with or failure to cooperate in the other party's performance."[7] The comments add that good faith

> is violated by dishonest conduct [in enforcing contract rights] such as conjuring up a pretended dispute, asserting an interpretation contrary to one's own understanding, or falsification of facts. [Good faith is also violated by] dealing which is candid but unfair, such as taking advantage of the necessitous circumstances of the other party to extort a modification of a contract for the sale of goods without a legitimate commercial reason. [Good faith is also violated by] harassing demands for assurances of performance, rejection of performance for unstated reasons, willful failure to mitigate damages, and abuse of a power to determine compliance or to terminate the contract.[8]

Good faith forbids parties from hiding behind indefinite contract terms, either by construing them in an excessively self-serving light or by claiming that the indefiniteness renders the contracts containing them void, *tout court*. Instead, where a contract leaves the particulars of performance to be specified by one of the parties, that party is constrained to make the specification in good faith,[9] which, as the comments to the U.C.C. say, entails that "the range of permissible variation is limited by what is commercially reasonable."[10] In the context of sales contracts that measure quantity by the output of the seller or the requirements of the buyer, good faith requires that the quantity a party orders or delivers not be unreasonably disproportionate to the legitimate expectations of the counterparty.[11] Contracts for exclusive dealings in some class of goods similarly require parties to use their best or at least reasonable efforts to supply or promote the goods in question.[12]

A comparable regime governs contracts in which terms essential to operating the contracts as circumstances have developed are not just left indefinite but are not included at all.[13] Where the parties have failed to make adequate arrangements for some contingency *ex ante*, they must employ good faith in making arrangements *ex post*. For example, termination is governed by good faith,[14] at least where the contract does not establish any specific regime. A party seeking to terminate may not do so before the nonterminating party has had "reasonable notification,"[15] which is to say a "reasonable time to seek a substitute arrangement."[16]

[7] Restatement § 205 cmt. [d]. [8] Restatement § 205 cmt. [e]. [9] U.C.C. § 2-311(1).
[10] U.C.C. § 2-311 cmt. 1. [11] U.C.C. § 2-306(1).
[12] *See* U.C.C. § 2-306(2); *Wood v. Lucy, Lady Duff-Gordon*, 118 N.E. 214 (N.Y. 1917).
[13] A similar principle may be found in English law, although not necessarily under the header "good faith." An example is the rule that "[w]here in a written contract it appears that both parties have agreed that something shall be done, which cannot effectually be done unless both concur in doing it, the construction of the contract is that each agrees to do all that is necessary to be done on his part for the carrying out of that thing, though there may be no express words to that effect." *Mackay v. Dick*, (1881) 6 App. Cas. 251 (H.L.) (Blackburn, J.).
[14] *See* U.C.C. § 2-309 cmt. 8. [15] U.C.C. § 2-309 cmt. 5. [16] U.C.C. § 2-309 cmt. 8.

The warranties concerning title that a seller provides her buyer are also governed by good faith. In particular, where a contract does not specify otherwise, a seller warrants that her title is good and its transfer is rightful, and that the buyer will not be unreasonably exposed to litigation based on third parties' colorable claims or interests in the goods.[17] Similarly, good faith requires a seller to disclose known material but hidden defects in goods sold.[18] The disclosure may be waived by a disclaimer that asserts that there may be hidden defects, but this of course puts the buyer on notice that goods may not be as they appear. And although contracting parties generally can, "if they consciously desire, make their own bargain as they wish,"[19] good faith precludes a party from using one clause to undo a promise made in another, at least in circumstances in which honoring the undoing cannot be understood except as implementing the manipulative term of a bait and switch. This principle applies with especial force to preclude sellers' efforts to disclaim warranties that their selling methods are designed to convey the impression of having given. The comments to one of the U.C.C. sections on warranties thus observe that "a contract is normally a contract for a sale of something describable and described. A clause generally disclaiming 'all warranties, express or implied' cannot reduce the seller's obligation for the description and therefore cannot be given literal effect."[20] Rather, "in determining what [the parties] have agreed upon good faith is a factor and consideration should be given to the fact that the probability is small that a real price is intended to be exchanged for a pseudo-obligation."[21]

In all these ways, the duty of good faith in performance regulates advantage taking within the contract relation. Unsurprisingly, therefore, good faith becomes particularly important where structural circumstances make it impracticable or even impossible for the parties to regulate such advantage taking directly and expressly, because prior agreements cannot effectively reach them.

Thus, although contracting parties generally remain free to renegotiate or rescind their contracts, good faith precludes one party from employing this freedom strategically, to exploit vulnerabilities of the other that are themselves created by (indeed creatures of) the contracts to be renegotiated.

For example, it is bad faith for an employer to discharge a sales employee who is paid on commission after the employee has obtained an extraordinarily large order but before completion of all the formalities required to make the commission come due.[22] Similarly, it would be bad faith for an employer to fire an employee just before the employee meets a performance quota that triggers a substantial bonus. In each case, the employee has expended effort that the employment contract contemplated and indeed was designed to induce and, by rendering this effort a sunk cost, eliminated her power to bargain for a share of the return to the effort. In refusing to pay the commission or the bonus, the employer has deprived the employee of the share of the return to her effort that the contract had allocated to her *ex ante* and exploited the employee's weakened bargaining position *ex post*. This is bad faith.[23]

[17] U.C.C. § 2-312(1) & cmt. 1. [18] U.C.C. § 2-314 cmt. 4. [19] U.C.C. § 2-313 cmt. 6.
[20] U.C.C. § 2-313 cmt. 6. [21] U.C.C. § 2-313 cmt. 6.
[22] *See Fortune v. National Cash Register*, 364 N.E.2d 1251 (Mass. 1971).
[23] Other cases display a similar, and similarly clear, pattern, in different fact settings. Thus, it is bad faith for a buyer who has contracted to purchase a specific asset from a middleman subsequently

Insurance contracts present similar patterns. Typically, an insurer assumes duties both to pay damage awards or settlements secured against the insured by injured third persons in connection with covered events, up to some limit, and to defend the insured against claims for such damages. This makes it bad faith for the insured to exploit the insurer's position by insisting on accepting unreasonably large settlement offers, and refusing to cooperate in any further defense, on the ground that this costs her nothing and saves her the burden of the lawsuit. And, much more practically important, it is bad faith for the insurer to reject reasonable settlement offers near the policy limit, on the ground that it bears none of the litigation risk associated with rejecting the offers.[24] In each case, one party exploits a strategic vulnerability of the other that arises inside the insurance contract (and indeed is caused by the contract) to secure its private advantage. Once again, this is bad faith.

Finally, good faith applies to create effectively mandatory duties in circumstances in which the parties' contractual relations have broken down in ways such that no prior agreement could reliably govern conduct. The most common such circumstances involve a party's response to his counterparty's breach, and thus in particular concern the party's efforts to recover damages. The parties cannot contract *ex ante* for the case in which a promisor denies her contractual obligations entirely, because this denial would cover any agreement that they had made for such a case. The promisor's denial of the contract does not, however, disentangle the parties from each other's affairs. The disappointed promisee will continue to insist on her contractual rights and to take steps to vindicate these rights. Insofar as the steps that she takes might impose costs on her promisor, the law must regulate her conduct (as the parties' agreement cannot). A mandatory duty of good faith figures prominently in this regulation.

For example, although a seller whose buyer has breached may, in appropriate circumstances, avoid the burden and expense of proving up market damages and instead resell the goods and recover damages based on the contract-resale price difference,[25] the resale must be made in good faith.[26] Relatedly, although sellers whose buyers breach may recover consequential damages, their recovery is limited according to their duty to make a good faith effort to minimize (including by resale) the consequential damages suffered as a result of the breach.[27] Analogous duties of good faith apply to buyers with respect to cover when their sellers breach[28] and to buyer's duties to mitigate (including by purchasing cover) their consequential damages from breach.[29]

These examples may be multiplied. And they all reaffirm the general lesson drawn earlier. The duty of good faith polices advantage taking within the contract relation. It seeks to prevent the frame of the contract relation—the fact that the parties to this relation rely on

to buy this asset directly from the middleman's supplier in order to save having to pay his profit. To do so would be to exploit the vulnerability to which the contract has exposed the middleman—the revelation of the asset to the buyer—in order to deprive the middleman of the very gain that the contract was designed to secure him. *See, e.g., Patterson v. Meyerhofer*, 97 N.E. 472 (N.Y. 1912). Similarly, it is bad faith for a financing-dependent buyer to fail to make adequate efforts to seek financing. *See, e.g., Fry v. George Elkins Co.*, 327 P.2d 905 (Cal. App. 2d 1958); *Goldberg v. Charlie's Chevrolet, Inc.*, 672 S.W.2d 177 (Mont. Ct. App. 1984).

[24] *See, e.g., Comunale v. Traders & General Ins. Co.*, 328 P.2d 198 (Cal. 1958) (en banc).

[25] U.C.C. § 2-706. [26] U.C.C. § 2-706(1). [27] *See* U.C.C. § 2-708 & cmt. 6 thereto.

[28] *See* U.C.C. § 2-712(1) & cmt. 4. [29] *See* U.C.C. § 2-715 & cmt. 2.

each others' expressed intentions—from becoming itself an opportunity for manipulation or exploitation. Good faith steps in to *require* contracting parties to respect each other's contractual intentions even where they, preferring manipulation, are disinclined to do so.

II. The Metes and Bounds of Good Faith

The examples all share the general sentiment that it is bad faith for one party to use the fact of the contract to exploit the other going forward. Thus it is said that good faith precludes a party from using its inevitable room to maneuver within the contract "to recapture opportunities forgone upon contracting."[30] Bad faith in performance, that is, "consists of an exercise of discretion in performance to recapture opportunities forgone at formation."[31] Most importantly, a party cannot use the very fact that after negotiations had concluded in an agreement, his counterparty took steps (pursuant to that agreement) that rendered her more vulnerable than she was in the negotiations, now to renegotiate aspects of the agreement on more favorable terms. In the words of a prominent early American opinion, "In every contract there is an implied covenant that neither party shall do anything which will have the effect of destroying or injuring the right of the other party to receive the fruits of the contract, which means that in every contract there exists an implied covenant of good faith and fair dealing."[32]

This formulation provides an important warning against an attractive error. It is tempting to think that the duty of good faith in performance *adds* to the content of contractual obligation—to this obligation's metes and bounds—concretely and in the context of particular contracts. Courts and commentators both occasionally succumb to temptation on this point. They treat good faith as what Allan Farnsworth and then-Judge Scalia, reciprocally quoting each other, have called "implying terms in the agreement."[33] Some even go so far as understanding the duty of good faith in performance to import one or another conception of what Todd Rakoff has called "exchange justice" into contract law.[34] On this view, now expressed in Daniel Friedmann's words, good faith imposes "restraints on self-interest in deference to a much heavier interest of another party."[35] Jack Beatson has offered a similar account of certain limits on advantage taking within contracts that have made their way into English law.[36] Even legislatures have gotten into this business, as in the

[30] Steven J. Burton, *Breach of Contract and the Common Law Duty to Perform in Good Faith*, 94 HARV. L. REV. 369, 373 (1980).

[31] Burton, *Breach of Contract*, at 387.

[32] *Kirke La Shelle Co. v. Paul Armstrong Co.*, 188 N.E. 163, 167 (N.Y. 1933). The case involved a silent-film era agreement to share "motion picture" rights to a play and the question whether rights to make a "talkie" based on the play were within the scope of the agreement. The court held that they were not. It has seemed to many that this is a mistake on the facts. *See L. C. Page & Co. v. Fox Film Corp.*, 83 F.2d 196, 199 (2d Cir. 1936) (words "motion picture" in pre-"talkie" contract held to include "talkies"); *see also Bartsch v. Metro-Goldwyn-Mayer, Inc.*, 391 F.2d 150 (2d Cir. 1968), *cert. denied*, 393 U.S. 826 (1968).

[33] *Tymshare Inv. v. Covell*, 727 F.2d 1145, 1152 (D.C. Cir. 1984); E. Allan Farnsworth, *Good Faith in Contract Performance, in* GOOD FAITH AND FAULT IN CONTRACT LAW 153, 161 (Jack Beatson & Daniel Friedmann eds., 1995).

[34] Todd Rakoff, *The Implied Terms of Contracts: Of "Default Rules" and "Situation-Sense," in* GOOD FAITH AND FAULT IN CONTRACT LAW 191, 195 (Jack Beatson & Daniel Friedmann eds., 1995).

[35] Daniel Friedmann, *Good Faith and Remedies for Breach of Contract, in* GOOD FAITH AND FAULT IN CONTRACT LAW 399, 400 (Jack Beatson & Daniel Friedmann eds., 1995).

[36] Jack Beatson, *Public Law Influences in Contract Law, in* GOOD FAITH AND FAULT IN CONTRACT LAW 263, 288 (Jack Beatson & Daniel Friedmann eds., 1995).

English Unfair Contract Terms Act, which (in Hugh Beale's words) has the "substantive content" that some clauses "cause such an imbalance that they should always be treated as being contrary to good faith and therefore unfair."[37] This approach adopts a substantive regime very similar to that which jurisdictions in the United States have imposed through substantive unconscionability; but it imposes this regime under the heading "good faith."

Such approaches possess a natural appeal. To understand good faith as inserting an additional, mandatory obligation into every contract would be to be able to use the duty to decide (close) cases. Being practical, lawyers and judges naturally seek guidance and assistance in resolving concrete disputes. Good faith understood as a distinctive additional contract term promises to provide both.

This promise is unlikely to be fulfilled, however.

To be sure, it is possible to fix the inner and outer bounds of good faith. On the one hand, it is commonly and rightly observed that "conduct that might not rise to the level of fraud may nonetheless violate the duty of good faith in dealing with one's contractual partners."[38] Good faith must require more of the parties than just that they abjure fraud, because good faith refers to rights established by a completed bargain rather than only to rights against being misused in bargaining.

On the other hand, it is equally familiar that good faith requires less than fiduciary loyalty and devotion.[39] A fiduciary, as it is sometimes said, is "required to treat his principal as if the principal were he."[40] In fact, a fiduciary must treat his principal more carefully still: there is any number of risks that a person might (even reasonably) take on his own account that he may not, acting as fiduciary, take on his principal's. Good faith, by contrast, does not require contracting parties to display substantive other-regard or altruism, preferring their partners' interests over their own, or even weighting the two interests equally, within their contracts. Good faith, in the words of one prominent opinion, "does not mean that a party vested with a clear right is obligated to exercise that right to its own detriment for the purpose of benefiting another party to the contract."[41] Another prominent American court draws the contrast between good faith and fiduciary loyalty more directly still. "'[G]ood faith,'" the court observes, "does not envision loyalty to the contractual counterparty, but rather faithfulness to the scope, purpose, and terms of the parties' contract."[42] English law takes a similar approach. As Jack Beatson has pointed out, "[o]ne of the hallmarks of English common law is that it does not have a doctrine of abuse of rights: if one has a right to do an act then, one can, in general, do it for whatever reason one wishes."[43] This has the consequence that "[e]xcept where the contracting parties are also in a fiduciary relationship, self-interest is

[37] Hugh Beale, *Legislative Control of Fairness: The Directive on Unfair Terms in Consumer Contracts, in* Good Faith and Fault in Contract Law 231, 245 (Jack Beatson & Daniel Friedmann eds., 1995). Beale points out that the statute "does not require that the significant imbalance be caused by the absence of good faith" (n. 91).

[38] *Mkt. St. Assocs. Ltd. P'ship v. Frey*, 941 F.2d 588, 594–5 (7th Cir. 1991).

[39] *But see Parev Prods. Co. v. I. Rokeach & Sons, Inc.*, 124 F.2d 147 (2d Cir. 1941), which comes close to taking a fiduciary duty view, seeking "the really equitable solution" as opposed to "a limited rule of good faith" (at 150).

[40] *Mkt. St. Assocs.*, 941 F.2d at 593.

[41] *Rio Algom Corp. v. Jimco Ltd.*, 618 P.2d 497, 505 (Utah 1980).

[42] *ASB Allegiance Real Estate Fund v. Scion Breckenridge Managing Member*, L.L.C., 50 A.3d 434, 440–41(Del. Ch. 2012) *aff'd in part, rev'd in part on other grounds*, 68 A.3d 665 (Del. 2013). I owe this reference to Andrew Gold.

[43] Beatson, *Public Law Influences in Contract Law*, at 266–7.

permissible, and indeed is the norm in the exercise of contractual rights."[44] Mere self-interest therefore cannot be bad faith.

Judge Richard Posner puts this point more colorfully, observing in *Market Street Associates Limited Partnership v. Frey*, that "[t]he contractual duty of good faith is thus not some newfangled bit of welfare-state paternalism or the sediment of an altruistic strain in contract law."[45] Similarly, "even after you have signed a contract, you are not obliged to become an altruist toward the other party."[46] Nor does good faith require contracting parties to adopt even an attitude of substantive impartiality between their contractual interests and the interests of their contracting partners. The duty of good faith in performance applies, after all, to every contract, including to contracts among sophisticated parties who can take good care of their own interests. The law does not seek, "in the name of good faith, to make every contract signatory his brother's keeper."[47] Good faith is not a principle of substantive fairness even just in the face of new contingencies that arise within the contract relation. Good faith thus leaves the parties free to be self-interested within their contracts—as self-interested as they were without them, subject only to honoring the terms of their agreements.

The inner and outer bounds of good faith are thus easy to discern. But it is not possible to say in general precisely where good faith falls in between these inner and outer bounds, at least not in a way that mechanically decides cases. In any concrete case, party conduct will slide seamlessly from clear bad faith, which undermines the contract, to clear good faith, which embraces the contract's purposes. The thought that good faith protects the reasonable contractual expectations of the parties cannot insert a seam.[48] The root reason why the idea that good faith in performance "protects the reasonable contractual expectations of the parties against *ex post* advantage taking" cannot fix the boundaries of good faith in a fashion that can decide close cases is that good faith is required precisely because the contractual intentions of the parties, and hence also their reasonable expectations, are not complete or clear. An account that understands good faith as a *rule of decision*, thus commits a circle: it supposes

44 Beatson, *Public Law Influences in Contract Law*, at 267.

45 *Mkt. St. Assocs. Ltd. P'ship v. Frey*, 941 F.2d 588, 595 (7th Cir. 1991).

46 *Mkt. St. Assocs. Ltd. P'ship v. Frey*, at 594.

47 *Mkt. St. Assocs. Ltd. P'ship v. Frey*, at 593.

48 A classic example of the problem appears in *E. Airlines, Inc. v. Gulf Oil Co.*, 415 F. Supp. 429 (S.D. Fla. 1975).

Eastern Airlines had contracted with Gulf Oil Corporation for Gulf to supply Eastern's requirements of jet fuel over a several-year period. The contract fixed the purchase price by reference to a price indicator called "West Texas Sour" reported in a trade publication called Platts Oilgram Service-Crude Oil Supplement. In the middle of the contract period, the 1973 O.P.E.C. oil embargo surprised world oil and fuel markets, causing prices to rise unexpectedly. However, and layering a second surprise on top of this first, the West Texas Sour price indicator did not reflect the hike in prices. (This was due to intricacies involving price controls implemented following the crisis.) The contract price therefore came to depart dramatically from the market price, and litigation ensued.

This raised the question how much fuel Eastern might demand consistent with good faith. In particular, Eastern's airplanes had taken on more fuel at certain airports than required to reach their next destinations, in order to refuel less frequently and to avoid refueling at certain other airports entirely. This practice, known as fuel-freighting, had allowed Eastern to avoid the inefficiencies associated with frequent refueling and with refueling at awkward locations. On the other hand, by increasing the flying weight of its airplanes, fuel-freighting had also increased Eastern's total fuel consumption. By lowering Eastern's fuel prices (through the anomalous West Texas Sour indicator), the contract with Gulf had shifted the balance of these costs in a fashion that increased the amount of fuel-freighting that was

what it purports to determine, that is, how much the terms of the contract allow each side to exploit subsequent developments to its unilateral advantage.

Good faith thus provides little help in drawing a line between permissible and impermissible conduct in between the outer and inner bounds (fraud on the one hand, and fiduciary loyalty on the other) just set out. Nor could it be expected to. Indeed, the additional duty conception of good faith does not simply initiate a fruitless quest but furthermore rests on a fundamental mistake. Good faith simply does not determine the *content* of contract obligation, and certainly not at the margins of performance (by adding an incremental duty or right to what the contract would have required in its absence). The Official Comment to U.C.C. §1-304 makes this plain:

> This section does not support an independent cause of action for failure to perform or enforce in good faith. Rather, this section means that a failure to perform or enforce, in good faith, a specific duty or obligation under the contract, constitutes a breach of that contract or makes unavailable, under the particular circumstances, a remedial right or power. This distinction makes it clear that the doctrine of good faith merely directs a court towards interpreting contracts within the commercial context in which they are created, performed, and enforced, and does not create a separate duty of fairness and reasonableness which can be independently breached.[49]

The U.C.C.'s formulation invites theoretical reflection. The task of legal theory is not simply to help decide (close) cases. Legal theory also seeks to illuminate the character of legal relations. It seeks, speaking a little loosely, to reveal the meaning of the law. An account of good faith might therefore have great theoretical value even if it provides only

optimal for Eastern. Gulf claimed that Eastern's fuel-freighting violated its obligation to set its requirements reasonably and in good faith.

As in general, the inner and outer bounds of good faith might be confidently identified in this case also. Thus it would have been clear bad faith, for example, for Eastern to use the contract to support fuel-arbitrage, buying at below market prices from Gulf and selling to its competitors at market prices. The contract, after all, unambiguously concerned Eastern's jet-fuel requirements as an *airline*, that is, for use in its airplanes, and not as a jet-fuel *dealer*. At the other extreme, it would have been clear good faith for Eastern to fuel and fly in precisely the patterns that it would have adopted, pursuant to the contract, had the contract and market prices not diverged. Eastern had no affirmative duty, under the contract, to adjust its fuels requirements downward to serve Gulf Oil's interests.

But these extremes mark out an immense middle ground, and assessing the extremes leaves it unclear where in this middle ground the line between good and bad faith lies.

Would it have been bad faith for Eastern to increase its requirements in connection with acquiring a competitor, where the acquisition was motivated exclusively by Eastern's access to cheaper fuel? Presumably so, since such an acquisition (with its exclusive motivation) looks like fuel arbitrage by other means. But if this is so, then surely the same argument applies to render it bad faith for Eastern to add airplanes or even just flights to its operations, at least where the growth is driven by cheap fuel. (The airplanes and routes, after all, will be won—and sometimes even literally bought—from Eastern's competitors; and it cannot matter to Eastern's good faith whether its expansion occurs by buying the competitor's stock or by acquiring its business assets.) And now it is only a small, and seemingly inexorable, step to calling it bad faith for Eastern to increase its fuel requirements in any way (or indeed to fail to decrease them in any way) on account of its advantageous price. This conclusion, however, cannot be right, as one of the points of a requirements contract—one of the benefits that the contract is intended to confer on a buyer and hence something that it must be good faith for her to insist on—is surely to allow a buyer to improve its business position (and hence among other things to grow) on account of having a reliable supply of inputs. The examples slide seamlessly from clear bad faith, at odds with the contract's purposes, to clear good faith, which embraces these purposes.

[49] U.C.C. § 1-304 cmt. [1].

limited assistance in deciding cases. An understanding of good faith thus does not so much help to decide cases as to understand what has been decided.

Good faith thus characterizes contract obligation's *form* and identifies an *attitude* towards contractual obligations: good faith supports the parties' contractual settlement, working to "effectuate the intentions of the parties, or to protect their reasonable expectations."[50] It is thus, fundamentally, an attitude of respect for the contract relation, and the measure of good faith is the contract itself. Good faith thereby establishes the character of the contract relation. It involves a distinctively contractual form of recognition and respect and fixes the character of contractual collaboration. A nonconclusory account of good faith explains, directly and without reference to other theory-laden terms, how contracting parties must balance self- and other-regard as they interpret, fill out, and implement their contractual arrangements.

III. Good Faith, Freedom of Contract, and Contractual Solidarity

Good faith requires contracting parties to vindicate reasonable contractual expectations but cannot be called on to fix the content of the expectations in whose terms it is defined. The measure of each party's good faith is the agreed purpose memorialized in the contract, which is to say the legitimate contractual expectation of the other. Good faith so understood is not a principle of substantive fairness in the face of new contingencies. The parties thus remain free to be self-interested within the contract—as self-interested as they were without it, subject only to the demand that they honor the terms of their agreement. A party may not use unanticipated contingencies to deprive his counterparty of a benefit that the contract allocated to her. But the parties equally need not sacrifice anything in the face of new contingencies that the contract does not require, nor need they assist the other parties in gaining from contingencies.

This feature of good faith—that it does not establish affirmative duties of other-regard so much as articulate respect among parties who remain at arm's length—will turn out to be essential to good faith's character, and indeed to the character of the contract relation generally.

The arms-length nature of good faith is itself rendered concrete in doctrine, for example, in the expectation remedy and the associated practice of "efficient breach."[51] The expectation remedy establishes a default that promisors insure their promisees against breach by guaranteeing the promisees' value of performance—through it, the law vindicates promisees' contractual expectations. At the same time, the remedy allows a promisor who confronts an opportunity to increase overall surplus by diverting the promised performance to a higher-valuing third party self-interestedly to appropriate the gains from dealing with the third party for herself.

[50] Steven J. Burton, *Breach of Contract and the Common Law Duty to Perform in Good Faith*, 94 HARV. L. REV. 369, 371 (1980). For cases, *see, e.g., Sessions, Inc. v. Morton*, 491 F.2d 854, 857 (9th Cir. 1974); *Ryder Truck Rental, Inc. v. Cent. Packing Co.*, 341 F.2d 321, 323–4 (10th Cir. 1965); *Perkins v. Standard Oil Co.*, 383 P.2d 107, 111–12 (Or. 1963) (en banc).

[51] The account of the expectation remedy that follows receives a more elaborate development in Daniel Markovits & Alan Schwartz, *The Myth of Efficient Breach: New Defenses of the Expectation Interest*, 97

As long as she transfers to the promisee an amount equal to the expectation remedy, a promisor who commits such an "efficient breach" surely displays no bad faith. The transfer vindicates the promisee's reasonable contractual expectations. After all, the parties, bargaining in the shadow of the remedy, will have reduced the contract price (and increased the promisee's contractual expectations) in light of the promisor's right to retain the gains from the "efficient breach."[52] The parties' contractual intentions will have contemplated that the promisor retains such gains *ex post*, and she will have paid for them *ex ante*. Her payment will have been memorialized in a lower price term, which is to say that the promisor's entitlement to the gains from efficient breach is made express in the contract, or at least implied in fact rather than in law. (This approach to the expectation remedy thus sounds in the parties' actual rather than ideal agreement, a point that will become important in a moment.) Indeed, given this arrangement, it would be bad faith for a promisee to insist on specific performance, as this would give the promisee a benefit that he did not pay for and deprive the promisor of one of the benefits that the contract expressly gave her.[53] The expectation remedy thus does not eliminate contractual sharing (including of the surplus generated by "efficient breach") but instead cabins contractual surplus sharing according to the parties' agreement, *ex ante*.[54]

In this way, the expectation remedy vividly embodies the attitude towards contractual obligation associated with good faith and brings the structure of the contract relation into line with this attitude. Good faith thus establishes a contrast to what the contract relation would be like were it governed by a regime of reciprocal fiduciary obligation between promisor and promisee. The fiduciary regime would require each party to display affirmative other-regard within the contract and to adjust its conduct not only to vindicate whatever expectations were fixed by the parties *ex ante* but also

Va. L. Rev. 1939 (2011); Daniel Markovits & Alan Schwartz, *The Expectation Remedy and the Promissory Basis of Contract*, 45 Suffolk U. L. Rev. 799 (2012) (symposium in honor of the 30th anniversary of the publication of *Contract as Promise*); and Daniel Markovits & Alan Schwartz, *The Expectation Remedy Revisited*, 98 Va. L. Rev. 1093 (2012).

52 The parties will generally prefer this, as the overall gains from trade (which the parties may divide however they can agree) will be greater under the expectation regime than under a property right regime.

53 Moralists who criticize the expectation remedy and "efficient breach" for, in effect, encouraging promisor bad faith miss this point. Examples include: Richard R. W. Brooks, *The Efficient Performance Hypothesis*, 116 Yale L.J. 568 (2006); Melvin Eisenberg, *Actual and Virtual Specific Performance, the Theory of Efficient Breach, and the Indifference Principle in Contract Law*, 93 Calif. L. Rev. 975 (2005); Melvin Eisenberg, *The Disgorgement Interest in Contract Law*, 105 Mich. L. Rev. 559 (2006); Daniel Friedmann, *The Efficient Breach Fallacy*, 18 J. Legal Stud. 1 (1989); Seana Shiffrin, *Could Breach of Contract Be Immoral?*, 107 Mich. L. Rev. 1551 (2009); Seana Shiffrin, *The Divergence of Contract and Promise*, 120 Harv. L. Rev. 708 (2007).

54 Specific performance is not different in this respect. Rather, it simply shifts the control over the contractual trade from the promisor to the promisee, whom it empowers to be self-interested within the contract in just the manner in which the expectation remedy empowers the self-interest of the promisor.

At least in the general run of cases, such a reallocation would reduce overall contractual surplus, for reasons having to do with transactions costs. The traditional specific performance remedy draws the promisee into the promisor's perform-or-breach decision, by giving the promisee a right to demand performance. But it does not exclude the promisor from that decision, as she retains her right simply to perform. This is an odd way of speaking, but it matters. Where a promisee entitled to specific performance demands too great a share of the gains from an efficient breach, a promisor will threaten to deprive the promisee of the gains entirely, simply by performing. The strategic setting associated with traditional specific performance thus requires a transactions costly, and hence inefficient, *ex post* renegotiation.

fairly to balance its and its counterparties' interests as these develop *ex post*. Such fiduciary arrangements are possible and indeed are recognized in law. But they remain starkly and expressly different from the contract relation.[55]

Contractual good faith is thus thin (being limited to respect for an antecedently and independently agreed surplus allocation) and flexible (being open to any surplus allocation on which the parties have so agreed). But it is neither inconsequential nor slight. Indeed, contractual recognition, although it arises at arm's length, possesses a value in which more intimate forms of recognition cannot share. Among other things, thinness reconciles the mandatory duty of good faith with freedom of contract. In addition, the structure of good faith corresponds to the formal equality that contract law embeds elsewhere in doctrine. Most importantly, good faith (rightly understood) establishes contract as a collaborative relation and places this relation at the center of the distinctive form of social solidarity established through market exchange.

The contrast between contractual good faith and fiduciary obligation—the principle that good faith does not establish intimacy or affection so much as articulate respect among parties who remain at arm's length—is worth exploring in the light of these claims. To begin with, this contrast illuminates the relationship between good faith in performance and freedom of contract—the fashion in which the duty of good faith serves as the core doctrinal expression of freedom of contract. Furthermore, the contrast reveals the character of contractual recognition and market solidarity.[56]

It is commonly said that the degree of other-regard required by contract is *less* than that required of fiduciaries. In one sense, the account just elaborated supports the commonplace view: if a beneficiary asks his fiduciary to walk a mile with him, she must, altruistically, walk with him twain; a contractual promisor, by contrast,

This reveals that in order to be as efficient as the expectation remedy, a specific performance rule would have to give promisees a right to *require* promisors to deal with third parties (committing an "efficient breach") and disgorge the gains from such dealing. *See* Brooks, *The Efficient Performance Hypothesis*; Markovits & Schwartz, *The Myth of Efficient Breach*. This requirement renders vivid that the entitlement to self-interest within the contract—and the associated insistence on sharing *ex ante* rather than *ex post*—survives the reallocation of gains associated with replacing the efficient expectation remedy with an efficient regime of specific performance.

[55] For more on the nature of fiduciary loyalty, including as it appears in contrast to good faith, *see* Daniel Markovits, *Sharing* Ex Ante *and Sharing* Ex Post: *The Non-Contractual Basis of Fiduciary Relations in* The Philosophical Foundations of Fiduciary Law (Andrew Gold & Paul Miller eds., forthcoming 2014).

Commentators do not always appreciate the structural difference between good faith and fiduciary loyalty and sometimes understand the two as what D. Gordon Smith calls "variations on a theme." D. Gordon Smith, *The Critical Resource Theory of Fiduciary Law*, 55 Vand. L. Rev. 1399, 1487 (2002). More specifically, Smith proposes that "[b]oth [fiduciary duty and good faith] are judicially imposed loyalty obligations designed to attack the potential for opportunism in relationships" (at 1487–8). Smith further asserts that good faith "requires each contracting party to consider the interests of the other contracting party when contemplating self-interested actions. To that extent, the duty of good faith is similar to fiduciary duty" (at 1488).

This is error, both about doctrine and about doctrine's deeper normative structure. Good faith, once again, looks backwards, to the contract and its allocation of benefits and burdens; fiduciary loyalty looks forwards, to balance the parties' interests as conditions develop.

[56] *See generally* Daniel Markovits, *Market Solidarity*, Inaugural Lecture as Calabresi Professor of Law, Yale University (Apr. 9 2012), *available at* <http://vimeo.com/40731104>.

may self-interestedly walk only the mile that she promised, and not an inch further. But contractual good faith is not simply a lesser version of fiduciary other-regard—altruism light, as it were. Rather, contractual good faith involves a distinctive form of recognition of the other to whom it is owned—a form of recognition that fiduciary altruism forecloses, or at least impedes.[57]

A fiduciary's obligation to take the initiative on her beneficiary's behalf is coupled with an entitlement to pursue the beneficiary's interests as the fiduciary sees them, including even where the beneficiary takes a different view. These are two sides of fiduciary intimacy's single coin, as altruism becomes quite literally a nonsense in the absence of a right, in the altruist, to promote the other's true interests rather than false ones. This thought is reflected in fiduciary law, through doctrines that limit the terms on which a beneficiary might engage a fiduciary. Broadly speaking, fiduciary arrangements must hold fiduciaries to standards of reasonable care on their beneficiaries' behalves and must give fiduciaries a right to pursue their independent judgments in their exercise of this care. Doctors must sometimes override the choices of their patients, for example, and lawyers must override the choices of their clients; at least, they must both sometimes refuse to go along with self-destructive or even just imprudent client initiatives. Beneficiaries cannot impose their unreasonable preferences or beliefs on their fiduciaries.

By contrast, a contractual promisor's entitlement to good faith self-interest comes with an obligation to take her counterparty's intentions at face value. Both are, equally, expressions of the contractual arrangement—to go only the distance, and only along the path, that the contract to which she and her collaborator agreed specifies. The contractual promisor's freedom from any altruistic obligation thus also deprives her of any entitlement to promote her perspective over her promisee's. Just as fiduciary altruism carries with it paternalism and associated limits on the freedom of the beneficiary, so good faith self-interest (the fact that a promisor may, within the constraints of the contractual agreement, remain as self-interested within the contract as she was without it) carries with it anti-paternalism. Anti-paternalism is, in fact, just another facet of freedom of contract, as a promisee subjected to the mercies of her promisor's paternalism within the promise would be deprived of promise as a reliable mechanism for pursuing her own purposes (a deprivation that the promisor's altruism reduces not one whit).

Finally, returning to the connection between good faith and freedom of contract casts the inter-subjective recognition involved in every contractual exchange in a revealing light. Fiduciaries, because of their altruism and the paternalism that this carries with it, recognize their beneficiaries in terms of their peculiar, idiosyncratic needs and interests—one might say, as the particular persons they are. Contractual promisors, by contrast, proceeding anti-paternalistically and in good faith, recognize

[57] Doctrine sometimes recognizes and implements this point. One can thus find cases that expressly associate certain rights to good faith in performance with arm's length contracts, by observing that these rights do not arise within joint ventures. *See, e.g., Ray-Tek Services, Inc. v. Parker*, 831 N.E. 2d 948, 953 (Mass. App. Ct. 2005). The fiduciary character of the joint venture entails rights and duties of its own, of course. But these squeeze out, rather than simply add to, certain of the rights and duties associated with contractual good faith.

their promisees for their general intentional capacities to pursue whatever interests and needs they have—one might say, for their generic moral personalities.[58]

In a nutshell, once again, good faith allows contracting parties to remain as self-interested, and as much at arm's length, within the contract as they were without it, *except* that they must accept, as a side-constraint, that the best interpretation of what they agreed to in contracting binds them to limit their self-interest. And the distinctive balance of self-interest and other-regarding constraint articulated by good faith elaborates a particular form of interpersonal recognition and respect.

This chain of characterizations—from good faith to self-interest to anti-paternalism to freedom of contract to recognition of generic personality–generates a striking conclusion, moreover. Contractual recognition (the basis of contractual solidarity) is not lesser but rather different from more intimate forms of recognition. Indeed, the contract relation—precisely because good faith is thinner, more generic, and more abstract than particular, concrete altruism—opens up possibilities for solidarity at arm's length that intimates cannot achieve. Good faith thus underwrites a distinctive form of recognition in which contracting parties recognize one another's expressed intentions, at face value. When they do so, the parties to contracts recognize one another as sovereign wills, whose freedom and hence also choices must be respected. Fiduciary relations lack this variety of respect, not in spite but rather because of the substantive other-regard that they involve.

The connection between good faith and freedom of contract—including through its emphasis that the boundaries of good faith in particular cases are determined by rather than determining the actual intentions and expectations of the parties—goes to the core of good faith and to its structural role in the contract relation. The duty of good faith in performance, once again, is not a separate undertaking of the parties to a contract but an attitude towards whatever undertakings the parties have adopted. To display good faith in contract performance is simply to recognize the authority of the contract, and hence the authority of one's counterparty to insist on performance according to the contract's terms.

The duty of good faith in contract performance thus expresses a commitment to a particular normative (and indeed legal) relation. Honoring the duty involves internalizing the authority structures of that relation and implementing them in one's own practical life. This, incidentally, is why good faith, even as its content may be varied almost arbitrarily by the parties (to take on any substance consistent with there being a contract between them), remains a mandatory rule that cannot be waived. Good faith in performance just is the attitude of taking contractual obligation appropriately seriously. To reject good faith is, in effect, to deny the contractual obligation to which good faith attaches. To make such a denial at the moment of contract formation, as would be involved in a waiver of good faith, is to forswear the intent to obligate. And that necessarily causes contractual obligation to fail from the get-go.

[58] I elaborate this thought in greater detail and argue that the structure of promissory recognition places promising at odds with intimacy in Daniel Markovits, *Promise as an Arm's Length Relation, in* PROMISES AND AGREEMENTS 295 (Hanoch Scheinman ed., 2011).

IV. Good Faith as a Pedestrian Ideal

Good faith, so understood, is a private analog—as between the contracting parties—of the public duty to obey the law that arises among citizens generally (and the rejection of good faith is a private analog of the revolutionary's denial of the political obligation to which the duty to obey the law attaches). The analogy between faithfully performing a contract and dutifully obeying the law reveals something important about good faith. The duty to obey the law is not simply a duty to act in accordance with justice or natural law, but rather attaches (defeasibly, of course) to *positive law*. Similarly, the duty of good faith in performance is not simply a duty to coordinate optimally but rather attaches to the *positive contract*—to the contract that was actually agreed rather than to some ideal alternative. Good faith in performance is thus a *pedestrian* ideal, which takes as its lodestar the actual contract that the parties' intentions established rather than the *utopian* contract that it would have been optimal for them to establish. Indeed, good faith underwrites a distinctive, intrinsically valuable relation among the parties, at all, *only* in respect of its pedestrian connection to their actual, concrete intentions.

This is not a trivial or obvious point, and it is not always understood. It is tempting to idealize good faith by connecting it not to what the parties intended—to their actual joint plan—but to what they ought, rationally or ideally, to have agreed, or even just to what they would have agreed *ex ante* had they known then what they have discovered *ex post*. But overlooking the actual in favor of the ideal—rejecting pedestrian good faith (based on the parties' actual agreement) in favor of a utopian alternative (that invokes the agreement that the parties ideally would have struck)—introduces confusions into discussions of good faith.

Natural justice has long tempted political thinkers towards skepticism concerning the authority of merely positive law. Similarly, the rational idealization of good faith has, at various times, attracted all manner of thinkers to resist the positive terms of actual contracts. In private law, the utopian approach to the contract relation is at the moment especially tempting to writers in the economic tradition.

Consider again, and in this light, Judge Posner's opinion in *Frey*. According to Judge Posner, the duty of good faith "is a stab at approximating the terms the parties would have negotiated had they foreseen the circumstances that have given rise to their dispute."[59] Good faith, on this approach, is thus just another "way[] of formulating the overriding purpose of contract law, which is to give the parties what they would have stipulated for expressly if at the time of making the contract they had had complete knowledge of the future and the costs of negotiating and adding provisions to the contract had been zero."[60] This is as clear a statement of the utopian approach as can be made: good faith, for Judge Posner, is the doctrinal pathway for making the ideal actual.

That vision of good faith cannot be the right one, however. At least, it cannot be right without in effect eliminating contract as a distinctive legal category, which expresses a peculiar face of human freedom and constructs a distinctive human relation.

[59] *Mkt. St. Assocs. Ltd. P'ship v. Frey*, 941 F.2d 588, 595 (7th Cir. 1991).
[60] *Mkt. St. Assocs. Ltd. P'ship v. Frey*, at 596.

As a shallow matter, the utopian conception of good faith simply does not fit the doctrine. According to the utopian view, the duty of good faith in performance *adds* to the substantive content of every contractual obligation. A utopian duty of good faith would entail that contractual promisors owe their promisees performance that they would not owe otherwise. The additions reflect the gaps between the perfectly efficient contracts that the parties would have made had they reasoned ideally without transactions costs and the inefficient contracts that the parties, given their positive transactions costs, actually did make. But doctrine, once again, expressly denies this: recall the U.C.C.'s insistence that good faith "does not create a separate duty of fairness and reasonableness which can be independently breached."[61] The doctrinal duty of good faith in performance is not a separate or additional undertaking of the parties to a contract but an attitude towards whatever undertakings the parties have adopted.

This feature of the doctrine is no accident, moreover. Rather, utopian conceptions of good faith would betray the deep structure of contract law.

To see why good faith cannot be understood in this utopian fashion, begin by observing that a gap inevitably exists between the ideal contract and the contract that the parties have actually made. In some cases, parties expressly adopt optimal terms. (Quantity terms set by sophisticated parties are likely optimal, for example.) In others, there exist good reasons to suspect that silent parties have in fact struck the optimal agreement. (One such case, familiar from earlier discussion, concerns the expectation remedy, which may profitably be understood in terms of a legal presumption that otherwise silent parties have, through a contract's price term, adopted an efficient liquidated damages clause.) But in many cases, it will be clear (or even just on balance the best view) that the parties are interacting on terms that are not optimal. In some cases, parties who have established no contractual relation at all would be better off had they established one. In others, parties have made a contract but on terms whose departure from the optimum has been undeniably memorialized in the express terms of their agreement. In still other cases, the parties' intentions receive only implicit expression, in the interstices of their express agreement, but the best reconstruction of the parties' real contractual intentions again departs from the ideal, optimal contract.

This is not just contingently but necessarily so. Parties to contracts, needless to say, do not reason perfectly or costlessly in their contractual practices; and the costs that they face are reflected in the divergence between agreements that the parties actually make and the ideal agreements. This divergence is inevitable and indeed a transcendental condition of the parties' contracting at all. If persons really could reason perfectly and costlessly in the manner that utopian good faith imagines, they would have no need of, and hence would not (and could not rationally) resort to contract. Rather than ordering their affairs by private agreements, perfectly and costlessly rational parties would engage in ideal public social planning to arrange all their affairs maximally well (efficiently, let us say) for all time. For perfectly, costlessly rational parties, private law, including contract law, is otiose: the only contract that they require is the social contract. Perhaps (and foreshadowing an argument to come) even the social contract

[61] U.C.C. § 1-304 cmt. [1].

would be otiose for such creatures, as they might all instantly agree to live by a unanimously affirmed principle of natural justice.

So actual contracts *necessarily* and indeed *constitutively* depart from the ideal. And in all cases in which the actual departs from the ideal—involving suboptimal failures to contract *tout court*, suboptimal express contract terms, and suboptimal implied in fact contract terms—good faith depends, at least partially, not on what would have been optimal for the parties to agree but rather on what they did agree. Whenever the actual depart from the ideal contractual intentions, the obligations that these intentions create turn not on what would have been optimal for the parties to agree but rather on what they did agree. Treating imperfectly rational parties as if they were perfectly rational, by giving good faith in their contractual relations a utopian bent, therefore undermines their actual contract practices in the service of an ideal whose content is fixed not according to the contracting parties' intentions, but rather according to the court or other lawgiver that determines what is ideal. A utopian standard of good faith, which looks to an ideal rather than to the parties' actual contract, thus violates the parties' contract under the guise of perfecting it. In this way also utopian good faith turns its back on contract.

This recounting of the good faith's insistently pedestrian character is not just a pedantic emphasizing of the contingent and concrete against the universal and abstract, moreover. The distinction between pedestrian and utopian is essential to the character of good faith—really, to the character of the contract relation elaborated in terms of good faith. A utopian standard of good faith, which looked to an ideal rather than to the parties' actual contract, would undermine rather than promote contractual values. Indeed, just as pedestrian good faith promotes freedom of contract and constitutes the contract relation as a site of recognition, so utopian good faith undermines both contractual freedom and recognition.

The connection between the pedestrian account of good faith and freedom of contract is easy to see (and reaffirms that good faith, in spite of being a mandatory rule, *promotes* freedom of contract). Pedestrian good faith protects the parties' actual contractual intentions against *ex post* exploitation, thereby allowing the parties to project their intentions into the future. Good faith is of a piece with contract law's negative libertarian elements. Pedestrian good faith serves rather than limiting freedom of contract by insistently refusing to require the parties' agreement to adopt any particular terms, or even to make any particular division of contractual surplus, but only to respect whatever division they have agreed. By contrast, utopian good faith imposes on the parties a bargain that they did not make. That the parties would be better off under the ideal bargain than under their actual one does by itself eliminate the imposition. Nor does the possibility that the parties would have chosen the ideal bargain had they perfected their deliberations. The fact that pedestrian and utopian good faith come apart entails that the parties did not perfect their intentions.[62]

[62] None of this is to deny that contracting parties might, *in some instances*, form the actual intention that gaps in their contractual understandings shall be filled in using ideal terms. Once again, the discussion of the expectation remedy illustrates just such a case. But there will also arise cases in which the parties' actual intentions either expressly or by clear implication depart from the ideal. And a contract

Utopian good faith thus necessarily encroaches on actual freedom, in the sense associated with negative liberty, in the name of ideal freedom, or positive liberty. This is just the private law analog of the more familiar public law thought that the utopian social contract—the idea that the state is constructed perfectly to instantiate ideal justice and that merely positive law can have no free-standing authority of its own—undermines collective political freedom, replacing democratic sovereignty with a tyranny of rights. The economic focus of utopian good faith in private law—the effort to attribute to the parties whatever intentions would have maximized the value of their bargain—is just a reference to positive liberty dressed up in negative libertarian clothes. That is the commonest apology of the paternalist.

The connection between pedestrian good faith and contractual recognition travels only slightly father afield. Utopian good faith, recall, reconstructs contracts according to ideal efficiency, that is, without reference to the actual intentions of the contracting parties. A party who applies utopian good faith to her own contractual performance can thus proceed without engaging her counterparty at all—she can reason in isolation rather than together with him. This is rendered vivid by imagining a world in which persons deliberate in the fashion that utopian good faith envisions. If persons could deliberate and coordinate *ex ante* in the perfect and costless style that utopian good faith attributes to them *ex post*, then all contracts would be unambiguously complete, so that it would be possible to perform and assess them purely mechanically, with no faith at all, either good or bad. Contracts would, literally, cease to involve a leap of faith. They would also cease to involve respect or recognition among the parties to them, or indeed to involve communication at all. The parties, being ideal and costless deliberators, would each know the other's intentions without needing to be told, just as ideal reasoners would all commonly know the entire truth without needing to communicate. This is why, as I observed earlier, persons who deliberated in the perfect and costless fashion imagined by utopian good faith would not pursue individual engagements with one another at all. Creatures capable of planning perfectly do not need private, obligation-based coordination mechanisms to supplement public coordination. They can simply make their public arrangements perfect, and then optimally achieve all their purposes by living perfectly within them.

Good faith is, in this respect, a practical analog to the principle of charity in interpretation of theoretical communications, a point that sometimes comes out in the cases.[63] Thus, Judge Posner observes that "whether we say that a contract shall be deemed to contain such implied conditions as are necessary to make sense of the contract, or that a contract obligates the parties to cooperate in its performance in 'good faith' to the extent necessary to carry out the purposes of the contract, comes to much the same thing."[64] Note, further, that the analogy to the principle of charity again rejects utopianism in favor of a pedestrian reconstruction of good faith. The principle

cannot arise simply out of a *general* intention in favor of optimal exchange, as this necessarily remains too abstract to resolve concrete questions. The analogy to the law is again helpful here. As a public order cannot be established simply by justice but requires positive law, so a contract cannot be established simply by ideal intentions but requires actual ones. Like utopian politics, so utopian contract is quite literally impossible—both practices are by their nature pedestrian.

[63] An exchange with Charles Fried helped me to recognize the importance of this analogy.

[64] *Mkt. St. Assocs.*, 941 F.2d at 596. The connection between good faith and contextual interpretation also figures in the history of the doctrine. Harold Dubroff thus observes that many of the earliest

of charity requires placing a favorable gloss on what has been said rather than assuming that the truth is always and already known. The utopian assumption would undermine the principle's connection to interpretation, by depriving it of a text to interpret. Once again, if the truth is always known even without being said, then communication becomes otiose.

These observations merely emphasize in an extreme case a basic objection to utopian good faith quite generally. By drawing its content out of the thin air of reason and quite apart from any concrete intentions or contractual engagements, utopian good faith replaces contractual recognition and solidarity *among the parties* with each party's substantively identical but wholly separate relation to right reason. Parties who operate their contracts according to utopian good faith might, to borrow a form of words from Hume, be *in agreement*; but there is not *an agreement* among them. And without a contractual agreement to serve as a substrate to sustain it, there can be no contractual recognition, either.

The analogy between private contracts and the social contract once again usefully develops this point, by illuminating the private contract relation in the brighter light of its more familiar public counterpart. Just as utopianism has tempted theorists of good faith in private contract, so it has been tempting for political philosophers to idealize the social contract. Indeed, the dominant strains of the social contract tradition have succumbed to and even embraced this temptation. The perfect social contract is not political but rather replaces politics, supplanting the actual (republican or democratic) exercise of collective sovereignty with an idealized or just social order (whose terms, enforced by technocrats or philosopher-judges) are designed precisely to constrain actual, concrete politics. The perfect completeness of the social contract thus eliminates the need for political action and agreement in the everyday sense. And the social contract enjoys its authority on the basis of its rationality or justice and not in virtue of having been adopted by any politically constituted sovereign. For the utopian, as Rawls admits, we "submit our conduct to democratic authority only to the extent necessary to share equitably in the inevitable imperfections of a constitutional system."[65]

Perfectly rational and reasonable creatures would not require politics or any political agreement—they would coordinate perfectly justly, but also perfectly separately, being once again in agreement without reaching an agreement on a constitution for their political life. Imperfectly rational and reasonable creatures subject to rule by an idealized social contract fail even to be in agreement and hence experience the constraints on their sovereignty that the social contract imposes as politically alienating.

American cases on good faith employ the doctrine "to avoid the sometimes harsh results that would otherwise have occurred under the conservative interpretation and gap-filling rules prevalent in the Nineteenth and early Twentieth Centuries." Harold Dubroff, *The Implied Covenant of Good Faith in Contract Interpretation and Gap-Filling: Reviling a Revered Relic*, 80 St. John's L. Rev. 559, 562 (2006). I would like to thank Paul MacMahon for pointing this argument out to me.

[65] John Rawls, A Theory of Justice 355 (1971). Rawls gives this thought practical effect in his theory of justice, by removing virtually all important collective decisions from politics in its ordinary sense. Justice, for Rawls, determines the substantive content of policy concerning not just basic liberties but the distributions of all primary goods, including income and wealth, powers and opportunities, and even the social bases of self-respect. *See* Rawls, A Theory of Justice, at 62.

That is why preventing political alienation in our imperfect world requires actual politics.

Politics, moreover, must proceed on formally rather than substantively egalitarian terms. More specifically, the formal equality of democratic citizenship is the only conception of public equality compatible with collective sovereignty in an open political community populated by imperfect moral deliberators and hence condemned to pluralist collective life subject to nonideal positive law. The utopian social contract—the idea that the state is constructed perfectly to instantiate ideal justice and that positive law can have no authority of its own—thus threatens to deny citizens the capacity to constitute themselves, communally, as a sovereign. And private contracts, once again, resemble the social contract. Good faith measures reciprocal recognition among formally equal private contractors just as the duty to obey democratic law measures reciprocal recognition among formally equal public citizens.

It is a mistake, for all these reasons, to treat our actual private law, which is very much required, as simply an effort (not very successful) to approximate the state of affairs in which it did not exist at all. Rather, private law establishes real relations among parties in their actual, imperfectly rational state. These relations have value—intrinsically—and not just as tools. They in fact have value precisely because they are relations of recognition among imperfectly rational creatures, who yet respect one another's rationality. (At the root of this thought is the insistence that the thing to be made sense of is *the contract* and not some idealization thereof—that the entities to be respected are the persons and not some idealizations thereof.) Utopian good faith thus disintegrates contractual recognition just as surely as pedestrian good faith instantiates it.

The contractual duty of good faith in performance is thus necessarily a pedestrian ideal rather than a utopian one, whose content is fixed according to the actual intentions of the imperfect parties rather than the counterfactual intentions that the parties would have formed had they deliberated perfectly.[66] This explains why, as doctrine makes plain, good faith cannot add much to deciding close cases: although the duty of good faith in performance requires the parties to respect each other's reasonable contractual expectations, good faith cannot be called on to identify the reasonable expectations in terms of which it is defined. Whereas utopian good faith might usefully decide cases, by specifying the content of reasonable contractual expectations

[66] Even those who propose utopian reconstructions of good faith in theory accept the ideal's pedestrian limitations in practice. Judge Posner, indeed in the very opinion, in *Frey*, that cast good faith in terms of "complete knowledge" and "zero" contracting costs, is a case in point.

The case concerned what good faith required in connection with a contract for the sale and leaseback of a shopping center. The contract expressly contemplated a further negotiation concerning financing to support additional improvements to the center and stipulated that, should this negotiation fail, the lessee might repurchase the property at roughly the original contract price. That turned out, given movements in the local real estate market, to be a very low price. The lessee initiated the financing negotiations without notifying the lessor of the repurchase option; the lessor refused financing; the lessee sought to exercise the repurchase option; and the lessor refused to convey the land on the ground that the lessee's failure to inform the lessor of the option when it initiated the refinancing negotiations constituted bad faith.

Judge Posner held that the lessee's duty of good faith, on these facts, required only that its silence concerning the repurchase option did not arise out of a subjective intention to trick the lessor into

according to its own free-standing substantive principle, pedestrian good faith simply directs a court to contractual intentions whose content must be gleaned from elsewhere, using other means.

V. Good Faith as Contract's Core

The thinness of good faith in performance—the fact that good faith does not require altruism or even modest affirmative other-regard but rather is consistent with remaining as self-interested within the contract as without it—connects good faith to formal rather than substantive conceptions of equality. And the fact that good faith nevertheless requires promisors to recognize the authority of their contracts, and hence also of their counterparties to insist on contract rights, connects good faith to equality of status—namely to the shared status of possessing full and equal contractual capacity.

Certainly contractual good faith remains possible even under conditions of substantive inequality. Nothing in the patterns of recognition and respect immanent in the contract relation depends on the substantive fairness of the division of contractual surplus. Even where one side to a contract has leveraged undeserved bargaining advantages in contract formation, so that the substantive terms of an exchange unfairly favor her over the other, she may perform her contract in good faith. Doing so requires only that she respect the contractual settlement, and hence her counterparty's authority to insist on that settlement, and so declines to exploit additional strategic advantages that arise within the contract (and are perhaps even obtained through it) to revise that settlement still further to favor her. In spite of the substantive unfairness that lies behind contracts in such cases, each party (including the exploiter) continues to assume duties to adjust, in good faith, to new contingencies, in order not to deprive the other party of the benefits that the contract was intended to secure. (That these benefits are unevenly, and indeed unfairly, divided, does not mean that the division has no normative force within the contract, or that either party may undo it to her unilateral advantage.) Contract obligation, one might say, does not depend on setting the world right before contracts are made, or improving the world through contracting, but can instead arise equally in nonideal as in ideal contracting. In this way, contract possesses the power to launder injustice, creating legitimate entitlements between parties where previously there were none and, moreover, inducing the parties to recognize these entitlements.

unwittingly triggering the option, which rendered the lessee's good or bad faith a question for the fact finder. He reached this conclusion even though subjecting the lessee to an affirmative duty to disclose would likely have been efficient, as it would have saved the costs of duplicative efforts by both sides to keep track of the terms of their agreement. Certainly the subjective (no trickery) standard of good faith that Judge Posner settled on is inefficient, as it makes assessing good faith require extensive and expensive fact finding, and hence dramatically increases litigation expenses *ex post*. These points follow Todd Rakoff, *Good Faith in Contract Performance: Market Street Associates Ltd. Partnership v. Frey*, 120 Harv. L. Rev. 1187 (2007).

One suspects that Judge Posner, in deciding the case, had at the back of his mind the actual commercial practices of sophisticated developers, which do not require affirmative other-regard but reject outright trickery. As the opinion says, good faith does not "make every contract signatory his brother's keeper." *Mkt. St. Assocs.*, 941 F.2d at 593. This is language steeped in the reconstruction of actual cultural practice rather than in critique aimed at rationalizing practice according to idealized reason.

Such a formal equality of status is likely the only conception of private equality compatible with freedom of contract in a dynamic open economy populated by nonideal costly economic deliberators. (Similarly, the formal equality of democratic citizenship is likely the only conception of public equality compatible with collective sovereignty in an open political community populated by imperfect moral deliberators and hence condemned to pluralist collective life subject to nonideal positive law.) Good faith is thus the measure of equal arm's length relations among free contractors in private law (just as the duty to obey democratic legislation is the measure of equal arm's length relations among free citizens in public law). Good faith in contractual performance thus connects the solidarity of the contract relation (solidarity within the contract, one might say) to the broader formal equality that lies at the bottom of the democratic, market-oriented societies in which contract typically flourishes. The doctrinal order and the economic structure thus converge.

The pedestrian account also returns the idea of good faith to its doctrinal beginnings. The discussion of good faith began by observing that it is a distinctively contractual notion, as opposed to an ideal from either tort on the one hand or fiduciary law on the other. This is what it means for good faith to be bounded below by fraud (which even tort law forbids) and from above by fidelity (which fiduciary law requires). Good faith applies not among strangers and is not owed to everyone (like tort duties) nor does it apply only among intimates (like fiduciary fidelity). Rather, it applies among persons who have forged a relationship with each other, structured around a shared understanding of a voluntary obligation, that they do not have with the general mass of humanity. Good faith applies only in respect of this obligation relation, and not in respect of other unrelated dealings and interests even among these persons. This, finally, is why good faith makes no independent contribution to the content of the contract obligation. The measure of good faith is the shared project of the contract; apart from this shared project, the persons' relation continues to be characterized by arm's length dealing.

Good faith thus takes the shared perspective of the contract—the joint activity of the contract's performance—as its lodestar. It is an attitude that the parties display towards each other in virtue of, one might even say (by) respecting, their agreement.[67] Good faith requires the parties to take a certain attitude with respect to whatever terms, whatever division of surplus, they have adopted (to honor these terms, roughly). A promisor cannot, that is, abandon her contractual intentions, including the intention to adjust to unanticipated contingencies in a fashion that secures the success of the contractual collaboration's shared plan. To return to the language of Judge Posner's opinion in *Frey*, and this time to agree with it, contracts "set in motion a cooperative enterprise, which may to some extent place one party at the other's mercy. The parties to a contract are embarked on a cooperative venture, and a minimum of cooperativeness in the event unforeseen problems arise at the performance stage is required even

[67] Note that the account here rejects the long-dominant (but perhaps now more generally retreating) view that good faith "has no general meaning or meanings of its own," but instead merely "serves to exclude many heterogeneous forms of bad faith." Robert Summers, *"Good Faith" in General Contract Law and the Sales Provisions of the Uniform Commercial Code*, 54 Va. L. Rev. 195, 196 (1968). Good faith does have a general content, which is set out in the main text.

if not an explicit duty of the contract. The office of the doctrine of good faith is to forbid the kinds of opportunistic behavior that a mutually dependent, cooperative relationship might enable in the absence of the rule."[68]

This thought underlies the common view that good faith is essential for preventing the contract relation from becoming a locus of exploitation. In fact, good faith plays a more fundamental role still in contract obligation, although this role remains unacknowledged. Good faith does not just prevent exploitation; it is essential for contract to exist at all. For imperfect planners, who cannot plan clearly for every contingency but whose plans inevitably involve haziness and have gaps, good faith is required to make joint planning possible. Good faith in performance is the attitude that imperfect planners must adopt towards their plans in order for the plans to be joint plans at all. It is, quite literally, the matrix in which a shared perspective is possible.[69]

One is tempted to say, in light of all of this, that good faith is the very essence of contractual solidarity, and hence of contract's contribution to social solidarity overall. To make a contract with another *just is* to adopt attitudes of solidarity in favor of the joint project fixed by the contractual intentions. To make a contract *just is* to accept the duty of good faith in its performance.

[68] *Mkt. St. Assocs.*, 941 F.2d at 595. (internal quotation marks and citation omitted).

[69] It is not coincidence, then, that good faith was often used to overcome the requirement of mutuality of obligation, *See, e.g., Imperial Ref. Co. v. Kanotex Ref. Co.*, 29 F.2d 193 (8th Cir. 1928). That requirement reflects the fact that contracts must be joint endeavors. Good faith is the measure of the *ongoing* jointness.

15

The Nature of Vitiating Factors in Contract Law

*Mindy Chen-Wishart**

At common law, agreements between parties that satisfy the requirements of contract formation generate contractual rights and obligations; but only presumptively so. Such rights and obligations may be defeated, wholly or partially, by recognized vitiating factors such as misrepresentation, mistake, duress, and undue influence. What is the nature of these vitiating factors and how do they relate to the arguments in favor of enforcing contracts? Do they merely negate the conditions for finding an enforceable contract in the first place, or do they express other values that qualify, trump, or otherwise interact with the pro-enforcement values? If the latter, what values are in play, how do they relate to each other, and how are they accommodated in legal reasoning and adjudication? The answer goes to the very nature and scope of contractual obligations and the conceptual apparatus for determining them.

Section I sets out the orthodox defective consent account of vitiating factors derived from the centrality of personal autonomy (also described in terms of voluntariness, liberty, freedom, choice, or consent)[1] in contract law. Section II puts this orthodoxy to the test by examining the constituents of recognized vitiating factors. Attention is certainly directed to the complainant's vulnerabilities, as proxies for otherwise unascertainable defective consent, in determining the enforceability of the contract. But it is also directed to other factors; namely: the reasonableness of the complainant's conduct; the quality of the enforcing party's (enforcer's)[2] conduct, knowledge, and belief; the subject matter and the fairness of the exchange; the protection of community values and interests, and considerations relating to the administration of justice. These, in turn, express five legitimate concerns in determining the scope of contractual liability, namely: (i) responsibility in contract formation; (ii) refusal to assist wrongdoers or exploiters; (iii) protection of vulnerable parties from harsh outcomes; and two general concerns that apply to any area of law, (iv) public policy; and (v) the demands of administrability. In Section III, I identify the three main techniques employed by the orthodox account to tame the evidence of Section II and so preserve the primacy of the consent-based account. These are perfectly legitimate up to a point but, taken to extreme, they present a picture that fails the primary test of a good theory—a good enough fit with the law. Section IV then creates conceptual space for the operation of the concerns beyond consent by reference to a two-step defeasibility approach to legal rules. Applied to the validity of contracts, they operate, where

* Thanks to my Philosophical Foundations of the Common Law classes at Oxford over the years. Thanks also to Prince Saprai, participants of The Philosophical Foundations of Contract Law Conference, the Hong Kong University Staff seminar, Lusina Ho, and Robert Mullins for valuable comments.

[1] I use these as synonyms in this article.

[2] Henceforth referred to as the "enforcer."

relevant, at stage two after the qualifying conditions for a presumptive contract are met at stage one. Section V then begins to explore how the principles in play at stage two might relate to the voluntariness principle operating at stage one in determining the enforceability of contractual undertakings. I conclude with an outline of the advantages of this pluralistic two-stage approach.

This chapter resists monistic extremism and for integrated, complementary, and limited pluralism. The orthodox defective consent interpretation gives a straitjacketed account of the vitiating factors. It assumes a one-step "consent-in, lack-of-consent-out" picture of vitiating factors that is normatively skewed, lacks fit with the law, lacks transparency, and takes an unrealistic and disrespectful view of the complainant's rationality. Identifying the principles at work in the vitiating factors and accommodating them within the two-step defeasibility approach redresses the normative imbalance of an overemphasis on the complainant's state of mind, enhances transparency, provides better fit with the law, and affirms the importance of the human faculties of reason and responsibility. Instead of obscuring the relevant concerns behind the façade of qualifying consent, the path is cleared for an open examination of them at stage two. Crucially, these turn out to be principled and limited; most can be seen, not as conflicting with, but as inherent to the consent principle at stage one or as complementary with it. In opposition to extremism, these operative principles draw on one another in generating defensible and meaningful limits to the scope of their, and that of personal liberty's, operation.

I. The Orthodox Interpretation of Vitiating Factors

A. Defective consent

Aside from illegal and immoral contracts, which are accepted as policy motivated, the vitiating factors are generally explained in terms of some defect in the essential voluntariness condition of contract formation. As such, it has even been discussed alongside contract formation. For example, the discussion in Part 2 of *Chitty*[3] on formation of contract includes the majority of vitiating factors (mistake, misrepresentation, duress, and undue influence) alongside offer, acceptance, consideration, and form. Likewise, Adams and Brownsword's[4] chapter on agreement includes discussion of the "reality of agreement," which covers ignorance, mistake, and duress. While most commentators and courts deal with the vitiating factors independently of formation, they nevertheless treat them as generally going to, or significantly overlapping with, the same issue of voluntariness. The implicit assumption is that the vitiation factors interrogate voluntariness at a higher level of detail, specifically, whether it is "full, free and informed."[5] Thus, mistake is said to *negative* or *nullify*

[3] Chitty on Contracts 171, 485–751 (Hugh Beale ed., 31st ed., 2012).

[4] John N. Adams & Roger Brownsword, Understanding Contract Law 47 (Sweet & Maxwell 5th rev. ed., 2007).

[5] *Zamet v. Hyman*, [1961] 1 W.L.R. 1442 (C.A.) 1446 (U.K.); *see, e.g.*, Konrad Zweigert & Hein Kötz, An Introduction to Comparative Law 327–8 (Tony Weir trans., Oxford University Press 3d ed., 1998).

consent;[6] duress[7] and undue influence[8] negate the freeness (or independence) of consent; and incapacity, the *fullness* of consent. While often overlooked in such discussions, misrepresentation can be seen in like terms as targeting the lack of *informed* consent.

Eminent unjust enrichment lawyers take the same view of the vitiating factors. These are simultaneously[9] causes of action to reverse the unjust enrichment conferred in purported performance of the now void, voidable, unenforceable, or discharged contract. Thus, illegal and immoral contracts aside, Birks explains why enrichment in such circumstances are unjust:[10] "It might be that he [the complainant] had given no consent at all, as where his pocket had been picked, or that his consent had been impaired, or that his consent had been qualified and the qualification had not been purged." Burrows[11] adopts the same taxonomy of the unjust factors; that is, those concerned with:

> non-voluntariness (ie, problems with the claimant's consent) and those concerned with "policy-motivated restitution." The former corresponds to the simple idea "I did not mean it" and can be further broken down... into "impaired consent" (mistake, duress, undue influence, exploitation of weakness, human incapacity), "qualified consent" (failure of consideration, which includes termination and frustration of contract), and "no consent" (ignorance). Policy motivated restitution comprises a number of different policies which, even though the claimant may have consented, call for restitution... [and include] illegality.

B. Rationale for the defective consent approach

Given the moral, political, and economic importance of personal autonomy in our current socio-historical context, its preservation is a ready justification for state action. Its core idea is that of self-authorship; that there is something intrinsically valuable in pursuing freely chosen goals and relationships. The rival to the autonomy theory of contract, that of maximizing utility (efficiency or welfare), likewise elevates individual choice to prime position since this provides the best test of welfare. Thus, the primacy of private ordering receives widespread support from classical liberals and libertarians such as

[6] E.g., *Bell v. Lever Bros., Ltd.*, [1932] A.C. 161 (H.L.) 217 (appeal taken from Eng.) (U.K.); Michael Furmston, Cheshire, Fifoot and Furmston's Law of Contract 314 (16th ed., 2012); Edwin Peel, Treitel on The Law of Contract [8-001] (13th ed., 2011); Stephen A. Smith, Atiyah's Introduction to the Law of Contract 175 (6th ed., 2006).

[7] *Pao On v. Lau Yiu Long*, [1980] A.C. 614 (P.C.) 636 (appeal taken from H.K.) (U.K.); Neil Andrews, Contract Law [11.03] (2011); Jack Beatson et al., Anson's Law of Contract 351 (29th ed., 2010); Furmston, Cheshire, Fifoot and Furmston's Law of Contract, at 337; Jill Poole, Textbook on Contract Law 552 (11th ed., 2012).

[8] Beatson et al., Anson's Law of Contract, at 360; Peel, Treitel on The Law of Contract, at 448; Smith, Atiyah's Introduction to the Law of Contract, at 175, 290–1.

[9] The exception is mistaken assumption, which requires a much higher threshold to vitiate a noncontractual transaction.

[10] Peter Birks, Unjust Enrichment 105 (2d ed., 2005); *see also* Peter Birks, An Introduction to the Law of Restitution chs. 6–7, 9 (rev. ed., 1989) [hereinafter Birks, Introduction].

[11] Andrew Burrows, The Law of Restitution 199 (3d ed., 2010).

Mill,[12] von Hayek,[13] Friedman,[14] Nozick,[15] and Fried.[16] If contractual liability is justified on the basis that parties have freely undertaken (consented to) such liability, or that freely assumed liabilities maximize welfare, then it makes sense to negate such liability if the complainant has not, after all, validly consented. The apparently inexorable logic is that if voluntary consent gets you into a contract then some defect in the voluntariness of the consent should get you out. The contract is vitiated because the consent is.

Moreover, vitiating the contract for reasons other than lack of voluntariness is generally regarded with suspicion. Classical liberal theorists give autonomy a *negative* bent by stressing freedom *from* external interference. The correlative demand is for state restraint in democratic and pluralistic societies in which disagreement is widespread and intractable. Legal paternalism and legal moralism should be avoided; the state (through its laws) should not impose its view of the good, but should remain neutral between different understandings of the good. Consistently, John Stuart Mill's famous "harm principle" permits the use of state power only to prevent harm to others.[17] Applied to contract, this confines the state's role to that of providing the necessary framework for making and upholding transactions. Accordingly, Nozick insists that a consistently libertarian society would allow an individual to sell himself into slavery, rejecting the notion of inalienable rights.[18] This approach elevates the individual's autonomy, manifested by her consent, to the pivotal position and minimizes or shuts out other considerations.

This view of contractual liability has the attraction of conceptual simplicity, clarity, and easy marketability. It conforms to the demands of Occam's razor,[19] the principle of parsimony that urges selection from among competing hypotheses, that which offers the simplest explanation. However, the simplest explanation is not necessarily the best explanation for a set of empirical facts. Classical physics is simpler than more recent theories; nonetheless it totally fails when describing the internal workings of the atom. Occam's razor does not require adoption of the simplest theory *come what may*; the simplest should not be preferred over a more complex but more correct theory. In Einstein words:[20] "everything should be kept as simple as possible, but

[12] John Stuart Mill, On Liberty (1859).

[13] Friedrich August von Hayek, Individualism and Economic Order (1948); Friedrich August von Hayek, 1 Law, Legislation and Liberty: Rules and Order (1973); Friedrich August von Hayek, 2 Law, Legislation and Liberty: The Mirage of Social Justice (1977); Friedrich August von Hayek, 3 Law, Legislation and Liberty: The Political Order of a Free People (1979); Friedrich August von Hayek, The Constitution of Liberty (1960); Friedrich August von Hayek, The Road to Serfdom (1944).

[14] Milton Friedman, Capitalism and Freedom (1962).

[15] Robert Nozick, Anarchy, State and Utopia (1974).

[16] Charles Fried, Contract As Promise (1981).

[17] John Stuart Mill, Utilitarianism, Liberty, and Representative Government ch. 1, ¶ 9 (1910).

[18] Nozick, Anarchy, State and Utopia, at 33.

[19] *See generally*, Alan Baker, *Simplicity, in* The Stanford Encyclopedia of Philosophy (Edward N. Zalta ed., 2011), <http://plato.stanford.edu/archives/sum2011/entries/simplicity>.

[20] Albert Einstein, *On the Method of Theoretical Physics*, 1 phil. sci. 163, 165 (1934) ("[T]he supreme goal of all theory is to make the irreducible basic elements as simple and as few as possible without having to surrender the adequate representation of a single datum of experience"). This is normally taken to be a warning against too much simplicity. Dubbed "Einstein's razor," it is used when an appeal to Occam's razor results in an oversimplified explanation that leads to a false conclusion. *See also* Immanuel Kant,

no simpler." Closer to home, Hart cautioned that "uniformity of pattern," although "pleasing," may come at "too high a price."[21] There must be a proper tradeoff between simplicity and adequacy of fit.

The central problem with the defective consent view of vitiating factors is the absence of a stable and workable account of qualifying consent. Moreover, the objective test of consent treats contract parties' actual (subjective, psychological) state of mind as largely irrelevant. In any case, actual consent (intention) is a matter of degree. At one end is the agent who knows that its conduct will be interpreted as entering a contract; if this thin consent were sufficient, almost every exchange—short of automatism, sleepwalking, being pushed, and such like—would be enforceable. At the other extreme the law could demand the thickest threshold of "full, free, and informed" consent; but given the all-pervasiveness of scarcity, and the limits on endowments, information, and rationality, no contract would qualify; we need a cut-off point. In between these extremes, it is impossible to determine, *in principle*, how thick a consent is thick enough, and, in practice, whether *a particular* party's consent is thick enough. The concept of individual autonomy, standing alone, provides very little purchase on this problem.

The starting point should be an accurate description of the phenomenon that we are trying to explain. As Peter Cane observes:[22]

> The "topdowner" (it seems) dons theoretical spectacles before looking at the map, whereas the ("pragmatic") middle-leveller first picks out the topological high spots and then chooses a conceptual lens to bring them into theoretical focus. The middle-leveller is, we might think, more likely than the top-downer to produce a convincing theory *of* law, as opposed to a theory *about* law. But if that were the aim, an approach that started "at the bottom"—in the messy detail of the law and legal phenomena—might be even more promising.

II. The Contents of Vitiating Factors

The focus of the orthodox account of vitiating factors is on the vulnerability of the complainant as a proxy for defective consent. However, Table 15.1 shows that the recognized vitiating factors also direct attention to limited and principled factors external to the complainant's state of mind in entering the contract.

A. Responsibility in contract formation

First, the vitiating factors generally require complainants to act reasonably and responsibly in contract formation, unless: they are infants, mentally incompetent, or

THE CRITIQUE OF PURE REASON 92 (Norman Kemp Smith trans., Palgrave Macmillan 1929) (1781) ("The variety of beings should not rashly be diminished.").

[21] H. L. A. HART, THE CONCEPT OF LAW 38 (3rd ed., 2012).

[22] Peter Cane, *The Anatomy of Private Law Theory: A 25th Anniversary Essay*, 25 O.J.L.S. 203, at 207 (2005) (referring to JULES COLEMAN, RISKS AND WRONGS 8–9 (1992)); *see also* JULES COLEMAN, THE PRACTICE OF PRINCIPLE: IN DEFENSE OF A PRAGMATIST APPROACH TO LEGAL THEORY 5–6 (2001).

Table 15.1 The factors relevant to vitiating factors

	C's vulnerability	C's responsibility/ fault	Fairness/subject matter of contract	E's knowledge and conduct	Public policy	Remedy
Infancy	Infancy		Important to remedy			Reasonable payment for necessaries received Contract void or voidable
Mental incapacity	Mental incapacity		Relevant to remedy unless C is "patient" when content irrelevant	Knowledge of mental incapacity unless C is "patient"[a] when E's conduct/knowledge irrelevant		Reasonable payment for necessaries[b] received Contract voidable; void if C is "patient" or
Unconscionable Bargains.	Cognitive disability short of incapacity		Improvident to C	Active or passive exploitation		Contract voidable
Misrepresentation	Mistaken assumption induced by misrepresentation	No failure to take care		Relevant to remedy: fraud, negligence, Misrepresentation Act, 1967, §2(1) (Eng.)		Contract voidable Reliance damages, damages in lieu of rescission
Duress: To person To property	Pressure exerted by E	Impliedly has no practicable alternative	Unfairness is evidence of causation	Threat of unlawful conduct		Contract voidable
Salvage	Pressure from circumstance of threat to life or property on ship at sea	Impliedly has no practicable alternative	Extortionate	Exploitation of existing vulnerability		Substitute fair price
Economic duress	Pressure exerted by E	No practicable alternative	Is evidence of illegitimacy of threat and of causation	Illegitimate "threat" rather than "offer"		Contract voidable
Undue Influence	Relationship of influence with E		Transaction "calling for an explanation"	Active or passive exploitation	Protect trusting relationships	Contract voidable

(Continued)

Table 15.1 (*Continued*)

	C's vulnerability	C's responsibility/ fault	Fairness/subject matter of contract	E's knowledge and conduct	Public policy	Remedy
Etridge Noncommercial guarantees	Relationship of influence with primary debtor or other vitiating factor		Transaction for primary debtor's benefit	Knowledge C is acting noncommercially and transaction is for benefit of primary debtor	Protect noncommercial guarantors	Contract voidable
Illegality		Purpose and knowledge of illegality relevant	Proscribed subject matter	Purpose and knowledge of illegality normally relevant	Variety of community values	Contract void, voidable or unenforceable
Common mistaken assumption	Mistake as to background assumption	Must not be at fault	Mistake must be fundamental	E must also be mistaken		Contract void
Non est factum	Inability to read or understand document	Must not be careless	Fundamental mistake about nature of document	Misrepresentation normally present, but unnecessary		Contract void
Frustration		Must not be at fault (self-induced frustration)	Radical change to obligations undertaken			Contract discharged L.R.(F.C.)A.[c]
Mistake of terms	belief at variance with own literal offer or acceptance	Objective test of intention		Knowledge of C's mistake		No contract or contract void

[a] Under the Mental Incapacity Act, 2005, "patients" cannot make valid contracts. CHITTY ON CONTRACTS, at [8-073].

[b] Mental Capacity Act, 2005, c. 9, § 7 (Eng. & Wales); Sale of Goods Act, 1979, c. 54, § 3(3) (U.K.). The position is the same under the common law.

[c] Law Reform (Frustrated Contracts) Act, 1943, 6 & 7 GEO. 6, c. 40 (U.K.) (providing restitution of benefits conferred subject to some loss apportionment).

impaired in bargaining ability (a constituent of an unconscionable bargains), or the policy underlying the illegality or contravention of public policy is to protect a class of persons to which the complainant belongs.[23] Thus:

- a plea of common mistaken assumption[24] will fail if the mistake is attributable to the fault of the complainant;
- a plea of frustration will fail if the alleged frustrating event is self-induced;[25]
- *non est factum* cannot normally be relied upon by literate persons of full capacity, and even those sufficiently impaired to qualify for relief must still take such care as could be expected of persons in their condition;[26]
- a plea of misrepresentation fails if the complainant is too gullible[27] or should have taken care to check the accuracy of the statement;[28]
- complainants in duress cases must show that they had "no practicable alternative" to submission to the enforcer's demand;[29]
- undue influence complainants are unlikely to succeed if they have acted foolishly;[30] and
- the complainants' good or bad faith in entering an illegal or immoral contract (or timeliness in resiling from it) will determine whether they can enforce the contract on completing their performance, claim restitution, or avoid the contract,[31] unless it would subvert the policy underlying the illegality.

The requirement of responsibility in contract formation is unsurprising. Since a primary function of contract law is to facilitate planning, cooperation, and coordination, the complainants' want of care should not deny the enforcers their legitimate expectations. The requirement is necessary to protect the autonomy-enhancing institution of contract from abuse.[32]

B. The enforcer's conduct, knowledge, and beliefs

Second, since a contract involves more than one party, it makes sense that the vitiating factors should also be concerned with the quality of the enforcer's conduct, knowledge, and beliefs. This determines whether the law should lend its assistance to the

[23] E.g., *Ailion v. Spiekermann*, [1976] Ch. 158 (U.K.) (protecting tenants from demands of illegal premiums). The tenant can enforce the lease and get restitution of the premium.
[24] *Associated Japanese Bank (Int'l) Ltd. v. Crédit du Nord SA*, [1989] 1 W.L.R. 255 (Q.B.) (U.K.); *Great Peace v. Tsavliris*, [2002] E.W.C.A. (Civ.) 1407, [76], [2003] Q.B. 679, 703 (U.K.).
[25] *Monarch S.S. Co. v. Karlshamns Oljefabriker (A/B)*, [1949] A.C. 196 (H.L.) (appeal taken from Scot.) (U.K.).
[26] *Saunders v. Anglia Bdg. Soc'y*, [1971] A.C. 1004 (H.L.) 1016 (appeal taken from Eng.) (U.K.).
[27] "Puffs" are not actionable. *See Dimmock v. Hallett*, (1866) 2 Ch. App. 21 (U.K.).
[28] The court may find that the complainant was not induced into the contract by the misrepresentation. *Peekay Intermark Ltd. v. Austl. & N.Z. Banking Grp.*, [2006] E.W.C.A. (Civ.) 386 (U.K.).
[29] *Universe Tankships of Monrovia v. Int'l Transport Workers Fed'n*, [1983] 1 A.C. 366 (H.L.) 383–5, 400–1, 405–6 (appeal taken from Eng.) (U.K.).
[30] *Clarke v. Prus*, [1995] N.P.C. 41 (Ch. D.) (U.K.).
[31] E.g., *Taylor v. Bhail*, [1996] C.L.C. 377 (C.A.) (U.K.); *Ashmore, Benson Pease & Co. v. Dawson Ltd.*, [1973] 1 W.L.R. 828 (C.A.) (U.K.); *Shelley v. Paddock*, [1980] Q.B. 348 (U.K.); *Strongman (1945) Ltd. v. Sincock*, [1955] 2 Q.B. 525 (U.K.).
[32] Joseph Raz, *Promises in Morality and Law*, 95 Harv. L. Rev. 916, 932 (1982).

enforcer in enforcing her claim. The answer is "no" where the enforcer has created or exacerbated the complainant's vulnerability. Thus, the doctrines of misrepresentation, duress, undue influence by overt pressure,[33] and unconscionable bargains by active victimization[34] will deprive the enforcer of her bargain, *even if she has not acted in bad faith.*[35]

Even if the enforcer has not created or exacerbated the complainant's bargaining vulnerability, she may still be denied enforcement if she exploits the complainant's *known* vulnerability by obtaining or accepting a transaction that is improvident to the complainant without taking account of the latter's interests (by disclosing information or recommending independent advice). Thus:

- undue influence may be inferred[36] from the parties' relationship of influence and a transaction that "calls for an explanation" where the enforcer fails to take steps to emancipate the complainant from her influence;
- unconscionable bargain includes "passive victimization"[37] of a complainant known to be suffering a bargaining impairment by accepting a contract improvident to the latter without taking relevant steps to safeguard her interest;
- the *Etridge* doctrine[38] avoids guarantees where the lender, knowing that the non-commercial guarantor acts for the benefit of the primary debtor, fails to take reasonable steps to ensure that the guarantor understands the transaction; the mental incapacity doctrine only operates if the enforcer knows of the complainant's mental incapacity or if the bargain is unconscionable.[39]

Enforcers who have not created or exacerbated, and are ignorant of, complainants' fundamental mistaken assumptions will nevertheless lose the contract if they share the mistake since their expectations are then unreasonable and unworthy of protection. It is only in the case of policy-motivated invalidity based on infancy and illegality[40] that enforcers can be deprived of the contract although they neither knew of the invalidity nor participated in it.[41]

The concern of vitiating factors with the enforcer's conduct, knowledge, and beliefs is unsurprising since contract law must set out the terms of permissible engagement between contract parties, the rules of the contract game. In this context, the Kantian idea that all persons should be treated with respect comes to the fore. We are required

[33] Corresponding to the old "actual undue influence." *Allcard v. Skinner*, (1887) 36 Ch. D. 145 (C.A.) (U.K.).

[34] Victimization may be active or passive. *Earl of Aylesford v. Morris*, (1872–3) 8 Ch. App. 484, 490 (U.K.).

[35] As with innocent misrepresentation, good faith duress (e.g., threat to property mistakenly believing she is entitled to do it), and good faith undue influence. *See Jennings v. Cairns*, [2003] E.W.C.A. (Civ.) 1935, [40] (U.K.). Unconscionable bargain is the exception in requiring bad faith.

[36] Corresponding to the old "presumed undue influence" category. *Allcard*, 36 Ch. D. at 145.

[37] See *Earl of Aylesford*, 8 Ch. App. at 490.

[38] *Royal Bank of Scot. PLC v. Etridge (No. 2)*, [2002] U.K.H.L. 44, [2002] 2 A.C. 773 (appeal taken from Eng.) (U.K.).

[39] *Hart v. O'Connor*, [1985] A.C. 1000 (P.C.) (appeal taken from N.Z.) (U.K.); *Imperial Loan Co. v. Stone*, [1892] 1 Q.B. 599 (U.K.); *Gore v. Gibson*, (1843) 153 Eng. Rep. 260 (C. Exch.) (U.K.).

[40] I use "illegality" to include contracts against public policy.

[41] E.g., *Re Mahmoud & Ispahani*, [1921] 2 K.B. 716 (U.K.).

to treat others "never simply as a means but always at the same time as an end."[42] We must not treat others *merely* as if their only value is derived from their usefulness to us, but must also consider their interests and ends. The vitiating factors fix the content of that obligation.

C. Substantive unfairness to a vulnerable complainant

Third, the vitiating factors also reveal concern with severe substantive improvidence of the contract for the complainant; this entails but is not limited to inadequacy of consideration. Mere undervalue is insufficient, the contract must be overreaching and oppressive or entail such substantial undervalue that it "shocks the conscience of the court."[43] Thus:

- improvidence of the contract for the complainant is indispensable to a finding of unconscionable bargain;
- for undue influence to be inferred, the transaction must "call for an explanation;"
- while substantive unfairness is strictly unnecessary for active undue influence,[44] it is practically indispensable in distinguishing "due" from "undue" influence (given the ubiquitous nature of the types of pressure involved that would not register on the radar of the duress doctrine, e.g. harassment, emotional blackmail, or bullying);
- substantive unfairness also functions as evidence that the undue influence has *induced* the complainant into the contract;
- likewise, the unfairness of the "demand" is relevant in determining the legitimacy of the pressure in duress cases, and acts as evidence that the pressure *caused* the complainant to contract;[45]
- *Etridge* only applies in favor of a noncommercial guarantor who obtains no direct benefit from the guarantee;[46]
- the doctrines of common mistaken assumptions, frustration and *non est factum* require that the relevant mistakes render performance "fundamentally" or "radically" different from that supposed by the parties at formation;
- the effect of infancy depends largely on whether the contracts are broadly beneficial to the infant;[47]

[42] IMMANUEL KANT, THE MORAL LAW: GROUNDWORK OF THE METAPHYSICS OF MORALS (Herbert James Paton trans., Routledge 1991) (1947).

[43] *Alec Lobb (Garages) Ltd. v. Total Oil Gr. Brit. Ltd.*, [1983] 1 W.L.R. 87 (Ch.) 94–5 (U.K.).

[44] *CIBC Mortgs. PLC v. Pitt*, [1994] 1 A.C. 200 (H.L.) 208–9 (appeal taken from Eng.) (U.K.). *See* Mindy Chen-Wishart, *Undue Influence: Vindicating Relationships of Influence*, 59 CURRENT LEGAL PROBS. 231, 265 (2006).

[45] *See Barton v. Armstrong*, [1976] A.C. 104 (P.C.) (appeal taken from New S. Wales) (U.K.); *Huyton SA v. Peter Cremer GmbH & Co.*, [1999] 1 Lloyd's Rep. 620 (Q.B.) (U.K.).

[46] *Royal Bank of Scot. PLC v. Etridge (No. 2)*, [2002] U.K.H.L. 44, [2002] 2 A.C. 773 (appeal taken from Eng.) (U.K.).

[47] Thus, a reasonable price must be paid for "necessaries" received. *Peters v. Fleming*, (1840) 151 E.R. 314 (C. Exch.) (U.K.); *see also* Sale of Goods Act, 1979, c. 54 § 3(3) (U.K.) (codifying that employment and certain other contracts *beneficial* for the child as a whole are valid, and certain contracts which confer on the child an interest in permanent subject matter, such as land or shares, are binding unless the child repudiates the contract before or within a reasonable time of attaining majority). The minor's liability on an executory contract for necessaries is uncertain. CHITTY ON CONTRACTS, at [8-011].

- contracts with mental incompetents are voidable[48] if the contract is unconscionable (requiring improvidence to the complainant); and
- even if the enforcer knows of the complainant's mental incompetence, the complainant must still pay a reasonable price for "necessaries" received.[49]

This focus on protecting vulnerable parties from extreme substantive unfairness can be referable to Kantian respect, mentioned above, more controversially, to the concern with distributive justice,[50] or in terms of protecting the complainant's future autonomy, which promotes, rather than conflicts with, the value of autonomy. The law should not facilitate undertakings that can have the effect of unduly reducing an individual's overall autonomy; hence it should be reluctant to enforce contracts that will push the complainant below some social minimum. Grossly unfair contracts are often objectionable precisely because they have an adverse long-term effect on the autonomy of the complainant. This is but an extension of the facility of bankruptcy, which renders contracts unenforceable in order to give the bankrupt a fresh start rather than require her to live the life of quasi-indentured servitude.

D. Public policy and community interests

Fourth, various public policies may operate to avoid contracts despite the parties' unquestioned consent. Contracts found to be illegal or contrary to public policy demonstrate a wide range of concerns with the community interest, civic virtue, and human dignity. Examples include contracts: to commit a crime or civil wrong, interfering with the administration of justice, to oust the jurisdiction of the courts, prejudicial to the state, which further sexually immoral purposes, prejudicial to family life, that unduly restrict personal liberty, and that are in restraint of trade or anti-competitive. We can detect some overlap with the concern to protect future autonomy, for example in the invalidity of slavery contracts, the sale of certain body parts, unreasonable restraints of trade, and terms exempting liability for personal injury and death.[51] Another strand is the protection and promotion of the valuable social contexts in which the exercise of autonomy derives meaning. This accounts, for example, for the doctrine of undue influence,[52] breach of fiduciary duties, the *Etridge* doctrine, and the recent controversy over the force of pre-nuptial agreements.[53] As Raz observes, supporting autonomy justifies supporting social forms since "a person's well-being depends to a large extent on success in socially defined and determined pursuits and

[48] The contracts of those designated "patients" under the Mental Capacity Act of 2005 are void subject to judicial discretion. Mental Capacity Act, 2005, c. 9 §2, §18 (Eng. & Wales).

[49] Mental Capacity Act, 2005, c. 9, at § 7.

[50] Anthony Townsend Kronman, *Contract Law and Distributive Justice*, 89 YALE L.J. 472 (1980). Controversial because substantively fair contracts do not necessarily correlate with distributively just outcomes, and because it invites the charges of paternalism, and interference with autonomy.

[51] Unfair Contract Terms Act, 1977, c. 50, § 2(1) (U.K.).

[52] *See* Mindy Chen-Wishart, *Undue Influence: Beyond Impaired Consent and Wrong-Doing, Towards a Relational Analysis, in* MAPPING THE LAW: ESSAYS IN HONOUR OF PETER BIRKS 201 (Andrew Burrows & Lord Roger of Earlsferry eds., 2006); Chen-Wishart, *Undue Influence: Vindicating Relationships of Influence.*

[53] *Radmacher v. Granatino*, [2010] U.K.S.C. 42 (appeal taken from Eng.).

activities"[54] that give meaning to his activities.[55] It is not that whatever is practiced with social approval is, for that reason only, valuable; society can be mistaken just as individuals can be,[56] but, individuals cannot escape the social web of significance.[57] This chimes with the communitarians' claim that the social matrix is prior to the individual—that community contributes to the constitution of our self-understanding,[58] and is the necessary context for the meaningful exercise of autonomy.

E. Administration of justice

Fifth, the administrability of rules is a legitimate concern in any area of law. Thus the concern to overcome errors and gaps in fact finding, and to prevent a flood of claims that would destabilize the security of contracts is evident, for example, in the evidential presumptions in the doctrines of undue influence and unconscionable bargains, the high thresholds required in common mistake, frustration and *non est factum*, the bright line drawn in infancy, and the objective test of intentions.

III. The Empire Strikes Back

Confronted with the range of factors in play beyond the complainant's state of mind, those subscribing to the defective consent thesis of vitiating factors employ three main techniques to tame this empirical evidence in order to preserve the primacy of the voluntariness fixed point. Namely: subsuming them within an enlarged concept of consent, rejecting their legitimacy or downplaying their importance, and consigning them to some *ceteris paribus* proviso. The Empire strikes back. These techniques are perfectly legitimate *up to a point*, but taken to an extreme, as often happens, they entail significant distortions of the true picture.

A. Enlarging consent

The most common technique is to enlarge the concept of consent in two different directions in order to subsume the "other" factors within its folds. First, certain vitiating factors are said to merely express the parties' *implied* intention. For example, when contracts are set aside for common mistaken assumption and frustration, the claim[59] is that it is because the contract contains an implied-in-fact term to this effect; it is the parties themselves who implicitly stipulate such an outcome, although they have neither expressed nor likely even contemplated it. On this approach, there are no "true" vitiating factors or "excuses for nonperformance" called mistake or frustration

[54] Joseph Raz, Morality of Freedom 309 (1988).

[55] Raz, Morality of Freedom, at 312.

[56] Raz, Morality of Freedom, at 329.

[57] Raz, Morality of Freedom, at 342, 312–13.

[58] Michael Sandel, Liberalism and the Limits of Justice (2d ed., 1998).

[59] Smith, Atiyah's Introduction to the Law of Contract; Stephen A. Smith, Contract Theory 297–8, 315, 374 (2004); P. Atiyah & F. Bennion, *Mistake in the Construction of Contracts*, 24 M.L.R. 421 (1961); C. Slade, *The Myth of Mistake in the English Law of Contract*, 70 L.Q.R. 885 (1954); J. D. Smith, *Contracts—Mistake, Frustration and Implied Terms*, 110 L.Q.R. 400 (1994).

proper. They are merely part of the rules establishing the content of a contract in general, and on construction of the contract and implied terms in particular.

It is readily accepted that terms are interpreted and implied by reference to the background context.[60] The real issue is the scope of the "background context," to which the parties are taken to have impliedly consented. It clearly includes the specifics of the particular transaction (its past dealings, commercial practices, purpose, and background legal rules), but how much more? Once it includes shared normative understandings on general moral considerations such as fairness and efficiency,[61] the language of private intentions merely obscures the public nature of these values. That is, other normative considerations are smuggled in, behind the façade of what the parties have impliedly or hypothetically agreed to.[62] This is associated with the (virtually) no gaps in contracts school,[63] according to which, if enough background context is taken into account, you can *always* tell what the parties (impliedly) intended in the circumstances that have occurred. Indeed, on an extremist version of this argument, *all* vitiating factors can be collapsed into implied terms.

Moreover, there is something distinctly odd in saying that a contract is void for mistake (a nullity *from the beginning*) because an implied term inside that *void* contract says so; the contract's "self-destruct" program detonates *before* it comes into being. The reasoning also necessitates the fiction that parties have agreed what is to happen in a state of affairs that is completely different from the one that they both assumed at formation. Lord Atkins[64] recognized that talk of implied terms is a synonym for common mistake, which *does* exist and only kicks in *after* construction has exhausted the contract's ability to determine the consequences of the mistake.[65] Likewise, Lord Radcliffe said of the frustration doctrine: "there is something of a logical difficulty in seeing how the parties could even impliedly have provided for something which *ex hypothesi* they neither expected nor foresaw."[66] Even clearer are contracts that are frustrated *against* the parties' express agreement.[67] As Fried accepts: "as we move further from actual intention the standard

[60] *Att'y Gen. of Belize v. Belize Telecom Ltd.*, [2009] U.K.P.C. 11 (appeal taken from Belize); *Investors Compensation Scheme v. W. Bromwich Bldg. Soc'y (No. 1)*, [1998] 1 W.L.R. 896 (H.L.) (appeal taken from Eng.) (U.K.).

[61] E.g., SMITH, CONTRACT THEORY, at 300–3; Raz, *Promises in Morality and Law*, at 932.

[62] RONALD DWORKIN, TAKING RIGHTS SERIOUSLY 151 (1977). Ronald Dworkin explains: "Suppose that you and I are playing poker and we find, in the middle of a hand, that the deck is one card short. You suggest that we throw the hand in, but I refuse because I know I am going to win and I want the money in the pot. You might say that I would certainly have agreed to that procedure had the possibility of the deck being short been raised in advance. But your point is not that I am somehow committed to throwing the hand in by an agreement I never made. Rather you use the device of a hypothetical agreement to make a point that might have been made without that device, which is that the solution is so obviously fair and sensible… the fact that I would have chosen it myself adds nothing of substance to that argument."

[63] Brian Leiter, *Legal Realism and Legal Positivism Reconsidered*, *in* NATURALIZING JURISPRUDENCE: ESSAYS ON AMERICAN LEGAL REALISM AND NATURALISM IN LEGAL PHILOSOPHY 60, 62–3 (2007).

[64] *Bell v. Lever Bros., Ltd.*, [1932] A.C. 161 (H.L.) 224–5 (appeal taken from Eng.) (U.K.).

[65] *Bank of Credit & Commerce Int'l SA v. Ali (No. 1)*, [1999] 2 All E.R. 1005 (A.C.) 1020 (U.K.); *Grains & Fourrages SA v. Huyton*, [1997] 1 Lloyds Rep. 628 (Q.B.) (U.K.); *William Sindall PLC v. Cambridgeshire Cnty. Council*, [1994] 1 W.L.R. 1016, 1035 (C.A.) (U.K.); *Associated Japanese Bank (Int'l) Ltd. v. Crédit du Nord SA*, [1989] 1 W.L.R. 255 (Q.B.) 268 (U.K.).

[66] *Davis Contractors Ltd. v. Fareham Urban Dist. Council*, [1956] A.C. 696 (H.L.) 728 (appeal taken from Eng.) (U.K.).

[67] E.g., *Ertel Bieber & Co. v. Rio Tinto Co.*, [1918] A.C. 260 (H.L.) (appeal taken from Eng.) (U.K.).

of presumed intention tends to merge into the other substantive standards used to solve the problems caused by a failure in the agreement."[68] The courts have rightly rejected the implied terms view of both mistake[69] and frustration.[70]

The concept of consent can be enlarged in another direction, by demanding a thick threshold of consent with the vitiating factors identifying when they have *not* been satisfied, despite first appearances at contract formation.[71] The reasoning is that since "the intent of a man cannot be tried, for the Devil himself knows not the intent of a man,"[72] we can only define the *external* conditions of valid consent. Nevertheless, this interpretation fails the test of "fit with the law" in significant respects. For example, the logic of defective consent implies that no valid contract was made, but the vitiating factors do not negate any of the elements of formation[73] (offer, acceptance, consideration, certainty, even intention to create legal relations). Rather, they are variously described as "excuses for nonperformance," "defences," "relief," "policing the contract," all premised on the existence of a valid contract that is subsequently set aside. Thus, the defective consent approach obscures the distinction between failure to meet the conditions of liability on the one hand (leading to no contract in the first place), and defeating or overriding them on another (leading to void or voidable contracts). It also fails to explain why the burden of proving valid consent is not on the enforcer who asserts liability, but rather on the complainant who seeks to escape liability to prove its absence.

Indeed, if we were to take this baseline of thick consent seriously, no contract would stand, and it is impossible to generate a limit to the fullness, freeness, or informedness of the consent required by reference to the concept of voluntariness itself. "Full" consent requires rational judgment. But where do we fix a principled cut-off point when research shows that human decisions are generally tainted by "predictable irrationality."[74] It is clear that infancy, mental incapacity, and even bargaining impairment (of the "poor and ignorant" type required by the unconscionable bargain doctrine) undermine "full" consent. But *something else* is needed to explain other limiting features of vitiating factors, for example:

- why relief is limited to such extreme cases;
- why contracts so tainted are not absolutely invalid but result in a gradation of invalidity depending on a range of factors including the enforcer's conduct and knowledge, and the nature and fairness of the transaction; and

[68] Fried, Contract as Promise, at 61; Smith, Atiyah's Introduction to the Law of Contract, at 177.

[69] *Great Peace v. Tsavliris*, [2002] E.W.C.A. (Civ.) 1407, [76], [2003] Q.B. 679, 703 (U.K.).

[70] *Davis Contractors*, A.C. 696 at 728.

[71] E.g., Smith, Contract Theory, at 323.

[72] Y.B. 17 Edw. 4, fol. 1, Pasch, pl. 2 (1478) (Eng.).

[73] The exception is the so-called "mistake as to terms" doctrine, now better interpreted as negating the complainant's mistaken offer or the enforcer's acceptance when the latter knows of the former's mistake. *Smith v. Hughes*, (1870–1) 6 L.R.Q.B. 597 (U.K.); *Hartog v. Colin & Shields*, [1939] 3 All E.R. 566 (K.B.) (U.K.); *see* Mindy Chen-Wishart, *Objectivity and Mistake: The Oxymoron of Smith v. Hughes, in* Exploring Contract Law 341 (Richard Bronaugh et al. eds., 2009).

[74] *See, e.g.*, Dan Ariely, Predictably Irrational: The Hidden Forces that Shape Our Decisions (2008); Ori Brafman & Rom Brafman, Sway: The Irresistible Pull of Irrational Behaviour (2009).

- why relief for unconscionability and mental incapacity are premised on the enforcer's unconscientious conduct or knowledge.

The answers lie in the values of responsibility in contract formation, certainty and security of contract, prevention of exploitation, protection of complainants from improvidence, and the protection of the institution of contract.

The requirement of "free" consent raises the same predicament of finding a principled cut-off and necessitates resort to other values. External pressures impairing the freedom of contracts are ubiquitous; as Trebilcock observes:[75] "scarcity often explains the need to contract in the first place. If we all possess all the endowments we needed to pursue any life we wished, contracting would be unnecessary." We can readily understand why duress undermines "free" consent. But, again, *something else* is needed to explain why:

- the scope of the doctrine is effectively confined to duress to the person, to property, and to economic interests;
- the substance of the contract ("the demand") is relevant to the availability of relief;
- duress (or indeed undue influence or misrepresentation) by third parties or duress by necessitous circumstances[76] are generally irrelevant; and
- relief is barred when the complainant has a practicable alternative to submission to the enforcer's demands.

Again, the answers lie in the values of certainty and security of contract, protecting the enforcer's reasonable expectations and the institution of contract, requiring responsibility in contract formation and preventing exploitation. The common reasoning that the complainants' consent in duress cases is defective when the pressure is one that they "should not have to put up with"[77] merely begs the question and obscures the principles in play. The same applies to undue influence where, moreover, the complainants usually enter the contracts willingly. Here, the justification for invalidity has less to do with the complainant's lack of *free* consent than with the enforcer's abuse of the social form of trusting relationships.[78]

Fully "informed" consent also sets an impossibly high bar. It is clearly undermined by ignorance and mistake. But, *something else* is needed to explain why:

- there is generally no relief for ignorance unless the enforcer has a duty to disclose;
- mistakes as to background assumptions afford no relief unless they are shared, and of fundamental importance;
- mistakes about terms must be known to the other party or, in *non est factum* cases, be catastrophic and without carelessness by the complainant; and
- relief for misrepresentation (induced mistake) vary with the degree of the enforcer's fault and the substantive consequences of avoiding the contract.[79]

[75] Micheal J. Trebilcock, Limits of Freedom of Contract 79 (1997).

[76] Aside from the salvage doctrine.

[77] Birks, Introduction, at 183–4; Smith, Contract Theory, at 332–6.

[78] *See* Chen-Wishart, *Undue Influence: Vindicating Relationships of Influence*; Chen-Wishart, *Undue Influence: Beyond Impaired Consent and Wrong-Doing*.

[79] This is evident in the Misrepresentation Act's bar to rescission. Misrepresentation Act, 1967, c. 7, § 2(2) (Eng. & Wales).

The answer must refer to the value of responsibility in contract formation, the protection of reasonable expectations, the concern to prevent exploitation and the balance of equities between the parties.

Hart[80] explains that to describe all of this in the language of "defective consent" is misleading. It suggests "that there are certain psychological elements required by the law as necessary conditions of contract and that the defences are merely admitted as negative *evidence* of these." Rather, it is "a compendious reference to the defences with which claims in contract may be weakened or met." He continues: "the word 'voluntary' in fact serves to exclude a heterogeneous range of cases such as physical compulsion, coercion by threats, accidents, mistakes, etc., and not to designate a mental element or state; nor does 'involuntary' signify the absence of this mental element or state." Consistently, Lord Nicholls concedes in *Etridge* that whenever the defendant's procurement of the claimant's consent is judged improper, that consent will not be *deemed* an expression of the claimant's will.[81] Thus, talk of consent here is *conclusory* not explanatory; it is merely shorthand for the variety of factors rendering a transaction defeasible.

Lastly, by treating the complainant who has knowingly, intentionally, and sometimes willingly consented as having not *really* consented, the orthodox approach takes a disrespectful view of the complainant's rationality in entering the contract. For example, allegiance to the defective consent approach led Birks and Chin to describe undue influence complainants as "lacking the capacity for self-management" due to their "excessive" and "morbid dependency" on the enforcer.[82] Their "autonomy" or the "integrity of [their] judgment" is "markedly sub-standard" or "impaired to an exceptional degree."[83] This unrealistic and insulting description of the complainants denigrates the values of attachment and commitment that usually motivate their contracts. It ignores the fact that when the novice nun gave her worldly possessions to the Mother Superior in the classic case of *Allcard v. Skinner*[84] she did not lack autonomy—she exercised it.

B. Rejection of the "Other" Factors

The second approach deployed by some consent-based theorists to aspects of vitiating factors that deviate from their master principle is to reject them or downgrade their relevance. Thus, where the scope of relief appears under-inclusive[85] against the defective consent baseline, expansion is advocated by eliminating "unnecessary obstacles." For example, in the realm of duress, Smith[86] argues for a new "state of necessity" defense, which would dispense with the need to prove that the enforcer applied

[80] H. L. A. Hart, *The Ascription of Responsibility and Rights, in* Logic and Language, First Series 145, 180 (A. G. N. Flew ed., 1960).

[81] *Royal Bank of Scot. PLC v. Etridge (No. 2)*, [2001] U.K.H.L. 44, [7], [2002] 2 A.C. 773, 795 (appeal taken from Eng.).

[82] Peter Birks & Nyuk Yin Chin, *On the Nature of Undue Influence, in* Good Faith and Fault in Contract Law 57, 82 (Jack Beatson & Daniel Friedman eds., 1995).

[83] Birks & Chin, *On the Nature of Undue Influence*, at 67–8.

[84] *Allcard v. Skinner*, (1887) 36 Ch. D. 145 (C.A.) (U.K.).

[85] Birks & Chin, *On the Nature of Undue Influence*, at 72.

[86] Smith, Contract Theory, at 331, 336–40; Stephen A. Smith, *Contracting under Pressure: A Theory of Duress*, 56 C.L.J. 343, 344, 358–71 (1997).

illegitimate pressure. Likewise, Birks's single focus on the quality of the complainant's consent leads him to view the current requirements of enforcer wrongdoing (e.g., in misrepresentation or duress) or knowledge of the complainant's weakness (e.g., in improvident guarantees and unconscionable bargains) as either incidental and irrelevant, or as there only to prevent restitution being too readily given.[87] The latter of course, begs the question: why is contractual invalidity and restitution according to the proclaimed defective consent baseline would be "too much"? The answer, *sub silentio*, is that "other" principles such as responsibility in contract formation and protection of the enforcer's reasonable expectations must also be factored into the equation.

On the other hand, where the scope of relief appears over-inclusive against the defective consent baseline, consent theorists advocate its contraction by rejecting or downgrading the relevance of other relief-yielding concerns. For example, the court's evident concern with substantive unfairness is rejected as illegitimate or relegated as mere evidence of defective consent.[88] Fried describes a general unconscionability doctrine as "two parts sentiment and one part common sense,"[89] and Birks, again, explains the concern with substantive unfairness as there only to avoid "being too ready to order restitution."[90] Again, this begs the question that the "other" factors answer.

Insofar as this approach advocates a rejection of "other" factors, it offers a critique rather than an explanation of the vitiating factors. Insofar as it downgrades the relevance of the "other" factors, it obscures the operation of important principles and proffers a distorted picture of the law.

C. Relevant but consigned to a "*ceteris paribus*" proviso

The third approach is to concede the impact of factors beyond consent in determining the legal status of contracts, but to remove or downplay their role in "contract law." At the extreme, the "if it doesn't fit, cut it out" reasoning leads to their exclusion from the scope of "contract law" altogether. Accordingly, it has been suggested that vitiating factors (and remedies for breach) are not *really* part of contract law *proper* since they are not about agreement,[91] but rather, belong to the law of unjust enrichment based on defective consent and not assisting wrongdoers,[92] or belong in the general part of law of obligations.[93] This excludes too much that is conventionally regarded as part of contract law. Contract law would be sorely deficient if it lacked the rules to determine when contracts are enforceable. Even if we agree that the vitiating factors belong to the general part of the law of obligations, it does so at a high level of generality and must still be particularized to the aims of *contract* law and the contexts in which *contracts* typically occur.

[87] Birks takes this approach to misrepresentation and duress. Birks & Chin, *On the Nature of Undue Influence*, at 80–1, 88–9.

[88] Smith, Atiyah's Introduction to the Law of Contract, at 289–99.

[89] Fried, Contract As Promise, at 105–8.

[90] Birks & Chin, *On the Nature of Undue Influence*, at 82–3.

[91] Smith, Atiyah's Introduction to the Law of Contract, at 243; Stephen A. Smith, *The Limits of Contract*, *in* Exploring Contract Law 1 (Jason Neyer et al. eds., 2009).

[92] Smith, Contract Theory, at 316.

[93] Smith, Contract Theory, at 315.

A more accommodating approach is to accept that factors beyond consent *are* part of contract law and concede that they are not generated by the voluntariness principle, but give them a supplementary or residual role, to be performed only when the consent principle runs out;[94] when we do not know what the parties intended in the circumstances that have occurred. Thus Fried concedes that there *are* gaps in contracts, which can be filled with "residual general principles of law" (such as compensation for harm, restitution of benefits, loss sharing in respect of common enterprises,[95] civility, altruism, and humanity).[96] Fried claims that none of these contradicts the consent principle since "the parties are quite free to control the meaning and extent of their relation by the contract itself."[97]

This reasoning conceals a good deal of importance. The identification of "gaps" depends very much on the question being asked. There are no gaps if the question is simply "what did the parties undertake to do or not to do?" but much more likely if the question is "what did they agree should happen *if x and y occurs*?" The real issue is why *x* or *y* are singled out as legally significant; they determine whether the undertakings are enforceable *irrespective* of *x* or *y* (the losses lie where they fall), or become unenforceable *because* of *x* or *y* since the parties' failure to deal with these circumstances *creates* "gaps" for the operation of the residual principles. It becomes impossible to hold the line that the residual principles are operating in a supplementary fashion. Indeed, Fried recognizes that the objective test may hold parties to liabilities despite lack of actual (subjective) consent in order to facilitate care in contract formation, discourage fraudulent claims, and overcome the evidential problems in determining the parties' state of mind.[98]

The third approach openly recognizes that voluntariness, while having a core position in contract law, is not the only value legitimately accommodated in a liberal society, and indeed, may be trumped by other values in some circumstances.[99] Nevertheless, the serious and detailed normative discussions are heavily concentrated on the master principle of voluntariness, relegating the operation of "other" principles to "bit parts." The emphasis is on the master principle qualified by the expression "all things being equal"—this is the standard *ceteris paribus* "get-out." It amounts to saying that "*voluntariness rules*, unless it doesn't, other things being important." It is true, but only trivially so.

The *ceteris paribus* proviso conceals a conceptual "blank spot." Conceding the role of "other" principles, but leaving them insufficiently specified or analyzed, implies that they are not important enough to warrant such analysis in the normative account of contract liability. At the same time, it undermines the explanatory power of the voluntariness principle, which becomes merely one element in the normative account of contractual liability. Without explicitly identifying and justifying the relevant

[94] Fried, Contract As Promise, at 60, 63.

[95] Fried, Contract As Promise, at 69–70.

[96] Fried, Contract As Promise, at 109–10.

[97] Fried, Contract As Promise, at 73.

[98] Fried, Contract As Promise, at 62–3.

[99] E.g., Fried, Contract As Promise, at 62–3; Thomas Hill Green, *Liberal Legislation and Freedom of Contract*, *in* Lectures on the Principles of Political Obligation (Paul Harris & John Morrow eds., 1986); Dori Kimel, *Neutrality, Autonomy, and Freedom of Contract*, in From Promise to Contract ch. 5 (2003).

principles, and determining their relationship to the voluntariness principle, free appeal to them looks more like an *ex post* rationalization of contract law rules than a philosophical justification of them. This variant of the orthodox account of vitiating factors is not wrong so much as that it is not right enough. It runs out of steam, and paints an incomplete picture of what is in play; it depends on a proper analysis, *which has yet to be done.*

That analysis has two parts. First, we need to create the conceptual space for considering the "other" principles. Second, we need to consider how the factors in play may interact with the master principle.

IV. Creating the Conceptual Space for "Other" Principles: Defeasibility

The consent-bound approaches are manifestations of the intellectual hegemony of the idea that legal concepts should be capable of definition through a set of necessary and sufficient conditions. This yields the basic form of legal rules: "if *X* (legally defined facts, e.g., offer, acceptance, consideration, certainty and intention to create legal relations), then *Y* (the legally defined consequences, e.g., contractual rights and liabilities)." If consent is required for a valid contract, then absent consent, no valid contract ensures. This one-step, closed, formalist reasoning responds to the internal demand of law for legitimacy through consistency and coherence. But, taken to extreme, it does so at the expense of justice and transparency.

Hart[100] notes the "obstinate loyalty to the persuasive but misleading logical ideal that all concepts must be capable of definition through a set of necessary and sufficient conditions." He describes the line of reasoning that since consent gets you into contract, only lack of consent will get you out[101] as "a disastrous over-simplification and distortion" of the law governing the *vitiation* of transactions. It fails to recognize that the validity of a transaction is a *two-stage* inquiry, so that even when the language of consent is used in determining both the formation and vitiation stages, they deal with *qualitatively different* concerns.[102] In truth, all legal rules are a set of *presumptively* (or ordinarily) necessary and sufficient conditions that are *defeasible* in some circumstances. Applied to the validity of contracts, it means that a contract is presumptively valid if it satisfies the requirements of formation at stage one (including consent), *unless*, at stage two, the vitiating factors (invoking other values) operate to defeat it.

Evidence for defeasibility as a general feature of law is abundant. First, "[a]ll laws admit certain cases of just excuse;"[103] even expressed exceptions may be overridden in a particular case on grounds of mercy, justice, equity, purpose, or rights.[104] Common law rules are subject to equity and it "is the office of equity, to support and protect the common law from shifts and crafty contrivances against the justice of the law. Equity therefore does not destroy the law, nor create it, but assist [*sic*] it."[105] Unless ossified,

[100] Hart, *The Ascription of Responsibility and Rights*, at 173, 177–8.
[101] Hart, *The Ascription of Responsibility and Rights*, at 183.
[102] Hart, *The Ascription of Responsibility and Rights*, at 174–6.
[103] *Moore v. Hussey*, (1609) 80 Eng. Rep. 243 (K.B.) 246 (U.K.).
[104] Richard H. S. Tur, *Defeasibilism*, 21 O.J.L.S. 355, 361 (2001).
[105] *Dudley v. Dudley*, (1705) 24 Eng. Rep. 118 (Ch.) 119 (U.K.).

and denatured, equity resists closure. In Lord Denning's words: "If the law should be in danger of doing injustice, then equity should be called in to remedy it. Equity was introduced to mitigate the rigor of the law."[106] Moreover, it "is not past the age of child-bearing."[107]

Second, judges apply "policy" overrides. For example, policy has replaced equity as the open-ended category of defeasance in the English law of negligence. Lord Atkin's famous "neighbour principle"[108] measured by foreseeability and proximity establishes a duty subject to any countervailing policies that negative, reduce, or limit the scope of the duty or the class of persons to whom it is owed.[109] Later addition of the requirement that the duty itself should be "fair, just and reasonable"[110] merely imbeds the stage-two policy decisions in the definitional elements at stage one. The good faith override in continental civilian contract law manifests the same defeasibility structure, as do the principles of construction, which allow deviation from the ordinary interpretation of words when it is clear that "something has gone wrong with the language used" or where it would lead to very unreasonable results.[111] The structure of defeasibility explains the distinction made in criminal law between the definitional elements of the offense, and the defenses. The defenses come into play, if at all, only after the definitional elements are satisfied.

The justifications for this defeasibility structure are substantive and pragmatic in nature. The open-ended character of defeasibility relates to the omnipresence of the unforeseen in human activity, and to the ever-present possibility of judicial development of legal principles and values in the light of the accidents thrown up by life and litigation.[112] If we were to attempt to write down all the exceptions to statutory rules, we could not be confident of listing every necessary and sufficient condition for the validity of a determination. The limits of foresight and available information means that rules can never give complete certainty; this is what makes for "hard cases."

Even if it were possible to spell out every conceivable precondition of validity, it may be unhelpful to do so because there is a limit to the amount of detail you can write into a rule and still maintain sufficient clarity and intelligibility. There is an infinite variety of possible circumstances triggering the interaction of different parts of the law, but rules, principles, and values can only be stated in general terms. The common law routinely distinguishes between ordinary run-of-the-mill cases and exceptional or unusual ones. This allows the law to "transcend closure without embracing absolute discretion"[113] by reference to a structure that "accommodates both regularity and (independent) particularity."[114] In a mature and well-structured legal system, the defeasibility factors will be identified and expressed but they can never be completely closed. This preserves continuity and certainty while permitting legal evolution.

[106] *Re Vandervell's Trusts (No. 2)*, [1974] 1 Ch. 269 (C.A.) 322 (U.K.).

[107] *Eves v. Eves*, [1975] 1 W.L.R. 1338 (C.A.) 1341 (U.K.).

[108] *M'Alister v. Stevenson*, [1932] A.C. 562 (H.L.) 580 (appeal taken from Scot.) (U.K.).

[109] *Home Office v. Dorset Yacht Co.*, [1970] A.C. 1004 (H.L.) 1027 (appeal taken from Eng.) (U.K.).

[110] *Caparo Indus. v. Dickman*, [1990] 2 A.C. 605 (H.L.) 617–18 (appeal taken from Eng.) (U.K.).

[111] *Investors Compensation Scheme v. W. Bromwich Bldg. Soc'y (No. 1)*, [1998] 1 W.L.R. 896 (H.L.) 912–14 (appeal taken from Eng.) (U.K.).

[112] Neil McCormick, *Law as an Institutional Fact*, 90 L.Q.R. 102, 125 (1974).

[113] Tur, *Defeasibilism*, at 360.

[114] Bruce Chapman, *Law Games: Defeasible Rules and Revisable Rationality*, 17 L. & PHIL. 480 (1998).

Moreover, as a matter of procedural justice, it would be unfair to require the enforcer to prove both the positive conditions of the claim, and also to imagine and disprove all possible legal defeating conditions that might negate the claim. This would not only be expensive and time consuming for little return in the general run of cases, it would also require information that the enforcer may not be aware of (e.g. in cases of incapacity, impairment, or mistake). It makes sense for the enforcer to prove the positive conditions of her claim, leaving it up to the complainant to raise any objections to it.

This conceptual sequencing of the enforceability question contributes to the certainty and integrity of the rule of law by reducing the incidence of unacceptable outcomes attendant on closed rule-based reasoning, without going to the other extreme of open-ended discretion. It expresses the law's compromise between the need for security and the need to uphold principles of deep importance in a given view of socio-legal order. The values deployed in the override phase are not external to the law, but are values inherent in the law, which are imperfectly captured in closed-rule-based reasoning.

V. The Relationship between Relevant Principles

This chapter challenges the hegemony of the defective consent approach to vitiating factors, and creates the conceptual space for the operation of other justified concerns. Public policy and administrability apply to any area of law. Responsibility in contract formation, refusal to assist wrongdoers or exploiters, and protection of vulnerable parties from harsh outcomes are evident elsewhere in contract law and in private law in general. They are normatively justified (or at least heavily fought over) in political theory, and reflect the oft-observed tension in contract law between the intention of the parties, fairness, and certainty.

While I have criticized the excessive abstraction, reductionism, and simplification of the orthodox approach, recognition of the existence of multiple operative principles brings its own problems; foremost being how the various values interact with each other. One approach is to treat them as conflicting and jostling for position.[115] Accordingly, the vitiating factors designate when the complainant's voluntary consent (the positive reason for enforcement) is outweighed by one or more of the reasons against enforcement. On this view, contract law reflects the legal system's practical compromises over a multiplicity of values, and goals, contains apparent contradictions, is subject to competing norms and exceptions, and is fragmented by special rules applying to distinct kinds of contracts (e.g., commercial versus noncommercial or consumer). After all, it would be unrealistic to expect one unified theory to explain every aspect of a contract law that has evolved over hundreds of years through the hands of many individuals. At the core of contract law is a conflict between private ordering-based individual freedom, and public ordering by the state, in the name of

[115] *See* Robert Hillman, The Richness of Contract Law: An Analysis and Critique of Contemporary Theories of Contract Law (repr. ed., 1998); Stephen Waddams, Dimensions of Private Law: Categories and Concepts in Anglo-American Legal Reasoning (2003); John N. Adams & Roger Brownsword, *The Ideologies of Contract Law*, 7 Legal Stud. 205 (1987).

paternalism, and community interests, which infringes that freedom.[116] This approach is vulnerable to accusations of being anti-theoretical and unacceptably indeterminate; a largely ad hoc and unstable mix[117] that compromises contract law as a distinct legal domain; or overrides the concern for personal autonomy instantiated in the institution of contract.

An alternative to conflict and compromise is *integration and coherence*. Many of the "other" principles bearing on the practice of contract are either *inherent to that practice or intersect with it in such a way as to generate meaningful limits*. The issue is one of definition and degree. Conflict becomes inevitable if the content of each principle is taken to extreme: if "voluntariness" is defined as negative freedom to agree anything; if "responsibility in contract formation" renders irrelevant any impairment in bargaining power, howsoever caused; if "nonexploitation" requires acting in the other's interest analogous to a fiduciary duty; if "exploitation" describes *any* disparity in the values exchanged, irrespective of individual choices. On these extreme definitions, where several principles are in play, we *can* only give effect to one at the cost of one or more of the others; it implies that *we lose something of value* when compromises or tradeoffs are made.

However, these definitions are not inevitable. Liberty, responsibility, exploitation, fairness, and other such concepts are *interpretive* concepts.[118] Their scope depends on their importance to *human* concerns, ambitions, and needs in the activity of contracting. On this view, the apparent conflict between the values turns out to be largely illusory because the relevant concepts are complementary, drawing on one another, and not in conflict.

For example, in Raz's[119] influential work, the state's primary duty in "autonomy-respecting cultures" is to promote, protect, and foster the autonomy of all citizens. But crucially, this does not require or justify the upholding of all voluntary undertakings since the value of autonomy depends on the worthiness of its exercise. Autonomously undertaking something repugnant is worse than being compelled to undertake it. The law need not empower individuals to make through contracts arrangements that we would not otherwise want them to make. It should only facilitate undertakings that fall within the spectrum of obligations that is morally permissible for individuals to assume. The value of autonomy dictates that the law should err on the side of permissiveness and give a wide margin of tolerance to the conception of the worthwhile.[120]

On this view, the state has no duty of neutrality between all options. The autonomy principle "permits and even requires government to create and support morally valuable opportunities, and to eliminate or discourage repugnant ones."[121] The state's proper role is not limited to that of guaranteeing a neutral framework within which citizens are left to make their own choices. The emphasis is less on the individual's right to be free *from* interference, than on the right to be free *to* pursue "acceptable and

[116] Clare Dalton, *An Essay in the Deconstruction of Contract Doctrine*, 94 Yale L.J. 997, 1010 (1985).

[117] Jay M. Feinman, *The Significance of Contract Theory*, 58 U. Cin. L. Rev. 1283 (1990).

[118] *See* Dworkin, Taking Rights Seriously.

[119] Raz, Morality of Freedom.

[120] State action should be confined "to matters which command a large measure of social consensus." Raz, Morality of Freedom, at 381, 419, 427.

[121] Raz, Morality of Freedom, at 417.

valuable projects and relationships."[122] This contrasts with the type of individualism that would enforce a promise, independent of its social context, "as manifestations of the sovereign will of a monadic individual."[123] It denies that a person can bind herself just because she intends to or that all the normative consequences of a promise are to be found in the promisor's intention.

The law's concern with the "other" identified concerns can then be interpreted in a way that *complements* and *interlocks* with the concern to promote this conception of autonomy. Thus, for example, the concern to support the autonomy-enhancing institution of contract (taking account of the context in which the practice occurs, and generally reflecting its social conventions, norms, and intuitions)[124] *complements* rather than conflicts with the concern to ensure responsibility in contract formation, and the refusal to assist a wrongdoer or exploiter. The law's refusal to facilitate undertakings that can unduly reduce an individual's future autonomy *complements* the protection of vulnerable complainants from harsh outcomes.[125] These involve no necessary conflict with respect for autonomy if the latter does not demand the legal enforcement of every voluntary undertaking, regardless of content and implications.

However, the problems of pluralism cannot be wholly resolved by reference to a positive conception of freedom. Not everything that is valuable for human beings is worthwhile only because it enhances their autonomy. The promotion of some values and goals (e.g., protecting the environment, or promoting equality and distributive justice), or the prevention of some undesirable occurrences (e.g., trading with the enemy) or repugnant undertakings (e.g., drug dealing, exemption of liability for death) may justify actions that reduce freedom however conceived. At the same time, the value of negative freedom, which is inherent in the very idea of contract, will push back the scope of: impermissible exploitation, protection of the vulnerable, operative public policy, and the demands of the administration of justice.

Thus, while the different values may draw on and complement each other, no algorithm or abstract formula will provide the answer of how these complex principles interact. A moral judgment is required in each case. Inevitably, there will be disagreement about the precise scope of the principles in play and how they should be weighted in different circumstances. Moreover, the answers will vary over time, and from community to community. This is unsurprising when we are dealing with the social practice of contract. The important point is that the principles in play are neither unitary nor unlimited. They are limited in number, morally and practically justified, largely complement and draw from one another, and operate at stage two to defeat an otherwise valid contract.

Conclusion

It may be argued that all this is merely a matter of labeling; that so long as we understand "defective consent" as a fig leaf for the variety of factors and principles embodied in the vitiating factors, no change is necessary. Three responses can be made to

[122] Raz, Morality of Freedom, at 417. [123] Raz, *Promises in Morality and Law*, at 931–2.

[124] Raz, *Promises in Morality and Law*, at 934, 938.

[125] And some contracts that are illegal or against public policy (e.g. slavery, unreasonable restraints of trade).

this. First, while this is recognized by some,[126] the prevalence of the orthodox defective consent view in judgments and texts shows that it still has a strong hold on the collective understanding of the nature of vitiating contracts. The normative distortion of overemphasizing the complainant's defective consent must be redressed by making conceptual space for the operation of other important values. The proper understanding and principled development of the law require us to say what we mean. Doing so enhances transparency by bringing all the relevant principles and values out into the open. Instead of their posing as questions of fact under the cover of a vague, bloated, and, at times, denatured concept of consent, the pluralist defeasibility approach describes the appropriate sequence of reasoning, and sharpens the focus on the identity of operative principles and their interrelationship with the autonomy principle which individuates the legal domain of contract.

Second, the pluralistic defeasibility approach provides much better fit with the details of the law. It explains why vitiating factors do not necessarily result in no contract being made, as the logic of defective consent would dictate, but instead, generally render contracts voidable, leaving the complainant with the choice of rescinding or affirming the contract. Indeed, a more open recognition that the issue goes beyond that of qualifying consent would license a more flexible approach to the remedial consequences of vitiating factors, tailoring them to the reason/s for the invalidity. It would explain why salvage cases result in an adjustment downwards of the extortionate price charged,[127] and why rescission for nonfraudulent misrepresentation can be barred and damages awarded in lieu, where it is equitable to do so.[128]

Third, the defeasibility approach explains the burden of proof and affirms human responsibility. The enforcing party proves the conditions of liability at stage one, which stands unless the complainant can defeat it at stage two. The defeasibility structure goes beyond procedural fairness to the enforcer and the practicalities and ebb and flow of arguments in an adversarial system. It also reflects and affirms the importance of the human faculties of reason, responsibility, and speech. An agent's denial of consent is a denial of responsibility for her action in entering the contract; if there is *really* no consent and no responsibility, there is nothing to explain. Instead, responsible agents own their actions and affirm their rational competence by answering for, rather than denying, them. It is natural for human beings to want to stand up for their own reasonableness and to be judged accordingly. This is part of preserving one's self-respect. The justifications and excuses embodied in the two-step approach allow one to hold one's head up high in a way that denials of responsibility do not.[129]

The attempt to impose analytical rigor and a "pleasing uniformity of pattern"[130] can tempt us to take abstraction and reductionism too far. This chapter has identified the factors and underlying principles in play beyond consent, most notably: responsibility

[126] *See, e.g.*, John Cartwright, Unequal Bargaining: A Study of Vitiating Factors in the Formation of Contracts (1991); Collins, The Law of Contract (4th ed., 2003); Ewan McKendrick, Contract Law (rev. 9th ed., 2011); Trebilcock, Limits of Freedom of Contract.

[127] *E.g.*, *The Port Caledonia & the Anna*, [1903] P. 184 (U.K.).

[128] Misrepresentation Act, 1967, c. 7, § 2(2) (Eng. & Wales).

[129] John Gardner, *The Mark of Responsibility*, *in* Offences and Defences: Selected Essays in the Philosophy of Criminal Law 177, 180–2 (2007).

[130] Hart, The Concept of Law, at 37.

in contract formation, nonexploitation and protection of vulnerable parties against harsh outcomes. In a mature and well-structured legal system, the defeasibility factors will be identified and expressed but they can never be completely closed. The well-worn techniques deployed to square these principles with the consent-bound approach lose sight of their force or fail to take them seriously. This chapter is an admonition against extremism and a defence of an integrated, complementary and limited pluralism. However, the latter approach should not itself be tempted into extremism, to jump from one oversimplistic position to another; positive autonomy can only take us so far. It cannot eliminate all uncertainty nor generate all the answers from the paradigmatic value of personal freedom, but it gets us closer and more transparently to the truth.

16

Mitigation, Fairness, and Contract Law

*George Letsas & Prince Saprai**

I. Mitigation and Loss Sharing

A. Failure to act

Consider the following case:

> I. A promises B to drive him to the airport but he fails to turn up.

Few would deny that A has breached a moral duty owed to B, and that A has secondary obligations towards B as a result of that breach. At the very least, A has a duty to apologize and to express regret. This is so whether or not B suffers loss as a result of the breach. But now let's assume that the promisee has suffered loss:

> II. A promises B to drive him to the airport but he fails to turn up. B misses his flight, which costs him £1,000.

Do A's secondary obligations include the duty to cover the promisee's loss? Again, few would deny that, *other things being equal*, A is responsible for B's loss. But what if things are not equal? Consider this case:

> III. A promises B to drive him to the airport but he fails to turn up. B can take a £50 cab to the airport and make the flight. However, he chooses to do nothing and he misses the flight, which costs him £1,000.

Is A responsible for the whole of B's loss in this case? It seems far less clear that he is, because B could have easily made his flight by taking the cab. Let's stipulate that it makes no difference to B whether A drives him or whether he takes a cab. What seems to be important here is that the promisee can *easily* bring about the same state of affairs that A was under a promissory obligation to bring about. Had he done so, he would also have avoided the loss that would have occurred if he did nothing. This can be shown by contrasting III with cases where it is *difficult* for the promisee to bring about the promised state of affairs. Consider the following case:

> IV. A promises B to drive him to the airport but he fails to turn up. B can only get a cab by doing a two-hour walk (he lives in a remote location). He chooses to do nothing and he misses the flight, which costs him £1,000.

* Drafts of this chapter were presented to The Philosophical Foundations of Contract Law conference at University College London (2013), and to the U.C.L. Private Law Group Workshop (2014). Thank you to participants on both of these occasions for invaluable feedback. Special thanks to Rob Chambers,

Here it is clear that A does have to cover the cost of the flight. Although B could have brought about the same state of affairs that A promised, doing so would have been burdensome for B. It would have required him to undertake a two-hour walk. Moreover, we would not take a different view if the cost of the flight were to be substantially higher (say £10,000). The two-hour walk would not become less burdensome, the higher the cost of the flight. A two-hour walk is an unreasonable means of bringing about the promised state of affairs regardless of the size of the loss that would be avoided. By unreasonable we simply mean that this is not an alternative that most people would expect to take, given the nature of the promised performance and the effect that taking the alternative would normally have on people's plans. Even if the promisee were a marathon runner, for whom a two-hour walk is a piece of cake, it would still count as a burden since it is not a substitute that most people would expect to use for getting to the airport. Our notion of burdensomeness is, therefore, agent-neutral.[1]

This suggests that the operative principle here is not efficiency, since efficiency would require comparing the cost of walking, which we should quantify, with the cost of alternatives, including the alternative in which the promisee does nothing and suffers loss. Efficiency would *require* the promisee to walk, if walking was the most cost-effective option, or would impose the cost of any losses on him if he chose not to walk.

Still, there will be cases where the alternative way of securing performance is not at all burdensome, but its cost exceeds the cost of the losses that would otherwise flow from the breach. Consider this case:

> V. A promises B to drive him to the airport but he fails to turn up. The only way B could have made the flight was by hiring a £10,000 helicopter to take him to the airport. B chooses to do nothing, and misses the flight which costs him £1,000.

Here, the existence of an alternative way to secure performance whose cost exceeds the cost of the losses that flow from the breach, does not affect the responsibility of the promisor. So, the size of the loss appears to have some relevance for determining the responsibility of the promisor.

Cases I–V support the following mitigation principle:

> MP1: When a promise is broken, AND (1) there is an alternative way to secure the state affairs promised by the promisor, AND (2) it does not matter to the promisee whether the promisor or someone else performs, AND (3) the promisee can easily take that alternative, AND (4) the cost of that alternative does not exceed the loss

Andrew Dyson, Dori Kimel, Greg Klass, Daniel Markovits, Ben Mcfarlane, Charles Mitchell, Paul Mitchell, James Penner, Solène Rowan, Irit Samet, and James Shirley for their comments. We also thank Lord Lawrence Collins, Riz Mokal, and Seana Shiffrin for discussing some of the issues that this chapter raises with us. The usual caveat applies.

[1] Our approach may be conceived of as majoritarian in nature, appealing to whether the majority of people similarly situated would regard the alternative to be burdensome. Majoritarianism is often used to justify default rules in contract law. We are however not committed to standard normative justifications offered in favor of majoritarianism, such as that majoritarianism is a rule of thumb for maximizing efficiency.

that would occur if the promisee did nothing, AND (5) the promisee fails to take it, THEN the promisor is not responsible for covering the whole cost of the losses that flow from his breach.

There will also be cases however where there is no easily available alternative open to the promisee to secure the promised state of affairs, but there is an easily available means for avoiding the loss that would otherwise flow from the promisor's breach.[2] So, for example, imagine that after A's breach there was no available means for B to get to the airport, but he could easily phone the airline to cancel the flight and obtain a significant refund. This is a type of what we shall call a "pure loss avoidance" case. At the expense of completeness, but to avoid undue complexity, we will not discuss those cases here. Suffice it to say that we believe a similar mitigation principle applies in these cases, the main difference being that it refers to the promisee avoiding the loss that would be caused by the breach of promise, rather than to securing the state of affairs promised.

According to MP1, the existence of alternatives, which the promisee can easily take but fails to do so, mitigates the responsibility that the promisor has for the promisee's losses. In cases like III, the promisor is not responsible for the *entire* loss caused by his breach of duty. Surely however the promisor is not completely off the moral hook for these losses? He committed a wrong and he still has secondary obligations in relation to at least some of the losses caused by it. This leads to a loss-sharing principle:

LS1: When MP1 applies, the promisor shares some responsibility for the loss caused by the broken promise with the promisee.

MP1 mitigates the responsibility of the promisor for the loss, and LS1 requires the promisee, when MP1 applies, to share some of the responsibility for the loss caused with the promisor.

B. Action taken

So far, we have been considering cases where the promisee does *not* take an easily available alternative that would have secured the promised state of affairs. What if, however, the promisee *had* successfully taken such action?

VI. A promises B to drive him to the airport but he fails to turn up. B takes a £50 cab to the airport and makes the £1,000 flight.

Here it is clear that A is responsible to cover the cost of B's loss. After all, it is because A breached his promise that B had to take a cab. Though B would have lost £1,000 if he hadn't, his loss now is only £50. A is responsible for B's actual loss, not the loss he would have incurred had he acted otherwise. Normally one is not responsible for a loss that hasn't obtained. Few moreover would argue that A should pay B £1,000 even though he is not responsible for a loss of that amount.

[2] Thank you to Ben Mcfarlane and Seana Shiffrin for drawing our attention to these cases.

Consider now the following case:

> VII. A promises B to drive him to the airport but he fails to turn up. B could have taken a £50 cab to the airport, but instead hires a £500 chauffer-driven limousine to take him to the airport. B makes the £1,000 flight.

It seems clear that A is not responsible for the full cost of the limousine, because there was a cheaper alternative, easily available to B, to obtain the state of affairs that would have obtained had A performed his promise.

Now, consider the following case:

> VIII. A promises B to drive him to the airport but he fails to turn up. B could undertake a two-hour walk and then get a cab (he lives in remote location), but instead hires a £500 chauffer-driven limousine to take him to the airport. There were no other ways of getting to the airport on time. B makes the £1,000 flight.

Here A should cover the cost of the limousine, because it would have been burdensome for B to undertake the walk. The walk was not an easily available alternative means of securing the state of affairs that A had promised.

Cases VI–VIII suggest the following mitigation principle:

> MP2: When a promise is broken, AND (1) the promisee successfully takes action to bring about the state of affairs that would have obtained had the promise been performed, AND there was (2) an easily available, AND (3) cheaper alternative way of securing the promised performance, THEN the promisor is not responsible for covering the whole cost of the losses that flow from his breach.

A similar mitigation principle applies where it is no longer possible for the promisee to secure performance, and he takes action instead which avoids the loss that would otherwise be caused by breach. In such circumstances, the promisor's responsibility for the loss is mitigated, if there was, open to the promisee, an easily available and cheaper alternative way of avoiding that loss. So, for example, assume that after A's breach, there is no available means for B to catch the flight, but that he could easily obtain a significant refund on the price of the ticket by calling the airline to cancel the flight. Instead of calling, however, which is cheap, B hires an expensive cab to take him to the airport to cancel the ticket in person. In such circumstances, A's responsibility for the cost of the cab is mitigated. This is another type of pure loss avoidance case. To avoid making things too complex, we will not go into the detail of the mitigation principle that applies to this case.

Let's go back to the cases where the promisee takes action to secure the promised state of affairs. Consider the following case:

> IX. A promises B to drive him to the airport but he fails to turn up. The *only* way B could make the flight is by hiring a £10,000 helicopter to take him to the airport. B chooses to hire the helicopter and catches the flight on time. Had he missed the flight he would have suffered a loss of £1,000.

It is clear here that A's responsibility for the loss caused is mitigated. The promisor is not responsible for the entire cost of the course of action that the promisee took in order to secure the promised performance when the cost of that action exceeds the loss that would otherwise have been caused by breach.

This case suggests the following mitigation principle:

> MP3: When a promise is broken, AND (1) the promisee successfully takes action to bring about the state of affairs that would have obtained had the promise been performed, AND (2) the cost of the course of action taken by the promisee exceeds the loss that would have occurred had the promisee done nothing, THEN the promisor is not responsible for covering the whole cost of the losses that flow from his breach.

A similar principle exists in cases where the promisee can no longer secure the promised state of affairs, but instead takes action to avoid the loss that would otherwise be caused by breach, but the cost of that action exceeds the loss that would have occurred had the promisee done nothing. This is another type of pure loss avoidance case. Again, we will not go into the detail of these cases here.

Let's go back to cases where B *does* successfully take action to secure the promised state of affairs. We have seen that in these cases, A's responsibility for the loss caused by his breach of promise is mitigated if principle MP2 or MP3 applies.

However, in cases like VIII and IX should A be responsible for at least *some* of the loss caused to B? It seems fair that he should be. This leads to a second loss-sharing principle:

> LS2: When MP2 or MP3 apply, the promisor shares some responsibility for the loss caused by the broken promise with the promisee.

C. Summary

The MP and LS principles above tell us that when a promise is broken and loss caused to the promisee, responsibility for that loss is shared by the promisor and the promisee in three types of case. First, cases where the promisee fails to take some easily available course of action that would have secured the promised state of affairs. Second, where the promisee does successfully take action to bring about the promised state of affairs, but there was a cheaper and easily available alternative course of action that could have been taken to secure that state of affairs. Third, when the promisee does successfully take action to bring about the promised state of affairs, but the costs of that action exceed the loss that would have occurred had the promisee not acted.

So far this is all at the level of systematizing our intuitions about particular cases of breach of promise. What justifies having those intuitions and the principles to which they lead? We turn to this question in Section II.

II. Justification: Altruism vs. Fairness

In MP1, the promisee takes no action to bring about the promised state of affairs, even though he could have done so easily. According to MP1, the existence of easily available alternatives is relevant for determining the responsibility of the promisor for losses caused by his breach. MP1 however is silent on whether the promisee has a duty to take the easily available alternative. All that MP1 says is that *if* the promisee fails to take the easily available alternative, then the promisor's responsibility for the promisee's losses is mitigated. Now, one way to try and justify MP1 is to argue that the promisee has a moral *duty* to take the easily available alternative, and that breach of that duty mitigates the responsibility of the promisor. This is the view taken by Charles Fried. For Fried, the moral foundation of that duty lies in the idea of altruism: the promisee's position is analogous to that of a Good Samaritan; there is a relation of trust between the promisor and the promisee which makes "the two parties neighbors rather than strangers."[3] Fried argues that when such relations of trust hold, they give rise to duties to save the other party "from serious loss when the actor can do so with little trouble, risk of loss, or harm to himself."[4]

The logic of Fried's argument seeks to justify MP1 in two steps. First, it postulates a duty on the part of the promisee to act in order to reduce a loss for which, it is assumed, the promisor is *pro tanto* responsible. Second, it argues that the breach of that duty has the normative effect of mitigating the remedial responsibility of the promisor. Though the promisor remains responsible for the losses caused by not performing his promissory obligation, his responsibility is now outweighed, qualified, or cancelled by the fact that the promisee failed to act as a Good Samaritan.

Let's start by granting, *arguendo*, that the promisee has a duty of altruism to help the promisor by reducing the losses caused by the breach of his promissory obligation. So, let's assume that at *t1*, when A fails to turn up to drive B to the airport, B *ought* (in the sense of has a mandatory reason to) take a cab with a view to reducing the losses for which A is *pro tanto* responsible. At *t2*, the promisee has sat back and done nothing, breaching his duty to help the promisor and allowing losses to accumulate. How would the promisee's breach of his duty to help the promisor have the normative effect of altering the promisor's responsibility for the losses caused by nonperformance? The normative explanation would, we think, run as follows. Upon breaching his duty to help the promisor, the promisee would be under an obligation to do "the next best thing."[5] This normally involves putting the person to whom one owes the obligation into the position he would have been in had one not breached. In this case, had B not breached his duty to help A, i.e., had B taken a cab to make his flight, A would be responsible for the much smaller loss (£50), than the one he is now responsible for (£1,000). In order to put A in the position he would have been in had B complied with his duty of altruism, B would need to make it the case that A is responsible for £50 rather than £1,000. B can achieve this by exercising a normative power: he can waive the claim he has against B for missing the flight (a loss for which A remains responsible). So, B's secondary obligation would require him to waive his claim against A for the amount of £950.

According to the argument from the duty of altruism, the promisor is *pro tanto* responsible for the loss caused by his breach of promise but, at the same time, he has a

[3] Charles Fried, *The Convergence of Contract and Promise*, 120 HARV. L. REV. F. 1, 8 (2007).
[4] Fried, *The Convergence of Contract and Promise*, at 7–8.
[5] For the explanation why *see* Joseph Raz, *Personal Practical Conflicts*, in PRACTICAL CONFLICTS: NEW PHILOSOPHICAL ESSAYS 172 (Peter Baumann and Monika Betzler eds., 2004); and John Gardner, *What is Tort Law for? Part 1. The Place of Corrective Justice*, 30 LAW & PHILOSOPHY 1 (2011).

valid moral claim that the promisee waive his right to hold the promisor responsible for the difference between the actual loss and the one that would have occurred had the promisee complied with his duty of altruism. Both the promisor and the promisee are wrongdoers. By combining the secondary obligations they owe to each other, in virtue of their wrongdoing, we can conclude that the promisor's responsibility for the actual loss suffered is diminished and shared with the promisee, which is what MP1 and LS1 require. Moreover, the argument from the duty of altruism tells us exactly how the promisor and the promisee are to share the losses: the promisor's share of responsibility consists in the loss that would have arisen had the promisee complied with his duty of altruism. The rest of the losses stay with the promisee, as he is responsible for them.

The duty of altruism, if true, provides normative support for MP1 and LS1. It also provides normative support for MP2 and LS2, i.e., for cases where the promisee took action to bring about the promised state of affairs. Where there was an alternative course of action that the promisee could have taken to bring about the same state of affairs which was cheaper than the course taken, easily available, and not more costly than doing nothing, then the promisee is under an altruistic duty to take it. The promisee should avoid taking courses of action that needlessly impose costs on the promisor. If, in these circumstances, the promisee fails to take the cheaper alternative he is then under a duty to waive the responsibility of the promisor for the losses that accrue as a result of the promisee not taking the cheaper route. The promisor's responsibility is limited to the loss that would have arisen had the promisee taken the cheaper course of action. Finally, MP3 and LS2 would be explained as follows. When the cost of the only available action to secure the promised state of affairs exceeds the cost of inaction, the promisee has a duty of altruism not to do anything and to suffer the smaller loss. When the promisee fails to do so, taking the action that results in a loss whose cost is greater than inaction (in example IX by taking a helicopter), then he has a duty to waive his claim against the promisor by that amount which represents the loss that he could have avoided by not taking any action. The promisor's overall responsibility is then limited to the loss that would have arisen had the promisee taken no action at all. This is because the promisee having failed to comply with his altruistic duty, is now required to do the next best thing which is waive his claim to the losses that arose as a result of his failure to comply with that duty.

Many philosophers have challenged the claim that a duty of altruism exists in this context. Why should the promisee be under a duty to *help* the promisor by waiving the claim he has against him as a victim of his wrongdoing? Normally, altruistic duties to assist others hold between people who are in a special relationship like friendship, love, family, or membership of the same moral community. The idea that promises, as a matter of fact, trigger such relationships is questionable. The making of a promise may, but need not, bring the promisor closer to the promisee in terms of ethical values such as intimacy, friendship, or trust. Whether it does so is a contingent matter. Promising a stranger that I will watch his bag while he makes a phone call will not necessarily bring us closer together. I may not trust that he will return, and he may not trust that I will watch his bag.

Those who defend altruism may however have in mind a stronger, noncontingent connection between promise and the value of trust, according to which the very making of a promise invokes trust between the promisor and the promisee, thereby triggering altruistic duties of assistance, over and above the duty to perform what was promised. On this view, there is a necessary connection between the existence of a promissory obligation and the existence of a degree of trust between the promisor and the promisee.[6] The promissory obligation in part *consists* in there being a relationship of trust between two parties. For example, on Thomas Scanlon's view, there is no promissory obligation in cases where the promisee does not believe that the promisor will perform.[7] Nevertheless, even on the noncontingent account, it is not clear why the existence of trust between the promisor and the promisee should ground duties *in addition* to the duty to perform what was promised.

Moreover, there are further worries about the duty of altruism. Why should the promisor's responsibility for the losses he caused be capped by the amount of the least costly alternative available to the promisee? It seems harsh that the promisee, by failing to help the promisor, might end up shouldering the biggest part of the actual losses suffered.

Leaving aside for the moment whether the duty of altruism holds between promisor and promisee, we want to explore whether there can be an alternative justification for MP1–MP3 and LS1–LS2, which does not turn on there being a moral duty on the part of the promisee to act in a particular way, following the promisor's breach. Private lawyers sometimes say that the innocent party has no duty to mitigate but that, if he doesn't, then he loses the right to claim full damages.[8] We want to explore this intuition at the moral level.

Consider again *t1*, when the promisor has either breached or has informed the promisee that he will breach. Why would it follow, upon the fact of breach of promise, that the promisee has a duty to take a particular course of action? Surely, the promisee is free to decide that he no longer wishes to bring about the state of affairs promised. In our example, B may decide that he no longer wishes to travel but that he will not hold A responsible for his decision. Or he may decide that he now feels like taking a more expensive means of transport to the airport (a limousine), without expecting the promisor to cover it. Such decisions would not violate any duty on his part. In fact, it seems that he has a right to make these decisions. It would be odd to say that the promisee has a duty to travel, or a duty to take the cheapest means of getting to the airport. He has a right to treat himself, so to speak, as well as a right to change his preferences. What appears morally problematic is the case where the promisee decides to do those things *and* seeks to blame the promisor for the loss or claim the cost of it from the promisor. This suggests that there is a moral duty not to claim losses that the promisee

[6] We take this to be Fried's position. *See* CHARLES FRIED, CONTRACT AS PROMISE: A THEORY OF CONTRACTUAL OBLIGATION 8 (1981).

[7] THOMAS M. SCANLON, WHAT WE OWE TO EACH OTHER 312, 314 (1998) (using his famous example of the profligate pal to illustrate the point).

[8] *See, e.g.*, ROBERT STEVENS, TORTS AND RIGHTS 170 (2007). There are also plenty of judicial statements that support this view in the case law. *See, e.g.*, *Darbishire v. Warran*, [1963] 1 W.L.R. 1067 at 1075 (Eng.): "The plaintiff is not under any actual obligation to adopt the cheaper method: if he wishes to adopt the more expensive method, he is at liberty to do so and by doing so he commits no wrong against the defendant or anyone else." *See also The Solholt* [1983] 1 Lloyd's Rep. 605 at 608 (Eng.). Thank you to Andy Dyson for highlighting these case law references.

could have easily avoided, rather than a duty not to incur these losses. But what could the foundation of that moral duty be? Altruism is ruled out since altruism postulates a duty to avoid losses rather than a duty not to claim losses that one could have avoided.

We believe that the foundation lies in the principle of fairness. It would be unfair if the promisee were entitled to claim losses from the promisor that he could easily have avoided, while obtaining what was promised. A cannot complain when B fails to take a cab to the airport and misses the flight, if B makes no claim against A. He cannot tell B: "why didn't you follow through on what my promise was meant to help you achieve, when you could have done just that?" But it is unfair for B to choose to sit back and miss his flight, which he can easily make by getting a cab, *and then* blame A for it, seeking compensation. Upon passing up on less costly alternative ways of securing the promised performance that are easily available, the moral profile of the promisor and the promisee changes. The principle of fairness bars the promisee from blaming the promisor for those easily avoidable losses or claiming compensation for them, at the same time as extinguishing the promisor's responsibility for them. The promisee has no right to claim these losses and, correlatively, the promisor is not responsible for them. This is so even though the promisee was under no duty to minimize or not to exacerbate losses.

By appealing to the principle of fairness, we are availing ourselves of the well-known method of asking which normative principles people would choose if they did not know their position in the relevant normative relationship.[9] In the present case we are asking what principles promissory parties would choose if they did not know whether they are the guilty promisor or the innocent promisee. And we assume that this method may lead parties to select principles simply on the basis that they are fair and not on the basis of some other value, such as equality or efficiency.[10] In other words, the fairness-based approach is not just a heuristic device for discovering what other values require.

According to the fairness-based explanation, when passing up on less costly alternatives (as in MP1), the promisee is exercising a choice rather than suffering a loss.[11] The principle of fairness is indifferent on how the promisee exercises that choice. It simply bars a claim on the promisee's part and extinguishes part of the promisor's responsibility for losses caused following his breach. It's not the case that the promisee *assists* the promisor in any way, as the altruism-based approach suggests. This is because the cost of the choice not taken is not, from a normative standpoint, a loss for

[9] A method familiar of course in political philosophy, thanks to the work of John Rawls. *See* John Rawls, A Theory of Justice 15–19 (rev. ed., 1999).

[10] Goetz & Scott, for example, use joint-cost-minimization as a basis for determining which mitigation principle parties would select. *See* Charles J. Goetz & Robert E. Scott, *The Mitigation Principle: Toward a General Theory of Contractual Obligation*, 69 Va. L. Rev. 967, 973 (1983).

[11] It can be claimed that by exercising this choice, the promise "breaks the chain of causation" or constitutes an intervening cause. This claim relies on a common-sense notion of causation, according to which the test for whether the promisee's conduct is an intervening cause is whether his conduct is fully voluntary. But it would be a mistake to argue that the promisor is not responsible *because* the promisee has caused the relevant loss. In our view, this gets matters backwards. Whether the promisee's failure to act constitutes an intervening cause in this sense depends on the prior question of whether it is fair for the promisee to share losses with the promisor. Causation here tracks responsibility, not the other way around.

which the promisor is even *pro tanto* responsible. The promisor's position is therefore no better off if the promisee chooses action over inaction in a case like III. It is not that the promisor would be worse off if the promisee failed to take action, since if he were to do so, then the promisor would not be responsible for the loss resulting from inaction. Hence, the promisee's inaction is not a failure to assist the promisor, nor is his taking the easily available alternative a helping hand towards him. In a way, the promisee could not help the promisor even if he wanted to. If fairness is the correct normative explanation of MP1–MP3, and LS1–LS2 then mitigation has nothing to do with assistance.

We should also note here that if fairness is the correct explanation of mitigation, then the subject matter of the mitigation is the promisor's responsibility, rather than the losses caused by his breach. According to the fairness-based account, what gets mitigated when the promisee takes the easily available alternative is the promisor's responsibility for breaching his promise, rather than the losses caused as a result of the breach.

The normative explanation based on fairness has the same structure as arguments justifying estoppel. So, to use a common example, I see you building a house on my land, mistakenly thinking that the land is your own, and instead of informing you of your mistake I allow you to continue building. Although I had no duty to inform you of your mistake, it would be unfair for me to rely on my right over the land in order to benefit from what you built, say by acquiring property rights over it. Property lawyers would say that I'm estopped from relying on my property rights against you or that by not informing you I waived those rights. These are alternative ways of making the same point, namely that my failure to inform you changes our moral profiles and extinguishes rights that I would otherwise have had against you and creates new ones.[12]

III. Advantages of the Fairness-Based Approach

There are three advantages to the fairness-based explanation of mitigation. First, it explains the intuition that when a promise is broken in a case like example III above, the promisee is under no obligation to take the cab and make the flight. The promisee chose not to travel, even though he could easily have done so, and therefore is barred from claiming the cost of his choice from the promise breaker. So, by failing to take easily available alternative courses of action, the promisee does not breach a duty and hence has nothing to regret or apologize for. By contrast, on Fried's view, the promisee would have reasons to feel regret and to make an apology even when he complies with his secondary obligation to waive his claim against the promisor. This is because he ought not to have allowed the losses to accumulate in the first place.

A second advantage of the fairness-based account is that it doesn't presuppose any special duties between the promisor and the promisee. It therefore avoids all of the

[12] The argument does not rely on the property owner deriving any kind of benefit from his silence. The relevant normative concern here is not unjust enrichment. For an example in law of a successful estoppel claim even in the absence of such benefit, *see Jackson v. Cator*, [1800] 5 Ves. 688, which involved an owner remaining silent out of spite. Loughborough L.C. asked rhetorically "Is it not just as competent to the Court to prevent an injury arising from mere spite as to prevent him from doing it in order to put money in his pocket?" (at 691). Thank you to Ben Mcfarlane for the reference.

objections against Fried's account that promises do not create any special relationships between the promisor and the promisee. All that the principle of fairness requires is that promisees not claim compensation from the promisor for losses that they could have easily avoided. It's therefore compatible with many competing accounts of the nature of promissory obligation, and doesn't presuppose the view that promising creates, either contingently or intrinsically, close relationships of the kind that trigger duties of assistance.

A third advantage of this normative explanation is that it can justify mitigation in nonpromissory contexts. Mitigation and loss-sharing principles seem to apply in these contexts. Consider for example moral wrongs other than breach of promise. If you negligently injure me, and I choose not to treat my injuries even though it was easy for me to do so, then it is unfair for me to blame you for the resulting harm and seek to recover the cost from you. Here it would make no sense to argue that I have a duty of altruism towards you to reduce the extent of the harm you caused me. Though I do have a strong reason to reduce the harm you caused me, this is not because by doing so I comply with a duty I have to assist you. Duties of assistance arise only when there is a special or close relationship between the parties, and unlike promising, one could not even begin to argue that there is a special relationship of this kind between the negligent injurer and his victim. It is interesting, though of course not in itself an argument in favor of fairness, that mitigation in tort law works no differently than in contract law.[13]

Finally, we should also like to point out that the explanation from fairness, if true, forms part of promissory morality broadly conceived. Few, if any, would equate promissory morality with the single principle that promises ought to be kept other things being equal.[14] Such equation would give an incomplete account of promissory morality given that the promise principle interacts with a multiplicity of other moral principles, for example, principles against exploitation, undue influence, unreasonable reliance, and so on. Fairness is a foundational value that is *pro tanto* relevant each and every time a promise is made and, in the context of mitigation, it changes the moral position of the parties. The application of the principle of fairness doesn't presuppose any institutional background (for example, the existence of the state or courts). Nor is it limited to a practical concern about how to shift losses caused by a breach of promise. Recall, that the principle of fairness also requires the promisee not to *blame* the promisor for losses that he could easily have avoided.

In sum, unlike the duty of altruism, the structure of the explanation from fairness is one that applies to all cases where there are secondary obligations arising out of the breach of a primary obligation. It qualifies or cancels part of the wrongdoer's responsibility for the loss caused by his breach. Unlike the duty of altruism, it construes cases of failure to avoid losses as a choice on the part of the innocent party rather than as a

[13] *McAuley v. London Transport Executive*, [1957] 2 Lloyd's Rep. 500 (Eng.) (worker's injury to hand resulting from employer's negligence, but worker's unreasonable failure to get medical treatment meant that employer not responsible for loss that could have been avoided; worker could have avoided loss of earnings from point when injured hand would have recovered from medical intervention).

[14] It is a common misreading of Fried to think that he held this view. *See* Fried, *Convergence*, at 7.

breach of a duty. In that respect, it offers a more direct normative justification for principles MP1–MP3 and LS1–LS2, than the duty of altruism. What we aim to do now is show that, by and large, contract law satisfies these mitigation and loss sharing principles.

IV. Contract Law

The mitigation and loss-sharing principles that we find in morality are also present in the common law mitigation doctrine. When a contract is broken, the legal responsibility of the promisor for any loss caused by his breach is mitigated in two types of case. First, there are those cases that Andrew Burrows describes as cases of "unreasonable inaction." These are cases where the promisee is precluded from recovering any losses from the promisor that the promisee "could reasonably have avoided but has failed to avoid."[15] Second, there are cases where the claimant takes "unreasonable action" in avoiding losses caused by a breach of promise. The claimant cannot recover for expenses unreasonably incurred.

According to the common law doctrine, the promisor's responsibility for loss is limited to the losses that the promisee would have suffered had the promisee taken reasonable action to bring about the state of affairs that would have obtained had the contract been performed.

Burrows, as well as the other leading contract lawyers,[16] says that whether reasonable steps should have been taken "depends on the particular facts in question."[17] When lawyers say that this determination is a matter of fact, we are unclear about what exactly this means. If it means that it is an extralegal or purely factual question, and that no underlying legal principle determines whether or not the promisor's responsibility for loss in cases of this type is mitigated, then we disagree. If, on the other hand, the claim is that there is an underlying legal principle, but that we have to look at the facts of a particular case to determine whether the conditions for the application of that principle are satisfied, then we agree.[18] We think that the cases clearly demonstrate that the courts apply the mitigation and loss-sharing principles that we find in morality to determine at least in part the responsibility of the promisor for the loss caused by his breach of contract.

A. Unreasonable inaction

Recall, that we claim that in cases where the promisee has failed to act, the promisor's responsibility for the loss caused by breach is shared if the promisee could have taken

[15] Andrew Burrows, Remedies for Torts and Breach of Contract 122 (3d ed., 2004). Burrows cites for this proposition Viscount Haldane L.C.'s classic statement of the principle in *British Westinghouse Elec. v. Underground Elec. Ry. Co. of London*, [1912] A.C. 673. The law, said Haldane, "imposes on a plaintiff the duty of taking all reasonable steps to mitigate the loss consequent on the breach and debars him from claiming any part of the damage which is due to his neglect to take such steps" (at 689).

[16] *See, e.g.*, Mindy Chen-Wishart, Contract Law 510 (4th ed., 2012); and Ewan McKendrick, Contract Law: Text, Cases, and Materials 895 (5th ed., 2012).

[17] Burrows, Remedies, at 123.

[18] There is reason to think that Burrows does mean the latter. He says that examination of the cases demonstrates the presence of certain factors which are relevant to the question of whether the promisor's responsibility for the loss should be mitigated. Burrows, Remedies, at 123.

an easily available alternative course of action to secure the promised state of affairs (assuming that the cost of taking that alternative does not exceed the loss that results from the promisee's inaction). It is *unfair* for the promisee to place the entire burden of this loss on the promisor's doorstep. We will now show that this principle, or to be more accurate combination of principles MP1 and LS1, explains the legal cases where responsibility was shared from those where it wasn't.

Take, for example, the case of *Payzu Ltd. v Saunders*.[19] The defendant in breach of contract refused to deliver silk in installments to the claimants unless the claimants agreed to pay cash on delivery of each installment. The claimants declined these terms, and instead brought an action for breach of contract claiming the difference between the contract and market price of the silk. The market price of the silk had risen. The Court of Appeal, however, held that the defendant did not have to pay the difference, because the claimants should have accepted the defendant's offer to pay cash. Instead, the claimants were awarded damages to reflect the residual loss that they would have suffered had they accepted the offer. The defendant's responsibility was mitigated, because the claimants:

> [W]ere in fact in a position to pay cash for the goods, but instead of accepting the defendant's offer, which was made perfectly bona fide, the plaintiffs permitted themselves to sustain a large measure of loss which as prudent and reasonable people they ought to have avoided.[20]

In other words, the claimants had an easily available alternative course of action open to them for securing the state of affairs that would have obtained had the promise been performed. They had no difficulty paying cash, and that would have led to them receiving the performance due under the contract, i.e., receiving the silk.[21]

The critical issue is whether the alternative or substitute if available is *easy* for the promisee to take. This explains why the law tends to take what Tomlinson J. described as a "tender approach to those who have been placed in a predicament by a breach of contract."[22] The approach is tender, because if the alternative imposes any serious difficulty on the claimant, then the courts will not mitigate the defendant's responsibility. In such circumstances, it is not unfair for the promisee to place the burden for the loss onto the promisor. This is brought out in Scrutton L.J.'s judgment in *Payzu* when he distinguishes commercial contracts from contracts of personal service.

> In certain cases of personal service it may be unreasonable to expect a plaintiff to consider an offer from the other party who has grossly injured him; but in commercial contracts it is generally reasonable to accept an offer from the party in default. However, it is always a question of fact. About the law there is no difficulty.[23]

The reason why the defendant's responsibility is harder to mitigate in contracts of personal service is that usually it will be much more burdensome for the claimant to accept the defendant's offer to renegotiate in that context. The main reason being

19 [1919] 2 K.B. 581 (Eng.).

20 *Payzu Ltd. v Saunders*, at 586 (McCardie, J.).

21 *See also The Solholt* [1983] 1 Lloyd's Rep. 605 (Eng.) (buyer should have accepted late delivery of a ship, which was still perfectly suitable for buyer's purposes).

22 *Britvic Soft Drinks Ltd. v. Messer U.K. Ltd.* [2002] 1 Lloyd's Rep. 20 [46] (Eng.).

23 *Payzu Ltd. v Saunders* [1919] 2 K.B. 581 [589] (Eng.).

that the relationship between the parties may already have broken down, because, for example, the dismissal occurred in circumstances that were humiliating or an attack on the employee's integrity, and in that context re-employment may impose a significant burden on the claimant, who may have to continue to work with the defendant.

It is important, however, to stress Scrutton L.J.'s remark that the issue of burdensomeness is a question of fact to be determined on a case-by-case basis. There will be cases of commercial contracts where renegotiation would be burdensome,[24] and cases of personal service contracts where it would not be.[25] Scrutton L.J. is just making the point that, as a general rule, renegotiation is likely to be easier in a commercial, rather than personal service, context. The underlying principle is that mitigation of the defendant's responsibility for the loss depends on whether the claimant had an *easily* available alternative way of securing the promised performance.

A personal service case where the defendant's responsibility was not mitigated by an offer to renegotiate and which illustrates the application of this principle is the decision of Blain J. in *Yetton v. Eastwoods Froy Ltd.*[26] The managing director of a company was wrongfully dismissed by his employer, and then offered re-employment as an assistant managing director by the same company. The claimant's refusal to accept the offer did not reduce the defendant's liability. Blain J. stated the principle on which the case rested as follows:

> [T]he opportunity to reduce damages by finding reasonable (I repeat reasonable) alternative employment should be taken and, indeed, sought, whether such employment is by the same defaulting employer or by someone else; in either case the test being whether it is reasonable to refuse it or not in the circumstances of each case.[27]

This is the same principle that underpinned the decision in *Payzu*. The key issue was whether it was reasonable to expect the claimant to accept the revised terms offered. Blain J. repeated the point made by Scrutton L.J. in *Payzu* that renegotiation with the defendant may be much more of a burden in the context of an employment contract:

> [P]ersonal factors clearly are more likely to be of weight or are likely to be of greater weight in cases of personal services than in (for want of a better word) what I call soulless cases of sale of goods contracts where money may often be the only important factor.[28]

On the facts, Blain J. decided that it was not unreasonable for the claimant to refuse the offer. Key to this finding was that the new job offered by the defendant to the claimant was a significant step down from the position the employee had occupied, and that relations between the parties had broken down to such an extent that it

[24] So, for example, the claimant does not in a sale of goods context have to accept goods of a lower quality. *Heaven & Kesterton Ltd. v. Et Francois Albiac & Cie* [1956] 2 Lloyd's Rep. 316 (Eng.).

[25] *Bruce v. Calder* [1895] 2 K.B. 581 [589] (Eng.).

[26] [1967] 1 W.L.R. 104 (Eng.).

[27] *Yetton v. Eastwoods Froy Ltd.*, at 115.

[28] *Yetton v. Eastwoods Froy Ltd.*, at 118.

was unclear how they could now work together. It is clear from the decision that requiring the claimant to accept the offer would have imposed a significant burden on him.

B. Unreasonable action

Remember, that when considering the moral position we claimed that the promisor's responsibility for the loss caused by his breach of promise is shared in cases where the promisee successfully takes action after breach to bring about the promised state of affairs, but the promisee could have taken an alternative course of action to obtain that same state affairs which was easily available and cheaper than the course of action actually taken by the promisee.

This principle, or to be more accurate combination of principles MP2 and LS2, we believe, explains the decisions reached in the contract cases where the promisee takes action to secure the promised state of affairs. The common law rule is that the promisee cannot recover expenses that were unreasonably incurred, and the promisor's liability is capped at the loss that would have arisen had the promisee acted reasonably in bringing about the promised state of affairs.

The MP2 principle identified earlier determines when the courts find the promisee's action in these legal cases unreasonable. Take, for example, the case of *The Borag*,[29] where the claimant shipowners took out a very high interest rate loan in order to secure the release of a ship wrongfully detained, because of a breach of contract by the ship managers. Lord Templeman L.J. in his judgment said on the issue of mitigation that the ship managers were not liable to cover the expenses associated with the high interest loan, because the shipowners had easily available to them cheaper alternative ways of securing the release of the ship:

> [T]he owners could and should have adopted a form of mitigation which was reasonable either by refusing to pay the interest charges to their bankers or by seeking a guarantee elsewhere or by some other available form of securing the release of the vessel more cheaply.[30]

This is a clear application of the MP2 principle that we find in morality. Given the existence of easily available and cheaper alternative methods for securing the performance, the promise breaker is not responsible for covering the entire loss caused by the breach, and it is unfair for the promisee to claim damages for that loss from the promise breaker.

The same or very similar principles are applied in cases where the promisee's actions either to secure the promised performance or, where that is no longer possible, to avoid the losses caused by the promisor's breach are held to be reasonable. So, for example, in *Britvic Soft Drinks Ltd. v Messer U.K. Ltd.*,[31] ingredients contaminated with benzene, which is carcinogenic, were supplied to a soft drinks manufacturer. It was no longer possible to secure the promised performance, and instead the manufacturer took action to reduce the consequential loss caused by

[29] [1981] 1 W.L.R. 274 (Eng.).

[30] *The Borag*, at 285.

[31] [2002] 1 Lloyd's Rep. 20 (Eng.).

the breach. In other words, this was what we described earlier as a pure loss avoidance case.[32] Even though the levels of benzene in the ingredients did not pose a risk to health, the Court of Appeal decided that the manufacturer acted reasonably in destroying and withdrawing products that contained those ingredients, because that was the *only* way to preserve its commercial reputation. The supplier was responsible for covering the costs incurred by the manufacturer.[33] There was no easily available and cheaper alternative course of action that the manufacturer could have taken to preserve its commercial reputation, and, therefore, the courts refused to mitigate the responsibility of the supplier for the loss caused, and it was fair for the manufacturer to claim damages for that loss from the supplier.

Recall that we said earlier that in cases where a promise is broken and the promisee successfully takes action to secure the state of affairs that would have obtained had the promise been performed, there is a separate moral principle which we called MP3 which mitigates the responsibility of the promisor for the loss caused where the costs of the action taken exceed the loss that would have occurred had the promisee not taken any action to bring about the state of affairs. LS2 also applies in this type of case and requires loss sharing. According to *Treitel's The Law of Contract* the common law mitigation doctrine contains a similar principle. *Treitel* formulates the principle in the following terms: "he [the promisee] should not... spend more on curing a defect in performance than the subject matter without the defect would be worth."[34]

The principle was applied in *Grant v. Dawkins and Others*.[35] The case concerned a contract for the sale of a house free from incumbrances. However, the house was subject to two mortgages. The purchaser wanted specific performance, and an order to allow him to pay off the mortgages and claim as damages any loss that exceeded the purchase price. Goff J. granted the order but said that the damages recoverable to the extent that they could not be compensated by the purchase price of the house were capped by the value of the house.[36] This is a clear application of the MP3 and LS2 principles. Responsibility for loss caused by the broken promise is shared when the promisee takes action to secure the promised state of affairs, in this case the costs of discharging the mortgages, the costs of which exceed the loss that would have been suffered by the promisee had the promisee done nothing; in this case that loss is represented by the value of the house. It was unfair, in these circumstances, for the purchaser to claim the *entire* cost of discharging the mortgages from the vendor.

[32] Strictly speaking, therefore, this is not a case where MP2 would apply, because MP2 involves cases where the promisee takes action to bring about the promised state of affairs. However, as we said in Section I.B, a similar principle to MP2 applies to cover cases of action taken to reduce or avoid consequential loss. As with MP2, central to whether the promisor's responsibility is mitigated in these pure loss avoidance cases is whether there was an easily available and cheaper alternative course of action that the promisee could have taken. The main difference is that the promisee's action in these pure loss avoidance cases relates to avoiding or reducing loss, rather than securing substitute performance.

[33] *Britvic Soft Drinks Ltd. v Messer U.K. Ltd.* [2002] 1 Lloyd's Rep. 20 [114] (Eng.).

[34] Edwin Peel, Treitel: The Law of Contract 1064–5 (13th ed., 2011).

[35] [1973] 1 W.L.R. 1406 (Eng.).

[36] *Grant v. Dawkins and Others*, at 1411.

Another example of the application of these principles is the tort case *Darbishire v. Warran*.[37] The defendant negligently damaged the claimant's car. The claimant had the car repaired and claimed the costs of repair which were £192 (minus an £80 insurance payout that he had received) and the costs of a hire car which he used while his car was being repaired as damages from the defendant. However, the costs of repairing the car exceeded the market value of the car, which was £85. The Court of Appeal declined to award the claimant the cost of repairs on the basis that "the cost of repairs greatly exceeds the value in the market of the damaged article."[38] Instead, the market value of the car and the costs of the hire car capped the sum that could be recovered. Responsibility for the loss caused by the defendant's negligence was shared between the parties.

There may be cases where due to the unique nature of the good it may be reasonable to incur the cost of securing the promised performance, even though it exceeds the market value of the good. So, for example, the cost of repairing a car was awarded in *O'Grady v. Westminster Scaffolding Ltd.*, even though they massively exceeded the market value of the car.[39] The reason was that the car in that case was unique. Before the crash that led to the car being damaged the claimant spent £300–400 per annum maintaining the car, and he had replaced the engine three times, put in new coachwork, and among other things carried out work on the wheels, the hood, and the steering column. The decision in this case is compatible with the moral principle MP3. According to that principle, the costs incurred by the promisee in securing the promised performance should not exceed the loss that would be suffered if the promisee took no action. In a case like *O'Grady*, the loss that the claimant would have suffered had he not repaired the car would have been huge given the unique nature of the car. Therefore, even though the cost of repairs exceeded the market value of the car, they did not exceed the loss that the claimant would have suffered had he not undertaken them.[40] What this case shows is that the market value of the good in question does not exhaust the value of that good to the claimant, or the loss that the claimant would suffer if the state of affairs to which he is entitled does not materialize. In such cases, the defendant is responsible for all of the losses that flow from his breach of duty. MP3 is not satisfied in cases of this kind, which is why the decision in *O'Grady* does not contradict that principle.[41]

V. The Convergence of Contract and Promise

In Section IV we argued that the doctrine of mitigation as it is found in English law satisfies principles MP1–MP3 and LS1–LS2. The fact that it does is of course no

[37] [1963] 1 W.L.R. 1067 (Eng.). [38] *Darbishire v. Warran*, at 1071.

[39] [1962] 2 Lloyd's Rep. 238 (Eng.).

[40] Lawyers distinguish between pecuniary and nonpecuniary losses. We are making the same distinction here, and clearly it is very important in morality and law to see that pecuniary loss does not exhaust the category of loss. For other examples of where this point has been made in contract law *see Ruxley Electronics and Construction Ltd. v Forsyth* [1996] A.C. 344 (Eng.), and *Farley v. Skinner* [2002] 2 A.C. 732 (Eng.).

[41] Therefore, the comparison between the cost of repairs and the market value of the good in question in *Darbishire* was too narrow. *Treitel*'s formulation which focuses on what the subject matter would be worth, not just what it is worth on the market, is broader, and captures the *O'Grady* case where the focus was on what the subject matter was worth to the promisee rather than what it was worth on the market.

argument for the merits of those principles. In Section II of this chapter, we argued that these principles are morally defensible either on the grounds of altruism or on the basis of fairness. We opted for the fairness-based explanation on the basis that, first, it explains the intuition that the promisee has no duty to reduce losses, second, it does not presuppose any special or close relationship between the promisor and the promisee, and, third, it explains why mitigation principles apply to other moral wrongs and not just promise breaking. If fairness provides support for MP1–MP3 and LS1–LS2, and the doctrine of mitigation as it exists in contract law as we have it satisfies these principles, then there is convergence between morality and contract law.

However, in recent times a number of contract theorists have argued that the doctrine of mitigation *diverges* from what promissory morality would require. This alleged divergence is welcomed by those who deny that contracts are promises, whereas it is an anathema to some who claim that contracts are promises (who we will call "promise theorists"). These promise theorists reject the mitigation doctrine and call for law reform. As mentioned already, our own view is that there is convergence between contract law and morality. Our view however differs from Fried's in that we propose the principle of fairness as the best normative justification of the doctrine, rather than altruism. In this section we want to criticize both strands of the alleged divergence since we think that their objections are directed against Fried's account of mitigation, and can be successfully met by our fairness-based account.

We will begin with the promise theorist Seana Shiffrin's critique of the mitigation doctrine. Shiffrin's argument relies on a number of premises. First, she argues that morality does not normally impose a duty on the promisee to accept alternatives. Second, when morality exceptionally requires the promisee to accept an alternative, then it is usually the promisor's duty to provide it. Third, the exceptional cases, where it might be argued that the promisee has a moral duty to avoid losses by taking alternatives, turn on a limited range of factors such as "the closeness of the relationship, the history of the relationship, the reason for breach, the reason the promisor wants to shift the burden, and how cumbersome mitigation activities would be."[42] Shiffrin finds that the doctrine of mitigation in contract law diverges from all three of these features of promissory morality. On her view, contract law imposes a *general* duty on the promisee not only to accept alternatives but also to seek them out, and to do so whether or not there are exceptional circumstances that—morally speaking—would justify a duty of assistance. She concludes that the effect of this divergence is to make the doctrine of mitigation morally objectionable. This is because it enables the promisor who commits a wrong by breaching his promise to impose a duty on the innocent promisee, the aim of which is to benefit the promise breaker, i.e., the guilty party. Why would one have a duty to help the person who wronged one? This looks morally perverse. As Shiffrin puts it: "It is morally distasteful to expect the promisee to do work that could be done by the promisor when the occasion for the work is the promisor's own wrongdoing."[43]

[42] Seana V. Shiffrin, *The Divergence of Contract and Promise*, 120 Harv. L. Rev. 708, 725 (2007).
[43] Shiffrin, *The Divergence of Contract and Promise*, at 724–5.

Critiques like Shiffrin's above are motivated by hostility towards altruism-based accounts of mitigation, of the kind that Fried offered. Shiffrin finds it "distasteful" that the innocent party should be expected to be altruistic towards the person who wronged him, particularly in cases where he did so without any excuse or justification. If there is a reason to help promise breakers, this is usually because of a moral value (for example, friendship, charity, etc.) other than promise. Fried's response is to bite the bullet and say that the promissory bond is special enough to trigger general duties of altruism, and that the more in the wrong the promisor is, the more altruistic the promisee's act of loss avoidance would be.[44]

In our view, the Shiffrin–Fried debate presupposes that the candidate normative explanation for the doctrine of mitigation is an altruistic duty on the part of the innocent promisee to help the guilty promisor. Shiffrin disputes the existence of such a duty and criticizes contract law, whereas Fried argues in favor of the duty and defends existing doctrine. But what if the candidate normative explanation is not based on altruism, but is based instead on the principle of fairness? Recall that, according to the fairness-based explanation that we put forward, the promisee has no duty to avoid losses but rather is barred from claiming damages that could have been easily avoided. Would Shiffrin's critique of the mitigation doctrine apply, were the fairness-based account correct? We do not think so.

First, contra Shiffrin, it does not follow from the existing case law that the promisee has a moral duty to avoid losses. As we have shown above, principles MP1–MP3 and LS1–LS2, which underpin existing case law, are compatible with the view that the promisee has no duty to avoid losses. In fact, the dominant reading of cases amongst private lawyers is that the so-called "duty to mitigate" is a misleading label, because no legal liability attaches when this "duty" is breached.[45] It follows that it cannot be assumed that the question of whether the doctrine of mitigation diverges from morality turns exclusively on whether the *duty* to avoid losses is morally defensible. Another possibility is that the law's position is morally defensible, without assuming the existence of a duty on the part of the promisee to avoid losses, let alone a duty based on altruism.

Second, the fairness-based account renders redundant Shiffrin's complaint that the mitigation doctrine is morally perverse. The basis of this complaint is that the promisee is under a legal duty to assist the person who has wronged him, which in moral terms is indefensible. As we argued earlier, under the fairness-based account, there is no moral duty of assistance on the part of the promisee. The promisee is morally free to sit back and not to seek alternatives. All that he is prevented from doing is to claim damages for losses he could have easily avoided. In fact, according to the fairness-based account, the promisee is unable to help the promisor even if he wanted to. If it is true that the promisor is not morally responsible for losses that the promisee could have easily avoided, then by avoiding them the promisee helps no one but himself.

[44] Fried, Contract as Promise, at 131.

[45] *See, e.g.*, Jack Beatson, Andrew Burrows & John Cartwright, Anson's Law of Contract 555 (29th ed., 2010); Chen-Wishart, Contract Law, at 509; Peel, Treitel: The Law of Contract, at 1062; Stevens, Torts and Rights, at 170.

Third, Shiffrin takes Fried to task for proliferating the circumstances in which altruistic duties to assist arise. On her view, such duties are exceptional and depend on a number of factors that go beyond the mere existence of a promise. But this complaint has no bite against the fairness-based account, which does not presuppose the existence of a special relationship between the promisor and the promisee, let alone one in which duties to assist necessarily obtain.

In sum, none of Shiffrin's objections cut against the fairness-based justification of the doctrine of mitigation. Even if she is right to dismiss altruism as a morally defensible account of the mitigation doctrine, we should not assume that altruism is the only candidate justification. Moreover, we have shown that the principle of fairness not only supports principles of mitigation of the promisor's responsibility and loss sharing at the moral level, but also explains existing doctrines and cases that would otherwise appear morally problematic.

The claim that the mitigation doctrine diverges from what interpersonal morality would require is also made by those who claim that contract law is not based on the morality of promising. So, for example, Dori Kimel has claimed, making arguments that are similar to Shiffrin's, that Fried's altruism-focused account of the mitigation doctrine is defective. First, Kimel argues that the promissory relation alone cannot explain the existence of these kinds of duties, because in the promissory context they only arise when other relational facts obtain, for example, when the parties are friends.[46] The mitigation doctrine is, however, as we saw earlier, insensitive to the presence of these facts, i.e., responsibility for loss caused by the promise breaker may be mitigated even if the only way that the parties are connected is by the promise.

Second, Kimel argues, following Atiyah, that given that altruism has a limited role in contract law, it looks incongruous that when it does make an appearance it requires the promisee to render assistance to the promisor who has wronged him.[47]

Kimel's critique of Fried's account of mitigation suggests that there is divergence between promissory morality (broadly conceived, to include other interpersonal moral principles, that interact with the promise principle) and the mitigation doctrine. However, Kimel thinks that the mitigation doctrine may nevertheless be justified. The doctrine is justified in law by the harm principle which requires the courts to refrain "from the imposition of a certain remedial duty where this could not be justified as the least demanding or restrictive way of preventing or redressing a given harm."[48] Kimel's argument is that imposing responsibility for the entire loss on the breaching party, is an "unnecessary and excessive interference with this party's freedom" in circumstances where the harm caused by the breach can be easily avoided by the innocent party.[49]

We are not going to evaluate Kimel's own account of the mitigation doctrine here. Instead, we just want to point out that the suggestion that there is divergence between law and

[46] Kimel argues that these facts do typically obtain in the promissory context, because promises are usually made in the context of ongoing relationships. DORI KIMEL, FROM PROMISE TO CONTRACT: TOWARDS A LIBERAL THEORY OF CONTRACT 110 (2003).

[47] KIMEL, FROM PROMISE TO CONTRACT, at 110–11, citing PATRICK S. ATIYAH, ESSAYS ON CONTRACT 124 (1986).

[48] KIMEL, FROM PROMISE TO CONTRACT, at 111.

[49] KIMEL, FROM PROMISE TO CONTRACT, at 111.

promissory morality here presupposes Fried's claim that the candidate moral justification for the mitigation doctrine is the duty of altruism. Kimel's objections, like Shiffrin's, that the duty of altruism cannot explain mitigation in law, have no force against our fairness-based account of the mitigation doctrine. First, our account does not require there to be a special relationship like that of friendship between the promisor and the promisee. It is sufficient for the promisee's claim to damages to be barred that he had an opportunity to easily avoid the loss. Secondly, the fairness-based account involves no incongruity. The promisee, as we have argued, is under no duty to assist the promise breaker, but rather is blocked on the basis of fairness from claiming loss that he could easily have avoided.[50]

Therefore, although the objections made by Shiffrin and Kimel to the altruism-focused justification of the mitigation doctrine may well be sound, they are insufficient to establish that there is any divergence between the law and promissory morality. In particular, those objections have no bite against the fairness-based account of the mitigation doctrine that we defend here. That account, we believe, establishes that contract doctrine is morally defensible at the level of first-order moral principles. One can justify the doctrine of mitigation without appealing to considerations that apply uniquely in the context of institutional action or the taking of coercive measures.[51] This is another way of saying that there is no divergence between what promissory morality (broadly conceived) requires and what contract law enforces.

We should end with a brief comment about the divergence/convergence debate, which has taken center-stage in contract theory in the past decade. The doctrine of mitigation, just like, for example, the doctrine of expectation damages, punitive damages, the rule against penalty clauses, and the consideration doctrine, appears to contradict the claim that the promise principle is the foundation of contract. In response to the perceived contradiction, contract theorists have reacted either by rejecting these doctrines as morally unjustifiable (like Seana Shiffrin in relation to remedies,[52] and Charles Fried in his early work with respect to the consideration doctrine),[53] or by rejecting the view that contracts are promises (like James Penner,[54] Randy Barnett,[55] and Dori Kimel).[56] We find both of these reactions too quick. What the fairness-based account of mitigation can teach us is that seemingly divergent doctrines of contract law can be justified if one considers the interaction between the promise principle and other moral principles, at the level of first-order moral reasoning. We ought to

[50] It may be that Kimel's account is compatible with our own. However, his account is distinct. Kimel relies on an aspect of political morality, to do with liberal constraints on state coercion, to justify the doctrine. We claim that an appeal to political morality is unnecessary to justify the doctrine, and that it can be justified on the grounds of what interpersonal morality requires alone. Kimel seems, at least in the promissory context, to deny this. *See* KIMEL, FROM PROMISE TO CONTRACT, at 110.

[51] Fried in his chapter for this volume is tempted now by an institutional justification for the mitigation doctrine based on considerations relating to justice and the rule of law. He claims that mitigation can be explained by reasons to minimize judicial intervention (such as cost and availability of resources). Fried says: "The objective theory advocated by Barnett, like the regime of default rules, the requirement of mitigation and much else, are practical necessities if the government is to become involved in enforcing agreements at all." Charles Fried, *The Ambitions of* Contract as Promise, *in* PHILOSOPHICAL FOUNDATIONS OF CONTRACT LAW, 17, 34 (Gregory Klass, George Letsas, & Prince Saprai eds., 2014).

[52] Shiffrin, *The Divergence of Contract and Promise*.

[53] Fried, CONTRACT AS PROMISE, at ch. 3.

[54] James E. Penner, *Voluntary Obligations and the Scope of the Law of Contract*, 2 LEGAL THEORY 325 (1996).

[55] Randy E. Barnett, *A Consent Theory of Contract*, 86 COLUM. L. REV. 269 (1986).

[56] KIMEL, FROM PROMISE TO CONTRACT.

consider the interaction between the promise principle and other first-order moral principles without assuming that the promise principle has any special role to play in that interaction.[57]

Conclusion

In conclusion, we have argued that the principles MP1–MP3 and LS1–LS2 that we identified in the first section of this chapter are morally defensible on the grounds of fairness. Fairness requires that the promisor is no longer responsible for losses that the promisee could have easily avoided. We have also argued that these principles justify contract doctrine and case law, and that there is therefore no divergence between promissory morality (broadly conceived) and contract law. The argument that the mitigation doctrine diverges from morality has focused on the claim, famously made by Fried, that the point of mitigation is to get the promisee to assist the promise breaker on the grounds of altruism. We have offered an alternative justification of the mitigation and loss-sharing principles, based on the principle of fairness. This alternative account does not depend on the claim that the promisee has a duty of altruism to assist the promisor, and avoids the objections made to the altruism-based explanation of the mitigation doctrine. If successful, our account dissolves the apparent divergence between the mitigation doctrine and promissory morality, at the level of first-order moral reasoning.

[57] As we argue in our paper 'Contract Law without Foundations' (unpublished manuscript) (on file with authors).

17

Remedies for Breach of Contract

One Principle or Two?

*Stephen A. Smith**

The common law provides two kinds of judicial remedies for breach of contract. The first is an order that the defendant do the very thing he or she promised to do. "*In specie* orders" (as I will describe them) may take the form of an order that the defendant pay a sum due under a contract[1] or an order that the defendant "specifically perform" a contractual duty.[2] *In specie* orders are available only if performance of the contractual promise remains possible (albeit late) and, in the case of specific performance, if other conditions are met. The second kind of judicial remedy is an order that the defendant pay damages. Damages orders are normally available whenever a breach is proven (though the amount may be nominal), and may be awarded together with, or in lieu of, an *in specie* order.[3] This chapter seeks to better understand contract remedies by exploring two conceptions of the relationship between *in specie* and damages orders.

The first conception—the "one-principle model"—supposes that a damages order is a particular type of *in specie* order. According to this model, both *in specie* and damages orders confirm existing legal duties. Furthermore, the duties confirmed are in each case closely related to the defendant's original contractual duty. Specifically, the one-principle model supposes that the confirmed duties are transformed versions of the original duty. As will be explained, defenders of the one-principle model

* I am grateful to Prince Saprai and Hanoch Dagan for comments on an earlier version of this chapter, and to Jacqueline Madden and John-Andrew Petrakis for research assistance.

[1] In England today, all private law rulings other than declarations and constitutive rulings (for example, a divorce decree) are styled as "orders." Thus, the standard form for a ruling requiring the payment of a debt or other monetary sum (including damages) reads: "It is therefore ordered that [the defendant] must pay the Claimant [the sum of *X*]." Civ. P. R. para. C17-001, Form N30(1). Until relatively recently (and still the case today in most common law jurisdictions), only rulings that originated in the Chancery Courts (for example, specific performance) were styled as orders. Rulings that originated in the Royal Courts (for example, damages or payment of a debt) were expressed as impersonal "judgments," stipulating that a particular result must happen ("It is this day adjudged that the claimant recover against the defendant $. . .:" I. H. Jacob, Chitty & Jacob's Queen's Bench Forms 689 (19th ed., 1965)). The contemporary English terminology is adopted in this chapter, but the older terminology is examined where the difference might be significant.

[2] Specific performance, as understood in this chapter, includes injunctive relief.

[3] Courts may refuse to issue any kind of order, notwithstanding proof of a breach of contract, if a limitation period has expired, a necessary formality is lacking, or the defendant has legal immunity. The actions that constitute a breach of contract may also form part of the cause of action in a claim for restitution, but in such a case the basis of the claim is the defendant's unjust enrichment, not the defendant's breach.

differ according to whether they explain this transformation on the ground that the original duty lives on after the breach (albeit in a different form) or, instead, on the ground that the reasons underlying the original duty live on (and so give rise to a new duty). The model's defenders agree, however, that the explanations of contract breakers' post-breach duties to perform and to pay damages are found in the explanation of their original duties. No additional principles are required. According to the one-principle model, therefore, an order to pay damages for failing to deliver goods is fundamentally the same as an order to deliver goods late—and both are fundamentally the same as an order to deliver goods that is issued prior to the contract's delivery date. Each of these orders directs defendants to comply, in the best way possible in the circumstances, with their original contractual duty (or the reasons underlying it). In short, all remedies for breach of contract are essentially orders directing defendants to perform their contractual duties.

In contrast, the second conception of the relationship between *in specie* and damages orders—the "two-principle model"—supposes that these types of orders are fundamentally different. Specifically, while the two-principle model joins the one-principle model in holding that *in specie* orders confirm existing duties and, further, that these duties are transformed versions of defendants' original contractual duties; the two-principle model supposes that damages orders differ from *in specie* orders in two respects. First, rather than confirming existing duties, damages orders create entirely new duties (and give effect to new reasons). Second, the content of these duties cannot be explained on the same grounds as the original duties. Unlike *in specie* orders, which are responses to rights, damages orders, in this view, are responses to wrongs. According to the two-principle model, additional normative principles are therefore required to explain damages orders.[4]

The proposition defended in this chapter is that the two-principle model better explains judicial remedies for breach of contract than the one-principle model. More specifically, it will be argued that while both models can explain *in specie* orders and also damages orders that are set at the cost of obtaining substitute performance for a still-live contractual obligation ("substitutionary damages"), the two-principle model provides a better explanation for all other damage orders.

I. The One-Principle Model

The common-sense idea underlying the one-principle model is that you should do your best to comply with your duties even if perfect compliance is no longer possible.[5]

[4] As will be discussed, both models accept that further principles must be invoked if we want to explain why courts are willing to issue orders at all and, in addition, why in some cases courts have a preference for monetary over nonmonetary orders. The "explanations" of damages orders that the one-principle and two-principle models provide are basically explanations of the contents of damages orders.

[5] The leading contemporary defenders of the one-principle model write primarily about tort law damages. *See generally* Joseph Raz, *Personal Practical Conflicts, in* Practical Conflicts: New Philosophical Essays 172 (Peter Baumann & Monika Betzler eds., 2004); Ernest Weinrib, *Two Conceptions of Remedies, in* Justifying Private L. Remedies 3 (Charles Rickett ed., 2008); Arthur Ripstein, *As If It Had Never Happened*, 48 Wm. & Mary L. Rev. 1957 (2007); John Gardner, *What Is Tort Law for? Part 1: The Place of Corrective Justice*, 30 Law and Phil. 1 (2011). However, the model is clearly intended to apply to damage awards generally. Indeed, the typical example introduced to show

Suppose that you promise to come to my house on Saturday at 10:00 a.m. to help me plant a tree, but then you forget about the promise until Saturday at 10:15 a.m. What should you do? The obvious answer is that you should come to my house as soon as possible. You should do this for the same reason that you should have come at 10:00, namely that you promised to help me. Your failure to show up at 10:00 does not release you from the promise. Rather, your promissory duty is now a duty to show up as soon after 10:00 as possible. The one-principle model supposes that it is duties of this kind that *in specie* orders confirm. Thus—to continue with the example—if our arrangement was legally binding and if you were able to get before a court at 10:15 and convince it to issue an order commanding me to perform my promise, the model's explanation for this order would be the same as the explanation for why I should have shown up at 10:00: I promised to help you. Of course, to fully explain this or any other order it is necessary to account not just for its content, but also to explain why courts issue orders at all. Neither the one-principle nor two-principle model is intended to answer the latter question.[6] Once this question is answered, however, the one-principle model holds that the content on an *in specie* order can be explained without introducing any new normative principles. The fact that I promised to assist you explains why I ought to assist even if I am late in doing so.

This explanation of *in specie* orders, which is accepted by the two-principle model, is, I hope, uncontroversial. In any event, I will not defend it further here. Instead, I will focus on the distinctive contribution of the one-principle model, which is to suggest that a similar story can be told for why courts order contract breakers to pay damages. To return to my example, the one-principle model supposes that the best way for you to give effect to your promise after the original time for performance has passed would be not just for you to show up as soon as possible, but also for you to do something else for me, such as offering to help with other work or, if our arrangement was legally binding, paying me a sum of money.[7] Furthermore, if the example is changed so that you don't remember your promise until Monday (at which point the tree is already planted), then according to the model the best way of giving effect to your promise (assuming it is legally binding) would be for you to pay me a sum of money. In short, the one-principle model supposes that the best way of giving effect to your promissory duty once the time for performance has passed is either to perform late and to pay damages (in cases where performance is still possible) or simply to pay damages (in cases where performance is no longer possible or desired). Finally, the model assumes that if I were to successfully sue you the court's ruling would confirm the duties just described.

the model's prima facie plausibility is the duty to perform a promise after the date of performance has passed. *See* Gardner, *What Is Tort Law for?*, at 30. The focus on tort damages may explain, however, why these authors do not discuss the special circumstances raised by cases in which damages are awarded as a substitute for a still-live duty (such duties are typically contractual). I discuss these cases below.

[6] I explore this question in Stephen Smith, *Why Courts Make Orders (And What This Tells Us about Damages)*, 64 C.L.P. 51, 54–69 (2011).

[7] The extent to which the one-principle model is specifically focused on legal duties depends on which version of the account is adopted. However, both versions are presumably consistent with allowing that the law has a role in specifying the form of transformed duties. This is why the above examples assume that the post-breach duty takes the form of paying money only where the original duty is a legal duty.

The above description of paying damages as "giving effect" to your promise is deliberately imprecise because defenders of the one-principle model provide two explanations of how primary duties justify and determine duties to pay damages. According to the "Razian" version of the model, the explanation is that the reasons underlying the primary duty continue to apply after the duty has been breached. These reasons then give rise to a transformed, post-breach, duty to compensate:

> [W]hen we fail to conform fully to a reason we have reason to come as close to full compliance as we can, call it reason to do the next best act. It is the very same reason which we did not conform to which is, or becomes, reason for the next best thing... So if I have reason not to damage your property, and I do damage your fence, I have reason to compensate you, that is to mitigate the consequences of failure, and this reason is the very same reason I had initially (the reason not to trespass or not to disturb your peace). There is no need for an independent principle of compensation to establish the case for it.[8]

Raz does not say whether the duty to pay damages is a variant of the original duty or a new duty, but John Gardner, developing Raz's idea in more detail, explicitly adopts the latter position.[9] The important point, however, is that regardless of how it is described, the duty to pay damages is based on the same reasons as the original duty.

In contrast, the "Kantian" version of the one-principle model supposes that the original duty itself applies after the breach. According to this view, the breach causes the original duty to take a different form, namely as a duty to perform late and/or one to pay damages. As developed in the work of Ernest Weinrib and Arthur Ripstein,[10] the Kantian version explains the original duties' persistence as a consequence of the nature of rights. For Weinrib and Ripstein, rights protect individuals' abilities to choose how to live their lives, free from others' domination. The consequence of this understanding, they say, is that while rights can be waived, abandoned, transferred, or discharged, they cannot be lost by the wrongful actions of others. In Ripstein's words, "the right to what I had survives any wrongs committed against it."[11] Weinrib and Ripstein accept that compliance with a duty to deliver goods on a particular date is not strictly possible after the date has passed. Yet the original duty, they insist, transforms, post-breach, into a duty that can be fulfilled, namely to deliver as soon as possible and/or to pay damages. In Weinrib's words, "Like Descartes' famous piece of wax that remains the same piece despite its different qualities when heated and cooled, the same duty is continuously correlative to the same right before and after the tort."[12]

[8] Raz, *Personal Practical Conflicts*, at 191. Raz leaves open the extent to which the "conformity principle" explains the law governing damages, noting that the principle cannot explain punitive damages or damages for pain and suffering, and, more generally, that other principles may come into play when determining the legal response to a breached duty. John Gardner, who further develops Raz's idea, explicitly argues that the conformity principle explains duties to pay damages: Gardner, *What Is Tort Law for?*

[9] Gardner, *What Is Tort Law for?*, at 32.

[10] Weinrib, *Two Conceptions of Remedies*; Ripstein, *As If It Had Never Happened. See also* Ernest Weinrib, The Idea of Private law 135 (1995); Arthur Ripstein, Force and Freedom 304–5 (2009).

[11] Ripstein, Force and Freedom, at 304.

[12] Weinrib, *Two Conceptions of Remedies*, at 13.

Whichever version is adopted, the one-principle model is consistent with what I described earlier as "substitutionary damages." Substitutionary damages are monetary orders or parts of monetary orders that are assessed at the cost of engaging a third party to perform an unperformed, but still "live," nonmonetary contractual obligation. Though relatively rare in practice,[13] such awards are the default judicial remedy in cases where the claimant's action is founded on the breach of a still-live nonmonetary contractual duty.[14] Thus, if I seek specific performance of your still-live (or "unterminated") contractual obligation to paint my house, the court's normal response would be to refuse the request and instead order you to pay me the cost of hiring another painter.[15] Such an award is fairly described as requiring you to perform a transformed version of your original duty. By definition, the award is a substitute for a live contractual duty rather than a response to a wrong. To be sure, you have committed a breach, namely failing to perform on time. Further, I can recover damages for any losses that I suffer as a consequence of that breach (e.g., loss of profits). But the cost of hiring a third party to perform does not fall into this category because up to the moment of the order the law supposes that you have a duty to paint my house. That duty is alive until it is replaced by an order to pay damages. Any part of a damages award that is given in lieu of ordering specific performance of a still-live duty must be a substitute for that duty. And where this monetary substitute is calculated at the cost of third party performance, the natural inference is that the court is asking the defendant to do the closest or next-best thing to actually performing his or her contractual duty.

A court-ordered duty to pay a sum equal to the cost of hiring a third party to perform a live contractual obligation is therefore properly described as a transformed version of the defendant's original duty. Of course, this transformation takes place not at the time of breach, but at the moment the damages order is issued. In my example, it is the court's order that transforms your duty to paint my house into a duty to pay me money. Neither the one-principle nor two-principle model is meant to explain this transformation. Like the explanation of the judicial practice of issuing orders generally, the explanation of the judicial practice of transforming nonmonetary duties into monetary duties is basically institutional. The main reason that courts issue monetary awards in lieu of specific performance is that monetary orders put fewer demands on scarce judicial resources: monetary orders are less likely to give rise to additional litigation and they can be enforced by the relatively simple and inexpensive means of execution against the defendant's assets (as opposed to imprisonment for contempt in

[13] In most cases involving the breach of nonmonetary obligations the obligation is no longer live because it has become impossible to perform or because it was terminated by the claimant. Even where the obligation remains live, the court may assess damages at less than the cost of performance if that sum is disproportionately larger than the monetized value of performance. *See Ruxley Elec. and Constr. Ltd. v. Forsyth*, [1995] 3 W.L.R. 118 (HL) at 127, 136. And of course if the relevant obligation is live then in a limited range of cases the court may agree to order specific performance.

[14] Harvey McGregor, McGregor on Damages 685–87, 772–4, 857–9, 884–9 (17th ed., 2004). If the contract price has not been paid it will be deducted from this sum.

[15] It might be argued that a claimant's decision not to request specific performance of a live contractual obligation is also a decision to terminate that obligation, and therefore that an award of damages in such cases cannot be substitutionary. The counter-argument is that claimants may request damages rather than specific performance not because they no longer desire performance but simply because they know the court is unlikely to award the latter.

the case of nonmonetary orders).[16] The one-principle model has nothing to say about such considerations. The model can, however, explain why, when courts transform nonmonetary duties into monetary duties, they normally quantify the latter by reference to the cost of hiring a third party to perform the nonmonetary duty. Paying for the cost of performance is the closest monetary equivalent to actual performance. Of course, it is not always possible for third parties to perform the relevant duty or even a near substitute. And some nonmonetary duties are relatively easy to supervise and enforce, in particular negative duties and duties to do things like convey title to land. These and related reasons explain why courts sometimes order specific performance. Nonetheless, when courts do issue substitutionary damages orders, the natural inference is that they are directing defendants to comply with transformed versions of their original duties.

The question for the one-principle model, which is the focus of the remainder of this chapter, is whether it can satisfactorily explain the kinds of damage awards it is designed to explain, namely awards other than substitutionary cost-of-performance awards. The answer defended below is that with respect to such awards (which I will describe simply as "damages awards" unless noted otherwise) the one-principle model neither makes sense on its own terms nor fits the law. I begin with the first objection.

A. Duties and reasons may not survive a breach

Although the one-principle model is meant to explain the law governing damages, it is defended for the most part not by showing that it accounts for the positive law better than alternative accounts, but rather by showing that it follows from the nature of reasons or of legal rights. Thus, in the Razian version it is argued that a general feature of reasons is that they continue to apply even when the duties they support have been breached, whereas in the Kantian version the persistence of duties is said to follow from the nature of legal rights. It is not possible here to examine the broader philosophical foundations of these arguments. It is possible, however, to show that the arguments are not supported by the ordinary understanding of reasons and duties.

Defenders of the one-principle model frequently invoke such understandings in support of their arguments. John Gardner introduces his version of the one-principle model by discussing Neil McCormick's example of a parent who, having failed to keep a promise to take his children to the beach on Saturday, is now under a duty (so the example assumes) to take them to the beach on Sunday.[17] Gardner explains that the latter duty exists because the reasons underlying the original promise continue to apply after its breach. In a similar way, Arthur Ripstein introduces the example of an overdue debt to make the point that the duty to pay the debt does not disappear because it was breached.

[16] Other reasons, which are also institutional, include: (1) monetary duties can be fulfilled by third-party execution and, more generally, require minimal personal involvement by the defendant (thereby reducing the risk that a state-ordered and coercively enforced duty may be regarded as a kind of servitude); (2) the substitution of a monetary award for a requested nonmonetary award allows courts to limit the assistance they offer to claimants who have acted unreasonably in asserting their rights.

[17] Gardner, *What Is Tort Law for?*, at 28.

These examples are persuasive because they involve situations where both lawyers and laypersons would say that it remains possible, post-breach, to perform the original duty, albeit late. They are cases where late performance would ordinarily be described simply as performing the duty. Paying a debt late is described as paying a debt, albeit late. Yet precisely for this reason, these examples tell us little about damages orders. A court order to perform any of the post-breach duties described in these examples would be an *in specie* order. To show that duties (or reasons) live on after a breach in the kinds of situations where courts order damages, the examples must be of cases where it would not be possible, if the matter went to a court, for an *in specie* order to be issued. In other words, the relevant examples will be cases where performance, even late, of the action specified by the original duty is no longer possible. Examples of this kind do not support the one-principle model.

Consider your duty not to interfere with a particular chattel of mine, for example the wooden chair in my office. As the one-principle model asserts, your duty not to interfere with my chair is not negated if it turns out that in the past you intentionally damaged the chair or even stole it. Similarly, if you had promised me that you would polish the chair once a year (polishing chairs being one of your hobbies), then your failure one year to keep the promise does not release you from fulfilling the promise in the future. You remain under a duty to polish the chair in future years.

But now suppose that there is an accidental fire in my office and my chair is burnt to ashes. It would be nonsense to say that you still have a duty not to interfere with my chair or, in the second scenario, to polish the chair every year. It is nonsensical not because I have waived or abandoned my right—I did neither—but because the subject matter of the alleged duty does not exist. Having a duty not to interfere with something that does not exist is simply not possible. Nor is it the case that your duty not to interfere with the chair or your promissory duty to polish the chair are transformed, by the burning of the chair, into duties to do something else. The duties, and the reasons underlying them, simply disappear.

In the chair example, the duties disappear because of an accident rather than a wrongful act. Yet the one-principle model attaches no significance to the wrongful nature of a breach. To the contrary, it is essential to this model that the alleged duty to pay damages is not a response to the breach, qua breach, but simply to a set of circumstances that, as it happens, was brought about by the breach. In the one-principle model, the breach is a morally neutral fact. If it mattered that the change in circumstances was caused by a wrong, then a new principle would be needed to explain why it matters. From the perspective of the one-principle model, the question facing contractual wrongdoers is not how they should respond to their wrongdoing, but how they can best give effect to their original duty (or the reasons underlying it) given the present circumstances. Neither Gardner's assertion that "reasons persist" nor Weinrib's assertion that "rights live on" are qualified according to the reason that the object of the duty is no longer possible. Indeed, Gardner stresses the unimportance of wrongdoing by noting that in McCormick's example of the promise to take the children to the beach, the promisor's breach was a justified response to an emergency.[18]

[18] Gardner, *What Is Tort Law for?*, at 28. The fact that the wrongdoer committed a wrong is not entirely irrelevant in Gardner's account. He argues that wrongdoers who comply in the best way possible with

In the chair example, the chair's burning admittedly does not affect what might be described as your abstract duty not to interfere with my property, that is, your duty not to interfere with whatever property I happen to own. However, this abstract duty (or the reasons underlying it) is not the duty presumed by the one-principle model to be the basis for a subsequent duty to pay damages. Your abstract duty not to interfere with my property persists over time in exactly the same form. The only duty that could potentially transform, once breached, into a duty to pay damages would be one relating to a particular object (or person, activity, etc.).

In the ordinary understanding, then, your duty not to interfere with my chair (or the reasons underlying that duty) is contingent on the chair's existence. If the chair does not exist, for whatever reason, then it makes no sense to speak of a duty not to interfere with the chair or of reasons not to interfere with the chair. This observation does not deny that the wrongful destruction of an object, for instance my chair, might give rise to duties to do something in response. Such duties, however, would be responses to the wrong, not the original right (or the reasons underlying it). In short, the ordinary understanding of duties draws a sharp divide between situations in which it is still possible to perform one's original duty, albeit late or otherwise slightly modified, and situations where performance is no longer possible. The one-principle model's conflation of these situations is inconsistent with this understanding.

Finally, and as I discuss in more detail in sections B and C, the ordinary understanding of duties is mirrored in the conventional legal understanding of orders. Lawyers describe an order to deliver contractually promised goods, albeit late, as specific performance. In contrast, an order to pay damages is not described as specific performance, late performance, imperfect performance, or any other kind of performance; it is simply described as damages. The law does not present *in specie* orders and damages orders as points on a continuum. The law regards them as fundamentally different: *in specie* orders are responses to rights, whereas damages orders are responses to wrongs.

B. No duty to pay damages

The one-principle model fails to fit the law in two main respects. First, the model supposes that contracting parties' duties transform, on breach, either wholly or in part, into duties to pay damages. Yet the common law recognizes no such duty.[19] Failing to pay damages in advance of a legal ruling is not a legal wrong (claimants cannot recover losses arising from nonpayment) and payment in advance is no defense to a claim for damages. These rules are not mere technicalities. For most of the common law's history, the most fundamental distinction within legal actions—formalized in the classification of writs—was between actions where the "demandant" sought enforcement of

the reasons underlying a previously breached duty should still feel regret for their breach. However, this qualification is not part of Gardner's explanation of damages.

[19] I defend this proposition in more detail in Stephen Smith, *Duties, Liabilities, Damages*, 125 HARV. L. REV. 172, 174–9 (2012). The law is the same in the United States. *See* Nathan B. Oman, *Why There Is No Duty to Pay Damages: Powers, Duties, and Private Law*, 39 FLA. ST. U. L. REV. 137 (2011).

a right and actions where the "complainant" sought redress for a wrong.[20] In the first case, the defendant could avoid going to court by complying with the demand (for example, by paying a debt). But in the second case, where the action was founded on a wrong, this option was not available. Prepayment of damages was not an option because the complainant was not asking to enforce a right; he was seeking redress for a wrong. This explains why common law lawyers traditionally talk about liabilities (not duties) to pay damages. It also explains why lawyers refer to the rules governing damages as rules for "assessing" damages—damages are assessed because courts (not wrongdoers) are meant to apply the rules.

Indeed, the very idea of a duty to pay damages is implausible because wrongdoers could not reasonably be expected to determine the content of such a duty prior to a judge's ruling. Courts enjoy wide discretion with regard to damages for mental distress, loss of reputation, and punitive damages, and significant discretion when applying the rules regarding remoteness of damages. More importantly, many of the facts that wrongdoers would need to know to determine what amount of damages they ought to pay are in the hands of their victims. Only the victim knows the value of the contract, the expected profits, and so on. Indeed, in many cases only the victim will know that the contract has even been breached (as for example where the breach arises from a hidden defect in goods or services). The victim could provide this information to the breaching party, but there is no legal duty to do this and defenders of the one-principle model have never suggested that the duty to pay damages is conditional on such information. Additionally, even if the victim provides such information, how is the breaching party meant to assess the information's veracity? It would be unreasonable to expect the breaching party simply to trust the victim—and impractical to suppose that the victim must provide witnesses, and so forth.

This objection cannot be avoided by supposing that, precisely because of the difficulties just described, the duty to pay damages is a genuine but "inchoate" duty—inchoate, that is, until it has been fixed by a court order. Assuming that the idea of an inchoate legal duty makes sense at all, this suggestion is inconsistent with the idea, central to the one-principle model, that the duty to pay damages is a natural evolution of the original duty. If it is part of the very meaning of a duty or of the reasons underlying it that it transforms, on breach, into a duty to pay damages, it should be possible to specify this duty in a rule. There might be special considerations that the law should take into account when it comes time to enforce the duty (e.g., supervision costs), but such considerations should not, and elsewhere in the law do not, enter when lawmakers contemplate duty-imposing rules. In any event, defenders of the one-principle model have never suggested that there is something special about duties to pay damages that explains why the law does not recognize them.

Finally, the suggestion that duties to pay damages are inchoate until fixed by a court is inconsistent with the nature of damages rulings. If damages rulings were

[20] *See* J. H. Baker, An Introduction to English Legal History 67 (3d ed., 1990); S. F. C. Milsom, Historical Foundations of the Common Law 243–4 (2d ed., 1981).

intended to fix inchoate duties, then we would expect them to take the form of declarations. A declaration is the individualized counterpart to a rule: it declares the rights and duties of the individual litigants. Yet damages rulings are framed as commands, that is, as orders. It would be extremely odd, not to mention inappropriate, for courts to employ orders (or, in earlier times, "judgments"[21]) to specify inchoate duties. For obvious reasons, courts and other authorities do not generally order individuals to perform their duties unless those individuals have shown themselves unwilling to comply voluntarily. (Courts order individuals to pay fines in amounts that are unknown prior to the order, but, as I explain below, they do this precisely because such orders create, rather than confirm, duties.) Courts require proof that the defendant has breached the duty or is about to breach it. Neither type of proof is possible with respect to an inchoate duty to pay damages.[22]

C. Damages are awarded for a wrong

The one-principle model supposes that damages are awarded to give effect to a right. As we have seen, the model's explanation for why those who break their contracts should pay damages is that their victims' rights (or the reasons underlying them) live on after the breach. In this account, a breach of contract is significant not for what it does, but for what it doesn't do—namely to extinguish the victim's contractual right (or the reasons underlying it). The fact that the defendant's nonperformance was a wrong is, in this story, irrelevant. All that matters is that the best way for the defendant to comply with his contractual duty, in the current circumstances, is to pay a sum of money.

To be sure, the one-principle model accepts that claimants who seek damages for breach of contract must prove a breach of contract. The model accepts that the reason defendants' duties take their current form, namely as duties to pay damages, is because they did not do what they contractually agreed to do. However, the content of defendants' post-breach duties is explained by the post-breach state of the world, not by the earlier breach. Because the date for the wedding has passed, the defendant's duty to deliver a wedding cake becomes a duty to pay damages. It is not important, in this explanation, that the reason the defendant must pay damages is that the defendant earlier committed a wrong. All that matters is that the best way to give effect to the original duty (or to the reasons underlying it), under the current circumstances, is to

[21] As mentioned in note 1, the judgments that were formerly issued with respect to rulings that originated in the Royal Courts were in the form of impersonal pronouncements that the claimant shall "recover" a particular sum of money, land, or other property. In practical terms, the main difference between an order and a judgment is that while an order cannot be coercively enforced until after the date of performance, a judgment is in principle enforceable at the moment it is issued. It is therefore even less likely that courts would issue judgments for damages if such rulings were intended to fix inchoate duties. The defendant might have no opportunity to comply with her supposed duties.

[22] Defenders of the Kantian version of the one-principle model might respond that the original breach is a breach of the duty to pay damages because, in their view, the two duties are the same. Yet regardless of its connection to the original duty, the alleged duty to pay damages is in substance sufficiently different from the original contractual duty that breach of the original duty does not establish that the defendant is certain or even likely to breach the duty to pay damages. Further, the original duty may have been breached accidentally.

pay a sum of money. The breach is simply the causal explanation for why the current circumstances are as they are.

The defendant's breach—or more strictly the defendant's continuing breach—of her duty is presumably also part of the one-principle model's explanation for why a court would order the defendant to comply with this duty.[23] As demonstrated by the rules governing *quia timet* orders (orders issued to prevent a future breach), common law courts generally refuse to issue orders unless the defendant has breached a duty or is about to breach a duty.[24] For obvious reasons, courts do not think it appropriate to order citizens to comply with their legal duties unless they are unlikely to do so voluntarily. Thus, part of the one-model's explanation for why courts are willing to issue damages awards in the cases where they award them is presumably that the defendant's initial breach and then her ongoing failure to comply with her post-breach duty to pay damages shows that she is unlikely to pay damages voluntarily. This explanation attaches no particular significance to the wrongfulness of the defendant's breach. The breach is important merely because it is evidence that the defendant is unlikely to perform in the future. This unlikelihood could be shown in other ways. As noted earlier, courts sometimes order defendants to perform a duty (including a contractual duty) merely on proof that they are likely to breach it in the future.

Common law courts view damages orders differently. Although they accept that *in specie* orders give effect to primary duties, they suppose that damages are awarded *for* a wrong and not merely following a wrong. As mentioned earlier, for most of the common law's history this distinction was formally recognized by a fundamental division between the kinds of writs employed to commence actions. "Demandants" (as they were called) seeking to enforce a right, such as the right to payment of a debt or to possession of their land, would commence their action with a *praecipe* writ—a writ of "right." *Praecipe* writs took the form of demands that defendants comply with the asserted right or come to court to explain why they had not complied. By contrast, "complainants" (as they were called) seeking redress for a wrong, that is, seeking damages, would commence their action with an *ostensurus quare* writ—a writ of trespass or "wrong." *Ostensurus quare* writs took the form of complaints that the defendant had wronged the complainant, coupled with pleas that defendants come to court to explain themselves. The writ system was abolished in the nineteenth century, but the distinction it formalized underpins the contemporary law. Nominal damages are explicitly awarded to acknowledge that the defendant wronged the claimant. Punitive damages—available since the beginning of the common law—are awarded in recognition of the defendant's egregiously wrongful behavior. Neither has any connection to the breached duty other than the fact that it was breached. More importantly, the core rules governing the assessment of ordinary damages reveal a similar focus on wrongs.

[23] This issue appears not to have been explored in the literature defending the one-principle model. An alternative to the view discussed above is that duty-confirming orders are available in any case where a valid duty is established. To adopt this view, it must be assumed, following Roman law, that strictly speaking there are no legal duties to refrain from, for example, assaulting others or carelessly injuring others (because it is not generally possible to obtain orders forbidding such actions). The Roman law position is discussed in Peter Birks, *Definition and Division: A Meditation on Institutes 3.13, in* The Classification of Obligations 1, 11–12 (Peter Birks ed., 1997).

[24] Andrew Burrows, Remedies for Torts and Breach of Contract 544–5 (3d ed., 2004).

Consider, for example, the long-standing rule that only parties to a contract may recover damages for breach, and then only with respect to losses that they suffer themselves. Suppose you enter a contract with me in which you agree to paint my sister's house. You then fail to paint the house. It is possible that in some common law jurisdictions our contract might fit within an exception to the privity rule such that my sister could recover damages from you or even that I could recover substantial damages. But in many cases the traditional rule would apply, with the result that, exceptional circumstances aside, I would only recover nominal damages if I sued you. Damages would be nominal because I would be unable to show that I suffered a loss. This result poses a difficulty for the one-principle model because the obvious way to give effect to the original duty (or the reasons underlying it), assuming that an *in specie* order is not possible, would be for you to pay me (or my sister) a sum equal to the cost of hiring someone else to paint the house. The payment of nominal damages is hardly a substitute for painting a house.[25]

It is no response to this objection that your contractual promise was made to me rather than to my sister. According to the one-principle model, the question for those who break their contracts is not "who did I wrong," but "how can I best comply with my original duty (or the reasons underlying it) in the present circumstances?" The answer to this question does not depend on who owns the house. Suppose that the contract had been to paint two houses, one owned by my sister and one by me. If the best way to comply with your duty to paint my house is to pay me the cost of hiring another painter, then the best way to comply with your duty to paint my sister's house should be to make a similar payment. The law, however, responds to the breaches of these duties in radically different ways.

Arthur Ripstein's work suggests a possible response to this objection. Drawing again on Kant's work, Ripstein argues that the duty to pay damages is a duty to restore to claimants the "means" that they would have enjoyed had the defendants performed their duties.[26] The duty takes this shape, Ripstein says, because claimants' original rights are rights against interference with their means: "You are entitled to be made whole because I have interfered with your right to your means; you are entitled to equivalent means because the right I violated was to those very means."[27] The "right to your means" could refer to the right to particular instantiations of your means (your right to your car, bank account, promise made to you, etc.). Or it could refer to means in the abstract (i.e., a right to a universal "means" of exchange). The word "means" itself suggests the latter interpretation, as does Ripstein's assertion that paying damages can make the world "as if it [the wrong] had never happened."[28] Only if your right is to means in the abstract can the payment of such means make it as if the wrong

[25] On the assumption that I terminated your contractual duty to paint my house, the two-principle model explains nominal damages on the ground that the wrong for which damages are a response in such a case caused the right holder (me) little or no loss. Neither model, however, can explain an award of nominal damages in a case where the contractual duty remains alive at the time of judgment. The explanation of substitutionary cost-of-performance damages defended above (which is consistent with both models) suggests that the cost of performance should be available regardless of whether the beneficiary of the relevant duty is a third party.

[26] Ripstein, *As If It Had Never Happened*, at 1964.

[27] Ripstein, *As If It Had Never Happened*, at 1981.

[28] Ripstein, *As If It Had Never Happened*, at 1957.

never happened. If this interpretation is adopted, it can explain why, in the painting example, I would not recover substantial damages. Your failure to paint my sister's house does not interfere with my means, defined abstractly. Of course, this interpretation does not explain why I receive nominal damages. More importantly, this interpretation leads directly to the Holmesian view that contractual duties are disjunctive duties to perform *or* pay a sum of money. If my contractual duty is to ensure that you receive a quantity of abstract means, then I can fulfill that duty by paying you a sum of money. Neither Ripstein nor any other defender of the one-principle model purports to adopt Holmes's position. This is not surprising because the Holmesian position renders the one-principle model redundant. If our primary duties are duties to perform or pay a sum of money, then it is unnecessary to invoke this model to explain why those who break their contracts are ordered to pay damages. In the Holmesian model, paying damages is not a transformed version of the original duty; it is literal performance of that duty.

A second core rule that shows damages are awarded for a wrong, rather than as a substitute for a right, is the rule providing that victims may recover damages for "consequential losses." The consequences for which such awards are meant to provide redress are the consequences of the defendant's wrongdoing. If I hire you to deliver a machine to my factory, your contractual duty is to deliver the machine. It is not a duty to ensure that I obtain whatever profits I reasonably expected to obtain by virtue of the delivery. Nor are the reasons explaining your duty reasons to ensure that I obtain these profits; they are reasons to keep your promise—and your promise was simply to deliver the machine. Of course, your promise is linked to the profits I expected to make from receiving the machine, but the link is merely one of causal probability. It is not part of the meaning of your promise, nor is it a necessary consequence of the promise, that I will profit from its performance. Indeed, it is possible that, had you fulfilled your promise, I would not have made any profits.

Professor Ripstein explains consequential damages on the ground that your rights to your means include the rights to whatever means you could have realized through those means: "If you have something as your means, you thereby also have whatever further means follow from having them."[29] Yet even accepting for the sake of argument that your rights are rights to your means, it is not clear how you could be said to "have" further means unless they followed automatically from ownership of your present means—which, as we just saw, they don't. To be sure, once you obtain further means you will have those means in the same way you have your present means, but by definition a claimant seeking damages for consequential losses has not yet obtained the further means. More broadly, the idea that we somehow own or have a right to the profits, etc., likely to be obtained from our present means is inconsistent with the rule that claimants can only recover damages for harm to their future prospects where such harm is consequent to an injury to their present assets (or person, etc.). If it were true that we "have" the fruits of our means in the same way that we "have" our means, then interfering with the former should be a legal wrong. Yet it is basic common law that, exceptional circumstances aside, losses of this kind (so-called "pure economic

[29] Ripstein, *As If It Had Never Happened*, at 1974.

loss") are not recoverable. The standard explanation for this principle is that damages are only available on proof of a rights infringement—and we have no rights to make profits, etc. Professors Ripstein and Weinrib support this explanation.[30] The explanation is inconsistent, however, with their view that paying consequential damages fulfills the defendant's original duty. There is no original duty not to interfere with expected profits.[31]

II. The Two-Principle Model

The two-principle model of contract remedies joins the one-principle model (and the law) in supposing that *in specie* orders command defendants to perform transformed versions of their original contractual duties and, furthermore, in supposing that these transformed versions are justified on the same grounds as the original duties.[32] The two-principle model accepts, therefore, that no additional principles are required to explain why parties who fail to make timely delivery, for example, have a duty to deliver as soon as possible. The two-principle model also joins the one-principle model in assuming that the content of substitutionary damages awards is explained by the content of the defendant's original contractual duty. The model accepts, therefore, that orders directing defendants to pay the cost of performance in response to proof of an unfulfilled, but still live, contractual duty, transform nonmonetary duties into close monetary substitutes and, further, that the transformation is justified on broadly institutional grounds. However, in contrast to the one-principle model (though not the law), the two-principle model assumes that other damages orders are different. Rather than responding to the claimant's alleged continuing right (or to the reasons underlying the original right), an order to pay nonsubstitutionary damages (hereafter "damages"), in this view, is a response to the defendant's wrong. In this model, the aim of damages is to provide redress for wrongs.

In theory, the two-principle model might explain the way in which damages *orders* respond to wrongs in two ways. First, it might suppose that such orders confirm wrong-responding substantive duties. In this view, the commission of a civil wrong gives rise, at that moment, to a legal duty to make redress, which takes the form of a duty to pay damages and which orders to pay damages confirm. If this view is correct, then, like *in specie* orders, damages orders merely direct defendants to do things that

[30] Ripstein, *As If It Had Never Happened*, at 1974–8; Weinrib, *Two Conceptions of Remedies*, at 134.

[31] There is also no free-standing duty not to interfere with others' expected "happiness." The absence of such a duty provides a further reason, in addition to the impossibility of putting a monetary figure on happiness, that damages for mental distress are difficult to explain using the one-principle model.

[32] The two-principle model expresses the conventional legal understanding of contract law remedies. It is reflected, *inter alia*, in the sharp distinction traditionally drawn between specific relief and damages in textbooks (not to mention in the existence of books and articles that focus exclusively on specific relief or damages). Within contemporary theoretical writing, the most developed two-principle account (though not described in these terms, and focused primarily on tort law) is John Goldberg and Ben Zipursky's theory of civil recourse. *See, e.g.*, John Goldberg & Benjamin Zipursky, *Rights and Responsibility in the Law of Torts*, *in* The Rights of Private Law 251 (Donal Nolan & Andrew Roberston eds., 2011); John C. P. Goldberg, *The Constitutional Status of Tort Law: Due Process and the Right to a Law for the Redress of Wrongs*, 115 Yale L.J. 524 (2005); Benjamin C. Zipursky, *Civil Recourse, Not Corrective Justice*, 91 Geo. L.J. 695 (2003).

they already had legal duties to do. In this view, *in specie* orders and damages orders differ not in the reason for issuing the order—in each case the reason is the existence of an outstanding substantive duty—but rather in the explanation of the duty that the order confirms. Thus, like the one-principle model, this version of the two-principle model regards the rules governing the quantification of damages as part of the substantive law; the difference is that in the two-principle model the substantive law in question is focused on duties arising from wrongs, not rights.

The idea that wrongs give rise to substantive duties to make redress is the traditional civilian understanding of damages.[33] As we have seen, however, the common law contains no such duty. The common law has never recognized a duty to pay damages prior to the issuance of a damages order.[34] This observation leads directly to the second way that the two-principle model might—indeed must—understand the role of damages orders. In this understanding, damages orders create, at the moment of their issuance, new duties.

The fact that damages orders create new duties is critical to understanding the form and rationale of the redress they provide. I noted earlier that the duty-creating nature of damages orders cannot be explained on the ground that damages orders are intended to fix uncertain or otherwise inchoate duties. If damages orders were intended to specify inchoate duties, they would not take the form of orders (or judgments): they would be declarations. Rather, the conclusion to draw from the duty-creating nature of damages orders is that the law must suppose that the actions required by such orders are not an appropriate subject matter, even in principle, for a substantive legal duty.[35] Why else would the law use orders, not substantive rules (or declarations), to impose duties to pay damages? Of course, there is no logical limit to the kinds of actions that lawmakers might stipulate as the subject matter of a duty-creating substantive rule. In practice, however, there is a limit because part of the very meaning of a rule-based duty is that the actions it requires reflect moral reasons applying to the subject.[36] Saying that there is a rule prescribing a "legal duty" to do X is saying that, in the eyes of the law, X reflects a moral duty. This understanding explains why legal duties are described as duties.

Orders are different. Although orders may direct defendants to do things that the law regards as a moral duty (as is true of *in specie* orders), the expression of moral duties is not part of the meaning of orders. This difference is most clearly illustrated by considering punitive orders, such as an order to pay a fine or to pay punitive. The reason that fines and other punitive actions are always mandated by orders, not by duty-imposing rules, is that wrongdoers do not have moral duties to punish themselves. If the law imposed a legal duty to pay a fine for, say, double-parking ("Anyone

[33] *See* Birks, *Definition and Division*, at 17–18 (arguing that the model also fits the common law); *see also* Rafal Zakrzewski, Remedies Reclassified 165–77 (2005).

[34] It does not follow from this observation that the common law denies that wrongdoers have moral duties to make amends for their wrongs. It merely follows that the common law does not recognize a legal duty to make such amends. *See* Smith, *Duties*, at 1751–5.

[35] I explore this idea in more detail in Smith, *Duties*, at 1746–8.

[36] *See generally* H. L. A. Hart, The Concept of Law 82–91 (1961); Joseph Raz, The Authority of Law 3-232 (1979); Joseph Raz, Ethics in the Public Domain 210–37 (1994).

who double-parks has a duty to pay the city $100"), it would send the wrong message. The law would be interpreted as imposing a price or a tax on double-parking, because this is the only way to make sense of the idea, implied by the use of a substantive rule, that there is a legal *duty* to pay the sum. Defendants do of course have legal duties to comply with court orders. However, these duties arise because of a general duty to comply with orders, not because the orders themselves express duties. Orders merely direct defendants to do particular actions ("it is ordered that the defendant pay the claimant $100"). The only reason orders provide for doing what they command is that they are orders. In contrast, substantive rules explicitly declare duties ("everyone has a duty to perform their contractual obligations"); indeed, the only reason provided by the law to follow rules qua rules is that the actions they require are duties.

The observation that damages orders create rather than confirm duties suggests, therefore, that such orders are structurally similar to orders to pay fines. Specifically, it suggests that the law does not view the required actions—the payment of damages—as based on moral reasons applying to their subjects, that is, on moral reasons applying to defendant wrongdoers. It suggests, in other words, that damages orders are meant to reflect other kinds of reasons. In principle, such reasons could take many forms, but in the remainder of this chapter I briefly explore an idea that is again inspired by the model of punitive orders.

Orders to pay fines and other punitive orders are clearly responses to wrongs. So far as I am aware, no one has ever suggested that paying a fine is a transformed version of the substantive duty that the defendant was fined for breaching. The characterization of punitive responses to wrongs has been debated, but taken on its own terms—namely on terms supposing punishment is required as a matter of justice—punishment is something that is imposed *for* a wrong and not merely as a consequence of a wrong. The general idea, which is captured in the traditional understanding of punishment as a matter of retributive justice, is that punishment restores a balance that the criminal's wrong has upset. By exercising a liberty—breaking the law—from which others, following the law, have refrained, the criminal gains an undue advantage. Erasing the wrong's physical effects is not possible, but it is possible, by removing from the criminal a proportionate liberty, to restore the balance of advantages and so to affirm that the law applies equally to everyone.[37]

My suggestion is that damages orders are intended, in broad outline, to do the same thing. The main difference is that whereas criminal punishment aims to restore a balance between wrongdoers and society, private law damages aim to restore a balance between wrongdoers and their victims. The payment of court-ordered damages affirms the legal equality of the claimant and defendant. In short, the suggestion is that damages are the private law equivalent of punishment. This idea is explored below by addressing three questions.

The first question asks how paying a sum of money—a tangible act in the real world—could serve to affirm the parties' equality (and, further, why the payments should be of the magnitudes specified by the courts). The short answer to this question

[37] For a fuller exposition of this (conventional) understanding of the core idea underlying retributive justice, *see, e.g.*, John Finnis, Natural Law and Natural Rights 262–4 (1980).

is that there is none. More precisely, there is no answer if one is looking for a tidy formula explaining why and in what amount damages are awarded in particular cases. This is exactly the response we should expect if, as I have suggested, damages are analogous to punishment. Even the most ardent defenders of retributivist theories of punishment do not suggest that they can explain the particular forms and magnitudes of the punishments levied by courts. In Western societies today, punishment is normally imposed by fine or imprisonment, but in previous times and still today in other societies, punishment takes different forms. Convention dictates to a large extent the forms and the magnitudes of individual punishments. Of course, the courts must respect the rule of law, avoid cruel and inhuman measures, seek proportionality between the wrong and the punishment, and so on. External considerations of these kinds explain why thieves are no longer drawn and quartered, why there are sentencing guidelines, and why the magnitude of the punishment increases with the seriousness of the crime. Yet at the end of the day, no one supposes that it is possible to explain why sentencing a thief to, say, five years in prison, or imposing a fine of, say, $10,000 on a polluter is the uniquely appropriate retributivist response to these crimes.

The same story is true, in general terms, of damages for civil wrongs. The law of damages attempts, in broad outline, to respond to civil wrongs by responding to the two main aspects of such wrongs. The first aspect is the breach itself—in the case of contract, the breach of contract. In cases where *in specie* orders are not possible (and where, therefore, substitutionary awards are also not possible), the law's usual response to a breach is to award a sum equal to the market value of the promised goods, land, or service (minus the contract price if payment was made in advance). Market value is an appropriate measure because it is an obvious, easily calculated, and conventionally recognized indicator of the seriousness of the wrong. In some cases, there is no market value, or the value is clearly inappropriate in proportion to the nature of the wrongdoing. This explains why nominal damages are available, why courts occasionally refuse to award the market price (e.g., where the actual loss is minimal and the breach unintentional), and why particularly egregious breaches may attract punitive damages.

The second aspect of a breach is its consequences—its effects on the defendant's well-being. Part of providing redress for a wrong is providing redress for its consequences, which the law does by, roughly, shifting them to the wrongdoer or, more strictly, by shifting to the wrongdoer those consequences which the wrong can fairly be said to have caused. In contract law cases, these consequences are primarily financial, and so the law's response, again, is to make the defendant pay the market value of the consequences. The detailed rules for assessing the extent and value of these losses reflect the special importance, in this field, of rule of law concerns. Civil wrongs are often unintentional, so it is important that citizens be able to predict the legal consequences of committing them. It should not be supposed, however, that the foundations of these rules are similarly determined. There is no uniquely appropriate way to establish how far the defendant's responsibility should extend down the chain of causation. Nor is there a uniquely appropriate way to put a monetary figure on the consequences of a breach. This is illustrated most clearly by cases in which the relevant loss or harm takes the form of mental distress or loss of reputation. When setting damages in such cases, the courts have no choice but to pick a random figure. Finally, only the person to whom the wrongdoer owed a duty can recover damages for either aspect of the wrong committed because that person alone was wronged.

A second question raised by the above suggestion is why the duty to pay damages is imposed by an order and not a substantive rule. If paying damages can do the things just described, why not require parties to make such payments automatically upon commission of a wrong? The short answer, which has already been alluded to, is that like the actions required by punitive orders, the actions required by damages orders are not appropriately the subject of a legal rule because they are not intended to reflect moral reasons applying to the subject. If there were a rule-based duty to pay damages, the payment of damages would carry a different meaning than it does now. There are a myriad reasons that one person might have a duty to pay a sum of money to another. To be sure, if a rule stated that such and such sums must be paid in the case where, say, goods are not delivered in accordance with a contract, then it would be clear that the payment is required because goods were not delivered in accordance with a contract. But the condition for the payment—the nondelivery of goods—would be represented, in the law, as just another duty-creating fact. A rule imposing such a duty would be no different in form—or meaning—from a rule requiring that citizens who earn income must pay the government a percentage of that income. Both rules merely specify facts giving rise to duties to pay money. In contrast, the payment of court-ordered damages carries a particular meaning. Damages are ordered in response to a wrong. Not coincidentally, the same distinction is seen in the case of punishment. As noted earlier, the law does not contain rule-based duties to pay fines partly because the fines would be interpreted as taxes.

Still, we might ask why it is the law's job to provide a means to affirm and restore the parties' equality? Why does the law not confine itself to upholding those moral duties, such as they may be, arising on commission of a wrong? The answer, in broad outline, is that redressing wrongs is part of the quid pro quo for the law's claim to authority. Together with *in specie* orders, the availability of damages orders (and provisions for enforcing them), gives such assurance as the law can provide that others will comply with their duties and, where they don't, that they will be required to make amends. Without such assurance, the law cannot reasonably ask citizens to comply with the duties stipulated by the law.[38] This explanation does not deny that wrongdoers may also incur moral duties to make amends for their wrongs. However, the circumstances in which those duties arise and the ways of making amends often bear little resemblance to the law's response to wrongdoing. Sometimes an apology is sufficient, sometimes a bottle of wine may be appropriate, and sometimes making proper amends requires a lifetime of effort. More importantly, private amends is a private matter. An order to pay damages publicly confirms that the law applies equally to both parties.

The third and final question raised by the two-principle model concerns its relationship to corrective justice. Weinrib and Gardner present the duty to pay damages as an instantiation of corrective justice. Indeed, each writer presents the one-principle

[38] For two very different justifications for this proposition (which draw, respectively, on Locke and Kant), *see* Goldberg & Zipursky, *Rights and Responsibilities*, at 269–71; Ripstein, *As If It Had Never Happened*, at 159–68.

model not merely as consistent with corrective justice, but as the outcome of a reflection on the meaning of corrective justice.[39] This characterization is puzzling because the two-principle account defended above presents itself as the private law analog to retributive justice—and corrective justice is widely assumed to be the private law analog of retributive justice. The question, then, is whether the two-principle model is indeed an account of corrective justice and, if it is, whether the one-principle model is also an account of corrective justice. The answer, I suggest, is that the two-principle model is an account of corrective justice and, further, it better fits the conventional Aristotelian understanding of corrective justice—which both Weinrib and Gardner endorse—than the one-principle model.

On the first page of the essay where his account of damages is most fully developed, Weinrib endorses the following account from Aristotle of the operation of corrective justice in a civil suit:

> [P]eople have recourse to a judge when they are engaged in a dispute. To go to a judge means to go to the just, for to be a judge means, as it were, to be the embodiment of what is just ... The judge restores equality. As though there were a line divided into two unequal parts, he takes away the amount by which the larger part is greater than half the line and adds it to the smaller part.[40]

Three aspects of Aristotle's account fit poorly with the one-principle model. First, Aristotle's account supposes that a judge brings about the result required by corrective justice. As Weinrib observes later in the same essay, "The point of Aristotle's account is to draw attention to the relationship between the particular injustice of the causative event and the particular response ordered by the judge."[41] This observation is problematic for the one-principle model because in that model's account of damages, the judge plays only an incidental role. As we have seen, the model assumes the existence of a rule-based substantive duty to pay damages. To be sure, the model presumes that judges will support this duty with duty-confirming orders, just as it presumes that judges will support duties to perform original contractual promises by issuing *in specie* orders. But the one-principle model has nothing to say about why judges should issue orders. The model is entirely an account of why there is a duty to pay damages.[42] If the duty to pay damages is fulfilled, there is no need to go to a judge. It is a mystery, therefore, why, if the one-principle model is meant to express Aristotle's conception of corrective justice, the judge figures so heavily in that conception. In contrast, Aristotle's focus on the judge fits the two-principle account of damages perfectly. The two-principle model supposes that

[39] Weinrib, *Two Conceptions of Remedies*, at 3; Gardner, *What Is Tort Law for?*, at 2.

[40] Weinrib, *Two Conceptions of Remedies*, at 1 [quoting Aristotle, Nicomachean Ethics V, 1132a19–29 (M. Ostwald trans., 1962)].

[41] Weinrib, *Two Conceptions of Remedies*, at 4. Throughout his writings, Weinrib highlights the judge's role in bringing about corrective justice. In The Idea of Private Law, Weinrib writes: "[t]he agent of this rectification [the rectification required by corrective justice] is the judge;" *Two Conceptions of Remedies*, at 65.

[42] Even if it were the case that part of the role of judges is to specify previously inchoate duties to pay damages, the one-principle model does not explain the importance of judges within the Aristotelian account of corrective justice because the model assumes that *in-specie* orders are also instantiations of corrective justice.

duties to pay damages are, and must be, created by judicial orders. In the two-principle model, damages can only achieve their ends when and because they are ordered by a judge.

The second problematic aspect of Aristotle's conception for the one-principle model is that it is an account of *corrective* justice, that is, it is an account of what is required to correct a wrong. Weinrib highlights this aspect of Aristotle's account when he observes that "what makes the judge's action corrective, *diorthotikon*, [is that] it is 'literally righting' a wrong."[43] Gardner makes a similar point when he observes that corrective justice always involves the reversal, undoing, or counteraction of a transaction.[44] This focus on correction fits uneasily with the one-principle model because the model views duties to pay damages as transformed versions of the original duty. Paying damages for a breach of contract is treated as similar in kind to late performance and, indeed, to performing on time. In the one-principle model, wrongdoers must pay damages not for correcting a wrong—the wrong is strictly irrelevant—but rather to comply as best they now can with their original duty or the reasons underlying it. Yet neither the original duty nor the reasons underlying it are directed at correcting or even responding to a wrong. The duty to perform a contract arises from the nonwrong of making a contract. Aristotle's image of the judge redividing a line when ordering damages is inapt if paying damages just continues the original duty. Damages, in the one-principle model, aim not to restore a balance but to attain a goal—namely the fulfillment of the object of the original duty or the reasons underlying that duty.

It is true that elsewhere in his work Weinrib downplays the corrective aspect of corrective justice. Though he never adopts Aquinas's terminology of "commutative justice," Weinrib follows Aquinas in supposing that corrective justice can explain not just duties to correct wrongs but also primary duties.[45] According to this view, contracting parties' duties to perform their contracts are duties of corrective justice. It may be queried whether corrective justice retains a distinctive meaning in this formulation—certainly it loses the distinctively arithmetic form described by Aristotle—but in any event Weinrib describes the payment of damages, at least, as an aspect of correction in the Aristotelian sense. Gardner similarly supposes that paying damages is an instance of Aristotelian corrective justice. Yet neither of their accounts explains the reason for paying damages in this way. For each of them, paying damages is fundamentally a way of satisfying a right (or the reasons underlying it). Indeed, if the one-principle model is correct, then "correction" is not only not the exclusive concern of corrective justice, it is not a concern at all. In contrast, it is essential to the two-principle model that damages are intended to correct a wrong.

The third reason Aristotle's account fits the two-principle model better than the one-principle model is that it is an account of justice. The concept of justice can be understood in different ways, but in the usual understanding it is concerned, as

[43] Weinrib, *Two Conceptions of Remedies*, at 5.

[44] Gardner, *What Is Tort Law for?*, at 9. It is not clear if Gardner thinks the reversal must always be a reversal of a wrong, but certainly it must be a reversal of something that stands in need of correction and, in the case of damages, he thinks this thing is a wrong.

[45] Weinrib, *Two Conceptions of Remedies*, at 56, 64–5.

John Gardner notes, with "moral norms of a distinctive type."[46] Specifically, and as Gardner again explains, norms of justice are traditionally understood to be concerned with matters of allocation.[47] This is why it is unusual, Aquinas notwithstanding, to say that we are required as a matter of justice to perform our contracts or to refrain from committing torts. Rather, we say that we should do these things simply because they are the right thing to do. However, issues of justice are raised once a judge becomes involved in a dispute. For example, if a judge refuses without good reason to order a defendant to pay a valid contractual debt or to refrain from infringing a valid restrictive covenant, then an obvious injustice has occurred. Because the resolution of a dispute is necessarily an allocative task, it is also necessarily a matter of justice.

This understanding poses a problem for the contention that the one-principle model is a model of justice because the duties (or reasons underlying them) that are the model's concerns are duties to do things like perform contracts, not commit assaults, and so on. If paying damages is basically a means of fulfilling a promissory duty (or the reasons underlying that duty), it is not clear how it is connected with justice, at least as conventionally understood. To be sure, if the duty is not performed, then the matter may end up in court, at which point it becomes a matter of justice that the dispute be resolved appropriately. Yet as was noted earlier, the one-principle model is fundamentally an account of rule-based duties to pay damages; the judge's only role is to rubber-stamp the duty.

Admittedly, the concept of justice is understood by some writers, including Professor Weinrib, to apply to actions like the fulfillment of contractual promises. Again, it may be queried whether the one-principle model gains anything from its association with such a broadly defined concept. For present purposes, however, it is sufficient to observe that, in contrast to the one-principle explanation, the two-principle explanation of damages neatly fits the conventional and traditional understandings of justice and, indeed, of corrective justice. This is exactly what we should expect if damages are the private law equivalent of criminal punishment. Damages play the role in corrective justice that punishment plays in retributive justice.[48]

[46] Gardner, *What Is Tort Law for?*, at 6. [47] Gardner, *What Is Tort Law for?*, at 6–10.

[48] If space permitted, a fourth question would be whether the two-principle model is consistent with the common law position that liability for breach of contract is strict. Briefly, it might be thought that the two-principle model's focus on wrongdoing sits uneasily with strict liability and, further, that the one-principle model's focus on the original duty easily explains strict liability (the latter claim is made explicitly by Raz, *Personal Practical Conflicts*, and indirectly by Gardner in *Obligations and Outcomes in the Law of Torts, in* RELATING TO RESPONSIBILITY: ESSAYS FOR TONY HONORÉ (Peter Cane & John Gardner, eds., 2001)). But the issue is more complex. To begin, for the one-principle model to explain strict liability, strict liabilities must reflect strict duties. Yet if contractual duties are indeed strict, then breaching them is by definition a wrong. And if the liability to pay damages arises from a wrong, then it is consistent with the two-principle model. A further complication is that it is not clear that the law actually recognizes strict duties. Strict duties impose patently unreasonable demands on citizens. (The best way to make sure that you do not breach a strict duty not to trespass is to never move your body.) Thus, it may be better to interpret strict liabilities along the lines suggested by their label, namely as pure or "free-standing" liabilities to damages orders (that is, as liabilities to pay damages that are not conditional on a breach). Neither model explains such liabilities. I discuss strict liabilities in *Strict Duties and the Rule of Law, in* PRIVATE LAW AND THE RULE OF LAW (Denis Klimchuk and Lisa Austin eds., forthcoming).

18

Efficient Breach

*Gregory Klass**

The most widely known, and widely criticized, economic claim about contract law is the theory of efficient breach. The simplest version of the theory recommends expectation damages because expectation damages give parties a reason to perform when and only when performance will increase overall social welfare. Oliver Wendell Holmes famously wrote that "[t]he duty to keep a contract at common law means a prediction that you must pay damages if you do not keep it,—and nothing else."[1] The simple theory of efficient breach advances a prescriptive version of the Holmesian Heresy. Where Holmes attributed the disjunctive view of contract obligations to the "bad man," the efficient breach theory attributes it to the law. A contractual duty is a duty to perform or pay damages because, having priced breach correctly, the law wants the promisor sometimes to choose breach.

Many contract theorists find this theory of efficient breach deeply unsatisfactory. To those who adopt nonwelfarist approaches, the theory's prescriptive claim can look like a *reductio ad absurdum* of welfarism. Any theory that claims that contract law should encourage the moral wrong of breach must be based on a false premise. Thus contract theorists who emphasize promissory obligations, principles of corrective justice, autonomy, or other nonwelfarist principles commonly either take the theory of efficient breach as their foil or simply ignore it.

This is unfortunate. An adequate theory of the functions or justifications of contract law requires a clear understanding of what contract law can do, which demands thinking about legal design. Economic work on design questions, including the theory of efficient breach, has produced significant results. Those results are independent of the social welfare principle that early proponents of efficient breach employed, and contract theorists should attend to them.

In fact, despite the attention the simple theory of efficient breach still garners, few economically oriented scholars would today defend it.[2] But many noneconomist contract theorists have paid little attention to subsequent economic work in the area.

* This chapter benefited from comments at the Bentham House Annual Conference 2013: The Philosophical Foundations of Contract Law, at University College London, May 10–11, 2013, as well as conversations with my colleague Josh Teitelbaum.

[1] Oliver Wendell Holmes, *The Path of the Law*, 10 Harv. L. Rev. 457, 462 (1897), *reprinted in* 110 Harv. L. Rev. 991, 995 (1997).

[2] As Richard Craswell explains: "Because these arguments are so simple, they are easily reproduced (and also easily criticized), so it is not surprising that they continue to loom large in much of contracts scholarship. . . . In point of fact, though, most economists have long since moved on to a much more complex analysis of efficiency and contract law." Richard Craswell, *Two Economic Theories of Enforcing Promises*, *in* The Theory of Contract Law: New Essays 19, 26 (P. Benson ed., 2001).

This chapter provides an overview. I begin by recounting the simple theory of efficient breach, the theory noneconomist scholars most often criticize. After describing the common criticisms, I canvass four economic critiques of the simple theory. Contemporary economic analyses of contract remedies, though they leave room for efficient breach, are far more nuanced than the simple theory suggests. I then identify three important lessons contract theorists, no matter what their orientation, can learn from a revised, more sophisticated theory of efficient breach. First, remedies often affect other terms, including the price. Second, as a result, parties themselves often want efficient remedies. Third, lawmakers must decide whether, when, or how parties should be able to choose the remedy. These lessons about the design of contract remedies pose questions that any theory of contract law should be equipped to answer. They also suggest design options nonwelfarist theories might find useful.

I. The Simple Theory of Efficient Breach

The simple theory purports to solve a puzzle posed by Lon Fuller and William Perdue in their 1936 article, *The Reliance Interest in Contract Damages: 1*.[3] Fuller and Perdue famously distinguish three "interests" of the nonbreaching party in obtaining relief, each corresponding to a damage measure. In a contract between A and B that A breaches, protecting B's restitution interest requires the return of any benefit that B directly provided A.[4] Protecting B's reliance interest requires compensating B for any change in B's position based on the expectation of A's performance, thereby putting B in the place B would have occupied had B not entered the contract. Protecting B's expectation interest requires providing B its expected gains from the transaction, putting B in the position B would have occupied had A performed the contract. The expectation measure typically exceeds the reliance measure, which is often greater than the restitution measure. Fuller and Perdue argue that the reasons for providing restitution and reliance-based damages are easy enough to intuit. The reasons for expectation damages not so much. "[T]he promisee who has actually relied on the promise, even though he may not thereby have enriched the promisor, certainly presents a more pressing case for relief than the promisee who merely demands satisfaction for his disappointment in not getting what was promised him."[5] The puzzle is why the law should " 'compensate' the plaintiff by giving him something he never had."[6]

The simple theory of efficient breach has an answer: the expectation remedy maximizes social welfare. As Richard Posner put the major premise, "contract remedies should... give the party to a contract an incentive to fulfill his promise unless the result would be an inefficient use of resources."[7] Of the three measures, only expectation damages provide an incentive to perform if and only if performance is efficient. The reason can be explained with an example.

[3] L. L. Fuller & William M. Perdue, Jr., *The Reliance Interest in Contract Damages: 1*, 46 Yale L.J. 52 (1936).

[4] "Directly" to distinguish restitution from disgorgement, which requires the breaching party to turn over all of the benefits from breach.

[5] Fuller & Perdue, *The Reliance Interest in Contract Damages*, at 56.

[6] Fuller & Perdue, *The Reliance Interest in Contract Damages*, at 52–3.

[7] Richard A. Posner, Economic Analysis of the Law, 56 (1972).

Suppose on January 1, Seller enters into a contract to sell goods to Buyer. Seller is to provide Buyer 100 units on or before July 1. Buyer is to pay $10 per unit, or $1,000 total, due 30 days after delivery. Seller is going to manufacture the goods in question, and expects to spend $8 per unit on production, shipment, and overhead. Buyer is going to use the units to manufacture other goods. On top of its $10 per unit payment to Seller, Buyer's costs of production, resale, and overhead are $6 per unit, and it will sell its product for $18 per unit. For each unit, therefore, the transaction generates $4 in new value: Buyer and Seller together invest a net $14 to produce a product worth $18 to willing purchasers. Out of this $4 surplus, Buyer takes $2 and Seller takes $2. If their relative bargaining strength were different, Seller and Buyer might divide that surplus differently. At a price of $9 per unit, Seller would take $1 and buyer $3; at a price of $11, the division would go the other way. The limiting factors are that Seller is unwilling to sell for less than $8, and buyer to buy for more than $12. Neither will agree to a losing deal.

Although the transaction looks like it will create value when the parties agree to it, things could change before the time of performance. A good deal in January might look much less attractive in April. The efficient breach theory considers two types of changes: good news and bad news.[8]

The more common scenario in the literature involves good news. Suppose on April 1, Third Party contacts Seller and offers to purchase 100 units for $1,300, or $13 per unit. Third Party is a competitor of Buyer and is willing to pay more for the goods because it has a new, less expensive production method. Whereas Buyer's production costs are $6 per unit, Third Party's costs are $3. Seller does not have the capacity to produce more than 100 units and so can sell to Third Party only if it breaches with Buyer. To keep things simple, suppose on April 1, Buyer has not yet invested any resources in the transaction and if Seller breaches, Buyer will not be able to get replacement goods elsewhere.

Sale to Third Party is more efficient than sale to Buyer. The transaction between Seller and Buyer creates $4 of value for each unit sold ($18 market price – $8 Seller costs – $6 Buyer costs). Sale to Third Party, on the contrary, will produce $7 per unit ($18 market price – $8 Seller costs – $3 Third Party costs). If we want to maximize social welfare (as measured in dollars), we want Seller to breach the contract with Buyer and sell to Third Party.

If Seller is a purely self-interested rational utility maximizer and has no other reason to perform or breach, expectation damages produce that result. The expectation measure requires Seller to pay Buyer for the profits Buyer would have earned from the transaction plus any costs Buyer has already incurred. On the facts, this means a transfer from Seller to Buyer of $2 per unit. If Seller sells to Third Party, Seller earns $5 per unit ($13 price – $8 production costs). Seller will therefore choose to breach, pay Buyer the $2 per unit in damages, and emerge with $3 per unit net profit, one dollar more than Seller would have made by performing.

[8] Economic analyses typically treat the good-news and bad-news scenarios as functionally equivalent, which accords with the assumed equivalence of opportunity costs and out-of-pocket costs. For an account of how the scenarios can differ, *see* Steven Shavell, *Specific Performance Versus Damages for Breach of Contract: An Economic Analysis*, 84 Tex L. Rev. 831 (2006).

Observe that if Third Party had offered Seller only $11 per unit, Seller would have chosen to perform, even though Third Party's offer is higher than the contract price. At $11, Seller initially earns $3 per unit. But after paying Buyer $2 per unit in damages, Seller emerges with only $1 net profit, making performance the preferred option. This too is the right result. Third Party's $11 offer does not indicate that Third Party values the goods more than Buyer does. Third Party might, for example, have the same production costs as Buyer's, but be willing to take $1 profit rather than Buyer's $2. Only if Third Party offers more than $12 per unit do we know that Third Party is the more efficient recipient of the goods. More generally, in a contract between A and B, the expectation measure gives A a reason to breach in favor of C's offer only if C's price indicates that C values A's performance more than B values that performance.

Expectation damages also provide the right incentives when the unexpected change involves bad news. Suppose instead of an attractive offer from Third Party, Seller's production costs unexpectedly go up, say as the result of a fire in its factory. Do we still want Seller to produce the goods for Buyer?

If we are concerned only with maximizing social welfare, it depends on the magnitude of the cost increase. Suppose Seller's per-unit costs increase from $8 to $11. The transaction is now a losing one for Seller. Seller will expend $11 to produce a good for which Buyer will pay $10. But the transaction as a whole remains welfare enhancing. With Seller investing $11 and Buyer investing $6, they together spend $17 to generate $18 in value. If, alternatively, Seller's per-unit costs go up to $13, performance is inefficient. Seller and Buyer are together spending $19 per unit to produce $18 in value.

Again the expectation measure gives Seller the right incentives. With no legal remedy, Seller experiences only its own costs of performance or breach. With the expectation remedy, Seller also experiences the costs of breach to Buyer. As a result, Seller will choose performance so long as the transaction as a whole creates value. If Seller's per-unit performance costs go up to $11, Seller loses $1 per unit on performance ($11 costs – $10 contract price). Because breach would cost seller $2 per unit in expectation damages, Seller will choose efficient performance. If Seller's performance costs go up to $13, Seller loses $3 per unit. Now Seller will choose to breach and pay damages.

Adding Buyer reliance does not change the result. Suppose on April 1, when Seller is considering breach, Buyer has invested $200 in preparing its own production facilities, an investment that will be wasted should Seller breach. The social cost of breach now includes destroying the value of Buyer's investment. A sale to Third Party for $13 per unit therefore results in only a $3 per-unit net gain from the transaction ($13 sale price – $8 Seller costs – $2 Buyer lost investment), which is less than the $4 net gain from performance. Again expectation damages get us the right result. Buyer's reliance means that the expectation measure is now $4 per unit ($2 wasted investment + $2 lost profit). Facing those payments, Seller will breach only if Third Party offers to purchase for more than $14 per unit, the point at which Seller's gain from breach equals its gain from performance ($14 price – $8 production costs – $4 damages = $2). This is correct. Only an offer of more than $14 clearly indicates that a sale to Third Party will generate more value than will performance.

Adding a prepayment to the hypothetical also does not change the result. Expectation damages give efficient incentives in all the scenarios for the same reason: In a contract between A and B, the social gain from A's performance is the sum of A and B's expected profits. If there is no legal remedy, when A decides between performance and breach A considers only its own expected profits. Expectation damages force A to internalize the effect of breach on B's expected profits. The measure thereby forces A to weigh all the welfare effects of performance against all the welfare effects of breach. A will perform when performance creates more value and will breach when breach creates more value. As Robert Cooter and Melvin Eisenberg put the point, "expectation damages place on the promisor the promisee's loss of his share of the contract's value in the event of breach, and thereby sweep that loss into the promisor's calculus of self-interest."[9]

We now have an answer to Fuller and Perdue's puzzle. Only expectation damages give parties efficient incentives. Because neither the reliance nor the restitution measure incorporates the gains of trade, both are typically lower than the expectation measure. Under either, therefore, a self-interested rational party will sometimes breach when performance would be more efficient. Supercompensatory remedies, such as disgorgement or punitive damages, are similarly inefficient. They give a party too much reason to perform and will sometimes result in performance when breach would be more efficient. Only the expectation remedy gives parties an incentive to perform if and only if performance maximizes social welfare.

II. Criticisms from Outside the Model

The efficient breach theory was first introduced by Robert Birmingham in his 1970 article, "Breach of Contract, Damage Measures, and Economic Efficiency," though the theory's influence is due to its promotion in the 1972 first edition of Richard Posner's *Economic Analysis of Law*.[10] By the 1983 publication of the *Restatement (Second) of Contracts*, the theory was widespread enough to receive a tentative endorsement in the Introductory Note to the Remedies chapter.[11] But the drafters also added a caveat:

> [The efficient breach theory's] focus on the pecuniary aspects of breach fails to take account of notions of the sanctity of contract and the resulting moral obligation to honor one's promises. The analysis of breach of contract in purely economic terms assumes an ability to measure value with a certainty that is not often possible in the

[9] Robert Cooter & Melvin Aron Eisenberg, *Damages for Breach of Contract*, 73 Calif. L. Rev. 1432, 1463 (1985).

[10] Robert L. Birmingham, *Breach of Contract, Damage Measures, and Economic Efficiency*, 24 Rutgers L. Rev. 273, 284, 288–9 (1970); Posner, Economic Analysis of the Law, §§ 3.8–3.11, 55–61. Douglas Baird has identified efficient breach theory as "Posner's most important contribution in contracts," with no mention of Robert Birmingham's earlier contribution. Douglas G. Baird, Reconstructing Contracts (2013). Birmingham's 1970 article bears reading by anyone interested in contract theory and economic analysis. In addition to introducing the idea of efficient breach, Birmingham discusses the relationship between contract law and nineteenth-century free market thinking, the Scholastic just price theory, and the application of efficient breach to labor contracts.

[11] *Chapter 16: Introductory Note, in* Restatement (Second) of Contracts 99–100 (1983).

judicial process. The analysis also ignores the "transaction costs" inherent in the bargaining process and in the resolution of disputes, a defect that is especially significant where the amount in controversy is small.[12]

This compressed statement gestures toward two strands of criticism. The first argues that the efficient breach theory is morally problematic, the second that it relies on empirically false assumptions.

The moral criticism begins with the simple theory's apparent celebration of efficient breach. Early advocates wrote that efficient breach should be "encouraged," that when performance is no longer efficient, there should be "an incentive to commit breach," and that "a contractual obligation is not necessarily an obligation to perform, but rather an obligation to choose between performance and compensatory damages."[13] These claims run contrary to common understandings of the moral force of a promise. A promise that is neither disjunctive nor conditional in form is neither disjunctive nor conditional in effect. A contractual promise creates a moral obligation to perform, not an obligation to perform if performance is efficient, or an obligation to perform or pay damages. An efficient breach remains a breach and therefore a wrong, and the law should not be in the business of encouraging wrongful behavior. The efficient breach theory commends acts that the law should condemn.[14]

Nor are the distributive outcomes of efficient breach morally attractive. Efficient breach theorists emphasize that when expectation damages work correctly, the obligee is indifferent between performance and breach. So long as damages put the non-breaching party in the position she would have occupied had performance occurred,

[12] Restatement (Second) of Contracts, at 100.

[13] Birmingham, *Breach of Contract*, at 284, 288–9; Posner, Economic Analysis of the Law, at 57; Charles J. Goetz & Robert E. Scott, *Liquidated Damages, Penalties and the Just Compensation Principle: Some Notes on an Enforcement Model and a Theory of Efficient Breach*, 77 Colum. L. Rev. 554, 558 (1977). Other early advocates adopted less charged formulations. John H. Barton, *The Economic Basis of Damages for Breach of Contract*, 1 J. Legal Stud. 277, 282 (1972) ("In the situation of changed circumstances, it may well be economically inefficient to complete the transaction. The changes may make the total cost of the transaction greater than the total benefits. Consequently, one is properly chary about requiring the enforcement of what I have called the 'non-market' contract, through injunction or through damages of a form that always induces performance."); Thomas S. Ulen, *The Efficiency of Specific Performance: Toward a Unified Theory of Contract Remedies*, 83 Mich. L. Rev. 341, 342 (1984) ("The law... should not hinder the breaching of contracts where the breach offers a Pareto-superior outcome.")

[14] *See, e.g.*, Douglas Laycock, *Holmes, Posner and Efficient Breach*, *in* The Death of the Irreparable Injury Rule 245 (1991); Daniel Friedmann, *The Efficient Breach Fallacy*, 18 J. Legal Stud. 1 (1989); Frank Menetrez, Comment, *Consequentialism, Promissory Obligation, and the Theory of Efficient Breach*, 47 U.C.L.A. L. Rev. 859 (2000); Seana Valentine Shiffrin, *The Divergence of Contract and Promise*, 120 Harv. L. Rev. 708, 732–3 (2007). For an ambitious attempt to argue that sophisticated parties do in fact intend their promises to be disjunctive, *see* Daniel Markovits & Alan Schwartz, *The Myth of Efficient Breach: New Defenses of the Expectation Interest*, 97 Va. L. Rev. 1939, 1973–7 (2011); Daniel Markovits & Alan Schwartz, *The Expectation Remedy and the Promissory Basis of Contract*, 45 Suffolk U. L. Rev. 799, 808–12 (2012). For criticisms of Markovits and Schwartz's argument, *see* Gregory Klass, *To Perform or Pay Damages*, 98 Va. L. Rev. 143 (2012); Seana Valentine Shiffrin, *Must I Mean What You Think I* Should *Have Said?*, 98 Va. L. Rev. 159 (2012)..

This criticism of the efficient breach theory should be distinguished from criticisms of expectation damages as insufficiently attuned to parties' moral obligations. Many authors assume or argue that the morality of promising recommends specific performance, disgorgement, or punitive damages for breach. Such claims are not directed at the efficient breach theory as such. I suggests some responses to such criticisms of the expectation remedy in Gregory Klass, *Promise Etc.*, 45 Suffolk U. L. Rev. 695 (2012).

what does it matter if her counterpart chooses to efficiently breach rather than perform? This attitude treats damage payments as an indulgence that washes away the wrong of breach.[15] As such, it misunderstands the function of damage payments. An unexcused failure to perform a promise often produces secondary obligations, such as the duty to apologize or to somehow make it up to the promisee. Damage payments might track or satisfy those obligations. They do not, however, make the wrong of breach go away, even if the promisee is fully compensated. Promissory obligations are about more than ensuring that the promisee achieves a certain level of welfare. They are about trust and moral authority. Post-breach redistribution does nothing to undo the moral wrong of breach.

In fact, the theory's recommended distribution gets things exactly wrong, for it advocates rewarding breach.[16] In the good-news scenario described above, the original contract promised $4 per unit in net gains from performance, $2 profit to Seller and $2 profit to Buyer. Third Party's offer to pay $13 for the goods created the opportunity for the parties to realize between them a $5 per-unit gain ($13 price – $8 Seller costs = $5). If, as the efficient breach theory recommends, Seller breaches, pays expectation damages, and sells the goods to Third Party, Seller pockets the $1 difference ($3 profit vs. $2 profit) and buyer comes out even ($2 expectation damages). If, on the contrary, Seller delivers the goods, Buyer might sell them to Third Party. Now, as compared to the first transaction, Seller comes out even ($2 profit), whereas Buyer receives the extra $1 from the sale to Third Party ($13 resale price – $10 contract price = $3). The theory of efficient breach is morally problematic not only because it encourages a moral wrong, but also because it would allocate all the gains from that wrong to the wrongdoer. The morally optimal remedy for a good-news efficient breach, according to this line of thinking, is disgorgement: return to the nonbreaching party of the Seller's gains from reallocating resources that had been promised to the buyer.[17]

In addition to these moral deficiencies, the simple theory rests on a false picture of the world. To begin with, as the drafters of the Second Restatement suggest, the theory largely ignores transaction costs.[18] The simple theory offers no account of how it is that breaching parties come to pay expectation damages. In the real world, payment often happens only after litigation or private settlement, which consume judicial and party resources that might otherwise be used to increase social

[15] "The indulgence which the preachers proclaim the 'greatest grace' is truly that, insofar as it brings great profit." Martin Luther, 95 Theses, Thesis 67.

[16] I believe this was first noticed in print by Goetz & Scott, *Liquidated Damages, Penalties and the Just Compensation Principle*, at 559, 568.

[17] *See* Richard R. W. Brooks, *The Efficient Performance Hypothesis*, 116 Yale L.J. 568, 572–3 (2006); John P. Dawson, *Restitution or Damages?*, 20 Ohio St. L.J. 175, 186–7 (1959); Melvin A. Eisenberg, *The Disgorgement Interest in Contract Law*, 105 Mich. L. Rev. 559, 578–81 (2006); Daniel Friedmann, *Restitution of Benefits Obtained through the Appropriation of Property or the Commission of a Wrong*, 80 Colum. L. Rev. 504, 513–27 (1980).

[18] This paragraph barely scratches the surface of the many sorts of transaction costs that are involved in enforcing contracts. For a richer descriptive account, *see* A. A. Leff, *Injury, Ignorance, and Spite—The Dynamics of Coercive Collection*, 80 Yale L.J. 1 (1970). *See also* Daniel A. Farber, *Reassessing the Economic Efficiency of Compensatory Damages for Breach of Contract*, 66 Va. L. Rev. 1443 (1980) (emphasizing both transaction costs and uncertainty of recovery).

welfare. Because litigation and settlement costs are deadweight losses, they can render an otherwise efficient breach socially inefficient. Litigation and settlement costs can also destroy the efficient incentives expectation damages would otherwise create. Depending on how the costs are allocated, they can result in undercompensation for nonbreaching parties and overdeterrence (from an efficiency perspective) of prospective breachers. Finally, litigation and settlement costs sometimes deter the victims of breach from even filing a lawsuit. Though efficient breach theory assumes that the obligee is indifferent between performance and breach, we know from experience that this is rarely the case.

The simple theory also unrealistically assumes perfect information. In the actual world, meritorious lawsuits sometimes fail due to lack of evidence or mistakes of judgment. And even where there is a finding of breach, a monetary award might not match actual losses. The plaintiff's burden of proof and legal rules that limit recovery mean that damage awards are systematically undercompensatory.[19] Nor do parties have the knowledge that the simple theory requires of them. In the above example, to know whether performance is efficient or in its interest, Seller must know both Buyer's present investment in the transaction and Buyer's expected profits from performance. In the actual world, one party rarely knows what its breach will cost the other. The efficient breach theory assumes transparency in an opaque world.[20]

Finally, the simple theory employs a false picture of how contracting parties decide between performance and breach. First, the theory assumes that parties are perfectly rational, or at least rational on average. Cognitive science and behavioral economics have demonstrated that even sophisticated parties can be systematically irrational. If this is so, we cannot be sure that even if the expectation remedy creates efficient incentives, parties will respond to them as the theory predicts.

Second, the simple theory assumes that the threat of legal liability is the only reason to perform. Opportunities for repeat play and reputational effects can give even an amoral self-interested rational utility maximizer nonlegal reasons to perform. A party who expects that she might have a long-term opportunity to transact with her counterpart again might not want to sacrifice it for a short-term gain from breach. And a party who regularly engages in similar transactions with others might worry about the reputational costs of breach.[21] Nor should we accept the premise that parties are purely self-interested. Many contracting parties have other-regarding preferences. Whether these come from friendship, moral responsiveness, a sense of honor, or somewhere else, such preferences provide additional reasons to perform. Only by assuming away such reasons can the

[19] *See, e.g.*, Charles J. Goetz & Robert E. Scott, *Enforcing Promises: An Examination of the Basis of Contract*, 89 YALE L.J. 1261, 1288–91 (1980).

[20] The costs of observing the nonbreaching party's expectation interest are rarely emphasized in the literature. An exception is Melvin A. Eisenberg, *Actual and Virtual Specific Performance, the Theory of Efficient Breach, and the Indifference Principle in Contract Law*, 93 CALIF. L. REV. 975, 1000, 1015 (2005); Eisenberg, *The Disgorgement Interest in Contract Law*, at 572. *See also* Barton, *The Economic Basis of Damages for Breach of Contract*, at 282 (mentioning that the efficient breach model "assumes a rather complete knowledge by the parties of each other's utilities… seldom warranted in practice").

[21] *See* Goetz & Scott, *Enforcing Promises*, at 1289 ("[A]n optimal legal sanction may also include a discount for the effects of extra-legal factors—such as reputational losses or social restraints on breach—that independently reward the performing promisor for taking into account some of the social effects of promising.").

simple breach theory conclude that expectation damages perfectly calibrate a party's reasons to perform.[22]

There are therefore two problems with the simple theory of efficient breach, one normative and the other descriptive. The theory judges whether breach is desirable and what the consequences of breach should be in ways that cannot be squared with common understandings of the parties' moral obligations. And the theory gets its results only by assuming away facts that we know to be true of most parties, most contractual transactions, and most contract disputes.

III. Criticisms from within the Model

The above common criticisms are, I think, enough to reject the simple theory of efficient breach as a complete explanation or sufficient justification of the common law's apparent attachment to expectation damages. The question is whether those criticisms aim at a theory worth criticizing. Although the simple theory enjoys some sway in the legal imagination, no serious economic thinker today propounds it. In fact, as soon as the simple theory appeared, economically oriented scholars working within the same neoclassical and welfarist model began raising significant questions about it. Over 40 years later, it is clear that even granting the assumptions of neoclassical economics, the simple theory simplifies much too much. It fails to recognize that some breaches are not only inefficient, but opportunistic. It does not provide a defense of expectation damages as against other possibly equally efficient remedies. It focuses on the single perform-or-breach decision, when in fact remedial rules provide incentives to act more or less efficiently across the whole of a transaction. And it ignores other functions remedies serve, such as risk allocation and signaling.

Even within the simplifying assumption of the model, expectation damages are a second-best tool for welfare maximization. In a first-best world, parties would enter into efficient complete contingent contracts. A complete contingent contract anticipates every contingency that might affect the desirability of performance and instructs the parties what to do in those circumstances.[23] An efficient complete contingent contract between Seller and Buyer, for example, would stipulate that if a third party offers

[22] For some initial attempts to make the empirical case specific to contract, *see* Tess Wilkinson-Ryan & David A. Hoffman, *Breach is for Suckers*, 63 VAND. L. REV. 1001 (2010); Tess Wilkinson-Ryan, *Do Liquidated Damages Encourage Breach? A Psychological Experiment*, 108 MICH. L. REV. 633 (2010); Daphna Lewinsohn-Zamir, *The Questionable Efficiency of the Efficient-Breach Doctrine*, 168 J. INSTITUTIONAL & THEORETICAL ECON. 5 (2012).

[23] *See* Steven Shavell, *Damage Measures for Breach of Contract*, 11 BELL J. ECON. 466, 468 (1980) ("[A] damage measure for breach of contract may create incentives for parties who have made a contract which does not provide for various contingencies to act in a way that is close to (and in the example is actually identical to) what they would have agreed upon under a Pareto efficient complete contingent contract"); *see also* Barton, *The Economic Basis of Damages for Breach of Contract*, at 283–7 (anticipating Shavell's notion of a complete contingent contract); Steven Shavell, *On the Design of Contracts and Remedies for Breach*, 99 Q. J. ECON. 121, 147 (1984) (further elaborating the idea). George Triantis has recently argued that many contracts are partly complete. "Real-world contracts, of course, are not complete. However, they may be partly 'complete' with respect to a subset of future states of the world. In particular, the parties may complete that portion of their contract by using conditions, and thereby assign efficient obligations to different states of the world." George G. Triantis, *The Evolution of Contract Remedies (and Why Do Contracts Professors Teach Remedies First?)*, 60 U. TORONTO L.J. 643, 646 (2010).

more than $12 per unit for the goods or if Seller's production increases to over $12 per unit, Seller shall be excused from delivery. Depending on the parties' risk preferences, the contract might also require that in that event Seller pay money to Buyer. In short, a complete contingent contract describes all of the circumstances in which performance is efficient and imposes a duty to perform in and only in those circumstances. Because the breach of such a contract is by definition inefficient, it should not be priced but punished. If parties were able to write complete contingent contracts *ex ante*, or if courts were able to construe them *ex post*, there would be no need to "encourage" efficient breach. Efficient breach would not exist.[24]

Although complete contingent contracts are a theoretical fiction, it is often possible to say with certainty that one or another breach is inefficient. A breach is opportunistic when one party attempts to reap "the benefit of the bargain without bearing the agreed-upon cost."[25] Suppose in the above hypothetical that Seller delivers the goods as promised, Buyer uses them to make and sell its own product, and Buyer then refuses to pay Seller the price. In the model, Buyer's breach is not even arguably efficient. It does not shift productive resources to a more valuable use, but merely alters the distribution of wealth. In fact, if unremediated the breach will impose social costs. Future sellers will be less likely to extend credit to buyers, reducing the number of value-creating transactions; those who do sell on credit will invest in value-sucking precautions to ensure payment. The efficient breach theory provides no argument against punishing such opportunistic breaches. As Posner puts the point in later editions of *Economic Analysis of Law*, "[i]f a promisor breaks his promise merely to take advantage of the vulnerability of the promisee... we might as well throw the book at [him]."[26] Even on the premises of the simple theory, some breaches are beyond the pale.

All of this is of a piece with the familiar economic claims about when the law should attempt to prevent wrongful behavior and when it should put a price on it. As Robert Cooter has formulated the point:

> If lawmakers can identify socially desirable behavior, but are prone to error in assessing the cost of deviations from it, then sanctions [that provide full deterrence] are preferable to prices. However, if officials can accurately measure the external cost of behavior, but cannot accurately identify the socially desirable level of it, then prices are preferable to sanctions.[27]

There exist whole categories of breach that are always opportunistic or otherwise inefficient. From a purely welfarist perspective, the socially optimal level of such behavior

[24] If parties could write efficient complete contingent contracts they would do so, since such contracts maximize the potential gains of trade. I discuss this point further in Section IV.

[25] *Patton v. Mid-Continent Sys., Inc.*, 841 F.2d 742, 751 (7th Cir. 1988) (Posner, J.).

[26] Richard A. Posner, Economic Analysis of Law 105 (3d ed., 1986). For extended discussions of opportunistic breach, *see* Richard Craswell, *When is a Willful Breach "Willful"?: The Link between Definitions and Damages*, 107 Mich. L. Rev. 1501 (2009); William Dodge, *The Case for Punitive Damages in Contracts*, 48 Duke L.J. 629, 654–62 (1999).

[27] Robert Cooter, *Prices and Sanctions*, 84 Colum. L. Rev. 1523, 1524 (1984); *see also* Guido Calabresi & Douglas Melamed, *Property Rules, Liability Rules, and Inalienability: One View of the Cathedral*, 85 Harv. L. Rev. 1089 (1972).

is zero. Bad faith breach of an insurance contract is a well-known example. An insurer who knowingly denies or delays payment of a valid claim is not shifting resources to more valuable uses, but simply taking an unbargained-for piece of the pie.[28] And on the model, extracompensatory remedies might be necessary to provide an incentive to perform. Or consider duties designed to make it easier for one party to recover for the other's breach, such as the duty to keep records, to share information about performance, or to permit audits. Because such terms are designed to ensure payment for breach of the underlying duty, their breach is rarely efficient.[29] Economic theory recommends punishing rather than pricing such opportunistic breaches.

But that is not all. Even if we restrict ourselves to efficient breaches of incomplete contracts, the simple theory fails to show that only expectation damages will do. The simple theory demonstrates at most that expectation damages are one way to incentivize efficient performance decisions. It does not show that expectation damages are the only way to do so.

The problem is Coase. The Coase Theorem says that if legal entitlements can be cheaply traded, then who gets them in the first instance does not affect their ultimate allocation, which will always be efficient.[30] Entitlements assigned to low-value holders will be traded up to higher-value holders because higher-value holders will be willing to pay more for them. The initial assignment has distributive effects, but does not affect allocative efficiency. It affects who gets how much, but the entitlement eventually ends up where it creates the most value.

The simple theory of efficient breach does not consider the possibility of post-contractual Coasian bargains. Suppose courts award specific performance wherever practicable and Buyer sues as soon as Seller indicates an intent to breach.[31] In the good-news scenario above, Seller no longer has the option to breach, sell the goods to Third Party for $13 per unit, and pay Buyer $2 per unit expectation damages. It does not follow, however, that Seller will perform. Third Party's offer gives Seller and Buyer the opportunity to jointly gain $1 per unit, or $100 total, from nonperformance. If Seller is rational, it will offer to pay Buyer to release it from the contract. Buyer, who stands to net $200 from performance, will demand at least $201 for the release. Seller, who can earn up to $300 more from selling to Third Party ($1,300 offer price – $1,000 contract price), will not pay more than $299. The simplest solution is a $250 payment, which splits the gains from nonperformance. Seller sells to Third Party for $1,300, pays Buyer $250, and ends up netting $250 after its own production costs. Each party comes out $50 ahead as compared to performance.

Specific performance plus renegotiation provide a similarly efficient result in the bad-news scenario. If Seller's costs jump to $13 per unit, Seller stands to lose $300 on

[28] *See* Nicholas J. Johnson, *The Boundaries of Extracompensatory Relief for Abusive Breach of Contract*, 33 CONN. L. REV. 181, 187–8 (2000); Roger C. Henderson, *The Tort of Bad Faith in First-Party Insurance Transactions after Two Decades*, 37 ARIZ. L. REV. 1153 (1995).

[29] *See* Gregory Klass, *Contracting for Cooperation in Recovery*, 117 YALE L.J. 2 (2007).

[30] R. H. Coase, *The Problem of Social Cost*, 3 J.L. & ECON. 1 (1960).

[31] *See* Alan Schwartz, *The Case for Specific Performance*, 89 YALE L.J. 271 (1979). The basic idea was identified by Robert Birmingham a year before he introduced the theory of efficient breach. Robert L. Birmingham, *Damage Measures and Economic Rationality: The Geometry of Contract Law*, 1969 DUKE L.J. 49, 70 (1969).

performance ($1,300 cost – $1,000 contract price), and so will be willing to pay Buyer up to $299 for the release. Again Buyer will grant the release for a payment of $201 or more. Because the parties can bargain to a mutually beneficial exit price, inefficient performance will not happen. As in the good-news scenario, the parties end up sharing the gains from breach, though now Seller's gains take the form of losses avoided.

Once we allow for the possibility of post-contractual Coasian bargains, other remedies become equally plausible. Suppose courts impose punitive damages for any willful breach. So long as paying the punitive damage award costs Seller more than Seller's benefit from breach, Seller would rather perform than pay damages, even if performance is inefficient. But again there is a third option: Seller can offer to purchase Buyer's release. Buyer now prefers breach plus recovery to performance. But when negotiating for a release Seller can credibly threaten to perform, making payment for the release Buyer's preferred alternative. Again we can expect the parties to arrive at an exit price that benefits both relative to inefficient performance.[32]

We even get efficient outcomes with subcompensatory remedies. Suppose the remedy is reliance damages and that Buyer has not yet invested anything in the transaction when Third Party offers Seller $11 per unit. At that price, we cannot be sure whether breach is efficient, and because the reliance measure gives us a damage payment of zero, we might worry that Seller will take the higher offer. But faced with the threat of breach, Buyer can offer to pay Seller something more to perform. Because Buyer stands to gain $200 from performance at the original price and nothing from breach, Buyer will be willing to pay up to $199 more to secure performance. Seller, who stands to earn an additional $100 from the sale to Third Party, will demand an additional payment of at least $101. Again, so long as post-contract renegotiation is possible, the remedy gets us the right outcome.

If this last result seems odd, that is partly due to the exclusive focus on the perform-or-breach decision.[33] Even if subcompensatory remedies, or no remedies at all, are compatible with efficient performance decisions, it is not obvious that they give parties enough reason to enter into contracts in the first place. I return to this issue later in this section. For the moment, the point is merely that in the frictionless model the simple theory occupies, all remedies are created equal. To show that expectation damages are the *more efficient* remedy, we need to add transaction costs to the model. The real question is which remedy provides an efficient outcome at the lowest cost.

Economically oriented legal scholars have not ignored transaction costs. Something approaching a consensus view has emerged about the variables that matter in the choice between, on the one hand, remedies that attempt to incentivize efficient unilateral performance decisions, such as expectation damages, and on the other, remedies

[32] William Dodge has argued the efficiency of punitive damages for all willful breaches. Dodge, *The Case for Punitive Damages in Contracts*, at 663–87. For a parallel argument applied to party-specified penalties, *see* Goetz & Scott, *Liquidated Damages, Penalties and the Just Compensation Principle*, at 567. For a thorough discussion of how and when parties might threaten inefficient performance, *see* Ian Ayres & Kristin Madison, *Threatening Inefficient Performance of Injunctions and Contracts*, 148 U. Pa. L. Rev. 45 (1999).

[33] Another reason it is odd is that the Coase theorem assumes that Coasian bargains are always performed. The theorem therefore assumes a solution to a problem that contract law is designed to solve. That, however, is a topic for another forum.

that rely on post-contractual Coasian bargaining.[34] The principle cost of expectation damages is determining the nonbreaching party's losses in the case of nonperformance, that is, the magnitude of its expectation interest. This cost is borne first by the party deciding between performance and breach, and later, if the issue goes to litigation, by parties and the courts.[35] Coasian bargains avoid those measurement costs. In post-contractual negotiations, each party uses what it already knows about its own interests to arrive together at a mutually beneficial exit price. But those negotiations can themselves be costly. Parties to a contract find themselves in a bilateral monopoly: each is negotiating for a benefit it can only get from the other side, and each is likely to be ignorant of the other's reserve price. With no outside alternatives, the parties might expend considerable resources haggling over an exit price. Those negotiation costs are deadweight losses, and might even prevent the parties from reaching a deal.[36]

Even if Coasian bargains are too expensive or impracticable, there are yet other efficient options within the model. The efficient breach theory recommends giving the obligor, Seller in the above example, the choice to breach and pay damages. This is effectively a call option: Seller has the ability to purchase nonperformance for a price. It might be equally efficient to give the obligee something like a put option.[37] On this approach, Seller would have an absolute obligation to perform, enforced by specific performance, penalties, or the like, and Buyer would have the unilateral power to cancel the contract and collect from Seller some or all of Seller's potential gains from nonperformance. Now if Seller gets an offer from Third Party, Buyer can decide whether performance happens. Buyer will choose to exercise its option to cancel only if Third Party's price is high enough that Seller will pay Buyer more than Buyer would receive from performance. If Third Party offers $11 per unit, Buyer will not exercise the put. Seller's gains from nonperformance, $1 per unit, are less than Buyer's gains from performance. If Third Party offers $13 per unit, Buyer will exercise the option so long as it can extract at least $2 of the higher price. Again, from an efficiency perspective, the choice turns on transaction costs. If the goal is to have one or another side make an efficient unilateral performance decision, the question is who is the cheapest inefficiency avoider.[38] This depends in part on which party is in a better position to seek out third-party offers or other wealth-creating alternatives to performance. It also depends on relative measurement costs. Giving Buyer a put option means that we

[34] For a basic introduction, *see* *Walgreen Co. v. Sara Creek Prop. Co.*, 966 F.2d 273 (7th Cir. 1992) (Posner, J.).

[35] Most writers on efficient breach emphasize only the latter, the costs of post-breach damage determinations. This is odd, since there's little reason to expect parties to know one another's cost functions. There is no reason to expect one party to be able to observe the other's expectation interest, though that knowledge is essential to the efficient breach story.

[36] *See* Robert Cooter, *The Cost of Coase*, 11 J. Legal Stud. 1, 16–20 (1982). For other costs associated with Coasian bargaining, *see* Markovits & Schwartz, *The Myth of Efficient Breach*, at 1973–7.

[37] *See* Brooks, *The Efficient Performance Hypothesis*; Ian Ayres, Optional Law: The Structure of Legal Entitlements (2005). *See also* Goetz & Scott, *Liquidated Damages, Penalties and the Just Compensation Principle*, at 559 (suggesting that the law need not allow the breaching party to keep all the gains of breach).

[38] *See* Richard Craswell, *Contract Remedies, Renegotiation, and the Theory of Efficient Breach*, 61 S. Cal. L. Rev. 629, 660 (1988).

avoid the costs of having Seller or a court figure out Buyer's expectation interest, but it adds the expense of measuring Seller's possible gains from nonperformance.

Though we have arrived at some fairly esoteric proposals, the above survey does not exhaust proposed efficient alternatives to expectation damages.[39] But it is enough to show the variety of remedies that can be efficient within the frictionless world of the simple theory. With respect to efficiency, the choice between remedial rules depends on their relative transaction costs. There is now a large theoretical literature on the relative transaction costs of different remedial schemes. That literature has not, however, converged on a single answer. As Ian Macneil observed over 30 years ago, "it is extremely easy to introduce selected transaction costs to show that the model 'proves' what the modeler wants it to prove, while ignoring countless other transaction costs of equal or greater pertinence in the real world—yielding different conclusions."[40] The question itself is at bottom an empirical one, for which we have very limited data.[41] Nor is there a reason to expect the same answer for all transactions. Different transaction types generate different types of transaction costs. A complete theory of efficient breach would provide an empirically grounded account of when and why expectation damages provide the cheapest route to an efficient performance decision. The simple theory does not.

A third internal criticism of the simple theory concerns its narrow focus on the choice between performance and breach. Remedial rules influence many decisions at various stages of a transaction. The simple theory's attention only to achieving efficient incentives to perform or breach risks providing inefficient incentives elsewhere in the transaction.

The point is made most easily with respect to the obligee's reliance decision. Recall again the January 1 contract between Seller and Buyer, in which Buyer is to pay $1,000 for goods delivered in July, which Buyer will then invest $600 in and resell for $1,800. Suppose now that Buyer has a choice: it can invest $200 in equipment in January and

[39] Another possibility is nested options. *See* Ian Ayres & J. M. Balkin, *Legal Entitlements as Auctions: Property Rules, Liability Rules and Beyond*, 106 Yale L.J. 703 (1996). Barry Adler has argued that on the efficient breach model, there is a case to be made for "negative damages," paid by the nonbreaching party to the breaching party, when the nonbreaching party benefits from breach. *Efficient Breach Theory through the Looking Glass*, 83 N.Y.U. L. Rev. 1679 (2008). I have suggested specific performance plus giving the obligor an option to avoid performance by voluntarily paying a price. Klass, *To Perform or Pay Damages*, at 147–8. Even tortious interference has been proposed as an efficient rule, on the theory that in a good-news scenario it requires fewer transactions to get to an efficient allocation. Fred S. McChesney, *Tortious Interference with Contract Versus "Efficient" Breach: Theory and Empirical Evidence*, 28 J. Legal Stud. 131, 148–56 (1999).

[40] Ian Macneil in *Efficient Breach of Contract: Circles in the Sky*, 68 Va. L. Rev. 947, 961 (1982); *see generally* at 951–7. For a recent example of what I consider a selective accounting transaction costs, see Markovits & Schwartz, *The Myth of Efficient Breach*, at 1973–7. Markovits and Schwartz do not explain why they include some transaction costs ("relax some of the model's assumptions," at 1973) in their analysis but not others.

[41] *See* Paul G. Mahoney, *Contract Remedies and Options Pricing*, 24 J. Legal Stud. 139, 142 (1995) (arguing that a transaction cost approach "yields… no persuasive conclusion when transaction costs are low (unless we can measure them with extreme precision)"); Eric A. Posner, *Economic Analysis of Contract Law after Three Decades: Success or Failure?*, 112 Yale L.J. 829 *passim* (2003); Schwartz, *The Case for Specific Performance*, at 294 ("On the basis of information currently available, it is impossible to say whether [specific performance's efficiency] gains would exceed the increase in administrative and judicial opportunity costs that the availability of specific performance would engender.").

shave $40 off its total costs, or it can buy the same equipment after Seller delivers the goods and expend the full $600 to improve and resell the goods. If Seller is certain to perform, the value-maximizing choice is to buy the equipment in January. By spending $200 six months early, Buyer nets an extra $40. But suppose there is a 20 percent chance that Seller will efficiently breach, in which case Buyer's $200 January investment will be wasted. We can now express the risk-adjusted value of Buyer's early investment as follows:

$$V = (.8)(\$40\,\text{gain}) + (.2)(\$200\,\text{loss}) = \$32 - \$40 = -\$8$$

Under these circumstances it is better for Buyer to wait until performance is certain before relying. By relying early, Buyer risks sunk costs that produce no value. But this is not the result we get with the expectation remedy. Because expectation damages fully insure Buyer against nonperformance, including its reliance costs, Buyer will invest as if Seller's performance is certain and purchase the $200 equipment in February.[42]

One example does not prove the rule, but it illustrates the moral hazard expectation damages create. Steven Shavell and others have used formal models to show that "[t]here does not exist a damage measure which leads to Pareto efficient decisions concerning both breach and reliance independent of the type of contractual situation."[43] Optimally incentivizing A's performance often means giving B the wrong incentives with respect to reliance. Similarly, giving B an incentive to rely efficiently can mean providing A suboptimal incentives with respect to performance. Where the simple theory lavishes all its attention on the one variable, efficiency requires attending to at least two.

In fact, it requires attending to many variables at once. In the past 40 years, economically oriented scholars have identified many other overlapping decisions remedial rules can affect. These include the number of transactions,[44] potential promisors' pre-formation investigations,[45] the selection of contracting partners,[46] quantity terms,[47] post-formation search for other opportunities,[48] post-formation reliance by the obligee,[49] precautions against one's own breach,[50] and post-breach mitigation by the nonbreaching party.[51] No single remedial rule is likely to provide optimal incentives

[42] *See* Shavell, *Damage Measures*, at 478 ("[U]nder the expectation measure the buyer is in effect guaranteed his expectancy, and hence he sees reliance as an investment with a certain payoff. Therefore, he engages in reliance up to the point where its marginal product conditional on performance is driven down to one.").

[43] Shavell, *Damage Measures*, at 472; *see also* Robert Cooter, *Unity in Tort, Contract and Property: The Model of Precaution*, 73 CALIF. L. REV. 1 (1985); Lewis A. Kornhauser, *Reliance, Reputation and Breach of Contract*, 26 J.L. & ECON. 691 (1983).

[44] David Friedman, *An Economic Analysis of Alternate Damage Rules for Breach of Contract*, 32 J.L. & ECON. 281 (1989); Goetz & Scott, *Enforcing Promises*, at 1283.

[45] Richard Craswell, *Precontractual Investigation as an Optimal Precaution Problem*, 17 J. LEGAL STUD. 401 (1988).

[46] Craswell, *Contract Remedies*, at 650.

[47] Barton, *The Economic Basis of Damages for Breach of Contract*, at 293–300.

[48] Peter A. Diamond & Eric Maskin, *An Equilibrium Analysis of Search and Breach of Contract, I: Steady States*, 10 BELL J. ECON. 282 *passim* (1979).

[49] *See* note 42.

[50] Craswell, *Contract Remedies*, at 645–50.

[51] Craswell, *Contract Remedies*, at 657.

across these many decisions. More to the point, as Richard Craswell has argued, there is "no reason to suppose that the totality of economic effects will always favor an award of expectation damages."[52] More likely is "some hybrid or intermediate number."[53] Efficiency-minded theories must balance and satisfice, seeking out the remedy that, in combination with other rules, creates the most value across the lifetime of a transaction.

Finally, the simple theory paints too simple a picture of what remedies do. According to the simple theory, the legal remedy for breach serves only to create efficient incentives. Even within the neoclassical model, remedies can serve several other functions as well. By ignoring them, the simple theory again simplifies too much.

Most obviously, contract remedies also serve to allocate risk. Generally speaking, parties enter into contracts for two sorts of reasons: to give one or both a new reason to perform and to shift risk among them. In some contracts, the incentive to perform looms larger. Think of a homeowner's contract with a builder to renovate a kitchen. It is true that the homeowner wants to recover damages should the builder walk off the job. But what she really wants is a new kitchen. The homeowner wants a contract primarily because she hopes that the threat of legal liability for breach will give the builder a new reason to perform. In other contracts, risk allocation is the more salient function. Insurance contracts are an obvious example. Because the insured is risk averse, it is willing to pay a premium to shift risks of loss to the insurer. Or consider forward contracts among nonproducers in a thick market. A contract to sell a commodity at a specified price two years hence allocates the risk of price shifts. The buyer avoids the risk that the spot price will be above the contract price, the seller the risk that the spot price will be below it. There is no such thing as an efficient breach of a pure risk-shifting contract. The goal in allocating risk is not to move resources to a more productive use, but to satisfy each party's risk preferences. Satisfaction requires strict enforcement of the agreed-upon allocation with specific performance or simple market damages.[54]

Both contract terms and contract remedies can function to allocate risk. In a forward contract, the price term allocates the risk of price changes. In the example kitchen-renovation contract, though not its primary function, the remedy insures the homeowner against the risk of the builder's nonperformance. More generally, because contract remedies almost always redound to the benefit of the nonbreaching party, they serve not only to incentivize performance, but also to allocate the risk of nonperformance.

[52] Richard Craswell, *Against Fuller and Perdue*, 67 U. Chi. L. Rev. 99, 109 (2000).

[53] Craswell, *Against Fuller and Perdue*, at 110. Many authors have made similar points. *See, e.g.*, Robert Birmingham, *Notes on the Reliance Interest*, 60 Wash. L. Rev. 217, 260–1 (1985); Cooter & Eisenberg, *Damages for Breach of Contract*, at 1462; Craswell, *Contract Remedies*, at 660–1; Craswell, *Two Economic Theories of Enforcing Promises*, at 28–32; Aaron S. Edlin & Alan Schwartz, *Optimal Penalties in Contracts*, 78 Chi.-Kent L. Rev. 33, 52–3 (2003); Avery Katz, *Reflections on Fuller and Perdue's The Reliance Interest in Contract Damages: A Positive Economic Framework*, 21 U. Mich. J.L. Reform 541, 558–9 (1988); Lewis A. Kornhauser, *An Introduction to the Economic Analysis of Contract Remedies*, 57 U. Colo. L. Rev. 683, 706 (1986); Posner, *Economic Analysis of Contract Law*, at 834–8; Samuel A. Rea, Jr., *Nonpecuniary Loss and Breach of Contract*, 11 J. Legal Stud. 35, 36 (1982); Robert E. Scott & George G. Triantis, *Embedded Options and the Case against Compensation in Contract Law*, 104 Colum. L. Rev. 1428, 1447–52 (2004).

[54] *See* Barton, *The Economic Basis of Damages for Breach of Contract*, at 277–9; Scott & Triantis, *Embedded Options*, at 1466, 1479–80.

Because different parties have different attitudes towards risk, this risk-allocation function further complicates the efficient breach story. To return again to the example, if Buyer is risk averse and Seller is risk neutral or risk preferring, expectation damages properly allocate the risk of nonperformance by shifting it from Buyer to Seller. In the model, Buyer knows it will get its $2 per-unit profit no matter what happens. Seller both bears the risk of loss in bad-news scenarios and enjoys the risk of an upside gain in good-news scenarios. More generally, expectation damages shift the risk of nonperformance to the breaching party.[55] In a frictionless world, they assure that the party who is owed a duty will occupy the same position whether the duty is performed or breached.

If, however, it is Seller who is risk averse and Buyer who is risk neutral or risk preferring, expectation damages provide the wrong allocation of risk. Suppose Seller has a nonlegal incentive, such as an interest in maintaining its reputation, to perform and that the only function of a damage payment is to allocate risk. Suppose further that the parties are especially worried about bad-news scenarios, in which Seller's out-of-pocket costs unexpectedly go up. If Seller is risk averse and Buyer risk neutral or preferring, setting damages at zero might achieve the optimal allocation of the risk.[56] In case Seller's costs go up, Seller can minimize its losses by choosing not to perform, coming out as close as possible to its original expectation. Buyer, of course, will suffer by getting neither the profits it expected nor payment for its lost expectation, or even reliance, costs. Buyer bears the risk of a bad-news scenario. But Buyer will have benefited *ex ante* in the form of a lower contract price. Think of reduction in the contract price as an insurance premium Seller pays Buyer to bear some or all of the risk of Seller's nonperformance.

There is much more one might say about how remedies can be used to shift risk between parties who have one or another combination of risk preferences. But the example demonstrates the problem for the simple theory. If we now drop the assumption that Seller has nonlegal reasons to perform, the remedy for breach serves two functions at once. It serves to incentivize performance and to allocate risk. The problem is that there is no reason to expect the remedy that provides the optimal incentives also to optimally allocate the risk of breach.[57]

[55] *See* Shavell, *Damage Measures*, at 488.

[56] *See* Kornhauser, *Reliance, Reputation and Breach of Contract*, at 701. In fact, if incentives are truly beside the point, the optimal allocation might be a reverse damage payment, in which Buyer fully insures Seller against Seller's own breach.

[57] The first article to make the case for a possible divergence between efficient incentives and the risk-shifting function of contract remedies was Barton, *The Economic Basis of Damages for Breach of Contract*, at 293–300 (identifying "differences between the optimum-allocation and the incentive-maintenance approaches"). A systematic examination of the efficient allocation of risk through remedies can be found in A. Mitchell Polinsky, *Risk Sharing through Breach of Contract Remedies*, 12 J. Legal Stud. 427 (1983); *see also* Jeffrey M. Perloff, *Breach of Contract and the Foreseeability Doctrine of* Hadley v. Baxendale, 10 J. Legal Stud. 39 (1981) (examining the efficiency of *Hadley* and its alternatives for various party risk preferences); Rea, *Nonpecuniary Loss and Breach of Contract*, at 37 ("The theory of optimal insurance suggests that nonpecuniary losses should not necessarily be compensated, but lack of such compensation may affect the seller's incentive to honor the contract."); Scott & Triantis, *Embedded Options* (arguing that damages are better viewed as option prices utilized to shift risk between the parties, and that such prices bear no relationship to compensation); Shavell, *Damage Measures*, at 487–8 (noting that "in most contractual relationships, both the allocation of risk and the allocation of resources will need to be considered with respect to the role of damage measures").

Incentives and risk allocation are not the only functions remedies serve in economic models. Richard Posner long ago observed that penalty clauses can perform a positive signaling function.[58] New entrants in a market, for example, might find themselves disadvantaged against established participants with reputations for performing. A lower cost new entrant who is a reliable contracting partner can signal its reliability by agreeing to a penalty for breach. The penalty might deter some efficient breaches. But if it makes a value-creating transaction possible, the result can be a net gain. Or consider Paul Mahoney's argument that in the sale of unique goods or in auctions, specific performance serves to assure buyers that the sale is final.[59] Without specific performance, a seller might use a bid simply to elicit information, or might keep looking for higher offers. Knowing that, potential buyers will be less likely to bid to their reserve price. The buyer can always wait for the seller to make a contract with another, then make a higher offer herself. Sellers can avoid this unattractive result by binding themselves to the mast with specific performance, thereby credibly communicating that the bidding deadline is real. Even if the remedy were to deter some efficient breaches, there might again be a net gain, here by eliciting correct prices and reducing transaction costs.

In short, the simple theory's exclusive emphasis on incentivizing the perform-breach decision ignores not only incentive effects elsewhere in the transaction, but also other functions remedies can serve within the model. These gaps in the theory, together with the simple theory's inattention to nonefficient breaches and uncertainty about the transaction costs that attach to different remedies, make it difficult to disagree with Eric Posner's conclusion that efficiency alone "does not explain why expectation damages are the standard remedy."[60]

IV. A More Interesting Theory of Efficient Breach

The simple theory neither explains nor justifies the common law's apparent attachment to expectation damages. Viewed from within the neoclassical economic model it occupies, the theory is radically incomplete. Viewed from outside that model, the theory rests on empirically questionable assumptions and for many is morally unsatisfactory.

But contract theorists should not ignore efficient breach theory. Early proponents presented the theory as a policy argument for expectation damages and a solution to Fuller and Perdue's puzzle. The theory is inadequate to that task. A revised, more sophisticated theory, however, reveals important features of contract remedies. This revised theory is not a policy argument for or defense of existing uses of the expectation measure. Instead, it constructs a stripped down, idealized model to identify

[58] Posner first makes this point in the second edition of his book. Richard Posner, Economic Analysis of the Law 93–4 (2d ed., 1977).

[59] Mahoney, *Contract Remedies and Options Pricing*, at 155.

[60] Posner, *Economic Analysis of Contract Law*, at 880; *see also* Richard R. W. Brooks, *What Efficiency Demands: The Efficient Performance Hypothesis Defended*, 117 Yale L.J. Pocket Part 14, 20 (2007), <http://yalelawjournal.org/images/pdfs/578.pdf> ("Any tie-breaker must be an empirical one. I am deeply skeptical of our capacity and willingness to search out that empirical answer.").

several features of contract remedies that too often escape notice. The revised theory is comparable to the prisoner's dilemma in game theory, to trolley problems in moral philosophy, or to brains in vats in theories of reference. It is a theoretical construct that isolates for analysis phenomena that exist in the world but can be difficult to disentangle from other facts or factors. Isolating these phenomena serves to dispel some common mistakes about contract remedies and to clarify a few basic questions that any adequate theory of contract law must answer.

The revised theory operates within the simplifying model of neoclassical economics but makes three changes to the simple theory. First, it observes that remedies for breach are likely to affect other terms parties choose. In particular, they are likely to affect how the parties allocate the gains of trade. Suppose when negotiating their contract, Seller and Buyer must choose between two remedies for Seller's breach: expectation damages and specific performance. Keeping for the moment the simplifying assumption of no transaction costs, the two remedies are equally efficient. But they have different *ex post* distributive consequences. All else being equal, Seller prefers expectation damages, which allow it to keep all of the gains from nonperformance, whereas Buyer prefers specific performance, which gives Buyer a chance to appropriate some of those gains by forcing Seller to buy a release. In negotiating the remedy, Seller and Buyer will each demand concessions to give up its preferred choice. For simplicity's sake, suppose Seller and Buyer know there is a 10 percent chance that a third party will offer Seller more than $12 per unit, and that on average such an offer will be for $14. In the sale of 100 units, there is therefore a 10 percent chance of an average $200 gain to the parties from nonperformance. If the remedy is expectation damages, Seller gets to keep that entire gain for itself, for a risk-adjusted benefit of $20 ($200 average gain × 0.1 probability). If the remedy is specific performance, the parties will negotiate a release. Suppose the parties expect that any such negotiations will result in an even split. Seller and Buyer will in that case each realize on average $100 from efficient nonperformance (half the $200 total), for a risk-adjusted present benefit of $10 each ($100 average gain × 0.1 probability). At the time of formation, therefore, Seller will demand at least, and Buyer will be willing to pay at most, $10 extra for a contract that includes the specific performance remedy rather than expectation damages. The price takes account of the remedy.

In competitive markets we can expect the same price effect even if parties do not have the power to choose the remedy. If Seller knows in advance that the remedy is specific performance, rather than expectation damages, Seller will charge a somewhat higher price for the goods. That increase in price will correspond to the increased costs to Seller in the case of Seller's nonperformance, discounted by the probability of its nonperformance. As Robert Cooter and Melvin Eisenberg put the point, "the exchange of legal rights is no different than the exchange of ordinary commodities."[61]

[61] Cooter & Eisenberg, *Damages for Breach of Contract*, at 1461. Scholars have long recognized the effect of remedial rules on price. Before the idea of efficient breach had entered the literature, Richard Hartzler made the point in his analysis of Fuller and Perdue's categories. H. Richard Hartzler, *The Business and Economic Functions of the Law of Contracts*, 6 Am. Bus. L.J. 387, 392, 394 (1968). The effect was quickly recognized by efficient breach theorists. *See, e.g.*, Goetz & Scott, *Liquidated Damages, Penalties and the Just Compensation Principle* (integrating the price effect into their analysis of the penalty rule); Anthony T. Kronman, *Specific Performance*, 45 U. Chi. L. Rev. 351 (1978) (integrating the price effect into the

The more costly to one party the remedy for breach, the higher the price that party will charge up front.

We can now return to the objection that the theory of efficient breach advocates giving the gains of breach to the party in the wrong. But if the remedy is built into the price, expectation damages simply give the nonbreaching party the remedy it paid for. In the above example, expectation damages mean that Buyer pays less for the goods. In exchange for that lower price, Seller is able to keep for itself all of the gains of nonperformance. Complaining about the fairness of this arrangement is like complaining about having to pay the deductible on an insurance policy after receiving the benefit of a lower premium. Any gains that efficient breach gives to the wrongdoer *ex post* have been paid for *ex ante* in the form of more favorable contract terms.[62]

Of course the distributive objection might not be about the fairness of allocating the gains of breach to the breaching party, but about whether the law should "reward" the party in the wrong by allowing it to keep the profits of breach. If this is the objection, the price effect at least identifies an important wrinkle. Sticking with the example, a legal rule that recommends specific performance, disgorgement, or punitive damages for breach will benefit those Buyers who are victims of breach. But that rule will often cost all Buyers at the time of formation. In many market conditions, increasing the cost of breach results in all Buyers paying a higher price for their contracts. Buyers in transactions in which there is no breach pay a price that subsidizes the recovery of Buyers in transactions in which there is a breach. Theorists who advocate these remedies should also be prepared to justify these price effects and the resulting cross-subsidy.

The price effect illustrates a distinctive feature of contract law. Unlike the duties imposed by, say, tort or criminal law, contractual obligations are created by the same individuals who are subject to them. As a result, the legal rules that govern contractual obligations affect not only decisions about their performance or breach, but also decisions, at the time of formation, about what those obligations will be.[63] Economic analysis, with its relentless attention to incentives, has given that fact more attention than have other theories. But an adequate theory of remedial rules, no matter what its principled commitments, cannot ignore the effect of remedies on contract terms. A theory of contract remedies should attend not only to how remedies impact parties' post-formation relationships, how they affect the parties' performance decisions, and the remedies' moral or other post-breach functions. It should also attend to the effects of remedial rules on the formation of contracts.

The price effect provides the starting point for a second and more fundamental modification to the simple theory. Early proponents of the efficient breach theory

analysis of specific performance). For a detailed analysis of price effects, *see* Mahoney, *Contract Remedies and Options Pricing*. For recent treatments, *see* Richard Craswell, *Promises and Prices*, 45 Suffolk U. L. Rev. 735 (2012); Markovits & Schwartz, *The Expectation Remedy and the Promissory Basis of Contract*, at 1961–77.

[62] I believe Richard Craswell was the first to make this point in response to the moral objection. *See* Craswell, *Contract Remedies*, at 642.

[63] As Goetz and Scott put the point, "a decision to enforce promises, and the subsequent choice of remedy, does not merely mold the performance behavior of contracting parties; it also shapes both the nature and amount of promise-making activity." Goetz & Scott, *Enforcing Promises*, at 1266.

based their case on principles of social welfare. Efficient breach, it was argued, is desirable because it results in an allocation of resources that increases aggregate individual welfare. The simple theory occupied the same space in this respect as Guido Calabresi's argument for strict liability in tort[64] or Gary Becker's deterrence-based account of criminal law.[65] Once the price effect is added, the theory no longer needs a social welfare principle. The price effect means that parties themselves want efficient remedies. All that is needed to get the theory off the ground is assigning some weight to the remedies that parties themselves prefer or would choose.

The idea can be illustrated by adding differential transaction costs to the above story. Suppose again that at the time of contracting Seller and Buyer can choose expectation damages or specific performance, but that when performance becomes inefficient, the remedies produce different transaction costs. For simplicity's sake, let us say that under the expectation remedy Seller will breach and voluntarily pay damages whenever nonperformance is more efficient at no additional cost to the parties, and that with specific performance, it will cost each party $20 to negotiate a release that divides the gains evenly. If there is $200 to be gained from nonperformance, with the expectation remedy Seller will breach and keep the entire $200. With specific performance, the parties will negotiate a release and each end up only $80 ahead. Other things being equal, Buyer again prefers an $80 gain from nonperformance to Seller receiving all the gains of breach. But the price effect means that other things are not equal. Suppose again that at the time of contracting both parties expect an average $200 potential gain from nonperformance 10 percent of the time. With the specific performance remedy Buyer and Seller each stands to garner only a risk-adjusted $8 from nonperformance ($80 average gain × 0.1 probability). That is $12 less than Seller's risk-adjusted $20 gain from expectation damages ($200 average gain × 0.1 probability). Seller will therefore happily reduce the price by up to $12 in exchange for the expectation remedy. Buyer comes ahead with any price reduction of more than $8, creating a price range in which expectation damages are both Buyer's and Seller's preferred remedy.

The phenomenon is a general one. By definition, efficient remedies increase the total gains of contracting across all possible futures. If in some futures one side ends up with those gains, the other side can benefit at the outset in the form of price or other concessions. As Alan Schwartz has put the point, "[a] promisee who cannot affect the size of his share will want to maximize the size of the pie."[66] So long as efficient

[64] Guido Calabresi & Jon T. Hirschoff, *Toward a Test for Strict Liability in Torts*, 81 YALE L.J. 1055 (1972).

[65] Gary Becker, *Crime and Punishment: An Economic Approach*, 76 J. POL. ECON. 169 (1968).

[66] Alan Schwartz, *The Myth that Promisees Prefer Supracompensatory Remedies: An Analysis of Contracting for Damage Measures*, 100 YALE L.J. 369, 377 (1990); *see also* Cooter & Eisenberg, *Damages for Breach of Contract*, at 1360 ("The *price* term of a contract controls the distribution of the value that the contract creates. Revision of an inefficient nonprice term can produce an increase in value, and this increase can be distributed between the parties by adjusting the price term so that each party is better off."); Craswell, *Contract Remedies*, at 633 ("[The] attempt to mimic the result of a perfect bargaining process is equivalent to identifying the remedy that is most 'efficient' in the sense of maximizing the sum of the parties' expected welfare."); Goetz & Scott, *Liquidated Damages, Penalties and the Just Compensation Principle*, at 578 ("*In the absence of evidence of unfairness or other bargaining abnormalities, efficiency would be maximized by the enforcement of the agreed allocation of risks embodied in a liquidated damages clause.*" (emphasis in original)); Shavell, *On the Design*, at 131 ("[O]ne remedy is Pareto superior to a second if given any contract price and use of the second remedy, both parties would prefer to make some

remedies increase the size of the pie without affecting the proportion that each party gets, both parties prefer efficient remedies.

The path to this result requires some heroic assumptions. I have simply stipulated higher transactions costs under specific performance than under expectation damages. As I observed above, the transaction costs that attach to various remedies depend on empirical facts about which there is considerable disagreement among theorists and on which we have limited data. More generally, the model assumes that the parties are risk neutral, fully informed, and perfectly rational, features that do not describe many actual transactions.

But the point of the revised theory is not to argue that legislators or courts should adopt one or another remedial rule. It is to illustrate the relevance of efficiency to almost any theory of contract remedies. That relevance follows from what I take to be three relatively uncontroversial premises. First, one function of contract law is to enable parties to better achieve their individual ends. Second, many parties enter into contracts to maximize their individual gain from a transaction. Third, remedies often affect prices. The three premises together make a prima facie case for efficient remedies. Where the price effect exists, efficient remedies enable both parties to increase their individual gain from the transaction. The argument for efficient remedies does not require a principle of social welfare, but only some deference to what, at the time of formation, the parties want from their transaction.[67]

None of this is to say that efficiency should be the sole, or even principal, guide in the choice of remedies. If enabling parties to achieve their individual ends is one purpose of contract law, it need not be the only purpose or sole governing principle. And some parties might happily pay a higher price for inefficient remedies that they prefer for other reasons. But we need an argument that one or the other is the case. Many theories of contract argue for the theorist's preferred remedy with limited attention to its efficiency. Such theories are incomplete unless they also demonstrate either that the theorist's reasons for imposing her preferred remedy are

adjustment in the price and to employ instead the first remedy."); Shavell, *Specific Performance Versus Damages for Breach of Contract*, at 841 ("[I]f the contractual 'pie' the parties have to divide would be increased by a change in the remedy for breach, there has to be a way to slice the pie (by means of a price adjustment) so that each has more pie to enjoy and thus is happier.").

[67] The point can be found in the efficient breach literature as early as 1972. Barton, *The Economic Basis of Damages for Breach of Contract*, at 285–6. Writing on another topic in 1977, Richard Posner and Andrew Rosenfeld make it as follows:

> If the purpose of the law of contracts is to effectuate the desires of the contracting parties, then the proper criterion for evaluating the rules of contract law is surely that of economic efficiency. Since the object of most voluntary exchanges is to increase value or efficiency, contracting parties may be assumed to desire a set of contract terms that will maximize the value of the exchange. It is true that each party is interested only in the value of the contract to it. However, the more efficiently the exchange is structured, the larger is the potential profit of the contract for the parties to divide between them.

Richard A. Posner & Andrew M. Rosenfeld, *Impossibility and Related Doctrines in Contract Law: An Economic Analysis*, 6 J. Legal Stud. 83, 89 (1977); *see also* Shavell, *Damage Measures*, at 489 ("The utility of damage measures to contracting parties themselves is no doubt a and perhaps *the* major aspect in which the social advantage of damage measures adhere. Furthermore, it affords a more appealing explanation of the observed use of damage measures than an explanation based on the notion that they are in the diffuse social interest.").

sufficiently important to sometimes defeat party preferences, or that parties themselves are likely to prefer the recommended remedy notwithstanding its potential inefficiencies.

The third modification to the simple theory builds on the second. The simple theory, like Fuller and Perdue's puzzle, treats the remedy question in contract as similar in kind to the question in tort or criminal law. It identifies a legal wrong and asks what legal consequence lawmakers should attach to it. But in contract law there is a prior question. The duties of tort and criminal law are established by legislatures and judges. Contractual obligations are established by parties who are then subject to them. Because contract law delegates to parties the power to create the duty, it might also delegate to them the power to choose, at the time of formation, the remedy for its breach. In contract law, the first question is not what the remedy should be, but who should have the power to choose it. Should the remedial rule be a mandatory one, picked by officials and binding on the parties, or a default plus altering rule, designed to allow the parties to decide? The simple theory elides that question. Like Fuller and Perdue, it simply assumes that the remedial choice will be made by legal officials, not by the parties.

In the model, the who-decides question transforms economic criticisms of the simple theory—it simplifies too much—into reasons for delegating to parties the choice of remedy. The argument is one of relative competence. In the model, parties at the time of formation are likely to know more than legislators or courts about which breaches are obviously inefficient, and so should be punished rather than priced, about which remedies will allow the parties to avoid inefficient performance most cheaply, about how one or another remedy will influence the many decisions the parties will take in the transaction and the relative importance of each, and about how to balance such incentive effects against risk allocation and other functions the remedy might serve in their transaction. For reasons canvassed under the previous point, parties themselves prefer more efficient remedies. In the model, therefore, both principles of social welfare and a commitment to helping parties achieve their ends recommend allowing the parties to choose the remedy.[68] Hence the observed convergence between efficiency and autonomy theories of contract.[69]

This final revision to the simple theory transforms it from a theory of efficient breach to a theory of efficient remedies more generally. In some transactions the parties might choose expectation damages because the expectation measure gives a party the option to perform or pay damages. In other transactions, or for certain types of breaches, the parties might pick other remedies. The most the revised theory can now offer is an argument for setting the default at expectation damages. Such an argument might, for example, be that most parties prefer expectation damages. In that case, it

[68] For a classic deployment of this argument, *see* Schwartz, *The Myth that Promisees Prefer Supracompensatory Remedies*.

[69] *See, e.g.*, Charles Fried, *The Ambitions of* Contract as Promise, *in* PHILOSOPHICAL FOUNDATIONS OF CONTRACT LAW 17, 21–4 (Gregory Klass, George Letsas, & Prince Saprai eds., 2014). The convergence is the result of assumptions baked into the neoclassical model such as individual rationality and knowledge and the exogeneity of preferences. Those assumptions are consistent with the priors of many autonomy theories, and are also contestable.

will involve empirical claims about relative transaction costs, the relative importance of various incentive effects and remedial functions, and the like.[70]

The above case for party choice relies on assumptions baked into the model. First, it assumes parties who have perfect knowledge and are perfectly rational. In the actual world, often neither is the case. Where parties are ill-informed or imperfectly rational, legislatures or courts might do a better job at picking the remedy that maximizes value or best realizes the parties' own goals. Again, this is an empirical question.

Second, the argument makes strong assumptions about society's reason for providing a remedy for breach. Deciding who should choose involves an inquiry into the relative competence and proper incentives of different institutional actors, which in turn depends on the design goal. If contract law's only purpose is to maximize social welfare, expand individual autonomy, or some combination of the two, the choice of remedies should be given to knowledgeable rational parties at the time of contracting.[71] If, on the contrary, we enforce contracts in order to protect the nonbreaching party's reliance, restitution, or expectation interests, that is an argument for mandatory limits on parties' ability to choose remedies that do not serve that end, such as penalties for breach.[72] If we believe contracts create a natural property right in performance, that is a reason for mandating disgorgement for some breaches, no matter what the parties' preferences.[73]

Although the revised theory does not integrate these alternative accounts of the functions of and justifications for contract law, it contains lessons for them. The first is simply to attend to the question of who chooses. Too often contract theorists reason directly from an account of contractual rights to conclusions about the proper remedy for breach. To the extent such theories advocate giving the choice of remedy to judges or legislators, they neglect an essential step. We need an argument why, when we allow the parties to make so many choices about their transaction, we should take this one away from them. Without such an argument, the remedial question is about only defaults and altering rules: What remedy when parties have not expressed an intent one way or another, and what expressions of a contrary intent suffice to defeat the default? If that is the only question, principled debates about contract remedies become much less interesting.[74]

The second lesson concerns design options. I have been speaking as if the who-chooses question has only two possible answers: parties or legal officials. Attention to economic analyses of contract design reveals a number of intermediary possibilities.

[70] *See, e.g.*, Markovits & Schwartz, *The Expectation Remedy and the Promissory Basis of Contract*. Alternatively, the argument for one or another default might involve nonmajoritarian considerations, such as the desirability of creating new incentives to reveal information through the process of contracting around the default. Proposals for bargain-forcing default remedies are rare, but *see* Scott & Triantis, *Embedded Options*, at 1476–90 (recommending "a bargain-forcing default that not only maximizes the freedom to contract for termination rights but indeed also encourages the parties to bargain explicitly over these provisions").

[71] *See, e.g.*, Jody S. Kraus, *The Correspondence of Contract and Promise*, 109 Colum. L. Rev. 1603 (2009).

[72] Ian R. Macneil, *Power of Contract and Agreed Remedies*, 47 Cornell L. Rev. 495, 496–8 (1962); *see also* Birmingham, *Notes on the Reliance Interest*, at 220 (suggesting that contract serves both compensation and efficiency goals).

[73] *See, e.g.*, Friedmann, *Restitution of Benefits*.

[74] The first to emphasize the implications for contract theory was Richard Craswell, *Contract Law, Default Rules, and the Philosophy of Promising*, 88 Mich. L. Rev. 489 (1989).

First, and most obviously, mandatory limits on the power to pick the remedy can leave room for party choice. The penalty rule, while prohibiting certain remedial choices, leaves many options to choose from. More subtly and importantly, lawmakers can tailor defaults to particular types of transactions or parties, they can pick defaults that are more or less sticky, and they craft altering rules that make it more or less costly to contract around the default.[75] These design options provide mechanisms for giving different weight in different circumstances to the various competing principles and purposes of contract law. Suppose, for example, a theorist holds that the point of contract law is to achieve some measure of corrective justice, and that corrective justice requires that the breaching party provide the monetary equivalent of performance. This suggests setting the default at expectation damages. Depending on the importance of that goal, on the value the theorist also attaches to party autonomy, efficiency, or other purposes, on her assessment of the effects of a mandatory rule on the formation of contracts, and so forth, the theorist might want to make it more or less difficult to contract around that default. More generally, as I have written elsewhere:

> Stickier defaults, and by implication costlier opt-outs,... can mediate between the sometimes conflicting interests the law has in, on the one hand, granting parties the power to control the scope of their legal obligations and, on the other hand, imposing liability on parties because of extralegal wrongs they have committed, harms they have caused, or other considerations.[76]

Economic analyses of the design question provide new tools for understanding what is possible in contract, and especially how remedial rules can respond to the multiple functions contract law might serve. Only by attending to the design literature can contract theorists know what principles and purposes contract law is able to advance.

There is more to say on the complex distributive effects of remedies, the prediction that many parties would choose efficient remedies, and the various ways to design remedial rules to incorporate party choice. I hope I have said enough, however, to convince that contract theorists, no matter what their other commitments, should pay attention to the revised theory of efficient breach. Whether or not the model describes the world, it reveals aspects of contract remedies that we might not otherwise see and provides a deeper understanding of the principles and purposes contract law might serve.

Conclusion

Many common criticisms of the efficient breach theory attack a theory no one holds. Sophisticated economic accounts of contract remedies have moved far beyond the simple theory of efficient breach. But a revised theory holds important lessons for contract theory. The revised theory illustrates special difficulties in evaluating the distributive consequences of contract remedies, given that the remedy is likely to affect the price or other contract terms. It predicts that many parties will want efficient remedies,

[75] *See* Ian Ayres, *Regulating Opt-out: An Economic Theory of Altering Rules*, 121 YALE L.J. 2032 (2012).
[76] Gregory Klass, *Intent to Contract*, 95 VA. L. REV. 1437, 1472 (2009).

putting the burden on theorists who do not consider efficiency to explain why their preferred remedy should sometimes trump party preferences. And it calls attention to the option of delegating the remedial decision to the parties themselves and suggests new tools for doing so.

More broadly, the revised theory of efficient breach illustrates the interplay between, on the one hand, the functions and justifications of contract law and, on the other, its design. Contract theorists should attend not only to the general distinguishing feature of contract law—that it provides for the private enforcement of voluntary obligations—but also to the special set of design challenges and options that result. The rules of contract law affect parties' behavior in distinctive ways. And contract law's delegation to parties of a limited law-making power provides design options not available elsewhere. Only by attending to the details of contract design can contract theorists understand what functions contract law can serve and what principles might justify it.

Index